Robert Bresson

Cinematheque Ontario Monographs

Shohei Imamura, no. 1
Robert Bresson, no. 2

Funding for this publication was provided by
the Toronto International Film Festival Group
and by Le Service Culturel du Consulat Général de France à Toronto

A DIVISION OF THE TORONTO INTERNATIONAL FILM FESTIVAL GROUP

Robert Bresson

Edited by James Quandt

TORONTO INTERNATIONAL
FILM FESTIVAL GROUP

Toronto, 1998

Toronto International Film Festival Group
2 Carlton Street, Suite 1600
Toronto, Ontario M5B 1J3
Canada

Canadian Cataloguing in Publication Data

Main entry under title:

Robert Bresson

(Cinematheque Ontario monographs ; no. 2)
Includes bibliographical references.
ISBN 0-9682969-1-2

1. Bresson, Robert – Criticism and interpretation.
I. Quandt, James   II. Cinematheque Ontario.   III. Series.

PN1998.3.B755R62 1998   791.43'0233'092   C98-900930-0

Distributed in Canada by Wilfrid Laurier University Press
75 University Avenue West, Waterloo, Ontario N2L 3C5 Canada
www.wlu.ca/~wwwpress
Telephone orders: (519) 884-0710, ext. 6124
Fax orders: (519) 725-1399
E-mail orders: press@wlu.ca

Distributed outside Canada by Indiana University Press
601 North Morton Street, Bloomington, Indiana 47404-3797 USA
www.iupress.indiana.edu
Telephone orders: (800) 842-6796
Fax orders: (812) 855-7931
E-mail orders: iuporder@indiana.edu

First published October 1998
Reprinted February 2000
Book design by Gordon Robertson
Printed in Canada

Acknowledgements

The Bresson project is an undertaking of Cinematheque Ontario to make Robert Bresson's work available to a wide audience. It involves two closely related endeavours. In co-operation with various organizations, distributors, producers, and other cinematheques, Cinematheque Ontario has ensured that new 35mm prints of all of Bresson's feature films were struck, and has organized a North American tour of over a dozen sites to present the retrospective. Designed to accompany the retrospective, the present volume modestly addresses the marked lack of recent English language scholarship and criticism of Bresson's work.

The Bresson Project has been made possible by the exceptional generosity, efforts, and encouragement of many individuals and organizations, particularly Robert and Mylène Bresson; the Bureau du Cinéma, Ministère des Affaires Étrangères, Paris (Pierre Triapkine; Laurent Burin des Roziers; Janine Deunf); and le Service Culturel du Consulat Général de France à Toronto (Fabyène Mansencal). All have supported the project since its inception, and their patient assistance throughout its often arduous development has been unstinting.

Also important in making the retrospective possible were New Yorker Films, New York (José Lopez); La Cinémathèque Française, Paris (Dominique Païni, Alain Marchand, Jacques Aumont); Canal + International, Paris (Ron Halpern); Véronique Godard, New York; Paramount Pictures, Paris; Éditions Gallimard, Paris (Prune Berge, Julien Laffon); Netherlands Government Information Service, The Hague (G. A. van Leeuwen); Gian Vittorio Baldi; Pacific Film Archive, Berkeley (Edith Kramer, Judy Bloch); Catherine Gauthier, Filmoteca Española, Madrid; Alliance Française, Toronto; Nicole Jouve, Interama, New York; John Minchinton; Argos Films (Anatole Dauman, Florence Dauman, Barry Edson).

I salute two friends and colleagues who inspired and assisted me throughout the organization of the retrospective: Lara Fitzgerald and Dorina Furgiuele, both of whose fineness of spirit was matched by their tenacity. Part "les dames" (in their mettle), part "les anges" (in their understanding and assistance), they contributed more than they know to the success of the project.

Similarly, Catherine Yolles guided the assemblage and editing of this volume with such radiant intelligence, rigour, patience, and great good humour, that she deserves a large part of the credit for its existence. (Whatever faults the book has are mine.)

My gratitude to all of the contributors, particularly those who wrote pieces especially for the book, and to the writers and copyright holders who granted the necessary permissions for the reprints. Gerry O'Grady of Harvard University did exceptional early research, and I also profited from the advice of Thomas Elsaesser, Raymond Bellour, Jonathan Rosenbaum, Kent Jones, and David Bordwell. The many directors who wrote commentaries on Bresson deserve warm appreciation, especially those I badgered throughout the making of their new films. Robert Gray contributed superb, discerning translations of several key articles, particularly that of René Prédal, a major contribution to English studies of Bresson. Lara Fitzgerald also contributed fine translations of complicated texts, and generously advised me on my own. David Kilgour expertly copy edited one section of the book. And Gordon Robertson accomplished the elegant design with a veteran sense of calm and refinement. Rosemary Ullyot of The Film Reference Library offered her usual unflagging, informed research assistance, and Robin MacDonald compiled the bibliography with her customary intelligence and magnanimity. Chris Gehman brought his fine eye, diligence, and acumen to the planning of the book.

I am, of course, also indebted to my colleagues at Cinematheque Ontario and the Toronto International Film Festival Group.

And, as in all my ventures and obsessions, the understanding and support of Richard Nordahl makes every endeavour possible.

James Quandt
Senior Programmer
Cinematheque Ontario

Note to the Reader

Assembling a collection of essays such as this poses problems of consistency. For example, the titles of Bresson's films vary from essay to essay; some retain the original French titles, others employ the English translations (which also vary), and some mix both. Similarly, the dates assigned to Bresson's films deviate; some use the year of production, others the year of release. In a number of cases, we have standardized these details, but have largely observed the original intentions of the writers, which accounts for the variances. A glaring inconsistency in Bresson studies is the translation of his *Notes sur le cinématographe*, which has appeared in at least two editions, one titled *Notes on the Cinematographer*, the other *Notes on Cinematography*. Less important but worth noting is that the title of the Tolstoy story on which *L'Argent* is based is translated three different ways. In both cases, we have chosen not to standardize these references.

This volume was prepared and published over a year before the death of Robert Bresson on December 18, 1999. A few minor references have consequently been changed in this reprint of the original edition. As well, we have taken the opportunity to update the bibliography.

Contents

Robert Bresson

Introduction

> It is with something clean and precise that you
> will force the attention of inattentive eyes and ears.
>
> — ROBERT BRESSON, *Notes on Cinematography*

THE FILMS OF ROBERT BRESSON comprise a sparse canon of daunting beauty and difficulty. Aside from a short musical comedy, *Affaires publiques* (1934), a substantial part of which was recovered a decade ago, the French master made only thirteen films over forty years, a corpus of unparalleled stylistic consistency and influence. This collection of essays, the first in English on the director since Ian Cameron's *The Films of Robert Bresson* published in 1970, explores many aspects of Bresson's oeuvre, perhaps the most singular and uncompromising in the history of narrative cinema.

Designed to accompany a retrospective of Bresson's films, the book surveys various interpretive approaches to his work, beginning with the Christian humanism of André Bazin and the Brechtian reading of Susan Sontag, which, along with the fine, influential limning of "Bresson's universe" by Amédée Ayfre, form a kind of *locus classicus* of Bresson criticism. Many of the subsequent articles refer to these three seminal works, and illustrate various recent approaches to Bresson's films: philological (P. Adams Sitney), semantic or semiotic (Allen Thiher, T. Jefferson Kline), Lacanian (Keith Reader), and neoformalist (Kristin Thompson). This section of the book, which includes several pieces either written or translated especially for it and reprints of numerous important articles on Bresson, is bracketed by two recent exegeses of Bresson's work: the first, René Prédal's magisterial account of what he calls Bresson's "interior adventure," which also serves as a review of French literature on Bresson (Agel, Ayfre, Estève, Deleuze, Arnaud, Bergala et al), most of which awaits translation; the second, Raymond Durgnat's omnivorous, eccentric (and exciting) traversal of the diverse philosophical, theological and artistic precepts that inform Bresson's style and vision. These twin explications, with similar structures, oddly seem to echo and contend with each other—on the subject, for instance, of Zola's and Courbet's affinities with Bresson, or the lack of human touch in his cinema—though Durgnat is more speculative and ecumenical, Prédal more circumstantial.

Accompanied by three of the most significant interviews with Bresson (by Jean-Luc Godard and Michel Delahaye, Paul Schrader, and Michel Ciment respectively), and commentaries by over thirty filmmakers on his work, this survey encompasses most of the important subjects and issues that are central to Bresson criticism.

The Early Films

The discovery of Bresson's musical comedy *Affaires publiques*, long thought lost, has produced a small body of critical work, most of it descriptive. In his concise account of the film, William Johnson notes the incipience of certain elements—a "clipped" rhythm, non-expressive acting, simplicity and detachment—of Bresson's mature style. Critics are paying increasing attention to Bresson's first two features, *Les Anges du péché* (1943) and *Les Dames du Bois de Boulogne* (1945), the latter recognized by Richard Roud in his study of Jean-Marie Straub as a "universally seminal film." Long treated as works "apart" from Bresson's corpus—see, for instance, the essays of P. Adams Sitney and R. Bruce Elder—*Les Anges* and *Les Dames* are stylized, literary films, elegantly written by Giraudoux and Cocteau respectively, their highly wrought language the opposite of the spare, intoned speech Bresson would subsequently employ. Both are shot with noirish contrasts by Philippe Agostini (as compared to the muted greys of Bresson's succeeding films, shot by L.H. Burel); and acted with swank authority and—in the case of the indelible Maria Casarès in *Les Dames*—high theatricality (again as opposed to the inexpressive simplicity of the non-professional actors Bresson called "models" in his later works). Recently, critics and scholars have reinterpreted these early works, despite their marked differences from the rest of Bresson's oeuvre, as either foreshadowings of his mature style and vision, or as the first substantial expressions of the same, emphasizing their interiority and economy—Raymond Durgnat here calls them "relentlessly precise"—and their themes of sacrifice and redemption. (Even P. Adams Sitney, who sees them more as products of the French cinema of that period than of an auteurial impulse, writes: "If we scrutinize them, we can find embryonic traces of some of Bresson's later achievements.") Tony Pipolo's complex interpretation of *Les Anges du péché* (a chapter of his upcoming book on

Bresson), while careful not to impose a Bressonian design on the film with the benefit of hindsight, demonstrates that it "is the first instance of the theme and moral imperative that drives all of Bresson's narratives." Similarly, René Prédal finds in *Les Dames du Bois de Boulogne* the first marked instance of what he calls "the parable of closed space" or imprisonment that is so central to Bresson's vision; and Gregory Markopoulos notes Bresson's use of "exaggerated sound" in the film, a prefiguration of Bresson's process of selecting and "orchestrating" natural sounds in his later work.

The Emergence of the Bresson Style

Les Anges du péché and *Les Dames du Bois de Boulogne* can now be seen as part of the "unified field" of Bresson's work, but it was with *Diary of a Country Priest* (1951) that Bresson developed the severe, minimalist style with which he became identified and which altered only slightly over the years, though his subjects and sources ranged widely. David Bordwell writes elsewhere that Bresson established a "pre-existent stylistic system which can reduce almost any subject to its own terms." This "system," which Bresson called *le cinématographe*, arose out of his desire to make the cinema express the ineffable, to give it what he called "an interior movement." Bresson's determination to inscribe in the profane imagery of the cinema the spiritual quandary of isolated people in search of grace led him to remove from his films everything he considered extraneous and false. The concept of *dépouillement*, with its connotations of stripping or paring away—sometimes to the point of deprivation—best describes this ascetic process.

The Pascalian aphorisms Bresson gathered in his book, *Notes on Cinematography*, distinguish between his system of *le cinématographe* which he associated with abstraction and precision, with music and painting, from that of *cinéma*, which he associated with theatre, with fraudulent realism, vulgarity, and facile psychology. Bresson's terse, runic observations are, as J.M.G. Le Clézio asserts in his introduction to the *Notes*, "for the invention of a new language, for perfection." (Many have mistaken Bresson's strictures as scripture, taking their counsel as a kind of spiritual doctrine, when he seems to have written and assembled them in a pragmatic spirit of self-exhortation.)

The style Bresson evolved to express his vision of the quest for redemption in a barbaric world, the "new language" Le Clézio refers to, can be defined in terms of denial, renunciation, and avoidance. (Bresson wrote admiringly of Debussy's playing the piano with the lid down, an apt metaphor for his own approach.) His images are starkly composed, flattened, and stress frontality in a manner that has been compared to Byzantine iconography, and to the paintings of Piero della Francesca,

Giotto, and Vermeer. (In his *Notes*, Bresson writes: "Flatten my images (as if ironing them), *without attenuating them*.") He scrupulously avoids establishing shots, minimizes the movement of both camera and players, limits camera angles and distances, and severely reduces the number and types of settings, abstaining at all costs from pictorialism and the traditional "landscape shot." (Bresson: "Not beautiful photography, not beautiful images, but necessary images and photography.") The resulting environment becomes a neutral ground, a *cantus firmus*, for Bresson's charged images of gestures and glances, of isolated objects and empty spaces, of parts of the body (hands and feet especially) and the oft-remarked doors he frequently fixes on—never merely doors in Bresson's cinema, but portals for the soul.

Sound

Bresson's use of sound is similarly unique, and one of the most admired and analyzed in all cinema. His statements on sound have become a kind of theology for some filmmakers, so contrary are they to the conventions of traditional cinema. Bresson instructs: "When a sound can replace an image, cut the image or neutralize it. The ear goes more towards the within, the eye towards the outer." From *Diary of a Country Priest* onwards—most markedly in the employment of natural sounds in *A Man Escaped* (1956) and the celebrated jousting tournament in *Lancelot du Lac* (1974)—Bresson increasingly uses sound as a replacement for, rather than an adjunct to or reinforcement of, his images. (Bresson's aesthetic emphasizes the process of divination, here sensory intuition.) Just as he often focuses on "vacant" spaces, the camera lingering after a character has departed, for example, Bresson emphasizes silence: "Be sure of having used to the full all that is communicated by immobility and silence." André Bazin famously asks: "Is *Journal* just a silent film with spoken titles?"

Though almost every writer on Bresson comments on his use of sound—it is all but unavoidable—Sitney's discussion is exceptionally specific and intelligent, and the clarity and suggestiveness of Lindley Hanlon's analysis of Bresson's use of "sound as symbol," as a source of emblematic meaning, in *Mouchette* (1967) reveals why her book on Bresson is so indispensable.

Voice is one of the central uses of sound in most cinema, and, again, Bresson's employment of voice is both unique and complex. Corresponding with the gradual elimination of music in his films, his dialogue becomes increasingly laconic; the austere *Diary* seems positively loquacious compared to the taciturn late films. (It requires over 850 subtitles, where *Mouchette* and *L'Argent*—both admittedly shorter films—require 225 and 256 respectively.) Bresson's use of voice-over, particularly in such films as *Diary* and *Pickpocket*, is also singular, even strange, and has prompted considerable analysis. André Bazin's essay on the radical "aesthetic principles"of *Diary* explores the "originality and boldness" of Bresson's stylistics with such noble lucidity that it has become a classic of film criticism. Bazin's is one of the first and most observant analyses of what became a distinguishing feature of Bresson's cinema—a strange one in a process of ascesis, in that it involves a repetition, a doubling: the pleonastic duplication of text and image (the curé's journal in voice-over describing what the images show us). Nick Browne's essay on *Journal* (unfortunately less well known than his excellent work on the "rhetoric"of *Au hasard Balthazar*) examines this peculiar device and how "disjunction, independence, interrogation, and even negation of the image, by the sense of the text, is as much a feature as illustration or duplication." T. Jefferson Kline's ingenious analysis of *Pickpocket* emphasizes the unreliability of the voice-over, how the image or the inferred narrative often directly contradict what the eponymous petty criminal tells us.

Models

Perhaps the most controversial element of Bresson's "system" is his use of what he calls "models": non-professional actors trained in neutral line readings, automatic gestures, and emotional inexpressiveness. (The "Bresson face"—hieratic, impassive, androgynous if not sexless—is famous.) Jean-Pierre Oudart has referred to the "Sadeian rapport" between Bresson and his models, which can be inferred from the director's note on his acting ideal: "Models who have become automatic (everything weighed, measured, timed, repeated ten, twenty times) and are then dropped in the medium of the events of your film—their relations with the objects and persons around them will be *right*, because they will not be *thought*." Bresson puts his models through dozens of takes to achieve just the right lack of inflection in a line, the precise downcast look, the exact automatic (therefore "natural") movement. (Like Mizoguchi, Bresson is a cardinal case of great art being born of cruel perfectionism. The reminiscence of L. H. Burel, cinematographer on four of Bresson's films, attests to this fact.)

Though Claude Laydu, indelible as the curé in *Diary* whose attempts to assuage the suffering of others meet with malice and indifference, and François Leterrier, his visage as blank as the prison walls that enclose him in *A Man Escaped*, are the initial instances of Bresson's use of "virginal" models, it is in *Pickpocket* that the practice reached its first apogee. Of the many discussions of the aesthetic impulse behind and the effect of Bresson's approach to performance, Kline's analysis of *Pickpocket* has some of the most illuminating perceptions, particularly about its service in Bresson's attempt to "detoxify" his art and therefore to avoid the inevitable intertextuality that conventional acting involves. Susan Sontag sees Bresson's singular use of actors as a neo-Brechtian device striving for "an effect of strangeness," while Sitney regards that distancing as a function of Bresson's duplication of "the visual experience of memory." Kent Jones's materialist reading of the comportment of Bresson's models emphasizes the way "Bresson isolates and elevates one of the most constant and beautiful of all human characteristics, curiosity about one's fellow men and women, by practising it with his camera, and reminds us in the process that such curiosity is active rather than passive." Babette Mangolte's evocative screenplay for her new film explores the profound effect the making of *Pickpocket* had on one of its non-professional actors. And in his essay on *Au hasard Balthazar*, Michael Haneke claims the film, in its use of a donkey as protagonist, is "the clearest and most coherent expression"of Bresson's much-criticized "model theory," the blankness of Balthazar transforming him into a tabula rasa "for the viewers' thoughts and feelings."

Music, Painting, Literature

Bresson is frequently praised as one of the few directors to have raised cinema to the level of the other arts (cf. the comments of Duras, Tarkovsky, L'Herbier). Schooled in painting, philosophy, and the classics, he reveals a profound love for and knowledge of the history of music, painting and literature in both his writing and his films. His *Notes on Cinematography* are full of musical metaphors, and references to musicians (Lipatti) and composers (Purcell, Vivaldi, Debussy). Perhaps surprisingly then, he uses music sparingly in his films, particularly after *Diary of a Country Priest*. In one of the most quoted of his *Notes*, he instructs: "No music as accompaniment, support or reinforcement. *No music at all*," and then modifies the command: "Except, of course, the music played by visible instruments." As with Bresson's use of sound, almost every commentator included here touches upon his employment of music—Sontag, Sitney, Hanlon, Ayfre, and Allen Thiher, for example—frequently treating it as a semantic code. Others (Rivette, Malle, Jones) compare him to composers (Bach, Webern). Sitney's passing comparison of Bresson to Messiaen is astute and reminds one of the analogy between the former's *A Man Escaped* and the latter's "Quartet for the End of Time," both products of their respective maker's experience in prisoner of war camps. Donald Richie succinctly explores three of the most famous instances of Bresson's use of music: Mozart's Mass in C Minor in *A Man Escaped*, Monteverdi's Vespers in *Mouchette*, and Schubert's piano sonata no. 20 in *Au hasard Balthazar*.

Bresson turned from painting to filmmaking—Prédal and Durgnat both have much to say about the connection between the two—and, again, the *Notes on*

Cinematography are replete with comparisons of film to painting: "We have to paint, and it is through painting that everything will emerge," etc. Many critics have discerned art historical references in his compositions, among them Ayfre and Thiher, both of whom see the influence of Georges de la Tour in his work. (One easily countenances the comparison to painters of "flatness" or "minimalism" such as Vermeer, Mondrian, and Giotto, but the baroque chiaroscuro of de la Tour, and the "mannerist" attenuations of El Greco and Modigliani, which Robert Droguet has posed as analogies, are surprising references.)

Much Bresson criticism has centred on his adaptations of literature: a section of a Diderot novel, two Bernanos novels, four works by Dostoevsky (if one includes *Crime and Punishment*, the unacknowledged source of *Pickpocket*, and *The Idiot*, which inspired *Balthazar*), a Tolstoy short story, André Devigny's autobiographical account, the Arthurian legends, and so on. Several essays included here concentrate on Bresson's adaptations, many of them in a highly original way. In an excellent example, Kline reads Bresson's disavowal of the Dostoevsky and Barrington texts in *Pickpocket* as one of the film's suppressions. In another, Kristin Thompson compares *Lancelot du Lac* to its source material, noting that Bresson's many amendments accentuate his despairing vision. Mireille Latil Le Dantec compares the works and worlds of Dostoevsky and Bresson, cataloguing their similar images, motifs, and concerns. Though according primacy to three films derived from the Russian writer—*Pickpocket, Une femme douce,* and *Four Nights of a Dreamer*—she provocatively discerns "Dostoevskian elements" in many other Bresson works, including the first two features. And in a patrician, epigrammatic critique of *L'Argent*, Alberto Moravia contrasts Tolstoy's and Bresson's notions of good and evil, and how both embody national characteristics.

A Cinema of Paradox

Bresson's obdurate vision and style produced a cinema of paradox, in which the denial of emotion creates emotionally overwhelming works, minimalism becomes plenitude, the withholding of information makes for narrative density, fragmentation evokes a sense of the world's wholeness, and attention to "the surface of the work," as Bresson called it, produces inexhaustible depth. Physical imprisonment becomes a metaphor for spiritual release and a chaste aesthetic generates potent sensuality. Interiority is manifested in a "language of things," an intense materialism transforms objects and gestures into signifiers of the transcendent, and documentary naturalism becomes abstract formalism. "All is Grace," as the ending of *Diary* states, yet suicide is heretically posited as a redeeming way out of a bare, cruel world (*Mouchette* [1967]; *Le Diable probablement* [1977]), and that barbaric world can become a place suffused with spiritual mystery and the possibility of redemption.

Bresson's work is riven by other paradoxes and contradictions: for example, between his almost neorealist method and its demand for authentic settings, and his extensive use of studio shooting in *A Man Escaped*; between his literary sources and the musical or painterly quality of his films (words are mistrusted in ways that not even Godard could imagine); and his rejection of "supporting" music and the analogical use of Schubert in *Au hasard Balthazar* (1966). Despite Bresson's avoidance of pictorial effects and traditional landscape shots, the desolate world of *Diary of a Country Priest*, with its glowering skies and barren trees, and the radiant nocturnal Seine in *Four Nights of a Dreamer* (1971) both have an unearthly beauty that has earned them a place among cinema's instantly recognizable terrains. His impeccable editing, with shots of individual solidity that abut and conjoin—that feel like *objects* laid hard and neat side by side—produces the crisp, clipped cadences of a clavichord (perhaps playing his beloved Bach), but the films often seem to flow (dream-like in *Diary* and *Four Nights*, inexorably, with the dark undertow of a nightmare, in *Le Diable probablement*). Conversely, the editing is often quick and analytical—shots come in flurries, their interstices missing—but the films always maintain a grave corporeality. They also feel premeditated, highly finished in their precision, but Bresson apparently worked instinctively, often with little planning: "My manner of working has stayed the same," he said in one of his last interviews, "nothing's calculated in advance. Art doesn't exist without surprises."

With the introduction of colour in his films, beginning with *Une femme douce*, Bresson's vision darkened, his growing pessimism disclosed in an increasingly voluptuous rendering of the world. (One might say sobriety invites intoxication.) The flatness of his compositions and his emphasis on dedramatization place Bresson in the tradition of modernism, yet his universe often seems archaic. Bresson's Arthurian tale, *Lancelot du Lac*, seems oddly contemporary, while his ethereal *Four Nights of a Dreamer* with its dreamy beatniks, *bateau-mouche*, and bossa nova, appears less voguish than courtly, medieval. (Frequently in Bresson, anachronism coincides with obsessive, documentary-like realism.) Given these many paradoxes, it is little wonder that commentary on Bresson's films often has a provisional quality, and frequently focuses on the simultaneity of opposites in his work (e.g. absence and presence—of characters within the frame, of hope, of God).

In his dense, elegant essay, Keith Reader enumerates other examples of paradox in Bresson's cinema, and inventively employs Lacan to discuss this interplay of absence and presence in three of his films.

Pascal and Jansenism

Bresson was greatly influenced by Jansenism, the ascetic school of Catholicism concerned with free will and predestination, most commonly identified with Pascal. (Pascal's wager will be known to cinephiles as the philosophical crux of Rohmer's *Ma nuit chez Maud*; the German critic Peter Buchka named his study of Bresson after the wager, emphasizing the theme of predestination in his work.) Long uncontested, an article of faith for many Bresson commentators, the Jansenist influence, both acknowledged and disputed by the director, has been challenged by many recent critics. For instance, Jonathan Rosenbaum and Kent Jones both forcefully argue that Bresson is less a Jansenist than a modernist and materialist. After examining many philosophical and theological tenets, Raymond Durgnat seems to settle on a kind of dark Christian existentialism, rather than Jansenism, to define what he calls Bresson's "negative vision." But there is no denying that Pascal exerted a major influence on Bresson, in both the substance of his thought and the rhetorical forms he chose to express it. (Louis Malle: "The construction of *Pickpocket*? Reread Pascal.") In a largely overlooked essay, Mirella Jona Affron convincingly argues that "the consistency of Bresson's position and expression, of syntax and vocabulary (on questions of theatre and film, narrative, acting, editing, sound, spectatorship), from his first extensive published pronouncements (1946), to the publication of his observations on filmmaking, *Notes sur le cinématographe* (1975), to the most recent interviews, maintains an unbroken link to his films and to Pascal's art of persuasion."

Transcendentalism versus Materialism

No art form would seem less suited to expressing the transcendent, of eliciting and refining what Calvin called the *sensus divinatus*, than film. Its fealty to narrative and realism, the high cost and collaborative nature of its "apparatus," and its reliance on complex technology all dictate against the pure, individual expression of the "holy" that one can find in painting, music, or literature. As noted above, Bresson attempted to force its instruments and intransigent realism to yield the numinous (what he named "the divine"), developing his "cinématographe" to those ends. Because of his "spiritual" subjects and monastic aesthetic, his Jansenist influences, and the often mysterious, ethereal quality of his imagery, Bresson has long been identified as a "transcendental" filmmaker. Paul Schrader's influential book, *Transcendental Style in Film: Ozu, Bresson, Dreyer*, in which the author's Calvinism finds a parallel in Bresson's Jansenism, sealed and certified this interpretation. (Recently republished, it remains a central work in English on Bresson.) However, because "transcendentalism" is so inchoate and capacious a concept, it has become increasingly suspect, particularly when applied to Bresson. (What does the "transcendentalism" of such disparate directors as Brakhage, Tarkovsky, Yanagimachi, Sokurov, Ozu, and Bresson have in common?) Criticism that focuses on Bresson's transcendentalism often tends to be vague, elusive, lacking in detail and visual evidence. T. Jefferson Kline, who manages to be both semiotically precise and philosophically abstract, notes, for example, that the critics who argue that the ambiguous ending of *Pickpocket* denotes Michel's spiritual conversion regrettably reject visual evidence "in favour of the invisible and the inexplicable." (But then, as with Pascal's wager and its leap of faith, how could such "evidence," which is of this world, be used to prove something as "invisible and inexplicable" as spiritual conversion? Raymond Durgnat poses some answers to this vexing question.)

Against this transcendentalist approach, several critics cite Bresson as a clear and supreme example of a materialist filmmaker, one whose images are solid and ineluctable as facts, whose use of sound places us in a dense, *material* world, and whose editing is based on principles of the relations between things, not abstractions. (The title of *Pickpocket* was originally *Incertitude*; the former, shorn of its modifying article, has a solidity, a thingness, where the latter is abstract, indistinct.) Ironically, like transcendentalism, materialism can mean many things (including historical materialism, with its emphasis on economic substructures—something few critics have broached in Bresson, even in analyses of the ostensibly Marxist *L'Argent*), and each critic's sense of Bresson's materialism differs. The neoformalism of Kristin Thompson's superb work on *Lancelot du Lac* and the semiotic approach of Lindley Hanlon in her examination of sound in *Mouchette* reflect such a difference.

The transcendental and the materialist are not necessarily contentious or mutually exclusive. Bresson said of *A Man Escaped*: "I was hoping to make a film about objects which would at the same time have a soul. That is to say, to reach the latter through the former." In his Lacanian analysis of three Bresson films, Keith Reader interprets the voice-over device in *Diary of a Country Priest* not as "nebulously metaphysical," but as "material . . . in one sense at least not metaphysical at all. The priest's simultaneous writing and reading . . . place before us language in its materiality, with its hesitations and the instruments of its production." But Reader insistently makes compatible the theological (here "mystical," as in Pascal and Weil) and the psychoanalytical (here materialist, as in Lacan). His convergence of the "transcendental and the immanent" in *Pickpocket*, for example, underscores his dialectical approach; this and other similar dichotomies are, for him, "not one[s] which can find no synthesis or resolution."

René Prédal and Mireille Latil Le Dantec both offer catalogues of images, gestures, and motifs in Bresson's cinema—inventories, in their palpability and emphasis on *things* as evidence, indicate a materialist orientation. (Durgnat hints that Bresson's cinema has affinities with the *chosisme* of the *nouveau roman*, with its obsessive description of objects.) But how often in Bresson's films are objects and gestures—perceptible, factual, seemingly unambiguous—suddenly, mysteriously transformed into something ineffable: signifiers of an absent force or being? (That "absent" need not be inferred as spiritual; Kline reads the absent in *Pickpocket* psychologically, as something suppressed.) And Bresson's notoriously ambiguous endings—think of *Les Dames du Bois de Boulogne*, *Pickpocket*, *Mouchette*, *L'Argent*—obstruct materialist readings, though their physical details are often precise.

Bresson's montage lends itself to both interpretive approaches. Working intuitively and precisely—he rarely shoots more than he needs, and edits in a screening room, not at an editing table—Bresson structures his "modest" images into a unique syntax or "écriture," as he calls it, that emphasizes relationships between images. "The flatter an image is, the less it expresses," he says, "the more easily it is transformed in contact with other images." And: "It is necessary for the images to have something in common, to participate in a kind of union." (His ideas about "relationships" or "unions" have strange parallels with Eisenstein's theory of montage, a materialist manifesto if ever there was one.) Adhering to his adage, "Not artful, but agile," Bresson's montage stresses vigour, rhythm, elision, compression. Transitions are often left out, narrative "climaxes" suppressed, and important events reported, alluded to, or left offscreen. A few enigmatic shots—the table falling over and the scarf drifting down from a window in *Une femme douce* (1969), for example—signify a key incident (in this case, the wife's suicide) which the viewer discerns only by decoding the conjunctions of images. This elliptical style demands of an audience an act of divination. Bresson: "Hide the ideas, but so that people find them. The most important will be the most hidden."

Bresson's montage, in its immaculate precision, elicits close analysis. But, as with much great cinema (Mizoguchi, Murnau), effect ultimately eludes analysis. Meaning, generated by a detailed "attention to surface," becomes mysterious, unfixed, ineffable. Which can lead one back to transcendentalism. Several pieces here, including those already cited, determinedly and successfully merge the two approaches, as the very title of Allen Thiher's study of *A Man Escaped*, "The Semiotics of Grace," suggests.

Grace, Pessimism, Despair

A central issue in Bresson criticism, closely related to the debates over his Jansenism, is his pessimism. Early Bresson commentators, though noting the bleakness of his world, with its emphasis on spiritual and physical confinement, focused on the possibility of grace, taking the famous final phrase of *Diary of a*

Country Priest, "All is Grace," as the definitive statement of his vision. After the twin masterpieces of *Mouchette* and *Au hasard Balthazar*, with their almost unbearable compendiums of cruelty against innocents, belief in Bresson's redemptive faith seemed increasingly untenable. His pessimism deepened in the colour films that followed, becoming "global" in the ecological anxiety of *Le Diable probablement*—its very title signalling a kind of abdication to despair.

Bresson's final film, *L'Argent*, transposes a Tolstoy story to contemporary Paris, and turns it into a terse and chilling indictment of capitalism and modernity. A young man's unwitting crime sets off "an avalanche of evil" that leads to mass murder. Whether there is the chance of expiation at the end is debatable—visual "evidence" is more cryptic here than in any of Bresson's other films—but the possibility of grace seems utterly remote. Little wonder that René Prédal, who offers some of the best writing extant on *L'Argent*, bluntly states: "The bleakness of Bresson's films is total."

Many critics have had problems with the films of Bresson's "late period," beginning with *Une femme douce*. It is no accident that this period coincides with his use of colour. Sontag states in her essay, written in the early sixties, that "it is almost impossible to imagine a Bresson film in colour." I have already noted the paradox that with the introduction of colour in his films, Bresson's vision seemed to darken; the greater the pessimism, the more sensuous his rendering of the world. (Magny suggests that "sexuality occupies a stronger place in [his] work the more [it] becomes pessimistic.") Many writers included here struggle with this paradox, and with his pessimism. Michael Dempsey, an ex-seminarian, writing about the "abounding despair" in Bresson's late period, worries that the pessimism of *Le Diable probablement* is so utter as to invite a kind of paralyzing "creative sterility." Dempsey's piece was written before *L'Argent*, a film that more than one critic has compared to Pasolini's *Salò*. (In an essay published elsewhere, Mark Le Fanu contrasts the pessimism of Tarkovsky [in *Nostalghia*] with that of Bresson [in *L'Argent*] and finds the latter unconvincing.) One of the best and most committed Bresson critics, Richard Roud, argues that *Le Diable* offers, in its sheer beauty and new-found emotion (as opposed to formal abstraction), a "redemption of despair." And Raymond Durgnat, though attending less to the late films in which Bresson's pessimism is most apparent, masterfully explores the darkness of his "negative vision."

Bresson and Other Filmmakers: Affinity and Influence

Perhaps because Bresson has been contradictory or elusive about his knowledge of cinema, not much has been written about the influence of other directors on his work. (His partiality to Chaplin and to *Brief Encounter* gives one pause, as does, in a different way, Jane Sloan's intriguing contention in her invaluable book, *Robert Bresson: A Guide to Sources and References*, that he was influenced by the films of Germaine Dulac.) André Bazin, Tony Pipolo, and P. Adams Sitney credit Renoir's influence on Bresson, the latter citing *La Règle du jeu* as "an abiding inspiration to Bresson." Sontag suggests that "Bresson is really more like Cocteau than appears—an ascetic Cocteau, Cocteau divesting himself of sensuousness, Cocteau without poetry." Several critics note Bresson's early similarities to René Clair, including Durgnat, who situates Bresson as one of "four poets of solitude," the other three being Tati, Melville, and Franju. And André Bazin suggests, in one of the more famous controversies regarding Bresson's "voice-over" device, that Melville used it first in *Le Silence de la mer*.

If direct influence is too fraught a subject, that of affinity is less so; one could propose a number of directors to whom Bresson might be profitably compared: Eisenstein, Hitchcock, Rohmer spring to mind, but there are many others. (The Becker of *Le Trou* is frequently invoked.) Though often classified with Yasujiro Ozu and Carl-Theodor Dreyer, as in Paul Schrader's study of the three directors, Bresson is in fact more rigorous than either. (Even Schrader seems reluctant to turn his Bresson/Ozu diptych into a triptych by appending Dreyer, finding the purity of the former directors' respective styles sullied by psychological and stylistic expressionism in Dreyer's work. On the other hand, Durgnat sees many formal similarities between Dreyer and Bresson.) One need only compare Bresson's version of the trial of Joan of Arc with Dreyer's to perceive the rigour of the French master's approach; as spare as it is, Dreyer's film can seem melodramatic when compared with Bresson's. The parched, parsimonious quality of Bresson's *Procès de Jeanne d'Arc* (1962) is indicated in its absence of water or fluids, where Dreyer's topography of mortified flesh sluices with ablutions of blood, tears, and spittle. "For want of truth," Bresson notes dryly, "the public gets hooked on the false. Falconetti's way of casting her eyes to heaven, in Dreyer's film, used to make people weep." (Bresson's Joan keeps her eyes down, not just to signify her modesty before God, but to signal that she is *not* Falconetti.) Ironically, Bresson's *Procès* is both the *ne plus ultra* of his aesthetic and his least liked film, as the negative comments of Sontag and Burel here, and the marked lack of critical scrutiny of the film, aside from Jean-Pierre Oudart's widely anthologized essay on "the suture," attest. Conversely, Dreyer's *Gertrud*—its compositions derived from "the Danish Vermeer," Hammershøi—seems sparer than its counterpart in Bresson's cinema, *Une femme douce*. (In her exceptional analysis of the latter, Mirella Jona Affron argues that it constitutes Bresson's *ars poetica*, and *Gertrud* has much the same status in Dreyer's work.)

Rather than a fellow "spiritualist" like Dreyer, one might suggest Rainer Werner Fassbinder as a director whose vision frequently coincides with Bresson's.

(He revered Bresson, and included a clip from *Le Diable probablement* in his *The Third Generation* as an hommage.) Dissimilar in most ways—the one a prolific melodramatist, the other a frugal minimalist—the directors shared a sense of the world in which the spurned, exploited and afflicted are as inclined to iniquity as are their tormentors. (Bresson may see both persecutor and persecuted—Balthazar aside—as similarly "immersed in sin," while Fassbinder would be more "profane" in his appraisal of their debility, but both would consider human disposition to cruelty as pervasive and inevitable.) One could readily pair certain of their films: Fassbinder's *Martha* with Bresson's *Une femme douce*, *In a Year of 13 Moons* with *Au hasard Balthazar*, *Fox and his Friends* with *L'Argent*, *The Merchant of Four Seasons* with *Diary of a Country Priest*. Bresson's contention that his lucidity is often mistaken for pessimism could just as well apply to Fassbinder; they are both like Charles in *Le Diable probablement*, whose "sickness" is that he "sees too clearly."

As the connection with Fassbinder reveals, Bresson's influence on other directors is easily demonstrable. Indeed, as the final section of the book, "Filmmakers on Bresson," illustrates, aside from Godard, Bresson is probably the most influential post-war French director. The introduction to that section explores his influence, which has extended across several generations, numerous countries and disparate cultures, and incompatible aesthetics.

Biography

Much Bresson criticism invokes "the Absent"—or what Keith Reader calls "the unsayable"—as a controlling metaphor of his cinema, and one must resort to it out of frustration when dealing with the most recalcitrant area of Bresson studies: his biography. Bresson is as renowned in his way for his vehement privacy as Chris Marker. He states in the famous interview with Jean-Luc Godard and Michel Delahaye: "Must one look at the life of someone to judge his work? This is his work. And that is his life." In directing critics' attention away from his life to his films, Bresson has secreted and concealed even basic details of his biography. For example, his birthdate fluctuates in reports between 1901 and 1911. (Some have speculated that the youthful looking Bresson hoped that vagueness about his age would make producers more inclined to fund his films, especially his long cherished project, *La Genèse*.)

The memories of such collaborators as L. H. Burel (included here) and Roland Monod give us some idea of his working methods, his unyielding control and intransigent perfectionism. But, aside from conspicuous lineaments—two marriages, the latter to his assistant director, Mylène van der Mersch, after his first wife died; the abandoned projects, including a life of Ignatius of Loyola and a chapter of

Dino de Laurentiis's film *The Bible*—there are few biographical details that help illuminate his art. One longs, for instance, for a commentary on his painting, which he abandoned because it made him "too nervous,"and how it might have influenced his filmmaking. (Can one infer that it falls into the tradition of Cézanne or even of cubism, given Bresson's aesthetic penchant for fragmentation and arrangement?) Also valuable would be a complete account of his experience as a prisoner of war during World War II, which shaped *A Man Escaped*. (Typically, he relied more on the experiences of another P.O.W., André Devigny, for the film's narrative.) One wonders too about the striking parallels between Bresson and fellow Catholics Messiaen and Julien Green, the latter of whose *Journals* have been compared to Pascal's *Pensées*, and whose sombre purity of style seems to share an affinity with Bresson's. (Bresson has disputed that Green worked with him on a script about Ignatius, though Green writes at length about this collaboration in his *Journals*. René Prédal suggests these were parallel, not collaborative, projects.)

Numerous critics have noted that Bresson was long in psychoanalysis, and even cast his analyst as the curé of Torcy in *Diary of a Country Priest*. But there have been precious few readings of his films which attempt psychological inquiry. While René Prédal contends that "his films bear no trace of the phantasms of his imagination, nor of a plunge into the arcana of the unconscious," Richard Roud frequently noted the "sexual substratum" of Bresson's cinema, but never hazarded a full investigation of this provocative theme. As T. Jefferson Kline suggests in his reading of suppression and fetishism in *Pickpocket*, that film has often been interpreted as a work in which the spiritual and the erotic coincide, indeed seem equivalent.

As often is the case, the void of Bresson's biography has been filled by speculation, apocrypha and supposition. Glancing details, for example regarding his correspondence with George Cukor about *Lancelot du Lac*, become magnified in importance because of the dearth of other information. Bresson's dictum, "Hide the ideas, but so that people find them. The most important will be the most hidden," suddenly takes on new meaning in this context. Any biographer of Bresson will certainly face a struggle—no doubt less spiritual than materialist—in face of this deterring lack of personal detail.

One might see Bresson's resolve to avoid scrutiny of his private life as part of his determination to "force the attention of inattentive eyes and ears": psychology is, after all, anathema in his *cinématographe*, and he no doubt saw, even before the cult of celebrity became as pervasive as it is, that biography is often the refuge of the indolent or glib critic. In its every aspect, Bresson's art is an entreaty away from distraction to a kind of composed, penetrative intelligence, and his obstinate search for this precision produced among the most exalted poetry in all cinema.

Lancelot du Lac

JONATHAN ROSENBAUM

The Last Filmmaker:
A Local, Interim Report

Two types of film: those that employ the resources
of the theater (actors, directors, etc.) and use the camera
in order to *reproduce*; those that employ the resources
of cinematography and use the camera to *create*.

Cinematography: new way of writing, therefore of feeling.

— ROBERT BRESSON, *Notes on Cinematography*

MONG THE PEOPLE of my acquaintance who know the most about film,
I doubt there are many—if any—who do not consider Robert Bresson to
be the greatest of all living filmmakers. Because Bresson is currently in his
nineties, the possibility of his making another movie—the last was *L'Argent* in
1983—is highly unlikely. And the issue of whether his work will survive at all, in
spite of its major importance, is worth discussing, because it is highly doubtful
that most of it "translates" to video.

The issue of why Bresson's work doesn't register on video is difficult and
complex, but for starters I would suggest that two central determining factors are
sound presence and the framed image. A friend has pointed out that in optimal
home viewing situations, both of these obstacles can be overcome with a good
projection system and a good set of speakers, but the fact remains that few viewers
have this sort of equipment at their disposal; and even if they do, few Bresson
films are available on laserdisc, and only a handful of his major works can be seen
on video. I can only report that *L'Argent*—a shocking and devastating work like
few others—all but ceases to exist on video; and though both *A Man Escaped*
(1956) and *Pickpocket* (1959) seem to fare somewhat better in that format, this may

be the case only for people who have already seen these films in theatres. I should also mention that a recent opportunity to see *A Man Escaped* on a big screen had more impact for me than all the Bresson movies I've ever seen on video combined, including *A Man Escaped*. (Part of this difference is surely tied to the disparate formal relationships between sound and image in the two media which no amount of high-tech equipment can ever fully overcome—the fact that film sound is experienced as being in the "background," "behind" the image, and video sound is experienced as being in the "foreground.")

A retrospective of Bresson's films in 35mm prints therefore offers a rare opportunity to come to grips with a master whose awesome power is virtually inaccessible to most people nowadays. For those not yet acquainted with this giant, I can guarantee that an extended look at his work will transform their understanding of what the art of film can be and do—and incidentally explain why any browsing of that work on video could never begin to function as an adequate substitute.

It's worth noting that the current dominance of the star system and the practice of home viewing are intimately intertwined. If a fundamental formal element in film art is the framed image, the absence of a clearly demarcated frame in most videos virtually rules out certain kinds of visual content that are dependent on frames. Stars tend to survive this loss because they usually need only to be recognized in order to register and because they traditionally are placed in the centre of frames, making the precise conditions of the space around them secondary. But if shots are designed as complex expressive units to be juxtaposed with other shots that precede and follow them (an art that Bresson calls "cinematography"), paring away portions of those shots—the necessary corollary of most video viewing, which entails eliminating the space around the edges of the film frame—interferes with that design. (It's worth adding that Bresson started out as a painter, and many of his notions about his art seem derived from painting.) And the fact that Bresson's complex designs depend on a refusal to use actors of any kind, much less stars—a decision that winds up affecting everything else about his work—already begins to explain why his art is so removed from the options of commercial movies in general and video in particular.

In place of actors, Bresson uses what he calls "models"—people with no acting experience who are rigorously trained by him to express as little as possible, in their movements, expressions, gestures, and line readings. The reasons for this procedure are actually quite simple, though so much at loggerheads with usual moviemaking practice that they require some getting used to and initially may appear simply perverse. For Bresson, the expressiveness willed by actors, appropriate and necessary to theatre, competes with the expressiveness of sounds and images that are under the control of a filmmaker. They also compete with the expressiveness of what people *are* as opposed to how they wish to represent themselves—their material and spiritual essence as human beings as opposed to their cover stories. Although the choice of models is of paramount importance to Bresson—and many of his models, as luminous and memorable as most stars that one could name, have gone on to become actors and even stars with other directors (most notably, Dominique Sanda after her appearance in Bresson's *Une femme douce*)—the beauty and power of these individuals are qualities that emerge from the films themselves; they are never a matter of willed "performances." As Bresson expresses it himself in his *Notes on Cinematography*, a slim volume of reflections that resemble Chinese fortune cookie messages in their brevity, "BEING (models) rather than SEEMING (actors)."

This doesn't mean that Bresson downplays his models or "plays up" his sounds and images. On the contrary, his approach toward the brute reality of sounds and images is every bit as elemental as his approach toward people. Like his usual practice of filming in natural locations rather than studio spaces, it points to an old-fashioned sense of craft and a fundamental trust in—and reliance on—material reality. The second aphorism in his *Notes on Cinematography* reads, "The faculty of using my resources well diminishes when their number grows." In other words, the fewer the elements that he uses, the more he can do with them. By the same token, the less his sounds, images, and models express individually, the more he can control them; and the more he can control them, the more they can express—especially in tandem with one another. ("The flatter an image is," Bresson states in his book, "the less it expresses, the more easily it is transformed in contact with other images.")

More an essentialist than a minimalist, Bresson can nevertheless yield a maximal emotional effect with a minimum of means. From *The Trial of Joan of Arc* (1962) on, all of his features, with the arguable exception of *Four Nights of a Dreamer* (1972), are essentially tragedies, brimming with despair and often shattering in their effect; many of his late films—most notably *Mouchette* (1967), *Une femme douce* (1969), and *The Devil Probably* (1977)—are preoccupied with suicide (and the latter film was once banned for teenagers in France as "an incitement to suicide"); yet it is not unexceptional to find him focusing on an actor's feet or hands for long stretches. The mystery of human—and in *Au hasard Balthazar* (1966), the life story of a donkey, non-human—personality lies at the heart of his work, but his means of arriving at that mystery is always concrete and precise.

Another central principle of economy that Bresson follows is to replace an image with a sound whenever possible. (Two of his reasons are cited in his 1966 interview with Jean-Luc Godard: because "the ear is much more creative than the eye" and "you must leave the spectator free.") In *A Man Escaped*—a meticulous account of a prison escape by a French resistance fighter in Lyon, based on an autobiographical account by André Devigny—this principle extends to the hero's offscreen narration, which alludes to certain narrative developments occurring over weeks and months (in contrast to the present-tense quality of all the seen material), as well as the remarkable use of offscreen sounds to convey Devigny's sense of the world outside his cell, sounds that become part and parcel of his relentless and obsessive will toward freedom.

The greatest of all prison-escape movies (and, not coincidentally, the biggest popular success in Bresson's career)—as well as the greatest Bresson film for me after *Balthazar*—*A Man Escaped* is to my mind an ideal introduction to Bresson's work. Much the same case could be made for *Pickpocket*—an existential tale about crime, urban solitude, and redemption with uncredited lifts from Dostoevsky's *Crime and Punishment*. Some of these lifts are banal, and the hero's sudden redemption at the film's end is unbelievable—even though both of these aspects of the film have become cornerstones in the scripts and films of Paul Schrader, from *Taxi Driver* to *American Gigolo* to *Light Sleeper*. But the poetry found in the urban solitude of the hero and his self-education in becoming a pickpocket remains ethereal and oddly uplifting; and one sequence in which he consorts with other pickpockets in the Gare de Lyon has the exhilaration of a breathtaking ballet.

As luck would have it, these two films are the first Bresson features I saw, back in the sixties, and I've been a passionate Bressonian ever since. But I couldn't claim that everyone who sees them feels the same way—or even that everyone who likes them does so for the same reasons. In her ardent defence of Bresson in *Against Interpretation*, Susan Sontag argues that "Ideally, there is no suspense in a Bresson film," pointing out that the very title *A Man Escaped* does away with it by telling us that the hero succeeds in his escape attempt. This sounds fine in theory, but in *my* experience at least, *A Man Escaped* is just about as suspenseful as any prison-escape movie gets, and the suspense hardly ever stops in *Pickpocket* either.

Maybe it all depends on one's involvement in the stories and characters. For me, Bresson's *Diary of a Country Priest* (1951) and *The Trial of Joan of Arc*—two of his most austere works—generate hardly any suspense at all, but that's probably because they've never fully engaged me, perhaps because I don't think I have seen either film in a decent print. But for someone more attuned to these films' subjects, they may seem positively Hitchcockian.

A similar difficulty for some is the dialectical use of offscreen narration in *Diary of a Country Priest*, *A Man Escaped*, *Pickpocket*, and *Une femme douce*. It is so contrary to commercial norms—at times entailing an anticipation, an echo, a modification, or even an outright contradiction of the visual information being offered—that one may have to get past one's first knee-jerk responses (that is, one's deeply ingrained Hollywood training) in order to appreciate all the expressive and formal functions it has for Bresson. (As Manny Farber noted of *Une femme douce*, "the movie is a brain-twister in which few sentences connect to the image they accompany. A young bride jumps up and down on her new bed, and her husband, the ultimate in prissiness and mundaneness, says, 'I threw cold water on her ecstasy.'")

But the main disagreement I have with a good many other Bresson fans regards the religious and spiritual aspects of his films. Despite Bresson's alleged and at times avowed Jansenism—a sectarian form of Catholicism that believes in predestination—it seems to me that what his best films are doing has more to do with materialism than with the "transcendental" qualities most critics have written about.

Asked in a 1962 interview whether he believed "in a spiritual domain," Jacques Rivette replied, "Maybe, but only through the concrete. If that means being materialist, I think that's what I am more and more." The same attitude and development clearly informs Bresson's career, to such a degree that I believe his last three films—*Lancelot du Lac* (1974), *The Devil Probably*, and *L'Argent*—could properly be described as atheist. There is also a powerful and wholly material eroticism in his work that makes a quantum leap around the time of *Pickpocket* and continues, more or less unabated, through *L'Argent*—an eroticism so interactively dependent on other material elements of sound and image that in *Lancelot*, for example, the rattle of armour—a nearly constant sound—plays a central role in defining and even creating our sense of the softness and vulnerability of flesh, Guinevere's as well as Lancelot's. (First conceived in the early fifties, *Lancelot* registers in its opening and closing sequences as a horrified testimony to the savagery of war, and in its handling of this theme comes across as resolutely modern—in striking contrast to *Une femme douce*, an updated adaptation of a Dostoevsky story, whose title heroine comes across as strangely medieval, like a maiden in a castle waiting to be rescued.)[1]

Bresson's last five features are his only films in colour, and as a teacher friend recently observed, his uses of colour lead to a radical reformulation of what his films are like; as my friend put it, you're not always sure what to look at in the shots, which never happens in the black-and-white films. This is less true of *Lancelot*, where the colour mainly functions like black-and-white in his other films (apart from serving as a cue for recognizing certain characters in armour through the colours of their banners or tights). But in the other four features, a dreamy and mannerist kind of slickness enters Bresson's world for the first time, with consequences that aren't always beneficial—despite a lyrical kind of abstraction in some of the images that are highly evocative. (I haven't seen *Une femme douce* in about a quarter of a century, but I've never forgotten the flurry of elliptical shots depicting the heroine's suicidal leap from a balcony—a montage that is briefly recalled during the suicide that occurs near the beginning of Bill Forsyth's *Housekeeping*.)

These are the films in which Bresson appears to be commenting most directly on what he finds hateful about the contemporary world. (The same emotions are clearly present in *Au hasard Balthazar* and *Mouchette*, but the rural settings of both pictures make their social critiques seem more attenuated.) And when it comes to *The Devil Probably*—a potent but difficult tale of adolescent suicide in which mannerisms associated with both poker-faced non-acting and French fashion periodically threaten to overcome the deeply felt sense of tragedy—one is better off seeing it only after one has seen some of Bresson's work in black-and-white or *Lancelot*. As a first taste of his work, it may simply prove to be too weird for comfort—unless one responds to it as directly and as viscerally as a whole generation of French cinephiles did back in 1977, on whom it exerted a lasting and continuing influence.

The only Bresson feature apart from *Balthazar* based on a story of his own that is completely original, *The Devil Probably* more or less begins with five disaffected youths going off to a political rally, where a leader appears before a microphone to say, "I'm calling for destruction. . . . Destruction is for everyone," and the crowd wildly cheers after each phrase. Soon afterward, one sees other students watching newsreel footage about diverse ecological disasters across the globe, culminating in the clubbing of baby seals; then some of the youths go to a church, where an angry discussion about the modern world and religion is brutally interrupted by the sounds of a vacuum cleaner and an organ being tuned. The rage being expressed here, combined with the spooky precision of the pared-down, almost neutralized style, turns many of the lines into *non sequiturs*—a sense of mortification combined with sensationalism that suggests the improbable fusion of Bresson with a headline-mongerer like Samuel Fuller. (The rage is still present in *L'Argent*, Bresson's most compressed indictment of the modern world—a contemporary adaptation of a story by Tolstoy—but there it becomes fully mastered and consummately measured.)

Bresson has steadfastly kept his personal life hidden from the public, and I can think of few reasons for trying to invade that privacy. But it seems entirely possible that Bresson's hallmarks as a filmmaker—including his use of offscreen sounds to replace images and the sense found in all his films of souls in hiding, of buried identities and emotions—might be traceable in part to his nine months (1940-41) as a P.O.W. in a German internment camp and his subsequent experience of the German occupation of France. I'm thinking not only of *A Man Escaped*, but also of *Les Dames du Bois de Boulogne*, made during the Occupation itself. Speaking last year to film historian Bernard Eisenschitz, Godard provocatively called *Les Dames*—a contemporary melodrama adapted from an incident in Denis Diderot's eighteenth-century novel *Jacques the Fatalist*, and the last Bresson film to employ professional actors—the "only" film of the French Resistance. (Specifically, Godard was alluding to Élina Labourdette's penultimate line in the film, "Je lutte," uttered around the same time that Charles de Gaulle proclaimed "Il faut lutter" in a speech.) Such an interpretation can of course be debated, but it seems to me a far more fruitful approach to Bresson's style to see it growing out of a concrete and material historical experience than to treat it as a timeless and transcendent expression of abstract spirituality.

For a couple of consecutive nights in 1970, I had the opportunity to watch Bresson direct, by virtue of being an extra on *Four Nights of a Dreamer* (a lovely minor film, though it contains one of the most ravishing lyrical passages in all his work, charting the passage of a tourist boat on the Seine). The most striking characteristic about him in relation to other directors I've seen working was his absolute isolation: most of his instructions were relayed through his assistant—a Belgian woman, Mylène van der Mersch, who has subsequently become his wife—with the result that many of the other extras thought she was the picture's director. Furthermore, a surprising number of people on the crew seemed to have little or no sense of who Bresson was, apart from the fact that he was old and "difficult"— walking off location in a huff one night after midnight while everyone stood around shivering in the October cold, waiting for him to come back.[2] Even when it came to shooting most of the indelible *bateau-mouche* sequence the following night, there was absolutely no way of perceiving what Bresson had in mind until I wound up seeing the film in Cannes the following year. The mishaps of the crew while boarding a boat for one of its normal nocturnal excursions—such as dropping a heavy piece of equipment on an unsuspecting tourist's foot—created a general atmosphere of pandemonium that had nothing to do with the sublime serenity and mystery of what finally unfolded on screen, accompanied by a gentle bossa nova tune. In the same fashion, when I had an opportunity years later to read the shooting script of *Lancelot du Lac* prior to seeing the film, there was no way I could glean anything substantive, even from a close reading, about what the experience of the film would be like. The encounter of sound and image taking place first inside his head and eventually on a strip of film wasn't anything that a *tournage* or a shooting script could even begin to suggest, and clearly the image we have of Bresson as an imperious filmmaker stems above all from his aloneness with his materials.

This prickly side of Bresson can be traced all the way back to his very first effort as a director—a sarcastic, surrealist slapstick short film with songs called *Les Affaires publiques* (1934), set in a mythical country, with shades of Jean Vigo and *Million Dollar Legs*. A curiosity that was lost for years until the Cinémathèque Française discovered a slightly shortened print a decade ago, it has the same raw physicality as his increasingly bleak features, as well as the same spirited anger about pomp and hypocrisy, greed and artifice, that informs his work all the way through *L'Argent*. Before the film was found, Bresson once described it as being "like Buster Keaton, only worse"—though he was reportedly pleased when it finally came to light years later. For critics who've expressed difficulty in squaring this rude farce with his subsequent work, I can only suggest that it conveys struggle, the theme that binds all his work together. "Je lutte": the ultimate Bressonian motto.

If film—not to be confused with star vehicles and video—is currently in the process of disappearing, it seems more than likely that the work of Robert Bresson will disappear as well. A Bresson retrospective gives you some idea of what the world is currently getting rid of, and allows you to take a good, hard look at some of its last traces—traces of an art that, appropriately enough, is as apocalyptic as any modern work I can think of.

Chances are, twenty years from now, you'll be grateful for having had a chance to pay these final respects.

Notes

1. For a lengthier discussion of *Lancelot*, see "The Rattle of Armor, The Softness of Flesh: Bresson's *Lancelot du Lac*" in my collection *Movies as Politics* (Berkeley: University of California Press, 1997, pp. 201-207).
2. For a fuller account of this experience, see "Four Nights of an Extra: Working With Bresson," *The Village Voice*, 29 April 1971, pp. 76, 86.

Une femme douce

Journal d'un curé de campagne

Le Journal d'un curé de campagne and the Stylistics of Robert Bresson

I F *Diary of a Country Priest* impresses us as a masterpiece, and this with an almost physical impact, if it moves the critic and the uncritical alike, it is primarily because of its power to stir the emotions, rather than the intelligence, at their highest level of sensitivity. The temporary eclipse of *Les Dames du Bois de Boulogne* was for precisely the opposite reason. This film could not stir us unless we had, if not exactly analyzed, at least tested its intellectual structure and, so to speak, understood the rules of the game.

While the instantaneous success of *Journal* is undeniable, the aesthetic principles on which it is based are nevertheless the most paradoxical, maybe even the most complex, ever manifest in a sound film. Hence the refrain of those critics, ill-equipped to understand it. "Paradoxical," they say, "incredible—an unprecedented success that can never be repeated." Thus they renounce any attempt at explanation and take refuge in the perfect alibi of a stroke of genius. On the other hand, among those whose aesthetic preferences are of a kind with Bresson's and whom one would have unhesitatingly thought to be his allies, there is a deep sense of disappointment in proportion as they expected greater acts of daring from him.

First embarrassed, then irritated by the realization of what the director did not do, yet too long in accord with him to be able to change their views on the spot; too caught up in his style to recapture their intellectual virginity which would have left the way open to emotion, they have neither understood nor liked the film.

Thus we find the critical field divided into two extreme groups. At one end those least equipped to understand *Journal* and who, by the same token, have loved it all the more without knowing why; at the other end those "happy few" who, expecting something different, have not liked it and have failed to understand it. It is the strangers to the cinema, the men of letters, amazed that they could so love a film and be capable of freeing their minds of prejudice, who have understood what Bresson had in mind more clearly than anyone else.

Admittedly Bresson has done his best to cover his tracks. His avowal of fidelity to the original from the first moment that he embarked on the adaptation, his declared intention of following the book word for word conditioned us to look for just that and the film only serves to prove it. Unlike Aurenche and Bost, who were preoccupied with the optics of the screen and the balance of their drama in its new form, Bresson, instead of building up the minor characters like the parents in *Le Diable au corps*, eliminated them. He prunes even the very essentials, giving an impression as he does so of a fidelity unable to sacrifice one single word without a pucker of concern and a thousand preliminary twinges of remorse. Again this pruning is always in the interest of simplification, never of addition. It is no exaggeration to say that if Bernanos had written the screenplay he would have taken greater liberties with his novel. He had, indeed, explicitly recognized the right of the adaptor to make use of his book according to the requirements of the cinema, the right that is "to dream his story over."

However, if we praise Bresson for his fidelity, it is for the most insidious kind of fidelity, a most pervasive form of creative license. Of course, one clearly cannot adapt without transposing. In that respect, Bernanos was on the side of aesthetic common sense. Literal translations are not the faithful ones. The changes that Aurenche and Bost made to *Le Diable au corps* are almost all entirely justified in principle. A character on the screen and the same character as evoked by the novelist are not identical.

Valéry condemned the novel for being obliged to record that "the Marquis had tea at five o'clock." On his side, the novelist might in turn pity the filmmaker for having to show the marquis actually at the table. It is for this reason that the relatives of the heroes in Radiguet, peripheral in the novel, appear important on the screen. The adaptor, however, must be as concerned with the text as with the characters and with the threat of their physical presence to the balance of the story. Having transformed the narrative into visuals, the filmmaker must put the rest into dialogue, including the existing dialogue of the novel although we expect some modification of the latter—since spoken as written, its effectiveness and even its meaning will normally evaporate.

It is here that we see the paradoxical effect of the textual fidelity of *Journal*.

While the characters in the book are presented to the reader in high relief and while their inevitably brief evocation by the pen of the curé of Ambricourt never gives us a feeling of frustration or of any limits being put both to their existence and to our knowledge of their existence, Bresson, in the process of showing them to us, is forever hurrying them out of sight. In place of the powerfully concrete evocations of the novelist, the film offers us an increasingly impoverished image which escapes us because it is hidden from us and is never really developed.

The novel of Bernanos is rich in picturesque evocations, solid, concrete, strikingly visual. For example: "The Count went out—his excuse the rain. With every step the water oozed from his long boots. The three or four rabbits he had shot were lumped together in the bottom of his game-bag in a horrible-looking little pile of bloodstained mud and grey hair. He had hung the string bag on the wall and as he talked to me I saw fixed on me, through the intertwining cords, a still limpid and gentle eye."

Do you feel you have seen all this somewhere before? Don't bother to look where. It was probably in a Renoir film. Now compare this scene with the other in which the count brings the two rabbits to the presbytery—admittedly this comes later in the book but the two could have profitably been combined, thus giving them a style in common—and if you still have any doubts, Bresson's own admission will remove them. Forced to throw out a third of his final cut for the exhibitor's copy he ended, as we know, by declaring with a delicate touch of cynicism that he was delighted to have had to do so. Actually, the only "visual" he really cared about was the blank screen at the finale, which we will discuss later.

If he had really been faithful to the book, Bresson would have made quite a different film. Determined though he was to add nothing to the original—already a subtle form of betrayal by omission—he might at least have chosen to sacrifice the more literary parts for the many passages of ready-made film material that cried out for visualization. Yet he systematically took the opposite course. When you compare the two, it is the film that is literary while the novel teems with visual material.

The way he handles the text is even more revealing. He refuses to put into dialogue (I hardly dare to say "film dialogue") those passages from the novel where the curé enters in his diary the report of such-and-such a conversation. Here is a first discrepancy, since Bernanos at no point guarantees that the curé is giving a word for word report of what he heard. The odds are that he is not. In any event, supposing he *is*, and that Bresson has it in mind to preserve, along with the objective image, the subjective character of something remembered, it is still true that the mental and emotional impact of a line that is merely read is very different from that of a spoken line.

Now, not only does he not adapt the dialogue, however circumspectly, to the demands of a performance, he goes out of his way, on the contrary, whenever the text of the novel has the rhythm and balance of true dialogue, to prevent the actor from bringing out these qualities. Thus a good deal of excellent dramatic dialogue is thrown away because of the flat monotone in which the director insists that it be delivered.

Many complimentary things have been said about *Les Dames du Bois de Boulogne*, very little about the adaptation. The critics have, to all intents and purposes, treated the film as if it was made from an original screenplay. The outstanding quality of the dialogue has been attributed to Cocteau, whose reputation has little need of such praise. This is because they have not reread *Jacques le fataliste*, in which they would have found if not the entire script, at least the evidence of a subtle game of hide and go seek, word for word, with the text of Diderot. While it did not make one feel one ought to go back to verify the fact at close quarters, the modern version left one with the impression that Bresson had taken liberties with the story and retained simply the situation and, if you like, a certain eighteenth-century flavour. Since, in addition, he had killed off two or three writers under him, so to speak, it was reasonable to suppose that he was that many steps away from the original. However, I recommend fans of *Les Dames du Bois de Boulogne* and aspiring scenarists alike to take a second look at the film with these considerations in mind. Without intending in any way to detract from the decisive part played by the style of the direction in the success of the film, it is important to examine very closely the foundations of this success, namely a marvellously subtle interplay—a sort of counterpoint between faithfulness and unfaithfulness to the original.

It has been suggested in criticism of *Les Dames du Bois de Boulogne*, with equal proportions of good sense and misunderstanding, that the psychological make-up of the characters is out of key with the society in which they are shown as living. True, it is the mores of the time that, in the novel of Diderot, justify the choice of the revenge and give it its effectiveness. It is true again that this same revenge seems to the modern spectator to be something out of the blue, something beyond his experience. It is equally useless on the other hand for those who defend the film to look for any sort of social justification for the characters. Prostitution and pandering as shown in the novel are facts with a very clear and solid contemporary social context. In the film of *Les Dames* they are all the more mystifying since they have no basic justification. The revenge of an injured mistress who forces her unfaithful lover to marry a luscious cabaret dancer seems to us to be a ridiculous gesture. Nor can the fact that the characters appear to be abstractions be explained by deliberate cuts made by the director during the filming. They are that way in the script. The reason Bresson does not tell us more about his characters is not because he has no desire to, but because he would be hard put to do so. Racine does not describe the colour of the wall paper in the rooms to which his characters retire. To this one may answer, of course, that classical tragedy has no need of the alibis of realism and that this is one of the basic differences between the theatre and the cinema. That is true enough. It is also precisely why Bresson does not derive his cinematographic abstraction simply from the bare episodes but from the counterpoint that the reality of the situation sets up with itself. In *Les Dames du Bois de Boulogne*, Bresson has taken the risk of transferring one realistic story into the context of another. The result is that these two examples of realism cancel one another out, the passions displayed emerged out of the characters as if from a chrysalis, the action from the twists and turns of the plot, and the tragedy from the trappings of the drama. The sound of a windshield-wiper against a page of Diderot is all it took to turn it into Racinian dialogue. Obviously Bresson is not aiming at absolute realism. On the other hand, his stylized treatment of it does not have the pure abstract quality of a symbol. It is rather a structured presentation of the abstract and concrete, that is to say of the reciprocal interplay of seemingly incompatible elements. The rain murmur of a waterfall, the sound of earth pouring from a broken pot, the hooves of a horse on the cobblestones, are not there just as a contrast to the simplification of the sets or the convention of the costumes, still less as a contrast to the literary and anachronistic flavour of the dialogue. They are not needed either for dramatic antithesis or for a contrast in decor. They are there deliberately as neutrals, as foreign bodies, like a grain of sand that gets into and seizes up a piece of machinery. If the arbitrariness of their choice resembles an abstraction, it is the abstraction of the concrete integral. They are like lines drawn across an image to affirm its transparency, as the dust affirms the transparency of a diamond; it is impurity at its purest.

This interaction of sound and decor is repeated in the very midst of elements which seem at first to be completely stylized. For example, the two apartments of the women are almost totally unfurnished but this calculated bareness has its explanation. That the frames should be on the walls though the paintings have been sold is undoubtedly a deliberate touch of realism. The abstract whiteness of the new apartment is not intended as part of a pattern of theatrical expressionism. The apartment is white because it has just been repainted and the smell of fresh paint still hangs about. Is there any need to add to this list the elevator or the concierge's telephone, or, on the soundtrack, the tumult of male voices that follows the face-slapping of Agnès, the text for which reads totally conventionally while the sound quality of it is absolute perfection.

I have referred to *Les Dames* in discussing *Journal* because it is important to point out the profound similarity between the mechanics of their respective adaptations.

The style of *Journal* indicates a more systematic searching, a rigour that is almost unbearable. It was made under very different technical conditions. Yet we shall see that the procedure was in each case basically the same. In both it was a matter of getting to the heart of a story or of a drama, of achieving the most rigorous form of aesthetic abstraction while avoiding expressionism by way of an interplay of literature and realism, which added to its cinematic potential while seeming to negate it. In any case, Bresson's faithfulness to his model is the alibi of liberty in chains. If he is faithful to the text this is because it serves his purpose better than taking useless liberties. Furthermore, this respect for the letter is, in the last analysis, far more than an exquisite embarrassment, it is a dialectical moment in the creation of a style.

So it is pointless to complain that paradoxically Bresson is at one and the same time the slave and the master of his text because it is precisely from this seeming contradiction that he gets his effects. Henri Agel, for example, describes the film as a page of Victor Hugo rewritten in the style of de Nerval. But surely one could imagine poetic results born of this monstrous coupling, of unexpectedly revealing flashes touched off by a translation made not just from one language into another (like Mallarmé's translation of Poe) but from one style and one content into the style of another artist and from the material of one art transposed into the material of another.

Let us look a little more closely now at *Journal* and see what in it has not really come off. While not wishing to praise Bresson for all his weak spots, for there are weaknesses, rare ones, which work to his disadvantage, we can say quite definitely that they are all an integral part of his style; they are simply that kind of awkwardness to which a high degree of sensibility may lead, and if Bresson has any reason here for self-congratulation, it is for having had the sense to see in that awkwardness the price he must pay for something more important.

So, even if the acting in general seems poor, except for Laydu all the time and for Nicole Ladmiral some of it, this, provided you like the film, will only appear to be a minor defect. But now we have to explain why Bresson who directed his cast so superbly in *Les Anges du péché* and *Les Dames du Bois de Boulogne* seems to handle them in this film as amateurishly as any tyro with a camera who has roped in his aunt and the family lawyer. Do people really imagine that it was easier to get Maria Casarès to play down her talent than to handle a group of docile amateurs? Certainly some scenes were poorly acted. It is odd however that these were by no means the least moving.

The fact is that this film is not to be measured by ordinary standards of acting. It is important to remember that the cast were all either amateurs or simple beginners. *Journal* no more approximates to *Ladri di Biciclette* than to *L'Entrée des artistes*. Actually the only film it can be likened to is Carl Dreyer's *Jeanne d'Arc*. The cast is not being asked to act out a text, not even to live it out, just to speak it. It is because of this that the passages spoken offscreen so perfectly match the passages spoken by the characters onscreen. There is no fundamental difference either in tone or style. This plan of attack not only rules out any dramatic interpretation by the actors but also any psychological touches either. What we are asked to look for on their faces is not for some fleeting reflection of the words but for an uninterrupted condition of soul, the outward revelation of an interior destiny.

Thus this so-called badly acted film leaves us with the feeling of having seen a gallery of portraits whose expressions could not be other than they were. In this respect the most characteristic of all is Chantal in the confessional. Dressed in black, withdrawn into the shadows, Nicole Ladmiral allows us only a glimpse of a mask, half lit, half in shadow, like a seal stamped on wax, all blurred at the edges.

Naturally Bresson, like Dreyer, is only concerned with the countenance as flesh, which, when not involved in playing a role, is a man's true imprint, the most visible mark of his soul. It is then that the countenance takes on the dignity of a sign. He would have us be concerned here not with the psychology but with the physiology of existence. Hence the hieratic tempo of the acting, the slow ambiguous gestures, the obstinate recurrence of certain behavioural patterns, the unforgettable dream-like slow motion. Nothing purely accidental could happen to these people—confirmed as each is in his own way of life, essentially concerned either against the influence of grace, to continue so, or, responding to grace, to throw off the deadly Nessus-mantle of the old Adam.

There is no development of character. Their inner conflicts, the various phases of their struggle as they wrestle with the Angel of the Lord, are never outwardly revealed. What we see is rather a concentration of suffering, the recurrent spasms of childbirth or of a snake sloughing off its skin. We can truly say that Bresson strips his characters bare.

Eschewing psychological analysis, the film in consequence lies outside the usual dramatic categories. The succession of events is not constructed according to the usual laws of dramaturgy under which the passions work towards a soul-satisfying climax. Events do indeed follow one another according to a necessary order, yet within a framework of accidental happenings. Free acts and coincidences are interwoven. Each moment in the film, each set-up, has its own due measure, alike, of freedom and of necessity. They all move in the same direction, but separately like iron filings drawn to the overall surface of a magnet. If the word tragedy comes to one's pen, it is in an opposite sense since we can only be dealing here with a tragedy freely willed. The transcendence of the Bernanos-Bresson universe is not the transcendence of destiny as the ancients understood it, nor yet the transcendence of Racinian passion, but the transcendence of grace which is something each of us is free to refuse.

If nevertheless, the concatenation of events and the causal efficiency of the characters involved appear to operate just as rigidly as in a traditional dramatic structure, it is because they are responding to an order, of prophecy (or perhaps one should say of Kirkegaardian "repetition") that is as different from fatality as causality is from analogy.

The pattern of the film's unfolding is not that of tragedy in the usual sense, rather in the sense of the medieval Passion Play, or better still, of the Way of the Cross, each sequence being a station along that road. We are given the key to this by the dialogue in the hut between the two curés, when the one from Ambricourt reveals that he is spiritually attracted to the Mount of Olives. "Is it not enough that Our Lord should have granted me the grace of letting me know today, through the words of my old teacher, that nothing, throughout all eternity, can remove me from the place chosen by me from all eternity, that I was the prisoner of His Sacred Passion?"

Death is not the preordained end of our final agony, only its conclusion and a deliverance. Henceforth we shall know to what divine ordinance, to what spiritual rhythm the sufferings and actions of the curé respond. They are the outward representation of his agony. At which point we should indicate the analogies with Christ that abound towards the end of the film, or they may very well go unnoticed. For example, the two fainting fits during the night; the fall in the mud; the vomitings of wine and blood—a remarkable synthesis of powerful comparisons with the falls of Jesus, the Blood of the Passion, the sponge with vinegar on it, and the defiling spittle. These are not all. For the veil of Veronica we have the cloth of Séraphita; then finally the death in the attic—a Golgotha with even a good and a bad thief.

Now let us immediately put aside these comparisons, the very enumeration of which is necessarily deceptive. Their aesthetic weight derives from their theological value, but both defy explanation. Bresson like Bernanos avoids any sort of symbolic allusion and so none of the situations, despite their obvious parallel to the Gospel, is created precisely because of that parallel. Each carries its own biographical and individual meaning. Its Christ-like resemblance comes second, through being projected onto the higher plane of analogy. In no sense is it true to say that the life of the curé of Ambricourt is an imitation of its divine model, rather it is a repetition and a picturing forth of that life. Each bears his own cross and each cross is different, but all are the Cross of the Passion. The sweat on the brow of the curé is a bloody sweat.

So, probably for the first time, the cinema gives us a film in which the only genuine incidents, the only perceptible movements are those of the life of the spirit. Not only that, it also offers us a new dramatic form, that is specifically religious—or better still, specifically theological; a phenomenology of salvation and grace.

It is worth noting that through playing down the psychological elements and keeping the dramatics to a minimum, Bresson is left to face two kinds of pure reality. On the one hand, as we saw, we have the countenance of the actor denuded of all symbolic expression, sheer epidermis, set in a surrounding devoid of any artifice. On the other hand there is what we must call the "written reality." Indeed, Bresson's faithfulness to the text of Bernanos, his refusal, that is, not only to adapt it but also his paradoxical concern to emphasize its literary character, is part of the same predetermined approach to the direction of his actors and the selection of his settings. Bresson treats the novel as he does his characters. The novel is a cold, hard fact, a reality to be accepted as it stands. One must not attempt to adapt it to the situation in hand, or manipulate it to fit some passing need for an explanation; on the contrary it is something to be taken absolutely as it stands. Bresson never condenses the text, he cuts it. Thus what is left over is a part of the original. Like marble from a quarry the words of the film continue to be part of the novel. Of course the deliberate emphasis on their literary character can be interpreted as a search after artistic stylization, which is the very opposite of realism. The fact is, however, that in this case the reality is not the descriptive content, moral or intellectual, of the text—it is the very text itself, or more properly, the style. Clearly the reality at one stage removed of the novel and that which the camera captures directly, cannot fit or grow together or become one. On the contrary the effect of their juxtaposition is to reaffirm their differences. Each plays its part, side by side, using the means at its disposal, in its own setting and after its own style. But it is doubtless by this separating off of elements which because of their resemblance would appear to belong together, that Bresson manages to eliminate what is accidental. The ontological conflict between two orders of events, occurring simultaneously, when confronted on the screen reveal their single common measure—the soul.

Each actor says the same things and the very disparity between their expressions, the substance of what they say, their style, the kind of indifference which seems to govern the relation of actor to text, of word and visage, is the surest guarantee of their close complicity. This language which no lips could speak is, of necessity, from the soul.

It is unlikely that there exists anywhere in the whole of French cinema, perhaps even in all French literature, many moments of a more intense beauty than in the medallion scene between the curé and the countess. Its beauty does not derive from the acting nor from the psychological and dramatic values of the dialogue, nor indeed from its intrinsic meaning. The true dialogue that punctuates the struggle between the inspired priest and a soul in despair is, of its very nature, ineffable. The decisive clashes of their spiritual fencing-match escape us. Their words announce, or prepare the way for, the fiery touch of grace. There is nothing here then of the flow of words that usually goes with a conversion, while the overpowering severity of the dialogue, its rising tension and its final calm leave us with the conviction that we have been the privileged witnesses of a supernatural storm. The words themselves are so much dead weight, the echo of a silence that is the true dialogue between these two souls; a hint at their secret; the opposite side of the coin, if one dare to say so, of the Divine Countenance. When later the curé refuses to come to his own defence by producing the countess's letter, it is not out of humility or love of suffering. It is rather because no tangible evidence is worthy to play a part either in his defence or his indictment. Of its nature the evidence of the countess is no more acceptable than that of Chantal, and none has the right to ask God to bear witness.

The technique of Bresson's direction cannot adequately be judged except at the level of his aesthetic intention. Inadequately as we may have so far described the latter, it may yet be that the highly astonishing paradox of the film is now a little more evident. Actually the distinction of having set text over against image for the first time goes to Melville in his *Le Silence de la mer*. It is noteworthy that his reason was likewise a desire for fidelity. However, the structure of Vercors's book was of itself unusual. In his *Journal* Bresson has done more than justify Melville's experiment and shown how well warranted it was. He has carried it to its final conclusions.

Is *Journal* just a silent film with spoken titles? The spoken word, as we have seen, does not enter into the image as a realistic component. Even when spoken by one of the characters, it rather resembles the recitative of an opera. At first sight the film seems to be somehow made up on the one hand of the abbreviated text of the novel and illustrated, on the other hand, by images that never pretend to replace it. All that is spoken is not seen, yet nothing that is seen but is also spoken. At worst, critical good sense can reproach Bresson with having substituted an illustrated radiophonic montage, no less, for Bernanos's novel.

So it is from this ostensible corruption of the art of cinema that we begin if we are to grasp fully Bresson's originality and boldness.

In the first place, if Bresson "returns" to the silent film it is certainly not, despite the abundance of close-ups, because he wants to tie in again with theatrical expressionism—that fruit of an infirmity—on the contrary, it is in order to rediscover the dignity of the human countenance as understood by Stroheim and Dreyer. Now if there is one and only one quality of the silent film irreconcilable of its very nature with sound, it is the syntactical subtlety of montage and expression in the playing of the film, that is to say that which proceeds in effect from the weakness of the silent film. But not all silent films want to be such. Nostalgia for a silence that would be the benign procreator of a visual symbolism unduly confuses the so-called primacy of the image with the true vocation of the cinema—which is the primacy of the object. The absence of a soundtrack for *Greed*, *Nosferatu*, or *La Passion de Jeanne d'Arc* means something quite other than the silence of *Caligari*, *Die Nibelungen*, or *El Dorado*. It is a frustration not the foundation of a form of expression. The former films exist in spite of their silence not because of it. In this sense the invention of the soundtrack is just a fortuitous scientific phenomenon and not the aesthetic revolution people always say it is. The language of film, like the language of Aesop, is ambiguous and in spite of appearances to the contrary, the history of cinema before and after 1928 is an unbroken continuity. It is the story of the relations between expressionism and realism. Sound was to destroy expressionism for a while before adopting it in its turn. On the other hand, it became an immediate part of the continued development of realism.

Paradoxically enough it is to the most theatrical, that is to say to the most talkative, forms of the sound film that we must look today for a resurgence of the old symbolism while the pre-talkie realism of a Stroheim has in fact no following. Yet, it is evident that Bresson's undertaking is somehow related to the work of Stroheim and Renoir. The separating of sound and of the image to which it relates cannot be understood without a searching examination of the aesthetics of realism in sound. It is just as mistaken to see it as an illustration of a text, as a commentary on an image. Their parallelism maintains that division which is present to our senses. It continues the Bressonian dialectic between abstraction and reality thanks to which we are concerned with a single reality—that of human souls. In no sense does Bresson return to the expressionism of the silent film. On the one hand he excludes one of the components of reality in order to reproduce it, deliberately stylized on a soundtrack, partially independent of the image. In other words, it is as if the final rerecording was composed of sound directly recorded with scrupulous fidelity and a text postsynchronized on a monotone. But, as we have pointed out, this text is itself a second reality, a "cold aesthetic fact." Its realism is its style, while the style of the image is primarily its reality, and the style of the film is precisely the conflict between the two.

Bresson disposes once and for all of that commonplace of criticism according to which image and sound should never duplicate one another. The most moving moments in the film are those in which text and image are saying the same thing, each however in its own way. The sound never serves simply to fill out what we see. It strengthens it and multiplies it just as the echo chamber of a violin echoes and multiplies the vibrations of the strings. Yet this metaphor is dialectically inadequate since it is not so much a resonance that the mind perceives as something that does not match, as when a colour is not properly superimposed on a drawing. It is here at the edge that the event reveals its true significance. It is because the film is entirely structured on this relationship that, towards the end, the images take on such emotional power. It would be in vain to look for its devastating beauty simply in what is explicit. I doubt if the individual frames in any other film, taken separately, are so deceptive. Their frequent lack of plastic composition, the awkwardness and static quality of the actors completely mislead one as to their value in the overall film. Moreover, this accretion of effectiveness is not due to the editing. The value of an image does not depend on what precedes or follows it. They accumulate, rather, a static energy, like the parallel leaves of a condenser. Between this and the soundtrack differences of aesthetic potential are set up, the tension of which becomes unbearable. Thus the image-text relationship moves towards its climax, the latter having the advantage. Thus it is that, quite naturally, at the command of an imperious logic, there is nothing more that the image has to communicate except by disappearing. The spectator has been led, step by step, towards that night of the senses the only expression of which is a light on a blank screen.

That is where the so-called silent film and its lofty realism is headed, to the disappearance of the image and its replacement simply by the text of the novel. But here we are experimenting with an irrefutable aesthetic, with a sublime achievement of pure cinema. Just as the blank page of Mallarmé and the silence of Rimbaud is language at the highest state, the screen, free of images and handed back to literature, is the triumph of cinematographic realism. The black cross on the white screen, as awkwardly drawn as on the average memorial card, the only trace left by the "assumption" of the image, is a witness to something the reality of which is itself but a sign.

With *Journal* cinematographic adaptation reaches a new stage. Up to now, film tended to substitute for the novel in the guise of its aesthetic translation into another language. Fidelity meant respect for the spirit of the novel, but it also meant a search for necessary equivalents, that is to say, it meant taking into account the dramatic requirements of the theatre or again the more direct effectiveness of the cinematographic image. Unfortunately, concern for these things will continue to be the general rule. We must remember however that it was through their application that *Le Diable au corps* and *La Symphonie pastorale* turned out so well. According to the best opinions, films like these are as good as the books on which they are modelled.

In the margin of this formula we might also note the existence of the free adaptation of books such as that made by Renoir for *Une partie de campagne* or *Madame Bovary*. Here the problem is solved in another way. The original is just a source of inspiration. Fidelity is here the temperamental affinity between film-maker and novelist, a deeply sympathetic understanding. Instead of presenting itself as a substitute, the film is intended to take its place alongside the book—to make a pair with it, like twin stars. This assumption, applicable only where there is genius, does not exclude the possibility that the film is a greater achievement than its literary model, as in the case of Renoir's *The River*.

Journal however is something else again. Its dialectic between fidelity and creation is reducible, in the last analysis, to a dialectic between the cinema and literature. There is no question here of a translation, no matter how faithful or intelligent. Still less is it a question of free inspiration with the intention of making a duplicate. It is a question of building a secondary work with the novel as foundation. In no sense is the film "comparable" to the novel or "worthy" of it. It is a new aesthetic creation, the novel so to speak multiplied by the cinema.

The only procedure in any way comparable of which we have any examples are films of paintings. Emmer or Alain Resnais are similarly faithful to the original, their raw material is the already highly developed work of the painter; the reality with which they are concerned is not the subject of the painting but the painting itself, in the same way as the text of the novel is Bresson's reality. But the fidelity of Alain Resnais to Van Gogh is but the prior condition of a symbiosis of cinema and painting. That is why, as a rule, painters fail utterly to understand the whole procedure. If you see these films as nothing more than an intelligent, effective, and even a valuable means of popularizing painting—they certainly are that too—you know nothing of their aesthetic biology.

This comparison with films of paintings, however, is only partially valid since these are confined from the outset to the realm of minor aesthetic works. They add something to the paintings, they prolong their existence, they release them from the confines of their frames but they can never pretend to be the paintings themselves.* The Van Gogh of Alain Resnais is a minor masterpiece taken from a major work which it makes use of and explains in detail but does not replace. There are two reasons for this congenital limitation. First of all, the photographic reproduction, in projection, cannot pretend to be a substitute for the original or to share its identity. If it could, then it would be the better to destroy its aesthetic autonomy, since films of paintings start off precisely as the negation of that on which this aesthetic autonomy is based, the fact that the paintings are circumscribed in space and exist outside time. It is because cinema as the art of space and time is the contrary of painting that it has something to add to it.

Such a contradiction does not exist between the novel and the film. Not only are they both narrative arts, that is to say temporal arts, but it is not even possible to maintain a priori that the cinematic image is essentially inferior to the image prompted by the written word. In all probability the opposite is the case. But this is not where the problem lies. It is enough if the novelist, like the filmmaker, is concerned with the idea of unfolding a real world. Once we accept these essential resemblances, there is nothing absurd in trying to write a novel on film. But *Journal* has just proved to us that it is more fruitful to speculate on their differences rather than on their resemblances, that is, for the existence of the novel to be affirmed by the film and not dissolved into it. It is hardly enough to say of this work, once removed, that it is in essence faithful to the original because, to begin with, it *is* the novel. But most of all the resulting work is not, certainly, better (that kind of judgment is meaningless . . .) but "more" than the book. The aesthetic pleasure we derive from Bresson's film, while the acknowledgement for it goes, essentially, to the genius of Bernanos, includes all that the novel has to offer plus, in addition, its refraction in the cinema.

After Bresson, Aurenche and Bost are but the Viollet-le-Duc of cinematographic adaptation.

Translated from the French by Hugh Gray

---

* At least up to the time of *Le Mystère Picasso* which, as we shall see, may invalidate this criticism.

Les Dames du Bois de Boulogne

The Universe
of Robert Bresson

RESSON'S TOTAL OUTPUT is extremely limited compared to that of other filmmakers of his generation: in twenty years [this article was written in 1962] he has made only six films. But, despite his wide range of subject matter, there are perhaps no films more unified or deeply marked by their director's personality. Undoubtedly the idea of the importance of the auteur in the cinema has been exaggerated by deliberately ignoring the often essential contribution of scriptwriters and adapters, of the producer, the editor, the cameraman, and sometimes the actors. The attempt to react against an anonymous commercial cinema, against the privileged position of stars, or against literary prejudice, has resulted in the director being given not simply an important role, but an exclusive one. However, what is clearly an exaggeration in most cases—particularly as regards the American cinema—is the pure and simple truth for Bresson. From *Les Anges du péché* to *The Trial of Joan of Arc*, whatever the point of departure of the film and the personalities of the people involved, whatever the theme or the characters, we always deal with the same universe, even though a relative evolution can be traced from film to film.

This is why it is not at all artificial to attempt an analysis of this universe as a whole and to try to isolate the parts which create its unity, instead of dealing with each film separately. In order to do this, we shall not concern ourselves with Robert Bresson as a person, nor with his psychology, but with what I shall call his mythology as it is expressed through the medium of the cinema. This is in any case the best way of respecting the rich personality of a man who has always chosen to stay discreetly in the background and who hates nothing more than to make a public exhibition of himself. Besides, in so far as his universe constitutes a whole, it would be impossible to make separate studies of content and form. The subject matter as such is not particularly original: the cinema teems with stories of abandoned mistresses, reformed thieves, escaped prisoners, priests, or nuns dedicated to saving souls, and warlike heroines who fall into enemy hands. Nor does analysis of isolated elements of Bresson's cinematographic language, stripped of their contextual significance, reveal more than curious quirks. Only by respecting the unfailing unity of themes and style can we really hope to get inside this universe and discover its richness and originality. So we must approach it through categories which do not rely exclusively on signs nor on meaning, but on both. Such categories, we feel, are the concepts of abstraction and reality, of stage character and real person, of loneliness and communication, and of immanence and transcendence.

From Abstraction to Reality

Bresson's universe is not that of everyday reality. It is distinct from it not only because it is an artistic universe, but because as such it makes no attempt to pass for the everyday universe. In this Bresson takes a different aesthetic position from others, who claim that they are setting up true works of art, yet define the truth of these works by direct reference to everyday life. When Zavattini and De Sica show us Umberto D going to bed or, in the same film, the maid getting up, they do it in order that we should witness gestures, attitudes and words which are often boring and insignificant as details, but which are interesting when seen as a whole, as they reveal a concrete situation to us, one which had never before attracted our attention. There is nothing like this in films such as *Les Dames du Bois de Boulogne* or *Pickpocket*. Nor indeed is there anything in these—or in any of Bresson's other films—which could be closely or remotely compared to the "slice of life," to the documentary description of an environment or the concrete representation of a human reality. We are as far from *vérisme* and naturalism as from neo-realism. Are we then equally far from reality—in abstraction, for instance?

At this point it would be a good thing to define as closely as possible what is meant by reality and abstraction. Philosophers give the latter two quite distinct meanings. First, there is the abstraction which proceeds by extension and enables one to classify beings according to their most general characteristics: Man, Animal, Living, Being; or Commerce, Industry, Justice (the totality of judges). Then there is that which proceeds by intensification and which attempts less to classify beings than to reach that which makes a being what he is, his essence— let's say his soul. The first form of abstraction does not exist in Bresson's work. His *Les Anges du péché* does not show us different "types" of nun, his curé of Ambricourt is not The Priest—not even The Country Priest. He is not a type of country curé to which another type, the curé of Torcy, forms a contrast. Hélène is not The Betrayed Mistress taking revenge. Fontaine is no more The Member of the Resistance than Michel is The Pickpocket (note that the film's title does not include the definite article).

What we find is the second type of abstraction, at least so far as the artist is capable of producing an equivalent. He can, in fact, choose to show by various devices the essence or soul of concrete reality, rather than its more or less chaotic workings. Instead of telling us everything about Lieutenant Fontaine and giving all the whys and wherefores of his actions in the Resistance, we are only given the bare essentials—though this does not stop him being perfectly individualized. Similarly, the pastoral life of the curé of Ambricourt is not described in detail and a close look will reveal a lot of omissions; this does not mean that any other priest cannot feel the brother of this man of God, even if in human terms he in no way resembles him. What I am saying is that this abstraction is not in any way pejorative: it does not result in the creation of bloodless people, bereft of character and personality, nor of mundane situations. The people we are shown are very strange, even though they have a universal relevance.

How does Bresson manage to give us only the essence of people and events without any feeling of thinness? Largely through a very precise choice of details, objects and accessories; through gestures charged with an extremely solid reality. André Bazin noted this in a well-known article on Bresson's style: "All that was needed," he said, "was the sound of a windscreen-wiper with a text by Diderot to produce a Racinian dialogue." The sound of the windscreen-wiper has an equivalent in all Bresson's films, whether in the soundtrack or the visuals. For example, the raking of the paths in the park during the curé's conversation with the countess, or Joan of Arc's old shoes being consigned to the flames of her own funeral pyre. It is the stylistic arrangement of all these concrete details which ultimately delineates the soul of a character, a situation or a film. Bresson said somewhere that the director is a "*metteur en ordre*." He is isolating raw elements taken from real life and putting them together in a certain order. "Like a painting," he also said, "a film should be made of relationships. To create is not to deform things nor to invent them, it is to give existing things new relationships."

This aesthetic approach is analogous to that found in cubist or non-figurative painting, where the canvases are made of those rich, sensitive realities which are "patches of colour arranged in a certain order," to take Maurice Denis's famous formula, or even of the elements of crude matter. Isn't the abstraction thus obtained of a different kind and less questionable in the end than that of those nineteenth-century pictures representing "Vengeance in pursuit of Crime," or "Commerce and Industry crowning the Republic"? You will not find the equivalent of these works in Bresson, but, for example, in the Cayatte of *Justice est faite* or *Nous sommes tous des assassins*.

Bresson is quite conscious of his originality in this field. On the subject of *A Man Escaped* he said: "I was hoping to make a film about objects which would at

the same time have a soul. That is to say, to reach the latter through the former."
It is these objects presented in a certain order and in a certain style which reveal
the soul. Bresson also said: "I wanted all the factual details to be exact, but at the
same time I tried to get beyond basic realism." It is just the same in *The Trial of
Joan of Arc* where objects and events keep all their weight as matter or reality: the
chains, the ladder, the wood of the pyre, as well as the examination of Joan's virginity by the women—yet the demands of style are never forgotten. The balance
between abstraction and reality is as perfectly realized as in a painting by Vermeer.

Bresson's universe has evolved constantly in his increasingly controlled
achievement of this balance. With *Les Anges* and *Les Dames*, abstraction definitely
predominated. The simplification of story-line, decor, and drama with the aim of
making the essence clear did not occur without a certain complacency. We were
meant to know that this simplicity was a style and that the style was not achieved
without effort. The objects or concrete details which were intended, as we have
just said, to concentrate on themselves a certain coefficient of reality, were chosen
more for their elegance than for their effectiveness. One would have thought this
choice was made by the dialogue writers, Giraudoux or Cocteau, rather than by
the director. The danger is that the result may be lack of substance, coldness, or an
ethereal atmosphere. Too many things, too perfect, in too rarified an atmosphere.

With *Diary of a Country Priest* there is a complete change. Supreme elegance
and a slightly decadent refinement are no longer sought after to cover up the simplicity and bareness. Now coarse red wine, mud, and vomit are there to remind
us that even when men have reached the highest degrees of mysticism or the most
subtle forms of art, they are never angels. In *A Man Escaped* the slop pails are emptied to music by Mozart, but this does not make the scene lose any of its "realism," even if it gains new significance through the music.

Bresson as director is often reproached for extreme "Jansenism." He won't
permit cheap display or vulgarity; he rejects spontaneity and the direct approach of
daily life, but he does not go so far as to despise the humblest—even the lowest—
things. It is true that under his direction they are never sordid; without appearing
to touch them, he transfigures them. *Pickpocket* provides a particularly convincing
illustration of this power. Nothing could be nastier or more mediocre than the
character, his immediate surroundings and his environment. Just think for a
moment of the image a Clouzot or an Autant-Lara could have made of it. Yet,
without obviously changing anything in this mediocrity and apparent filthiness,
without expressionistic lighting or musical effects, simply through the precision of
directing and acting, everything is turned inwards and takes on a different meaning. Beyond the surface, which is still as sordid as ever, one can glimpse another
dimension: that of the soul.

With reality as the starting point—happily often a less mediocre reality—the
rest of Bresson's films are the same: it is always souls that one finds. So it would now

be appropriate to examine how, through this universe where abstraction and reality harmonize, these souls are revealed through the characters which incarnate them.

From Character to Person

In the cinema as in the theatre and, by extension, even in "the social comedy," one talks of characters. Basically the character is the likeness of a human being, the one which is exhibited to its fellow-creatures, the one which lives to be looked at. So for those who watch them, films are by definition peopled by characters. But within the worlds which are evoked, it is quite possible that for each other, too, they are characters. Such is frequently the case with comedy films which show human "types" reduced to their outer skin; also with the sort of film known as "commercial," where the superficial treatment is not susceptible to deeper psychological interpretation; it is even the case sometimes with those films whose ideological basis obliges them to admit to no human dimension other than that shown in society. By contrast, there are other works which claim to offer us something deeper, something beyond the social mask of their characters: either psychological "characters" which are justified by their credibility and their inner cohesion, or "symbols" charged with moral or metaphysical significance, or "existences" of which a concrete description will enable one to grasp the sense or non-sense of human reality.

Bresson's characters show none of these things. Certainly there is, particularly in the first two films, *Les Anges du péché* and *Les Dames du Bois de Boulogne*, some psychology of character. But apart from the fact that this diminishes progressively in importance in later films, it is significant to note that the fundamental traits— even in women—are not compassion or imagination, but will-power and lucidity, energy and obstinacy. Think of Anne-Marie and Thérèse, of Hélène, and even more of Fontaine and the little curé of Ambricourt. The legionnaire on his motor-cycle makes no mistake when he says to the latter: "You could have been one of us." He is able to fight with the countess and with Chantal "soul for soul," with an obstinacy similar to that of Fontaine or of Chantal herself, who declares: "I shall go to hell if I want to." And even Michel the Pickpocket, who is apparently more passive, has a wild energy—"I had made up my mind"—and a coldly calculating intelligence. Joan of Arc is tenacity itself. Not the obstinate peasant who refuses to give up her superstitious beliefs, but the clear-minded aristocrat who knows what she wants and why she wants it. But aren't the qualities of firmness and intelligence rather more of a moral than a psychological order?

Yet the characters which embody them are certainly not pure symbols or archetypes. Joan of Arc is not quite an Antigone, and Fontaine is only a Hamlet in reverse. Although they are not described in minute detail in a given situation in the neo-realist manner, they nonetheless attain, similarly, a certain area of meaning beyond psychology yet this side of symbolism. They open up a literally endless perspective on themselves, on the universe, even on the whole of existence. In fact there is always something fundamental and mysterious in them which escapes us. They emanate a sort of discomfort which means that they can never be truly sympathetic. The phenomenon of projection and identification has no part in them. They make us feel uncertain and uneasy. Where they are concerned, every ambiguity, if not equivocation, is possible. Who is Thérèse? Who is Hélène? Who are Chantal, the curé, Fontaine, Michel, Joan? "The closer we get, the more they reveal themselves and the more obscure they become . . . instead of becoming clearer" (J. Arbois). In other words, they are more than characters, more than souls, they are people: "the most perfect thing in nature" (S. Thomas), but also the most ineffable if it is true that in them is concentrated, in its almost pure state, the entire being of the universe.

This is why, even in their most extreme confidences, they never fundamentally reveal anything but their mystery—like God himself. Thus one can see them again and again without wearying of them, for they enrich but never satiate. Like Wisdom, "They that eat me shall yet be hungry, and they that drink me shall yet be thirsty" (Ecclesiastes XXIV, 21).

This is even truer of the later films than of the early ones. In *Les Anges du péché* as in *Les Dames du Bois de Boulogne*, while there is a certain facility in the stylistic elegance, there is also something too mechanically intellectual and too obvious in the character make-up. Dare I say that the ambiguity has too little weight and one often brushes against the old analytical novel. In *Diary of a Country Priest*, however, the turning point has been reached and from there on the director, as though aware of Sartre's famous criticism of Mauriac, avoids giving the impression that he knows everything about his characters on the pretext that he has created them. They are people whose ultimate secret is beyond him too.

Basically Bresson's style is an amalgam of strict but relatively simple means of achieving this end. There is always, for example, an increasing tendency towards inexpressiveness in the acting: anything which could be construed as direct communication through facial expression or gesture—in fact anything which might recall the theatre or even Elia Kazan's famous Actor's Studio—is avoided. In this way Bresson manages to achieve a genuineness which is finally more convincing than the impression produced by naturalistic acting. You would have to be a lawyer or prosecutor in a court of law before you could affect to believe (or be naive enough to believe) in the facial expression of feeling, or the well-known sincere tone of voice. Instead, by asking his actors—more often than not non-professionals—not to "act," or even, as has been said in comparison with standard technique, to "act" or "speak falsely," he endows the characters which they represent

Procès de Jeanne d'Arc

with a sort of aura of strangeness, as though one were dealing with people escaping in some way from our world. But this does not make them any less human, because he always takes special care to load them, their environment and the objects which surround them, with a sufficient weight of reality. Bresson even increasingly avoids giving too important a place to music, which would tend to increase dangerously the feeling of unreality; the music he chooses is intermittent and very pure: Mozart in *A Man Escaped* and Lully in *Pickpocket*. In *The Trial of Joan of Arc*, there is only a drum-roll at the beginning and the end, and the occasional distant sound of church bells. But more apparent than ever is the immobile mask and the neutral tone which give the film's heroine, over and above the social or moral aspects, an extraordinary resemblance to the other Jeanne—of *Pickpocket*—and even to Chantal in *Diary of a Country Priest*, just as one already existed between the curé, Lieutenant Fontaine, and the pickpocket himself; this also endows the admirable historical text, to which Bresson wanted to be absolutely faithful, with a distinction and a spiritual relevance which realistic or expressive speech would have been unlikely to achieve to such a degree.

But if this strange tone seems to give an extra dimension to the character who uses it—and, taken in context, it is in fact the aesthetic equivalent of the mystery in the person—it also apparently makes communication, to which speech is normally devoted, not just problematical, but improbable. It is this further aspect of Bresson's universe which we must now consider.

From Loneliness to Communication

Many modern works, in the cinema and elsewhere, cultivate more or less successfully the theme of loneliness, preferably in a crowd, and produce variations which do not always manage to avoid a certain romantic complacency. By contrast, there is nothing less romantic than the loneliness of Bresson's characters. Theirs is not a sentimental attitude and it would be impossible to reveal the slightest complacency. On the contrary, they are fighting a constant, ruthless battle to reach each other by one means or another. They seem to know that their isolation is only apparent and that mysterious opportunities of meeting do exist, if one knows how to grasp them. They are like forest trees seen at eye-level, their smooth, stiff trunks well-spaced, always protected with bark, while underground, invisibly, their roots intermingle, and at the same time, high in the sky, their topmost branches lean towards one another in the hope that a breath of wind will enable them to touch. These people see each other, address each other, reproach each other, but even after they have been trying for a long time, communication is always a leap into the unknown, almost a miracle. Think of Anne-Marie and

Thérèse in *Les Anges du péché*, of the curé and Chantal and the countess, of Fontaine and Jost, of Michel and Jeanne. And the exchanges between Joan of Arc and her judges are more than a dialogue, they are a duel; yet a strange understanding is to be forged on the pyre between the executioners and the victim in the presence of the cross which they hold out to her and which she contemplates: an understanding in which all human contradictions are condensed and resolved.

Here again Bresson's style translates with perfect control a world in which neither communication nor loneliness are taken for granted, where, because of a fundamental discontinuity, meeting remains possible. In particular the spatio-temporal structure of all these films is also perfectly suited to this aspect. Thus we are always dealing with privileged areas, cut off from the rest of the world, as monasteries or prisons can be. We already have both in *Les Anges du péché*. In *Les Dames du Bois de Boulogne*, Agnès's and her mother's flat is a true prison to which Hélène has the key. In *Diary of a Country Priest* everyone remembers the castle and presbytery bars, and even more the "prisoner of the Holy Agony." *A Man Escaped*, *Pickpocket* and *The Trial of Joan of Arc* deal with prisons in the strictest sense.

Furthermore, these enclosed spaces which encompass the people who live in them do not have only one part: they are subdivided into juxtaposed cells, which are not without association but without links. You cannot go directly from one to another; there is always a space to be crossed, a staircase to go up or come down, corridors to be walked along. Think, for example, of the cells in the convent and of those in the prison in *Les Anges du péché*, of those in *A Man Escaped*, where the systematic absence of establishing shots serves to underline the partitioning. In *Les Dames du Bois de Boulogne*, the two flats perform the same function and the waterfall is a sort of neutral cell where the meetings take place. The cars seem like moving cells which each character takes with him and in which he is separated from the others, even if only by a window. Even the famous sequence of the lift and the staircase becomes profoundly significant when seen from this angle. So does the pickpocket's lonely room, simultaneously connected with and separated from the outside world by a sordid staircase. But it is with *The Trial of Joan of Arc* that the cellular universe reaches its final paroxysm: here the whole film is set in the rooms of the Château de Rouen which have been turned into a prison.

How can one help thinking of the space which Bresson, the erstwhile painter, may have meditated upon, the space of cubist paintings, where one is dealing not with an unique perspective which binds together and unifies everything but with a partitioning of facets which are entangled with each other without intermingling because they are always separated by rigid edges. But here the intervention of a temporal dimension allows for a more complete orchestration of discontinuity. In the first place, this is because time in the film is shown as being firmly bounded by a beginning and an end, with no extension into an hypothetical future. What Thérèse or Michel are going to do at the end of *Les Anges du péché* and *Pickpocket* or what Fontaine will do after his escape, is of no interest to us. In the other films, death definitively closes off the flow of time, even though it may open up new horizons. Moreover, this enclosed time itself is made up of a succession—almost a juxtaposition—of moments with no quality of duration. For instance, in *Les Dames du Bois de Boulogne*, the fade-outs are not sufficient to bind together the separate moments: the taxi, Hélène and Jean, Hélène alone, Madame D's cabaret, the waterfall . . . Nor is there more flowing duration in *A Man Escaped*. The escape plan which should unite everything in fact only justifies each element. "The door had to open," says Fontaine, "I had no plans beyond that," and André Bazin comments: "His fate and his liberty are sufficient to each moment, indeed to each shot." *Pickpocket* is no different: its extremely fragmented outline, with unusually abrupt cuts and ellipses, has often surprised and disconcerted both spectators and critics. And in *Diary of a Country Priest*, Bresson has managed to edit out entire sequences without causing any irritation. Everyone knows that the number of Stations of the Cross, which has been fixed at fourteen, is purely arbitrary. It can be done validly with one small cross. The whole of Bresson's film is that cross which summarizes it as much as ends it. And in *The Trial of Joan of Arc*, each scene, each interrogation, even each question and answer could be self-sufficient, at least to the extent that the whole film is latent in each exchange.

The very striking discontinuity of space and time in Bresson's universe and the loneliness of the characters which it expresses, seems to be supported by the hidden inclusion of everything in each part and of everyone in each person. Because of this, neither loneliness nor communication is taken for granted, and both create problems. Even so, it has been pointed out that the stress moves from the former towards the latter from one film to the next, from *Les Anges du péché* to *The Trial of Joan of Arc*. Bresson's people, we were saying, are like forest trees side by side, seeming not to notice that their roots intermingle, but stretching their branches across the space towards each other in order to make contact when a chance breath of wind helps them. This parallel is valid from *Les Anges du péché* to *The Trial of Joan of Arc*, but a fundamental fellowship seems to become more apparent: roots bare themselves and the wind blows more often.

Les Anges du péché is summed up in Anne-Marie's and Thérèse's attempt to communicate. Failures and pseudo-successes follow each other, but each stays in her prison—a prison of hate or of self-sufficiency. The only things which can close the gap are Anne-Marie's sacrifice and death: Thérèse leaves the convent which has been her prison and voluntarily enters the prison which will prove a true convent for her, the place where she regains her inner freedom. The four characters in *Les Dames du Bois de Boulogne* are no less shut up in themselves, and the attempt by one woman to reunite the other two is seen by her as a method of separating them even further. Agnès's death is apparently a success, but is in fact a drastic failure.

The curé, though trying with all his might to communicate, finds his own loneliness forming a constant barrier between him and the loneliness of others. He makes souls close up; Chantal here wears the same mask as Maria Casarès in the previous film. In the last resort, he with his humility is as impotent as Anne-Marie with her pride. Still, we do find here, unexpectedly, souls which open up: the countess, Séraphita, Dufréty's friend, and perhaps Chantal herself . . .

But it is above all in *A Man Escaped* that isolation—I mean real isolation within apparent communication—gives way to solitude—apparent isolation where there is real communication. Fontaine in his cell is apparently alone; in reality, in truth, he is not alone. The prison is a world of communication, even of communion. If he escapes, it will be thanks to all those who surround him: the prayers of some, the advice of others, and the experience of all. The sign of this real communion in apparent solitude is the music from Mozart's Mass, heard each time they walk round the yard with their slop pails. People have seen life, liberty, and God in this music. I see all those, but also unity, brotherhood, and communion. The music does not express the rather facile side to brotherhood, "the too human human," as seen by De Sica, but perhaps it has greater depth. If Fontaine had held out his hand to Jost in the first place, like a rather stupid big brother, instead of originally considering killing him—yes, killing him—their community in adventure would certainly not have been so complete. Bresson explained this aspect in an interview: "Fontaine finally holds out his hand to Jost in spite of himself, not to perform an act of generosity—quite the contrary—but because of that fellowship which binds us to each other, without our knowledge (and whether we want it or not) across life's partitions, as across the partitions of Montluc prison. It is a chance which leads Jost into Fontaine's cell, or the wind which bloweth where it listeth . . ." In Bresson's work there are always partitions, but thanks to human energy and the mysterious breath which animates them, these partitions seem to become less hermetically sealed.

Like *A Man Escaped*, *Pickpocket* is also a story of communication, but it begins with one of the most impenetrable cases of loneliness ever shown on the screen. Of all Bresson's characters, this one is certainly the most of an "outsider"—and they all are to a greater or lesser degree. He is isolated by his vice even among his equals. "He is alone with them, alone in the crowd, happy. Alone with his hands" (Jean Collet). The theme of the hands has a role here which is antithetical to that in *A Man Escaped*. While the Lieutenant uses his to win his liberty, to get rid of his handcuffs and communicate with others, the diabolical dexterity of Michel's hands, "the marvellous beating of wings" (René Guyonnet) ultimately serves only to rebuild the enclosed space, all-enveloping and lonely, of which he is the sovereign lord, because he is alone there: this situation could only end with handcuffs and prison. But a series of apparently unconnected meetings—of the mother, the woman and the child—will one day quite suddenly release him from his inner prison. Finally he discovers that someone else besides himself exists, and, through the bars which still cut him off from her, he hugs this unique person whose kiss reconciles him with the universe.

This is a happy ending which in another context could have been melodramatic, but here, although surrounded by apparent coherence, everything is so strange, so obviously predetermined by external forces, that one is obliged to accept it like the rest. Still, perhaps it would be a good thing to analyze this type of justification and see how those things which are of man and those which are beyond him work in this special universe.

From Immanence to Transcendence

So far it has been impossible to avoid referring constantly to an invisible dimension which can be felt in each character and even more strongly in their connections with each other. But this dimension is not on the same plane or even in direct extension of the others. Transcendence here is only an additional element which intervenes from outside by some means or other. We are dealing with immanent transcendence, or even, one might say, with radical invisibility. For the invisible world remains invisible, or rather appears only as invisible. When Bresson was offered a four millimetre cross to distinguish the priest in *A Man Escaped*, he said: "I'm afraid it may be a bit big." This is not timidity and fear of allowing too much importance to the Absolute. On the contrary, it is concern that it should not become relative, not just have a place among other things, when it should be everything, the soul of everything. And it turns out that, far from being obscured by so much caution, the mysterious presence of the "wind which bloweth where it listeth," becomes all the more hauntingly irrefutable by remaining impalpable. So much so that one may well wonder whether the word God is ever spoken in any of the films, even *Les Anges du péché* or *Diary of a Country Priest*. It is there like the other side of the world, or rather like the real place of which we know the other side, what André Bazin nicely terms *le côté pile de la face de Dieu* (the tails side of the face of God). It is situated in discontinuity, in the void we were talking about earlier. In other words, it is confused with freedom, for each free action seems a leap across this void, a true miracle. The Absolute does not influence men in the way that one thing acts upon another. It is simply at the heart of their freedom—its soul. On the subject of *A Man Escaped*, Bresson said: "I want to show this miracle: an invisible hand on the prison directing events and making something succeed for one person and not for another . . ." An invisible hand which never acts except by the hand of Fontaine, by that obstinate hand that makes tools and forces doors. "Help yourself," said the original title of the film.

There is even an invisible hand in *Diary of a Country Priest*, in *Les Anges*, in *Les Dames*, in *Pickpocket*, and of course in *The Trial of Joan of Arc*. It is this which made Henri Agel write: "Bresson, like Pascal and the true poets, lifts the moment from its temporal framework and transfigures it into a piece of eternity."

How does this eternity appear, while remaining invisible? Mainly through the inexpressiveness of faces and through death. By expressing nothing, the masks express precisely that which is beyond expression. Think of the faces of Thérèse, Hélène, Chantal, Michel, Joan . . . The whole point is that behind these inexpressive faces lies death. Jacques Prévert wrote: "how vague, inconsistent and disturbing a live face would seem to us if there was not a death mask inside it." But even if Bresson's characters do not always see their own death, they have no difficulty in seeing death around them and in seeing in it the sign and the gate to the beyond. In *Les Anges*, Thérèse's conversion takes place between the murder of her lover and Anne-Marie's death. In *Diary of a Country Priest* there is the baby's death, the countess's, the doctor's, and finally the curé's. Even *Les Dames* loses all its point if one does not admit Agnès's death at the end of the film. In *Pickpocket* the death and burial of the mother are the episodes which appear to correspond to an experience peculiar to Bresson; they are at the centre of Michel's drama, and will be the point of departure for his final evolution. "I believed in God for three minutes," he says to Jeanne. But when you've believed like that for a moment, it goes on for ever. That's why this "outsider" in contrast to Camus's (although he, too, sees his mother die) will receive grace and his diabolical hands will be purified.

But it is with *The Trial of Joan of Arc* that death takes on its true face of eternity, that of sacrifice, foreshadowed in *Diary of a Country Priest*. Joan, in spite of her courage in armed combat and even in the more terrifying battle of words, is afraid of death and in particular of death by fire: she thinks her virgin body has not merited this ultimate purification. It is really only at the end, when there can be no more hope of any other sort of liberation, that she will finally agree to see in it the predestined means of meeting Him whose Voices have never deceived her. The shots of the pyre which end the film translate with a simplicity and beauty rarely attained in other sacred art this accession through death to eternal life. This very pure body literally fades away into the sky and only a half-burnt stake is left to mark for the people who remain one of those mysterious points in time when the paths of history and eternity have crossed.

Yet again, in Bresson's work, it is never one thing sacrificed to another, neither history to eternity, nor grace to freedom. The two mysteriously coexist, or rather interpenetrate, rather as the soul and body do. It is significant that Bresson hesitated a long time between two titles for the film which eventually became *A Man Escaped*: *"Le Vent souffle où il veut . . .*—The wind bloweth where it listeth" and *"Aide-toi*—Help yourself . . ."* ("heaven will help you" is understood). This is why a partial study of Bresson's universe can always produce differing interpretations.

For example, one could perfectly well refuse to see in it anything but man, his will and his history. In that case, it would be stressed that decisions and events are formed by minds and resolute spirits. If you are a prisoner, you are told, use your brain and your hands. Your freedom lies in your human hands. And if your companion fails, although he may be "courage itself," it's because he didn't reflect for long enough. But if you are an unfortunate, lonely and despairing priest, fight yourself with all your strength, fight the evil that is in you and around you. Fight without hope or logic, just for the beauty of the gesture, just as, on a different plane, a young Legionnaire does. Then, even if God remains silent, you will attain peace. If, on the other hand, you are what society calls a thief, don't think yourself marked with some indelible blemish which will be either your shame or your pride, but know that you yourself have chosen to be like that. All you must do is simply look out for other things in you and around you, other forces which surround you and which can be as strong, if you wish, as your vice: the dying look of your mother; the child you find by the way; the woman you have not yet been able to see. It is there that your freedom lies. In you and around you, in your human universe. If, however, you have given all your strength to the service of your country and your enemies have defeated you and have you in their power, then renounce none of your ideals, die in hope, for the example of your sacrifice may perhaps serve your cause better than your most outstanding actions would have done.

Why, then, seek grace in a world where prisoners can attain freedom simply by brute force; where a young priest finds peace by fighting despair alone; where a proud thief ends by accepting a humble form of communication with his fellow creatures, after very subtle but very definite and profound preparation; where a heroine finally sacrifices herself without showing weakness because she has faith in the future? Why seek grace? Because, if you look more closely, grace is there, powerful even while invisible. In fact there is nothing but grace—its sovereign omnipotence obscures everything else. Because "the wind bloweth where it listeth," one prisoner will escape and another will be killed; one thief will recant, another will die in sin; one priest will retain a strong and unfailing hope, another will know the depths of complete moral and spiritual abandonment. Why? Doubtless one can provide vague human reasons, but they are always insufficient, and in the end only God knows. "All is grace," but that is why nothing is freedom. Should we not say of those who think they can escape from its grasp—of Chantal in *Diary of a Country Priest*, the executioners in *A Man Escaped* and *The Trial of Joan of Arc*, and even more of Hélène in *Les Dames*—that they are literally "graceless" in the manner of certain Racinian characters (this is not the first time that the relationship between Bresson and Racine has been underlined), that they are Christians without grace. In other words, to the Jansenism that Bresson is so often accused of in his direction, he adds an undeniably Jansenist way of thinking.

The fact that two such contradictory interpretations can reasonably be upheld at the same time shows only one thing: we are dealing, as Pascal would say, with two faces of the same truth. Instead of choosing, then, we must agree that in Bresson's universe "all is grace" but simultaneously "all is freedom." No formula could be more orthodox if the Doctor of grace, Saint Augustine, is to be believed: ". . . as the law is not made void but established through faith, since faith procures the grace whereby the law is fulfilled, so the freedom of the will is not made void through grace, but rather is thereby established . . ." (*"De spiritu et littera,"* xxx, 52). Seen in this light, it is perhaps significant that it has proved possible to make the Jeanne of *Pickpocket* simultaneously a symbol of grace and of freedom. When she embraces Michel through the prison bars, she is grace bringing freedom.

These are some of the aspects of Bresson's universe which seem essential. Although he saw the light almost twenty years ago—a relatively long time in the brief history of the cinema—one cannot fail to be struck by his youthfulness. While the old guard of the cinema persist in repeating endlessly the old formulae on which their youthful success was based—when they are not trying, with touching willingness to please, to borrow the trappings of the latest fashions from the more turbulent of their young disciples—Bresson, with an imperturbable disregard for the cinema around him, has only to be himself to gain quite naturally a place in the vanguard—the only valid section—of what has been too complacently called the New Wave. The films of Alain Resnais, of Truffaut, of Chris Marker or of Agnès Varda, whatever their inner differences may be, are all involved in the same search as Bresson.

The superseding of analytical psychology, which had scarcely evolved since Paul Bourget; the extreme importance given to the text and its dissonances with the picture; the entirely new evaluation of the different forms of temporality; the recognized value of empty space and absence; a certain hieratic quality in the acting, the rejection of theatrical performances and traditional dramatization, not to mention the all too well known "distanciation": all these constitute, even more than the thematic element, a common climate which is that of the true modern cinema. If Bresson can be seen as the precursor, chronologically, and if the whole younger generation respects him because of this, he is not reduced as a result to the honorary role of venerable ancestor; far from it, he remains a contemporary and an equal. Besides, in our epoch of speeded up history, one no longer bows to age, but only to mastery.

Translated from the French by Elizabeth Kingsley-Rowe

Un condamné à mort s'est échappé

SUSAN SONTAG

Spiritual Style in the
Films of Robert Bresson

S OME ART aims directly at arousing the feelings; some art appeals to the
feelings through the route of the intelligence. There is art that involves,
that creates empathy. There is art that detaches, that provokes reflection.

Great reflective art is not frigid. It can exalt the spectator, it can present images
that appall, it can make him weep. But its emotional power is mediated. The pull
toward emotional involvement is counterbalanced by elements in the work that
promote distance, disinterestedness, impartiality. Emotional involvement is always, to a greater or lesser degree, postponed.

The contrast can be accounted for in terms of techniques or means even of
ideas. No doubt, though, the sensibility of the artist is, in the end, decisive. It is a
reflective art, a detached art that Brecht is advocating when he talks about the
"Alienation Effect." The didactic aims which Brecht claimed for his theatre are
really a vehicle for the cool temperament that conceived those plays.

2

In the film, the master of the reflective mode is Robert Bresson.

Though Bresson was born in 1911, his extant work in the cinema has all been
done in the last twenty years, and consists of six feature films. (He made a short film
in 1934 called *Les Affaires publiques*, reportedly a comedy in the manner of René Clair,
all copies of which have been lost;* did some work on the scripts of two obscure

---

*This article was originally published in 1964; a substantial fragment of *Les Affaires publiques* was
discovered in 1987 at the Cinémathèque Française. *Ed.*

commercial films in the mid-thirties; and in 1940 was assistant director to Clair on a film that was never finished.) Bresson's first full-length film was begun when he returned to Paris in 1941 after spending eighteen months in a German prison camp. He met a Dominican priest and writer, Father Bruckberger, who suggested that they collaborate on a film about Bethany, the French Dominican order devoted to the care and rehabilitation of women ex-convicts. A scenario was written, Jean Giraudoux was enlisted to write the dialogue, and the film—at first called *Béthanie*, and finally, at the producers' insistence, *Les Anges du péché* (The Angels of Sin)—was released in 1943. It was enthusiastically acclaimed by the critics and had a success with the public as well.

The plot of his second film, begun in 1944 and released in 1945, was a modern version of one of the interpolated stories in Diderot's great anti-novel *Jacques le fataliste*; Bresson wrote the scenario and Jean Cocteau the dialogue. Bresson's first success was not repeated, however. *Les Dames du Bois de Boulogne* (sometimes called, here, *The Ladies of the Park*) was panned by the critics and failed at the box-office, too.

Bresson's third film, *Journal d'un curé de campagne* (*Diary of a Country Priest*), did not appear until 1951; his fourth film, *Un condamné à mort s'est échappé* (called, here, *A Man Escaped*), in 1956; his fifth film, *Pickpocket*, in 1959; and his sixth film, *Procès de Jeanne d'Arc* (*The Trial of Joan of Arc*), in 1962. All have had a certain success with critics but scarcely any with the public—with the exception of the last film, which most critics disliked, too. Once hailed as the new hope of the French cinema, Bresson is now firmly labelled as an esoteric director. He has never had the attention of the art-house audience that flocks to Buñuel, Bergman, Fellini—though he is a far greater director than these; even Antonioni has almost a mass audience compared with Bresson's. And, except among a small coterie, he has had only the scantest critical attention.

The reason that Bresson is not generally ranked according to his merits is that the tradition to which his art belongs, the reflective or contemplative, is not well understood. Particularly in England and America, Bresson's films are often described as cold, remote, overintellectualized, geometrical. But to call a work of art "cold" means nothing more or less than to compare it (often unconsciously) to a work that is "hot." And not all art is—or could be—hot, any more than all persons have the same temperament. The generally accepted notions of the range of temperament in art are provincial. Certainly, Bresson is cold next to Pabst or Fellini. (So is Vivaldi cold next to Brahms, and Keaton cold next to Chaplin.) One has to understand the aesthetics—that is, find the beauty—of such coldness. And Bresson offers a particularly good case for sketching such an aesthetic, because of his range. Exploring the possibilities of a reflective, as opposed to an emotionally immediate, art, Bresson moves from the diagrammatic perfection of *Les Dames du Bois de Boulogne* to the almost lyrical, almost "humanistic" warmth of *Un condamné à mort s'est échappé*. He also shows—and this is instructive, too—how such art can become too rarefied, in his last film, *Procès de Jeanne d'Arc*.

3

In reflective art, the *form* of the work of art is present in an emphatic way.

The effect of the spectator's being aware of the form is to elongate or to retard the emotions. For, to the extent that we are conscious of form in a work of art, we become somewhat detached; our emotions do not respond in the same way as they do in real life. Awareness of form does two things simultaneously: it gives a sensuous pleasure independent of the "content," and it invites the use of intelligence. It may be a very low order of reflection which is invited, as, for instance, by the narrative form (the interweaving of the four separate stories) of Griffith's *Intolerance*. But it is reflection, nonetheless.

The typical way in which "form" shapes "content" in art is by doubling, duplicating. Symmetry and the repetition of motifs in painting, the double plot in Elizabethan drama, and rhyme schemes in poetry are a few obvious examples.

The evolution of forms in art is partly independent of the evolution of subject-matters. (The history of forms is dialectical. As types of sensibility become banal, boring, and are overthrown by their opposites, so forms in art are, periodically, exhausted. They become banal, unstimulating, and are replaced by new forms which are at the same time anti-forms.) Sometimes the most beautiful effects are gained when the material and the form are at cross purposes. Brecht does this often: placing a hot subject in a cold frame. Other times, what satisfies is that the form is perfectly appropriate to the theme. This is the case with Bresson.

Why Bresson is not only a much greater, but also a more interesting director than, say, Buñuel is that he has worked out a form that perfectly expresses and accompanies what he wants to say. In fact, it *is* what he wants to say.

Here, one must carefully distinguish between form and manner. Welles, the early René Clair, Sternberg, Ophuls are examples of directors with unmistakable stylistic inventions. But they never created a rigorous narrative form. Bresson, like Ozu, has. And the form of Bresson's films is designed (like Ozu's) to discipline the emotions at the same time that it arouses them: to induce a certain tranquillity in the spectator, a state of spiritual balance that is itself the subject of the film.

Reflective art is art which, in effect, imposes a certain discipline on the audience—postponing easy gratification. Even boredom can be a permissible means of such discipline. Giving prominence to what is artifice in the work of art is another means. One thinks here of Brecht's idea of theatre. Brecht advocated strategies of staging—like having a narrator, putting musicians on stage, interposing filmed scenes—and a technique of acting so that the audience could distance itself, and not become uncritically "involved" in the plot and the fate of the characters. Bresson wishes distance, too. But his aim, I would imagine, is not to keep hot emotions cool so that intelligence can prevail. The emotional distance typical of Bresson's films seems to exist for a different reason altogether: because all identification with characters, deeply conceived, is an impertinence—an affront to the mystery that is human action and the human heart.

But—all claims for intellectual coolness or respect for the mystery of action laid aside—surely Brecht knew, as must Bresson, that such distancing is a source of great emotional power. It is precisely the defect of the naturalistic theatre and cinema that, giving itself too readily, it easily consumes and exhausts its effects. Ultimately, the greatest source of emotional power in art lies not in any particular subject-matter, however passionate, however universal. It lies in form. The detachment and retarding of the emotions, through the consciousness of form, makes them far stronger and more intense in the end.

4

Despite the venerable critical slogan that film is primarily a visual medium, and despite the fact that Bresson was a painter before he turned to making films, form for Bresson is not mainly visual. It is, above all, a distinctive form of narration. For Bresson film is not a plastic but a narrative experience.

Bresson's form fulfills beautifully the prescription of Alexandre Astruc, in his famous essay "Le Caméra-Stylo," written in the late forties. According to Astruc, the cinema will, ideally, become a language.

> By a language I mean the form in which and through which an artist can express his thoughts, however abstract they may be, or translate his obsessions, just as in an essay or a novel . . . The film will gradually free itself from the tyranny of the visual, of the image for its own sake, of the immediate and concrete anecdote, to become a means of writing as supple and subtle as the written word . . . What interests us in the cinema today is the creation of this language.

Cinema-as-language means a break with the traditional dramatic and visual way of telling a story in film. In Bresson's work, this creation of a language for films entails a heavy emphasis on the word. In the first two films, where the action is still relatively dramatic, and the plot employs a group of characters,* language (in

---

* Even here, though, there is a development. In *Les Anges du péché*, there are five main characters—the young novice Anne-Marie, another novice Madeleine, the prioress, the prioress's assistant Mother Saint-Jean, and the murderess Thérèse—as well as a great deal of background: the daily life of the convent, and so forth. In *Les Dames du Bois de Boulogne*, there is already a simplification, less background. Four characters are clearly outlined—Hélène, her former lover Jean, Agnès, and Agnès's mother. Everyone else is virtually invisible. We never see the servants' faces, for instance.

the literal sense) appears in the form of dialogue. This dialogue definitely calls attention to itself. It is very theatrical dialogue, concise, aphoristic, deliberate, literary. It is the opposite of the improvised-sounding dialogue favored by the new French directors—including Godard in *Vivre sa vie* and *Une femme mariée*, the most Bressonian of the New Wave films.

But in the last four films, in which the action has contracted from that which befalls a group to the fortunes of the lonely self, dialogue is often displaced by first-person narration. Sometimes the narration can be justified as providing links between scenes. But, more interestingly, it often doesn't tell us anything we don't know or are about to learn. It "doubles" the action. In this case, we usually get the word first, then the scene. For example, in *Pickpocket*: we see the hero writing (and hear his voice reading) his memoirs. Then we see the event which he has already curtly described.

But sometimes we get the scene first, then the explanation, the description of what has just happened. For example, in *Journal d'un curé de campagne*, there is a scene in which the priest calls anxiously on the vicar of Torcy. We see the priest wheeling his bicycle up to the vicar's door, then the housekeeper answering (the vicar is obviously not at home, but we don't hear the housekeeper's voice), then the door shutting, and the priest leaning against it. Then, we hear: "I was so disappointed, I had to lean against the door." Another example: in *Un condamné à mort s'est échappé*, we see Fontaine tearing up the cloth of his pillow, then twisting the cloth around wire which he has stripped off the bed frame. Then, the voice: "I twisted it strongly."

The effect of this "superfluous" narration is to punctuate the scene with intervals. It puts a brake on the spectator's direct imaginative participation in the action. Whether the order is from comment to scene or from scene to comment, the effect is the same: such doublings of the action both arrest and intensify the ordinary emotional sequence.

Notice, too, that in the first type of doubling—where we hear what's going to happen before we see it—there is a deliberate flouting of one of the traditional modes of narrative involvement: suspense. Again, one thinks of Brecht. To eliminate suspense, at the beginning of a scene Brecht announces, by means of placards or a narrator, what is to happen. (Godard adopts this technique in *Vivre sa vie*.) Bresson does the same thing, by jumping the gun with narration. In many ways, the perfect story for Bresson is that of his last film, *Procès de Jeanne d'Arc*—in that the plot is wholly known, foreordained; the words of the actors are not invented but those of the actual trial record. Ideally, there is no suspense in a Bresson film. Thus, in the one film where suspense should normally play a large role, *Un condamné à mort s'est échappé*, the title deliberately—even awkwardly—gives the outcome away: we know Fontaine is going to make it.* In this respect, of

---

* The film has a co-title, which expresses the theme of inexorability: *Le Vent souffle où il veut.*

course, Bresson's escape film differs from Jacques Becker's last work, *Le Trou* (called, here, *Nightwatch*), though in other ways Becker's excellent film owes a great deal to *Un condamné à mort s'est échappé*. (It is to Becker's credit that he was the only prominent person in the French film world who defended *Les Dames du Bois de Boulogne* when it came out.)

Thus, form in Bresson's films is anti-dramatic, though strongly linear. Scenes are cut short, and set end to end without obvious emphasis. In *Journal d'un curé de campagne*, there must be thirty such short scenes. This method of constructing the story is most rigorously observed in *Procès de Jeanne d'Arc*. The film is composed of static, medium shots of people talking; the scenes are the inexorable sequence of Jeanne's interrogations. The principle of eliding anecdotal material—in *Un condamné à mort s'est échappé*, for instance, one knows little about why Fontaine is in prison in the first place—is here carried to its extreme. There are no interludes of any sort. An interrogation ends; the door slams behind Jeanne; the scene fades out. The key clatters in the lock; another interrogation; again the door clangs shut; fade-out. It is a very dead-pan construction, which puts a sharp brake on emotional involvement.

Bresson also came to reject the species of involvement created in films by the expressiveness of the acting. Again, one is reminded of Brecht by Bresson's particular way of handling actors, in the exercise of which he has found it preferable to use non-professionals in major roles. Brecht wanted the actor to "report" a role rather than "be" it. He sought to divorce the actor from identifying with the role, as he wanted to divorce the spectator from identifying with the events that he saw being "reported" on the stage. "The actor," Brecht insists, "must remain a demonstrator; he must present the person demonstrated as a stranger, he must not suppress the '*he* did that, *he* said that' element in his performance." Bresson, working with non-professional actors in his last four films (he used professionals in *Les Anges du péché* and *Les Dames du Bois de Boulogne*), also seems to be striving for the same effect of strangeness. His idea is for the actors not to act out their lines, but simply to say them with as little expression as possible. (To get this effect, Bresson rehearses his actors for several months before shooting begins.) Emotional climaxes are rendered very elliptically.

But the reason is really quite different in the two cases. The reason that Brecht rejected acting reflects his idea of the relation of dramatic art to critical intelligence. He thought that the emotional force of the acting would get in the way of the ideas represented in plays. (From what I saw of the work of the Berliner Ensemble six years ago, though, it didn't seem to me that the somewhat low-keyed acting really diminished emotional involvement; it was the highly stylized staging which did that.) The reason that Bresson rejects acting reflects his notion of the purity of the art itself. "Acting is for the theatre, which is a bastard art," he has said. "The film can be a true art because in it the author takes fragments of reality and arranges them in such a way that their juxtaposition transforms them." Cinema, for Bresson, is a total art, in which acting corrodes. In a film,

> each shot is like a word, which means nothing by itself, or rather means so many things that in effect it is meaningless. But a word in a poem is transformed, its meaning made precise and unique, by its placing in relation to the words around it: in the same way a shot in a film is given its meaning by its context, and each shot modifies the meaning of the previous one until with the last shot a total, unparaphrasable meaning has been arrived at. Acting has nothing to do with that, it can only get in the way. Films can only be made by bypassing the will of those who appear in them; using not what they do, but what they are.

In sum: there are spiritual resources beyond effort, which appear only when effort is stilled. One imagines that Bresson never treats his actors to an "interpretation" of their roles: Claude Laydu, who plays the priest in *Journal d'un curé de campagne*, has said that while he was making the film he was never told to try to represent sanctity, though that is what it appears, when viewing the film, that he does. In the end, everything depends on the actor, who either has this luminous presence or doesn't. Laydu has it. So does François Leterrier, who is Fontaine in *Un condamné à mort s'est échappé*. But Martin Lassalle as Michel in *Pickpocket* conveys something wooden, at times evasive. With Florence Carrez in *Procès de Jeanne d'Arc*, Bresson has experimented with the limit of the unexpressive. There is no acting at all; she simply reads the lines. It could have worked. But it doesn't—because she is the least luminous of all the presences Bresson has "used" in his later films. The thinness of Bresson's last film is, partly, a failure of communicated intensity on the part of the actress who plays Jeanne, upon whom the film depends.

5

All of Bresson's films have a common theme: the meaning of confinement and liberty. The imagery of the religious vocation and of crime are used jointly. Both lead to "the cell."

The plots all have to do with incarceration and its sequel. *Les Anges du péché* takes place mostly inside a convent. Thérèse, an ex-convict who (unknown to the police) has just murdered the lover who betrayed her, is delivered into the hands of the Bethany nuns. One young novice, who tries to create a special relationship with Thérèse and, learning her secret, to get her to surrender herself voluntarily to the police, is expelled from the convent for insubordination. One morning, she is found dying in the convent garden. Thérèse is finally moved, and the last shot is of her extending her hands to the policeman's manacles. . . . In *Les Dames du Bois de Boulogne*, the metaphor of confinement is repeated several times. Hélène and Jean have been confined in their love; he urges her to return to the world now that she is "free." But she doesn't, and instead devotes herself to setting a trap for him—a trap which requires that she find two pawns (Agnès and her mother), whom she virtually confines in an apartment while they await her orders. Like *Les Anges du péché*, this is the story of the redemption of a lost girl. In *Les Anges du péché*, Thérèse is liberated by accepting imprisonment; in *Les Dames du Bois de Boulogne*, Agnès is imprisoned, and then, arbitrarily, as by a miracle, is forgiven, set free. . . . In *Journal d'un curé de campagne*, the emphasis has shifted. The bad girl, Chantal, is kept in the background. The drama of confinement is in the priest's confinement in himself, his despair, his weakness, his mortal body. ("I was a prisoner of the Holy Agony.") He is liberated by accepting his senseless and agonizing death from stomach cancer. . . . In *Un condamné à mort s'est échappé*, which is set in a German-run prison in occupied France, confinement is most literally represented. So is liberation: the hero triumphs over himself (his despair, the temptation of inertia) and escapes. The obstacles are embodied both in material things and in the incalculability of the human beings in the vicinity of the solitary hero. But Fontaine risks trusting the two strangers in the courtyard at the beginning of his imprisonment, and his trust is not betrayed. And because he risks trusting the youthful collaborationist who is thrown into his cell with him on the eve of his escape (the alternative is to kill the boy), he is able to get out. . . . In *Pickpocket*, the hero is a young recluse who lives in a closet of a room, a petty criminal who, in Dostoevskian fashion, appears to crave punishment. Only at the end, when he has been caught and is in jail, talking through the bars with the girl who has loved him, is he depicted as being, possibly, able to love. . . . In *Procès de Jeanne d'Arc*, again the entire film is set in prison. As in *Journal d'un curé de campagne*, Jeanne's liberation comes through a hideous death; but Jeanne's martyrdom is much less affecting than the priest's, because she is so depersonalized (unlike Falconetti's Jeanne in Dreyer's great film) that she does not seem to mind dying.

The nature of drama being conflict, the real drama of Bresson's stories is interior conflict: the fight against oneself. And all the static and formal qualities of his films work to that end. Bresson has said, of his choice of the highly stylized and artificial plot of *Les Dames du Bois de Boulogne*, that it allowed him to "eliminate anything which might distract from the interior drama." Still, in that film and the one before it, interior drama is represented in an exterior form, however fastidious and stripped down. *Les Anges du péché* and *Les Dames du Bois de Boulogne* depict conflicts of wills among the various characters as much or more than they concern a conflict within the self.

It is only in the films following *Les Dames du Bois de Boulogne* that Bresson's drama has been really interiorized. The theme of *Journal d'un curé de campagne* is the young priest's conflict with himself: only secondarily is this acted out in his relation with the vicar of Torcy, with Chantal, and with the countess, Chantal's mother. This is even clearer in *Un condamné à mort s'est échappé*—where the principal character is literally isolated in a cell, struggling against despair. Solitude and interior conflict pair off in another way in *Pickpocket*, where the solitary hero refuses despair only at the price of refusing love, and gives himself over to masturbatory acts of theft. But in the last film, where we know the drama should be taking place, there is scarcely any evidence of it. Conflict has been virtually suppressed; it must be inferred. Bresson's Jeanne is an automaton of grace. But, however interior the drama, there must be drama. This is what *Procès de Jeanne d'Arc* withholds.

Notice, though, that the "interior drama" which Bresson seeks to depict does not mean *psychology*. In realistic terms, the motives of Bresson's characters are often hidden, sometimes downright incredible. In *Pickpocket*, for instance, when Michel sums up his two years in London with "I lost all my money on gambling and women," one simply does not believe it. Nor is it any more convincing that during this time the good Jacques, Michel's friend, has made Jeanne pregnant and then deserted her and their child.

Psychological implausibility is scarcely a virtue; and the narrative passages I have just cited are flaws in *Pickpocket*. But what is central to Bresson and, I think, not to be caviled at, is his evident belief that psychological analysis is superficial. (Reason: it assigns to action a paraphrasable meaning that true art transcends.) He does not intend his characters to be implausible, I'm sure; but he does, I think, intend them to be opaque. Bresson is interested in the forms of spiritual action— in the physics, as it were, rather than in the psychology of souls. Why persons behave as they do is, ultimately, not to be understood. (Psychology, precisely, *does* claim to understand.) Above all, persuasion is inexplicable, unpredictable. That the priest *does* reach the proud and unyielding countess (in *Journal d'un curé de campagne*), that Jeanne *doesn't* persuade Michel (in *Pickpocket*) are just facts—or mysteries, if you like.

Such a physics of the soul was the subject of Simone Weil's most remarkable book, *Gravity and Grace*. And the following sentences of Simone Weil's—

> All the natural movements of the soul are controlled by laws analogous to those of physical gravity. Grace is the only exception.
>
> Grace fills empty spaces, but it can only enter where there is a void to receive it, and it is grace itself which makes this void.
>
> The imagination is continually at work filling up all the fissures through which grace might pass.

supply the three basic theorems of Bresson's "anthropology." Some souls are heavy, others light; some are liberated or capable of being liberated, others not.

All one can do is be patient, and as empty as possible. In such a regimen there is no place for the imagination, much less for ideas and opinions. The ideal is neutrality, transparence. This is what is meant when the vicar of Torcy tells the young priest in *Journal d'un curé de campagne*, "A priest has no opinions."

Except in an ultimate unrepresentable sense, a priest has no attachments either. In the quest for spiritual lightness ("grace"), attachments are a spiritual encumbrance. Thus, the priest, in the climactic scene of *Journal d'un curé de campagne*, forces the countess to relinquish her passionate mourning for her dead son. True contact between persons is possible, of course; but it comes not through will but unasked for, through grace. Hence in Bresson's films human solidarity is represented only at a distance—as it is between the priest and the vicar of Torcy in *Journal d'un curé de campagne*, or between Fontaine and the other prisoners in *Un condamné à mort s'est échappé*. The actual coming together of two people in a relation of love can be stated, ushered in, as it were, before our eyes: Jean crying out "Stay! I love you!" to the nearly dead Agnès in *Les Dames du Bois de Boulogne*; Fontaine putting his arm around Jost in *Un condamné à mort s'est échappé*; Michel in *Pickpocket* saying to Jeanne through prison bars, "How long it has taken me to come to you." But we do not see love lived. The moment in which it is declared terminates the film.

In *Un condamné à mort s'est échappé*, the elderly man in the adjoining cell asks the hero, querulously, "Why do you fight?" Fontaine answers, "To fight. To fight against myself." The true fight against oneself is against one's heaviness, one's gravity. And the instrument of this fight is the idea of work, a project, a task. In *Les Anges du péché*, it is Anne-Marie's project of "saving" Thérèse. In *Les Dames du Bois de Boulogne*, it is the revenge plot of Hélène. These tasks are cast in traditional form—constantly referring back to the intention of the character who performs them, rather than decomposed into separately engrossing acts of behaviour. In *Journal d'un curé de campagne* (which is transitional in this respect) the most affecting images are not those of the priest in his role, struggling for the souls of his parishioners, but of the priest in his homely moments: riding his bicycle, removing his vestments, eating bread, walking. In Bresson's next two films, work has dissolved into the idea of the-infinite-taking-of-pains. The project has become totally concrete, incarnate, and at the same time more impersonal. In *Un condamné à mort s'est échappé*, the most powerful scenes are those which show the hero absorbed in his labours: Fontaine scraping at his door with the spoon, Fontaine sweeping the wood shavings which have fallen on the floor into a tiny pile with a single straw pulled from his broom. ("One month of patient work—my door opened.") In *Pickpocket*, the emotional centre of the film is where Michel is wordlessly, disinterestedly, taken in hand by a professional pickpocket and initiated into the real art of what he has only practised desultorily: difficult gestures are demonstrated, the necessity of repetition and routine is made clear. Large sections of *Un condamné à mort s'est échappé* and *Pickpocket* are wordless; they are about the

Les Dames du Bois de Boulogne

beauties of personality effaced by a project. The face is very quiet, while other parts of the body, represented as humble servants of projects, become expressive, transfigured. One remembers Thérèse kissing the white feet of the dead Anne-Marie at the end of *Les Anges du péché*, the bare feet of the monks filing down the stone corridor in the opening sequence of *Procès de Jeanne d'Arc*. One remembers Fontaine's large graceful hands at their endless labours in *Un condamné à mort s'est échappé*, the ballet of agile thieving hands in *Pickpocket*.

Through the "project"—exactly contrary to "imagination"—one overcomes the gravity that weighs down the spirit. Even *Les Dames du Bois de Boulogne*, whose story seems most un-Bressonian, rests on this contrast between a project and gravity (or, immobility). Hélène has a project—revenging herself on Jean. But she is immobile, too—from suffering and vengefulness. Only in *Procès de Jeanne d'Arc*, the most Bressonian of stories, is this contrast (to the detriment of the film) not exploited. Jeanne has no project. Or if she may be said to have a project, her martyrdom, we only know about it; we are not privy to its development and consummation. She *appears* to be passive. If only because Jeanne is not portrayed for us in her solitude, alone in her cell, Bresson's last film seems, next to the others, so undialectical.

6

Jean Cocteau has said (*Cocteau on the Film*, A Conversation Recorded by André Fraigneau, 1951) that minds and souls today "live without a syntax, that is to say, without a moral system. This moral system has nothing to do with morality proper, and should be built up by each one of us as an inner style, without which no outer style is possible." Cocteau's films may be understood as portraying this inwardness which is the true morality; so may Bresson's. Both are concerned, in their films, with depicting spiritual style. This similarity is less than obvious because Cocteau conceives of spiritual style aesthetically, while in at least three of his films (*Les Anges du péché*, *Journal d'un curé de campagne*, and *Procès de Jeanne d'Arc*) Bresson seems committed to an explicit religious point of view. But the difference is not as great as it appears. Bresson's Catholicism is a language for rendering a certain vision of human action, rather than a "position" that is stated. (For contrast, compare the direct piety of Rossellini's *The Flowers of Saint Francis* and the complex debate on faith expounded in Melville's *Léon Morin, prêtre*.) The proof of this is that Bresson is able to say the same thing without Catholicism—in his three other films. In fact, the most entirely successful of all Bresson's films—*Un condamné à mort s'est échappé*—is one which, while it has a sensitive and intelligent priest in the background (one of the prisoners), bypasses the religious way of posing the problem. The religious vocation supplies one setting for ideas about gravity, lucidity, and martyrdom. But the drastically secular subjects of crime, the revenge of betrayed love, and solitary imprisonment also yield the same themes.

Bresson is really more like Cocteau than appears—an ascetic Cocteau, Cocteau divesting himself of sensuousness, Cocteau without poetry. The aim is the same: to build up an image of spiritual style. But the sensibility, needless to say, is altogether different. Cocteau's is a clear example of the homosexual sensibility that is one of the principal traditions of modern art: both romantic and witty, languorously drawn to physical beauty and yet always decorating itself with stylishness and artifice. Bresson's sensibility is antiromantic and solemn, pledged to ward off the easy pleasures of physical beauty and artifice for a pleasure which is more permanent, more edifying, more sincere.

In the evolution of this sensibility, Bresson's cinematic means become more and more chaste. His first two films, which were photographed by Philippe Agostini, stress visual effects in a way that the other four do not. Bresson's very first film, *Les Anges du péché*, is more conventionally beautiful than any which have followed. And in *Les Dames du Bois de Boulogne*, whose beauty is more muted, there are lyrical camera movements, like the shot which follows Hélène running down the stairs to arrive at the same time as Jean, who is descending in an elevator, and stunning cuts, like the one which moves from Hélène alone in her bedroom, stretched out on the bed, saying, "I will be revenged," to the first shot of Agnès, in a crowded nightclub, wearing tights and net stockings and top hat, in the throes of a sexy dance. Extremes of black-and-white succeed one another with great deliberateness. In *Les Anges du péché*, the darkness of the prison scene is set off by the whiteness of the convent wall and of the nuns' robes. In *Les Dames du Bois de Boulogne*, the contrasts are set by clothes even more than by interiors. Hélène always wears long black velvet dresses, whatever the occasion. Agnès has three costumes: the scant black dancing outfit in which she appears the first time, the light-coloured trench-coat she wears during most of the film, and the white wedding dress at the end. . . . The last four films, which were photographed by L. H. Burel, are much less striking visually, less chic. The photography is almost self-effacing. Sharp contrasts, as between black-and-white, are avoided. (It is almost impossible to imagine a Bresson film in colour.) In *Journal d'un curé de campagne*, for instance, one is not particularly aware of the blackness of the priest's habit. One barely notices the bloodstained shirt and dirty pants which Fontaine has on throughout *Un condamné à mort s'est échappé*, or the drab suits which Michel wears in *Pickpocket*. Clothes and interiors are as neutral, inconspicuous, functional as possible.

Besides refusing the visual, Bresson's later films also renounce "the beautiful." None of his non-professional actors are handsome in an outward sense. One's first feeling, when seeing Claude Laydu (the priest in *Journal d'un curé de campagne*),

François Leterrier (Fontaine in *Un condamné à mort s'est échappé*), Martin Lassalle (Michel in *Pickpocket*), and Florence Carrez (Jeanne in *Procès de Jeanne d'Arc*), is how plain they are. Then, at some point or other, one begins to see the face as strikingly beautiful. The transformation is most profound, and satisfying, with François Leterrier as Fontaine. Here lies an important difference between the films of Cocteau and Bresson, a difference which indicates the special place of *Les Dames du Bois de Boulogne* in Bresson's work; for this film (for which Cocteau wrote the dialogue) is in this respect very Cocteauish. Maria Casarès's blackgarbed demonic Hélène is, visually and emotionally, of a piece with her brilliant performance in Cocteau's *Orphée* (1950). Such a hard-edge character, a character with a "motive" that remains constant throughout the story, is very different from the treatment of character, typical of Bresson, in *Journal d'un curé de campagne*, *Un condamné à mort s'est échappé*, and *Pickpocket*. In the course of each of these three films, there is a subliminal revelation: a face which at first seems plain reveals itself to be beautiful; a character which at first seems opaque becomes oddly and inexplicably transparent. But in Cocteau's films—and in *Les Dames du Bois de Boulogne*— neither character nor beauty is revealed. They are there to be assumed, to be transposed into drama.

While the spiritual style of Cocteau's heroes (who are played, usually, by Jean Marais) tends toward narcissism, the spiritual style of Bresson's heroes is one variety or other of unself-consciousness. (Hence the role of the project in Bresson's films: it absorbs the energies that would otherwise be spent on the self. It effaces personality, in the sense of personality as what is idiosyncratic in each human being, the limit inside which we are locked.) Consciousness of self is the "gravity" that burdens the spirit; the surpassing of the consciousness of self is "grace," or spiritual lightness. The climax of Cocteau's films is a voluptuous movement: a falling down, either in love (*Orphée*) or death (*L'Aigle à deux têtes*, *L'Éternel retour*); or a soaring up (*La Belle et la bête*). With the exception of *Les Dames du Bois de Boulogne* (with its final glamorous image, shot from above, of Jean bending over Agnès, who lies on the floor like a great white bird), the end of Bresson's films is counter-voluptuous, reserved.

While Cocteau's art is irresistibly drawn to the logic of dreams, and to the truth of invention over the truth of "real life," Bresson's art moves increasingly away from the story and toward documentary. *Journal d'un curé de campagne* is a fiction, drawn from the superb novel of the same name by Georges Bernanos. But the journal device allows Bresson to relate the fiction in a quasi-documentary fashion. The film opens with a shot of a notebook and a hand writing in it, followed by a voice on the soundtrack reading what has been written. Many scenes start with the priest writing in his journal. The film ends with a letter from a friend to the vicar of Torcy relating the priest's death—we hear the words while the whole screen is occupied with the silhouette of a cross. Before *Un condamné à mort s'est échappé* begins we read the words on the screen: "This story actually happened. I have set it down without embellishment," and then: "Lyons, 1943." (Bresson had the original of Fontaine constantly present while the film was being made, to check on its accuracy.) *Pickpocket*, again a fiction, is told—partly—through journal form. Bresson returned to documentary in *Procès de Jeanne d'Arc*, this time with the greatest severity. Even music, which aided in setting tone in the earlier films, has been discarded. The use of the Mozart Mass in C Minor in *Un condamné à mort s'est échappé*, of Lully in *Pickpocket*, is particularly brilliant; but all that survives of music in *Procès de Jeanne d'Arc* is the drum beat at the opening of the film.

Bresson's attempt is to insist on the irrefutability of what he is presenting. Nothing happens by chance; there are no alternatives, no fantasy; everything is inexorable. Whatever is not necessary, whatever is merely anecdotal or decorative, must be left out. Unlike Cocteau, Bresson wishes to pare down—rather than to enlarge—the dramatic and visual resources of the cinema. (In this, Bresson again reminds one of Ozu, who in the course of his thirty years of filmmaking renounced the moving camera, the dissolve, the fade.) True, in the last, most ascetic of all his films, Bresson seems to have left out too much, to have over-refined his conception. But a conception as ambitious as this cannot help but have its extremism, and Bresson's "failures" are worth more than most directors' successes. For Bresson, art is the discovery of what is necessary—of that, and nothing more. The power of Bresson's six films lies in the fact that his purity and fastidiousness are not just an assertion about the resources of the cinema, as much of modern painting is mainly a comment in paint about painting. They are at the same time an idea about life, about what Cocteau called "inner style," about the most serious way of being human.

L'Argent

RENÉ PRÉDAL

Robert Bresson:
L'Aventure intérieure

1. A Rare Oeuvre: The "Cinematograph"
Critical Work

Bresson and His Time

FOR OVER THIRTY-FIVE YEARS, Robert Bresson has been nurturing his project *La Genèse*, spanning the creation of the universe to the Tower of Babel. Philippe Arnaud correctly writes, at the conclusion of his work,[1] that the project is comparable to Carl-Theodor Dreyer's on the life of Christ, which he never completed. A sort of matrix or Vauclusian spring that irrigates Bresson's entire work, this reflection on the origins of humanity is perhaps not destined to become reality, but it presents the dimension of the artist's work and defines its deeper nature: Bresson is not proposing an *entertainment*, but a world view that the majority of critics acknowledge as Christian.

Bressonian Exegesis

As early as the 1950s, Henri Agel, Amédée Ayfre, and even André Bazin had pointed to the transcendent not only in Bresson's Christian subjects (at the time, *Les Anges du péché, Journal d'un curé de campagne*; later, *Procès de Jeanne d'Arc*), but also in the most profane ones (*Un condamné à mort s'est échappé*; then *Pickpocket* or *Au hasard Balthazar*), thereby demonstrating that neither the characters' psychology nor the context—that is, the individual and the society—can provide the key to these exceptional destinies. Because "There's an Absolute in this universe. But it lies beyond language and even being."[2] Its originality lies in its not weighing on individuals from the outside. On the contrary, the Absolute is inextricably connected with each individual's free will: "The Absolute does not influence people in the way that one thing acts on another. It is simply at the heart of their freedom; it is its soul."[2] This is the same as the "Heaven helps those who help themselves" demonstrated in *Un condamné à mort s'est échappé*, and this self-consciousness also explains the importance of each person's death, which points to the deeper meaning of destinies and determines the precise essence of every individual.

But Bresson's spirituality is not a carefree Christianity, and his work rarely corresponds to what the hierarchy of the Catholic Church or writers of the upstanding press would wish for. Bresson questions, doubts, and communicates his anguish as a believer: "His ambiguity, his austerity obviously do not flatter Christians looking for a simple apologetic, a smiling and warm religion, an easy harmony between the corporeal and the spiritual. Placing the accent on the sin that divides us and the sinner's solitude, Robert Bresson offers us an earnest meditation of exceptional sincerity. . . . He is a filmmaker and a moralist, not a prophet and a mystic."[3]

In fact, this rigour is applied essentially to his religious subjects, or those laden with cultural references. In a sense, one could say that there are so many things "behind" the existence of a curé of Ambricourt, a Joan of Arc or a Lancelot du Lac, that it is what the director holds back that reveals the unshowable, the unfathomable expressed by these mystic or mythical figures. But with his contemporary secular subjects, Bresson takes great pains to capture the *Zeitgeist* (*Quatre nuits d'un rêveur*, *Une femme douce*) or plastic beauty (*L'Argent*), in a way compensating for the loss of subliminal substance by ensuring a certain openness of the films—if not the characters—towards the outside world. When the cultural substratum no longer bears them, Bresson's heroes are nourished by the world around them: the number of locations and characters multiplies; the images are less spare.

Above all, Michel Estève[4] rightly rejects those too often repeated ideas of DISINCARNATION and ABSTRACTION. On the contrary, Bresson never separates the spirit from its corporeal envelope (which would be disincarnation): the curé of Ambricourt's stomach pains, and Joan of Arc's fear of fire humanize these "saintly" figures. In the same way, the images never seek to lead to the concept (which would be abstraction). Instead, the director isolates the detail from its context, distils it, pulls it from the chaos of reality, and thus stylizes its description. The world does indeed exist on screen (landscapes in *Au hasard Balthazar*, *Mouchette*, or *Journal d'un curé de campagne*, the quays along the Seine in *Quatre nuits d'un rêveur*. . .), but Bresson retains only what is strictly necessary for his purpose, creating a highly representative system of objects and sounds that seeks to be autonomous. As early as 1951, André Bazin pointed out that Bresson's films do not correspond to conventional psychology or dramatic principles, but present themselves as veritable meteors outside the cinema (be it auteur or commercial cinema).[5] Carrying on and extending the spiritualist analysis of the earliest Christian commentators, but placing greater emphasis on aesthetics, Michel Estève also shows that Bresson is unclassifiable ("On his own in this awful profession," as Jean Cocteau wrote in 1957 in his *Prefatory Letter* to René Briot's essay)[6], for "by his sense of modesty, his use of ellipsis, his rejection of effect too highly applied, his desire to underline construction, his sense of visual composition, he is a 'classic.' But this 'classic' shows himself to be absolutely 'modern' by other characteristics that are just as essential to his aesthetic system."[4] Bresson's modernity resides primarily in his rejection of conventions and negation of the spectacular: in opposition to the theatre and the novel, his cinema is primarily poetry and music, the creation of new relationships between things, beings, sounds and images, as in the succession of shots.

This cinema of montage and rhythm is not the concern only of theological critics; the intensity of his work also appeals to analysts not usually attracted to the themes that Bresson develops. Characteristic of the approach of a non-unconditional admirer who would forego elitist snobbery to analyze the films rather than the intentions ascribed to the filmmaker, Robert Droguet proposes that "once past the initial novelty, vigour overtakes rigour. Once past the 'process,' or that which appears as such on a first viewing, there remains energy. . . . And within this vigour, what surfaces first upon a second viewing is the profundity. We are accustomed to the dry 'picturesque' quality of his manner, we are accustomed to Bresson's mannerism, which is as flagrant as the 'elongations' of El Greco or Modigliani, yet it is the energy of the material that dominates."[7]

Philippe Arnaud[1] also discusses the vivid experience of the "first time." Accordingly, the absence in the films of specifics about locations—the withholding of all geographic indications—stem not from a desire for abstraction but "on the contrary the means of giving us these locations with their greatest ORIGINAL FORCE. . . . Whence the sensation, upon watching these films, of never having seen this—the force of the first time"—of elements that are recreated "with the intensity of a GENESIS."

Auteur Cinema, Modern Cinema

Bresson came to feature films during World War II. Arriving at the twilight of Poetic Realism, and fifteen years before the New Wave, he was not borne by any aesthetic movement, and forged his own cinema alone. He entered through the main door of professionalism with *Les Anges du péché*, based on an idea by Father Brückberger, the almoner of Saint-Germain-des-Prés, with dialogue written by Jean Giraudoux a few months before he died, when this playwright was at the zenith of his glory (for *La Duchesse de Langeais*, directed by Jacques de Baroncelli in 1942, and *Sodome et Gomorrhe*, staged at Jacques Hébertot in 1943, with Edwige Feuillière starring in both the stage and film versions).

Bresson's first feature, along with the next one, constitute only initial approaches to the "Bresson system"; they carry over from the cinema of the period a certain ponderous dramatic mechanism, a taste for psychology, and an occasionally laboured aesthetic. But, conversely, his obstinate quest for truth is already discernible. For him, truth dictates where the camera is placed; the actor must be almost surprised into being unself-conscious, and not create his character. As well, the actual sounds are recorded live rather than being produced by foley artists.

With these characteristics distinguishing him from the predominant "French cinema of quality," Bresson will have the formidable honour—shared only by Renoir, Tati, Cocteau, and, to a lesser extent, Becker—of symbolizing in the 1950s, to the writers of *Arts-Cahiers du cinéma*, the essence of auteur cinema ("la politique des auteurs"). Worshipped by the critics of the young generation, Renoir and Bresson will, unfortunately, be quickly caricatured by their followers and trapped in a schematical opposition: the humanist versus the Jansenist, the lover of life and of man versus the spiritualist pessimistic about the future of the human race.

In any event, after the universal acclaim he achieved with *Journal d'un curé de campagne* (1951), and even more with *Un condamné à mort s'est échappé* (1956), Bresson navigates, with a certain panache, the transition to the New Wave, at a time when other luminaries are faltering, esthetically and commercially: Delannoy, Autant-Lara, Duvivier, Carné, Clément, Clouzot . . . Bresson, in contrast, embarks on his most fertile period, directing five films in the decade between 1963 and 1973, one film every two years.[8] Indeed, *Pickpocket*, released in 1959, along with *Hiroshima mon amour* (Alain Resnais), *L'Avventura* (Michelangelo Antonioni) and *À Bout de souffle* (Jean-Luc Godard) constitutes the quartet of germinal works of the modern cinema; together they mark a clear rupture with the existing conception of the seventh art. The film club favourite becomes a filmmaker who is closer, more intimate, and even warmer.

In terms of dramatic continuity, the interpretation and direction of a specifically cinematographic space and time, *Pickpocket* proves to be "more New Wave" than the most typical films of the day. It appears to have adopted before the fact, in fiction cinema at least, the fundamental conquests of "cinéma vérité." When both movements—the "New Wave" and "cinéma vérité"—run out of steam, Bresson stages a superb return to literature, adopting a Bernanos text (*Mouchette*) and two Dostoevskys (*Une femme douce*, *Quatre nuits d'un rêveur*), shot quickly, with almost no artificial lighting, and a certain amount of improvisation in the streets . . . which the directors of the "late New Wave" had long ceased dare to do! Paradoxically, in these works, Bresson appears to be less moralistic and somewhat more sociological, alert to his time.

Indeed, Bresson's films offer a paradigm of modern cinema both as to their aesthetics and thematic preoccupations: Louis Malle, Jean-Luc Godard, Eric Rohmer, and Jacques Rivette have repeatedly acknowledged their debt to Bresson. And what of Gérard Blain, Jean Eustache, Luc Moullet, Marguerite Duras, and all the others who, in one film or another—or even in one sequence or one shot—suddenly turned "Bressonian" when some necessity overtakes their style.

The 1970s and 80s, on the other hand, witnessed a relative waning of Bresson's influence, and the publication in 1975 of his book (*Notes sur le cinématographe*, Gallimard) was received with a certain indifference, especially since it had been long awaited. That notwithstanding, *L'Argent* (1983) still testifies to the radical difference of his vision. Repeatedly postponed or uncompleted projects abound throughout his career: as early as 1947 he wrote a script on Ignatius of Loyola for an Italian production company (d'Angelo-Universalia), with Julien Green also working on an adaptation for the same producer. Neither script was ever produced, but Bresson picked up the theme again in 1960, for, as he stated, "his life is a surprising blend of coincidence and predestination,"[9] thereby synthesizing the entire dialectic of his work. In 1952 Bresson penned his first script of the *Graal* (shot twenty-two years later, in 1974, after nearly being shot in black-and-white in 1960), *Au hasard Balthazar* (finally made fourteen years later), and *La Genèse* (never produced, but twice revived: in 1963 for Dino de Laurentiis, with whom Bresson soon clashed, and in 1985, thanks to his receiving an exceptional pre-production grant). In 1953-54 Bresson attempted an adaption of Madame de La Fayette's *La Princesse de Clèves*; Alain and Odette Virmaux relate that he turned successively to Jules Supervielle, Albert Camus, and Paul Morand, but was unable to reach an understanding with any of these three prestigious collaborators. As it happens, Jean Delannoy was at the same time writing a version with Jean Cocteau that was finally produced in 1960. Bresson has still not abandoned hope of making *La Genèse*, although he now acknowledges the difficulties involved, and in 1986 he received "advance on box-office" funding for a new project, *La Belle vie*, which still hasn't materialized.

The Art of the True

Bresson states: "I am a maniac of the TRUE, for the slightest detail. A false use of lighting is just as dangerous as a false word or a false gesture."[10] Yet he also warns against an excessively blind respect of the natural: "Unfiltered reality will not of itself create truth."[11] Consequently, if one is to preserve the beauty of the true ("Your film shall have the beauty, or sadness, etc., that one finds in a city, a countryside, a house, and not the beauty, or sadness, etc., that one finds in the photograph of a city, a countryside, a house"), it cannot be achieved simply by recording things, but by capturing their artistic reality: "You shall make with the beings and things of nature, cleansed of all art, especially dramatic art, an art."[11]

Indeed, Bresson's universe is quite foreign to the notion of realism, the realistic vision being to some extent that of the happy medium. Bresson thus situates himself more—depending on the film, or occasionally at the same time—on the side of verism (*Mouchette*) or of symbolic abstraction, as he never presents the viewer with a raw document, but rather a purified vision, where the central conflicts stand out in sharp focus. In sum, if Bresson thirsts for the real, he does not cultivate it like Zola or Courbet, but seeks it rather in the manner of Van Gogh or Cézanne. What he is really seeking is truth rather than reality itself, and as Jean-Pierre Oudart states, "it is no longer for the *character* to SAY it, or for a subjective *fiction* to PRODUCE it, but for the literal *image*, as a cinematographic construct, to EXPRESS it."[12] Thus Bresson surprises by his framing, soundtracks, his editing and very unusual sound mixes; although his work does not go as far as the aggressive sound collages of a Jean-Luc Godard, it always takes great liberty with respect to realism. Similarly, this director never shows what we expect. In *Au hasard Balthazar*, for example, Gérard, the motorcycle gang tough, is suspected of murder, and called to the police station. However, we never learn anything of this presumed crime, Bresson using the scene only to show the starting point for the relationship between Arnold and Gérard, and to show that the latter is protected by the baker's wife.

To reveal the essence of a soul, the director can nuance his naturalistic palette: there are the rarefied films (*Les Dames du Bois de Boulogne*, *Procès de Jeanne d'Arc*, *Lancelot du Lac*) and the films of the gutter (*Journal d'un curé de campagne*, with its cheap wine and vomit, *Mouchette* and its clogs, *L'Argent* and its blood). In sum, if Bresson insists on his constant preoccupation with reality, the viewer is instead aware of how the real is fabricated, somewhat as in the cinema of Dziga Vertov, who also proposed to portray the real by means of an extremely elaborate formalism. To the realism of the details corresponds the aesthetics of the composition of fragments, how they are placed in relationship to one another by the constant practice of paring away: the director is able to concentrate the maximum of meaning by removing from each shot everything that may impede our grasping these subtle relationships.

Consequently, to speak of Bresson and his times might appear paradoxical if we were to limit ourselves to seeking in his films traces of the major events of the last forty years. While the atom bomb, the war in Algeria, and the economic mutations of French society crop up directly or as undercurrents in several of Resnais's films, it is quite obvious that these events have no bearing on Bresson's universe, any more than do the problem of the Third World, North/South conflicts, the relationship between socialism and freedom, or—on an entirely different plane—the famous middle-class triangle (wife/husband/lover or mistress) that daily nourishes our literature, theatre and cinema.

In short, however one takes it, examines, analyzes or psychoanalyzes it, his work refuses to play the role of the mirror—be it realistic, true to life, reassuring, or even distorting, revealing, or caricatural . . . And yet Bresson is not really isolated, since he expresses himself in his films, and thus reaches thousands of viewers, provoking numerous and profound critiques and raising hundreds of millions of [old] francs to create his works (even if economic realities have prevented him from making more films). An artist of his stature could not but have a relationship with his time. What's more, in other countries, Bresson is seen to be "typically French," which means that while some of us do not wish to recognize him as one of our own, the distance of the "outsiders'" gaze results in their seeing him as characteristic of our state of mind and our cinema. This, then, is the heart of the problem that allows us to pose with relative clarity the "Bresson phenomenom": Though he is of no interest to the historian, and concerns the sociologist only moderately, cinephiles and moralists are passionately interested in Bresson.

His work has reality only as a work of art that conveys a thought that expresses itself through a specific language. It can in no way be reduced to some document for study in social science laboratories, as it already functions as a filter of reality, a considered synthesis, a reflexive gaze. Which is to say that it is the quintessence of its time and that, far from turning its back on life, it draws the moral of the latter, providing its most perfect representation. Not to say that it resists being studied, but it demands other approaches than technological objectivity. It requires, in order to be penetrated, a certain connivance, a willingness to share, and the belief in a cinema capable of signifying more than the literal meaning of its soundtrack. Thus, it quickly becomes obvious that, even when presenting Joan of Arc or Lancelot, Bresson is confronting his times. But, a bit like Godard, Bresson speaks to his age rather than of his age; a visionary, not an echo, he inspires more than he draws inspiration; a vision, not a sponge, he paints what he understands, leaving to others the simpler task of filming what they see.

Bresson thus maintains with his times profound relationships that touch on the expression of feelings, self-awareness, the sense of mortality, or the quest for spiritual fulfillment. These may not be issues that are addressed very often in the popular press or on talk shows, but who would claim that they are of no importance? For Bresson cinema is "perhaps capable of capturing this . . . thing that words cannot say, that forms and colour cannot render,"[9] though it is certainly not by stressing the "specific means" determined by professionals (camera movements, use of particular lenses . . .), for the director defines style precisely as "everything that is not technical."[11]

Challenging in his words the rest of cinema, Bresson says he alone practises the "cinematograph" that cannot be compared to any other audio-visual expression: whereas "cinema draws on a common fund, the 'cinematograph' embarks on a voyage of discovery to an unknown planet."[11] Thus, he distinguishes between "two kinds of films: those that employ the means of theatre (actors, staging, etc.) and use the camera in order to REPRODUCE, and those that employ the means of the 'cinematograph' and use the camera in order to CREATE."[11]

Few are the filmmakers who have given us a theory of cinema that accounts for both their own creation and cinematographic expression in general. S.M. Eisenstein devoted several volumes to the subject. Bresson does the same in his *Notes* with a series of extremely dense aphorisms. But far from living on a foreign aesthetic planet, the Bressonian "cinematograph" constitutes instead the farthest extreme of this cinema, which he pushes to its very limits. Rather than deny it, he exploits it to the maximum, that is, makes more and better use of it than almost any other films, past or present.

2. Solitudes in Action: Pride and Passion
Incommunicability and Communion of Characters

Bresson the Psychologist

I N 1968, Bresson spoke of "the absence of psychology and analysis" in his films, cultivating this paradox by adding, "As far as I'm concerned, I have always considered the supernatural to be exact reality" and "incommunicability is what makes union, communion possible."[13] One can clearly sense the intellectual provocation and the linguistic quarrel the filmmaker relishes, being anxious to provoke reactions, and wary of any all-encompassing consensus. Indeed, when he states that "there should be no psychological analysis. We have to paint, and it is through painting that everything will emerge,"[14] Bresson is quite simply defining the behaviourist attitude that was contemporary to the beginnings of cinematography.[15] In opposition to the novelistic introspection of Victor Hugo's famous "storm inside a skull," Bresson is defending a behavioural psychology of which cinema seems to be particularly effective. But this is certainly a question of favouring one method of observation over others and is in no way a total rejection of the psychological approach that has always characterized French cinema, and in particular the work of Bresson, which is rich in powerfully defined characters.

Isolated Beings Reaching Out

In Bresson's films, a being lives, feels, acts, and reasons in a way that is quite particular in relation to those around him. He is as if in another world, governed by a different system of values and thought. In *Au hasard Balthazar*, Marie's father exemplifies this: with an energy and a lucidity that border on arrogance, he continues on his way, sure that he is right. But Marie and the leader of the motorcycle gang are also close, out of communication with others. Often the feelings of the hero are confused or at the very least special (the curé of Ambricourt with his vow of celibacy, the latent homosexuality of the pickpocket, Joan's desire to remain dressed as a man), and this abnormal state increases the character's solitude. For example, in *Balthazar*, relations between Marie and the donkey are strange: she decorates it and kisses it in the barn in plain view of the astonished motorcycle gang.

When Jacques Doniol-Valcroze and Jean-Luc Godard tell him that they see in each of his films the overriding theme of solitude, Bresson indeed acknowledges: "Yes, and it is dangerous, because on the screen it appears as coldness and indifference. It must be surrounded with a lot of tenderness and love to succeed in having it accepted."[9] The style, therefore, echoes the personalities of the characters: "Bresson creates a void around his heroes, as if his heroes consent to see in the world only what they want and seek."[16] This is the reverse of the "data files" that Resnais asks his scriptwriters to write, and nothing is known of the past or future of the protagonists except their precise role in the chosen events. It is because the characters are loners that "never do we encounter with Bresson the figure of a transmission, either pedagogical or familial."[17] No mentor (not even the curé of Torcy in *Journal d'un curé de campagne*) is powerful enough. The mothers are ridiculous (*Quatre nuits d'un rêveur, Les Dames du Bois de Boulogne*) or die (*Pickpocket, Mouchette*). The fathers abdicate their responsibilities (the alcoholic in *Mouchette*, the middle-class man in *L'Argent*, the teacher in *Au hasard Balthazar*). As for the couple in *Une femme douce*, they exemplify the encounter of two profound solitudes. Of course, one might think that "the young woman's suicide-sacrifice redeems the monstrous egotism of the husband, giving him access to the consciousness of the other,"[18] but more than anything else, the film recounts a horrible mess in which the man's resentment and bitterness are transferred to the woman. Also, the curé of Ambricourt (*Journal d'un curé de campagne*) and the vagabond Arnold (*Au hasard Balthazar*) were seeking in wine "annihilation of the ego,"[19] like Arsène in *Mouchette* or the father of the little woman, the former piano teacher—now a drunk—who plays Bach's "Chromatic Fantasia" until the glass sitting on the instrument vibrates, and falls and breaks (*L'Argent*). In fact, the role of alcohol is as important as that of money in the director's work.

Bresson loves to break with classical clichés: his Joan of Arc is neither a disembodied mystic, nor a coarse peasant. He sees her as simple, yet noble, beautiful, elegant, and natural in her relations with the great (after all, was she not said to be the half-sister of Charles VI?). Beyond any dramatic structure and any psychology, individual isolation is also combined, on the one hand, with a transcendence that unites them from above (one could say that men are all sons of God), and on the other hand a sort of human solidarity that links them from below (they are all brothers). In any case, these films are discreet in terms of the physical expression of feelings and emotions. There is little laughter, hardly any tears, and there are never great outpourings of sentimentality. Skin contact is rare; all the aloofness that walls in and isolates the hero runs counter to the violent emotions of the soul.

Fulfilment, therefore, can only be found in the self. Outside is the prison of the world. Already apparent in *Les Anges du péché* ("Thérèse comes out of the convent, which has been her prison, to go voluntarily to prison which will be her true convent, where she rediscovers her inner freedom"),[20] the image of the prison world, of man as captive being, is materialized by being anchored in reality in *Un condamné à mort s'est échappé*, and continued in *Pickpocket*, *Procès de Jeanne d'Arc*, and *L'Argent*. The parable of closed space begins with *Les Dames du Bois de Boulogne* when Agnès cries out, when she discovers the place she will have to inhabit to obey Hélène: "I call this a prison." From then on, apartments, châteaux, convents, presbyteries, and jails separate the Bressonian character from the daily lives of others. Wide shots are rare and the open spaces in *Journal d'un curé de campagne* are filmed in such a way (low, grey skies) that, far from opening up towards somewhere else, they separate even more the priest and his village from the rest of the country.

Moreover, Bresson's heroes are young, never more than thirty years old. Old age is not a subject that interests him and he endows his imaginary creatures with a few qualities that are inherent to that youthfulness: "Intransigence, pride, sense of the absolute and of hope."[21] This tenacious, indomitable character is all the more astonishing given that all these creatures have an unassertive physical character and that some even appear weak (the curé of Ambricourt). But these are beings who choose—or have chosen—and never leave the initiative to others. Jean Sémolué defined them in 1957 as elite souls, persons possessed, around whom the films are structured.[16] If this strength is very visible from the outside, earthly failure, that is, death, awaits his protagonists (Anne-Marie in *Les Anges du péché*, Joan of Arc or Lancelot du Lac), but inner victory remains essential.

His unshakeable will placed at the service of a passion (sainthood, theft, jealousy . . .) pushes the being beyond his human limits to the affirmation of his own existence. For Michel Estève they are "prisoner beings who reach out all their energy towards liberation."[21] While it is true both materially and psychically at the beginning of Bresson's career in film, it seems that this idea of liberation is less clear in the later films where there is something like a yielding to evil, with a seeming impossibility of extrication. The rigour of the characters is, of course, echoed in that of the directing.

Like Lancelot and Bresson himself, everyone is on a quest for the grail. All are reaching out—including Yvon Targe in *L'Argent*—with the desire to attain something that is formulated in the key scene, usually close to the end, towards which the whole aesthetic construction of the film has been working: Fontaine's escape (*Un condamné à mort s'est échappé*), the conversion of the former criminal (*Les Anges du péché*), Jean learning that he has married a girl of easy virtue (*Les Dames du Bois de Boulogne*), the mortal agony of the curé of Ambricourt (*Journal d'un curé de campagne*) . . .

André Bazin also talks about the "stubborn repetition of behaviours,"[22] and this term seems essential for characterizing these beings, who are in fact stubborn in good and in evil. "The confinement of characters in their obsession and in their pride" is just as clear among the secular protagonists as among the religious ones.[19] They are not without a certain narcissistic complacency in carrying out actions that defy common sense and watching themselves act (voice-over narration of *Un condamné à mort s'est échappé*, of the country priest, and of the pickpocket). Madmen of God (the religious protagonists) or tormented rebels (the others), they are blocked in terms of the least attempt at exchange or dialogue, still seeming to talk to themselves without really trying to address anyone in a world of tormentors and victims in which each wants to use the other until suicide constitutes a logical end, which is sometimes terribly sweet. A yielding to death more than a fascination with it, suicide is devoid of its sordid character: a white scarf fluttering down from a window and the screech of tires in *Une femme douce*; childish wrestling and a noise of falling into water for *Mouchette*—the only way, it seems, to find peace.

It is possible to see in almost all of Bresson's films a way of the cross, the passion of Christ appearing as the common lot in which men find their fulfilment, that is, the understanding of the world and the place they occupy in it. The plots move forward, in a syncopated rhythm, through successive episodes that are like the stations of the cross (such as the different masters Balthazar endures) and not through a fatal chain of events as in ancient tragedy. The allusions to the life of Christ in Bresson's work are obvious, starting with *Journal d'un curé de campagne*. These are not, however, facile references to Jesus, because, for any Christian, every man carries his cross, different from that of others, but finally always comparable to the cross of the Son of God. With the curé of Ambricourt, Joan of Arc, or even the donkey, the parallel is easy because they are all innocent. But the pickpocket is a thief. As for Yvon, he is completely corrupted by the evil that has struck him unjustly. Both these men realize the same spiritual path as the "saints," but their redemption is relegated to the final scene.

An Inner Path

The diary of the country priest is the diary of the inner life of a clergyman, exclusively "of the art of his life related to God," in the words of André Malraux in the preface he wrote for the novel by Bernanos. The details of his physical existence or his contacts with others are given only as they relate to that search for God carried out by a being inhabited by voices and visions. The next two films—*Un condamné à mort s'est échappé* and *Pickpocket*—repeat this same subjective structure, and although Bresson comes back less systematically to the process, the "'cinematograph' films" are necessarily made, for him, "of internal movements THAT ARE SEEN."[11] The struggle that is recorded is always essentially spiritual. It is natural for the curé of Ambricourt and for Anne-Marie, who sets for herself the goal of saving a soul (*Les Anges du péché*), but the same is true of Lieutenant Fontaine (*Un condamné à mort s'est échappé*), who has a passion for freedom like Hélène does for love (*Les Dames du Bois de Boulogne*), or Joan for God (*Procès de Jeanne d'Arc*). The condemned man does not try to escape because of a need to accomplish on the outside any particular action, but because of his absolute craving for freedom.

In all interviews, Bresson emphasizes the fact that he wants to describe an inner journey: "The external adventure is the adventure of the pickpocket's hands. They lead their owner into internal adventure," which is always the discovery of the meaning of *his* existence, if not the discovery of the meaning of *life* itself.[14] But this quest becomes more and more difficult starting with *Au hasard Balthazar*. Of course, each individual is always responsible for the constitution of his own being, but the depths become more and more murky (*Le Diable probablement*) and man is, therefore, less and less able to find his way (*L'Argent*). The curé of Ambricourt manages to impose his will on the girl, and the pickpocket finally discovers love by way of "a strange road," but Balthazar only finds nature for a brief moment. The inexpressiveness of faces and the atonal dialogue, therefore, convey the part of the individual that is never revealed.

The clash of souls constitutes the only subject of *Les Anges du péché*: Thérèse and Anne-Marie confront each other and yet, in the end, Thérèse surrenders to the authorities after having said the vows on behalf of Anne-Marie, who is too weak to do it. Each has found the peace of renunciation, recognizing the love of the other and giving hers in turn: Anne-Marie accepts her failure and death; Thérèse renounces revolt and goes to meet punishment. The unbelievable has occurred, and not one fold has been disturbed in the costume of appearances in the indefinite present in which each sequence forms a block joined to the next one, with the viewer never knowing how much time has passed between them. Chronological marking is of no interest in metaphysics and it is not very important to know how long Fontaine's preparations for escape or Joan's trial last, nor the number of years that have gone by before the end of *L'Argent* or *Lancelot du Lac*. Bresson is not attached to dates. Only continuity is important to him, the order of things, but not at all the time it takes to carry them out.

Bresson illustrates the convention that one goes from the specific to get to the general. His portraits are surprising, in fact, in their specifics (the wine on the curé of Ambricourt's table), and yet the characters acquire a truth that goes beyond them:

"They are indeed uncommon beings, even if they have a universal impact . . . through the very precise choice of extremely specific details, objects, props and gestures," remarks Amédée Ayfre, who recalls Bresson's own words about *Un condamné à mort s'est échappé*: "I would like to create both a film of objects and a film of the soul: that is, attain the latter through the former." Bresson indeed makes faces filmed as objects the gateway to those souls.

Bresson's relentless work to make his "cinematograph" run counter to cinema has sometimes been difficult to accept, even for his most loyal collaborators. For example, his director of photography, L.H. Burel, did not understand why, after having chosen a beautiful young woman to play the part of Joan of Arc, he did everything possible to make sure that the "purity" of her eyes, "their clarity, their naivety, and even their mysticism" were never seen.[23] Her eyes are downcast, her gaze furtive. Bresson does not make her a Zorro-like heroine: she is beaten, subject to the law of the judges, and does not even defy them, but her fulfilment is of another kind. Her anti-heroism is close to that of Lancelot. Bresson demystifies these figures of legend the better to emphasize their internal beauty. But for Burel, "in this film, Bresson has hidden too much of the spirituality of the girl, like the majesty of the judges. Everything has become dry, lifeless." Nor did he use for dramatic effect the splendid archways underneath the Meudon Observatory which could have suggested the weight of history through the power of the decor. Everything is reduced, made commonplace.

In short, Bresson has given a contradictory image of Joan through her words. She speaks like a fanatic, a visionary of God, someone with explosive power . . . but she behaves like some poor wretch defeated from the start. This dichotomy between the WORD and the FLESH is very anti-cinematographic but it is one of the strengths of Bresson's system, because it touches the paradox for the human condition: it is often said that the spirit is strong but the flesh is weak. Bresson prefers to invert the process by declaring that the flesh is weak but the spirit is strong. His cinema prompts the viewer to first see the weakness in order to better understand the strength, and not the other way around.

This intrusion of the role of bodies as responsive natural things and elements (wind, rain) occurs in *Pickpocket* when Michel takes pleasure in the theft, not only psychologically but also physically. Many psychoanalysts have likened theft to love and there is, in fact, a veritable eroticism of theft, just as one can speak of an eroticism of objects. Bresson eroticizes *Pickpocket* through his concern for contact; his approach of using the sense of touch is all the more troubling since it is precisely, along with smell, the only one—in principle—that cannot come into play in cinema. From this point on, eroticism becomes progressively more present in the work. Barely glimpsed in *Au hasard Balthazar* (Marie's body), female nudity is quickly revealed several times in *Une femme douce*. In *Quatre nuits d'un rêveur*, Marthe looks at herself for a long time in a large mirror, while the tenant lurks, invisible, soon to knock on the wall. Later, the young people will be shown undressed as we hear the sound of the footsteps of the mother looking for her daughter. It is obvious that Marthe is divided between an erotic desire that drives her towards the tenant and a sincere desire to feel love from Jacques, the warm companion of her four nights. Never do the reactions of the body hide the spiritual development; rather, they mark the stages in the image through a sort of perverse antiproof.

Exchange

While it is appropriate to speak of solitary beings and incommunicability, we must also note, in contrast, that the central subject of the majority of Bresson's films is, as Amédée Ayfre[24] points out in "The Miracle of Communication": beings walled in on themselves manage once with a great deal of difficulty to communicate with others (Anne-Marie and Thérèse in *Les Anges du péché*: the curé and Chantal in *Journal d'un curé de campagne*; the pickpocket and Joan . . .). This is so extraordinary that it constitutes the event that is sometimes enough to fill a life, and this, indeed, is what appealed to the filmmaker in *White Nights* by Dostoevsky. Lucid, energetic, and obstinate, the Bressonian characters collide with their wishes. Their reconciliation can, therefore, only be very short and abrupt, although extremely violent and profound. Those hard personalities do not reveal themselves much and maintain their opaqueness even for the viewer, which runs counter to the process of identification. But when they succeed in communicating, the exchange is so strong that it then takes on the appearance of a veritable communion. The communion of souls constitutes in Bresson the only remedy for incommunicability, but it is as rare as, in contrast, this incommunicability is common.

Contrary to Eric Rohmer, whose major concern is to clearly situate his action (*Place de l'Étoile, Les Nuits de la pleine lune* . . .), Bresson neglects topography as much as he does chronology: no establishing shots, places juxtaposed without the least sign that might help the viewer to locate himself. On the other hand, the concepts of journey, of movement, and of entrance and exit are fundamental. While Bresson prefers not to show spectacular actions, he augments the number of comings and goings: stairways, leaving and returning to the cell in *Procès de Jeanne d'Arc*; shots of buses, taxis, the subway, departures and arrivals to and from Michel's home or his mother's in *Pickpocket* . . .

These journeys could enable the hero to communicate with others, but each time, it is a labyrinthine route poorly controlled by the character, who is dominated by this symbol of the modern era. Ill-suited to this world of communication, he moves, but does not create contact, journeys, but does not communicate.

Gazes and Visions

We know that Bresson systematically uses a 50mm lens, which is very "uncinematic," framing as little as possible and capturing as much as possible the view of the eye. Because of this, he does not like laboured dolly or panoramic shots, which do not correspond to our way of seeing because they separate the eye from the body.[25] The human gaze constitutes, in fact, a basic element, both for the characters and for the director and the audience. During filming, one of Bresson's primary concerns is to capture gazes correctly, which must be both as precise and as natural as possible. In order to do this, he likes to isolate the face from the context: "Your backgrounds (boulevards, squares, public gardens, subway) must not absorb the faces you apply to them."[26] The same concern for using the gaze as a medium of exchange with the viewer is found in the editing, by which Bresson sets up the audience to follow the narrative guided by the eyes of the characters: "Editing a film means linking the characters to each other and to the objects through their eyes."[26]

The world recorded by the camera is first and foremost that seen through the eye of the character: if in *Pickpocket* it is mostly pockets, handbags, watches, hands, looks, it is because that is what interests Michel. As for Lieutenant Fontaine, he is concerned only with the elements of his cell that are useful to him or which resist (door, bars . . .). *Un condamné à mort s'est échappé* does not include a single establishing shot, in order to respect as much as possible the perceptions of the protagonist. The first two features still have a true dramatic story line in several parts, but the subsequent ones eliminate any overall structuring that would suggest a "satisfactory" reading with its explanatory reference points and links. Cinema presents a world governed by "psychological time (that is, the subjective passing of time) and interior time,"[21] hence the role of diaries or voice-overs, which determine the cinematic construction.

In *Journal d'un curé de campagne* and *Pickpocket*, Bresson even parallels the diary, which is seen, with the reading voice, being a play on the process that permits in *Journal d'un curé de campagne* a true passage of the soul. Often, in fact, the image shows reality, and the dialogue shows the state of consciousness of the curé (he hears and sometimes participates in the conversation, in particular with the curé of Torcy). But suddenly, he switches off and withdraws into himself. The image then remains (usually his face) and the real sound fades, replaced by the voice-over: "The superficial words of another person are in a way erased by the interior commentary, which conveys the double perception of the priest: perception of an exterior silence in spite of the voice of the other (or the external noises); perception of an interior duration, which is itself permeated with the supernatural. At these precise moments, Bresson succeeds in making us aware of an ontological time in which the true destiny of man is played out, and the mystery of the human being shows through."[21]

The pace of *Pickpocket* is irregular in order to parallel the completely subjectivized time of the voice-over, which several times alludes to Michel's heart beating violently, during both the thefts and the discovery of love. Therefore, sequences made up of brief shots (the beginning) are alternated with others made up of longer ones (the theft at the racetrack). On the other hand, Fontaine's tension leads Bresson to construct *Un condamné à mort s'est échappé* in a single movement. The voice-over hurries time. Amidst the interminable slowness of the life of prisoners, punctuated with a few identical operations that are repeated every day, shot in "objective" images framed quite wide, Fontaine's point of view imposes a breathless pace on the succession of medium or close-up shots of the preparation for the escape: a few hours more would mean failure and execution. It is, therefore, never the events that impose their pace, but the interior development of the characters.

Too often a contrast has been drawn between noises, which are considered real, and images, which are almost always essentially subjective. Such observation must be qualified since, although Bresson does record real sounds, the way he uses them subsequently matches the requirements of the psychology of the protagonists and not those of reality. Michel Estève points out, for example, that when, in *Pickpocket*, Michel runs away from what he believes to be the trap laid by the commissioner by jumping onto the Paris-Milan train, the screech of the wheels on the rails during departure constitutes for the thief "the very expression of his (temporary) deliverance; consequently, for the audience, it had to be amplified to create an awareness of its subjective value. Bresson recorded the noise of wheels on real rails, but in a particular circumstance that provided him with a characteristic contrast, in the middle of the night, in a silent station, and with a train that was going to the depot."[21] It was, indeed, real sound, but detached from everything else so that it would assert itself, that is, give it an unreal tonality. The filmmaker wants to express all the components of man and he prefers to accentuate his psyche more than his appearance, his inner life more than his social relationships.

But when Bresson states that "there is only one point in space where a thing, at a certain instant, asks to be looked at," or that he does not want the audience to be aware of the camera movements because "it is not an eye that is moving, but a view,"[26] it is clear that the suggested point of view goes somewhat beyond the gaze of the character in order to convey more precisely that of the filmmaker, the master of the filming and editing. Paradoxically, it is in *Au hasard Balthazar* that the superimposition of Bresson's gaze on that of the protagonist—the donkey—is the most precise, since the two beings share the same incomprehension of the maliciousness of men. Able to talk to a post or a milestone, Arnold sometimes has attitudes close to that of the donkey, while all the others are gauged both by the animal, which they are hardly concerned about, and by the demiurge (Bresson? God?) whom they ignore even more.

In fact, the shift of point of view from the central character to the view of the filmmaker is not at all systematic since there is, of course, still a lot of proximity and flexibility in the process of both identifying with his character—often—or of giving them an autonomous character—sometimes—of this double gaze. In various other films, the distance increases or else disappears. In any case, it is never very great since Bresson is only concerned with heroes who fascinate him. Without merging completely with them (the films are never autobiographical), he loves them, understands them and attempts to present them in the best light possible by rehabilitating for this purpose—although he hates theatre—the old rule of classical unities: a single closed space, linear action, limiting of participants, stripping away of the anecdote, and images concentrated on the most significant elements. Since these are characters who are completely oriented towards a goal, this form of narrative precisely conveys the state of mind of the hero, because his gaze and that of the filmmaker are going in the same direction and making identical choices: the decor of Joan's prison or Anne-Marie's convent constitute spaces that are characteristic of their personalities, as is Bresson's *mise en scène*, of which the aesthetic is the reflection of his protagonists' state of mind. Just as these beings speak little, the filmmaker repudiates dialogue. On the other hand, the interiority of the religious world precisely matches his moral and formal preoccupations.

3. Manipulation: Grace, Chance, and the Devil
Evolution of a Spiritual Thematics

Bresson the Moralist

*P*ickpocket was first entitled *Incertitude*, which would have evoked *The Wind Bloweth Where It Listeth*, the subtitle of *Un condamné à mort s'est échappé*, while also announcing the *Au hasard* or *probablement* of the following works. The fact that the wind blows where it likes indeed raises the question of individual destiny, and everyone's responsibility in modelling his or her own life. But the Bressonian hero can scarcely hope to find in the sky precise signs of destiny. If Bresson's cinema is a Christian cinema, it is not in the sense of *The Ten Commandments* or *Monsieur Vincent*, but of Dreyer and Rossellini . . . or Pascal or Teilhard de Chardin, had the latter been filmmakers.

The Incertitudes of Fate

On the subject of *Au hasard Balthazar*, Bresson commented: "Our life consists of both predestination and chance . . . you don't even have to choose."[27] The Bressonian hero is thus not the absolute master of his destiny; the director allows in his films for individual freedom and predestination, while leaving a place for chance, that is, the three contradictory aspects of fate. This flexible approach is situated halfway between the heavy fatalism of Muslims (everything is written) and the total freedom of materialism. For a Christian, man is nothing without God, but that does not mean he is a simple plaything in the hands of the creator.

The short tale drawn from Diderot, on which Bresson based *Les Dames du Bois de Boulogne*, illustrates the entire philosophy of *Jacques le fataliste*: "We believe we control our fate, but it always controls us." For, as Mallarmé wrote, "A throw of the dice shall never abolish chance." This chance (encounter in *Quatre nuits d'un rêveur*) is taken as a sign of destiny, which places the dialectic of freedom-predestination at the centre of the work. Bresson sets it up so that fate is full of surprises, and the pick-pocket finds himself being punished at the very moment he resolves to turn honest. Thus the films never adopt a classical dramatic structure: their abrupt endings often astonish. In this "strange road," which sometimes brings together apparently irreconcilable people or places, are we to see the hand of God? For Philippe Arnaud, this chance-beset fate is the locus of meaning, and the essayist adds: "This locus—some call it God."[17] This is clear in the religious films, where the hero finds the gate to heaven, but it is less obvious when the character finds his will annihilated by the evil force of destiny, when he is acted upon, more than he himself acts, self-destructively, unaware of the repercussions (*Le Diable probablement*, *L'Argent*). As soon as one can put self-conscience—or affirmation—and justice in place of notions of salvation or grace, ambiguity enters, but at the same time it enhances the debate that makes for the richness of the films; no one has ever been able to prove divine intervention in life, and Bresson does not seek to provide in his films proof for the existence of God.

A Phenomenology of Salvation

André Bazin described it thus on the release of *Journal d'un curé de campagne*, which ends with the words "Everything is grace." In the incredible scene of the medallion between the curé and the countess, the dialogue could never render what transpires, for which there are no words. Indeed, "the words spoken are only pauses," and everything is in the silences between the words: it is here, for Bazin, that grace is found. Freedom and coincidences give rise to aberrant behaviour that answers to no rules of works of art: "The transcendence in the universe of Bernanos-Bresson is not that of the classical *fatum*, or even Racinian passion; it is that of grace, which everyone can refuse." Therein is the justification of the refusal of every logical composition. Never does an important event appear as the foreseeable consequence of another. The story does not arise from a psychological chain of events, and never makes use of any classical mechanism of narration. Thus, Bazin, referring to the two nocturnal fainting spells comparable to Christ's falls on the road to Calvary, speaks of the stations of the cross (Séraphita's rag taking the place of Veronica's veil). But Bresson does not insist on these references; on the contrary, he instead blurs resemblances by his barely allusive direction, drowning in the misty greyness of the landscape any symbolist temptation: "His resemblance to Christ is only secondary by projection on the higher level of analogy. . . . Thus, for the first time no doubt, cinema offers us not only a film whose sole realistic events, whose sole perceptible movements, are those of inner life, but, still more, a new, specifically religious—better yet, theological—dramatic structure: a phenomenology of salvation and grace."[22]

This type of analysis can be applied—more or less perfectly—to all the films from *Les Anges du péché* to *Procès de Jeanne d'Arc*. Although Bresson has never portrayed the bliss that faith can instil (there are no outbursts of joy in his works), his world view is clearly of Christian inspiration because the help of grace is accorded to the hero, who is struggling with evil in accordance with the adage "Heaven helps those who help themselves," which could apply just as well (or even better) to *Un condamné à mort s'est échappé* as "the wind bloweth where it listeth."

Au hasard Balthazar marks a turning point in the oeuvre, for from this point on suffering seems to gain the upper hand, grace is withheld, and free will collides with monstrous injustice. In *Les Dames du Bois de Boulogne*, the evil is the work of Hélène. In *Journal d'un curé de campagne*, it is incarnated for a time by Séraphita and Chantal. Identifiable, it can be combatted: the match is even, the collision between man and man conceivable. But in *Au hasard Balthazar*, Gérard, a perverse being, appears dominated by evil, one could almost say "possessed by the devil." Nonetheless, he alone is not responsible for the misfortunes of Marie or the donkey, and he has nothing to do with the teacher's suffering. The origin of evil becomes indistinct, and it is spread everywhere. The blows rain down, and we cannot discover from where. As a result, it is impossible for the individual to combat this evil. One no longer has a choice, and is plunged into a vicious circle that transforms victims into tormentors, for instance in *L'Argent*, where Yvon cannot understand why he thus attracts misfortune.

With the progression from film to film, but also with some bifurcations or exceptions, evil, which from 1943-63 was the work of man, becomes from 1963-83 progressively autonomous, and the "manipulator" is no longer visible. Who? God being more and more absent, it's *Le Diable probablement* ["The Devil Probably"], but he seems to be mostly an independent entity who circulates freely and arbitrarily, blindly striking the good and the evil. He is now a leper who devours everything.

Evil on the Loose

If in 1957 Jean Sémolué maintained that Bresson's films were not "depressing" but "oppressing," three years later, at the end of his book, Sémolué was already asking "Is Bresson's universe indeed pessimistic?" thus answering his own question by underlining the tragedy of the incommunicability of consciences.[28] From *Au hasard Balthazar* on, it becomes harder and harder for grace to impose itself in the end. A viewer would search for it in vain in that film or in *Lancelot du Lac*, and are those who would find it in *L'Argent* or *Une femme douce* not forcing the meaning deliberately on the basis of the filmmaker's earlier films? But this would probably not occur to the viewer who knows nothing of the pre-1960 films: the transcendence is not apparent, the void becomes quite terrifying, and the neutrality of the director's gaze icier and icier—the spectator no longer always being invited to see everything through the protagonist's eyes. The construction of *Une femme douce*, for example, leaves little room for any sort of hope. True, the first shot of the white scarf fluttering while the body lies crushed on the sidewalk evokes the flight of the birds in *Mouchette*, or the two white doves that escape from Joan's pyre. But these possible representations of the soul flying up to heaven come at the end of those films. *Une femme douce*, on the contrary, ends with the heavy lid of a casket closing on the dead woman's body, and answers in the negative the question of the opening sequence: has she found freedom in death? No, concludes the last sequence, after the hour-and-a-half long inventory. What's more, if the Bresson-Bernanos association has often been examined, [29] the connection to Dostoevsky proves to be just as worthwhile, Bresson having twice based adaptations on the Russian writer (*Une femme douce*, *Quatre nuits d'un rêveur*), that is, just as many as on Bernanos (*Journal d'un curé de campagne*, *Mouchette*). The dialectic of Good and Evil is strong in both novelists, but in the Russian it lies within each individual, whereas it is in a way exterior—coming from above AND below—in the Frenchman. The bleakness of Bresson's films is total. Trapped in the iron-clad armour of predestination, his characters find no way out of their despair and die miserably. His heroes are left without ties, abandoned by all: everyone drifts in a world without warmth or values, and they no longer find any meaning in their lives.

This aridity, this coldness, this sense of a void that nothing and no one can fill, truly constitutes the most negative image that can be given of the modern world. There is no more strange road; on earth, the exits are blocked, and the heavens remain mute. From this point on, the quest for the grail is doomed to failure. The wandering typical of all figures in the later films, whether it be Lancelot's companions or the youths in *Quatre nuits d'un rêveur* and *Le Diable probablement*, leads only to the madness of men: the heap of the vanquished knights' flesh and iron on which Lancelot collapses is that of the Apocalypse, yesterday, today, and tomorrow.

Encircled by the cacophony of existence, the silence of the essence is all the more terrifying. Of course, these are not the conclusions of an opinion poll, or a journalistic enquiry, or a scientific study, but the vision of a Christian questioning himself *ad nauseum*. His intimate impressions are very different than many of today's artists, as his condemnation is total, global.

Situated in a Judeo-Christian society, we nonetheless sense that his dissection is not limited to that context. We can wager that other Christians—the mayor of Tours, the Cardinal of Ancona, or the current tenant of the Vatican—would not share his pessimism, or at least would have scapegoats to point to (other than the Devil), and solutions to offer. Already in *Balthazar*, a gang of hoodlums was responsible for the death of the donkey (killed on a smuggling raid) and Marie's irredeemable downfall. Since then, evil has only enthralled people a little more.

Many viewers and critics reject what they perceive to be an accusation, whereas it would be more correct to speak of a vision. A new Saint John, Bresson would open the eyes of his contemporaries; he harangues them not with intricate baroque flourishes, but with the icy clear-sightedness of death. He has been in psychoanalysis all his life (even having his analyst, Dr. Armand Guibert, play the role of the curé of Torcy) but his films bear no trace of the phantasms of his imagination, nor of a plunge into the arcana of the unconscious.

Never do recklessness nor uncontrolled passion ripple the sea of appearances. From time to time, however, an aborted gesture or the furtive revealing of a patch of skin causes the smooth surface of things to shudder, hinting at the titanic subterranean combats being waged behind the faces and deep inside the bodies.

To try to understand, Bresson goes back to the origins: that of each person, that is, childhood, but also that of all humanity, "Genesis." And whereas, around the planet, people are killing themselves, or, at best, in states of nervous depression, or in psychoanalytic therapy, who would affirm that the existential questions posed by Bresson are not topical? It's just that Bresson does not make delicately allusive dramatic comedies (Claude Sautet): he plunges in with violence and, more recently, despair.

For him, the emptiness of the heavens and the victory of Evil are not subjects one can "use." One must embrace them completely, analyze the source and not the results (war, hunger, social injustice . . .), for the worm is no longer in the fruit. It has eaten into the roots, that is, man, and not just society.

Bresson is certainly not a disciple of Rousseau: man is not good . . . though he can become good, and we shouldn't be surprised at the "strange road" one must take to do so. Most viewers don't want to hear this, for they don't like to be thrown back on themselves. At best, they can accept that hell is other people, but they refuse to acknowledge it within their hearts and minds, as Bresson suggests. Twentieth-century man far prefers big public trials over simple, individual examinations of conscience. People like to think that a ballot can change everything: they love political crises.

As it is, when the issue of a social crisis is raised (Antonioni, Godard), they find it harder to go along. When Bresson says that before we change governments or society, we must modify man, his message scares people. Hence, they reject him and attempt to reduce him to silence. "The Devil Probably." From "Genesis" to *L'Argent*, by way of sweetness and dream, this is the transcript of a trial without possibility of appeal of an itinerary to perdition. Yes, Bresson judges and condemns, concluding that evil triumphs over good.

What is surprising is that he does so with the quiet force of the self-evident, by means of framing rather than speeches, images more than dialogue, that is, as an artist rather than a politician. But people today have lost the habit of seeking from the artist subject for reflection, the opportunity to withdraw, to find oneself. Art is no longer educational, is no longer an object of knowledge. Thus the spectator is deaf to the explicit dialogue in the bus in *Le Diable probablement*. One passenger asks: "Who enjoys making humanity look foolish?" Another continues: "Who is subtly manoeuvring us?" The first passenger answers: "The Devil, probably." Upon hearing this, the driver spins around suddenly . . . and his vehicle crashes into the car ahead: the black humour of a Bresson conscious of the enormity of these words (which would be easier to accept spoken from the pulpit), and who disarms them with a pirouette that brings on a smile. Thus Bresson occasionally covers his tracks with a sort of irony of despair, even allowing himself to joke about death twice: in *Pickpocket*, Michel tells his mother, "Yes, of course you're going to get better," yet the next shot opens on her funeral mass; in *Au hasard Balthazar*, the man dies immediately after the woman prays, "God, don't let my husband die." But if Bresson can thus invite the viewer to establish a certain distance, he nonetheless retains the blackness of his gaze.

In his book, Michel Estève accepts the evidence of this evolution towards a totally desperate vision: "From *Une femme douce* to *Le Diable probablement*, Bresson's second universe appears fraught with pessimism and even despair. Faith in the Redemption seems to have disappeared . . . suicide is frequent . . . love is no longer possible . . . solitude imposes itself on the hero. The world seems comparable to a prison from which one can escape only by voluntary death. . . . From *Au hasard Balthazar* on, with the exception of course of *Mouchette*, tragedy no longer seems able to open on to a Christian transcendence."[30]

But a few pages later, in his conclusion, underlining that, were it not for the uncertainties of the film business, *Lancelot du Lac* and *Au hasard Balthazar* would have been made before *Un condamné à mort s'est échappé*, Estève comments that, in this case, there would not be the same impression of evolution towards despair. Bresson's filmography "would then be characterized by a world view of a dichotomous type, within the cycles of evolution. On the one hand, faith in the Redemption, communion with the saints, the alliance of freedom, man's efforts, and grace, invincible hope. On the other hand, the ascendency of evil, sacrificed innocence, impossible love, pessimism, despair, suicide . . . This ambivalence finds a certain unity not only in the existential reality of the tragic that is characteristic of all the director's films but also in the theme of the presence or absence of God."

The analysis is indeed seductive, and also explains Bresson's denials when asked about the despairing character of his films. But this reading of the work remains hypothetical. Obviously a project conceived twenty years earlier is never made exactly the way it was originally planned. In fact, it seems likely that if *Balthazar* and *Lancelot* had been made when first conceived, they would not have had the hopelessness that Bresson gave them in the mid-sixties and seventies. No doubt there would be a glimmer of hope or transcendence. But, revisited at a time when despair had overcome his world view, they were reworked in the sense of despair consistent with Bresson's state of mind at the time.

The filmmaker's statements are so important that Joël Magny places them front and centre in his analysis of the films, affirming that, above all, Bresson says SOME-THING ELSE, and that the fact that he says it differently is only secondary—the consequence of the radical newness of his subject.[31] But while Magny writes this early on, the rest of his essay is almost exclusively devoted to style, proof that even when one wants to extricate the WORD, the extreme purity of the ACTION dazzles the observer, all the more since the evolution of the form these past few years has accompanied the radicalization of the themes. It is true that too often the aesthetic judgement sometimes eclipses the reading of the message, and that the praise heaped on the images sometimes mask the uneasiness felt upon hearing the subject. But believing that we have now identified the latter, we, in turn, can decipher the fascinating plastic system patiently elaborated by the filmmaker.

4. You Must Paint the Bouquet from the Side It Wasn't Arranged
The Pictorial Aspect of the Work

Bresson the Visual Artist

I N *Quatre nuits d'un rêveur*, Bresson amuses himself by putting into the mouth of the former classmate from the fine arts school an abstruse speech on the world of painting. As for the painters who talk about art on their way to the waterfall with the donkey (*Au hasard Balthazar*), they exchange words that might, in a different context, be considered reasonable, but, said as they are, appear stupid.

So the filmmaker applies his irony to a very intellectual manner of experiencing the visual arts. Let's wager that the filmmaker is thereby settling scores with critics in general (including film critics), but that he is also warding off some evil spell with regard to the specific practice of painting. In fact, the director only stopped painting a few years ago. For a long time he believed that after his death people would realize that his production as a painter outweighed that as a filmmaker. Somewhat like Leonardo da Vinci wished to be recognized as a scholar rather than hailed as an artist, Bresson has thus invested an enormous amount in one means of expression while communicating in another, such an unbearable separation of the two functions of art finally having led him to abandon this schism, for fear of losing his own identity.

An Aesthetic of Framing

The theme of the prison that we pointed out springs from a visual need to circumscribe the subject by a frame . . . unless it's the other way around.[32] In Bresson, framing is so determinant because the composition that it delimits stands against the chaos of the offscreen. There is not only a choice, but also the organization of reality, and the characters themselves are determined by this frame. The prison-like room with no exit is above all the set where fate rather than action is played out. In the circumscribed space, there's little air, objects are rare, the backgrounds are blurred, and solitude is a given, while each sound takes on its own resonance. Prison is thus both a metaphor for existence and the necessary condition for any activity as a "cinematograph."

The scene of the murder of the little woman near the very end of *L'Argent* is exemplary of this visual sense, where the composition of each shot is made more dynamic by the image being photographed within a changing continuity. All the figures are admirable, but created only so as to be perceived just long enough to establish their aesthetic link to those that follow or precede them: the dog howls after walking over a corpse in the stairway, then stops at the door to the bedroom. The woman is sitting on her bed, lit by the small lamp. From offscreen Yvon asks, "Where's the money?" The two hands gripping the axe handle cross the frame from right to left with a whistle, then stop, the blade pointing towards outside the frame. Cut to the dog, barking and howling. The axe falls on the lamp, breaking it, and plunging the room into blackness. The axe is thrown into the dark water.

These are not shots conceived as tableaux and Bresson often emphasizes that he improvises a great deal on set: he doesn't storyboard beforehand at the drafting table, but his intuitive work is always preceded by long reflection. That said, Bresson prepares his shots visually as well as thematically. His gaze is that of a painter, and this not only by his sense of framing and his sculpting with light, but also by a taste for composition that includes the dimension of sound. Thus, in the scene in *Une femme douce* where the protagonist, coming out of the bathroom, walks by the television set, her attention is caught by the images and sound of an air battle. She drops the large towel she's wrapped herself in—Jean-Claude Rousseau notes astutely that "the violent images and sounds of the television in the room reveal the woman's fragile nudity."[33] This contrast between the softness of the flesh and the metallic hardness belies an extremely sensual visual sensibility, which we also find in many of the more intimate scenes in *Lancelot du Lac*, whereas the tournament sequence, orchestrated around fragmentary close-ups, resembles the sensibility of *L'Argent*. The inclusion of sound and movement as constituent elements of the visual direction means that a shot never resembles a static composition. Like Antonioni, Bresson practises an action painting, but if the Italian filmmaker is interested primarily by colour, our director's attention is concentrated on the brushstroke.

This taste for the visual dimensions in their entirety is shown by the fact that, according to Jean-François Naudon, who edited *L'Argent*, Bresson never watches a film on the editing table. He does all his work in a movie theatre, the film being projected on the big screen, with its surface and exact proportions and all its luminosity. Similarly, Bresson never "covers" himself while shooting: he films the shot at the angle he wants, with the framing that seems aesthetically right to him. He doesn't "protect" himself with various back-up shots because he knows full well he won't use them. If a scene doesn't work, he will shoot it again. He's one of the rare directors who will redo certain shots after a rough cut; that is, he doesn't adapt his vision to his material, but on the contrary imposes modifications on his first sketch. That said, Bresson isn't content with the approximate image of the editing table, which is only good enough for editing the film in terms of meaning, narration, and acting. He prefers to assemble the shots as visual components, and he gives priority to considering the aesthetic relationships that may arise between the images.

Often, an interior is framed through an open door or window. Thus, in *Le Diable probablement*, where the behaviour of the young people is very strange— quasi-unreal, supple, light, elastic, almost in slow motion, and airy (angels of death?)—Charles looks through the half-closed shutters of an apartment on the way to the Père-Lachaise cemetery. He hears the sound of a piano probably coming from the television whose blueish light we see. What does he perceive through this music, coming from inside the room, when he is near the end of his road to an expected death? He is outside, far from everything, rejected both by shade and light, already dead. This depth of field that suddenly opens up is typical of a visual composition, but it occurs during a movement (not really interrupting Charles's walk) and is introduced by a sound dimension that springs up from we know not where.

Lancelot du Lac

The function of the Bressonian close-up is also difficult to reduce to a specifically visual or cinematographic effect. It is not the equivalent of a magnifying glass over a detail, but functions as a veritable metaphor. Never subservient to a wide shot to provide detail, it replaces a number of wider views (the few shots in *Lancelot* that "summarize" the tournament), for Bresson knows how to define an entire story with a few brushstrokes and at the same time open a reflection on this story. What's more, the close-up immediately points to the essential, that is, the conclusion: in *Lancelot*, this is the ground where the knights end in the dust.

Inseparable from any systematic use of the close-up, the role of the off-camera seems to be determinant: onscreen, the symbol; off-camera, the entire realistic and psychological fabric—everything that the cinema had till then held to be eminently cinematographic, neglecting the essential, to which Bresson returns. Beginning with *Citizen Kane*, the cinema lived off the myth of depth of field. Here, again, Bresson breaks with the style that had become predominant, and refocuses our attention on the frame rather than movement, by stressing lines over forms, flat surfaces over relief, but also by reconciling the perceptible and the ideological.

Objects, Looks and Hands

These three elements provide Bresson support for his filmic construction. He doesn't employ them for themselves, but as links for the web of relationships they command: objects are immobile, hands are mobile, and looks indicate movement. On the basis of this triad, rhythm determines direction: "Rhythms are all-powerful. That is the first thing. . . . Then, there is a colour (it may be cold or hot), then a meaning. But meaning comes last."[34] Conceptualization occurs only at the end of the creative process, after the images have been produced.

Bresson also states: "Painting taught me that it's not about pretty images, but about necessary images," that is, the essential constituent elements of a whole.[35] If the latter is not possible without the former, reciprocally each shot is nothing if not placed in the precise spot where it is to mesh. The same holds for the narration, which does not constitute the matrix of the images, but "is a rhythm. Above all it is one more element that acts on all the other elements of the film and modifies them."[34] The composite whole of the work forms an equilibrium where nothing takes primacy, and where each part depends on this whole, but also influences it.

This is why Bresson's close-ups do not violate the intimacy of the protagonists, who remain withdrawn, secretive. The shots do not reveal or underline. They simply—or should we say, on the contrary, with all their ambiguity?—indicate one interpretative approach, suggesting to the viewer a reflection ON the character instead of revealing what he or she is thinking. The intellectual distance remains, despite the physical closeness: the aesthetic emotion suggests a perceptual knowledge that is never reductive.

But, if he is a proponent of montage, Bresson also knows how to work within the shot. In *Pickpocket*, Michel, Jacques, and Jeanne go out one Sunday. A medium-shot frames the three of them sitting, immobile, at a sidewalk café. A merry-go-round with planes on it is reflected in a mirror. We hear carnival music in the background, laced with the sound of cars driving by in the street in the audio foreground. Everything is said before the few explanatory shot/countershots and the young woman's biting words ("You're sad, you're not in real life, you're not interested in anything that interests others"); there is a foreground of boredom (the shot of the three youths, the noise of traffic), and a celebration that reaches the characters only in the form of reflections and an indistinct echo. The scene is set up so that when Jacques takes Jeanne to the fair, Michel seizes the occasion to steal a watch, finding personal pleasure in the theft and not in the carnival distractions he is unable to share with the others.

However, from *Un condamné à mort s'est échappé* to *Pickpocket*, the relationship is clear: the hands, skillful in both cases, furnish the link. But in *Pickpocket*, they lead to the theft: "With theft, I entered . . . BACKWARDS into the rule of morality.[36] Immediately my pickpocket was there."[37] This idea of entering backwards (a physical notion) into morality (an ideological notion) is interesting, as Bresson likes to talk of things in conceptual terms, and on the contrary to reason with words—and images—in the domain of the perceptible to assist the passage from one shot to another.

From a practical point of view, filming someone from the back is nothing new, and classic cinema resorted to it quite often to avoid the shot/countershot, provided that the back or neck didn't completely block the perspective. But Bresson likes to quote Renoir's advice to Matisse: "You must paint the bouquet from the side it wasn't arranged." Alain Bergala reminds us that it was probably Rossellini who first used this method in film in shooting a scene of *Viaggio in Italia* in Capri, where he places the camera on the side of the bay to film a simple wall![38] Godard does the same thing, first in *Sauve qui peut (la vie)* ("I tried to shoot the landscape from the back") and above all in recreating the *tableaux vivants* of *Passion*. He arranges his models like they are in the real painting, but films them from a different angle than the one chosen by the painter in order to "see the story rather than tell it," as he put it. Bergala comments that Bresson does the same when, instead of submitting to the real, he wants, like a painter, "to create the visible by looking."[26] An arrangement is indeed the pre-visible, what is seen before, the snapshot. But cinema must track the unforeseen, the perverse; consequently Bresson does not allow himself to decide anything ahead of time, leaving instead the possibility of attacking the shot differently from what he'd prepared.

According to Bergala, one sometimes gets the impression Bresson has put everything into place in a certain way, and that at the last minute he's changed ideas and filmed from the other side to suddenly create an obstacle to legibility.

That said, the filmmaker has an obsessive concern for visibility, installing the camera, for example, facing doors to show whoever is coming in. But in some shots he works differently, going as far as to block the screen with an actor's back that suddenly obstructs communication. This distortion between the arrangement (preparation of the shot) and the attack (filming) culminates in the systematic use of false leads in the narration as well as within the image. In *L'Argent*, the first meeting of Yvon with the old lady coming out of the post office is filmed deliberately to suggest to the viewer that Yvon—waiting in ambush as she handles her money—has the intention of robbing her. And indeed the young man begins to follow the woman, whom the viewer automatically believes will be the next victim. But the reality is quite different: this is a genuine case of love at first sight between someone who unconsciously wants to be killed and the person who will perform the murder. The exchange between these two individuals is unbearable, and the fact that Bresson has set things up so that the viewer is at first mistaken as to the exact nature of their relationship increases the extraordinary— one could almost say monstrous—character of this veritable call to be put to death that would be completely incomprehensible in a classic narrative.

The first conversation takes place in the kitchen, and this sort of impossible communication will occur, as Bergala notes, through the mediation of an object. Bresson shows the woman busy with the dishes, then uses a shot of Yvon's head framed between two pots, one of unglazed terra cotta, the other of gleaming metal. The viewer's gaze can't help but travel from one to the other, past the protagonist's eyes, rapidly oscillating from the matte to the shiny surface. The pots, set out on the table, aggressively take up the foreground, and the face of the seated young man is less well lit. This composition, which runs counter to the rules of clarity, imposes an effort on the viewer, rupturing the banal appearance of normalcy, preventing the meaning of the shot from being self-explanatory. Here, the masking is produced by the use of an object with a surprising status, which goes neither in the sense of the story, nor in fact against it. It suspends the story, leads without seeming to (no symbolism or cinematographic effect) to the anticipation of some unspeakable event.

The Music of Sounds

If Bresson is a visual artist, he is also a music lover. In *Les Dames du Bois de Boulogne* Hélène first plays on the piano the fugue from the *Musical Offering* by Jean-Jacques Grünenwald, which constitutes the theme of vengeance that recurs throughout the film. The Kyrie from Mozart's C Minor Mass lifts the very material story of *Un condamné à mort* towards a Christian reflection on life and death. The robberies in *Pickpocket* take place to music by Lully, and the donkey's adventures in *Balthazar* are accompanied by the second movement (andantino) of Schubert's Piano Sonata no. 20.

But over the years the musical score occupies progressively less space in the films. True, Claudio Monteverdi's *Magnificat* bursts forth during the credits in *Mouchette*, just after the images of the suffering mother, but we will have to wait for the last shot showing the surface of the pond, now still, after the adolescent girl has drowned, to hear it again—this song of joy providing a poignant counterpoint. In *Une femme douce*, Bresson attempts the juxtaposition of a sonata by Mozart with a song by Purcell and some jazz composed by Jean Wiener. The patchwork effect is even more pronounced in *Quatre nuits d'un rêveur*, which is accompanied by fragments of contemporary international juke-box pop that cannot be linked to the specific itinerary of any one character. With *Procès de Jeanne d'Arc*, the score disappears, with the exception of the drum rolls composed by Francis Seyrig that accompany the credits and final shots. Similarly, Philippe Sarde's work on *Lancelot du Lac* takes up quantitatively little room, and, finally, in *L'Argent*, the only music heard is a fantasia by Bach played onscreen by the father of the little woman.

In his *Notes sur le cinématographe*, Bresson acknowledges that it took him a long time to use silence as a compositional and emotional element. Just as one shouldn't seek the poetry of his films in the dialogue, but in the images, the musicality should not be found in the soundtrack, but should reinforce the filmic construction. If he is a painter on set, Bresson is a musician during editing in his quest for a rhythm that owes nothing to the rules of the dramatic spectacle.

About his use of sound in *L'Argent*, the director thinks that "while music flattens a surface, makes it into an image," sound, on the contrary, "lends space, relief. It arrives and the screen deepens, thus bringing in the third dimension."[39] The idea is that one must never duplicate an image with a sound ("a sound must never come to the aid of an image, nor an image to the aid of a sound. . . . The image and sound must never reinforce each other, but must each work in turn in a sort of relay,") and if, in *Au hasard Balthazar* the first car accident is seen, the second will only be heard. What's more, for fear of giving in to the seductive ease of the image, Bresson accords special importance to sound: "When a sound can be replaced by an image, leave the image out or neutralize it. The ear tends towards the inside, the eye towards the outside."[26]

His work with sound is thus rather ambiguous with respect to the notion of realism.[40] True, Bresson has several times said that sound increasingly interests him because he believes that the tape recorder captures true sounds, whereas the camera greatly deforms the real. But then why are his images more and more beautiful? And again, is it really out of a taste for realism that, when the knights meet in the forest, each of their lines is punctuated by the sound of the visor as they raise it before and lower it after speaking (*Lancelot du Lac*)? This punctuation borders on irony, and breaks any realistic effect.

As we have seen, however, with the example of the Paris-Milan train that Michel takes in *Pickpocket*, the director is more interested in conveying the subjective impression of a sound than capturing its real impact.[41] This is why—explaining that what we think we hear is not what we really hear—Bresson recommends one "go over [the unorganized sounds] one by one in silence" to "mix them in the correct proportion."[26] In fact, if the soundman had recorded the real sounds of the Lyon train station where the thieves operate, he would have obtained only a blurred cacophony corresponding to the mechanical realism of what the machine picked up. But humans know how to focus their ears selectively, and while one person will make out through the din the striking of a clock because he or she wants to know the time, another will hear the sound of the wheels on the tracks of the train he or she is waiting for. For neither of them will the sounds form an auditory "hubbub." This is why Bresson records all sounds separately to be able to use them to compose a true score occasionally placed in the service of rhythm, but at other times in that of meaning, such as when he presents the consequence before its cause: in *L'Argent*, we are in the cell with Yvon, and can make out a strange noise coming from behind the door. It's only in the next shot that Bresson shows the corridor, enabling the viewer to identify the sound of a vacuum cleaner.

Doing away with the music, and placing on the sound-effects track all efforts at sound composition thus constitutes a clear evolution in Bresson's style. But we could also have examined other modifications. In his essay, Philippe Arnaud notes, for example, the disappearance of dissolves starting with *Une femme douce* because the director finds that, in colour, they lose all their beauty. Similarly, camera movements become less and less frequent, and the lighting is not the same in films photographed by L. H. Burel (*Journal d'un curé de campagne*, *Un condamné à mort s'est échappé*, *Pickpocket*, *Procès de Jeanne d'Arc*), Ghislain Cloquet (*Au hasard Balthazar*, *Mouchette*, *Une femme douce*) or Pasqualino De Santis (*Lancelot du Lac*, *Le Diable probablement*, *L'Argent*).

True, certain constants remain, such as a taste for rays of light piercing the dark, but to Burel's sculptural mastery of greys, one could juxtapose Cloquet's softer palette, or De Santis's very particular way of making the light move within the motionless frame imposed by Bresson. What's more, between the very "Nouvelle Vague" shooting style on *Pickpocket* (quasi-improvised on the street, with at times only a small fill-in light) and the studio work with its meticulously prepared effects on *Un condamné à mort s'est échappé*, we see that, even without changing his director of photography, Bresson modifies his formal approach as a function of places, stories, and above all, intention. Thus, as rigorous as the "Bresson system" is in its principles, it remains flexible in its application, reflecting a director who theorizes about cinema in general, but always leaves room for inspiration at the moment of shooting.

5. Create and Do Not Represent: The "Bresson System" Fragmentations, Models, Understatement

Bresson the Filmmaker

BRESSON'S MAJOR CONCERN is economy of means: "When one violin is enough, don't use two. . . . One doesn't create by adding but by subtracting. Developing is something else (not showing off)."[26] In *Au hasard Balthazar*, the noise of water falling drop by drop conveys both the donkey's thirst and the grain merchant's avarice.

Blanks, Silence and Immobility

In his preface to *Notes sur le cinématographe*, the novelist Jean-Marie Le Clézio emphasizes "the need for economy, but also the sensual delight of creation."[42] If we set aside the second part of the remark, we completely miss the Bressonian search and fall back into the "accusations" of barrenness that are born out of an inadequate interpretation of Jansenist tendencies. Bresson's simplicity also signifies richness, as his rigour excludes emptiness. His spareness is a requirement of writing that tends to enhance the force of the utterance. The message, therefore, is not impoverished but is stoked to incandescence through the precision of terms and the precision of hard images that hit home every time. First proposed by Henri Agel, the term "Jansenist" quickly caught on, because Christian, aesthetic criticism found, to define the work of another Christian aesthete, a word that applies both to morality and form, that is, that proposes an authentic cinematographic and extremely demanding world view, based on precision and self-abnegation.

In opposition to the civilization of the media, which carries live the death of a girl trapped by an earthquake in Mexico, Bresson practises a salutary withholding of information, image, and emotion. Preferring tragedy to melodrama, eroticism to pornography, and analysis to accumulation of knowledge, he struggles against the voyeurism of the times, sometimes augmenting the violence of what he has to say by hiding from view part of the act taking place. For example, instead of showing the final massacre in *L'Argent*, he suggests an idea of it that is much more horrific than any realistic reconstitution.

In contrast, in the face of all the images of death that are withheld in the work of Bresson, the film that Marthe goes to see in *Quatre nuits d'un rêveur* indulgently depicts a gangster's slow agony. *Une femme douce* also includes several elements from other media: theatre, excerpts from television shows and from Michel Dev- ille's *Benjamin ou les mémoires d'un puceau*, which was released a few years earlier. Without being pushed to the ridiculous (except shots from the film *Amour, quand tu nous tiens* destined in *Quatre nuits d'un rêveur* to be the counterpart of the intel- lectual discourse of another kind of stupidity uttered by the painter friend), these real or false images from other forms of expression seem to always miss their target through excess. By concentrating his idea, Bresson goes to the essential and his aesthetic tends towards the linear purity of the necessary.

A Narrative *Sotto Voce*

Whether the film strains to the maximum (*L'Argent, Procès de Jeanne d'Arc*) or whether it breathes more freely (*Quatre nuits d'un rêveur, Le Diable probablement*), Bresson always presents his narrative with the greatest possible intensity. His mini- malist art gives the close-up two superimposed functions that make it the linchpin for all levels of the narration: first it expresses the maximum with the minimum of effect, then it tends towards symbolism, even to parable. A rhetorical device, it is also a creator of meaning and participates in discourse in as much as it is an integral part of the grammatical system. This double articulation gives it a real complexity under the appearance of natural simplicity. But one of the most effective charac- teristics of the persuasive strength of a Bressonian sequence is that everything is said in hushed voices. The author hides or only halfway reveals, in order to pro- voke an explosive contrast between the restraint of the expression and the vio- lence of the message. In *Au hasard Balthazar*, Bresson films neither the seduction of Marie by the motorcycle gang member nor Jacques's conversation with the father of the girl, in spite of the major significance of these episodes. In fact, those images would not have contributed anything more to the psychology of the characters present, and the author did not consider it useful to film those scenes.

This preference for minimalist expression comes from Bresson's desire to stim- ulate the imagination of the public. Consequently, "each time I can replace an image with a noise, I do it," because, if "the eye is lazy, the ear, on the other hand, invents. . . . Hearing is a much more profound sense, and very evocative,"[34] which increases the viewer's freedom with regard to the film. In *Au hasard Balt- hazar*, the image presents a section of wall while we hear the braying of the donkeys that Arnold is beating. In this way, the effect (the animals' cries of pain) refers back to the cause (the blows they are receiving).

Bresson's aesthetic is, therefore, based essentially on the linguistic system called asyndeton, which consists of eliminating the links between terms or groups of terms that are closely related. More precisely, understatement, ellipsis, and metonymy are the figures used most often. With respect to dialogue, the pickpocket's final line is addressed to the young woman ("Oh Jeanne, what a strange road I had to take to find you") and constitutes an understatement that is every bit as exemplary as the justifiably famous reply of Chimène to Rodrigue: "Go, I do not hate you." Moreover, with Bresson, understatement is integral to all descriptions of love relations: one look in *Pickpocket*, a gesture in *Lancelot du Lac*, the furtive image of a part of naked body in *Quatre nuits d'un rêveur* express desire with a totally drastic economy of means.

As for the ellipses that purely and simply omit many elements of the thing or the idea to be transmitted, they completely cut out the return from the carnival in *Pickpocket*: Michel has gone there with Jeanne and Jacques, but he suddenly leaves them. Next shot: he is home, his clothing soiled, and blood on his hands, commenting via voice-over: "I had run, I had fallen." Jacques then enters saying, "I was so afraid..." Michel: "Afraid of what?" Jacques: "Fear." Michel: "Explain." But the friend explains nothing. Alone again in the next shot, Michel takes an object from this pocket while remarking by voice-over: "The watch was very beautiful." It would be difficult to be more elliptical in explaining how Michel had sneaked away from the young couple, disappearing without saying a word to go steal. Things obviously went badly for him, but he succeeded in keeping the stolen watch.

Finally, Bresson excels in metonymy, often providing one element instead of another whose meaning he wishes to convey, advocating specifically "that the cause follow the effect and not accompany or precede it."[26] In *Lancelot du Lac*, the image of a foot leaving the stirrup or a helmet rolling on the ground replaces the view of the blow delivered in the tournament by Lancelot to his adversary. In the final scene of *L'Argent*, the lamp that falls and breaks represents the death of the old woman. Then the axe is thrown in the water. It was the instrument of the murderer, and the blood that stains it is the metonymic figure of the murder. By abruptly bringing together this sequence of sharp-edged fragments, the asyndeton augments the expressive force of the narrative, the meaning of which emerges from the heart of the action without any reflective slowing.

An Arranger

The Bressonian universe has a discontinuous structure. Not only are the beings there isolated, but space and time are themselves compartmentalized. In *Au hasard*

Balthazar, in fact, it is difficult to grasp the exact location of Marie's house, of the bakery, and of Arnold's cabin because there are never large camera movements or wide establishing shots to make links between these distinct cells, which are juxtaposed, but which maintain their individuality. Similarly, the passage of time takes place in selected moments presented successively and not in a homogeneous duration. This elliptical construction, which excludes any clear geographical vision of the places, is felt as a frustration by the viewer of *Un condamné à mort s'est échappé* because it precisely provokes a comparable lack in Fontaine, who must escape, not only from his cell, which he knows so well, but also from the prison which he sees poorly. Like the audience, he therefore must imagine, almost scout out, the route he will have to take to the prison wall.

We know that Bresson hates the theatre arts and loathes theatrical REPRESENTATION. It is in opposition to that that he considers fragmentation indispensable. While theatre necessarily presents a whole, cinema must "see beings and things in their separable parts, isolate these parts, make them independent in order to give them a new dependence."[26] His book *Notes sur le cinématographe* is presented in short phrases, Bresson having eliminated the transitions that would have provided the articulations of reasoning, exactly as he does in his films by disposing of any explanatory link. This practice of asyndeton, this time in the domain of literature, keeps his essay from appearing to be an arrogant and castrating cinematographic instruction manual, because he arranges between each aphorism a space for reflection for the reader-viewer.

For his own reflection no doubt, too, to the extent that Bresson is not a giver of lessons. On set, the filmmaker is still searching for his form and specifically poses himself problems on the scale of the shots that will determine how they are edited together. The tournament scene in *Lancelot du Lac* was apparently initially conceived a bit more classically, that is, chronologically and with a more encompassing topography. It was during editing that the decision to retain only a discontinuous series of close-ups of details was finally made, leading to one of the most famous sequences in Bresson's cinema, born of the practice of images and not of a pre-established theory.

In short, the director is not really at ease in relation to the two obligatory godparents of cinema, theatre and painting, which for him are arts of RE-PRESENTATION. Bresson is in fact loath to present a second time the reality that he prefers to destroy—fragment into basic units—to then recompose it in a different way (by arranging as he sees fit those elements during editing). This is then an authentic act of cinematographic creation instead of simple reproduction, copy or filmed theatre. The fragmentation is not an end in itself. The goal of the artist is not to show that our world is divided or to create himself a world in pieces. This is only a moment in his creation: he starts from a compact whole (reality) to arrive at another globality (fiction), and, in order to do this, he has to go through a phase of fragmentation.

But the result is actually a whole. Bresson insists on this at every opportunity: "Bring together things that have never been brought together and did not seem predisposed to be."[26] It is here that his gaze imposes a certain strangeness, since the relationships established in his films are different from those of traditional dramatical construction. The brutal obviousness surprises, freed of the psychological cautions and certain duplicities of behaviour. Bresson sees more clearly into his creatures than do the characters themselves and the relationship between shots reconstructs unity from pieces: "A film is born first of all from COMPOSITION. . . . Indeed: we take elements that already exist. Therefore, what counts is the coming together of things, and through that, finally the composition."[27]

The beauty of a Bresson film comes from harmony, not so much of the image and the detail itself, but from the arrangement of the fictional continuity. Through that, the author imposes the proof of an order (higher? divine?) in spite of the evil and horror of a substantial number of its components. Bresson loves to call himself a *metteur en ordre* [arranger] rather than a *metteur en scène* [director], since the essential part of his creative work resides in that very concrete, but intellectually thought-out operation in which things and people are placed wherever the author decides to put them.

The "I" of the Actor

In 1951, André Bazin remarked in his famous study of *Journal d'un curé de campagne* that the words, "even actually spoken by a character" are given "in the manner of an operatic recitative. . . . The actors are not asked to play a text—whose literary aspect in any case makes unplayable—nor even to live it: only to *say* it. That is why the text recited as a voice-over in *Journal d'un curé de campagne* connects so readily with that actually spoken by the protagonists. There is no essential difference between them in style or tone." The actor does not play an emotion, does not convey a psychological situation: "What we are required to read on his face is not at all the uninitiated reflection of what he says, but a permanence of being. . . . Bresson is naturally interested in the most carnal qualities of the face which, to the extent that it does not act at all, is not the privileged imprint of the being, the most readable trace of the soul."[22]

At this time, Bresson had almost completely given up on actors, who were present in his first two features, and his direction of non-professionals began to cause problems. As the years went by, we see a little more with each decade that the author's wager on interpretation is moving steadily towards the standards recognized by the public. Although in total discord with the 1950s, the famous "tone" of non-actors no longer surprises anyone.

A comparison between Rouch and Bresson will no doubt, on this point, be captivating. What indeed is the "interpretation" of a Nadine Ballot (*La Pyramide humaine, La Punition, Gare du Nord* . . .) in comparison with that of a François Leterrier (*Un condamné à mort s'est échappé*), or a Claude Laydu (*Journal d'un curé de campagne*)? Of course, the former is perceived as herself while the latter two perform, but, in both cases, the cinematographic life of the "interpreters" has nothing to do with the work of actors.

The play of the non-actors actually operates in the opposite way to the "*nouveau naturel.*" It is a body that denies itself in the face of the spirit. The supposedly expressive "grimace" has become useless: faces are taken for what they are and not what they seek to convey.

In sixty years, cinema has not been able to forge a method of interpretation that is radically different from that of the stage, while codified expressions can only distract from the essential. Bresson—and many with him today—therefore pays close attention to gesture and attempts an exterior approach. More than in the gesture per se, the filmmaker is interested in the indication of a direction that has barely begun, wanting to establish not exactly the action but rather the idea preceding it.

In *Une femme douce*, the couple has gone to see *Hamlet* at the theatre. When they come home, the woman takes out the play to show her husband how the actors cut the passage in which Hamlet advises the actors: "Speak the speech, I pray you, as I pronounced it to you, trippingly on the tongue: but if you mouth it, as many of your players do, I had as lief the town-crier spoke my lines" (Act III, scene 2). Quite mischievously, Bresson makes Hamlet a kind of precursor of his own way of directing actors! It should be noted that this is not a coy concern for his "trademark," since his obstinacy is quite suicidal. Cinema is ruled by the star system, and his refusal to use stars has condemned Bresson for more than a half-century to only rarely being able to realize his projects. He knows this, but his aversion to professionals is such that he insisted on using an untrained donkey in *Au hasard Balthazar* . . . which he then had to work with for two months, stopping the shooting to teach it to do what he wanted for the circus sequence!

We know that Bresson never talks about actors, using exclusively the term MODEL taken from the visual arts: a painter uses a model—and not an actor—to make his painting. But the term does not convey exactly what Bresson is looking for, because those models are often professionals, especially those who pose nude. Amédée Ayfre has in any case many times referred to Georges de La Tour in reference to the inexpressive asceticism of Bressonian models, emphasizing their way of being there, heavily, beyond any notion of expressiveness in the painter as in the films of the filmmaker.

Bresson cannot accept the actor's interpretation of an actor because the actor "operates a projection. That is his movement: he projects himself outward. Whereas your non-actor character must be absolutely closed, like a vessel with a cover. Closed. . . . We are extremely complex, and what an actor projects is not complex."[27] Bresson criticizes actors for exteriorizing their feelings instead of interiorizing them. For him, the actor must be CLOSED and COMPLEX, full of mystery and contradictions ("It is what I cannot know about F. and G., models, that makes them interesting for me")[26], because he thinks that "it is by playing in the most steady and mechanical way possible that emotion is caught."[27] This is obviously a very personal point of view not shared by a majority of directors. Bresson believes that instead of giving the exact thing, the actor tacks on his emotion to impose on the audience how to react. The author wants the emotion to be felt directly by the viewer and not mediated by the actor. Consequently, the line has to be said as mechanically as possible: "Nine tenths of our movements follow the dictates of habit and automatism. It is unnatural to subordinate them to will and thought." On the contrary, it is preferable to find "the automatism of real life."[26]

For Bresson, all playing is theatrical, exaggerated, the exact opposite of the natural. There is no specifically cinematographic playing, and any actor, therefore, pulls a film towards "photographed theatre." In fact, quite disturbed by the rarefied movements, which break with the gesticulation of the stage, critics had long taken him to task for the flat tone in which all the lines are said, made even more pronounced by the immobility of the faces, which mask the interior emotion. This very specific quality is obtained by post-synchronization done in rather unusual conditions: while post-synchronization is normally done with the actor watching his image on the screen in order to recapture the mood, Bresson's model does not see the film. Sitting in the dark, he hears over headphones his line spoken by Bresson, and has to find—by starting over twenty or thirty times—the intonation and rhythm of the *filming* instead of conforming to a pre-existing *image* that he would see and attempt to illustrate.

This distillation had already required filming with long, numerous and fastidious rehearsals because, without ever telling him, Bresson attempts to grasp the truth of the model more than the character. Everything that is played materially on the set rather than with reference to a pre-existing idea that the "interpreter" might have of the film and the role he thinks he will have to play in it. Bresson banishes "play" and looks for the "I," that is, "the man through and beyond the interpreter," affirming, for example, "the primacy of the human being," as noted by Estève who adds in his book: "The author of the film asks them to reach, through asceticism, towards the truth of their being by stripping away the masks of 'appearance.' 'Become what you are,' said Nietzsche."

The problem is that this anti-play breaks so much with accepted codes of acting that it takes one by surprise on first viewing and one must wait for a second viewing for its authenticity to become apparent and to be able to fully appreciate the "interior, unique, inimitable way of being" of the model whose voice, unstudied, reveals "his innermost character and his philosophy, better than his physical appearance," to the extent that the important thing is not what they show but what they are hiding "and especially what they do not suspect is in them."[26]

Of his models he asks, "Talk as if you're talking to yourselves," that is, as if they allowed a few scraps of murmured interior monologue to escape, but as dialogue, coming out all at once without looking at the conversational partner, to whom, apparently, the speech is not addressed.

When he expresses himself, the character seems caught up in a private conversation, a face-to-face with himself in which each character is searching deep inside for the words he hears himself say more than actually saying them: "The Bressonian model talks the way you listen, by gathering as he goes along what he has just said to himself," writes Michel Chion in his essay on *La Voix au cinéma*, published in 1985. He then immediately adds, "So well that he seems to close off his discourse as he says it, without giving it the possibility of resonating inside a partner or the audience." The characters are not really engaging in dialogue. There is neither theatrical exchange nor novelistic communication, but poetic creation, a raw poetry that is aimed at the essential, in the atonal simplicity of someone who would scrupulously repeat the words spoken in another circumstance. These are words that come from some place where the form and diction are not in sync with present time.

Gilles Deleuze notes in *L'Image-temps*, also published in 1985: "The character talks as if he is listening to his own words repeated by another in order to attain a LITERALITY of voice, cutting it off from all direct resonance, and making it produce a free indirect discourse." If using the expression of Pier Paolo Pasolini ("free indirect discourse") hardly suits the Bressonian style, since it was forged by the filmmaker-theoretician to apply to authors (Godard, Bertolucci, Antonioni) in the 1960s interested mostly in exercising their camera movements, this idea of reading, of text rather more than words, is nonetheless essential. Since the impression is very perceptible in the flashback in *Quatre nuits d'un rêveur*, Deleuze aptly notes that "Dostoevsky already gave his heroes strange voices ('I began as if I were reading from a book . . .'; 'When you speak, it is as if you were reading a book . . .')." In fact, the acting in Bresson's films is not tacked on the outside to distinguish it from the actor's doing his thing. It is a way of approaching realities differently, which, certainly, eludes cinematographical representation, but precisely not its power of expression.

It should also be noted that while a few observers have not hesitated to write that the actors "play" badly—a remark that can only delight the filmmaker—no one disputes, however, the remarkable choice of models. Even if he was surprising at times, we will never again see the curé of Ambricourt other than with the features of Claude Laydu, although he does not correspond to Bernanos's description of him. Similarly, Mouchette is marvellously personified by Nadine Nortier. As for the pickpocket, a character created from scratch by the filmmaker, he literally is Martin Lassalle. Although they do not all resemble one another, Bresson chose them because "they all do have something in common: an inner life, mystery."[43] Doubtless Florence Carrez and Luc Simon stand out less as Joan of Arc and Lancelot.

This probably because these films were not looking for a face but rather a concept of sainthood and knighthood, Bresson recording with perhaps even more intransigence than usual their illogical, irrational, and, therefore, nonconformist "turmoil."

Not only does the director want to reveal his actors to themselves, but he also expects them to surprise him. That is why he likes to create during filming conditions that are favourable to great spontaneity. Hoping for strokes of inspiration, he does not want the models to have prepared their texts. This desire for discovery is more and more intense, so much so that he no longer searches so much, in *Le Diable probablement* or *L'Argent*, for actors with a moral resemblance to the characters, since such an identity would not contribute anything new. He now prefers to set off on the adventure of filming starting from a rather vague physical correspondence and an interesting tone of voice, anticipating a revelation that would be all the more exciting since it creates a contradiction with what he had imagined. Of course, Bresson does not practise *cinéma-vérité* and he takes great care in "drawing the limits within which" he seeks to be surprised, speaking of "infinite surprises in a finite frame."[26] But his discovery of the possibilities of the tape recorder incited him to identify the more and more subtle vibrations of an "expression that can go unnoticed, obtained through slowing down or speeding up what is almost imperceptible, and through the matte and glossy of the voice," which leads him back to his concerns as a plastic artist in order to model sound. [26] Cinema lives in all the stages of its production, because Bresson innovates by seeking to test his convictions.

We have even observed that when Bresson empties the image, it is to load the sound, which is still very present, very material, both in *Un condamné à mort s'est échappé*, when the filmmaker had the cell rebuilt in the studio but with real materials to capture the authentic noises, and in *Lancelot*, in which the metallic sounds of the armour saturate the soundtrack and sometimes obliterate the words. Like Godard, also in the habit of accentuating the sound, Bresson has thus contributed to advancing mixing techniques towards greater expressiveness of the soundtrack, something very characteristic of a modern cinema that no longer accepts the tyranny of images.

As for his relationship to the text, it is profoundly altered under falsely classical exteriors. In general, Bresson takes short works (*Mouchette*, or the two Dostoevskys, Tolstoy, or the story by Devigny, even a few dozen pages of Diderot), which he develops as it suits him, while maintaining the dense, compact character of the original texts. Only twice (*Journal d'un curé de campagne* and the trial transcript of Joan of Arc) would he have to pare down a text, that is, undertake the traditional work of adaptation. But *Procès de Jean d'Arc* is his shortest film since he retains only the essence of a long debate.

The author quite simply takes the opposite direction of eighty years of cinema-literature relations which say that one must keep to the spirit and not to the letter. Bresson sticks precisely to the letter, especially if it is the atonal letter of the dry, cold transcript (the "minutes" of Joan's trial), thereby revolutionizing the relations between the written and the image. It is quite evident that everything important being done today in this area goes exactly in the same direction, whether it is René Allio working with the story of the Camisards or Pierre Riv-ière, and in particular Jean-Marie Straub in his reading of difficult texts for which the image provides an ideal support.

By citing the work of these two filmmakers (but we could also have men-tioned *La Cecilia* by Comolli or the films of Marguerite Duras, though the latter added an additional parameter by transposing her own texts), we see that the work of Bresson not only stimulates pure experimentation (Straub) but also new attempts at a narrativity intended for a broader audience, since the Bressonian lab-oratory fertilizes the whole field of the "cinema-tographiable."

In the world of the filmmaker, therefore, SUBVERSION and TRANSGRESSION are always at work, the rigour leading not to fluidity but, instead, to respect for com-plexity. In fact, Bresson's cinema is much less systematic than are his theoretical pronouncements. For example, while he has stated many times that each shot is only an empty form and that meaning emerges only from the relationship among the images, the beauty of those images means that they first of all assert them-selves, then take on their role as links. Certainly Bresson has gone to the logical extreme of his reasoning in *Le Diable probablement,* in which certain framings (the famous shots that cut above the shoulders and below the knees) are frankly ugly. But those in *Journal d'un curé de campagne* or *Lancelot du Lac* are among the most beautiful in the history of cinema, and as such hold the viewer's attention.

In addition, the neutrality of the first level at which he films things cannot remain transparent once caught up in the tight interlacing of directive editing, and everything quickly acquires a symbolic meaning. It is not possible to erase, cut out, that is, to distil and clarify without forcing the meaning, giving rise to interpretation and the spinning of parable. There is, in the most obvious way, the meticulous choice and then highlighting of a detail taken from the welter of real-ity which induces the exegete—but also the cinema buff or the simple filmgoer—to look for the why: what does this element that is accented in this way signify more than all those that have been eliminated?

We can bet that in spite of the positions he has taken on preserving a certain purity of the gaze, Bresson is aware of that inevitable tendency, which he takes into account and even plays with. However much he takes away and empties to the maximum, each viewer easily finds all kinds of references and rich backgrounds, which are all the easier to identify since they belong to the most widespread cul-tural heritage: Christianity, classical painting, and music, history, mythology . . .

Thus, each film gains by being appreciated as a complete work rather than seen as the statement of an aesthetic or even a stage in a moral quest. These dimensions exist, as we think we have shown in this preliminary essay. But the pleasure of savouring the films remains. Because the pleasure provoked by the Bressonian "cinematograph" is, in the end, similar to that provided by the masterpieces of cinema for the last ninety years. Yes, it is possible to love Bresson and the greatest of other filmmakers, and while one sometimes encounters film buffs who do not like Bresson, I know of none whose admiration for Bresson blinds them to such an extent that they hate the rest of cinema . . . fortunately.

Translated from the French by Robert Gray and Howard Scott, Kinograph

Notes

Numbering of notes follows the style of the original French text. *Ed.*

1. Ph. Arnaud, *Robert Bresson*, Cahiers du cinéma, 1986.
2. A. Ayfre, "L'univers de Robert Bresson," *Télé-Ciné*, no. 70-71, November/ December 1957. It is important to place his text in context: Ayfre would not have been able to speak the same way about the films of the last twenty years, where predestination increasingly replaces free will.
3. Jean Collet on *Pickpocket*, *Télé-Ciné*, no. 88, March/April 1960.
4. M. Estève, *Robert Bresson: La passion du cinématographe*, coll. Ça Cinéma, Albatros, 1983.
5. A. Bazin, "*Le journal d'un curé de campagne* et la stylistique de Robert Bresson," *Cahiers du cinéma*, no. 3, June 1951.
6. René Briot, *Robert Bresson*, Éditions du Cerf, 1957.
7. R. Droguet, *Robert Bresson*, coll. *Premier Plan*, no. 42, Serdoc, Lyon, 1966.
8. Three books were written about him in five years: those by René Briot, published by Éditions du Cerf (1957), Jean Sémolué (Éditions universitaires, 1960) and Michel Estève (Seghers, 1962).
9. Robert Bresson, *Cahiers du cinéma*, no. 104, February 1960.
10. Robert Bresson, *Cahiers du cinéma*, no. 178, May 1966.
11. Robert Bresson, *Notes sur le cinématographe*, Gallimard, 1975.
12. J.-P. Oudart, "Bresson et la vérité," *Cahiers du cinéma*, no. 216, October 1969.
13. Robert Bresson, *L'Avant-Scène cinéma*, no. 80, April 1968.
14. Robert Bresson, *Cahiers du cinéma*, no. 178, May 1966.
15. Thorndike's book on *Animal Intelligence* was published in 1898, and J. B. Watson's studies in the United States, like those of Bekhterev in the USSR, date from immediately after World War I.
16. J. Sémolué, "Les personnages de Robert Bresson," *Cahiers du cinéma*, no. 75, October 1957.
17. Ph. Arnaud, *Robert Bresson*, Cahiers du cinéma, 1986.

18. J. Magny asks himself this question in *Cinéma 83*, no. 294, June.

19. J. Magny "L'expérience intérieure de Robert Bresson," *Cinéma 83*, no. 294, June.

20. A. Ayfre, "L'univers de Robert Bresson," *Télé-Ciné*, no. 70-71, November/December 1957.

21. M. Estève, *Robert Bresson*, coll. Ça Cinéma, Albatros 1983.

22. On *Le journal d'un curé de campagne*, *Cahiers du cinéma*, no. 3, June 1951.

23. L.-H. Burel, *Cinéma 74*, no. 189, July/August.

24. "These beings see each other, touch each other, speak to each other, but communication between them always remains a miracle, a true leap into the unknown." (A. Ayfre, *Télé-Ciné* no. 70-71, November/December 1957.)

25. As he wrote more or less in his *Notes sur le cinématographe*.

26. Robert Bresson, *Notes sur le cinématographe*, Gallimard 1975.

27. Robert Bresson, *Cahiers du cinéma*, no. 178, May 1966.

28. J. Sémolué, "Les personnages de Robert Bresson," *Cahiers du cinéma*, no. 75, October 1957.

29. Perhaps because Michel Estève, one of the most perceptive commentators on Bresson, is also one of the leading specialists on Bernanos's literary output.

30. *Robert Bresson: La passion du cinématographe* appeared in 1983. It was thus written just before the release of *L'Argent*, which perhaps goes even further into blackness.

31. J. Magny, "L'expérience intérieure de Robert Bresson," *Cahiers du cinéma*, no. 75, October 1957.

32. See above, "Isolated Beings Reaching Out."

33. J.-C. Rousseau, "Bresson, Vermeer," *Robert Bresson*, Camera/Stylo, no. 5, Ramsay-Poche-Cinéma, 1989.

34. Robert Bresson, *Cahiers du cinéma*, no. 178, May 1966.

35. Robert Bresson, *Les Lettres françaises*, May 24, 1962.

36. Our emphasis.

37. Robert Bresson, *Cahiers du cinéma*, no. 104, February 1960.

38. In his paper delivered at the Rencontres Jacques Cartier in Lyon, December 1989.

39. Robert Bresson, *Cahiers du cinéma*, no. 104, February 1960.

40. See the whole of "Solitudes in Action" above.

41. See above, "Gazes and Vision."

42. "Build your film on white, on silence and immobility." Robert Bresson, *Notes sur le cinématographe*, Gallimard, 1975.

43. Robert Bresson, *Cahiers du cinéma*, no. 104, February 1960.

Une femme douce

P. ADAMS SITNEY

The Rhetoric
of Robert Bresson

From *Le Journal d'un curé de campagne* to *Une femme douce*

T
HERE ARE TWO irreconcilable critical paths open to the film critic. One takes cinema to be the heir to the nineteenth-century literary tradition, specifically the novel with its popular base. According to this tradition Alfred Hitchcock, John Ford, Jean Renoir, and Josef von Sternberg are among the greatest artists of the cinema. I subscribe to the other view that sees cinema as a modern art and values it for its freedom from traditional fictional forms and for its intensity. The pantheon of this approach is more contestable, because the critics who share it are less willing to accept an orthodoxy. Nevertheless, the early Buñuel, some Russians from the twenties (Eisenstein, Dovzhenko, Vertov), Vigo, and some of Dreyer would probably be universally acknowledged.

For a formalist critic of the cinema, narrative is interesting to the extent that it can be stretched and/or subverted. Dreyer, who approached cinema through the dramatic tradition, intuitively radicalized his forms through sheer intensity. *La Passion de Jeanne d'Arc*, *Vampyr*, *Vreden's Dag*, *Ordet*, and *Gertrud* constitute together the greatest achievement of an individual within the history of the cinema.

Bresson has been more conscious than Dreyer in his application of form. His approach has been from a novelistic perspective, and the intensity he has achieved has depended upon the way in which he extends and abstracts narrative. As I will suggest in this article he analyzes the elements of his narrative through the very means by which he presents it. So the experience of a Bresson film simultaneously combines both mechanisms and their illusions.

Although I recognize the value of thematic and character analysis for Bresson's work, I have preferred to adapt a philological approach to the problems of filmic style, in the hope of defining broad principles of construction such as the linear style, and overall unaccented rhythm, as well as specific cinematographic figurations such as synecdoche, hysteron proteron, binary contexts, the two-part shot, ellipsis, and elision. Less precise definitions, for example, the first person or the subjunctive as it applies to film, have been necessary to make distinctions of stylization among Bresson's films. I believe this method of criticism is justifiable in his case; the high frequency of figuration in all of his later films demands it.

But let me summarize some of the more familiar thematic approaches. The most exhaustive and readily available study on Bresson in English has been a medium-length article by Susan Sontag, "Spiritual Style in the Films of Robert Bresson," included in her book of essays, *Against Interpretation*. I refer the reader to it for a detailed discussion of the first six films, *Les Anges du péché* (1943), *Les Dames du Bois de Boulogne* (1945), *Journal d'un curé de campagne* (1951) *Un condamné à mort s'est échappé* (1956), *Pickpocket* (1959), and *Procès de Jeanne d'Arc* (1962).

Sontag accurately observed, "All of Bresson's films have a common theme: the meaning of confinement and liberty." That article, written at the turning point of his career, preceded his masterpiece, *Au hasard Balthazar* (1965) and subsequently, *Mouchette* (1966) and *Une femme douce* (1969). After seeing these three recent films, we must revise our picture of his overall concerns which clearly have been shifting during the last decade. Bresson criticism demands a philosophical or literary analogue, preferably a parallel text with the same radical formalism and religious orientation. Sontag gives us a quotation from Simone Weil, the contemporary French author of gnomic, tortured aphorisms in the negative route to God. The title of the book from which she quotes, *Grace and Gravity*, might well describe the visual dilemma of Bresson's imagery: a concentration on objects and gestures, always concrete, yet evoking spiritual landscapes and hierarchies. Nevertheless there is a medievalism about Weil's writing, as there is in Kierkegaard, that opposes the absolute modernity of form in everything Bresson does, that gives tension to his art.

By implication Sontag is reminding us of the persistence of Jansenism in France. Thus she quotes Weil, the contemporary instance, rather than Pascal, the source of that tradition, whose thoughts of predestination and the acquisition of grace are essentially the same as Weil's. These concerns, the fruit of Weil's thought, are for Bresson only the matrix, but the *focus* of his energies has been the construction of a specifically abstract cinematographic form to contain and dissect these traditional principles. The ambiguity of formal operations, moment by moment—e.g., reversal of effect and cause, attenuated ellipses, schematic constructions, and synecdoche—registers in the Bressonian context as the unfathomable process of God's will (or, free will) while his firm architectonic suggests the inexorable workings of a superimposed (divine) destiny.

Bresson says as much in a lengthy interview with Godard and Delahaye (*Cahiers du cinéma*, no. 178; *Cahiers du cinéma in English*, no. 8) "You know, to my mind, Pascal is so great but he is so great to everyone's . . . Well, in Jansenism there is perhaps this, which is an impression that I have as well: it is that our lives are made at once of predestination—Jansenism, then, and of chance (*hasard*)."

But there are other philosophic approaches as well. Jean-Luc Godard responded to *Au hasard Balthazar* with "The Testament of Balthazar," (*Cahiers du cinéma*, no. 177; *Cahiers du cinéma in English*, no. 6) a page of excerpts from Maurice Merleau-Ponty altered in part to refer directly to the film. There may be an abstract justification in equating existentialist revelations with Bresson's implicit concept of identity (an ambivalent perspective that alternates between presenting the self in direct first person and as an object in the narrative) but the statements from Merleau-Ponty throw no light on the problems Bresson presents to the serious critic. Ultimately Godard succumbed to the magic of the film by marrying into it.

The composer Olivier Messiaen comes to mind as the closest parallel to Bresson in the other arts. A devout Catholic, the organist of the Trinité in Paris, Messiaen has always been a radical modernist and a seminal figure in the evolution of modern music (in addition to his compositions, he deserves the credit of teaching both Stockhausen and Boulez). Nevertheless, the material of Messiaen's art, pure sounds, submits to simultaneous modernism and theophany more flexibly and more readily than narrative film.

All music participates in the philosophical mode; cinema does so rarely, Bresson's work being an unusual case. (His recognition and use of music as a metaphysical analogon will be explained more fully in my discussion of *Un condamné à mort* and *Pickpocket*.) The contradiction between his form and his themes rejects philosophical resolution. One cannot properly say that he puts a radical form to traditional content, as Resnais does to Cayrol's *Muriel* script. The films are too well fused for that; in their nuclear distillation, the individual shot, one sees Jansenist and modern spirit mingled.

One speaks of "narration" in discussing the films of Robert Bresson rather than "plot." He replaces the conventional outline of events with a sense of the process by which events are arranged on the screen. That substitution indicates the modernist approach to fiction, in which specific imagined situations have less importance than the way in which those situations are perceived by the author and the reader. Essentially, narrative becomes interesting in those works from which it almost disappears. It turns into a formal element when it diminishes as the focus of interest in a work. The modern cinema, particularly in France, has made much of this transference, redeeming the process of adaptation from its reactionary tradition by using cinematography to analyze the structure of the adapted work.

Robert Bresson has rigorously explored the formal perimeters of the contemporary fiction film. Others have been more radical in their reduction of narrative, but no one has sustained a tension between story and abstraction for as long or as consistently as he.

The distinction between the geometric and the linear in film editing is essential to an analysis of Bresson. For the most part, radical formalism in cinema has been geometrical: Eisenstein, L'Herbier, Kuleshov, Vertov, Kubelka and most other formalists use the alternative positions of the camera, one following the other, to articulate a solid geometry of cinema in which the various angles at which an action is shot, and the interaction of close-ups and long shots, combine to give the illusion of a cubic spatial field from which the camera is capable of extracting an infinite series of perspectives.

In the vision of filmmaking, metonymy is essential. For Roman Jakobson, who has most clearly articulated the difference between metaphor and metonymy, cinema in general is basically metonymic:

The development of a discourse may take place along two different semantic lines: one topic may lead to another either through their similarity or through their contiguity. The metaphoric way would be the most appropriate term for the first case and the metonymic way for the second, since they find their most condensed expression in metaphor and metonymy respectively.

In poetry there are various motives which determine the choice between these alternants. The primacy of the metaphoric process in the literary schools of romanticism and symbolism has been repeatedly acknowledged, but it is still insufficiently realized that it is the predominance of metonymy which underlies and actually predetermines the so-called "realistic" trend, which belongs to an intermediary stage between the decline of romanticism and the rise of symbolism and is opposed to both. Following the path of contiguous relationships, the realistic author metonymically digresses from the plot to the atmosphere and from the characters to the setting in space and time. He is fond of synecdochic details.

The alternative predominance of one or the other of these two processes is by no means confined to verbal art. The same oscillation occurs in sign systems other than language. A salient example from the history of painting is the manifestly metonymical orientation of cubism, where the object is transformed into a set of synecdoches; the surrealist painters responded with a patently metaphorical attitude. Ever since the productions of D.W. Griffith, the art of the cinema, with its highly developed capacity for changing the angle, perspective and focus of "shots," has broken with the tradition of the theater and ranged an unprecedented variety of synecdochic "close-ups" and metonymic "set-ups" in general. In such pictures as those of Charlie Chaplin, these devices in turn were superseded by a novel, metaphoric "montage" with its lap dissolves—the filmic similes.

The most systematic employment of filmic metonymy is geometrization. The linear style, on the other hand, suggests tapestry or bas-relief as the pictorial metaphor for cinema, not sculptural space. For the most part, linearity has been the preference of filmmakers unconcerned with form; Bresson has deliberately developed an antigeometrical approach; he has linearized the metonymic principle by discrete movements of the camera which change carefully set-up long shots to significant close-ups, and vice versa, in an effort to attain maximal economy of means. In so doing, he has further emphasized the isolated "take," or camera set-up, as an independent molecule of narrative, rather than as a facet (or angle) of an illusory crystal. Bresson's choice seems to be directly related to his serious effort to "adapt" the space of the novel to a cinematic medium that has historically sought its essence in the elaboration of the dramatic arena.

The greatest problem for the critic is the difficulty of maintaining an analytical perspective while watching a film. Although Bresson deliberately distances the viewers by emphasizing the structure of events rather than their emotional vectors, he holds his films together with ritualistic rhythms that lead the viewer's consciousness from the texture of his formal mechanisms to an involvement with the ambiguities of the narrative and the sense of inextricable fate common to all his films. The formal mechanisms Bresson employs are not spectacular; he avoids metaphor, parallel cutting, geometrization, and antichronology—all of which would call attention to themselves; his art proceeds instead by indirection, allusion, ellipsis and the elision of disjunctive scenes. This distinction cannot be overemphasized. A Bresson film devolves with as much formal rhetoric as that of the most radical avant-gardists. Yet he concentrates on those figures of cinematography which produce a sense of fluidity and condensation and avoid strong ruptures and interjections. In recent literary history, the method of Virginia Woolf, in contradistinction to that of James Joyce, would compare with Bresson's; Woolf brings the reader from the specifics of narrative to more abstract considerations without letting her reader detect the locus of transition. In Bresson as in Woolf, the most extreme formal devices coincide with, *are*, the essential developments of the narrative. Thus, from moment to moment, demands on the critical observer are extreme.

The following eleven shots from *Mouchette* are described to remind the reader of what he has already seen (I am afraid the description would be hopelessly inadequate, if he has not yet seen the film).

1. *Mouchette, a young adolescent girl, poorly dressed, stands facing the camera before a church. She turns her back to us and walks toward the church as the camera pans slightly down to see her feet. She splashes her shoes in a mud puddle and climbs the church stairs out of the frame. Others follow her, among whose feet we recognize the shoes and pants of her father. He is running.*

2. *From inside we see her enter the church with other people. Her father catches up to her and gives her a violent shove from behind. She lunges forward to*

3. *A side view of her, still propelled by his shove, reaching the holy water basin. A quick fade-out as loud circus-like music comes in. The music continues with different intensities mixed with the calls of barkers throughout the sequence of shots described below.*

4. *Medium shot of hands washing glasses in a bar; the camera dollies back to reveal it is Mouchette. She dries her hands on her apron, takes the apron off, arrogantly tosses the sponge into the sink and comes forward so that her middle again fills the screen. In the foreground, before Mouchette, someone opens a cash register, gives her a few coins in payment, and closes it. She comes forward and leaves the screen by the left.*

5. *From inside the bar we see Mouchette go out the open door and*

6. *From outside, sit with her father who is drinking with her brother and other men outside the bar. She gives him the coins she has just earned. He says nothing, but hands her his half-finished glass of white wine, which she drinks. She leaves and the camera lingers on her father and brother who neither move nor speak.*

7. *From behind, we see her make her way through a crowd of a small amusement park.*

8. *In the foreground, some people get into amusement cars that move, revealing Mouchette approaching from behind. She watches for a moment and leaves the frame.*

9. *A crowd of people are seen watching an offscreen amusement. Mouchette pushes her way through them toward the camera and comes forward to dominate the shot. The torso of a woman holding a baby passes her.*

10. *Close-up of hand buying a token for a ride. After the exchange we see that it is the woman with the baby.*

11. *Same situation as #9, but the camera is closer on Mouchette's torso. The woman with the baby gives her the token. The camera pans to Mouchette's face. The woman is gone without Mouchette having thanked her. Mouchette leaves the frame to take a ride in a bumper car.*

This passage typifies the visual rhetoric of the later Bresson films. In the overall schema of *Mouchette* it is not a crucial episode, nor does it occur in *Nouvelle histoire de Mouchette*, the Bernanos novel which Bresson adapted. Foremost we should consider the amount of information conveyed in these eleven shots which take less than two minutes of screen time. Although there is no dialogue, the recurrent themes of the cruelty of Mouchette's father, his drunkenness, her poverty, and the arrogance it imparts to her, are all instanced here. In a few seconds Bresson makes his statements on the relevance of church going. (In *Au hasard Balthazar* he uses a mass as the setting for a forecast of the sexual relationship the heroine and the juvenile delinquent choirboy. And in *Pickpocket* we have a glimpse of a mass during the funeral of the protagonist's mother—an equally unsatisfying religious experience. There is a persistence of the antiliturgical in Bresson's Catholicism as in that of Bernanos, two of whose novels he adapted to film.)

Bresson prefers to use a single take for both a close-up and medium shot, rather than two. The first shot establishes Mouchette in front of the church and shows us the details of her splashing in the mud. The fourth take performs several functions: it begins with a close-up, *in medias res*, which leaves the performer in ambiguity. We suspect it is the regular bar mistress and learn immediately it is Mouchette. Just as immediately we notice that we are watching the end, not the beginning, of an episode, and we have a final close-up of the girl getting her pay. The eighth shot changes from a tight middle view to a wide shot of Mouchette when the foreground characters leave their car. Finally, the eleventh shot combines a close-up of Mouchette receiving the token and a medium shot of her reaction. In a brief and almost randomly chosen passage from Bresson, then, there are four shots with a change of scale and emphasis.

In at least two others there is a simple change of emphasis. The second shot begins as Mouchette enters the church and becomes dramatic and violent when she is pushed, and the ninth shot appears to be an establishing shot of a crowd until the girl pushes her way through, towards us.

The tenth shot from our breakdown exemplifies a textural ambiguity Bresson loves to use. On the one hand, we do not know whose hands we see in the close-up. Even later we never see her face; she is characterized by the fact that she holds a baby. That's all. The sequence of shots ten and eleven reverses cause and effect, so that the "meaning" of the former is unknown until we see the latter. This shot is abstract while we watch it and concrete, in a narrative matrix, only halfway into the next shot. Although this is only a matter of seconds, or fractions of a second, the effect of the two shots involves an engagement of the viewer's mind and an immediate satisfaction which is characteristic of the sensual experience of seeing a Bresson film.

Split seconds are crucial to his art. The first, fourth, eighth, tenth, and eleventh shots are all held for an instant after the essential action within the field is completed, while conventional editors would cut just before the end of a gesture for "continuity." This tiny affirmation of the empty space of action, reaffirmed several times a minute in all of his later films, gives the cumulative impression of a tremendous retardation of action, a contemplative vision, and extreme formalization. The sixth shot is an exaggerated example of the same principle whereby the camera lingers on the blank alcoholic faces of Mouchette's brother and father after she leaves the table.

Finally, it should be mentioned that the brief fifth shot is an example of a camera position that recurs periodically throughout the film. The cyclical recurrence of frames of action is another device Bresson uses in all of his films after *Les Dames du Bois de Boulogne*. Like the previous trope, this retards the dynamics of action, for Bresson's uniqueness does not consist in the minimalization of the schemata of his films (they are rich and often complex plots), nor in the retardation of the action itself, which is compressed and accelerated if anything, but in the careful employment of the subtle mechanics I have instanced here to undermine the dynamics of action and give simultaneously the impression of stasis and the movement of narrative.

The absence of dialogue to which I referred above is characteristic of long stretches in Bresson's films. In such passages one is not conscious of a lack of sound: Bresson fills the ear with a collage of noises, vividly suggesting expanses of space outside of the cramped frame. But in the films after *Journal d'un curé de campagne*, with one exception, dialogue is concentrated in widely separated episodes. These episodes tend to be cut with functionally alternating shots of the speaker and listener. A long monologue, such as the pornographic story in Bergman's *Persona*, would be antithetical to the condensed narrative Bresson uses. If he eschews such radical formalizations as long monologues so popular with Bergman, Godard, Resnais, etc., why do his films give the impression of tremendous restraint and deliberate alienation from the drama of his characters? I believe it is because he uses dialogue primarily as an exchange of information and ideas, albeit personal information at times. Even at its most psychologically oriented, Bresson's dialogue is merely the conjoined utterances of two isolated creatures. No one, in later Bresson films, has a particle of faith in persuasion or the cathartic value of speech.

Having outlined the principles of Bresson's style in the first section, we shall now consider how that style evolved, through a chronological survey of his works as the loci of gradually accumulated tropes. In respect to our present concerns his first two feature films, *Les Anges du péché* and *Les Dames du Bois de Boulogne*, are almost outside the case; although they complement one another, they distinctly form a preface to his later work. In the six years that lie between *Les Dames du Bois de Boulogne*, and *Journal d'un curé de campagne*, Bresson must have re-evaluated his idea of the cinema. Both early films follow the conventional dramatic conception of the medium with complex motivations, a balance of parallel contrasting scenes elaborating intricate intrigues, and, above all, with an emphasis on dialogue. Jean Giraudoux wrote the speeches for *Les Anges* and Jean Cocteau for *Les Dames*. The former film is less interesting in itself than as an indication of the degree to which Bresson was rooted in the traditional French cinema when he started to make films. Before that he had made a short comedy, *Les Affaires publiques*, which is now lost or, possibly, hidden by the maker, and he assisted René Clair on an aborted project.

In both films the camera work of Philippe Agostini, the "movie music" of Jean-Jacques Grünenwald, and the sets of René Renoux (*Les Anges*) and Max Douy (*Les Dames*) give the works a sumptuous, almost decadent texture, typical of the

French cinema in the forties, and yet within that baroque milieu they are both restrained, even ascetic films. If we scrutinize them, we can find embryonic traces of some of Bresson's later achievements. In the scene of Hélène's visit to the club, where Agnès dances, there is a preview of the *subjunctive* method which the film-maker later perfected: the spectator looks from the point of view of the protagonist (here Hélène) at a scene of highly evocative images. Bresson leaves these evocations ambiguous, but the ambiguity does not encourage the viewer to imagine alternative possible situations. Rather he witnesses the merest fragment of what seems to be a concrete, ongoing reality. The ambivalence of Antonioni and the fragmented hint-dropping of Hitchcock are instances of the same method used for completely different psychological ends. They engage the viewer with the idea of a solution; Bresson distances him with the experience of contiguous privacies. Further examples of the subjunctive method would be the use of letters to convey narrative information, and offscreen sound (Agnès's cry, when entertaining her customers) to determine the emotional signature of a scene.

Another typical feature of Bresson's style expressed in the first two films is the ambiguous end of *Les Dames*: we do not know whether Agnès lives or dies. This is not posed as a hanging question. For years, I saw the film and thought it clear that she would live. Yet Ken Kelman told me he has always assumed she was about to die. We surprised each other with our assumptions, but we should not have. A re-consideration of many episodes in Bresson's oeuvre, inspired by the above conversation, has suggested to me that there is a deep core of ambiguity in several of his films. He underplays and elides the ambiguities so that the viewer can make assumptions of fact rather than contingency. This becomes especially dramatic in the construction of *Au hasard Balthazar*, and we shall return to it when considering that film.

One would like to know what Bresson's thoughts were in the period between *Les Dames du Bois de Boulogne* and *Journal d'un curé de campagne*; he has not discussed them in his numerous, but reticent, interviews. He had planned to shoot a film about Ignatius of Loyola, the founder of the Jesuit order—a script was written with Julian Green. The shooting never started. One suspects, from all the interviews and the tales about him, that Bresson did not *suddenly* turn his back on the conventions of French filmmaking. *Les Dames* was a masterpiece in those terms. It remains the greatest achievement of its decade in France; and, although it had no financial success, Bresson must have realized the extent of his mastery of the cinematic aesthetic of his times. When we look over his career, there emerges a pattern of continual attempts to pose and master new formal problems in the schema of each new film. Perhaps the extent of his success with *Les Dames* necessitated the search for a new form.

In any case by 1950 Bresson had radicalized his formal interests. At the same time he acquired a new set of assistants: Léonce-Henry Burel as cameraman, Pierre Charbonnier as the set decorator, who were as dry and lean in their work as

Agostini, Renoux, and Douy were fluid and rich; Grünenwald remained as the composer for one last film; and, above all, Bresson wrote his own script and dialogue. The scope and consistency of these changes placed beyond credence the suggestion that he might have been influenced significantly by his new crew.

The rejection of professional actors coincided with the change of collaborators. This may be the most famous and obvious of his stylistic traits: the stripped, almost mechanical acting of his amateur protagonists. For the passions of his characters Bresson substitutes his obsession with form and formalization. He does this by reducing their psychological perspectives to a pattern of behaviour, cinematically to a type of movement. When we compare his first two films (in which the characters are identical with their passions, and the actors professional) with the later seven, or when we compare these later films with their literary sources, the extent of Bresson's formalization becomes evident. The obsessive and sympathetic psychologies of characters in Dostoevsky and Bernanos (or in *Les Anges du péché* or *Les Dames du Bois de Boulogne*) disappear in Bresson's later adaptations. He transfers this level of intensity to the mechanical activities of the characters and to the total rhythm of the films. The primary means of this substitution has been simply repetition of movements and behaviour.

All these elements are a part of a total recasting of his form, which begins with *Journal d'un curé de campagne*, to continue through all his subsequent films. A cinematic first person has replaced the conventional third. This has long been an aspiration and pitfall of the narrative cinema. In the best known example of the so-called subjective camera, Robert Montgomery's *The Lady in the Lake*, the camera substitutes for the body of the hero who is heard but, of course, not seen. Orson Welles planned a similar treatment of Conrad's *Heart of Darkness* which, like most of his ambitious projects, was never realized. In any event, *The Lady in the Lake* proves the impossibility of a crude equation between a fictional *I* and the camera lens.

In cinema the lyrical first person has succeeded where the narrative failed. The sensually responsive camera of Stan Brakhage, for instance, directly mediates between the eye of the filmmaker and that of the spectator. Its instrumentality remains apparent. Its activity responds to the material seen. The lyrical mode captures the rapture of the present moment by imitating the movements of the eye in the process of seeing. But narrative differs from lyrics in that even in the present tense a narrative work assumes the continuous sequence of time, that is, the projection of our past experience into the present. While we watch, we remember. Montgomery's film confused the visual aspect of memory with the dynamics of present experience. The result is a clumsy static camera incapable of the instantaneous changes and variations that characterize the act of seeing.

In *Journal d'un curé de campagne*, Bresson confronted the problem of transposing the first-person novel, written in the form of a diary, to the cinema. His solution, a subtle one, altered the entire course of his career and gave birth to the style by which he is now recognized. Consciously or unconsciously, Bresson realized the superiority of representing the first person, as it appears in the eye of the memory, over the existential *I*. Traditionally, writers have intuited the near impossibility of representing the existential present, and have preferred the convention of the first-person imperfect (or past) tense. Certainly Proust gives us a conscious index of the accuracy with which the subjective can be rendered when relegated to the past.

In the eye of the memory the *I* is passive. One cannot overestimate the importance which *remembered vision* plays in all of Bresson's films since the forties. He has consistently chosen amateur actors, as I have noted, to play his protagonists; his direction of them eliminates subjectivity. This, in fact, has been the major criticism levelled against him: that his actors are wooden. His method of directing has been mocked by conventional critics precisely because they are unwilling to consider the possibility of a quality of observation superior to what we are normally given in the cinema. Bresson has instinctively found a visual correlative for the self in a narrative context by eliminating "expressiveness" from the standard vocabulary of acting.

Extreme examples of the same reduction can be found within the avant-garde tradition, especially in those films where the protagonists are actually somnambulists and the form of the whole film a trance. Similarly the recurring figure in Magritte's paintings of the man with a bowler hat seen in a landscape from behind, as if he were our mediator in looking at the scene before him, and us, partakes of the same observation of the self in a dream. Bresson's does not extend into dream. But then, Bresson is not an avant-gardist. The avant-garde has declared a perpetual revolution against established modes of thought and expression. Thus the avant-garde casts off aesthetic systems and methods which form the modernist tradition. A priori all avant-gardists are modernists, but not all modernists share the avant-garde sensibility. Bresson is a good example of a non avant-garde modernist. One feels that his rejection of the conventional cinema arises less from principle than from the futility of trying to use the conventions while maintaining a fierce accuracy of observation. To judge from his themes and metaphysics one would suspect that his sympathies lie with tradition, but to look carefully at his films is to see the modernist.

In the *Cahiers du cinéma* (no. 178) interview Bresson describes his method of pictorial composition:

> . . . you must know what you want to do plastically—and do what is necessary
> to have it. The image you have in your mind, you must foresee, that is to say,
> see it in advance, literally see it on the screen (while taking into account that
> there risks being a disparity, and even an entire difference, between what you

see and what you will have) and you must make the image exactly as you want to see it, as you see it, as you create it . . .

Even Bresson's apologists, preferring a philosophical justification of the acting style required in his films, have neglected to mention this formal and observational principle: that he makes his characters more distant, and thereby closer to the visual experience of memory, by his restraining direction. The philosophical argument added to this principle reunites his methodology to his doxology, so that one sees each protagonist as the agent of greater (spiritual) forces, directed as if in the grip of power beyond himself (he is literally in the grip of Bresson). Thus it seems appropriate to view his films as aesthetic demonstrations within which his actors are true performers in a more profound game.

I do not want to make a case for a systematic formula in all of Bresson's work of mental/visual memory translation into cinema. He detests systems in the imaginative process. From the same interview based on *Au hasard Balthazar*, we find: "In the end, you see what I sought to do, and it was very difficult, for it was necessary that the two schemata [of the film's plot] about which I have just spoken to you not give the effect of a system, it was necessary that they not be systematic." The margin of contradiction, small as it is, in Bresson's work makes it all the more difficult to define systematically his aesthetic position. He is a practical formalist, not a rigorous one.

Nevertheless the evidence for a first-person orientation in the films since *Les Dames du Bois de Boulogne* is irrefutable: nothing happens in *Journal d'un curé de campagne* that the priest does not experience himself; the same is true for the prisoner of *Un condamné à mort s'est échappé*. (Throughout the shooting, Bresson kept on set as an advisor the man upon whose experience the film was based.) Likewise for Michel the Pickpocket; Jeanne d'Arc; Mouchette; and the man of *Une femme douce*.

However the rigidity of the single perspective is disturbed in almost every film (Chantal peers in a window undetected by the curé in *Journal*; Michel's friends find him missing in *Pickpocket*; Joan's guards whisper, perhaps out of her range of hearing; we see Mouchette's father and brother delivering bootleg liquor; the suicide of *Une femme douce* is seen from the maid's point of view, while the husband is out). But in every case, the events unseen by the protagonist are present to his memory, as the logical extension of an act of his or as told to him. In any case, the scenes "behind the back of the protagonist" are never crucial, nor do they ever occupy a significant part of the total film.

I have already claimed that *Journal d'un curé de campagne* marked an essential break with the style of Bresson's two earlier films. Without retracting that statement, I should qualify the extent of his formal revolution, for, in addition to retaining Grünenwald as a composer (and therefore using music conventionally as a "support" for the images), Bresson included at least two merely dramatic scenes which are without cinematic distinction. They are the medallion and the summer house scenes. In the former the priest confronts the countess. It is a splendid moment in itself, the climax of the countess's life and the central episode of Bernanos's novel, but it violates the intense identity of the protagonist and the narration (which I have called the first-person sense) to the detriment of the film as a whole. The scene between the priest and the vicar, equally damaging to the principle of first-person narration, is not even redeemed by the dramatic excellence of the medallion episode.

The equation of narration and protagonist is a function of Bresson's peculiar and brilliant adaptation of Bernanos's novel. Long conversations on theology and faith fill the book, which scrupulously records dialogues and scenes of confrontation. Bresson faced the problem of transposing the action of the novel to filmic images while at the same time retaining the perspective of the priest which Bernanos renders through language.

Normally the cinema of adaptation limits itself to the recreation of the omniscient perspective. The writer holds an advantage over the filmmaker in his ability to use the first person and habits of language to refract narrative action through the point of view of a character. Bresson could not use the camera as flexibly as a pen to suggest the priest's personality; he solved the problem by employing a severe *subjunctivization* of the action. He selected elliptical fragments from the novel's continuity which would distract the viewer's attention from the action itself and direct attention to the way the action was perceived, or more accurately, remembered.

He emphasized this indirection with short interludes of the priest actually writing in his journal, his voice speaking contrapuntally over these scenes. Sometimes the priest writes out a scene before it appears on the screen, sometimes after; yet a tension always obtains between the journal, read or heard, and the experiences we share with him. This tension is heightened by carefully selected instances of description which we do not see. In *Pickpocket* as well, Bresson concentrates the subjective expression of emotion in the writing, and prefers to leave the visualization in a state of "demonstration" and objectivity.

It is within this formal matrix that the dramatic episodes constitute flaws. They substitute direct experience for the subjunctive. In all of Bresson's later films, such substitutions have been eliminated. In narrative films, as in plays, we have been trained to expect the alternation of accented and unaccented scenes, of the comic and the pitiful, of suspense and release. Bresson gives us the contrary, an unaccented succession of short episodes; he postpones the emotional synthesis until the very last shots of *Un condamné à mort s'est échappé* and *Pickpocket*; in *Procès de Jeanne d'Arc*, *Au hasard Balthazar*, *Mouchette*, and *Une femme douce*, that synthesis occurs after the last image. In *Journal* he reversed his tactics following the priest's departure from Torcy. That film ends, as his later works do, with an unbroken chain of brief, fragmented scenes, whose power is cumulative rather than tonic.

The subjunctive method does not diminish the emotive power of the priest's progress toward death, but it substitutes a reflective experience of it for the sympathetic dynamics of a dramatic film. In the novel, the priest records a detailed scene with his doctor who tells him he has cancer. In the film, Bresson cuts immediately from a shot entering the doctor's office to one of leaving, as he tells us over the soundtrack: "It was cancer of the stomach." The sequence indicates the basic method of distillation Bresson employs in the process of adaptation.

It is known that the original editing of *Journal* exceeded the screen time the producer would permit and that Bresson cut it down. It would be ironic if the elliptical style by which he has become distinguished were born of this economic contingency. I think we can trust Bresson when he says that he was ultimately grateful for the forced condensation. From the priest's departure from Torcy on the back of a friend's motorbike to the final image of the cross, the end of the film (a litany of brief scenes, *in medias res*) especially benefited from extreme ellipses and the subjunctive method, whether by initial design or as a result of the order to shorten the film. It becomes a poem of dying, an elongated sequence of glimpses of his last days. Bresson has equalled this ending in some of his later films, never has he surpassed it.

He began to use fragments of classical music, instead of Grünenwald's musical underlinings; in *Un condamné à mort s'est échappé*, he quoted moments from the Kyrie of Mozart's C Minor Mass over the titles, during repetitive actions (the prisoners descending the stairs to the exercise yard, or emptying their slop buckets), and at the end of the film, *following* the minutes of maximum tension, the climax of the escape, which are silent. As Bresson employs it, the music functions not as a support to the visual occasion, but as an allusion: it is a metaphysical vector which reminds us of the essential determinism of the filmmaker's theme. It also suggests the guidance of a presence beyond the immediately visible. In all his subsequent films when Bresson uses music at all, he follows the principle used in *Un condamné à mort*.

The shift from accompanying to allusive music was part of an overall evolution in Bresson's consciousness of the function of sound in films. Natural sounds, heard from offscreen areas, play as important a role in the definition of the form of this film. When we hear the sound of rifle shots, we know this is the execution of his fellow prisoners; the sound of a key rattled against stairs warns him of the approaching guard; a church or prison bell tells him the time (the elliptical use of this is remarkable at the end of the film when the one o'clock bells are immediately followed by the four o'clock). As in *Journal*, the protagonist's voice reports on what we are seeing, what we will see or have not seen. His comments are brief, and concentrate on his feelings which, of course, have no visual reflection; he does not keep a diary.

Although the signal innovation of *Un condamné à mort* in the Bressonian formal repertoire was his use of music, I have noted the film also initiated a purification of Bresson's camera style by generalizing the methods used for the end of *Journal*. Bresson keeps his camera close to the actors—a feature of the cramped prison space as well as a formal device—and inserts long passages of close-ups, without establishing long shots. Most of the screen time details Fontaine's escape, a day book of his meticulous labours with ingenious cell-made tools.

It is a mark of Bresson's genius that he transferred an involvement with the suspense of escape to a fascination with the means of doing so. The filmmaker could have gone further in the elimination of suspense (and does so in his later work), but compared with other escape films, *Un condamné à mort* severely reduces the means and elements of suspense. According to the conventional demands of the genre, details are supposed to accumulate before the climax to elongate the time of maximum tension. Therefore such details become negative spaces in the film, keeping the viewer from what he desires most to see, while he responds to the conditioning of what he has already seen. Conversely, in Bresson's film the details are even more fascinating than the situation, and the filmmaker dwells on them to the satisfaction of the viewer. If *Un condamné à mort s'est échappé* can be called a suspense film, it is one of sensual fulfilment rather than postponed release.

Bresson underlines the sensual aspect of Fontaine's preparations, rehearsals, and procedures of escape in three ways: by magnifying the *scale* of his operation with the close-ups; by including numerous tracking shots and pans in these cramped scenes, which conflict with the fixity of the frames in the rest of the film and in the rest of Bresson's work in general; and through an extensive use of synecdoche, i.e., offering passages of close-up as complete and logical sentences, rather than as detailed interruptions of a wider space.

The last aspect deserves some elaboration. The Bressonian close-up has the same uniqueness as his first-person narrative. Traditionally, that is, since D. W. Griffith, the close-up has been an interruption in the time flow of a film for a significant "detail," precisely as the term is used in the photographic reproduction of parts of paintings. Bresson seldom gives us both the detail and the wider space. He prefers a cinematic synecdoche whereby the close-up implies the wider space, which is unseen. As I have endeavoured to show in the first part of this essay, when he presents a wide view followed by a close-up (or vice versa), he does it in one shot, through a discrete camera movement. He employs this combination, however, only when the action is bipolar and the occurrence of the wide shot is different from the close-up. In the scenes of the preparation of tools, scraping, etc., before Fontaine's escape, Bresson prefers the synecdoche as he does generally throughout his work. A hand gesture (he seems particularly fond of them) inevitably occurs in a field of vision which suggests the space outside the frame, when a portion of the body occupies a corner of the image of which the hand (say) is central, or when some movement occurs within the close-up, often leaving the frame empty.

The flow of synecdoches has a stronger, more metrical rhythm than the alternation of long and short scenes, such as forms the basis of the timing of *Journal* and of the other sections of *Un condamné à mort s'est échappé*. Another development in rhythmetics originating with this film is the repeated use of fades and dissolves. Often a scene fades or dissolves onto another occurring in the very same space, signifying an ellipse of time. He does this predominately with shots of Fontaine at his barred window, as seen from outside.

Pickpocket continues and extends the formal evolution of the earlier films. Here Bresson's visual rhetoric reached maturity for the first time. The film may not be as deeply moving as *Journal* or as dynamic in the application of its tropes as *Un condamné à mort*, but is more sustained, balanced, consistent, and perfected than anything in his previous work. Together with the two subsequent films, *Procès de Jeanne d'Arc* and *Au hasard Balthazar*, it defines the most ambitious phase of Bresson's career.

In *Pickpocket*, Bresson transformed his conception of the synecdochical sequence; he employed long passages of close-ups, as in *Un condamné à mort s'est échappé*, but in this case to retard or redirect the narrative line. The process we see illustrates the craft of picking pockets. The narrative, however, does not depend upon Michel's success as a pickpocket or upon the outcome of any given burglary. The story, which is very loosely related to Dostoevsky's *Crime and Punishment*, although Bresson does not acknowledge it, initially revolves around Michel's cat and mouse game with a police inspector, and ultimately his love for a girl with a small child. The scenes in which we see Michel teaching himself his trade, practising it on subways, or in the breathtaking passage showing an orgy of robbery with two accomplices at the Gare de Lyon, where wallets are lifted, passed on, emptied, passed again, and even returned to the owner's pocket amid the rush of people catching trains, all these scenes are tangential to the central narrative ideas of the film. A great deal of tracking and panning passes unnoticed in these episodes because of the excitement with the material and the closeness of the camera to the subject.

In addition to formalizing the "process sequence" Bresson has virtually eliminated suspense from this film. There is no build up to Michel's final capture. A detective slips handcuffs on him as he is picking a pocket at the racetrack. The music, here Lully, comes in during connective scenes not to underline drama but to recall the sense of a greater order, as in *Un condamné à mort*. The protagonist's voice narrates discretely, and he is seen keeping a diary. The repetition of situations and locations (picking pockets in the Metro, climbing the stairs to his room, discussing the theory of moral superiority in the café) reinforce the rhythmic montage and give the film a ritualistic tone that is even more pronounced than in the earlier films. Indeed, in its insistence on a cycle of locations it is almost oneiric. As a whole

Pickpocket surpasses all of Bresson's other films in the construction of a first-person narrative that refuses identification (as with Fontaine) or pity (as with the priest).

All the elements are abstracted and sublimated to the whole. There are no pivotal scenes, no suspense as I have noted, no climax. The divorce of the plot from the rhetoric of the "process sequence" makes for a reflective viewing of the most intense passages of the film, and that reflectiveness in turn encourages a formalistic approach to the rest of the work.

I have already spoken of Burel, the cameraman, and the use Bresson has made of him; a word should be said for Pierre Charbonnier who made the sets for all of his films except the initial two. Their starkness ideally complements the style of acting and the unhighlighted quality of the photography. Charbonnier is particularly good at creating a bare and cramped room, be it the country priest's cottage, Fontaine's cell, the pickpocket's tiny room, Joan's dungeon, or the cabin of Arsène in *Mouchette*.

Generally, Bresson is at his most conservative in passages of dialogue. With one exception, he employs a functional shot/countershot of speaker and listener in all of the films I have discussed so far. The exception, of course, is *Un condamné à mort s'est échappé* where the situation in which prisoners were forbidden to talk with each other necessitated covert and swift exchanges. Bresson responded to this limitation with an elaborate choreography of speakers at the prisoners' water trough. In *Procès de Jeanne d'Arc*, his most elaborate experiment, he tried to make long interrogation as abstract as Fontaine's scrapings or Michel's robberies. The film has a breathing rhythm born of the alternation of speakers which formally contradicts the established expectations by showing listener when speaker is anticipated or vice versa. The varying length of episodes, separated by fades, reflects the respiratory alternation of the shots.

The film is the one exception to the paucity of dialogue in Bresson's work. It is essentially a re-enactment of the speeches from the original trial. The minimalization of expression is more extreme here than in any of his other films. Joan and her inquisitors speak in the tones of the faithful reciting familiar prayers, even though the content of their speeches is at odds with this form of delivery. The speed or slowness with which they recite their lines and the pace of the alternation of speakers determines the rhythmic value of each scene, which ends with an interlude of her return to her cell or with a direct dissolve to a subsequent interrogation. The film proceeds with a musical structure, an irregular respiration of quick/slow shots and of protracted/curtailed scenes.

In the first confrontation of Joan with her judges the camera remains fixed upon her as she answers questions from an offscreen voice. Only towards the end of the scene does the image cut to the judge when he speaks. In the second exchange the tempo is different. The views shift between the chief interrogator and Joan as they engage in a swift alternation of short questions and answers. Bresson builds up the visual expectation of changes of shots only to formally contradict those expectations. The camera does not directly face either Joan or her judges. It frames both of them at a slight angle from a point equidistant from each. The sequence of speakers describes a triangular space with the camera at the apex and the actors at either end of the base. In the courtroom the camera always frames Joan to the right and the judges to the left, but when they come to her cell to question her the directions are reversed. The alternation of scenes, between courtroom and cell, involves a chiastic placement of the interrogators and interrogee. At no point in the film do Joan and her judges appear in the same shot. The emphasis on shot/countershot may draw the attention away from the first-person perspective. But Bresson does not replace it with an intersubjective situation. Joan is the absolute centre of the film.

In the enumeration of his films in the first person, I was careful to exclude *Au hasard Balthazar*. It gives the impression neither of a first-person diary nor of the objective eye of omniscient third-person narrative On the one hand, it initiates a general breakdown of the first-person perspective which can be seen in the fluctuation between first and third person in his subsequent films. Yet *Mouchette* and *Une femme douce* are fundamentally first-person accounts despite the deviations. *Balthazar* is much more extreme.

No other Bresson film traces as complex a development as *Au hasard Balthazar;* perhaps it is because of its supreme complexity that I find it the most satisfying, the most ecstatic, of his films. The intricacy emerges from the ambition to use a donkey, Balthazar, as the central character without making the film either a fable or an allegory. In other words, it was Bresson's desire to make a film virtually without a protagonist. *Au hasard Balthazar* defines a society, the earlier films define a psyche; both definitions devolve through indirection, but *Au hasard Balthazar* compounds Bresson's customary formal abstraction with the structural device of a donkey with a series of owners who are the periphery (and real subject) of the film. A complex network of parallels and near parallels primarily between the donkey and Marie, his first owner, and secondarily between a round of other owners, amounts finally to a novelistic vision of provincial society. (It is an abstract novel to be sure.) Again Bresson's acute power of observation holds in tension his genius for formal abstraction, preventing the film from the pitfalls of a "systematic" schema or a moralistic thrust.

As in all his films, except *Une femme douce*, Bresson maintains linear time (no flashbacks or flashforwards) in elliptical conglomerations, beginning with the donkey's birth and ending with his death. The animal's life, like the stations of a saint or even Christ himself, is punctuated by encounters, cumulatively suggesting the deadly vices of humanity: the lust and sadism of Gérard, a juvenile delinquent, his sometime owner; the avarice of the old miller, who refuses him hay for his labour; the sloth, drunkenness and wrath of Arnold, who uses him to carry

Au hasard Balthazar

tourists; the pride of Marie's father, refusing to disprove a false accusation of larceny. Marie and her childhood boyfriend baptize him in loving blasphemy, and he dies among sheep from the bullet of a border patrolman aimed at Gérard, turned smuggler with the stolen ass.

Marie herself shares the donkey's fate in human terms, the more pathetic because she possesses "free will" under which she collapses: Gérard seduces her, makes her his gang's woman, and abandons her, naked, humiliated; she gives herself to the miller in return for shelter and jam to eat; yet she rejects her earlier boyfriend, a bourgeois student who will marry her. These two creatures, Marie and Balthazar, seem to have one soul between them. What happens on the screen to one affects them both. That the ass's human persona be a girl, not a man, is not surprising when we consider the moral superiority of the female in all of Bresson's most recent films. Joan, Marie, Mouchette, "the gentle creature" far surpass the men they encounter in spiritual intensity. And they are all creatures of strong erotic presence, raped even when they give themselves.

The music in *Au hasard Balthazar*, Schubert's 20th Piano Sonata, serves the same aesthetic purpose as the quotations in the earlier films (*Procès de Jeanne d'Arc* has no music aside from an initial and a final drum roll); it is used in fragments eleven times, usually during connective scenes; it never guides the emotions; yet twice it serves another function (in addition to suggesting a metaphysical continuity, reminding us of the design): when Gérard chases Marie in circles around the donkey before seducing or raping her, the music changes a basically ridiculous event, the chase, into formal choreography; later, the music assists in one of the most remarkable moments in the film: when Jacques proposes to Marie, she turns away saying that terrible things have happened since they were childhood friends. Bresson cuts to a shot of Balthazar who stands near them. The music comes in with the shot of the donkey and ends when that shot does. In the next image, Marie says, "Now you know everything." The film remains ambiguous about whether the image with the music stood for a short silence during which Jacques realized her situation or whether it elliptically represents a long passage in which Marie has told her story.

That is just one of many kinds of ambiguity in the film. The most elaborate surrounds a mysterious murder which we learn of in the most subjunctive way although it affects several characters: first we see a gun in Gérard's room; next he receives a summons to the police station; as he enters it with his gang, he passes an ambulance framed in the corner of the image (a synecdochical reference to the body). He denies guilt. Later he accuses Arnold, the town drunk, who guiltily fears he has murdered without remembering it. Who was murdered, how, and why, we never learn.

Bresson extends the ambiguity to the very identity of the characters. When I first saw the film, I assumed without question that the woman living with Marie's father late in the film was an intimate housekeeper. It was only after I heard her referred to as the mother by a critic of the film that I considered that possibility. According to the script, published in Italian translation, she is Marie's mother, yet subsequent reviewing of the film does not clarify this ambivalence within the context.

A similar ambivalence attends the woman in whose house Gérard lives. She could be his mother, remarried to a baker hostile to her son. She could be simply a maternal employer.

Marie's mother (I shall identify her as such for convenience) tells Jacques near the end of the film that Marie has gone away and will not return. I took her literally. However, many believe she meant Marie had died after the beating from Gérard and his gang. Does Marie sleep with the miser? At one point she slaps away his hands; she refuses his money, but later she sits on his lap dressed only in a blanket. These are fundamental ambiguities about which it is impossible to assume a definite answer. Other scenes are more obviously obscure. When Arnold says, "Goodbye, old friend" and falls from Balthazar to his death, did he know he would die? and was the cause of death the fall on his head? Was he addressing the donkey or the milestone on the road which resembled a grave?

The progress of the film is totally elliptical; it covers twenty years, far longer than any other Bresson film. We do not see Marie's initial rape, or beating, or her disappearance. The rape is shown by Gérard's chase, followed by a dissolve to him blowing his delivery boy's horn triumphantly. The beating occurs in a spectacular ellipsis between shots of Marie wandering in the empty house where she is to meet Gérard for a last time and a shot of the gang leaving the house, scattering her clothes in a field. The disappearance has been described.

The scenes follow a temporal order, but not a logical one; emphasis shifts, characters alternate. We are left with a chain of essences: the baptism of Balthazar; the children on swings repeating each other's names lovingly; the departure of her boyfriend; Gérard and motorscooter gang coming upon the adolescent Marie, in a nightgown, crowning Balthazar with flowers; Gérard pouring oil on the road to make cars skid and crash; Marie's hands; Gérard burning Balthazar's tail; dancing to rock and roll; Balthazar in the circus counting with his hoof; Arnold falling dead from the donkey, etc. My sequence is certainly inaccurate, but the spirit of the cutting is clear. As in *Journal d'un curé de campagne* the film builds to an excruciating climax, the final humiliation and disappearance of Marie; Balthazar's death makes the coda.

There are scenes of the donkey at work, pulling logs, grinding grain, and counting in the circus, but Bresson does not make any emphatic use of "process sequences" as in *Pickpocket* or *Un condamné à mort s'est échappé*. Instead, his strategy in this film was to create short episodes, often only one shot long, which reverse their contexts. In the first quarter of the film we learn that Jacques's father has accused Marie's father of cheating him. When Marie's father refuses to speak to

Jacques who has come to apologize for his father's behaviour, such a series with a binary context occurs as follows:

> Marie and her father enter Balthazar's stall (dissolve)
> Marie's father puts down his accounts, enters the stall, where he finds his wife and tells her that he is selling the donkey since Marie never leaves her room any more, even to take care of the animal (dissolve)
> Marie rushes into the empty stall (dissolve)
> Gérard's employer has Balthazar.

The last element in this series, centering around the donkey is also the first shot of a new context involving Balthazar's relations with Gérard. Each element of the narrative information reveals itself separately without explicit interaction among the characters. We learn indirectly that Marie is sulking and we infer it is because of her father's treatment of her old boyfriend, then directly that he plans to sell the animal. In the next shot we realize the animal is gone and have a hint of Marie's unhappiness over it. Finally we discover to whom he was sold. The fragmentation of information directs the attention to the individual shot as a module of narrative and ruptures the ease of story continuity. A more explicit use of binary context can be found after the scene in which Marie hit Gérard for beating up Arnold and is in turn slapped by him. They go off, his arm around her, playing pop music on his portable radio. There is a dissolve to the following series:

> The radio and Balthazar's chain (dissolve)
> Balthazar's bread basket, soaking in the rain, followed by a shot of his hoofs in a puddle (dissolve)
> Balthazar in the snow. Marie and Gérard come out of an abandoned house they use for lovemaking. Marie notices that the donkey is trembling (dissolve)
> A sledge hammer is unwrapped and Gérard prepares to kill the sick donkey when Arnold comes and rescues him.

The three scenes of the donkey alone (the first suggested only by his slightly moving chain) are synecdoches and symbols informing the viewer basically that Gérard and Marie remained lovers through the winter, for every time the donkey is hitched and the radio abandoned it is to make love. If this were not immediately evident, the later shot of them emerging from the empty house would confirm it. The first shot in the series, following their fight, simply alludes to the fact that they made love immediately afterwards. By extending this synecdoche into a series, Bresson adds an ambiguity to the function of the first shot after we have seen it. It stands for the whole spring as well as the specific afternoon of the fight. Similarly, the shot of Balthazar in the snow seems at first like another element in the seasonal sequence. It immediately develops into the first element of a new theme, the donkey's illness.

As the reader might infer from the images quoted, Bresson makes considerable use of the dissolve in this film, both to elongate contiguous episodes and to condense widely separated ones. He reduces the fade here almost exclusively to transitions from daytime to night and vice versa.

The binary contexts and abstract series of synecdoches disorient the direction of the narrative and reinforce the ambiguities of the film's structure. When the viewer is disoriented, he pays more attention to the individual shot. Bresson brings him to the brink of his art, which is an analysis of the means of narrative while simultaneously creating the narrative. Another device in Bresson's repertoire for the same effect is hysteron proteron, putting the last first, which most commonly means a reversal of cause and effect. In the scene between Marie's father and the lawyer, the filmmaker reaches the height of his subjunctive involution. The scene begins with a shot of the lawyer's doorplate to identify his profession; immediately we see Marie's father listening to the lawyer reading aloud a letter in which Jacques's father gives him management of his property without the obligation of rendering accounts. From the images immediately following we realized that Marie's father had just brought this old letter to the attorney as evidence of a transaction a decade old after Jacques's father has formally accused him of financial misconduct. Thus we experience the shot first as if Marie's father were hearing the letter for the first time, and suddenly our sense of time and order is inverted, the roles reverse, and in one subjunctive stroke we jump ten or more years into a new situation.

On a lesser scale, the shot which begins with a pool of oil on the road and pans to show Gérard pouring it (our first meeting with this juvenile delinquent) employs the same principle. After an interval of a few shots, it becomes evident that he poured the oil maliciously to make cars skid and crash. Like the other tropes we have catalogued here, hysteron proteron redeems narration from the somnolent logic of storytelling by forcing the viewer to engage his active intelligence in the devolving of the plot.

The change of cameraman from Burel to Ghislain Cloquet attended minor changes in the visual texture of this film. There is more outdoor photography in the three films Cloquet photographed and subsequently a higher contrast in the image tones. Bresson pans the camera more than he did with Burel. In *Au hasard Balthazar* and in *Mouchette* he increases his use of the two-part shot (long shot becoming a close-up, and the opposite). Thus the shot of the oil and then Gérard pouring it, or Marie sitting in her nightgown watching Balthazar when the camera pans to her hand as Gérard sneaks up on her to grab it, are typical of this film's style, which is the most extreme example of the linear approach in all of Bresson.

A complex example of linearity appears in the long scene in which Gérard declares a party at the local bar when Arnold inherits some money. The scene begins with firecrackers, tossed out the café door by gang members, which explode and scare Balthazar who is chained outside. All through this scene there are cyclic repetitions of the lighting, tossing, and explosion of firecrackers followed by a shot of the ass's reaction. Yet the spatial relation between the explosion and the donkey is vague. When Marie's mother calls her out from the party to beg her to return home, she refuses. Meanwhile Gérard breaks up the bar, smashing bottles and mirrors, without reaction on the part of the dancing couples or the stoically drunken Arnold. The simultaneous elements of the scene are intercut in rhythmic cycles with overlapping sounds, but no attempt was made to unite the scenes geometrically.

At the end of the party the local miser tries to dance with Marie, but one of the gang boys stops him, saying that he must pay for the privilege. Then Bresson dissolves to a hand paying out a large sum of money, but it is the lawyer paying the bar owner from Arnold's inheritance for the damage Gérard did. This is not the sole example of a tangential word/image montage in the film. Earlier when Arnold awoke from a dream of guilt over the murder and promised the moon he would never drink again, Bresson faded to a shot of a glass on a bar, filled and drunk; then, once he is drunk, Arnold viciously attacks Balthazar.

Because of the possibility that a scene might be only one shot or as long as the bar scene, the periphrasis of the plot outline (it is the one film completely written by Bresson without literary models, and he indulges his love of intricacy), the ambiguity of events and of character, the ellipses of decades or minutes, reversal of cause and effect, the subjunctive narration, and because of the sudden changes in emphasis and scale, *Au hasard Balthazar* continually vibrates with a visual rhetoric and aura of evocations. Both moment by moment and as a whole work it excites my mind and passions as no other narrative film ever has.

In *Mouchette* Bresson adds nothing to his repertoire of formal innovations. He does refine and redistribute the mechanisms I have been studying. The film begins exactly as *Procès de Jeanne d'Arc* had. Then Jeanne's mother testified that her daughter had been tried and burned; now it is Mouchette's mother who predicts a significant fact to come, her own death, and wonders what will become of her children. From this the film moves immediately to the exploration of a process in the familiar close-up method. We see Arsène, the poacher, making wire traps to catch quail. The birds come and are caught. Then Mathieu, the game warden, who had been spying on Arsène, frees them. By opening the film with a process sequence Bresson set up a metrical rhythm which dominates the whole film, insisting on the abstract nature of the images that follow.

In no other film, even *Au hasard Balthazar*, has the filmmaker so mastered the cumulative structure. Even while Mouchette is killing herself (it takes three tries for her to roll down the hill into the lake), the viewer is hardly aware of what she is really doing; it seems possibly a game. Then when the body falls in the water, Bresson brings in music for the first time, Monteverdi's *Magnificat*, and we realize we have seen the last shot. Suddenly the whole film coalesces.

In a way *Au hasard Balthazar* was the turning point of Bresson's career. In *Mouchette* and *Une femme douce* he seems to be retracing his former successes. The first recalls *Journal d'un curé de campagne;* both are adaptations from Bernanos, both balance a first-person approach with an overview of a provincial town as a microcosm. Despite the brilliances of the film, *Mouchette* does not explore its own shape as vigorously as the preceding five films. Bresson seems to have terminated one front of his formal explorations and to have accepted his own repertoire as the perimeters of his style.

Une femme douce innovates in the Bressonian context colour photography and an alternation of time levels, since the film proceeds through a series of flashbacks, a device he had avoided before. Yet colour and flashbacks are pale innovations when compared with the high level of figurative cinema in the earlier films. It too looks back to the previous achievements of the filmmaker for its inspiration. This time he has doubled back on *Pickpocket*; again the source is Dostoevsky, though much more explicitly in the later film, and the conjugal situation of the earlier film is elaborated in the latter.

Bresson and his cameraman Cloquet have not mastered colour as effectively as they had black-and-white. The tones are muted and controlled, but the image is not as sure and monumental as in the six previous films. The colour is not an overwhelming disaster; it is a handicap. His images lack the essential reinforcement that the lucid photography gives his other films. For example, the distinction in tone between artificially lit scenes and exteriors, of which the filmmaker had been so proud, evaporates with the need for excessive studio lighting required for all colour shooting.

One isolates the colour easily; the involutions of time raise more problems. Unlike the previous films, *Une femme douce*, following its literary source, utilizes two times: the present of the narration (in the film by the husband to his maid, in the story to the reader), and the past of the narration visualized (unnecessary, of course, in the story). *Une femme douce* hyperbolizes two aspects of the structures of his earlier films (putting the conclusion first, and narration which duplicates and offsets what we have seen or will see) with, unfortunately, less formal invention than in any of his previous essays.

Near the beginning and near the end we see the same sequence of shots: the opening of a windowed door, a metal table falling over on a balcony, a scarf floating in the air, and the body of the heroine dead on the sidewalk. Every other shot relates to the visual experience of the narrator, the husband of the suicide. He is a pawnbroker who takes an interest in a beautiful young girl, who brings her belongings to him for money to buy books. He marries her, almost in spite of her will, then "throws cold water" on her love and enthusiasm (a paraphrase translation of his own words). He jealously follows her with a gun when she leaves the shop. One morning he glimpses her, with the gun in hand, thinking of murdering him, deciding against it. He buys a new bed for her; henceforth they sleep separately. She grows ill, approaches death, recovers. They reconcile, and in her first moment of solitude she jumps from the balcony.

Despite the flaws I have mentioned, the film has the same effective architecture as the other Bresson films, the same piling of molecular events. Their reconciliation is one of the ecstatic moments of Bressonian ambiguity: at night, the husband disowns his unemotional, studied objectivity, embraces her, and promises to take her away from the pawnshop, away from Paris; next morning, she offers him coffee and tells him she will respect him dutifully. Both gestures, cut one after the other, satisfy their partner's need to an abnegation of their own, making the tragedy, which we have known from the beginning of the film, excruciating. The minutes subsequent to this reconciliation, then, partake of the purest and tensest cinema; with suspense and psychology removed, we watch concentratedly the process of the ineluctable.

The greatest of many surprises in *Une femme douce* must be its abundance of intellectual quotations. They do not protrude from the film (Godard's philosophical reflections, by comparison, seem as if postered on the walls of his plots), but reveal its essence. In some ways, *Une femme douce* intellectualizes the polarities visualized in *Au hasard Balthazar*. For instance, Bresson insists on a speculation about the similarity of man to beast, implying again the burden of "free will" in a progressively secular culture. In their first conversation the pawnbroker, to prove his education, quotes from Goethe the introduction of Mephisto to Faust. An extraordinary ellipsis follows: school books thrown into the back seat of a car, then the two of them are at the zoo. Later in the film, during her recovery, they visit the paleontology exhibits of a natural history museum, to study the virtual identity of the human skeleton to those of animals.

In all the other films time appeared sequentially, sputtering forward in irregular units. It was a plastic quality, invoked but not defined. With *Une femme douce* Bresson joins the many modernist filmmakers who explicitly confront opposing currents of time. His resolution is not extraordinary; yet it is consistent with his earlier presuppositions and it explains his unexpected cornucopia of quotations. The male protagonist of the film compulsively searches his memory for everything he can recall of his wife. Here Bresson has transferred the psychotic need of Dostoevsky's speaker to analyze his own guilt to a need to explore the past simply to discover who his wife was and what was his relationship to her. The effect stylistically is as if a typical Bresson film were buried in the context of a more conventional work, for the fluid, leisurely elaboration of time present contrasts markedly to the elliptical, figurative images from the flashbacks. This confirms certain arguments put forward in this article about Bresson's dedication to the imagery of memory, if nothing else.

The earlier diary films depend upon the natural persistence of memory; *Une femme douce* describes the forcing of recollection. If we take the flashbacks as a whole to accurately represent memory as Bresson has observed it, then the quotations become focal points around which the memories turn. These are fixed images, in common domain, to which he can refer to refresh his memory. In our recollection of the past, artistic and intellectual experiences can have a permanence that is denied to the daily events which have to be reconstructed backwards in an analysis of the steps leading to a tragedy. I do not offer this viewing of the film to deny the polemical force of the specific quotations, but to orient the fact of the quotations in the historical evolution of Bresson's art.

Mouchette

P. ADAMS SITNEY

Cinematography vs. the Cinema:
Bresson's Figures

"THE IDEAS, hide them, but so that one can find them. The most important will be the most hidden."[1] Sometime between 1950 and 1958 Robert Bresson wrote that note to himself. In 1975 he published the slim but thrilling volume of *Notes sur le cinématographe* which he had accumulated between 1950 and 1974. In a style recalling Joubert's journals, he revealed his painterly approach to filmic issues and he provided several hints about his theoretical orientation toward his medium, most importantly, his distinction between "le cinéma," a debased version of theatre, and "le cinématographe," a high art in which "intelligence" is defeated by "automatisme," sound invents silence, emotion takes precedence over representation, and one sees "models" rather than "acteurs."

Suture

In 1969 Jean-Pierre Oudart introduced the term "suture," from Lacanian psychoanalytic theory, to film criticism, extolling the unique use of shot/countershot in Bresson's *Procès de Jeanne d'Arc*.[2] He argued that the emphasis on reversed fields in the exchanges between Jeanne and her judges, with the camera often placed at an oblique angle to the heroine, demonstrated Bresson's peculiar understanding of cinema's illusionary space. "Suture" is the act of joining the matched fields of shot/countershot which the viewer automatically performs.

Oudart's thesis was developed in a number of articles he wrote in the early seventies for *Cahiers du cinéma*. Soon it became the basis for a theory of identification in cinema in general, which Stephen Heath, among others, elaborated. Oudart claimed, in his initial article, that Bresson lost sight of the discovery he had made in editing *Pickpocket* and turned into a structural principle in *Procès de Jeanne d'Arc*, when he made his next film, *Au hasard Balthazar*, in which shot/countershot plays a diminished role.

Oudart ignores the fact that the style of *Procès de Jeanne d'Arc* reflects the unusual prominence of verbal exchanges in that film. Generally, shot/countershot in Bresson's films underscores the significance of acts of seeing. In this chapter, I shall concentrate on two of Bresson's films in which the process of seeing demands special attention. In the first, *Mouchette*, I shall compare what Mouchette sees in shot/countershot to what we sometimes see of her and about her through camera movement and framing. Then, I shall consider the centrality of seeing in *Pickpocket*.

In 1969 I wrote an article on Bresson's films for the magazine *Changes* which I revised and published in *The Essential Cinema* in 1975 before reading *Notes sur le cinématographe*. Rereading my essay, I am surprised and disappointed in my unwillingness or inability to pursue the implication of the stylistic features I had pointed out as typical of the filmmaker. The most hidden ideas remained securely out of sight in that article. For example, I described a sequence from the middle of *Mouchette* which I had chosen because of its neutrality, its apparent segregation and autonomy from the movement of the film's plot. That sequence and my obtuseness to it will be the starting point for a reconsideration of Bresson's narrative style and its relationship to the questions of form, cinematic language, and modernity I have been exploring in this book. Of modernity, the filmmaker has published only one remark, in the negative mode: "Novelty is not originality nor modernity," to which he footnoted a line from the opening of Rousseau's *Confessions*, "I did not try to conform to others nor the opposite." Here Bresson proudly joins company with a great original and radical modernist; the negative mode is often his most forceful means of expression, as when he writes, "Cinematography, the art, with images, of *representing* nothing."[3]

Synecdoche and Imitation

I had described eleven shots from the moment Mouchette deliberately splashed mud on herself before entering church until an anonymous woman gave her a token for a bumper car ride. Here is my description of the fourth shot in the sequence:

> A quick fade-out as loud circus-like music comes in. The music continues with different intensities mixed with the calls of barkers throughout the sequence of shots described below.
>
> 4. Medium shot of hands washing glasses in a bar; the camera dollies back to reveal that it is Mouchette. She dries her hands on her apron, takes the

apron off, arrogantly tosses the sponge into the sink and comes forward so that her middle again fills the screen. In the foreground, before Mouchette, someone opens a cash register, gives her a few coins in payment, and closes it. She comes forward and leaves the screen by the left.[4]

I had terminated my description of the sequence with the eleventh shot because it is followed by a dramatic scene and an important innovation by Bresson to the plot of Bernanos's *Nouvelle histoire de Mouchette*, which he adapted rather closely: Mouchette engages in an innocent flirtation with a teenage boy in another bumper car. He waits for her after the ride, but before she can speak to him her father suddenly descends upon her and slaps her face. We never see the boy again in the film. Shortly after that, the barmaid Louisa and the poacher, Arsène, are seen enjoying the rides of the fair together.

The plot itself can be quickly summarized. Mouchette's mother lies dying at home with an infant to care for. Her father and brother, both alcoholics, deal in illegal wine, which we see them delivering to the bar where Louisa works. She has an ambiguously defined relationship to Arsène, the poacher, while M. Mathieu, the gamekeeper, who is married, pursues her. After school, where Mouchette is ostracized by the other pupils, she witnesses a fight between Arsène and Mathieu, gets lost in the woods during a downpour, and is eventually found and raped by Arsène. In a fit that may be alcoholic or epileptic he believes he has murdered the gamekeeper. Mouchette comforts him and agrees to cover up the murder with him before returning home. There her mother dies before she can tell her what has happened to her. The next morning she is given something to eat by a prying shopkeeper and a shroud for her mother by an old woman obsessed with death. After visiting Mathieu's home and telling him and his wife that she is Arsène's lover, she wraps herself in the shroud and commits suicide by rolling down a hill into a pond. It takes her three tries, and seems, to the viewer, like a game until her body disappears under the water.

Within this sordid and squalid drama of provincial life, the brief sequence I had described in detailed shots seemed an insignificant interlude. Yet when examined in the light of the whole film the details of the cinematic construction, even in this passage, can tell us a great deal about Bresson's interpretation of Bernanos's novel. The fourth is particularly revealing. When the fourth begins, the viewer naturally assumes that he is watching Louisa, because she is the only person we have seen behind the bar before this. Yet before the camera has tracked back very far we realize that Mouchette is working there instead. Is there a significance to this momentary deception by the filmmaker? Now it seems to me that that complex and exciting shot embodies a subtle insight into Mouchette's psychology[5] and a clue to the mystery of her suicide; and that the ambiguity prods the viewer to recognize it. Her suicide is a mystery not because it lacked motivation; the poverty, cruelty, ostracism, loss of her mother, and, above all, rape provide an overabundance of causes. Yet it is mysterious because Bresson, unlike Bernanos, gives us no warning of its occurrence and no exposition of the girl's mental acts leading up to it. The same is true for his next film, *Une femme douce* (1969), in which the narrator compulsively recounts the history of his wife's suicide in the vain hope of finding sufficient cause. In *Le Diable probablement* (1977) the situation is somewhat transformed: a young man, fixed upon the idea of killing himself, cannot find a sufficient reason for living while testing the sexual, political, and moral passions of his peers.

Mouchette kills herself essentially because of the utter collapse of the crude hopes her world offered her. Bresson invented Louisa from an unexplained remark in the novel by Mathieu to Arsène during their fight—"Stay away from Louisa"—he cast her as a plain and physically unremarkable woman, whose age, perhaps thirty, is difficult to read; yet, for Mouchette, she must have been the only model for an erotically attractive and somewhat independent woman. The rivalry of Arsène and Mathieu invested her with that value. The only indication Bresson gives us of the tenuous identification of Mouchette with Louisa is the momentary ambiguity of the fourth shot from the sequence I have isolated. The image of Arsène and Louisa on the fair ride takes on an added significance after this hint of identification between the two women. *She* is able to enjoy the fair publicly with her lover, but Mouchette is brutally humiliated and stopped before even speaking to a boy who was attracted to her in the bumper cars.

Furthermore, if Louisa is invested with sexual value, so is Arsène, if only because of his success with her. He too has none of the physical attributes we associate with erotic heroes in films. Surely, an identification and a rivalry with Louisa is behind Mouchette's acceptance of his sexual violence toward her. When he collapses in a fit, she tries to soothe him by singing the very song her disgusted schoolteacher chastised her for singing off-key. The next morning she tests the social value of her experience by boasting to Mme Mathieu that she has become Arsène's lover. But that defiant declaration fails to secure for her the status of maturity and sexual desirability she had unconsciously anticipated as Louisa's successor. Instead, she receives the less than generous attention of two women who pity her for the loss of her mother. Her suicide occurs when she feels the poverty of her aspirations and the vacuity of their fulfilment.

Bresson illustrates the collapse of her illusionary values with a metaphor derived from *La Règle du jeu*, a film of erotic triangles and social values quite remote from the world of *Mouchette*. Just before her death Mouchette sees a hare, shot by a hunter, writhing and finally dying. The montage of the hunt recalls the opening of the film in which Mathieu spies on Arsène as he sets his snares for small game birds. Together the two sequences, with their meticulously detailed compositions and rhythmical editing, pay homage to the magnificent central hunt scene of Renoir's film in which the shooting of hares is coupled with the killing of birds by huntsmen in blinds.

The death Mouchette accepts for herself shares a quality of sport or game with the hunt she watched. After the dismantlement of her models for imitation, the dying hare presented the first impression Mouchette could grasp with vigour. The montage and isolation of the episode, together with the shot/countershot of Mouchette's immediate reaction to it, underline the importance the filmmaker gave to it. Unlike the subtlety of the identification with Louisa which belongs to the occulted infrastructure of the film, the graphically depicted shooting of the hare concedes the sudden consciousness of a new option. In killing herself Mouchette acted again upon her need to imitate. This last touch was another of Bresson's additions to Bernanos's story. It fulfils cinematically the demands of Bernanos's pessimistic naturalism, demonstrating the awful power with which the patterns and perspectives the individual inherits and discerns in his or her world curtail freedom.

Bernanos's Frighteningly Sudden Exit

Only readers of Bernanos's novella would know that the old woman who gave Mouchette the dress had encouraged her suicide. Bresson has eliminated the story she told Mouchette about the original owner of the dress, a young girl who died. Out of the simile which ends Bernanos's description of the old woman, the film-maker seems to have made his hunting episode: "She had curled up in her chair, and her fingers were moving so restlessly and quickly along her black dress that her hands were like two small grey animals hunting invisible prey." Again, in the last chapter, which describes Mouchette alone in the quarry where she will kill herself, there is a version of that simile: "At that moment, the deep, secret impulse toward death seized her again. It was so violent that she was almost dancing with anguish, like an animal caught in a trap."[6]

By transforming these metaphors into a concrete situation and giving them the status, not of cinematic analogies as Eisenstein might have done, but of elements in a shot/countershot encounter, Bresson has found a filmic substitution for the access to interiority that Bernanos's language has. Passages such as the following would find no place in Bresson's cinema:

> And now she was thinking of her own death, with her heart gripped not by fear but by the excitement of a great discovery, the feeling that she was about to learn what she had been unable to learn from her brief experience of love. What she thought about death was childish, but *what could never have*

touched her in the past now filled her with poignant tenderness, as sometimes a familiar face *we see suddenly* with the eyes of love makes us aware that it has been dearer to us than life itself for longer than we have ever realized . . .

People generally think that suicide is an act like any other, the last link in a chain of reflexions, or at least of mental images, the conclusion of a supreme debate between the instinct to live and another, more mysterious instinct of renouncement or refusal. But it is not like that. Apart from certain abnormal exceptions, *suicide is an inexplicable and frighteningly sudden event*, rather like the kind of rapid chemical decompositions which currently fashionable science can only explain with absurd or contradictory hypotheses.[7]

Bresson so thoroughly empties out the projection of intention, conflict, and other signs of interiority that would require interpretation from the actors he calls "models" that the sort of elaboration and even editorializing that characterizes the passages from Bernanos's final chapter seems very remote from his art. Nevertheless, the phrases I have emphasized indicate how closely he has followed the text, or rather, how he has found correlatives to his own epistemological model in it. The sudden sight of the dying hare, which would not have touched Mouchette in the past, now motivates her suicide, which seems "an inexplicable and frightening event" on the screen. His narrative style is so radical because he invests the act of seeing—and therefore the shot/countershot structure—with the full burden of fictional psychology. This radicalism has the effect of making events, which are inexplicable and frightening, seem like the natural consequences of previous events in the chain of images. Furthermore, the very ascesis of psychological projection by the actors gives to each image an equal, neutral value which accentuates this appearance of logic. He gnomically says this when he writes:

Flatten my images (as with an iron) *without attenuating them.* . . .

To edit a film is to join persons to one another and to objects by glances.[8]

Again, the *Notes* suggest an important nuance:

Because you do not have to imitate, like painters, sculptors, novelists, the appearance of persons and objects (machines do that for you), your creation or invention confines itself to the ties [liens] that you knot between the various bits of reality caught. There is also the choice of the bits. Your flair decides (p. 35).

For Bresson the art of cinematography is not simply that of pictures and sounds; it is the art of making connections (*liens*) or montage. He grants to the mechanical reproduction of the camera a crude access to reality that is denied to human perception. However, he acknowledges that the truth (*le vrai*) immanent in cinematographic reality emerges when the machines correspond to human perception. The filmmaker must first give himself over to the machinery and then, through montage and fragmentation, construct his film according to the emotional dimensions of the images and sounds he has recorded. This process implies an employment of intuition and improvisation on the level of shooting and a willingness to let the camera "correct" the errors of the script. The problem, he writes, "is to make seen what you see through the mediation of a machine which does not see as you see. And to make heard what you hear through the mediation of another machine which does not hear as you hear."[9] Without the middle term, submission to and redomination by the intervention of the machinery, there is no cinematography.

Bresson's addiction to shot/countershot editing puts him at the opposite pole to Dreyer. In *Mouchette*, for example, he built an episode in a shop of a woman, who offers Mouchette breakfast just after her mother's death, around a long take of the girl intercut with seven countershots. Here, as often in his films, he seems to have reduced direction to a matter of telling the "models" to look up, look left, look down, etc., so that the sequence could be constructed in the editing. The principle is the same as Hitchcock's, but the effect is more like Kuleshov's in that Bresson's montage elicits an emotional reaction to figures who do not mime emotions.

Framing the Hand

The flattening and accentual neutrality of Bresson's images increases their potential for exchange within the rigours of his visual economy. But economy, in the literal sense, is also a central issue for him. Both *Pickpocket* and *Une femme douce* (in which the husband is a pawnbroker) offer elaborate versions of the ambiguous sexuality of the exchange of goods and money. In the eleven-shot series I mentioned at the beginning of this chapter there are four apparently casual exchanges. In the fourth shot—which is crucial to the identification of Mouchette with Louisa—Mouchette receives money for her work at the bar. She passes the money to her father in the sixth. In the tenth a woman buys a token for a ride which she slips to Mouchette in the eleventh. She uses it immediately afterward to ride the bumper car.

Earlier, Mouchette's father had responded to her automatic surrender of the money by passing his wine glass to his daughter. The interchange of wine and money describes the parameters of his economy; for it reverses his illegal labour. In strict adherence to the confines of naturalism, which emphasizes the determinism of heredity, Mouchette's brother repeats the patterns of his father.

Correspondingly, the woman with the infant who buys the token for Mouchette is a countertype of her mother, who also has an infant. It is important to keep in mind that the viewer cannot know the woman's intention until her act is completed. Such attention to manual, undramatic action is a variation on the significant framing of Mouchette when we first see her at the bar. The close framing of her purchase in shot ten of the series does not isolate her from the figures who constitute the bustling environment of a fair. Only in shot eleven do we realize what she has done. This ambiguity is of a different order from that of shot four; we cannot assume, even for a moment, that the person buying the token is her mother. The association with the mother, which the presence of the infant reinforces, is purely formal; it calls our attention—if we notice it at all—to what the mother *cannot* do for her daughter. The ellipsis of the framing and the consequent anonymity of the benefactor separates this woman from those malicious and sinister women who will later offer gifts on the morning after her mother's death.

Even this innovation of Bresson's can be traced to a very different source in the novella. Returning to the final chapter, we find that the involuntary memory of a single act of kindness returns to the girl just before she kills herself. The paragraph is worth quoting in full because it demonstrates the extent of the filmmaker's transposition:

> It had happened one holiday-time at Trémières. She was taking back to Dumont's café the fish which the old man had caught during the day—a basketful of eels. On the way a big fair-haired girl had bumped into her, and turned around and asked her her name. Mouchette had not answered and the girl had gently and absent-mindedly stroked her cheek. At first Mouchette had thought nothing of it, and indeed, the memory had been painful until evening and she pushed it out of mind. It had returned suddenly, changed almost unrecognizably, just before dawn when she was asleep on the ragged mattress Madame Dumont, on evenings when the café was full, put down for her in the narrow corridor littered with empty bottles and cans and smelling sharply of sour wine and heavily and greasily of paraffin. In some strange way, while she was half-asleep, she felt herself cushion her face in the crook of her arm and smell the imperceptible perfume of that warm hand, and indeed she seemed to feel the hand itself, so near and so real and living that without thinking she raised her head and put up her lips to be kissed.[10]

This memory is prefaced in the book by the assertion that "Her mother had never been affectionate and Mouchette had never received many caresses from her hands," and followed shortly by an essential link: "Until her chance meeting with Arsène she had never, despite such fleeting moments, been able to overcome the strange rebellion against tenderness which made her so solitary."

The anonymous woman with the baby receives none of the emphasis that Bernanos gives to the girl who stroked Mouchette's cheek. Through the film-maker's art, that woman is absorbed within seconds back into the crowd from which she scarcely emerged. Furthermore, her kind act ironically instigates her father's sudden attack, more violent than his earlier shove in the church; for after seeing her flirting with the boy in the bumper car, he rushes at her, pushes her, and slaps her. Another factor in Bresson's systematic orchestration of gestures would be the bumper car scene itself, in which the superficially violent bumps become signs of play and eros.

More crucial than the quick disappearance of the woman with the infant is the withdrawal of Mouchette's own mother. Her intense pain and imminent death prevent her from listening to her daughter's urgent wish to disclose her rape. The mother's death abandons Mouchette to her unformulated mimesis of Louisa. Instead of responding to her daughter as a child, traumatized by the brutality of her sexual initiation, the mother asks the girl to play another role beyond her age by warming the baby's bottle, which she does against her breast.

The Self-Correction of the World's Fragility

Pickpocket is Bresson's prime example of the moral value of perception freed from the confines of intelligence.

Georg Lukács in *The Theory of the Novel*, invoking an intricately developed yet useful Hegelian argument, identified the ironization of subjectivity characteristic of the novel in the following way:

> The self-recognition and, with it, self-abolition of subjectivity was called irony by the first theoreticians of the novel, the aesthetic philosophers of early Romanticism. As a formal constituent of the novel form this signifies an inte-rior diversion of the normative creative subject into subjectivity as inferiority, which opposes power complexes that are alien to it and which strives to imprint the contents of its longing upon the alien world, and a subjectivity which sees through the abstract and, therefore, limited nature of the mutually alien worlds of subject and object, understand[s] these worlds by seeing their limitations as necessary conditions of their existence and, by thus seeing through them, allows the duality of the world to subsist. At the same time the creative subjectivity glimpses a unified world in the mutual relativity of ele-ments essentially alien to one another, and gives form to this world. . . .
>
> The irony of the novel is the self-correction of the world's fragility: inade-quate relations can transform themselves into a fanciful yet well-ordered

round of misunderstandings and cross-purposes, within which everything is seen as many-sided, within which things appear as isolated and yet connected, as full of value and yet totally devoid of it, as abstract fragments and as concrete autonomous life, as flowering and as decaying, as the infliction of suffering and as suffering itself.[11]

Perhaps more than any other filmmaker with a serious reputation, and certainly more than any discussed in this book [*Modernist Montage*], Bresson has adapted important novels and novellas to the screen. The most ambitious literary source he approached was the model for *Pickpocket*: Dostoevsky's *Crime and Punishment*. Perhaps the very scale of that ambition accounts for his refusal to acknowledge the intimate relationship between the novel and his film. Dostoevsky's novellas have been the bases for two of his other films, as have two novels of Bernanos. Visconti is the only other major modern filmmaker that comes to mind who has been confident in translating serious fiction into cinema. In discussing *Mouchette* I have attempted to show how Bresson implemented and interpreted his literary source and, more crucially, how he inflected it cinematographically by structuring both into the film, and into the film's fictional bearer of subjectivity, an openness to a privileged moment of audiovisual stimulation. That moment is the point at which the filmmaker as "the normative creative subject" "glimpses a unified world" within the duality he has reflected. Yet, apt as Lukács's brilliant description of novelistic creativity is for Bresson's self-conscious art, there are critical differences between the verbal modality of the novel and Bresson's cinematic fiction. It is in *Pickpocket* that these differences are most richly and complexly manifested.

The Function of Repetition

The nearly identical repetition of the film's beginning in its final minutes highlights the nullity of its central development. In the opening episode the pickpocket presents us with his first theft. Like Dostoevsky's Raskolnikov, he commits a crime in order to prove to himself his superiority over other humans and their law. He never intended to become a pickpocket, simply to commit a single crime to substantiate his theory. We find out all this only after the first theft has been accomplished and the thief apprehended but released because of insufficient evidence.

The presence of a racetrack is evoked elliptically by a composition of figures staring slightly beyond the camera, while on the soundtrack the sound of approaching horses grows louder and then begins to wane. Just as the sound intensity passes the crowd, the pickpocket, Michel, among them, glances to the left as if following the horses. Both at the beginning and at nearly the end of the film this configuration of image and sound is all we see of the actual race. In neither do we get the countershot.[12] Each time this elliptical trope occurs, Bresson intercuts details of the theft Michel commits while everyone's attention is diverted by the drama of the race. The first time, he gently snaps open a woman's purse as the race commences, and, just as the horses pass, he lifts out a wad of bills, pockets them, and turns away from the camera, exiting from the composition. During all of this, a voice-over commentary describes his emotional state: anxiety leading to elation.

When the trope recurs, Michel is the victim of a police plant. By now he has learned the fine points of picking pockets, so that he can unbutton a man's jacket at the start of the race, and remove his wallet with two fingers just as the horses pass. But this time, the man handcuffs him as he completes the operation. The virtual repetition of the earlier shot is a clue to the more elaborate repetition of the crime and its consequences. Both times he was caught by the police; both times the act failed to confirm the theory; both times the failure created a possibility for a visual stimulus to take on a meaning for him. The difference between his reaction to the first stimulus and the second breaks the chain of repetition and constitutes the meaning of the film. Its exposition will require some elaboration.

At the very beginning of the film, which purports to be the pickpocket's journal, he writes and tells us that there are two kinds of men: those who act and those who write about actions; he, however, claims to be both in one. The statement may be interpreted either as a simple boast of his uniqueness or, more profitably, as a paradox. The initial aphorism does not admit what follows it. Of course, taken literally his boast is a fiction, for Michel himself is a fiction who neither acts nor writes outside of the film in which the filmmaker disposes him.

The Journal

The pretext of the journal, here as in *Journal d'un curé de campagne*, justifies the voice-over which puts the action of the film into the past tense, emphasizing its finality at the start, and pretends to be an intimate or at least interior account. Maurice Blanchot astutely observed in the passage on "The Recourse to the Journal" in his essay, "Le Solitude essentielle," that journal writing involved a literary paradox:

> What does the writer have to remember? Himself, who he is when he is not writing, when he is living a daily life, when he is alive and real, and not dying and without truth. But the strange thing is that the means he uses to recall himself to himself is the very element of forgetfulness: the act of writing. . . .

The Journal shows that already the person writing is no longer capable of belonging to time through ordinary firmness of action, through the community created by work, by profession, through the simplicity of intimate speech, the force of thoughtlessness.[13]

Blanchot was writing of the journals kept by novelists and poets, but what he observed applies as well to the fictional journal, which as a novelistic form is, in Lukács's phrase, "a self-correction of the world's fragility." One of the ironical displacements of subjectivity characteristic of the novel is the notion that a person is the sum of what has happened to him. The fictional journal invites us to share the "well-ordered round of misunderstandings and cross-purposes," again Lukács's phrase, with the invented protagonist.

Bresson makes the case more complex by using a ploy common to the authors of fictional journals, the preface. Before the film actually introduces us to Michel, we read on the screen:

This film is not in the police genre. The author has to express himself though images and sounds.

The nightmare of a young man driven by his weakness into an adventure of picking pockets for which he was not made.

Only this adventure will reunite through some strange paths two souls who, without it, perhaps would never have known each other.

The difference between a film and a written text obliges Bresson to give up the convention, as old as the novel form itself, of pretending that the journal is a found object, unless he were to make the radical move of treating the images and sounds as found material. The words "This film" immediately underline the fictional status of the journal, which the preface never mentions. Furthermore, it diverts attention from the perspective of the first-person narration by referring to the intersubjectivity of the two souls. The key term "cauchemar" [nightmare] predicts the passive acting style of the "model" as well as the thematic recurrence of the initial theft and prepares us for the recognition—under the metaphor of waking—that distinguishes it from the cycles of repetition. Significantly this preface can only be understood retrospectively; for it predicts so much more than it can elaborate in a single paragraph.

The double inscription of preface and journal reflects the importance of reading in the film. The most obvious instance of the power of reading within the plot itself is the recurring allusion to the autobiography of a pickpocket called "Barrington" which Michel has read and which he recommends to the police inspector, with whom he plays a cat and mouse game. Barrington's book must be another example of the possibility of acting as well as writing. Michel's blindness to this is another way the filmmaker has of putting into question the opening aphorism. A more subtle, and metaphorical, variation on the theme of reading, however, is the event which turns Michel from being the executor of a single paradigmatic crime to a professional thief. Because he has picked one pocket, he sees differently. On the metro he sees a man reading a newspaper and his life is changed. He has "read" the newspaper reader figuratively. Rather than accepting the sight before him, as we see it in the shot, he interprets the newspaper not as something to read but as a tool. The reader, he realizes, is a pickpocket who covers his face behind the paper and uses the paper as an excuse for bumping into another rider. Folding up the paper, he has enclosed the snatched wallet within it. The film viewer, who has not directly experienced Michel's anxiety and elation at the first theft, cannot interpret the filmic image of the subway scene as he does. Only afterward, when the scene shifts to Michel's tiny room, do we realize how he read that scene; for he is practising the use of a newspaper to disguise the act of picking pockets. Fate, he tells us, directed his steps to that subway. What he figuratively read in the common sight began his education as a thief. Like the subjectivized images I discussed in *Mouchette* this sight of the man with the newspaper takes on a special meaning for the consciousness open to it.

Bildungsroman

Most of *Pickpocket* details Michel's education as a criminal; its form suggests the *Bildungsroman*. Eventually this subjective reader is himself read by other trained eyes. Another, more experienced thief has seen him and invites him to join him and an accomplice as they practise the art of picking pockets at its most elaborate and refined level. We must deduce this sequence from the fragmentary episodes Bresson gives us. One evening Michel notices a man pacing back and forth before his door. His manner suggests that of a cruising homosexual. Michel follows him onto a street car and, again in a scene suggesting an erotic liaison, tacitly becomes his partner as they enter a café. This suggestion of a pick-up extends the erotic tone of the thefts themselves, which resemble caresses and usually involve reaching into men's clothes.

A parallel development turns on another act of reading. Jeanne, who lives in the same building as Michel's mother, and who is the girlfriend of his friend, Jacques, has left a note for him telling of his mother's condition as she approaches death. Exhausted from a vigorous day of robbery, he steps over the note without seeing it. He reads it too late, the next morning. His mother has died. The police have known Michel since a robbery occurred at his mother's house. The unconfirmed suggestion is that Michel had committed this larceny before the period of the film began. We are led to infer that the theory of superiority and its practical consequences entail a self-justification of that initial crime against his own mother.

In the middle of the film Bresson presents us with a depiction of the team of thieves working the Gare de Lyon, an orgy of precisely calculated robbery which is matched by the choreographic precision of camera movements and a breathtaking rhythmic montage in a *tour de force* of cinematography. It functions analogously to the hunt scene in the centre of *La Règle du jeu* which I assume to be an abiding inspiration to Bresson.

An account of the sequence of twenty shots will illustrate the intricacy of the montage and camera movement, which in its precision and virtuoso timing corresponds to the combined skills of the thieves.

A close-up of a notebook entry (1): "I have become extremely daring . . ." dissolves into a moving sequence shot (2), which begins with Michel entering the train station and weaves among characters we take to be his possible victims after he passes out of the image, until it settles on a woman buying a ticket. The next three short shots (3-5) detail Michel deftly substituting a rolled newspaper for the purse under her arm, then passing it to an accomplice; the third dumps the empty pocketbook in a waste basket. Then another sequence shot (6) made up of a long shot and a moving series of close-ups shows an accomplice removing bills protruding from a victim's billfold and passing them to Michel. That shot ends with Michel's glance, matched by a countershot (7) of a plainclothes detective, while the voice-over asks "Where did I meet him?" before the tracking camera spots a new mark.

Eight more shots describe the elegant teamwork involved in taking this mark's wallet: A hand taps his shoulder (9), but when he turns to look, a thief from the other side lifts the wallet from inside his jacket, and drops it into Michel's waiting hand (10), as the man turns in the other direction (11). Next, in the most elaborate sequence shot of the film (12) Michel slips the wallet into a tourist's pocket (in close-up). The camera tracks back to identify the innocent carrier for us, and follows him through the ticket gate to the quays where it focuses on two detectives coming in the opposite direction. Panning to follow them, it swivels until it is 180 degrees from where it began, catching Michel passing through the ticket gate in pursuit of the tourist. There follow seven shots taken from inside a train coach. First, the carrier climbs on followed by Michel (13). In a compartment Michel removes the hidden wallet as the man lifts his baggage to the overhead rack, and passes it to an accomplice, who carries it down the aisle (15) to pass it to the third member of the team in a nearby compartment. No sooner has this wallet reached its final destination than attention shifts to a heavy man who had been in the background. In a breathtaking exchange of three short shots, the third man lifts a wallet from the breast pocket of the heavy man as he passes down the aisle. He holds it with three fingers against the inner window for half a second (twelve frames) (16), then removes the money which he passes to an accomplice and slips the wallet back into the same breast pocket as the man returns down the aisle (17-18). In the final three shots of the sequence, Michel helps a man onto the train (19), removes his watch and receives a purse passed to him (20), and climbs down from the coach to deposit the empty purse under the wagon (21).

The second, seventh, and the spectacular twelfth shots are long. They set up the actions which follow. The ninth, tenth, and eleventh shots follow each other rapidly: they describe the single, quick gesture of distracting the traveller by touching his shoulder. By the time he has looked in two directions, he has been robbed and the wallet has changed hands. The elegant tenth shot of Michel's hand catching the wallet sets up our expectations for the breathtaking sixteenth shot in which the stolen wallet hovers—as if in midair—visible only to the thieves and to us.

Fated Vision

Fate again provides Michel with an important sight, this time a stark and blatant one that we have no trouble interpreting with him: his two accomplices, who had preceded him to a railway station, are arrested before his eyes. He escapes from Paris for a couple of years. Bresson cuts from his departing train to an image of him returning. The interval allows for a complication in the plot. Jeanne has had a baby and refused to marry Jacques, who has disappeared. Michel takes a job and gives Jeanne most of his salary to support the child. The filmmaker loses little time in illustrating Michel's normal life. Soon we find him in a café, looking at a man reading the racing paper. This time he is unable to read the reader. When he tries to pick his pocket the next day at the track, we realize that he is a police agent who has entrapped Michel.

The story of a criminal who performs his act to confirm his superiority, discusses his theory with the police, and gets involved in helping an unfortunate, kind woman comes directly from *Crime and Punishment*. The variations are fascinating, because through them Bresson demonstrates the difference between "cinema" and "cinematography." Axe murders, like Raskolnikov's, abound in commercial films. Bresson has substituted a nearly invisible act (which the camera can unveil with great compression and even erotic power) for the lurid horror of a scene of blood and violence. Less brilliant, but nonetheless interesting, is his translation of Dostoevsky's saintly prostitute, Sonia, into Jeanne. Her situation is more believable; her decision, in Catholic France in the 1950s, to have her child out of wedlock is certainly not revolutionary, but it evidences behaviour according to principle more humanely than Michel's fusion of theory and practice. But more significantly, the substitution of Jeanne for Sonia reduces her dimensions in this film in order to enclose us in the solipsistic mind of the pickpocket while it withholds the crucial intersubjective moment to the very final shot.

Every shot of the epilogue is decisive. Even though it is the closest transcription of Dostoevsky in the film, it is uniquely and wholly Bresson's. Immediately after his arrest, the camera presents Michel sitting on his cell bed. But the cell is so like his tiny room that, for an instant, we might think he has been released and sits brooding at home. The sound of a metal door opening and the echoing corridor confirms that he is in jail. The epilogue to *Crime and Punishment* has two chapters. In the first, we learn of Raskolnikov's trial and sentence quickly, and then of the death of his mother and the correspondence between Sonia, who accompanied the murderer to Siberia, and his sister. Bresson moved the mother's death to the central narrative of the film. He did not want that to complicate Michel's solitude. But he did reproduce the behaviour of Raskolnikov in his model. Dostoevsky wrote:

> Sonia wrote simply that he had at first shown no interest in her visits, had almost been vexed with her indeed for coming, unwilling to talk and rude with her. But that in the end these visits had become a habit and almost a necessity for him, so that he was positively distressed when she was ill for some days and could not visit him.[14]

The first of Jeanne's visits to Michel produces the same hostility. When she suggests that the court will be lenient because of his confession, he tells her he will recant it, almost to upset her. Of the jail he says, "I do not see it." Here Bresson adapts his original closely. In the second chapter of the epilogue we read: "In prison, of course, there was a great deal he did not see and did not want to see; he lived as it were with downcast eyes" (p. 467).

But although the transposition is faithful, the sense is different. So much of *Pickpocket* turns on fortuitous moments of seeing, that Michel's declaration reveals the intensification of his solipsism in the formula, "I do not see it." For him the walls of the prison dissolve and only his "idea" of superiority, and consequently the sense of his inferiority at having blundered, remains visible. This too comes right out of the second chapter of Dostoevsky's epilogue:

> At least he might have found relief in raging at his stupidity, as he had raged at the grotesque blunders that had brought him to prison. But now in prison, *in freedom*, he thought over and criticized all his actions again and by no means found them so blundering and so grotesque as they had seemed at the fatal time. (p. 466)
>
> ". . . many of the benefactors of mankind who snatched power for themselves instead of inheriting it ought to have been punished at their first steps.

But those men succeeded and so *they were right*, and I didn't, and so I had no right to have taken that step."

It was only in that that he recognized his criminality, only in the fact that he had been unsuccessful and had confessed it.

He suffered too from the question: why had he not killed himself? (p. 467)

Michel repeats the question to himself after his first interview with Jeanne: "Why live?"

After a fade-out, the initial jail scene repeats itself. Michel is in the same position and we hear the same sounds but this time Jeanne does not come. Instead, he gets a letter telling him that the baby was ill and that Jeanne will come in a short time. This too parallels Sonia's illness and the letter in which she explains her absence. "His heart throbbed painfully as he read it," according to Dostoevsky. Michel informs us of the same reaction to reading Jeanne's note. Again, the isolation of the sequences, the paring down of the plot, and most crucially, the weight given to acts of reading in the film, make this admission of emotion much more dramatic in *Pickpocket* than in *Crime and Punishment*.

The scene fades again and in the next shot we see that Jeanne had kept her promise. As Michel sees her through the grating of the prison meeting room, he tells us "Quelque chose illuminait sa figure." This phrase was not in the original script. The American subtitler, for an unknown reason, remains closer to Dostoevsky than Bresson here; for the former had written: "But at the same moment she understood, and a light of infinite happiness came into her eyes" (p. 471).

Figura

The change is critical. It is with this phrase that Michel announces his conversion. The question, "Why live?" prepared him to read the letter with more meaning than its simple apology could contain; and the sight of the letter created the condition in which he could see Jeanne as the answer to his question. Literally, his description of the moment would be translated: "Something lit up her face." *Figure*, from Latin *figura* means, first, a shape or an outline. A French listener would hear it as "face" without difficulty. I take the change of Dostoevsky's line, and the choice of "figure" instead of "visage" as meaningful. The image of Jeanne is not significantly different from those we have seen of her before. Bresson did not literalize the line with a flood of light, as some conventional filmmakers might have.

Michel sees Jeanne's face and reads it *figuratively*. She is a trope for his redemption from the cyclic repetition, demonstrated by the two racetrack scenes, and demonstrated again by the sameness of the scenes in the jail cell. "Quelque chose illuminait sa figure," also refers to the cinematic image: it is an illuminated trope, a projection of light and shadow. Bresson has written in his *Notes:* "How hide from oneself the fact that it all winds up on a rectangle of white fabric hung on a wall? (See your film as a surface to cover.)"[15]

The viewer of "le cinématographe" is invited to read images figuratively, to escape from the nightmarish blindness to the commercial "cinema's" literalness, to see the two models, according to another of the metaphors of the preface, as "souls." *Figura* has a religious as well as a rhetorical dimension. In typology the Old Testament prefigures the New. Read from the pivot of the Christ event, the histories and the prophecies of Israel encode promises of salvation.

As film viewers, we had been forced to read the crucial repeated scenes figuratively. The very separation of picture and sound makes a trope of the composite. In the *Notes* this is the definition of economy:

Economy
Make known that we are in the same place by repetition of the same noises and the same sonority. (p. 41)

Once Michel has read the image of Jeanne figuratively, the grammatical person of the narrative changes. The recourse to the journal, which has dominated up to this moment, no longer functions. As Michel and Jeanne kiss each other's fingers through the bars, the voice-over addresses her for the first time: "O Jeanne, what a droll path we took to find each other."

This shift of person, to the almost prayerful mode of address, can even be found in the final entry in Bresson's short book to which I have referred so often.

DIVINATION, this word [*nom*], how can I not associate it with the two sublime machines which I use to work? Camera and recorder, take me far away from the intelligence which complicates everything. (p. 72; translation modified)

The obsessive Michel, throughout all of *Pickpocket* until the final shot/counter-shot exchange of the film remained a figure for the crippling intelligence which complicates everything. His redeeming vision of Jeanne is an act of divination. The space of Bresson's fictions is a trap for capturing meaning which, for him, is always figural.

Notes

1. Robert Bresson, *Notes on Cinematography*, p. 18. Hereafter cited as *Notes*; translation modified to follow Bresson's punctuation.

2. Jean-Pierre Oudart, "La Suture," and "Cinema and Suture"; Daniel Dayan, "The Tudor Code of Classical Cinema"; William Rothman, "Against the System of the Suture"; Stephen Heath, *Questions of Cinema*; Barry Salt, *Film Style and Technique*; David Bordwell, *Narration in the Fiction Film*; and Noël Carroll, *Mystifying Movies*.

3. Bresson, *Notes*, p. 63, translation modified; p. 59.

4. P. Adams Sitney, "The Rhetoric of Robert Bresson," in *The Essential Cinema*, pp. 186-89.

5. I use the word, keeping in mind Bresson's dictum: "No psychology (of the kind which discovers only what it can explain)." This is rather a case of what he identified as "Expression through compression. To put into an image what a writer would spin out over ten pages." *Notes*, p. 47. In my reconsideration of this film I am guided by a reading of René Girard's *Deceit, Desire, and the Novel*.

6. Georges Bernanos, *Mouchette*, pp. 115, 123.

7. Ibid., pp. 118-119, ellipsis and emphasis mine.

8. Bresson, *Notes*, p. 6, translation modified, my ellipsis.

9. *Notes*, p. 37, translation modified.

10. *Mouchette*, pp. 121-22.

11. George Lukács, *The Theory of the Novel*, pp. 74-75; ellipsis mine. I have corrected the apparent typographical error "understand" to "understands" to make the passage legible.

12. See David Bordwell, *Narration in the Fiction Film*. Bordwell argues perceptively that Bresson's inflection of "shot/reverse-shot" is "well suited for the neutral transmission of story information" (p. 293). As often, so it would seem, he and I are interested in the same cinematic phenomena, but we are never more in disagreement than when he writes: "*Pickpocket's* stubborn resistance to interpretation, its preference for order over meaning, reappears in the final four segments" (p. 306). In general, his description of what he calls "Parametric Narration" corresponds to several of the issues in this book, although he takes a very different approach. Note, in this regard, his discussion of "The Problem of Modernism," p. 310.

13. Blanchot, *The Gaze of Orpheus*, pp. 71-72.

14. Fyodor Dostoevsky, *Crime and Punishment*, p. 465. Hereafter page references given parenthetically in text.

15. Bresson, *Notes*, p. 13.

Une femme douce

MIRELLA JONA AFFRON

Bresson and Pascal:
Rhetorical Affinities

Hébrard: "Whatever is going to happen to us is going to happen,
and there is nothing we can do to stop it."

Pastor (pointing to Fontaine): "He can."[1]

I N THE FORTY YEARS that separate *Les Anges du péché* (1943) from *L'Argent* (1983), reflections of Christian thought in the work of Robert Bresson have received the close, sometimes devoted attention of numerous critics.[2] Bresson's Christian thematics have been analyzed (with more frequent reference to Jansenism and Pascal early in his career) not only in *Les Anges du péché, Journal d'un curé de campagne* (1950), *Procès de Jeanne d'Arc* (1961), *Lancelot du Lac* (1973), films based on explicitly Christian subjects, but in all of Bresson's films, including a project abandoned in its early stages: a life of Ignatius of Loyola.[3] The Jansenist doctrine of grace has in particular served as a filter for the explication of the Bressonian text: grace is a gratuitous gift of the hidden God who reveals himself only to those who seek Him with all their being; the good are not necessarily chosen, for without effective grace they are impotent to accomplish the commandments they practice; nor are the wicked necessarily lost; on God's charity alone depend salvation and damnation. Bresson's evolution with respect to these and attendant themes—free will and predestination, hope and despair, revelation and faith—has dictated the organization (and reorganization) of his films into cycles.[4] Of major critical interest has been the attention paid the manner by which these themes are translated into images and sound.[5]

But while Bresson's films reflect an evolving and increasingly dark understanding of Christian doctrine, what has remained unchanged, and indeed appears immutable, is that other aspect of his affinity to Pascal—the rhetorical affinity—as yet largely unexamined. The consistency of Bresson's position and expression, of syntax and vocabulary (on questions of theatre and film, narrative, acting, editing, sound, spectatorship), from his first extensive published pronouncements (1946), to the publication of his observations on filmmaking, *Notes sur le cinématographe* (1975),[6] to the most recent interviews, maintains an unbroken link to his films and to Pascal's art of persuasion. It is the continuous sympathy of Bresson's discourse on art, expressed in practice and theory, with Pascal's principles of rhetoric, most often gathered into the introductory section of editions of *Les Pensées*, that is the object of this study.

Les Pensées/Notes sur le cinématographe

The surface resemblance of *Les Pensées* and *Notes sur le cinématographe*, the similarity of the graphic design each dictates to the page, is that much more striking for the fact that both are outside class or genre. What is known as Pascal's *Pensées* is a collection of more than nine hundred fragments, some as short as a single word hurriedly scribbled on a scrap of paper, some as long as a dozen or more pages of structured and highly polished prose. These notes—reminders on style and content, sketches of an outline for the finished work, reflections on readings, maxims, passages of analysis of the human condition, extensive commentaries on scripture and faith—were meant to serve an undertaking interrupted in 1662 by Pascal's death: his projected *Apologie de la religion chrétienne*, an exhaustive defence of the Christian religion. *Les Pensées* were first published in 1670 in what has come to be called the Port-Royal edition. In the past century-and-a-half, they have appeared in numerous scholarly editions and have been organized occasionally by theme but most often according to the schema advanced by the editor as the one closest to Pascal's intention (sometimes even, it has been noted, closest to the intentions of a particular editor). Bresson's work, as the title implies, is also a collection of notes, about four hundred in all, written from 1950 to 1958 and from 1960 to 1974. *Notes sur le cinématographe* are reflections on the art of filmmaking—on acting, for example, directing, editing, sound—and intended, despite their title, to serve no ulterior project.

Thus, neither the "pensée" nor the "note" can be subject to any very clear conventions of genre. If these works, in spite of widely divergent origins (the first is a creation of editors, the intermediate expression of a work we do not have in its definitive form; the second a creation of the author, the definitive form of what is normally considered an intermediate expression), bear a resemblance, it is not to a common model but to each other. And furthermore (and here is the point on which the comparison, for the purpose of this essay, must be based), Bresson's "notes" are closest to Pascal precisely in those "pensées" that Pascal devotes to rhetoric (the subject not of the projected work's content but of its form) and which are clustered under the headings "order," "plan," and/or "style," according to the edition. In these sections, where Bresson's intention is closest to Pascal's, the form of *Les Pensées* most resembles that of *Notes sur le cinématographe:* short entries, reflecting in their concision, subtlety, and force the very rhetoric they propose. The resemblance of function between Pascal's "pensées" devoted to style and the art of persuasion and Bresson's *Notes sur le cinématographe* explains the affinities of the two works, the shared form.[7]

This function is double: autodidactic (to remind oneself of a certain number of principles and precepts) and didactic (to persuade others of these principles and precepts). Bresson, like Pascal, passes from the first person (self-admonition), to the second (the admonition of others), to the infinitive (which acts as an imperative for everyone). The clearest echo of Pascal's style, however, can be found in the elliptical fragments ("The terrible habit of theatre"),[8] in antithesis (*"Resemblance, difference"*),[9] in paradox ("An actor draws from him what is not really there"),[10] and in the occasional surprise of the aphorism ("Images and sounds like people who make acquaintance on a journey and afterwards cannot separate").[11] On the model of Pascal (and Montaigne before him), Bresson's arguments often rest on sources quoted. He borrows in order to confirm, contradict, rectify; his reading of others becomes a reading of himself. Pascal's method, illustrated in this assessment of the strengths and limitations of Montaigne ("Montaigne has seen that we are shocked at a fool, and that habit is all-powerful; but he has not seen the reason of this effect.")[12] finds its parallel in the notes of Bresson, among which the following: *"Every movement reveals us* (Montaigne). But it only reveals us if it is automatic (not commanded, not willed)."[13] Finally, the fragmentary nature of the entries sustains the sense that *Notes sur le cinématographe,* like *Les Pensées,* is, in spite of the fixity of its form, an intermediate work, that it serves another text: for Pascal, the unfinished *Apologie de la religion chrétienne,* and for Bresson, the thirteen films that in the course of forty years have carried his signature and those still to come.

Narrative

"All things conceal a mystery" (*Les Pensées*)

Les Anges du péché, Bresson's first full-length film, includes a number of scenes that document the practices of convent life among the Dominican sisters of Béthanie.

In one of these, the nuns gather to celebrate the joyous rite of the "miracle of the maxims." To each falls by lot the maxim that will be her emblem for the year. The drawing is random only in appearance: "There are no accidents in this lowly world. There are only signs," says Mother Dominique. The miracle of the maxims relies on the faith that to each celebrant of the ritual is destined a particular aphorism, and that during the lottery this aphorism is received by the one for whom it was divinely ordained. (Thus, Anne-Marie, the protagonist of *Les Anges du péché*, having drawn a dictate of Catherine of Siena—"Once you have heard the word by which God ties you to another being, your ears are no longer of any use. All other words are merely the echo of that word."—follows it to her death.)

To the first sister falls a maxim of Pascal ("All things conceal a mystery")[14] that echos throughout the film. Nothing is random; purpose lies hidden beneath incidence. *Les Anges du péché*, and more clearly still two of Bresson's subsequent films, *Un condamné à mort s'est échappé* (1956) and *Pickpocket* (1959), accommodate this mystery within the generic frame of the mystery itself—albeit radically transformed.[15] How radical is the transformation in Bresson's own view can be fathomed from the film-within-a-film sequence of *Quatre nuits d'un rêveur* (1972). The heroine and her mother attend a gala screening ("Gala screenings are a bore," says Marthe) of a movie of Bresson's invention that bears the melodramatic title, *Amour, quand tu nous tiens (The Bonds of Love)*. The bit of film we are allowed to watch (mother and daughter are the first to walk out) is in fact a Bressonian parody of the film noir. The shoot-out has just taken place. The young gangster is fatally wounded. As he lies dying, surrounded by a pool of blood, he pulls out a picture of the girl he loves (close-up of the gangster, close-up of the photo of the girl), and mumbles: "We fell into a trap." This series of caricatural shots is accompanied by the silences, grunts, and, finally, the burst of music that recalls a genuine Bresson ending. Bresson's joke, in charting the distance between the images and the sound, describes the abyss between his view of the Hollywood thriller and his transformation of the genre.

Yet, both in the case of *Pickpocket* and in that of *Un condamné à mort s'est échappé*, Bresson felt it necessary to confront the issue of genre directly. To divorce *Pickpocket* from the mystery he relies on an intertitle; for *Un condamné à mort s'est échappé*, he relies on the title itself.

The disclaimer that opens *Pickpocket* reads as follows:

The style of this film is not that of a thriller. The author attempts to explain, in pictures and sounds, the nightmare of a young man, forced by his weakness into an adventure in theft for which he was not made. Yet this adventure, by strange paths, brings together two souls, which otherwise might never have been united.

Bresson protests before the fact against the confusion of *Pickpocket* with the conventional thriller, its title, plot, and cast of characters notwithstanding. In a defence reminiscent of the classical preface, he cautions the viewer against expecting the style of the thriller, introduces his hero, and offers the "correct" interpretation of the dénouement. To guarantee the sincerity of the disclaimer, Bresson commits what would otherwise be an ultimately destructive act: he gives away the ending.

In *Un condamné à mort s'est échappé*, the title's second clause announces the climax, while the first retains the film's connection to the thriller. The two parts of the title undermine one another to define Bresson's recasting of the genre. The film has a subtitle, however, *Le Vent souffle où il veut*, itself part of a maxim drawn from the authority of the Old Testament.[16] "The wind bloweth where it listeth" serves as the title's emblem. Title and subtitle link the two mysteries: the one that can be uncovered and solved, and that gives its name to the genre; the other that covers all things in eternal enigma.

The tension between these mysteries has its parallel in the contrast of the two confessions in *Pickpocket*: confession as sacrament and confession as narrative device. The policeman who hounds Michel into admitting his crimes seeks a confession in the usual forensic sense, but he insists also that Michel submit to introspection, that he look within himself. The result is two confessions: one oral (which we do not hear and which is presumably transcribed onto a police register we do not see), which leads to Michel's punishment; the other written, the spiritual confession that documents his salvation. The latter closes with these words: "Oh Jeanne, what a curious path I have had to take in order to reach you."[17] The policeman is doubly confessor, doubly interrogator, instrument of the law and of God, cop and priest. Michel's adventure in theft, yet another cinematic illustration that crime doesn't pay, becomes an adventure in faith.

Can one then speak of suspense at all in Bresson's versions of the thriller? No, answers Eric Rohmer in his discussion of *Un condamné à mort s'est échappé*, if by suspense one intends the clever choice and placement of good and bad omens. Yes, if by suspense is understood that nothing can distract the spectator from the thought of escape.[18] The title and voice-over testify to the survival, indeed to the vigour of the narrator/hero. The image is in the past in relationship to the present of the voice; from the first intervention it is clear that the danger is long gone.[19] Yet the image remains in the present of the screen and of the viewing.[20] While we know that the man escapes in the end, the mode and, above all, the fact of the escape root our attention. The wind blows, but we do not know from where it comes nor where it goes. The enigma of the subtitle, the suspense of that other mystery, remains. In Bresson's hands, the mystery, the conventional mode of the hidden, becomes the privileged mode of the revealed. "All things conceal a mystery."[21]

"A curious path" (*Pickpocket*)

If *Un condamné à mort s'est échappé* and *Pickpocket* retain traces of their intersection with the conventional thriller, each of Bresson's narratives, whatever its generic affinity, charts a "curious path" of its own. The first entry of *Journal d'un curé de campagne* draws the distinction between the typology of *Un condamné à mort s'est échappé* and *Pickpocket*, and Bresson's other works. "I do not think that there can be any harm in noting down, day by day, with complete frankness, the very humble, the insignificant secrets of a life which is in any case without mystery." Secrets are opposed to mystery (understood in profane or narrative terms); that mystery is distinct from the sacred mystery frozen in the film's final image and present, with greater or lesser ambiguity, in all but Bresson's latest narratives, irrespective of genre. *Un condamné à mort s'est échappé* and *Pickpocket* are further distinguished by the happy and generically familiar endings to which their curious paths lead: the political prisoner manages the daring escape; the young man gone wrong is rehabilitated.

In narrative terms, there are no other happy endings in Bresson. But in Christian terms, the curious paths of Agnès, of Anne-Marie, of the country priest, of Joan, Balthazar, Mouchette, of the gentle creature (it can be argued), all of which end in death, all end happily. For each the "drôle de chemin" is the unfathomable way of grace; it culminates in redemption. The dénouement cannot be tragic for the saved.

The climax of *Au hasard Balthazar* (1965) serves as an example. Part way through a cruel trek across a mountain border, weighed down by the crushing burden of a load of smuggled goods, Balthazar's young tormentors are frightened off by the shots of frontier guards. The donkey has been hit; he is finally abandoned to himself. As morning breaks over a radiant plateau, circled by a flock of sheep, Balthazar dies in glory. So ends his "curious path," the winding narrative of the film, Balthazar's passage from the schoolteacher and the children, to other farmers, from Marie, to the baker, to Arnold, to the circus, to Arnold again, to the corn merchant, and finally, full circle, to the schoolteacher. These stages of Balthazar's life are random only in appearance. "Au hasard" translates the biblical metaphor of the wind that blows where it will into the command given a beast of burden: that it follow the route of chance wherever it leads, for that chance is actually—and mysteriously—the direction foreordained.[22]

Beginning with *Lancelot du Lac*, the direction of the Bressonian path shifts radically; so does its end. No longer is the narrative an uninterrupted progression towards salvation. *Lancelot du Lac* recounts a return; the long night of doubt and guilt begins in the forest of still-armoured, hanging skeletons. The hero finds his way back (with the help of the old woman who prophesies his death) at the point at which he has forsaken certitude. Lancelot, then Charles and Yvon, the protagonists of *Le Diable probablement* (1977) and *L'Argent*, are subject to historical and social forces of whose cruelty they are aware. These forces assume responsibility for the "curious path." *Lancelot du Lac* is the transitional film. The divine hand no longer guides chance. In Bresson's two most recent films, it is governed by the devil—probably.

"Deus absconditus" (*Les Pensées*)

Arthur is the first to realize that God has withdrawn from the kingdom of the Round Table. He retires into reflection and prayer, awaiting (in vain, it turns out) a sign from above that will show him the way. Lancelot too comes to understand that for his lifetime the holy adventure is over. He turns to the quest for his own salvation. But grace is gratuitous, of course, and while those who do not seek (at least not through their own practice of the sacraments) may be saved (Agnès, Michel, Balthazar, Mouchette, and the gentle creature, for example), those who do, like Lancelot, may lack the effective grace to find. Bresson translates the breach between seeking and finding by disrupting the narrative logic that supposes a visual effect to follow a verbal cause. At the beginning of the second night of *Quatre nuits d'un rêveur*, Marthe and Jacques are seated on a bench by the banks of the Seine. Marthe asks Jacques to tell her his story. He insists that he has no story to tell. The very next frame bears the intertitle: "Histoire de Jacques." There is no necessary consequence between what is said and what is done; word and fact, dialogue and image may or may not be consonant. We hear Arthur say: "Gawain killed by Lancelot. God will not allow it." Yet, seconds before, Lancelot, unknowing, had indeed slain Gawain. What is affirmed to be God's will (or thought to be in conformity with it), is subject to contradiction by that will made manifest in the image.

Towards the end of *Au hasard Balthazar*, shortly after the death of her daughter, Marie's mother is seated alone in front of the house. She prays aloud that God spare her husband. There is a tap on the window pane; she enters her husband's room. Without the smallest expression of shock, she acknowledges his death in the ritual gesture of crossing his hands over his chest. Her plea for intercession has gone unanswered; through the disjuncture between her words and their effect, she bears resigned witness to the hidden God. But only in *Les Dames du Bois de Boulogne* (1945), through the name of the square on which Agnès and her mother are lodged by Hélène, Square Port-Royal,[23] is reference made, however indirectly, to the God of Jansenism and of Pascal, the "Deus absconditus" who so tempers signs of Himself as to provide both sufficient light and sufficient obscurity: invisible to those He wills to blindness, He is visible to the chosen He wills to enlightenment.

With the exception of *Procès de Jeanne d'Arc*, and of rare moments in other films (the death of Anne-Marie in *Les Anges du péché* is one example, the conversion of the countess in *Journal d'un curé de campagne* is another), God is hidden, which is to say silent, in the world inhabited by Bresson's characters. His presence is sometimes audible to the spectator, however, through the intervention of music: Mozart's Mass in C Minor (*Un condamné à mort s'est échappé*),[24] Lully (*Pickpocket*), Schubert's Sonata no. 20 (*Au hasard Balthazar*), Monteverdi's *Magnificat* (*Mouchette*, 1966), and Bach's "Chromatic Fantasy" (*L'Argent*). That this music is non-diegetic (and that much more startling for the almost entirely diegetic nature of Bresson's soundtracks) guarantees that God, while revealed to the spectator, remains hidden from the characters. That there is no music in *Procès de Jeanne d'Arc* confirms the weight of its presence elsewhere. In *Procès de Jeanne d'Arc*, as Robert Droguet notes, "no music is necessary, nor worthy of Joan's words . . . the only words worthy of being heard, sacred."[25] Joan's universe is God's. To the faithful—witnesses to the action in the theatre as in the courtroom—God is revealed through her voice (as Joan's voices had revealed God to her). There is no breach between word and act, dialogue and image, cause and effect. To others, God will remain hidden. In either case, music is superfluous.

God in Bresson is thus both hidden and revealed, hidden to all but very few of Bresson's characters through silence, and revealed to Bresson's audience sometimes through film sound. The revelation of God through film image was suggested to François Mauriac by *Journal d'un curé de campagne*.[26] Unlike sound in Bresson (whose meaning emerges through its superimposition on the image at chosen moments),[27] the image carries in itself the potential of revelation. The analogy of the screen as veil—and the particular reference to Veronica—authorizes and advances Mauriac's speculation.

> This is the mystery: thanks to given devices, thanks to a method, the soul emerges truly, it appears, we see it, we can almost touch it, it shines all over the face of this crucified child. Each of you, if you wish, can observe this: the miracle is permanent . . . What if this God had left a living, almost blinding imprint of his presence on this world: the human face? What if the screen stretched out before the crowd were that cloth that had wiped the sweat and blood of his humanity just once and offers itself in vain to our unseeing eyes, to our closed hearts?[28]

The metaphor of the veil is invoked again, three years later, by André Bazin for his discussion of the descent in Marcel Ichac's *Annapurna*: " . . . this time cinema is there, Veronica's veil over the face of human suffering."[29] Three hundred years before Mauriac and Bazin, the analogy of the veil had served Pascal to translate one of the central tenets of his thought: the invisible made visible, the spiritual represented through the material. "All things are veils that conceal God."[30] The screen, suggests Mauriac, is that veil made manifest at last.

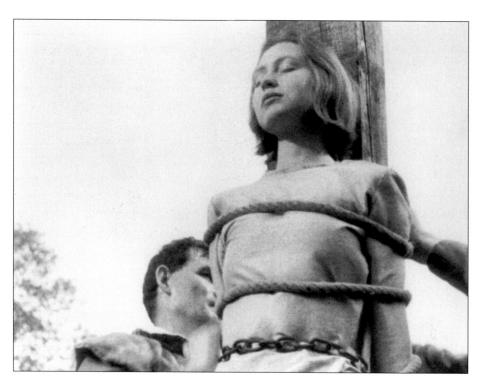

Procès de Jeanne d'Arc

Acting

"On automatism" (*Notes sur le cinématographe*)

The practice of acting for film is a principal preoccupation of Bresson's *Notes sur le cinématographe*. References to this problem appear throughout the text, though they are especially concentrated under the heading "ON AUTOMATISM."[31]

Two terms recur in those notes that combine to describe both an ideal and a method of screen acting: "model" and "automatism." The argument can be summarized as follows:

1. *Acting for film (and the direction of film actors) are activities distinct from acting and directing for the theatre. They demand a distinct vocabulary.*

   No actors.
   (No directing of actors.) No parts.
   (No learning of parts.)
   No staging.
   But the use of working models, taken from life.
   BEING (models) instead of SEEMING (actors).[32]

   Among the comments of Bresson's few professional actors, the most revealing are Maria Casarès's ironic asides on her experience in *Les Dames du Bois de Boulogne*.[33] (In this film Bresson used professionals in all the principal roles for the last time; he reduced their number in *Journal d'un curé de campagne*, and then eliminated them from his casts.) Often reported are the testimonials of Bresson's non-professional actors: the trials of Claude Laydu in preparing to play the country priest, for example, and the three-month period of training in impassivity undergone by Dominique Sanda, then a seventeen-year-old model, before the shooting of *Une femme douce*. The ideal Bressonian actors are Balthazar, devoid of facial expression (save for blinking), and Lancelot in armour, totally masked, though recognizable still by his prowess—and his horse.

2. *The distinction between acting for film and acting for theatre is in fact an opposition at the most fundamental level: that of externalization/internalization.*
   "HUMAN MODELS: Movement from the exterior to the interior. (Actors: movement from the interior to the exterior.)"[34]
   Bresson does not make upon his models the conventional demands of dramatic expression: that they cry, for example. He asks them instead—from

Agnès's mother in *Les Dames du Bois de Boulogne* to the good woman of *L'Argent*—to wipe away nonexistent tears, to find not the gesture through the feeling, but the feeling through the simplest and most stylized of gestures. "Talking of automatism, this also from Montaigne: *We cannot command our haire to stand on end; nor our skinne to startle for desire or feare. Our hands are often carried where we direct them not.*"[35] Because the physical, the discernible, reaction to intense feeling is independent of will, extreme manifestations, such as weeping, occur independently of the subject's attention. The priest of Ambricourt does not even make the automatic gesture of brushing away a tear. He recounts it. Stylization is carried one step further, removing emotion from the screen and placing it in the word: "I hadn't realized I was crying. I hadn't noticed."[36] For Fontaine, in *Un condamné à mort s'est échappé*, the distance between the consciousness of feeling and the consciousness of its expression is even greater. He can only note with uncertainty what—hidden from view—cannot be confirmed: "I think I lost courage for an instant and cried."

3. *Words must lead to thought, not thought to words. They must therefore be repeated mechanically until they can be emitted automatically. The model must not seem to have understood the lines.*

"Models who have become automatic (everything weighed, measured, timed, repeated ten, twenty times) and are then dropped in the middle of the events of your film—their relations with the objects and persons around them will be *right*, because they will not be *thought*."[37]

The vocabulary, syntax, accent of Bresson's characters vary little, in spite of wide difference of class, place, and time. The speech of one character (Mouchette, for example, the child of an alcoholic rural family) resembles that of another (Marthe, a daughter of the Parisian bourgeoisie, or Guenevere, the legendary queen) because the model for each is Bresson himself: " . . . I make every effort to give my characters a family resemblance . . . I ask my actors (all my actors) to speak in a given way, to act in a given way, basically always the same."[38]

4. *Automatism, born of constraint, breeds emotion. The model stripped of falsehood has the power to move the audience to thought and to feeling.*

"It is from being constrained to a mechanical regularity, it is from a mechanism that emotion will be born. To understand this, think of certain great pianists."[39]

In an interview with Jacques Doniol-Valcroze and Jean-Luc Godard, Bresson describes the adventure of *Pickpocket* as the adventure of Michel's hands which drag their proprietor into the adventure in theft. In time, they drag him further, beyond theft to the inner adventure, the adventure of the soul. In Michel's case, crime leads to the "reign of morality."[40] Fontaine also had able hands. Both characters are shown exercising their craft with patience and rigour (one picks pockets, the other picks at the cell door) until dexterity becomes automatism, and automatism gives way to grace for Fontaine through freedom and for Michel through imprisonment. The pickpocket perfecting his technique, the prisoner preparing his escape, the pianist submitting to the obligations of the music, and finally the filmmaker practising his art, have the discipline of hands in common: "Let people feel the soul and the heart in your film, but let it be made like a work of hands," writes Bresson.[41] The exercise of a highly developed craft needs no comment. The automatism of the spectacle will move the viewer to thought and feeling.

5. *The director's role is therefore to oblige his actors to return to themselves.*

"It would not be ridiculous to say to your models: 'I am inventing you as you are.'"[42]

This last contention, rejected by a number of Bresson's non-professional actors,[43] is developed by Pierre Klossowski—novelist, essayist, editor of Nietzsche—recruited to play the corn merchant in *Au hasard Balthazar*: "It was not a matter of treating us like unthinking objects, arbitrarily moved about, but of finding the natural in each of us, of ridding us of false intonations, corrupted gestures, of all the dregs accumulated through habit, through custom. It is a very difficult and very instructive process of paring away that he helped us undergo, we, his interpreters, by his masterful hand."[44]

"Nous sommes automate autant qu'esprit" (*Les Pensées*)

"Automate," which Bresson appears to borrow from Pascal, had been borrowed by Pascal from Descartes (together with its corollary, "machine") to serve his discussion of the practices of faith. Two celebrated passages contain the germ of the argument. The first is a reflection on the design of letters to be written to a friend, a non-believer, exhorting him to seek God. "A letter of exhortation to a friend to induce him to seek. And he will reply, 'What is the use of seeking? Nothing is seen.' Then to reply to him, 'Do not despair.' And he will answer that he would be glad to find some light, but that, according to this very religion, if he believed in it, it will be of no use to him, and that therefore he prefers not to seek. And to answer to that: The machine."[45] The other is part of the discourse on the uses to which the deceptive power of custom can be put by the Christian apologist. "For we must not misunderstand ourselves; we are as much automatic as intellectual; and hence it comes that the instrument by which conviction is attained is not demonstrated alone. How few things are demonstrated? Proofs only convince the mind. Custom is the source of our strongest and most believed proofs. It bends the automaton, which persuades the mind without its thinking about the matter."[46]

The argument can be summarized as follows: Whatever does not originate with the mind, with reason, obeys a mechanism whose origin is in the body. This mechanism prevents reason from penetrating the truth—in this case the truth of faith. In order to eliminate obstacles to belief, the body (the "machine") must be bent to a new form. This can be accomplished through systematic submission to the disciplines prescribed by the Church. Once the "machine" is bent, once the practices of faith have become habit, the "automate," persuaded of the truth of religion through the power of custom, will incline to itself the mind, persuaded through demonstration. Thus the heart of the non-believer will have been prepared by the body and the mind to accept grace.

"Models . . . capable of being divinely 'themselves.'" (*Notes sur le cinématographe*)

For the film director, then, no less than for the director of conscience, thought and will are feeble instruments with which to effect the conversion of the individual—from nonbeliever to Christian, from actor to model. "Nine-tenths of our movements obey habit and automatism. It is anti-nature to subordinate them to will and to thought."[47] The actor's body must be bent through the repeated discipline of word and gesture prescribed by the "cinématographe"; through automatism a new nature, that of the model, will replace the old, that of the actor. "Your models, pitched into the action of your film, will get used to the gestures they have repeated twenty times. The words they have learned with their lips will find, *without their minds' taking part in this*, the inflections and the lilt proper to their true natures. A way of recovering the automatism of real life."[48] The prescription of religion in *Les Pensées* is almost identical. "The external must be joined to the internal to obtain anything from God, that is to say, we must kneel, pray with the lips, etc. . . ."[49] At the moment of conversion, the diction of faith—divine, miracle—becomes appropriate to the practice of acting. "Models. Capable of eluding their own vigilance, capable of being divinely 'themselves.'"[50] "If, on the screen, the mechanism disappears and the phrases you have made them say, the gestures you have made them make, have become one with your models, with your film, with you—then a miracle."[51] This is the regimen that Arthur attempts to impose on his knights ("Pray Gawain. You must pray.") so that they will be prepared to receive God's word, should the privilege of this grace be theirs; it is the ritual gesture to which the countess returns (once the country priest has obliged her to repeat after him the liturgical formulas of acceptance of God's will), and which—miracle—from its first exercise signals salvation.

"Speak the speech . . . as I pronounced it to you." (*Hamlet*)

Soon after their marriage, the pawnbroker in *Une femme douce* (1968) is given two tickets to a performance of *Hamlet*. The play-within-a-film sequence begins during the preparation of the play-within-the-play (Act III, scene ii) and continues as *Hamlet* ends, that is during the duel scene (Act V, scene ii). The camera is fixed on the stage during two long takes, although from time to time there are shots of She seated in the first row of one of the balconies, and He behind her. Once home, She rushes to the bookshelf and opens a copy of the play to the passage that, as she had suspected, had been deleted from the version performed—Hamlet's advice to the players. Evidently, she concludes, alluding to the acting, "Speak the speech . . ." was excised so that the actors might shout to their hearts' content, "saw the air . . . with [their] hand," and "o'erstep . . . the modesty of nature," free of the inhibition of Hamlet's admonishment. Her reading of "Speak the speech . . ." becomes the occasion for a comment on acting in which the film's heroine, through the intermediary of Shakespeare, voices not only a Bressonian preoccupation but a Bressonian methodology.[52] Hamlet urges the players to speak the lines as he had pronounced them, to imitate his diction; Bresson has his actors repeat after him, again and again, until they have mastered his intonation, his rhythm, even the quality of his voice. In the version adopted for *Une femme douce*, "trippingly on the tongue" is translated by "au bout des lèvres," the very idiom that serves Bresson to describe an ideal diction (and that Pascal had used to define the mechanics of prayer). That the theatre sequence is the only major addition to the Dostoevsky novella which serves as the source of *Une femme douce* confirms its importance to the larger discourse on art that marks the film.

Editing

"No art without transformation" (*Notes sur le cinématographe*)

Numerous entries of *Notes sur le cinématographe* are devoted to reflections on this precept: "No art without transformation."[53] (While alternative solutions may mimic the natural, they fail to imitate nature, asserts Bresson after Chateaubriand.) Transformation depends in turn on fragmentation, placement, and absence, three principal functions of editing, although Bresson avoids this term, as he does the entire lexicon of filmmaking when he can.

"On fragmentation" (*Notes sur le cinématographe*)

The passage that follows, drawn from Pascal's considerations on the diversity of human beings, serves as footnote to "ON FRAGMENTATION,"[54] one of a handful of thematic headings that organize *Notes sur le cinématographe*: "A town or countryside at a distance is a town or a countryside; but as one approaches it those are houses, trees, tiles, leaves, grasses, ants, ants' legs, to infinity."[55] A variation on the celebrated demonstration of the terrors attendant upon the human condition (caught in its disproportion between the infinitely and incomprehensibly big and the infinitely and equally incomprehensibly small), the metaphor of the approaching city reminds the apologist of the variety of his interlocutor. That the analogy is optical serves Bresson particularly well. From afar all cities look alike; distance betrays them. The true nature of each will become apparent in its parts, and in the arrangement of the parts of its parts. Like any two cities, or any two persons (in another *pensée*, Pascal compares two grapes, and then two seeds), no two phenomena are identical. The rhetoric of persuasion needs to be adjusted to that truth. So does the rhetoric of film. Bresson's heading, "On fragmentation," is followed by an entry that echoes another of Pascal's thoughts on style:[56] "This [fragmentation] is indispensable if one does not want to fall into REPRESENTATION. To see beings and things in their separate parts. Render them independent in order to give them a new dependence."[57]

"C'est une même balle" (*Les Pensées*)

Bresson's considerations on transformation through placement have their source in another of the principles crucial to Pascal's rhetoric—subsumed in the metaphor of the "jeu de paume." Bresson returns to the question of placement both in *Notes sur le cinématographe* and in the film that is most explicitly his *ars poetica*, *Une femme douce*. (*Une femme douce*, it has been variously noted, includes a film-within-a-film sequence, a play-within-the-film sequence followed by a comment on the performance, three occasions in which the camera lingers quite deliberately over television images, visits to three different museums, a visit to the zoo, two reflections on natural history, images cluttered with books that are shown to be consulted or read and records of jazz and classical music whose playing constitutes the soundtrack, a heroine who wants to read, hear, and know everything, and a hero who prides himself on quoting Goethe.) On repeated occasions, Bresson makes an explicit comparison of the cinematic image (or shot) to words and colours. (In *Une femme douce*, the comparison is implicit yet insistent; the shot is to the sequence as the bone is to its larger structure.) The analogy of the "jeu de paume" has particular resonance in the comparison of the shot and the word. "Cinematographic film, where the images, like the words in a dictionary, have no power and value except through their position and relation."[58] The familiar *pensée* reads: "Let no one say that I have said nothing new; the arrangement of the subject is new. When we play tennis, we both play with the same ball, but one of us places it better. I had as soon it said that I used words employed before. And in the same way if the same thoughts in a different arrangement do not form a different discourse, no more do the same words in their different arrangement form different thoughts!"[59]

Towards the beginning of *Une femme douce*, there is an extended discussion between She and He of the similarities in skeleton between man and other animals. She is on the floor of the sitting room surrounded by books and records, eating sweets. She tells He of a recent visit to the natural history museum; opened before her is a book of photographs of skeletons. "It's the same raw material for all . . . the same bones, arranged differently, for a mouse, for an elephant, for a man," She observes. Towards the end of the film, He and She make a visit together to this same museum. They walk through rooms filled with skeletons of animals large and small, much like those that had served to illustrate the book on which She had commented earlier. "You were right. It's the same raw material for all," says He, taking up her point—and Pascal's almost to the word. For Bresson as for Pascal, in art as in nature, it is not so much a question of the matter at hand ("c'est la même matière"—He repeats after She) but of its editing ("la disposition des matières est nouvelle"—writes Pascal), not so much a question of which words one uses, which ball, which colours, which bones or which shots, or whether they have been used before, but of their placement. In nature, as in art, editing is the vital activity, for in the disposition of necessarily finite materials lie the infinite possibilities of invention. In cinema, of course, this activity (to which Bresson refers only rarely by its conventional name—montage) is, as Bresson insists in the variety of his analogies, especially privileged. To it is reserved a discrete phase of the process, the final moment that guarantees the work's integrity and distinction.

"Beautés d'omission" (*Les Pensées*)

There are several discussions of painting in Bresson's work (the director, it is often recalled, began as a painter), the most extended among these being the monologue of Jacques's classmate from the École des Beaux-Arts in *Quatre nuits d'un rêveur*. Despite the excessively intense—ultimately comical—tone of the student's pronouncements, Jacques's visitor makes two points similar to those repeated with clear seriousness by Bresson in other contexts: (1) What matters is not the subject painted nor the painter, but the disappearance of both in the encounter of the two (an observation very like that made during an exchange on "action painting," equally ambiguous in tone, conducted by two tourists riding donkeys in *Au hasard Balthazar*); (2) What matters is not what is shown but what is not shown. The smaller the spots on the canvas, the greater the world defined by the painting; one sees not what is but what is not. The student first rejects representation— Chardin's "brioche," Manet's peony, Van Gogh's chair—then embraces the ellipsis created by its disappearance. On the value of omission, Pascal's "Beautés d'omission,"[60] Bresson has remarked again recently: "Poetry slips in between the cuts."[61]

Shortly after He and She are married (*Une femme douce*), they attend a showing of Michel Deville's period film, *Benjamin* (1967). Unlike the treatment of the *Hamlet* sequence that follows a little later in the film, Bresson chooses here to hold the camera on the audience rather than on the entertainment, intercutting only two relatively short fragments from the sumptuous images of the film. Like the filming of the *Hamlet* sequence, Bresson's audience enters the theatre in the middle of the show. Despite lateness and the hidden screen, the viewer of *Une femme douce* understands at once the plot of the film-within-the-film, indeed becomes immediately immersed in the world of *Benjamin*. A few lines of dialogue accompanied by some lush strains of music suffice. It is instantly clear that either track, visual or sound, will show and tell all at every point. The evidence of that doubling (which, unlike Bresson's, is in fact redundancy), forces the question of editing or transformation—which Bresson posits as the question of art. It forces too the acknowledgment of the conflict between the first and the second screen. Bresson runs a considerable risk in his demonstration. Will the audience of the deliberately distancing *Une femme douce*, once it has grasped Bresson's point, not wish it could continue to see (even to hear) the welcoming, enveloping *Benjamin*? The easy loves of its charming young hero are not necessarily abandoned without regret for the continued sparring between the pawnbroker and the gentle creature. And the facility of Deville, and of his reading, may prove irresistible to an audience struggling to overcome the Bressonian ellipsis.

Spectators

"Sight and hearing" (*Notes sur le cinématographe*)

Deville's film illustrates one of Bresson's insistent claims: that the failure to acknowledge the irreconcilable conflict between theatre and film has produced "cinéma" (photographed theatre), rather than "cinématographe" (whose properties Bresson describes most often only in opposition to "cinéma"). The antithesis of "cinéma" and "cinématographe" determines many of Bresson's formulations on his craft: the director must cast models, not actors; the director's purpose is to create not represent; the director must reject mise en scène (together with "metteur en scène" to which Bresson prefers the designation "metteur en ordre"). Bresson extends the contrast of "cinéma" and "cinématographe": "CINÉMA films controlled by intelligence, going no further."[62] The reader is left to presume that in Bresson's own case the controlling authority is a faculty that surpasses reason without excluding or opposing its processes. The nature of that faculty can be defined through other contexts.

In a discussion of the climactic sequence of *Un condamné à mort s'est échappé*, René Briot proposes that while the spectator's intelligence is concentrated on the film's final images through sight, the soundtrack appeals directly to his or her sensitivity through hearing.[63] Briot's analysis is sustained by several reflections published by Bresson some years later in *Notes sur le cinématographe* under the heading "SIGHT AND HEARING,"[64] among these: "The ear goes more towards the within, the eye towards the outer,"[65] and "If the eye is entirely won, give nothing or almost nothing to the ear. One cannot be at the same time all eye and all ear."[66]

"Esprit de géométrie/Esprit de finesse" (*Les Pensées*)

These contrasting pairs—outside and inside, eye and ear, reason and sensitivity—recall the crucial Pascalian categories: "esprit de géométrie"/"esprit de finesse." Two paths to understanding allow the filmmaker a double entry into spectator response; the two divergent orders of comprehension which distinguish his interlocutor demand of the apologist a double strategy of persuasion. Reason is subject to persuasion through the understanding of origins and the rigorous methodologies of mathematical deduction, sensitivity through the grasp of consequences and the complex mechanisms of taste and intuition. Since the filmmaker's audience is hidden from him, Bresson will choose not one or the other route; rather, he will alternate between the two: "Image and sound must not support each other, but must work each in turn through *a sort of relay*."[67] But while the mind can be inclined to accept the truth (of religion or of images) through the proof of demonstration, the conquest of the spectator's inner being, the "dedans," cannot be achieved by a linear appeal to the eye alone. It requires the more immediate and synchronous appeal to the ear. In the end, the mission of persuasion can only be entrusted to the soundtrack, and particularly to music,[68] which, surpassing image and logic, speaks directly to the spectator's heart. Through the ear, through intuition, the spectator (like the incipient convert graced by the "esprit de finesse") is finally convinced. "It is the heart which experiences God, and not the reason. This, then, is faith: God felt by the heart, not by the reason," writes Pascal.[69] "Films de CINÉMA," controlled by intelligence alone, project the spectator towards the surface, outside the self. Reason is satisfied and the truth of what is proposed may even be granted. "Films de CINÉMATOGRAPHE," Bresson's films, are controlled by two faculties, one of which, more powerful than reason, projects the spectator within. There, what is proposed is understood at once and immediately accepted by the heart as true.

Rhetorical Affinities

The bonds of faith and dogma that unite Bresson to Pascal across the span of intervening centuries, already well documented, are no stronger than the unifying kinship of literary and dramatic sensibility, translated by the rhetorical affinities that define this essay. The points that follow summarize the argument.

In the crucial statements on craft that we owe to Pascal and Bresson, the rhetorical matrices are, if not identical, clearly related: the *pensée*, the *note*. Borrowing as a rhetorical method is at the basis of both; so are the stylistic strategies of persuasion—admonition, sententiousness, contradiction. Among the narrative modes available to him, the thriller is for Bresson the most likely receptacle for the transcendental; mystery, as genre, accommodates the spiritual mystery. The incongruous, very nearly the unfathomable, becomes the course of the narrative, and the revelation that in the end pierces the cinematic artifact may be as close as any art can come to a tracing of the hidden God. Automatism is at the source both of the practice of faith (as Pascal prescribes) and of the practice of acting (as Bresson dictates); the rhetoric of the director echos that of the confessor. And the power of the message borne by the varieties of diction is based not so much on its originality as on its transformation: through fragmentation, placement, ellipsis that is, through editing. Finally, the collective spectator, unseen and unheard, seeing and hearing, demands from the filmmaker not a choice between the appeal to reason and to the heart, but concessions to both. Not through "cinéma" but through "cinématographe," the uncorrupted medium, will Bresson's spectator, like the subject of Pascal's artful persuasion, be moved to the suspension of disbelief.

Notes

1. From *Un condamné à mort s'est échappé*. All dialogue from Bresson's films has been transcribed from the soundtracks. Unless otherwise indicated, all translations are mine.

2. See in particular the work of Amédée Ayfre, a summary of which is provided in the section on Bresson in René-Claude Baud, "Panorama critique," *Le Cinéma et sa vérité* (Paris: Éditions du Cerf, 1969), pp. 208-13. See also two works of Henri Agel: "L'Ascèse liturgique," in *Le Cinéma et le sacré* (Paris: Éditions du Cerf, 1954), pp. 29-42; and *Robert Bresson* (Brussels: Club du Livre de Cinéma, 1957). For an exhaustive review of the literature, see the indispensable annotated bibliography in Jane Sloan, *Robert Bresson: A Guide to References and Sources* (Boston: G. K. Hall, 1983).

3. In 1947, Bresson had asked Julien Green to prepare a scenario for *Ignace de Loyola*, which was to be a production of the Italian studio, Universalia. Green relates his

impressions of Bresson in diary entries of the period: "He seems inimical to picturesque effects, wants neither crucifix nor miracles . . . In the scene in which the Virgin appears to Saint Ignatius, he doesn't want the Virgin to be seen. (Oh, Hollywood, wouldst that you could hear these wise words of a great director!)" Quoted in "En Travaillant avec Robert Bresson," *Cahiers du cinéma*, no. 50 (August/September 1955), pp. 19-21.

4. Among the most current is Michael Dempsey's analysis of "the waning of transcendence and the rise of despair" between the black-and-white and the colour films. See "Despair Abounding: The Recent Films of Robert Bresson," *Film Quarterly* 34, no.1 (Fall 1980), p. 3.

5. See André Bazin, "*Le Journal d'un curé de campagne* and the Stylistics of Robert Bresson," in *What Is Cinema?*, trans. Hugh Gray (Berkeley: University of California Press, 1967), pp. 125-43; Susan Sontag, "Spiritual Style in the Films of Robert Bresson," in *Against Interpretation* (New York: Farrar, Straus & Giroux, 1966), pp. 177-95; and Paul Schrader, "Bresson," in *Transcendental Style in Film: Ozu, Bresson, Dreyer* (Berkeley: University of California Press, 1972), pp. 57-108.

6. Published by Gallimard, Paris. The English translation by Jonathan Griffin is *Notes on Cinematography* (New York: Urizen Books, 1975). All references are drawn from this edition.

7. Other authors share this function and form, of course, among them Paul Valéry, to whom Bresson has sometimes been compared. For Valéry, too, Pascal served as model (and as antagonist).

8. *Notes*, p. 2.

9. *Notes*, p. 37.

10. *Notes*, p. 31.

11. *Notes*, p. 20.

12. Blaise Pascal, *Pascal's Pensées*, trans. W. F. Trotter (New York: E. P. Dutton & Co., 1958), p. 69. All references are drawn from this edition.

13. *Notes*, p. 67. In the course of *Notes sur le cinématographe*, Bresson cites Montaigne three times, Pascal and Racine twice; he cites also Chateaubriand, Vivaldi, Napoléon, Auguste Renoir, Mozart, Corot, Purcell, Baudelaire, Leonardo, Proust, Bach, Debussy, Mme de Sévigné, Cézanne, and Montesquieu.

14. *Pensées*, p. 215.

15. *Les Anges du péché* is suffused with the conventions of two genres—the film noir and the hagiographic film. Two "mysteries" are merged as they are in the very particular mission of the congregation of Béthanie: the rehabilitation through convent life of women released from prison.

16. See John III: 4-8.

17. Michel's revelation will find an echo in the last tape recorder entry of *Quatre nuits d'un rêveur*: "Oh Marthe, what power makes your eyes shine with such fire, lights your face with such a smile? Thank you for your love . . . And be blessed for the

happiness you bring me." In *Quatre nuits d'un rêveur* as in *Pickpocket* all is grace in the end, but through the redemption of autobiography as ostensible fiction, not autobiography as ostensible fact.

18. Eric Rohmer, "Le Miracle des objets," *Cahiers du cinéma*, no. 65 (December 1956), p. 43. See also Susan Sontag, *Against Interpretation*, p. 183.

19. See David Bordwell and Kristin Thompson, *Film Art: An Introduction* (Reading, Massachusetts: Addison-Wesley, 1979), pp. 207-16, for a discussion of sound in *Un condamné à mort s'est échappé*.

20. Bresson notes (as have others) in his introduction to the published scenario, *Procès de Jeanne d'Arc: film* (Paris: Julliard, 1962), p. 7: "It is the cinematographer's privilege to put the past in the present once again."

21 Roland Monod in "En travaillant avec Robert Bresson," *Cahiers du cinéma*, no. 64 (November 1956), p. 20, states: "As Bresson himself has said: 'I would like to show this *miracle*: over the prison, an invisible hand directing the events and making one and the same thing succeed for one person and fail for another . . . The film is a mystery.'"

22. According to Bresson (quoted in Michel Estève, *Robert Bresson* [Paris: Éditions Albatros, 1983], p. 52.), "Au hasard, Balthazar" was the insignia of the counts of Baux who claimed descendance from Balthazar, one of the three magi.

23. One of the projected titles of *Les Dames du Bois de Boulogne* had been *Les Dames de Port-Royal*, its ambiguity surpassing that of the title finally chosen. The Bois de Boulogne is the haunt of twentieth-century prostitutes; Port-Royal the retreat of the Jansenist order in whose midst were to be found the most pious of seventeenth-century women. Reference to Square Port-Royal is absent from the literary souce of the film, the Mme de la Pommeraye episode of Diderot's *Jacques le fataliste*.

24. For a discussion of the relationship of Mozart's unfinished Mass in C Minor, K. 427, and synecdoche in *Un condamné à mort s'est échappé*, see Peter Schofer, "Dissolution into Darkness," *Sub-Stance*, no. 9 (1974), p. 62.

25. *Robert Bresson* (Lyon: SERDOG, 1966), p. 35.

26. See Michel Estève, *Cinéma et condition humaine* (Paris: Éditions Albatros, 1978), pp. 211-17, for a discussion of divine absence and presence in Bresson's adaptation of Bernanos's novel, *Journal d'un curé de campagne*. See also Dudley Andrew, "Desperation and Meditation," in *European Filmmakers and the Art of Adaptation*, ed. Andrew S. Horton and Joan Magretta (New York: Ungar, 1981), pp. 20-37.

27. See Bordwell and Thompson, *Film Art: An Introduction*, p. 211.

28. Quoted by Lo Duca in "Un Acte de foi," *Cahiers du cinéma*, no.1 (April 1951), p. 46, from the *Figaro* review (February 27, 1951).

29. *Qu'est-ce que le cinéma?* (Paris: Éditions du Cerf, 1981), p. 31.

30. *Pensées*, p. 215.

31. *Notes*, pp. 11-17.

32. *Notes*, p. 1.

33. Just two clauses of Maria Casarès's 430-page autobiography, *Résidente privilégiée* (Paris: Fayard, 1980), pp. 231 and 235, are devoted to her work on *Les Dames du Bois de Boulogne*, filmed during the Occupation: " . . . that brought me home one evening from one of the very long days spent submitting to the continuous paring down we suffered at the hand of the implacable Robert Bresson during the shooting of *Les Dames du Bois de Boulogne* . . ." and ". . . during long nights, interrupted only by failures of electricity, during which Bresson, by candlelight, paraded his slim and elegant silhouette in front of me, using the 'break' to find, for me, the precise intonation I was to give to the most spontaneous of lines: 'Oh! Jean! You frightened me . . .'"

34. *Notes*, p. 2.

35. *Notes*, p. 68.

36. See Nick Browne, "Film Form/Voice-Over: Bresson's *The Diary of a Country Priest*," *Yale French Studies*, no. 60 (1980), for a discussion of the relation of voice-over to the narrative strategies of *Journal d'un curé de campagne*.

37. *Notes*, p. 12.

38. Quoted in Michel Estève, *Robert Bresson* (Paris: Éditions Seghers, 1974), p. 111.

39. *Notes*, p. 128. See Monod, "En travaillant avec Robert Bresson," p. 18, for Bresson's extension of the analogy between screen acting and the technique of a great pianist: "A text must be spoken the way Dinu Lipatti plays Bach. His marvelous mechanism links the notes. Intelligence, emotion are born later."

40. "Entretien avec Robert Bresson," *Cahiers du cinéma*, no. 104 (February 1960), pp. 4-5.

41. *Notes*, p. 12.

42. *Notes*, p. 14.

43. See, for example, the remarks of François Leterrier, who plays Fontaine in *Un condamné à mort s'est échappé* ("Propos de Robert Bresson," *Cahiers du cinéma*, no. 75 [October 1957], p. 6) and of the novelist Marie Cardinal, who plays Mouchette's mother ("Mère Sainte Bob," *Arts et Loisirs*, no. 77 [March 15, 1967], pp. 24-26).

44. "Je suis naturellement cabotin," *Arts et Loisirs*, no. 37 (June 8-14, 1966), p. 10.

45. *Pensées*, p. 72.

46. *Pensées*, p. 73.

47. *Notes*, p. 11.

48. *Notes*, p. 32.

49. *Pensées*, p. 73.

50. *Notes*, p. 36.

51. *Notes*, p. 18.

52. Gordon Gow in "A Gentle Creature," *Film and Filming* 17, no. 3 (December 1970), p. 50, and Jane Sloan in *Robert Bresson: A Guide to References and Sources*, p. 27, draw the relationship between the Hamlet scene and Bresson's methods.

They are not concerned, however, with the extension of this discussion to the relationship between Bresson's principles and Pascal's.

53. *Notes*, p. 5.

54. *Notes*, p. 46.

55. *Pensées*, p. 46.

56. "Nature has made all her truths independent of one another. Our art makes one dependent on the other. But this is not natural. Each keeps its own place." *Pensées*, p. 7.

57. *Notes*, p. 46.

58. *Notes*, p. 5.

59. *Pensées*, p. 7.

60. *Pensées*, p. 331.

61. "Entretiens: Robert Bresson," *Cinématographe*, no. 29 (July/August, 1977), p. 29.

62. *Notes*, p. 24.

63. *Robert Bresson* (Paris: Éditions du Cerf, 1957), p. 90.

64. *Notes*, p. 27.

65. *Notes*, p. 28.

66. *Notes*, p. 28.

67. *Notes*, p. 28. In her essay on Bresson in *Against Interpretation*, pp. 177-78, Susan Sontag evokes the Pascalian categories of "esprit de géométrie" and "esprit de finesse." According to Sontag: "Some art aims directly at arousing the feelings; some art appeals to the feelings through the route of intelligence. There is art that involves, that creates empathy. There is art that detaches, that provokes reflection . . . In the film, the master of the reflective mode is Robert Bresson." Sontag approaches the question from the point of view of a work that assumes an audience commonly endowed with a single faculty of understanding, in the case of Bresson's audience, one that would be susceptible to an appeal through intelligence. The interlocutor in film is various, however, thus the double entrée at which Bresson aims—"géométrie" and "finesse," detachment and involvement—through image, on the one hand, and sound on the other.

68. See above, p. 13.

69. *Pensées*, p. 78.

Affaires publiques

Affaires publiques

ADE IN 1934, Bresson's short feature debut was believed lost until 1987, when a print came to light in the Cinémathèque Française. It was shown last year at New York's Museum of Modern Art along with other discoveries and rarities from the Cinémathèque's archives.

Bresson came fairly late to filmmaking. Born in 1907,[1] he studied classics and philosophy and became a painter before turning to the cinema. A British painter friend, Roland Penrose, lent Bresson the money to make *Public Affairs*.

Two members of Bresson's first creative team went on to collaborate on his feature films: Pierre Charbonnier was production designer on seven of them and Jean Wiener wrote the music for three. At first sight, however, *Public Affairs* has little else in common with Bresson's later films. Set in an imaginary country named Crogandie, it is a surreal satirical comedy—"un comique fou," as Bresson described it.

The chancellor of Crogandie (played deadpan by the then famous clown Béby) takes part in three public ceremonies (with Marcel Dalio—well known for his roles in *Grand Illusion*, *Rules of the Game*, and *To Have and Have Not*—playing a different part in each). When a statue of the chancellor is unveiled, its wide yawning mouth sends everyone in the country to sleep. At a fire fighters' demonstration, the building to be set on fire rolls offscreen and the chancellor's coat-tails smolder instead. At the launching of a liner, the champagne bottle refuses to break; when shot out of a gun it blasts through the metal plating and causes the ship to sink. Meanwhile the princess of neighbouring Mirémie, in love with the chancellor, has piloted a plane to Crogandie, pursued on horseback by the king.

While that brief synopsis may evoke the Marx Brothers or *Million Dollar Legs*, *Public Affairs* has a tighter organization, with transitions eliminated almost completely. Within the constraints of a short film, Bresson manages to present a remarkable variety of incident—what might be called a precise clarity of confusion. Here one can see the beginnings of the clipped style that would predominate in his mature work, even in the increasingly complex personal relationships of the later films, from *Balthazar* through *L'Argent*. And here, too, Bresson already shows the detachment, the refusal to cue emotion, that he would maintain in his serious films, most rigorously in *Pickpocket* and *The Trial of Joan of Arc*.

It may be little more than a coincidence that Bresson chose a genre that requires no expressive acting. "Since I considered that only the action was important," he said, "it was simply a matter of having [Béby, Marcel Dalio, et al.] perform it."[2] Coincidence or not, this approach certainly prefigures his later exfoliation of expressiveness from his players—or, as he preferred to call them, *modèles*.

As a zany comedy, *Public Affairs* interrupts its "story" with surprising bursts of action. Before the statue is unveiled, a circle of "high school girls," having demurely sung the Crogandian anthem, swirl into a chorus line and kick their legs out of slit skirts in a jazzy dance routine. (They were in fact from the Folies Bergères.) In a rapid one-two-three-four, the chancellor is presented with a bouquet, it's crushed in his embrace of the presenter, he tosses it aside, and it's swept into a street cleaner's pan. And when the cord is pulled for the unveiling, the cloth whooshes into the statue's open mouth.

Similar though less zany interruptions recur throughout Bresson's work—like the unexpected joy of the priest being taken for a motorbike ride in *Diary of a Country Priest* or the Afro-Brazilian music from the *bateau-mouche* in *Four Nights of a Dreamer*. And the bouquet sequence of *Public Affairs* is transformed into the reverberating effect that people can have on one another for good or evil: the pickpocket team passing the loot from one to another in *Pickpocket*; Mouchette being paid for her café work, immediately giving the money to her father, and being given a drink in return; and the passing of the counterfeit bill from boy to store clerk to Yvon to café owner in *L'Argent*.

Those comparisons may seem superficial, the kind that can too easily be found between films that are fundamentally dissimilar. The point, however, is not that *Public Affairs* contains the seed of Bresson's later moral concerns but that it reveals more than the seed of his later style—a style that proved as viable for high seriousness as it did for *comique fou*.

The strongest connection between *Public Affairs* and Bresson's later work is the complete assurance with which it is made. This is no tentative prentice work. "As I see it," said Bresson, "any errors one may commit in *mise en scène* arise from lack of foresight. Thus, before starting to shoot my film I made sure of knowing *Public Affairs* by heart. I hardly used a studio at all. I was quite content to look for outdoor settings, and I found them easily because all I needed was a wall, a tree and the sky. In other words, it wasn't a question of making an "artistic" film but of having the poetry emerge from a particular continuity of invention."[3]

In *Public Affairs* as in his mature films, Bresson relies on the simplest of technical means. Apart from some doctoring of the sinking liner, there are no visible trick shots, including slow or speeded motion. The use of sound, too, is simple and effective—as in the silence that takes over when everyone falls asleep. The film opens inside the Crogandian radio station with an announcer in the foreground and a soprano singing but unheard behind a soundproof studio window. The film ends as the chancellor's chauffeur lays waste to the studio, finally smashing the window so that the soprano's voice bursts forth.

Bresson's own voice bursts forth in *Public Affairs*—saying something different from what we've come to expect, yet just as compelling. This is a wonderfully enjoyable film in its own right.

Notes

1. Some sources give Bresson's birth year as 1901 or 1909, but most give 1907.
2. From an article by Paul Gilson in *Pour Vous*, quoted in Philippe Arnaud, *Robert Bresson*, Cahiers du Cinéma Collection "Auteurs" (Paris, 1986).
3. Ibid.

Les Anges du péché

TONY PIPOLO

Rules of the Game:
On Bresson's *Les Anges du péché*

If you hear the word that ties you to another human being,
do not listen to any others that follow—they are merely its echo.

— CATHERINE OF SIENA

To set up a film is to bind persons to each other and to objects by looks.

— ROBERT BRESSON

W HAT MIGHT WE INFER from the fact that Bresson's first feature is about the following and breaking of rules? Or, rather, about the conventional following of the rules as opposed to pushing them to the limit, testing their efficacy? None of Bresson's protagonists can be said to face such a situation more literally than the novice Anne-Marie in *Les Anges du péché*. Leaving the secular world to enter one within walls governed by strict codes of behaviour and ordered routines, she soon reveals an impatient tendency to take her vocation more earnestly than those around her, much to their chagrin. As with all such protagonists, her pride must be curbed; but when it is, it becomes clear that her fervour was but the sign of a deeper spirituality.

If Bresson can be said to have had a similarly impassioned novitiate, it would certainly comprise this film—and no doubt *Les Dames du Bois de Boulogne* made the following year—for while both abide by the rules of mainstream narrative cinema, they are unmistakeably fired with the genius of the true artist. One can clearly discern in *Les Anges du péché* not only themes that resonate throughout his work, but the emergence of the strong moral perspective that would come to define that work and that would tirelessly seek to discipline the form in which it is embodied. And, while it may be commonplace to observe that the coherence of a major artist's work is evident from the beginning, the traces of that evidence are often surprising. The catalyst for Bresson's subsequent preoccupation with form—his renunciation of acting, expository dialogue, and mandatory establishing shots; his perfecting of framing, editing, and the relationship of image and sound—is apparent not so much in his handling of the conventions he had inherited but in the film's subject and in the motto that determines his protagonist's *raison d'être*. The word which, once heard, ties one person to another, describes Bresson's vocation no less than it does Anne-Marie's. The pursuit of a purely cinematographic ideal through the chastening of the language of cinema is nothing less than the cornerstone of his aesthetics and his philosophy. He would hold narrative structure accountable to a particular scrutiny, curtailing its excesses, eliminating facile transitions, collapsing temporal relations. If editing increasingly became the most articulatory implement of this ambition, it is because Bresson considered it the paradigm for all relationships in film—as some early remarks made around the time of the production of *Les Dames du Bois de Boulogne*, anticipate:

> A film is entirely a matter of relationships [*en rapports*]. The subtlety . . . must be placed within these relationships. The relationships of actors with actors, of actors with objects and the decor that surrounds them, of action with the rhythm of images.[1]

Eventually, these relationships would be so impeccably conceived and executed that they would come to be called—whenever other filmmakers seemed to be imitating or striving to achieve them—Bressonian.

The Text

We must, of course, first deal with the obvious. The credits on the screen attribute the scenario for *Les Anges du péché* to "R.L. Bruckberger, 'dominicain,' Robert Bresson, Jean Giraudoux," in that order, and the "text" to Giraudoux. This has not prevented some scholars from crediting Bresson alone for the scenario, "from an idea" of Bruckberger's and attributing only the dialogue to Giraudoux. Jean Sémolué, for example, says that while in 1943, "the depth and extent of the subject was attributed to Father Bruckberger . . . in reality, it was conceived by Bresson with the help of a book which Father Bruckberger recommend he read: *The Dominicans of the Prisons* by Father Lelong," published in 1937.[2] While there is no footnote indicating how Sémolué came to this conclusion, one can read a certain ambiguity into Bruckberger's own account to support it. Bruckberger affirms that he originally thought of making a film about the Bethany community of nuns in 1940 after seeing a film about the Salvation Army (*Les Visiteurs du ciel*); and in 1941, in a fortuitous meeting with Bresson who was under contract to make a film but was looking for a subject, he suggested the Bethany idea. According to Bruckberger, although "Bresson knew nothing about the religious life and was ignorant of Bethany, he was immediately taken with the idea. We together wrote the scenario that remained intact until the completion of the film, and it was based on this scenario that Giraudoux agreed to do the dialogue."[3] Bruckberger insists that Giraudoux did not know anything of the religious life either and also appealed to him throughout the production.

If Bresson were "immediately taken by the idea," it strongly suggests that he was predisposed for personal, not only pragmatic reasons. It is also unclear just how the scenario could remain unchanged until the completion of the film while Giraudoux was writing the dialogue and "introducing the embellishments" that justified his being credited in third place.[4] Because correct attribution for a film's authorship is often such a thorny, irresolvable issue, many scholars simply draw their conclusions with the benefit of hindsight, as is the case here. Sémolué, René Briot, and others argue (and their assumption is reflected in many filmographies, including one provided in a recent publication[5]) that as one came to know Bresson's work in later years, one could go back and identify those thematic and stylistic preoccupations that emerged more plainly in the later work. While this tactic may be the only true test, it tends to ignore the question of sources, inspirations, and working alliances that profoundly affect even as singular a filmmaker as Bresson.

To be sure, the stronger and more integral the work becomes, the stronger the argument for attributing authorship by hindsight. In the case of *Les Anges du péché*, whatever Bresson did or did not know about the religious life of the Dominican nuns without Father Bruckberger's assistance, we do know that it became Bresson's habit to research areas of relevance to his films in order to give them as much authenticity as possible. In the case of *A Man Escaped*, his only film based directly on a contemporary nonfiction source, his own prison experience no doubt helped to reinforce the details of André Devigny's autobiographical account. For *Pickpocket*, he hired Kassagi, a professional pickpocket, as both actor and advisor on the film.

The proof of this authenticity is on the screen, and for that, neither Father Bruckberger nor Giraudoux can claim credit. Even Sémolué, who admires Giraudoux's dialogue, affirms that since the playwright had already written dialogue for an earlier, unexceptional film (*La Duchesse de Langeais*), the distinguishing personality behind the success of *Les Anges du péché* is really Bresson since it was he who created the "very particular atmosphere," to which Giraudoux "generously subordinated" his contribution. It is worth noting that despite the affinity the character of Anne-Marie has with Giraudoux's "fragile and inflexible heroines," the unabashed religiosity of the film is atypical of the writer's work, which usually hesitates between two ideas or beliefs rather than embrace a single-minded theme.[6] While that religiosity was no doubt affected by Father Bruckberger's influence, it was controversial enough to have generated disapproval by the Catholic community at the time of its release.[7]

Of course, we should not underestimate the dialogue of Giraudoux in the film, anymore than we should that of Jean Cocteau in *Les Dames du Bois de Boulogne*. Both texts do their work efficiently, even eloquently, though clearly since both are products of pre-eminent figures of the theatre, there is a great deal more—in the way of exposition and characterization—than would suit the later Bresson. Indeed, the structure of *Les Anges du péché* closely follows that of classical drama, complete with a given order of things, a protagonist who challenges it, rising action, conflict, climax, falling action, dénouement, and catharsis. While the story and setting, therefore, are fertile ground for Bresson's thematic interests to emerge, the dramatic structure and the dialogue that sustains it clearly posed a challenge—as we shall see—to his ambitions as a filmmaker.

Narrative/Structure

A prefatory note—the first of several in Bresson's work—informs us that the film will be about the "life of a French Dominican Community founded in 1867 by Father Lataste," and that the "images and details are close to the realistic atmosphere which rules in the convents and to the spirit which animates their mission." The mission of this particular convent is to rescue young women recently released from prison and offer them an alternative to the kind of lives and men that led them to the crimes for which they were imprisoned. While some go on to begin anew, others remain with the convent and become sisters. These objectives and the dangers of pursuing them are established in the opening sequence, which details the routine by which the nuns, led by Mother Prioress, conduct this night-time operation.[8] That they do it comfortably and competently not only demonstrates their unanimity, but immediately counters the stereotypical image most films offer of convent life. The evening's work done, Mother Prioress and her assistants return to the chapel with Agnès, their newest rescuee, where the entire community has been assembled in prayer for the duration of the operation. Their unfaltering solidarity confirmed, all bow reverently before the altar as the "Salve Regina" registers this harmonic cohesion, and a fade-out provides closure to this sequence.

The fade-in to the next shot, apparently the next morning, shows another young woman, Anne-Marie, arriving at the convent to join the order; it is followed by a close-up of the convent door as her shadow falls across it. A classic instance of ironic juxtaposition, the shot foreshadows the clash about to occur between the smoothly run regime we have just witnessed and—as will soon become evident—Anne-Marie's proud, independent spirit. Although from a bourgeois background, she is attracted to the work of this order and eager to engage in it. While her manner charms the Mother Prioress, it is apparent that Anne-Marie is ruled more by her impulses than by the convent's regimen. Though her pride blinds her to the wisdom and necessity of rules, she nevertheless poses a challenge to the spiritual integrity of the order, toward an examination of how rules serve the essence of the religious life.

The first manifestation of this conflict is when Anne-Marie insists on accompanying Mother Prioress to the prison even though she has been told by Mother Saint-Jean that she is too new for the venture, that she should pray at their founder's grave to bring "peace" to her "troubled soul." A few moments later, surprisingly, we see her arriving at the prison with Mother Prioress. Bresson registers this apparent exception to convent routine through one of two striking elliptic narrative tropes,[9] a strategy that will prove to be especially strong in his work. There is, to be sure, an important scene in the interim between Anne-Marie and her mother, who has come to persuade her to return home. Anne-Marie gently resists her mother's plea and upon returning to her cell, throws the letters and photographs connecting her to the world into the fireplace. A photo of her mother burns in close-up and the shot fades out on the image of its ashes. The next shot fades in on the Prioress and Anne-Marie at the prison. Thus, without explanation, Anne-Marie's denied request has apparently been granted.

At the prison they witness an incident in which a young woman, Thérèse, loses her temper when, while making her rounds with meals, she is mistreated by a guard; she hurls the food cart down the stairs and tries to escape, but is caught and placed in solitary confinement. Anne-Marie, who had already taken notice of her, sneaks off to visit her when she hears Thérèse screaming. Thérèse complains that she is paying for a crime she did not commit. Her efforts to calm her rebuffed, Anne-Marie leaves, but at the convent remains haunted by Thérèse's predicament. During the ceremony at which the sisters are given their "maxims"—randomly chosen quotes read to each of them and believed to "always fall right," i.e., to miraculously suit the personality and nature of each sister—Anne-Marie is given the motto that prefaces this essay. Upon hearing it, she stands in deep thought, and when a sister asks if she is feeling well, replies, somewhat enigmatically: "I hear the word. The word of my maxim. I had already heard it at the prison."

In the next shot we see her desperately urging Mother Prioress to meet Thérèse at the prison. Her abrupt manner startles both Mother Prioress and Mother Saint-Jean; the latter remarks "Mischievous child!" to which the former replies, "Which children should we listen to, the mischievous ones or the good ones?" The next shot fades in on a guard at the prison and it is only when he walks to the right and the camera follows that we see Mother Prioress and Anne-Marie awaiting Thérèse's release. Once again, an elliptic cut marks the absence of exposition, suggesting possibly that any explanation would be either inadequate or beside the point. It is clear that Anne-Marie's manner has won over Mother Prioress, that, mischievous or not, her spirit has once more triumphed over the rules.

Elliptic strategies of this kind can be found in many films, but their significance in Bresson, even at this early stage, is that they bear directly on the moral and thematic foundations of his work. Here, they appear to respond, as if by injunction, to the maxim which Anne-Marie is given—the "word that ties [her] to another human being"—and to make inevitable the effectuation of its directive. The narrative structure itself, in other words, is now committed to fulfilling the truth of the maxim. It is the moral conviction that underpins this connection between narrative trajectory and form that, I believe, gives Bresson's work such undeniable force. And it is for that reason that a subsequent parallel cut (following Thérèse's release from prison and refusal to go to the convent) from Anne-Marie praying for Thérèse in the chapel to the latter on her way to murder the man responsible for her imprisonment—despite any superficial irony in the contrast—registers a deeper bond as yet unclear to either of them.

The next shot confirms the emphasis on the bond between the two characters. The fade-out on Thérèse standing in the hallway after shooting the man (off-screen) segues into a fade-in on the nuns at work as Anne-Marie reads from the life of Saint Francis. At one point she stops, insisting that she has heard the doorbell and knows it is Thérèse. Since no one else hears it, she is directed to continue the reading, but cannot hide her distracted and excited state. The other nuns look at her somewhat critically while Anne-Marie exclaims, "The bell again. Why don't they open?," and finally, "I know it's Thérèse," as she closes the book, smiling radiantly, and as if by divination, says, "the door is open." Her intuition is confirmed in the next long shot of the convent hall in which we see Thérèse being conducted by one of the sisters to Mother Prioress.

Two striking details reinforce the structural implications of the bond. The first is how Thérèse's arrival is registered—i.e., not simply as the next step of the story, but *indirectly*, by way of Anne-Marie's telepathic sense; it is as if Thérèse has been summoned by the same "word" that now rules Anne-Marie's life. The other is that while Thérèse *has* arrived, she has come ostensibly to hide from the law; and, although this seems initially to mock Anne-Marie's naive and presumptuous faith, it turns out otherwise.

Oblivious to Thérèse's "real" motives, Anne-Marie persists in treating her as her special project, irritating her superiors and generating conflicting opinion: while many of the nuns think highly of her, others consider her a trouble-maker.

In a chorus-like scene set in the laundry, she is described both as the closest to sainthood and too proud to know her limits. The alternation of views is nicely mirrored in the *mise en scène* as the reflection of water from the large tubs wavers continually across the shots. In an exchange on the stairs, Thérèse warns Anne-Marie of the talk about her and tells her that while Mother Saint-Jean has forbid her to make any more prison visits, she remains Mother Prioress's favourite. Mother Saint-Jean reprimands Anne-Marie for devoting too much time to Thérèse and neglecting others, but Anne-Marie asserts that she would be betraying God and herself if she deserted Thérèse.

In keeping with the rule, Anne-Marie subjects herself to the community's judgment by going from cell to cell and asking each sister to assess her behaviour. Predictably, she receives conflicting responses: she is kind, but stubborn; simple, but conceited; clever, but hot-headed; she is quick-tempered and partial, but irascible; she lacks self-control, but is true and simple-hearted; she is selfish, touchy, coquettish, ambitious, obstinate, and doesn't understand people.

The situation reaches a climax during a communal gathering of work and readings when Anne-Marie disrupts the scene by protesting the presence of Mother Saint-Jean's black cat—whom Anne-Marie calls Beelzebub—and the attention given it by the sisters, particularly Thérèse, who deliberately caresses it to antagonize Anne-Marie. The cat's unfettered roaming across the tables from sister to sister is an apt symbol of the spreading, unruly tension of the entire situation. On an impulse, Anne-Marie picks up the cat and hurls it out of the room. In a meeting at which the nuns publically identify each other's transgressions and accept punishment, Anne-Marie accuses several sisters of caressing an animal until an impatient Mother Prioress makes her stop. Finally, at dinner, she defies her superiors by refusing to do her penance, after which the community decides that she must leave.

Nevertheless, since the maxim must be fulfilled, the parallel destinies of Anne-Marie and Thérèse continue to operate. While the police conduct the investigation that eventually leads them to suspect Thérèse of murder, Mother Prioress learns that Anne-Marie has not returned home. Shortly after, we see that she has not even left the convent grounds, but has lived outdoors, eating things from the garden. One night during a storm she prays by Father Lataste's grave and collapses, is found unconscious the next morning and carried into the convent. Declared too ill to recover, she spends her last hours repenting her recalcitrant behaviour and in a long scene tries to convince Thérèse that while she may have behaved stubbornly, her motives were sincere. In the final scene, Anne-Marie, near death, prepares to take her vows, surrounded by Mother Prioress, Thérèse, and others, as the entire community kneels in prayer. Too weak to continue speaking, she asks Thérèse to complete the words for her. As Anne-Marie expires, Thérèse suddenly rises from her place, a newfound peace and moral courage visible on her face, wends her way through the mass of nuns and delivers herself into the hands of the police. The word that has tied these two together has clearly been fulfilled: their parallel destinies now fused into one, death and surrender seem but two enactments of the same mandate.

The Text Cinematographic

The "inevitability" of this narrative structure, determined as it is by moral, philosophic, and thematic concerns, naturally affects the film *as a film*. Not having yet perfected the filmic strategies that would eventually match the intensity, precision, and rigour of his thought, Bresson relies here on established conventions of film construction with varying results. For example, since dialogue plays such a strong role in this first feature, it exerts a powerful effect not only on the life and atmosphere of the *mise en scène*, but even more emphatically on the editing and rhythm of the film. Nowhere is this more pronounced than in the lengthy shot/countershot exchange between Anne-Marie and Thérèse near the end. Compared to the carefully balanced rhythm between dialogue and cinematographic features of the opening sequence of the film, this scene is almost exclusively dependent on the verbal text—thirty-six of its thirty-nine shots include dialogue—to bring into focus many of the implied and subtler communications between the two characters in preceding sections of the film.

The scene sets several tasks for itself: it must, first of all, show us a considerably humbled Anne-Marie, fully aware of her pride and presumptuous behaviour and how they prevented her from reading Thérèse's character correctly. This confession is necessary to Anne-Marie's redemption and the way we perceive her death. But as it proceeds, Anne-Marie repeats herself to the point of seeming again self-absorbed, and indeed, Thérèse, as captive and involuntary listener, seems both impatient and bored. It is, in fact, supremely ironic that Anne-Marie tells Thérèse that she had completely misunderstood what Thérèse really needed—namely, "someone who wouldn't talk, whose silence would dry your tears and calm your pain." The viewer might well sympathize and understand when Thérèse, in reaction to this, leaves the room, saying: "I can't stand one more minute with you . . . you're lying, just trying another method. Prestige failed so you're trying friendship. You understood nothing!"

To the degree that this exchange is about contesting wills, it resembles the debates in Giraudoux between characters of opposing views. The difference lies in our awareness that despite Anne-Marie's awkward acknowledgment of her flaws, her aim is still consonant with the narrative's, namely, to move Thérèse from moral turpitude and isolation to release and salvation. This, of course, is a Bressonian concern, echoed in many films.[10] As such, the scene, also burdened with this task, must continue. Something impels Thérèse to return to the bedside (an earlier remark of Anne-Marie's that implies that she suspects Thérèse may be hiding from something has made her curious) and Anne-Marie temporarily shifts the subject to her illness, for which she also blames her stubborn nature. Finally, Thérèse appears to close all avenues when she says that one might cure a "wounded heart" but not a "dead one"—i.e., hers. To this, Anne-Marie replies that the hope that such a thing could be accomplished would keep her alive, even if it took one hundred years. Startled and apparently moved by this, Thérèse tenderly places her hand in Anne-Marie's, a gesture that Bresson might not have resorted to later in his career and that seems almost gratuitous, since the moment's importance has already been marked by the fact that the extreme close-up reaction shot of Thérèse to Anne-Marie's remark and the very next shot—also an extreme close-up—of Anne-Marie closing her eyes, are the *only* two of this entire sequence (except for the one that begins it) *without* dialogue. The scene ends with Anne-Marie's apt summation—of the moment, the scene, and the narrative's aim: as the camera moves in to a close-up, she says, "Perhaps this is the first day of those one hundred years."

To be sure, this scene, no less than the rest of the film, is beautifully lit, and as photographed by Philippe Agostini—who also photographed *Les Dames du Bois de Boulogne*—it achieves an ethereal quality, a luminosity to reflect its revelatory purpose. Its development, however—its emotional and thematic thrust, its stress on verbalized character interaction, its dramatic movement from distance to intimacy—is almost exclusively carried by the dialogue. In an ordinary film of the period, this would not be unusual—very typical, in fact, of the French tradition of quality which privileged writing over *mise en scène* and actors' expressions as the dominant feature of *mise en scène*. But seeing *Les Anges du péché* now, knowing what a "Bresson" film is, it is difficult not to react with surprise at the copiousness of the text, its virtual tyranny over the scene and its undeniable determinant effect on the editing structure. Given the length of the scene and Bresson's penchant—evident even in this first film—for cutting over long takes, it was inevitable that it would be broken down the way it is. It's easy to imagine that it was precisely this dominance of language—exceeding its place as one element among others—that led Bresson eventually to deny it any such privilege. That decision would affect all others: framing, camera angles, editing, narrative structure, rhythm.

Contrast this scene with the film's opening sequence, a wonderfully assured and realized example of the Bressonian style in the making. In twenty-seven shots—twelve fewer than the scene just discussed—we are introduced to the convent's regime and are apprised of the plans, preparation, and execution of the nuns' clandestine visit to the prison. In addition to Mother Prioress and other nuns, we see prison personnel, Agnès, the young woman being escorted safely away by the sisters, as well as the unidentified men they are trying to evade. All of this consumes six and one-quarter minutes of screen time, a mere one and one-half minutes more than the time devoted to the scene at Anne-Marie's bedside.

Of the twenty-seven shots of the opening sequence, fourteen of them employ camera movements. While some of these are slight, all complement the mobilizing activity of the nuns: first, as the community is summoned to prayer, then as Mother Prioress, informed that the chauffeur is ready to take her to the prison, convenes a brisk strategy meeting before setting out. This momentum is sustained even in shots without camera movement, in which internal subject movement is framed to achieve a dynamic effect: for example, the car taking the nuns to the prison approaches quickly from background to foreground, its headlights stopping directly in front of the camera in close-up. The movement of the lights across an otherwise dark night scene on a deserted Paris street also sustains the mood of danger and tension generated from the beginning. Movement is picked up and carried through in each shot. After they exit the car, Mother Prioress and her companion are seen approaching from background to middle ground in a shot again without camera movement, distant hooded figures in the night, their black habits fluttering from side to side in testimony to the hurried nature of their mission. The whole thing has the air of an operation of the French underground, which, given the time of the film's production and release under Vichy occupation, seems apropos. Indeed, the rescue of the woman and the evasion of the menacing unidentified figures in the streets confirm this impression. In such a context, the headlights which penetrate the darkness might also connote a beam of hope.

Dialogue is used in only nine shots, and much of it has that crisp, elliptical quality so distinctive to the filmmaker that it seems probable that Bresson insisted on tailoring it specifically in accord with the rhythm of the sequence in general. In the single shot of the strategy meeting, for example, Mother Prioress begins with a line—"I've drawn a sketch in order to avoid another failure"—that alludes to an unexplained prior event and provides only teasing suggestions of what is about to take place. The latter is also true of subsequent lines in the same shot, such as "Don't forget to take a torch, Mother" and "We'll go right back to the taxi if all goes well." While there is enough here and in a few other lines to spark curiosity and create suspense, it is certainly not a full exposition of the plan. In keeping with the sense of urgency that the meeting evokes, the camera moves in at two different points animating the discussion even further.

Last but not least, the structure of the operation is beautifully framed by two brief scenes in the convent's chapel, one as the nuns set out to the prison and the other when they return. The nuns have been gathered and directed by the Prioress to pray "until we come back, for the success of our venture." As Mother Prioress leaves, we hear the assembly singing "Salve Regina," and they are still singing it when Mother returns a short time later with another "ange du péché" from prison. Not only is the prayer hour a "good cover" for the militant activities of this particular convent, but in keeping with the spirit of the secret mission, it is something like the equivalent of "synchronizing one's watches." The "Salve Regina" rings out and times the rescue operation, thus assimilating it within the province of the order's vocational aspirations. The actions of Mother Prioress and her assistants, in other words, are simply another form of prayer, an equation Bresson affirms in many films and which imparts to the actions of his other characters—like the country priest and Fontaine (the condemned man who escapes)—that quality of sacred ritual.

If this opening sequence shows us glimpses of what is to come in Bresson, the bedside sequence shows us Bresson not yet able to contend with a voluminous verbal text in cinematographic terms. Perhaps unwittingly, the bedside sequence, in effect, was a test of the conventions—in particular, of the strength and/or limitations of shot/countershot as an expressive strategy when it is prolonged *primarily* to serve the dialogue.[11] This is an important point, for there are certainly examples of extended cross-cutting in Bresson's work, conceived wholly in cinematographic terms. In *A Man Escaped*, for example, we witness what might be described as an ongoing "dialogue" between the prisoner and objects in his cell (e.g., the door as he works patiently to dismantle it) in a similarly restricted physical situation. But because of the way shots are framed and cut and the way we are sensitized to the man's precarious situation through the meticulous use of offscreen sound, the experience of the film is total, one in which the mind and the senses are equally engaged in the act of perception. In the bedside scene the repeated cutting between Anne-Marie and Thérèse almost erases itself as cinema; one can comprehend the scene merely by listening to the words and not have to perceive it on any other level. It would not surprise me if just such an impression prompted Bresson to seek ways of rehabilitating a convention like shot/countershot editing and of rescuing the cinema from enslavement to the word.

Admittedly, the bedside scene, by its very nature (e.g., in requiring one character to be lying down throughout), would have taxed the efforts of any beginning filmmaker with serious ambitions. Other than severely trimming the dialogue itself, it is difficult to imagine what other options would have presented themselves to someone working within the traditional narrative system. An earlier ten-shot exchange between the same two characters, set on a staircase, illustrates how setting and camera angle alone can enhance the shot/countershot structure when dialogue is paramount.

That the text in general presented a considerable challenge to Bresson is evident in the many camera movements he employs to offset static or stagey compositions. There are many sequence which a lesser filmmaker would have simply shot as written, treating them as pro-filmic "scenes" requiring no cinematic intervention. Countless examples of the practice can be cited from within the French cinema of the 1930s alone—the decade preceding Bresson's entry into feature filmmaking. One need only recall Marcel Carné and Marcel Pagnol, whose work, notwithstanding its charms, exemplified the advocation that the sound cinema *should be* "canned theatre." It was, of course, Jean Renoir, who, in his films of the same period—notably, *Toni, Le Crime de Monsieur Lange, La Bête humaine,* and *La Règle du jeu*—liberated the camera from that fixed, contemplative stance and allowed it to be seized by the rhythm and dynamics of the action, capturing behaviour and events as if by chance.

While Bresson's mature style clearly differs from Renoir's, it can be argued that the small, but significant camera movements in *Les Anges du péché* owe something to Renoir's in that by reframing shots and scenes in progress, often in conjunction with the movement of characters, they physically destabilize the sense of a pro-filmic space. As a constant force within the space of action, the camera refuses to abandon the field to talking figures. A noteworthy aspect of many of its moves is its peculiar consciousness of sites, the way it both responds to and exploits the architectural properties specific to the convent setting—and, in the critical sequence of Thérèse's attempt to escape, to the prison setting as well. Indoors, the convent is lined with corridors off of which are the individual cells of the sisters. Because the camera is placed more or less at the juncture of two such corridors, the image is framed initially to stress a diagonal recession of space. Two or more figures often pause momentarily at this juncture to converse and then move on, their exit marked by the camera's pivoting toward the adjacent diagonally framed corridor. The effect, achieved even by a very slight move of the camera, is to authenticate the space in deep focus and to facilitate the recording of continuous movement toward and away from the camera.

Outdoors, there is a portico which runs along all four walls of the building, thus forming a square, columned-off extension of the convent, also enclosing an open-air garden in the centre. The situation, in other words, is similar in that the camera is often positioned as it is indoors or, as a variation, tracks straight back from approaching figures, pausing when they do to talk, then moving to the left or right when they move, only to reveal that it was momentarily poised once again at a dynamically pivotal juncture.

The Power of Grace

It is hardly surprising that Bresson's first feature should have a religious subject, the iconography and thematic aspects of which prefigure his later films. Nor is it surprising that he would find in the story and setting of this film a variety of characters who manifest the "seven deadly sins." While this palette is more comprehensively arrayed in *Journal d'un curé de campagne* and *Au hasard Balthazar*, it is already apparent in *Les Anges du péché* that Bresson's cosmos—whether it be set in a Dominican convent, a provincial village, a medieval forest, or the streets of Paris—is one in which human nature is inherently flawed, in which those characters who might, in someone's else's films, embody a state of innocence corrupted by others—are no less susceptible to the pettiness and weaknesses of the human condition than their tormentors. That anyone in a Bresson narrative seems to transcend this condition is not confirmation of their having escaped it, but of their having—temporarily—come under the benign influence of what the country priest would call "grace," a gift which may be given or taken away without reason and so not to be mistaken for an inherent virtue in the character him or herself. It can infuse a secular life as well as a religious one. The elevation of Bresson's camera above the deceased body of Sister Anne-Marie at the end of *Les Anges du péché* is a sign of this grace and its power of transmission, inspiring Thérèse to seize her own spiritual release. But that camera also rises above Agnès's bed at the end of *Les Dames du Bois de Boulogne* after her husband's plea brings her back from her death-like swoon. It is the gesture that tells us that human love, however alloyed, remains the only reflection we have of the divine. Lying near death and confessing her prideful excesses, Anne-Marie tells Thérèse that the only excuse for her stubborn behaviour was that she loved Thérèse. The same words are uttered by Agnès to excuse her part in Hélène's nefarious scheme to ruin the life of her former lover Jean. "My only excuse," she tells Jean, now her husband, "is that I loved you." We are meant to see the first as spiritual since the love that inspires Anne-Marie leads another to renounce her hate and pride and change her life. But while the setting and the situation in *Les Dames* is more worldly, the effect is the same.

Whatever one may think of the concept of grace and the religious convictions that underlie it—and clearly this is a dilemma many admirers of Bresson face—it is not an ignorable feature of his narratives. To analyze Bresson's style without accounting for the way it is significantly shaped by the filmmaker's faith is to devalue the moral conviction that gives it its unique force. This is not to say, however, that every story must end in redemption. Indeed, from *Au hasard Balthazar* (1966) to *L'Argent* (1983), it is at least arguable whether his protagonists experience this saving grace at the end.

Consider the final moments in *L'Argent*, for example, Bresson's last film, which recall those of *Les Anges du péché*. In the latter, Thérèse, having at last been moved by Anne-Marie, solemnly descends the stairs of the convent, its walls lined with nuns kneeling in mourning for Anne-Marie—and, coincidentally, in unwitting tribute to the newly awakened Thérèse—and walks determinedly into the arms of the waiting police, offering her hands to be cuffed. The feeling one has—reinforced by the expression on the actress' face, the trajectory of the narrative, the spiritual nature of the transformation, and, not least, by the surge of the march-like Grünenwald score—is, far from dispiriting, that an undeniable victory has been won, one shared by both the living and the dead.

In the final shot of *L'Argent*, Yvon is led away by the police, his hands visibly cuffed and held high in midframe as he walks toward the camera and offscreen, passing the curious onlookers who, without turning a head, continue to stare into the café from which the man has emerged, as if awaiting something more exciting. The man, having committed robbery and murdered at least five people, is, befitting his entire life, ignored. Having lost everything of any value to him—his wife, his child, his good name, his freedom—thanks to the malice and treachery of a host of perfect strangers, he has nothing to live for. In adapting Tolstoy's novella, "The Forged Coupon," Bresson ends his version halfway, discarding the story's second half which recounts the slow but powerful spiritual transformation which this character undergoes. No such regeneration, or even remorse, is implied in the final scene of Bresson's film, despite the fact that the man has confessed his crimes and surrendered.

What does such a difference import? Has Bresson's philosophy changed, his belief in the moral transformation of the individual no longer tenable? The tie that binds in *Les Anges du péché* and the word that reveals its spiritual genesis presume a view of the world and of human interaction that allows for the possibility of profound connections that lead to moral improvement—thus, to some degree, redeeming the otherwise fallen nature of the human condition. There are no comparable ties in *L'Argent*, no connections that spring from a moral or spiritual source; the one possible exception—an old woman who temporarily befriends the young murderer—ends as violently and fruitlessly as the others. As the title of the film indicates and as the Tolstoy story chronicles, the tie between people is money—and fake money at that. As a perversion of the very notion of exchange, the forged bill passed from person to person transmits an equally devalued humanity, devoid of decency, honesty, and compassion. Whether the film is taken as a parable about contemporary life or about the triumph of capitalism, its premise—like the maxim that writes Anne-Marie's "destiny" and dictates the structure of *Les Anges du péché*—orders its trajectory. The difference is that while that order appears to enchain the characters in both films, this enchainment ends in hopeless resignation to the world's flawed system of justice in *L'Argent*, while in *Les Anges du péché* it is an act of deliverance. Thérèse is freed internally; her surrender to the law is a sign of this, a confirmation that whatever the world determines cannot ultimately touch her soul.

L'Argent shows us the world as more nakedly materialistic and corrupt. But, contrary to what a superficial reading of Bresson's developing thought might suggest, there is no contradiction between this view and the Christian ethos, as held, for example, by Pascal, for whom the world—fallen by definition—is exactly as it is supposed to be; one not only cannot, but should not presume to change it. In reflecting on the weakness of human justice in one of his *Pensées*, Pascal—argues Erich Auerbach—asserts that "on this earth might represents not only actual positive right, but legitimate right as well."[12] Pascal basically accepted the Augustinian philosophy that "the world is fundamentally and necessarily evil, in dramatic opposition to the kingdom of God; one must decide whether to follow the one or the other."[13] Nevertheless, the way of the world, its custom, must be obeyed. "He demanded the determinate, the enduring and absolute; he could not abide fluctuations and compromises, which he identified with evil."[14]

This is the Pascal I see underlying Bresson's view of the world, not the easily misread Pascal of the wager, which sounds like an insincere game on the part of philosopher and filmmaker. There is no compromise in Bresson—not in *Les Anges du péché* and not in *L'Argent*. The image of the world may seem to have radically changed between the former and the latter, but this is too simplistic a conclusion. For one thing, Bresson explores a wider compass in *L'Argent*—a move perhaps first discernible in *Au hasard Balthazar* and clearly the case with *Le Diable probablement*. In *Les Anges du péché* we are presented with a very particular view in that the premise of the narrative is to set against one another quite pointedly the world and its vanities on the one hand, and on the other an ordered place within it, designed—however imperfectly—to cleanse the individual (whether the "angel of sin" or well-meaning souls like Anne-Marie) of worldliness. It can, nevertheless, be seen as a microcosm of the world itself in which rules must be obeyed and one's pride conquered. The situation graphically demonstrated in the bar scene in *Balthazar*, however, is that anarchy rules and money pays for the damages. In *Le Diable probablement* no system of rules—marxist, capitalist, atheist, religious—is categorical and no method of dealing with the consequences—politics, social action, psychoanalysis—carries any weight or conviction. In *L'Argent* money has become the rule—the basis of all social and familial interaction.

But this is to assert that the world is in crisis and that, in the absence of a strong system of values, the idea of living a morally disciplined life has been increasingly devalued. If art can still be seen to both reflect and counter the way things are, Bresson's seems the closest to having done so. While the statement at the head of this essay is included in his *Notes* dated 1950-1958,[15] *Les Anges du péché* demonstrates that "binding persons to each other and to objects by looks" was already the primary aesthetic stress for Bresson whether or not he had yet chastened the system—i.e., editing—which would infuse that aim with a moral force unlike any other filmmaker's. *Les Anges du péché* is the first instance of the theme and moral imperative that drives all of Bresson's narratives. What we see in *L'Argent* is how that theme and moral imperative have been perfectly embodied in the structure and form of the film itself. It is no longer only the direction and outcome of the narrative that inevitably ensues from the maxim, but the filmic object itself. Form and style here are indistinguishable from meaning and morality. Whatever the world has done, Bresson, as his last film clearly shows, is as strongly committed as ever to the word that has tied him to the singular pursuit of an essential, morally accountable cinema.

Notes

1. Bresson in an interview with Jean Queval, *L'Écran française*, no. 72, November 12, 1946 (my translation).
2. Jean Sémolué, *Bresson*, Flammarion, 1993.
3. Cited in René Briot, *Robert Bresson*, Collection 7th Art, Les Éditions du Cerf, Paris, 1957, pp. 15-16. The original title for the film was *Béthanie*; according to Briot, the producers preferred the more "melodramatic" *Les Anges du péché*.
4. Ibid.
5. *Robert Bresson: Éloge*, Cinémathéque française, Mazzotta, 1997.
6. See Jacques Guicharnaud, *Modern French Theatre from Giraudoux to Genet*, Yale Romantic Studies, revised edition, New Haven, 1967.
7. René Briot reports that it was not unusual for people attending screenings to complain about the film's showing of quarrels and jealousies within convents (*Robert Bresson*, p. 25).
8. According to René Briot, because of the terrible conditions imposed by the war, the entire film had to be shot at night (*Robert Bresson*, p. 15).
9. The adjective "elliptic"—defined as "of or related to extreme economy of oral and written expression" in *The American Heritage Dictionary*—is being used here instead of the noun "ellipsis" because the latter describes a very specific rhetorical strategy in poetry, whereby a word or term is omitted but clearly implied and grammatically consistent with the rest of the line or sentence. Ellipsis has been somewhat loosely applied to film structures, along with other terms derived from classical rhetoric, and no doubt, something akin to its linguistic model occurs in films, whereby certain rapidly edited "film phrases," usually depicting a single action, can be taken in as a syntactical unit equivalent to a line in verse. One thinks, for example, of such montage moments in Eisenstein as the cossack slashing the face of the woman in *Potemkin*, where the actual contact between sabre and face is omitted. But precisely because of examples like this, one would like to make clear distinctions between them and other less compacted instances where there is a sense that the ongoing logic governing a narrative has been deliberately disrupted by a strategical leap from one point to another that appears to omit something we have every reason to expect should have been included. While the kind of immediate comprehension that obtains in a literary context is not what occurs in *Les Anges du péché*, there is certainly a form of elliptic construction in the narrative. I would suggest that at least four conditions must be met to assert this.

The first is that one must be able to cut off the segment of the narrative in question and see it as a "unit" of some kind in order to recognize that a key part of it has been omitted. Secondly, that "part" should be as specific and as easily supplied by the viewer as the missing word or term in verse. Thirdly, the recognition that we are dealing with an elliptic film trope rather than a carelessly constructed scenario must be established by context, pattern, and purpose. Lastly, in order for the effect to register at all, there must be some element of surprise—even shock—and perhaps momentary confusion, a sense that some prior knowledge of things has been contradicted. All four of these, I believe, are evident in *Les Anges du péché*.

10. At its most succinct, in *Pickpocket*, a critical exchange between Michel the protagonist and the police inspector is reduced to a handful of words and a single gesture, condensing dozens of pages of Dostoevsky's *Crime and Punishment*.

11. One might cite *The Trial of Joan of Arc* (1962) as an example of this very thing, but I would argue that the results are quite different. First, the trial situation renders the context more dynamic; its interrogative nature is set against a very charged, though largely offscreen backdrop which bears upon the shot/countershot exchanges in unpredictable ways. Secondly, because of this context, the use of offscreen space and sound is far more complex than anything in the bedside sequence in *Les Anges du péché*. Thirdly, the framing and editing of the exchanges are far more pointed and assertive, every shot and cut as crisp and as tensely balanced as the dangerous questions posed by the judges and Joan's inspired answers themselves. In short, by this point in Bresson's career, the "cinematographic" has assumed control and the text given its proper place within it.

12. Eric Auerbach, "On the Political Theory of Pascal," in *Scenes from the Drama of European Literature*, Minneapolis: University of Minnesota Press, 1984, p. 103.

13. Ibid., p. 106.

14. Ibid., p. 104.

15. Robert Bresson, *Notes on Cinematography*, trans. Jonathan Griffin, New York: Urizen Books, 1975, p. 6.

Les Anges du péché

On Robert Bresson's Film
Les Anges du péché

HESE ANGELS haven't much to do with beasts or even devils: they are nuns who take in fallen girls just out of jail; they dress them in Dominican habits, house them, feed them, help them settle down, and occasionally a conversion or a vocation comes to reward such charitable efforts. Renée Faure, a little scatterbrain just emerging from her worldly bourgeois milieu, is one of these "couturiers of God"; she has a vocation, but pride too; she is ardent, but indiscreet; very gay, but a touch arrogant; cherished by certain sisters, she is envied by others; and it is with this electric character that she undertakes to save a lost soul. Jany Holt has furious black eyes, a stubborn forehead, a bitter mouth; after a term in the slammer, she has just knocked off her pimp who had squealed on her before she went in, and has figured out that a convent is a good refuge. She is a wolf in the sheepfold, and a devil for that imperfect angel Renée Faure. At all costs Renée Faure wants to save Jany Holt, but merely manages to get on her nerves; pursued, invaded, hurt, the fallen girl takes her revenge and, by the intermediary of a little black cat—devil-creature in the service of a devil-woman—manages to provoke the excellent but touchy Renée Faure to rebellion within the convent walls. The Angel leaves her paradise, though her heart remains attached: nightly she returns to prowl around it and—poor little bird tormented by pride and love, no longer sheltered by her blithe white wings—is assaulted one night by a storm; it is cold and rainy in the convent's dark garden; the next morning, the good sisters discover Renée Faure with pneumonia; this affliction will lead her to the convent infirmary, whence a fortunate death will lead her to heaven: such is the price paid for Jany Holt's soul, conquered at last by a charity so indiscreet as to lead to death.

This successful film had a lot of reasons for being unendurable: the title, the setting, the argument. The setting was dangerous: a convent full of nuns—we know what they become in a director's eye; and for all their talent, decorators can never produce a convincing chapel on the set: too many pillars, too many flowers, too many bells, all that organ music; and the stars, for all the elasticity of their temperament, never do nuns well: eyebrows too carefully plucked, lips too heavily rouged, a face which the efforts of sanctity turn merely hypocritical and from which the greasepaint cannot erase the stigmata of a highly secular existence (see the end of the film *Ramuntcho*). Here nothing of the kind: the convent is delicate, tender, clean; not too much chapel; from time to time a linear cloister; more often, a sunny little garden, a workroom, a kitchen, a corridor, no organ, and a bell only once or twice; a little evensong; the dialogue simple, decisive, quite virile. Bresson's nuns are reliable; they know how to wear their habits; they know how to walk, pray, speak; they don't keep raising their eyes to heaven, nor casting them down to the ground; they are fresh without being freshly painted; charming without being provocative; and the way Sylvie plays the Prioress, with her umbrella, her pursed lips, her big nose and her kind eyes, she really looks like a nun, for once, and not a madam in disguise. The quality of the images is high: the sackcloth dark and simple; the whitewashed walls vibrant, almost torrid; the lighting diffused as through muslin veils—these are the three dimensions of space in which the cameraman has operated, while dialogue takes us into a higher universe where the convent's intimacy is as warm as sackcloth and as restful; where pride and penitence glare as harshly as the whitewashed walls; and where tenderness and spirituality resemble the light's great aerial circuits.

The argument, too, was dangerous. Thesis-films are rarely successful, and films on religious subjects always painful, combining as they do the two most pathetic enemies of art: lack of talent and good intentions. *L'Appel du silence* (a film on Père Foucauld) makes the spectator squirm in his seat with shame and embarrassment. Here the scenario is by a Dominican, Father Bruckberger (author of *Watershed*, a study of the Thomism of Claudel, Maritain, and Bernanos). It seems to me that in the author's own mind the scenario makes no great claims; the point was to paint a picture, and therefore to concoct a plot which would bring together a few yards of canvas, and for two hours, these Angels of Sin. But the subject, though delicately conceived, is not without a certain depth; I particularly admire Father Bruckberger's understanding of the intolerable character of Sister Anne-Marie (Renée Faure) and of the after all quite legitimate rebellion of Thérèse (Jany Holt). Of course it is Anne-Marie who wins (for a Christian, to die well is to win), and Good triumphs in the end, but at what cost? And throughout the film, we have felt that Good was not so separate from Evil, that between these two powers there were certain espousals, so to speak, which united them to the point of creating a homogenous substance, as in life itself; this pessimistic vision might have linked the scenarist to the great tragic tradition, had he not been a Dominican. The scenarist's ecclesiastical condition afforded us the soothing ascension of the final "Salve

Regina," and there were a lot of tears in the house; but it no doubt also caused that childish storm which broke just in time over the nuns' orchard; after all, for Father Bruckberger, Anne-Marie had to die. But does one die of a storm? Of a defeat? Not likely, alas! But we know in what esteem—for different motives—Dominicans and directors hold the spectacle of a fine death.

The dialogue required of Giraudoux only his talent, not his famous manner; and such talent is enormous. To listen to this film is a great pleasure for both mind and heart. Not one sentimental sentence; not one pedantic sentence; no effusions, no catechism; a human dialogue, full of grandeur and kindness, which grips the soul and embraces it without any of the tricks of religious eloquence, and occasionally even insinuates the more exquisite nourishment of a certain, malice, a certain tenderness.

Translated from the French by Richard Howard

Journal d'un curé de campagne

NICK BROWNE

Film Form/Voice-Over: Bresson's *The Diary of a Country Priest*

HE STYLISTICS of the modern European cinema, insofar as its project is (still) the characterization of a figure in a certain milieu, are closely associated with the structural and compositional resources of the voice-over in certain key works. In Bresson's *Diary of a Country Priest* (1951), for example, the incorporation of extensive spoken material into the film alters the relations among the elements of the soundtrack (character speech and "effects"), reorganizes the usual relation of the profilmic material (the adapted text, Bernanos's novel) to the completed work, and restructures the relation of the camera (its placement and movement) to a style of acting and to character speech. Through reference to the conventions of writing, and by reconstructing the relation of sound to image, the film's voice-over perspicuous form, the vision "of," or "on," the interior life of its central character. Examination of the compositional role of the voice-over in the general structure and conduct of the narration, in, addition to clarifying the ground of the work's form and effect, has a special theoretical interest.

As an element of the narration, the priest's voice-over, like the sound "effects" themselves, is closely related to the construction of the system-character, the impression of a centre of "consciousness," and the mode of transcription of cinematic point of view. By clarifying the structural role of the voice-over in the narration of *Diary of a Country Priest*, we may see on what terms film continues its affinities with, and proclaims its discontinuity from literature, and beyond that, we may appreciate more exactly the mode by which cinema both maintains and limits its commitment to the assumptions of psychological realism.

The significant and expressive relations between the voice-over and image in the film are complex. Text is neither a simple commentary on the image, nor is image a simple illustration of the text. Disjunction, independence, interrogation, and even negation of the image, by the sense of the text, is as much a feature as illustration or duplication. Though the diary form calls of course for all events to be in the past, it does not precisely prescribe the forms of the presentation derived from that fact. The images need not simply present the remembered vision of what the text states. If the specifically formal and semiotic aspect of the film is the problematic of the narrative presentation of character by means of scene (character, dialogue, camera) conjoined with speech (the voice-over), even if the speech seems to take the lead, the analysis of the film calls for a model of narration different from the conventional. To the extent that there exists a contemporary theory of filmic narration, it is based largely on "classical" works, and articulated on the analogy, and dis-analogy, between narrative "voice," as that concept is developed in the theory of the novel and the framing and authority of the camera. Such theory has made several pertinent observations relating to the distinction between literal spatial positions of the camera (as in framing and composition), the mode of character vision, and narrative or authorial point of view. This is the essential distinction between shots, views, and point of view. Though the mechanism of cinematic exposition is typically invested in the appropriation and in the definition of a central character by authorial surrogation, the narrator, while retaining the power to critique character vision, also assumes the task of structuring that character's story and of presenting it to an audience. Such a form of agency involves inscribing an implied audience at an angle to the fiction. Narrative point of view in cinema then is not defined by literal camera position in relation to character, though it is based on such graphic configurations, but by the realization of a dramatically embodied scene, composed of a sequence of shots, organized by the assumption of an attitude formed and expressed by the manner of narrating the dramatic story to an implied audience.

An authorial narrative intervention in its classic form is typically displaced, or even hidden by the form of the *découpage*: as a result the story simply seems to tell itself through a sequence of natural camera placements. Bresson's innovation in narrative technique is linked neither to the foregrounding of authorial intervention (as it is in Godard's *2 ou 3 choses que je sais d'elle* (1966) in which the voice-over tends to merge—as in Cocteau's *Le Sang d'un poète* (1930)—with confession and autobiography), nor to the scrutiny or acknowledgement of the process of adaptation as an aim in itself, but is addressed rather to the problem of characterizing the subjectivity of the priest. The film's form is linked essentially to representation of character. The film does not substantially qualify the theory of conventional film narration in its general form, but suggests that an amplified model of representation or composition as "point of view" is necessary in order to account for the decisive function and effect of the system of sound in the film.

The voice-over is a performance of parts of Bernanos's text. For the most part it follows the past tense expected of the diary form, but does so in such a way that the derived effects of "pastness" are bracketed and modulated by a complex set of narrational and plastic strategies. Within the diary format, a hierarchy and structure of tenses is proposed and maintained. The "pastness" of the voice-over narration is qualified, to the advantage of the fiction of presentness of action, by including, on the level of the narrated story, the act of writing the diary. The first shot of the film, a dolly-in on the journal, discloses an already-written text that anticipates and programs the episodic structure of the film to follow: "I do not think I shall do any harm if I note down day by day quite frankly the humble and indeed insignificant secrets of a life which in any case is without mystery . . ." The form of pastness conveyed by the presentness of voice-over intervention is not that of a completed form. As a simple record of events, the journal might be "concluded" each day, but both the events' continuation and certainly their significance are open to inflection in the future. Often the described events are states of being (e.g. the priest's health) that are not concluded at the time of the diary entry. The quality of presentness of such spoken/written reports within the flow of the film, or what seems like the repetition of a visual scene by the voice-over, suggests the equivocal status of such written material in the narration. By a careful presentation of the first series of voice-over speeches, and by later uses in conformity with such codes, the film structures a way of reading/hearing such texts. The film presents the pair 'written text'/'performance by voice,' with voice-over as an independent entity, as *authorized* not primarily by the written text, but by the "lived" experience of the character represented by the text. At crucial points it establishes the text as the writing down of a lived experience, thought and felt by the character as an "inner monologue." The first time, for example, the voice-over appears in the story proper, after the credits, it appears without corresponding written text but with an image, a close-up, of the priest. The line, "My parish, my first parish," comes at the moment when the camera, which has at first permitted the priest ample scope for physical movement and investigation, dollies forward to frame the priest more tightly in a close-up, thus summarizing and concluding the psychological response to the moment. The voice-over, in other words, is integrated into the system or the psychology that motivates camera movement in the film.

The image is not as Bazin suggests the simply "objective" element of the film. The inflection given to the shot/countershot figure, the typical mode of representing dialogue, tends to characterize and develop an attitude toward the priest. Typically, this cinematic figure is constructed symmetrically, to represent each party in the same way (angle and scale) with a sort of equality, first one speaking then the other. In this sense, the shot/reverse-shot figure of cinema corresponds to the presentation of alternating dialogue—speech within quotations—in prose fiction. But the visual style of Bresson's film inflects this cinematic figure in particular ways, to underline the passivity of the priest. In conversation, the camera is

Journal d'un curé de campagne

often on the curé even when his interlocutor is speaking. Thus we see him responding—silently. In such exchanges, the priest is privileged by a shot of larger scale with tighter framing. At points of dramatic conclusion, the camera often alters its framing by a slow dolly forward so as to concentrate and personalize the reactions of the priest. In effect, the camera movement itself, apart from *mise en scène*, enacts, in plastic terms, a version of psychology not limited to manifest physiognomic signs. The intervention of the camera in the composition of the images of the dialogue system represents an authorial inflection and comment, favouring the priest as an organizing centre of consciousness that is probably best modelled theoretically by descriptions of the form of shared narrator/character authority found in "indirect discourse." While the images of the film rarely assume the form of representation of the character's literal vision, direct or remembered, the effect of his continual presence on the screen and the visual rhetoric of the presentation of his relations with others, renders certain subjective effects as if in the first-person mode. The action is set up plastically, however, to create the impression of his subjectivity without defining its particular contents. Conveying the sense of a form of subjectivity different from impressionism, that is different from a subject which records sights and sounds, is the specific contribution of the soundtrack in relation to the imagery. Sound creates an unreachable "depth" of feeling that is crucial to the overall structure and effect of the work. The system of sound "effects"—cars, hoofs, wagon wheels, a rake on stone, music from within the fiction, etc.—assumes a place within the overall system of the film that isolates character subjectivity and puts it as a distance from the weight and physicality of the "real world" that the sounds materially evoke.

The effect of "distance" is created jointly by camera movement, usually a dolly-in to close-up (signifying intensification and concentration) and the clear and distinct presentation of sounds "off" that do not register significance as such, but rather the sheer physicality of sensation. In this way, sound foregrounds the interior quality of the voice-over. Sound enters into the point of view system by defining a centre of consciousness as a meditative, not an impressionistic, subject. The clarity of this meditative, interior and emotional space of speech, the post-synchronous soundtrack, is defined by the way it enjoys a privileged environment possessing an aural space uncontested by other sounds. The effect, when early in the film the voice-over superimposes itself on the dialogue uttered by another, making it nearly inaudible, is to locate the authority and tense of the voice-over. It derives, implicitly, from an interior monologue contemporaneous to the event. The film's use of sound establishes a narrative framework. The performance of the voice, neutralizing to some extent the convention of the past tense and establishing a hierarchy of presence, determines a place for the action. While seeming to acknowledge that the handwritten manuscript refers to the fiction of a typographically printed novel as the source, the film declares in both formal and narrative terms that it is derived finally from the authenticity and uniqueness of lived thought.

The problem of the relation of the voice-over to imagery in *Diary of a Country Priest* is different from *Hiroshima mon amour* (1959), a film which in its filmmaking sequences and in the documents of the museum also has a self-referential form. In the Resnais film, however, the imagery, tonally, rhythmically and in particular syntactically (i.e., the series of four separated intercut shots of the dying German lover, or the series of Nevers's confinement in the basement), is controlled by the effort of Nevers to remember. The overall structure of narrative material (not only the flashbacks, but its avoidances, repetitions, etc.) like each of the individual shots, reflects the effort, and later the consequences, of remembering. The episodic and progressive narrative structure of *Diary of a Country Priest*, on the other hand, does not provoke questions of remembering. Neither in syntax nor in tonality does the construction of the images themselves, with the exception perhaps of the dream-like slow dissolves, make any allusion to memory as an explicit problem. Nothing in the images themselves suggests a narration of a remembered vision, or remembered sound. Indeed the form of the *découpage* suggests that the intervention of the third person, who takes the priest as his surrogate-subject, represents things in a manner (i.e., in relation to the "outside" via sound, where its significance is mediated by the camera) that the priest would not be in a position to narrate. His knowledge is circumscribed at several levels, but most significantly, for example, by the process of arriving at an understanding of his role in the larger and mysterious scheme of things or of the connection elaborated by the film between blood, wine, and ink. There are motifs, strategies of presentation, as well as overall design and interpretation, that belong to Bresson.

The relation between voice-over and image in the film is not essentially a difference in tenses, past and present. Within the framework of the film, there is a sense of movement between the pastness of the diary format and the presence of the unrolling image, whether accompanied by voice-over or not. Rather, the specific domains of speech and image are differentiated and integrated by the terms of the compatibility of "views" of character they offer. Within the narrative system of character, tense is only an aspect of the general problem of narrative distance. That linkage and control of two points of view is the underlying formal and compositional issue of the film, and the basis of its power, becomes clear not so much in sequences accompanied by speech-narration that repeats what the scenes show (transparency), but in the scenes of explicit disjuncture, when the priest says something to himself that is in conflict with what the image shows (character opaqueness). It is in these scenes that the voice-over technique works most effectively. Early in the film, we see the priest walk forward to a window, his face betraying no particular sign of discomfort. But the voice-over reveals a different state. "I would have given anything this morning for one human word of compassion, of tenderness." Such scenes are constructed, paradigmatically, on the difference between the opaqueness of visual appearances and the report of the depth of feeling of the interior world. Typically, such passages are devoted to the depiction of the pain of losing faith, the overall problem confronted by the character. For example: "I had not noticed that I was crying. It was without thinking. The truth is, it has always been on the Mount of Olives that I find myself when lost . . . I was the prisoner of the Holy Agony." The restrained acting style and the manner of delivery of dialogue is designed to support this opposition between appearance and voice which is valorized by the film as "spirituality."

The significance and power of the voice-over and the acting, however, are not separable from the presentation of the character through the precise visual forms of the *découpage*. The subjectivity implied by the construction of images is not that of remembered vision, but of an objectified drama. It is represented by a filmic perspective, and a form of filmic composition, designed as the very condition and support for the integration of the "truth" of the voice-over within the discourse of the film.

The theoretical model capable of representing the general structure of this sort of narration, divided between a form of first-person speech that sometimes turns against itself, and the complex discourse of a narrated story represented by a sound camera—of recordings of dialogue, sound, and action—must necessarily challenge and extend existing accounts of narrative theory in film. The form of such an explanation, presumably a complex mode of structure of authority within indirect discourse, must certainly be grounded in the distinction in the scope and province of the dramatic "I," the narrative "I," and the camera. The structure of the enunciation is not, to be sure, limited to the voice-over function. We have presented, in some detail, a description of the infrastructure of these relations, in terms of authority and tense. These perspectives that we have called inside/outside, narrative and dramatic, are linked finally to the overall rhetoric of Bresson's presentation of events to his audience by a form of characterization of spirituality which is another mode of authorial distance.

Un condamné à mort s'est échappé

ALLEN THIHER

Bresson's *Un condamné à mort*: The Semiotics of Grace

S TANLEY CAVELL tells us in *The World Viewed* that the material basis of the movies is "a succession of automatic world projections" and, moreover, "that the projected world does not exist (now) is its only difference from reality. (There is no feature, or set of features, in which it differs. Existence is not a predicate.)"[1] Although the film semiotician might well ask how the projected world then comes to signify or to possess a semantic dimension, this view of film ontology is probably more widely held than any other. The view seems to lie, for instance, behind Robert Bresson's repeated rejection of the ideas that film can be a form of representation, that an actor's mimicry can have a role in film, or that film can use in any sense the notion of *mise en scène*. But Bresson, who hardly intends for his films to be a mere appropriation of an absent world, would have a ready answer for the film semiotician. According to Bresson, it is through the creation of a system of relationships among the projected images that the filmic world comes to have meaning. Bresson goes so far, in fact, as to deny that a single image can have a meaning, for if it does, it risks destroying the signifying system that the filmmaker must create:

> If an image, looked at apart, clearly expresses something, if it includes an interpretation, it will not be transformed by the contact with other images. The other images will have no power over it, and it will have no power over the other images. Neither action nor reaction. It is complete in itself [*définitive*] and unusable in the system of the cinematograph. (A system does not decide everything. It is a beginning toward something.)[2]

The cinematograph—Bresson has only disdain for the "cinema"—thus derives meaning from a system of relationships predicated on the interaction of all elements in a film.

However, it is Bresson's final remark, in parentheses, that points to the need to think beyond the immediate visual system that orders a series of projected world views. For the filmic system can generate meaning only if the relations making up the system are semanticized in turn by a more general signifying context that is not directly present in the projected world. We would say, in fact, that the filmic signification is generated by the context provided by the film's narrative project, for narration is a privileged semanticizing agent for endowing the system of filmic elements with meaning. Perhaps it is in this sense that we might understand Bresson's remarks on how film can signify what most deeply concerns him: "Life must not be rendered by photographically recopying life, but by hidden laws in the middle of which one feels that your models move."[3] Models—Bresson has no use for the word "actor" either—must move in conformity with hidden laws that we might take to be the laws of narrativity or the narrative project that invests the filmic world with meaning. Thus the most fruitful critical approach to a film would be one that seeks to lay bare the film's fundamental narrative project, its hidden laws, so that all the elements in the filmic system can stand out in the full significance that they have derived from this semanticizing context.

The narrative project that endows the filmic system with meaning is rarely an autonomous structure, and perhaps it inevitably derives its semanticizing capacity in turn from the cultural context that gives rise to it. Even the most generically fixed narrative form is embedded in a cultural matrix that allows it to invest the image with a semantic dimension. In the case of a very complex film, such as Bresson's *Un condamné à mort s'est échappé* (1956), this cultural matrix is of the greatest importance. On the surface, Bresson's portrayal of a condemned prisoner's escape might appear to be an evocation of the French Resistance, for the film's opening titles tell us that *Un condamné à mort* is a "true" story dealing with the Montluc prison in which, of the ten thousand prisoners the Germans sent there during the Occupation, seven thousand died. On one level, then, it appears that the film is a historical adventure film, narrating how the prisoner Fontaine avoids death by escaping against impossible odds, and is thus a work that borrows its narrative conventions or signifying codes from a pre-existing cinematic genre.[4] The strength—and weakness—of genres is, of course, that they facilitate a quick recognition of the semantic codes the work uses and thus allow an easy "reading" of the film. But, as auteurists have stressed, the great director is one who uses the pre-existing forms in order to shape his own vision. Perhaps the greatest directors, then, are those who use genres as a point of departure for the creation of new cinematic codes, and in this respect, it is evident that only the relatively inexperienced viewer would attempt to view *Un condamné à mort* solely in terms of the canons of the adventure genre. The film uses the adventure genre only as a means for creating a new narrative structure, one whose significance is derived not so much from the heroic concerns of the Resistance, but rather from the cultural matrix provided by the Christian existentialism that was a dominant current in French intellectual life during the fifties.

It is, in fact, with a Kierkegaardian understanding of religious paradox that one must begin an interpretation of *Un condamné à mort*, for in one sense this is a film about an unmediated relationship between the particular and the absolute. The cultural context that grounds the narrative project is, in general terms, that system of existentialist religious values in which the oppositions of faith and despair, freedom and grace, or spirit and flesh establish a coherent semantic field. The film's full title is the first sign that we must look to this cultural matrix: *Un condamné à mort s'est échappé ou le vent souffle où il veut (A Man Escaped or The Wind Listeth Where It Will)*. In semantic terms, titles often direct the viewer toward a context that offers the first key to meaning, and in the case of Bresson's film the double title orients us toward the fundamental series of oppositions that provide a general context. The film's visible action—the escape—is informed by an absent spiritual drama that stands in opposition to the present material drama of resistance and escape. (*Opposition* is used here in the technical sense of "a correlational opposition of pertinent features.") Fontaine's escape from the German prison, the manifest struggle for freedom in the world, is doubled by a spiritual determinism, for it is grace that allows him to overcome his captors. This opposition, a paradox in the eyes of the world, gives rise to secondary oppositions that both inform the narrative and generate secondary levels of meaning. For example, Fontaine struggles in prison to vanquish isolation and to achieve fraternal communion. This opposition derives its full meaning from its relationship to the religious drama, especially insofar as this opposition is part of the religious paradox: The prison actually allows these prisoners to overcome isolation and to enter into true communion. To give another pointed opposition, one might consider the relation between the material presence of evil and the despair to which it might lead, on one hand, and, on the other hand, the seemingly gratuitous faith that never abandons the hero, a paradox that is expressed existentially as a constant leap of faith.[5]

The film's narrative project is thus grounded in a rhythm that alternately turns on solitude and communion, the absurd and faith, and freedom and grace, in a series of related oppositions that endow all elements in the film with meaning. The first shots presenting Fontaine, detached from his fellow prisoners after he has been captured, begin the presentation of solitude, for he then attempts to escape alone from the automobile that is taking him and another prisoner to Montluc. He is recaptured, though the camera here emphasizes how little importance his physical flight has by refusing to follow him as he tries to flee. Fontaine is then handcuffed and struck with a revolver by an anonymous agent; the dull thud of the blow reveals how evil must be born concretely in the presence of flesh. Bresson pursues this descent into evil and isolation in the next series of shots, which suggest that Fontaine undergoes the solitude of the Passion. Fontaine is spat upon by passersby and, as the following ellipsis suggests, beaten by his captors. Isolation is thus lived as degradation of the flesh, though, as the comparison with the Passion reveals, this is the converse of the absent dream of grace and communion.

Isolation and evil, those absurd absolutes, give way in narrative rhythm to Fontaine's first leap of faith, when he chooses to trust Terry, one of the men he sees walking in the courtyard, with the urgent message to the Resistance about his arrest and the Germans having seized their radio code. This leap of faith finds its complementary expression in the grace that allows Terry to bring Fontaine a pencil and paper; both Terry's act and the items he brings make possible the communion that might overcome the isolation imposed by prison walls. Communion as a transcending of the walls is realized paradoxically, in fact, when Fontaine uses the wall that separates him from a neighbouring prisoner as a means of communication. They tap out messages to each other, and when the other prisoner tells Fontaine how to remove his handcuffs, we see clearly that communion, faith, and, as shown in this image, freedom are bound together as the constants that inform the narrative's structure.

The narrative rhythm takes Fontaine back to solitude when he is moved to a cell on the top floor of the prison. His only neighbor here is Blanchet, the epitome of a man defeated by an absurd imprisonment and thus incapable, for the moment, of any kind of transcending communion. It is here that we see Fontaine closest to despair, as he speaks of his "frightening solitude." But it is also at this moment that we first see Fontaine and the other prisoners go down into the courtyard where, joined in their common humiliation, they enter into a silent communion as they empty their slop buckets. As the men go to gather up their pails, a brief chord from Mozart's Mass in C Minor stands in counterpoint to their abjection. In one respect, the music endows this humiliating routine with the solemnity of a religious service; at the same time, it recalls that the men's degradation, in spite of the daily drudgery that numbs the flesh and weakens the will, is the converse of the spiritual drama that stands behind every act. The music opens here onto the world of transcendence that stands in opposition to the material world of a drama that seemingly warrants only despair.

Mozart and the cesspool, like fraternity and torture, are two poles that structure Bresson's narrative project throughout the rest of the film. Equally important from this point in the narration until the end are the related poles of despair and lack of communion, on the one hand, and faith and willed action, on the other. Fontaine begins to use a spoon to remove fragments of wood from his cell door, a task demanding that he carefully dig away minute splinters, but also showing that he has assumed responsibility for his freedom. In opposition to this act of faith stands his neighbour's silence, the negation of communion, as well as the message given to him that Terry will be taken away and the news he receives of the condemnation of another prisoner. In existential terms, Fontaine has assumed his freedom, and by this act he has demanded the freedom of all men. In ethical terms, he has made freedom the universal value that vouchsafes all human activity. Though Blanchet quite correctly perceives that Fontaine's resistance could result in the punishment of all, Fontaine's continued affirmation slowly brings Blanchet out of his despair, for it opens a realm of future possibility in which Blanchet might again claim his dignity as a man and his worthiness as a self.

In religious terms, this affirmation is a paradox, recalling Kierkegaard's statement that faith surely implies an act of the will—even if grace be the most unmerited of gifts. This opposition of will and grace stands behind the scene in which Fontaine, now needing another spoon to finish dismantling the door, converses with the Pastor, who informs him that thanks to a miracle he has received a much-wanted Bible. Fontaine seems to know his own miracle of grace when he finds a much-needed second spoon lying on a ledge in the washroom. Yet this demonstration of grace is also a demonstration of Fontaine's determination to seize every available opportunity to continue his escape attempt, as Fontaine himself suggests when he later tells the Pastor, with a tone of remonstrance, that it would be all too easy if one were to let God take care of everything. Perhaps there is no way to resolve this paradox of freedom and grace, for, to borrow again from Kierkegaard, the man of faith is in such a relation to the absolute that nothing can mediate it. Freedom and providence stand semantically in opposition, and perhaps the great power of this film lies precisely in its power to maintain this opposition while showing how in Fontaine they are two manifestations of the drama of faith.

At this point the film's rhythm leads again to communion, for, having broken the door open, Fontaine can go into the corridor at night and bring a word of hope to a prisoner who has been permanently confined to his cell. The dialectic of communion and solitude then leads to destruction, for Orsini, the prisoner with the burning, sincere eyes, who has also been transformed by his contact with Fontaine, attempts to escape but is captured and executed. But now even Blanchet can see that the web of evil and grace is somehow connected, for it is Blanchet who tells Fontaine that Orsini had to fail so that through his failure he could tell Fontaine what he needs to get over the wall.

The final rhythm of this film is largely shaped by a series of leaps of faith, and by leap of faith we mean the Christian existentialist notion of an active affirmation of faith in the face of the absurd. For instance, Fontaine refuses to turn over a pencil he has, even though he can be punished by death if his captors find it. The absurdity of his act astonishes him, and yet Fontaine knows that this is another affirmation of faith and will. Even more important in this regard, once Fontaine has learned that he will soon be executed, is the arrival in his cell of Jost, the adolescent prisoner who has already become a traitor by volunteering for military service with the Germans. Bresson multiplies signs that point to Jost's being a potential

German agent, for he alone talks to the German guard, and he admits that he thinks the Germans will win the war. Moreover, in a striking series of poses in the washroom, Fontaine's friends hover about Fontaine to warn him to beware of the boy. Communion, in the sense of the most elementary trust, between these two prisoners can only be a leap of faith. The paradox of faith is made even more complex in this instance, for, having revealed his plans for escape, Fontaine finds himself obliged to consider killing this child to preserve his own struggle against evil. Fontaine's unswerving faith thus leads him to the extreme situation where faith appears to resemble the evil that it strives to overcome.

The escape itself is the final leap of faith. It hardly seems an exaggeration to say that the physical leaps the two prisoners undertake are so many material analogues doubling the existential leap itself. This seems especially true of the final, determined jump; Fontaine hurls himself into space, sustained only by his improvised rope, as he goes from the inner to the outer wall. The leap triumphs over the absurd presence of evil as embodied in the wall, and it is a leap achieved through the fraternal communion that the two men have come to know. Jost's presence is a mark of grace, for it is only through his help that Fontaine, too weak to scale the final wall alone, can succeed.

The leap of faith here achieves that communion that few of Bresson's characters succeed in knowing, though for nearly all of them some form of human community would be a sign to the viewer of grace and salvation. In this respect one might consider how the religious community of *Les Anges du péché*, Bresson's first major film, expels Anne-Marie during her novitiate. The expelling in turn leads to her sickness and death as she seeks to maintain furtive ties with the convent. Perhaps even more exemplary is Bresson's country priest in *Journal d'un curé de campagne*. He is isolated, scorned, and humiliated in the provincial community for which he should be the centre of communion in every sense of the term. Like Anne-Marie, he finds transcendence only in death, though it is an isolated death born of sickness. For Bresson's heroes often live their estrangement as a form of humiliation of the body, as we see when his Mouchette finds her only human contact by being raped. She is so isolated that only in this violation of her flesh does she seem to find a moment of paradoxical communion, though this is only a prelude to her final despair and suicide. In nearly all his works, be it *Au hasard Balthazar*, *Jeanne d'Arc*, *Pickpocket*, or *Une femme douce*, Bresson's narrative turns in one way or another on isolation and humiliation, on estrangement and the impossibility of a desired community. Only in *Un condamné à mort* does transcendence seem to be realized in the flesh.

This discussion of the cultural oppositions that endow the narrative with significance allows us in turn to see how each individual element in *Un condamné à mort* acquires meaning within the semanticizing context provided by the narrative. Let us consider in greater detail Bresson's use of music, in this case Mozart's

Mass in C Minor. On the level of immediate presence, the mass is present as a work of music and thus has meaning in terms of its own conventions and cultural codes. The naive viewer may, in fact, perceive this music only as a bit of *fioritura*, especially if he is accustomed to the standard filmic code by which film music often functions as a redundant marker, duplicating other elements of meaning within a shot or a scene. One will recall that in Bresson's film a chord or two of the mass recurs periodically, when the prisoners go down into the courtyard to empty their slop buckets or at the end of the film when Fontaine and Jost escape into the night. The music thus sounds at those moments when men find themselves together. Through this recurrence the narrative project appropriates the music and converts it into a signifier that has both its intrinsic meaning and a special meaning grounded in the filmic context. In *Un condamné à mort* the narrative principle of absence-presence specifically causes the music to signify the absent spiritual drama of communion that stands in opposition to the present drama of absurd degradation.

The religious drama of spiritual elevation is thus signified as doubling—though absent in physical terms—the action that we see on the screen. This oppositional relationship endows the music with a semantic dimension that is predicated on the music's intrinsic meaning but that fully exists only so far as the music is integrated into the narrative whole. Moreover, the music takes on full meaning only so far as it functions, if we may borrow a category from linguistics, as a paradigmatic option. Mozart's Mass stands, in other terms, in opposition to all other kinds of music that Bresson might have used, a patriotic piece or some kind of music signifying emotional distress. More importantly, it stands in opposition to the silence that exists most of the time. With no undue paradox we might say that it is the opposition between music and silence that endows silence with a semantic dimension, for in this context it comes to signify the absence of that revelation that the music offers. In a similar vein, the variety of natural sounds that Bresson uses on his soundtrack, such as the sound of a train whistle coming from beyond the walls, enter into a relationship with the silence and come not only to denote their source, but also to signify a transcendent world beyond the walls, an absent world that is the object of faith.

Another feature of the projected world for which it is difficult to find appropriate critical categories is the composition of this world achieved through lighting and the use of volumes, or, in other terms, the fact that the plastic values of Bresson's shots acquire meaning. Of course, the very fact that we perceive a projected world as being invested with these values indicates that some kind of fundamental conversion of the projected world has taken place. In theoretical terms, I should again maintain that it is primarily the narrative project that allows the viewer to see that a signifying intention lies behind framing, lighting, or composition, and that this transforming intentionality in turn allows the viewer to read these properties in function of the narrative context. It is again the narrative context that endows these purely "cinematic" elements (pure because they belong neither to the world nor to language) with semantic depth.

Bresson's composition of shots in *Un condamné à mort*, as in other of his works, is a more complex matter than in the case of many other directors, since he often draws upon well-known pictorial models. Like his use of music, then, his compositional values possess a semantic dimension that pre-exists the filmic context. The tensions Bresson creates between light and shadow in Fontaine's cell, the modelling he does with light volumes, are often based, for example, on the representational codes elaborated by baroque painters like Georges de la Tour or Philippe de Champaigne. The tension that exists between light and dark is thus already codified, for it designates a semantic space created by the opposition of flesh and spirit, free will and grace, or human and divine. The baroque code pre-exists the filmic context but is in turn appropriated by the film's action and integrated into the semantic whole. The film's primary narrative opposition of visible-invisible can thus appropriate the pictorial representational code and endow it with connotative values that are grounded in the film's narrative project.

Compositional values function, then, at several levels. They most immediately make up part of the image that sets forth the narration in its physical presence; at the same time, they signify through their own pictorial codes and through their being appropriated by the narration and given connotative values in the filmic context. Consider, for example, the shots near the end of *Un condamné à mort* when Jost and Fontaine climb through the skylight and edge along the prison roof, slowly making their way toward the precipice they must descend. The contrast between light and dark, in which Fontaine's face emerges intensely from the shadows, seems to suggest connotatively the spiritual drama of the escape while it also stresses the physiological tension caused by this nearly impossible enterprise. Moreover, the contrast portrays, in baroque terms, the drama between human will and destiny, in which man must triumph over darkness as he confronts the unknown in an unstable world. Fontaine does this literally when, after the descent, he enters the darkness and kills the German soldier who is standing guard. This baroque representational value comes to signify the specifically Christian drama that the film narrates, and in this context the light and darkness are physical analogues for the drama of the visible and the invisible, the present and the absent, that underlies the film's narration. These levels are, of course, integrated into one mimetic whole in which the prisoners' progress is as much progress toward physical liberation as it is a defeat of the darkness and an arrival at the final communion.

The same kind of considerations we have given to compositional values can be given to Bresson's use of framing and the field size of his shots. The close-up, for example, functions paradigmatically in opposition to the four or five other options the filmmaker has when choosing field size. A great deal of discussion has been given to the meaning of a close-up, but it seems adequate to say that, according to standard film convention, it is most often used to designate a moment of psychological intensity or to signify a revelation. It stands, then, in opposition to the normal narrative shot, and its meaning is generated precisely by this opposition. Bresson, however, uses the close-up as his standard shot in *Un condamné à mort*. As Fontaine spends hours, for example, using a spoon to carve away the wood of his cell door, Bresson shows the prisoner's perseverance by means of a series of insistent close-up shots concentrating on the prisoner's hands, the spoon, and the wood. This deviation from standard film convention can be explained only if it can be integrated into the semantic totality generated by the narrative project, which is to say that the viewer must read this use of the close-up as the expression of an aesthetic intentionality that gives rise to a new filmic code. Within the specific context of *Un condamné à mort*, it is apparent that this use of the close-up presupposes the conventional use, for by making the close-up his standard shot Bresson is showing how revelation springs from the most minute acts and how every gesture Fontaine undertakes as he cuts away the wood is an intense expression of will. The close-up as Bresson uses it can thus become the standard shot for advancing the narrative at the same time it recalls, through its intensity, that there are no indifferent acts in the material world of the narration. Every act, even the most repetitive, routine gesture, betrays the invisible drama of grace.

Bresson has been called the most elliptical director in film history, and it is true that his use of ellipsis provides another example of how Bresson converts standard signifying elements of film discourse into a new filmic code. Ellipses are usually part of what one might call a secondary narrative code in that they denote an absent element of episodic experience, and standard film codification usually designates them by a dissolve. But consider the series of shots that begin with Fontaine's being recaptured, brought to the prison for the first time, pushed into a room in which we see, through the open door, a row of shovels, and then . . . and then nothing, for Bresson interrupts the action with a dissolve before showing Fontaine transported to his cell on a stretcher. On a first viewing this ellipsis can be very disconcerting, for the adventure-film genre that seems to inform the film would call for a direct confrontation between the hero and his captors, between the good and evil whose opposition serves to generate narrative meaning.

In *Un condamné à mort*, however, it is evident that the ellipsis is not simply used to designate economically some bit of episodic experience or to bring about dramatic concentration. Since the narration is as much informed by what is absent as by what is present, by the invisible world of grace as by the present material world, the ellipsis can be read as a connotative signifier, referring to the absent world that informs the unfolding narrative. The ellipsis opens onto the invisible. This original use of ellipsis allows readings such as Peter Schofer's: "In seeing black, in seeing non-action, and inhuman nothingness, we enter Fontaine's world; we transcend the physical and participate in Fontaine's unconsciousness."[6] It is not the physical contact between the prisoner and his torturers that is of the greatest import, and the ellipsis signifies that this cruel moment itself must be seen as referring to another drama, the drama of grace in which Fontaine, perhaps unconsciously, must hold onto his faith in the face of the absurd.

Bresson has disturbed more than one critic—most notably André Bazin—by his use of a spoken text or commentary that, in accompanying the image, often seems to be a redundant element offering a kind of semantic duplication.[7] Or perhaps one might say that Bresson seems to take pleasure in violating that canon of prescriptive film theory that requires that the image should have the primary responsibility for meaning in film. The origin of this prescriptive rule concerning the genesis of meaning dates back to the beginning of the use of sound in film. However, as several decades of successful films should have demonstrated, there appears to be no a priori reason why a film should not integrate an overlaid spoken text into its semantic structures.

It is a dubious proposition, in fact, that text or image can ever be in any real sense redundant, since their juxtaposition within a narrative context would appear to semanticize them in ways that go beyond either's meaning when considered alone. In *Un condamné à mort*, for example, when Fontaine is thrown into his cell and is then shown trying to pull himself together, his overlaid voice tells us, "Nothing broken, but I must not have been a pretty sight to see." The shot presenting Fontaine with torn clothes and a bloodcovered face does, indeed, show that he is not a pretty sight to see. And if the viewer understands the spoken text as a mere interpretative commentary on the image, without considering their juxtaposition in the narrative context, then it might be taken to be redundant.

Yet this way of considering the spoken text hardly takes account of the way it functions within the specific context. Fontaine's spoken text is in the past tense. By its juxtaposition with the image it thus tells the viewer that the present image he sees designates a narrative past. It endows the image with a dimension of total completion or "pastness." This paradigmatic opposition of past-present is in turn appropriated by the film's primary narrative opposition of absence-presence. The voice, speaking from a present moment—since the act of enunciation can only occur in the present—thus signifies the presence of the word and the absence of the visual world or what we have called the material world of the physical narrative. We again confront a religious paradox, for the speaking voice essentially designates the pastness and thus the absence of what seems most physically present. The spoken word implies, then, the primacy of the absent spiritual drama, for the truly present drama is embodied in the word, and by *word* we might well understand the logos or Verb that reveals grace.

In conclusion, then, we might say that Bresson has informed his narrative by exploiting the ontological properties of the different elements of filmic discourse, for speech and image are not the same in this respect. Though present in a material sense, as a projection, the image signifies an absent world; the present instance of speech tells us the world is not only absent, but also in time past. The spoken word, even when recorded and mechanically reproduced, always surges forth as a present and, unlike the projected image, is as ontologically complete in its presence as if it were actually spoken. The full presence of the spoken word becomes significant, of course, only in the specific context of the narrative opposition of presence-absence that informs *Un condamné à mort*. In this context, Fontaine's speaking voice is semanticized in a way that has nothing to do with the immanent meaning of his words. The present voice of the absent speaker designates that locus of eternal presence, beyond the world, from whose vantage point the unfolding of *Un condamné à mort* can be seen as the work of the divine providence that has ordered the narrative. It is through such an understanding of film that Bresson has created one of the few truly Christian films that exist, and certainly no other film testifies so elegantly to the paradoxes of Christian existentialism.

Notes

1. Stanley Cavell, *The World Viewed: Reflections on the Ontology of Film*, pp. 24, 72.
2. Robert Bresson, *Notes sur le cinématographe*, pp. 17-18. (All translations are mine, unless otherwise indicated.)
3. Bresson, *Notes sur le cinématographe*, p. 78.
4. For a definition of the notion of codes, see Umberto Eco, *A Theory of Semiotics*. "One can then maintain that it is not true that a code organizes signs; it is more correct to say that codes provide the rules which *generate* signs as concrete occurrences in communicative intercourse" (p. 49).
5. Most of my references to Kierkegaard are drawn from *Fear and Trembling* and *Sickness unto Death*, as well as the *Journals*.
6. Peter Schofer, "Dissolution into Darkness: Bresson's *Un condamné à mort s'est échappé*," *Sub-Stance*, no. 9 (1974): p. 60.
7. André Bazin, "The Stylistics of Robert Bresson," in his *What is Cinema?*, trans. Hugh Gray (Berkeley: University of California Press, 1967), pp. 125-43.

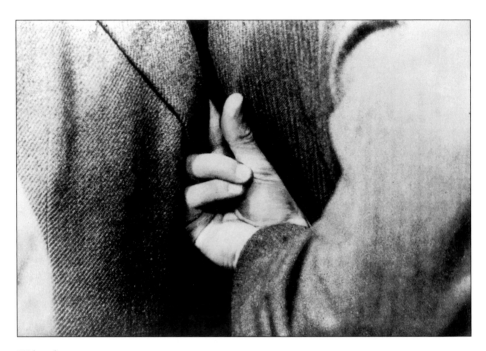

Pickpocket

Picking Dostoevsky's Pocket: Bresson's Sl(e)ight of Screen

> They want to find the solution where all is enigma only.
>
> — PASCAL, in Bresson, *Notes sur le cinématographe*

> Hide the ideas, but so that people find them.
> The most important will be the most hidden.
>
> — BRESSON, *Notes sur le cinématographe*

Like his contemporary Eric Rohmer, Robert Bresson has been called a Jansenist, and this by none other than Jean-Luc Godard.[1] But if the label has some usefulness in assessing the place of Pascal in Rohmer's work, it seems to serve more as an easy "solution" to Bresson's "enigma" than as a real hermeneutic strategy.[2] Bresson's own allusion to Pascal in his *Notes sur le cinématographe*, when juxtaposed to the more playful hide-and-seek attitude toward ideas in his films, seems more coy than transcendent.[3] The "purloined letter" effect may indeed be a better critical tack than Jansenist labelling when one is confronted with the deliberately enigmatic quality of Bresson's style, for his films are so constructed as to appear nearly invisible at first viewing and require an unusual effort of reconstruction for any satisfactory comprehension. The *cinematograph*, as Bresson was to label his work, is difficult to see precisely because its author conceived it against all of the norms of classical cinema. In reintroducing the normally dropped syllable *graph*, Bresson accentuated cinema writing (*écriture*) at the expense of *mise en scène*. "CINEMATOGRAPHY ['LE CINEMATOGRAPHE'] IS A WRITING ['UNE ECRITURE'],￼" Bresson writes, "WITH IMAGES IN MOVEMENT AND WITH SOUNDS" (NC, 2/12). Although this definition seems anodyne at first glance, its implications are far from insignificant. The first corollary of the theorem is: "A film cannot be a stage show ['un spectacle']" (NC, 3/12). And insistence on the unspectacular nature of the cinematograph led immediately to a second corollary: "An actor in cinematography might as well be in a foreign country. He does not speak its language ['Un acteur est dans le cinématographe comme dans un pays étranger. Il n'en parle pas la langue']" (NC, 3/13).

Pickpocket constitutes a perfect emblem of Bresson's entire project: its very title is a foreign word, isolated from definite or indefinite article, ambiguous. That ambiguity is to remain in force throughout the film. Indeed, it was not only Bresson's actor who was to feel like a stranger in the world of his film: often his collaborators felt as much "in the dark" as his actors and critics. Léonce-Henry Burel, Bresson's cameraman for *Pickpocket*, was to say later, "I didn't understand what he was trying to say. As a matter of fact I don't think anybody has ever understood, really. Who is this pickpocket, why does he steal and so on?"[4]

Analysis of the opening sequence of the film immediately suggests the degree of difficulty that faces us as viewers. Following the title of the film, Bresson addresses a caveat to his viewer: "The style of this film is not a thriller. The author attempts to explain in pictures and sounds the nightmare of a young man forced by his weakness into an adventure in theft for which he was not made. Yet this adventure, by strange paths, brings together two souls which might otherwise never have been united." The French term for such a text is *prière d'insérer*; a technique belonging to a long literary tradition of confessional literature, including not only Montaigne and Rousseau but numerous eighteenth-century novelists, of orienting the reader's attention in a particular way. It must be noted that this tradition includes a subtradition of subversion: modern examples of this technique are more often traps for the unsuspecting reader than sincere helps to the reader's progress.[5] In this particular case, a reading of the film's "plot" has been offered that will conflict with the visual evidence to be presented. The immediate effect of this notice, however, is of distanciation: the lowering of expectations of genre (the word "style" substituted for "genre" is, I would contend, a most revealing substitution, for it is Bresson's style itself that undermines the expectations of the genre), the destruction of suspense by revealing the general outcome of the story, and the insistence on the *explanatory* nature of the work all contribute to a flattening of the viewer's emotion.[6] The very substitution of a *text* for *images* is itself a sign of Bresson's insistence on cinema writing. The titles and credits that follow this announcement themselves constitute a throwback to a style adopted at the outset of the movies and seem consciously to reject years of evolving techniques in presenting credits. In and of themselves they function as a rejection of an entire tradition of cinema and announce a return to origins.

Pickpocket's first image offers little relief from this insistence on *écriture*. We see a close-up of a hand (with no identification of its "owner") writing what is clearly a diary or journal entry: "I know that normally those who have committed crimes don't talk about them or that those who talk about such things haven't done them. And yet I have done these things ['je les ai faites']." This image is accompanied by a voice-off, establishing a narrative voice for the film that is to recur at regular intervals some sixty times in the film, four times accompanied by an image of journal writing. Although there is generally little carry-over from film to film in Bresson's works, the image of the journal writing accompanied by voice-over narration immediately evokes its homologue in *Journal d'un curé de campagne*. In both works the image of the journal produces a complex and often ambiguous effect, establishing simultaneously a link with and a break from traditional literary technique. As Nick Browne has pointed out in an essay on Bresson's *Journal d'un curé de campagne*: "Text is neither a simple commentary on the image, nor is image a simple illustration of the text. Disjunction, independence, interrogation, and even negation of the image, by the sense of the text, is as much a feature as illustration or duplication."[7]

One of the immediate ambiguities, as Browne points out, is that between past and present narration.[8] Although a journal normally suggests events that have already taken place recollected in a meditative spirit, in *Pickpocket* Bresson's camera catches the as yet unidentified hand in the present act of writing. The past tense employed in the journal writing contrasts actively with the present tense of the camera, creating a tension between *knowledge* and *perception* that constantly disturbs our ability to trust the narrator. That is, the journal entry itself ("je les ai faites") implies a knowledge of the events of the whole film that seems to be negated by our perception that the journal writing occurs in the same chronological period as the other events pictured, a fact reinforced by three other journal "entries" that occur in the present tense of the film. At the very least the *place* of the narrator becomes highly suspect. That suspicion invades at least one other level of the film. At numerous times the voice-over narrator will actively mislead the viewer, stating attitudes or facts that are directly or implicitly contradicted by the images we see.[9]

Now, because the journal writer's activity is exactly parallel to the inscription, or *prière d'insérer*, that opens the film, the narrator's and the "image maker"'s activities are implicitly associated.[10] If the narrator becomes discredited, there is at least a suspicion that this unreliability extends to the image maker himself. By extension, writing itself comes to be put into question in ways that will have a profound effect on our understanding of the film.

Bresson moves from this highly problematic view of textuality to yet another image, which, because of his editing, further complicates our understanding. The close-up of the hand writing the journal dissolves into a close-up of another disembodied hand, this one female, holding a sheaf of hundred-franc notes. There is at least a suggestion that writing and money will occupy similar positions in the universe of this film. This seems all the more likely inasmuch as the editing of the entire first sequence leaves the viewer caught entirely off guard. Bresson's camera focuses on various people in a crowd without identifying either the locale or any figure with whom the viewer may identify. Finally, the words (*off*) "For several days my decision has been made. But will I have the courage?" coincide with the camera's frontal view of Martin Lassalle. Yet he is so expressionless as to resist our attention and only retains it because of the series of looks exchanged with others in the crowd.[11] He turns, and the camera follows him from behind as he trails a mass of people (toward what end?) and stops, as they stop, finding himself directly behind a woman in a large-brimmed white hat. Now as the character Michel faces the camera, the voice-off narrator (in reality, Michel's disembodied voice) says without a trace of emotion, "I should have just left ['J'aurais mieux fait de m'en aller']." The camera and editing now shift repeatedly from the actor's expressionless eyes to his hand as it slowly moves to unhitch the clasp of her alligator purse and removes another sheaf of French francs. The click of the clasp is immediately followed by the only facial expression Lassalle is to provide in the entire film: a wincing of his eyes, which has an almost orgiastic effect in the bleak facial desert of his expression. The hand movement and eye movement are accompanied by the sound of horses' hooves galloping by. We are at the Longchamp racetrack. Michel is a pickpocket.

The camera next follows Michel through the crowd, past some iron gates onto a wide alleyway, at which point he drones, "I was walking on air. I had conquered the world. But a minute later I was arrested ['Je n'avais plus les pieds sur terre. Je dominais le monde. Mais une minute après, j'étais pris']." But we do not see him taken; we see only two men walking behind him. A cut places Michel between two men in an automobile, and another cut places him (presumably) in the police station, where a detective is concluding their encounter with the words, "You're free to go ['Vous êtes libre']." Michel's eyes move to the sheaf of francs on the inspector's desk. The inspector hands him the money, and he stands as if to leave.

Bresson's camera work and editing in this sequence produce an effect of strangeness. On the one hand, with but three exceptions, the images we are privileged to see are virtually devoid of informational content (the three exceptions being the three images of money). On the other hand, again with those exceptions, the *actions* announced are not shown. Repeated viewings of this sequence lead to the impression that what Bresson has included in his film are those images that are normally consigned to the cutting-room floor. We do not see the horses racing. We do not witness the arrest of Michel. We do not hear the conversation between Michel and his captor. We experience only the transitions *between* those actions announced by the narrative voice-over. It is almost as though we were reading a sentence from which all of the adjectives and most of the substantives had been removed, leaving only prepositions and conjunctions.

As Alan Williams has noted, classic Hollywood cinema developed a "grammar" that was dedicated to making what is in fact an ontologically discontinuous art form appear seamless.[12] Through careful editing of transitions, classic directors succeeded in minimizing the gaps between shots and scenes, artfully removing "unnecessary" transitions by a montage of actions that appeared to bridge those transitions. Such a grammar of continuity allowed film to concentrate on the significant actions and manage an economy of gesture without any apparent discontinuity of movement. Bresson's work, on the other hand, and *Pickpocket* in particular, seems dedicated to maximizing our sense of discontinuity. This is reflected not only in this first sequence but in many others as well. The most remarkable of these discontinuities occurs in the sequence when Michel accompanies Jacques and Jeanne to an amusement park. The scene begins with an invitation from Jacques, who stands at Michel's door. A cut to Jeanne outside is followed by a dissolve to the three friends sitting at a café table. Jacques says to Michel, "You're sad ['Vous êtes triste']." Michel responds, "Non." Whereupon Jacques accuses him, "You're not really living. You're not interested in the things others are ['Vous n'êtes pas dans la vie réelle. Vous ne vous interessez à rien qui intéresse les autres']."[13] Jacques and Jeanne rise from their seats, and Jacques asks, "Are you coming? We're going to take a plane ride." (A curious juxtaposition with the accusation just levelled.)[14] Bresson's camera focuses on Michel sitting alone at the table. Michel stands. Bresson's camera fails to follow Michel and instead remains trained on the empty table. A dissolve moves us away from and back to the empty table, undoubtedly to indicate some passage of time. Another dissolve moves us to an empty staircase. Michel passes through the frame and enters his room, cloaked in shadows. He leans over a pitcher in the corner, produces a handkerchief, and wipes blood off his hand. "I had run and fallen ['J'avais couru. J'étais tombé']," the narrator's voice-over informs us. Later we are to "learn" that Michel has apparently stolen a watch and/or encountered some violent adventure during the time Bresson's camera and editing have been riveted on the empty café table. The connecting pieces are again displayed in place of actions normally considered worthy of the viewer's attention. Again we are compelled to accept Bresson's substitution of the voice-over narrative account for visual proof. Inasmuch as the voice "belongs" to Michel, and inasmuch as he has much to hide in this film, we are entitled to doubt what we hear.

Both of these sequences illustrate a shift of emphasis in Bresson's new *cinematograph* away from the image whose value normally derives from its power of representation to images and sounds that have a purportedly neutral value and are meant to function merely as elements in a relational system.[15] Although Bresson never mentions his work directly, Saussure's linguistic theory underlies this new language of film. Bresson prescribed a

> cinematographic film, where expression is obtained by relations of images and of sounds, and not by a mimicry done with gestures and intonations of voice. . . .

One that does not analyze or explain. That *recomposes*. . . . An image must be transformed by contact with other images, as is a color by contact with other colors. . . . No art without transformation. . . . Cinematographic film, where the images, like the words in a dictionary, have no power and value except through their position and relation. . . . No absolute value in an image. Images and sounds will owe their value and their power solely to the use to which you destine them. . . . IN THIS LANGUAGE OF IMAGES, ONE MUST LOSE COMPLETELY THE NOTION OF IMAGE. THE IMAGES MUST EXCLUDE THE IDEA OF IMAGE. (NC, 5/16, 5/17, 11/28, 33/71)

Reference to Saussure's theory of linguistic value will help clarify the radical nature of what Bresson is proposing here. In his *Course in General Linguistics*, the Swiss linguist proposed that given the arbitrary nature of the sign, individual units of language had no intrinsic value. "Language," he proposed,

is a system of interdependent terms in which the value of each term results solely from the simultaneous presence of the others. . . . All values are apparently governed by the same paradoxical principle. They are always composed: (1) of a *dissimilar* thing that can be *exchanged* for the thing of which the value is to be determined; and (2) of *similar* things that can be *compared* with the thing of which the value is to be determined. Both factors are necessary for the existence of a value. A word's content is really fixed only by the concurrence of everything that exists outside it. . . . The value of any term is accordingly determined by its environment. . . . Concepts as well are purely differential and defined not by their positive content but negatively by their relations with the other terms of the system. Their most precise characteristic is in being what the others are not.[16]

It suffices to substitute "image" for "word" or "phoneme" to understand how neutral Bresson would like his image to be: "*Images* (phonemes) are characterized not, as one might think, by their own positive quality but simply by the fact that they are distinct. *Images* (phonemes) are above all else opposing, relative and negative entities. . . . In language there are only differences . . . *without positive terms*. The idea or substance that an *image* (sign) contains is of less importance than the other signs that surround it. Proof of this is that the value of a term may be modified without either its meaning or its sound being affected, solely because a neighboring term has been modified."[17]

Bresson is explicit in his substitution of *image* for *word*: "The most ordinary word, when put into place, suddenly acquires brilliance ['éclat']. That is the brilliance with which your images must shine" (NC, 56/116). And he adds, "See your film as a combination of lines and of volumes in movement apart from what it represents ['figure'] and signifies. . . . To move people ['émouvoir'] not with images likely to move us ['images émouvantes'], but with relations of images that render them both alive and moving ['des rapports d'images qui les rendent à la fois vivantes et émouvantes']" (NC, 44/92, 43/90). The implications of this attempt to neutralize the value of the image become clear in the following passage from Saussure: "The value of any term is accordingly determined by its environment; it is impossible to fix even the value of the word signifying 'sun' without first considering its surroundings: in some languages it is not possible to say 'sit in the sun.' . . . If words stood for pre-existing concepts, they would all have exact equivalents in meaning from one language to the next; but this is not true."[18]

No one doubts the cultural value that can be attached to images, for every civilization has its own particular icons of beauty. Nor can we forget the experiments in image contexture carried out by the Russian director Kuleshov demonstrating that the same photograph of an expressionless face could be "read" as happy or sad according to the surrounding images.[19] Bresson seems intent, however, on moving beyond these positions to a notion, borrowed from Saussurean linguistics, of the absolutely arbitrary nature of the image. Such a move goes counter to everything we know about the ontology of the photographic image, of course.[20] Because the camera replicates exactly the reality that stands before it, it has an iconic value that is lacking to the word. And yet, consistently to deprive individual images of their normal narrational and/or cultural contexts, as Bresson has consistently attempted to do, has a *transgressive* function that cannot be denied. "Cinematography," insists Bresson almost doggedly, "the art, with images, of *representing* nothing ['de ne rien représenter']" (NC, 59/120). Representation, in other words, is nothing but repetition; presentation, by contrast, is the essence of creativity. The "image orderer," as Bresson prefers to call the director, thus becomes a kind of god. "Cutting ['Montage']. Passage of dead images to living images. Everything blossoms afresh ['Tout refleurit']" (NC, 43/91). Out of dead, flat images, new life is given by the particular combinations dictated by the image maker. "An old thing becomes new if you detach it from what usually surrounds it" (NC, 26/57). However much this may sound like Proust's writing on the nefarious effects of "habitude," Bresson's application of the theory seems entirely antithetical to Proust's. The filmmaker's emphasis on "dead" and "flattened" images (as opposed to Proust's metaphors) will likely strike the filmgoer at first viewing as, in fact, deadening—mere absences, such as the café table from which Michel's absence is the only justification for the presence of the image.

The implications of this theory for the actor are no less severe. Indeed, Bresson excised the very word "actor" from his working vocabulary and substituted the word "model" in order to eliminate any possible "pollution" from "the terrible habit of theater" (NC, 2/12):

The truth of cinematography ["Le vrai du cinématographe"] cannot be the truth of theater. . . . Nothing rings more false in a film than that natural tone of the theater copying life and traced ["calqué"] over studied sentiments. . . . The photographed theater or CINEMA requires a *metteur-en-scène* or director to make some actors perform a play and to photograph these actors performing the play; afterwards he lines up the images. Bastard theater lacking what makes theater: material presence of living actors, direct action of the audience on the actors. (NC, 3-4/13-14, 5/16)

Like his attempt to "neutralize" the image, Bresson's attempts to "detoxify" his models of any theatricality is by now legendary. His theory of the "model" culled from his *Notes sur le cinématographe* can be synthesized as follows:

No actors.
(No directing of actors.)
No parts ["rôles"].
(No learning of parts.)
No staging ["mise en scène"].
But the use of working models, taken from life ["modèles, pris dans la vie"].
BEING ["etre"] (models) instead of SEEMING ["PARAITRE"] (actors). . . .
Model. Reduce to the minimum the share his consciousness has ["Réduire au minimum la part de sa conscience"]. Tighten the meshing ["l'engrenage"] within which he cannot any longer not be him and where he can now do nothing that is not *useful*. . . . Model. Preserved from any obligation towards the art of drama. . . . To your models: "One must not act either somebody else or oneself. One must not act anybody ['Il ne faut jouer personne']."(NC, 1/10, 26/58, 29/63, 31/67)

This effectively *absent presence* was to be accomplished by a rigorous training requiring repetition of the model's lines until all theatricality had been eliminated.[21]

Your models, pitched ["lâchés"] into the action of your film, will get used to the gestures they have repeated twenty times ["les apprivoiseront à eux"]. The words they have learned with their lips ["apprises du bout des lèvres"] will find, *without their minds' taking part in this*, the inflections and the lilt ["la chanson"] proper to their true natures. A way of recovering the automatism of real life. (NC, 32/70)

Thus the model was to become a kind of blank that, like the other images in Bresson's creation, would draw its meaning from its juxtaposition. . . with other images:

A model. Enclosed in his mysterious appearance. He has brought home to him ["ramené à lui"] all of him that was. He is there, behind that forehead, those cheeks. . . . Over his features, thoughts outside or feelings not materially expressed, rendered *visible* by intercommunication and interaction of two or several other images. (NC, 7/21, 22/50)

In the sequences from *Pickpocket* we have just discussed, it is clear that Bresson has achieved the unexpressive facial image in at least two different ways: first he has expanded the role of voice-over narration, removing from his protagonist the need to appear to speak, thus minimizing the facial movement that occurs in reaction to one's own discourse; second, he has instructed Martin Lassalle to avoid all facial play. Thus the only life that seems to occur is the montage of glances from one character to another.

Further, in order to keep the presence of the model as neutral an image as possible, Bresson worked to ensure that his models, both male and female, would be as "virginal" as possible. This meant, among other things, that Bresson not only used non-professional actors as his models but never used the same actor in more than one film. Marjorie Greene reports that when asked whether he would use Claude Laydu of *Journal d'un curé de campagne* in another film, Bresson responded (almost as if he were replaying Michel), "No. . . . How can I? For *Journal* I robbed him of what I needed to make the film. How could I rob him twice?"[22] Such solicitude, however, does not at all correspond to Bresson's usual treatment of his models.[23] Nor is the question of inexperience really convincing; as Jean-Luc Godard repeatedly pointed out to Bresson, it matters little whether one uses a trained actor or not if ultimately one trains his actors as intensively as Bresson does.[24] It is more plausible that Bresson, consciously or unconsciously, avoided professional actors precisely because of their inevitably *intertextual* nature. As Georges Sebbag has noted, "As handsome as a lightning rod, the professional actor captivates our attention. He incessantly exerts a kind of blackmail of reincarnation. Every time he slips into a new skin, he manages to carefully retain something of his familiar intonation and customary silhouette."[25] Marlon Brando, for example, brought to each of his films the persona he had developed in previous ones. Recent filmmakers have explicitly exploited this tendency: Bertolucci exploring Brando's various film personae in *Last Tango in Paris* and Truffaut Jean Dasté's previous avatar in *La Chambre verte*.[26] By using "virgin" models, Bresson effectively isolated his films from this intertextual phenomenon.

Bresson's theory and practice of the cinematograph, however self-contradictory the proposed justifications may be, do, taken as a whole, propose a radical departure from the traditions of representation and film acting so basic to classic cinema. His theory of the *combinatoire*, coinciding as it does with Saussure's theory of linguistics and the arbitrary nature of the sign, tends to break down linear narration and chronological and spatial coherence in favour of the purely relational function of the image. In such a "zero degree" climate, the film viewer must attempt whatever coherence she or he can derive from the accumulation and repetition of images. The introduction of any emotional or allusive material into such a "climate" would of course generate no little heat. Such is indeed the case with the allusions to Dostoevsky's *Crime and Punishment* that punctuate this film.[27]

Purely at the level of anecdote, there are numerous parallels between film and novel. At the most superficial level, both authors recount stories of men who commit crimes, are "cornered" by a sympathetic police inspector, and go to jail, where they are comforted by a woman to whom they had confessed their crimes. The stories' protagonists, Michel and Raskolnikov, are both students living in the poorest of conditions. Raskolnikov's garret, "under the roof of a high five-storied house was more like a cupboard than a room. . . . It had a poverty-stricken appearance with its dusty paper peeling off the walls. . . . The furniture was in keeping with the room: . . . a painted table in the corner on which lay a few manuscripts and books; the dust that lay thick upon them showed that they had been long untouched. . . . It would have been difficult to sink to a lower ebb of disorder."[28] The dust on Michel's books, piled on a table in the corner of his slatternly room, attracts the police inspector's attention, causing him to run his index finger through it in a meditative gesture. Raskolnikov is, like his French counterpart, "above the average in height, slim, well-built, with beautiful dark eyes and dark brown hair" (CP, 4). Each receives an important letter from his mother and as a consequence develops an increasingly strained relation to her. Each decides, as an act of will, to commit a crime against a woman. Each seems to disdain the monetary gain from his crime and to be motivated instead by some other factor; each succumbs to "the condition that overtakes some monomaniacs entirely concentrated on one thing" (CP, 29). Each hides his stolen money "in a hole at the bottom of the wall" of his room (CP, 90). Each will return to the scene of his original crime and thereby ensure his capture (Raskolnikov to the old lady's apartment, Michel to the Longchamp racetrack). Each is haunted by repeated encounters with a police inspector who suspects him of the crime and who interrogates him about his theories of crime! To Porfiry Petrovitch, Raskolnikov exclaims, in reference to an article he has published on crime,

> I simply hinted that an "extraordinary" man has the right . . . that is not an official right, but an inner right to decide in his own conscience to overstep . . . certain obstacles, and only in case it is essential for the practical fulfillment of his idea (sometimes, perhaps, of benefit to the whole of humanity). . . . All legislators and leaders of men, such as Lycurgus, Solon, Mahomet, Napoleon, and so on, were all without exception criminals, from the very fact that, making a new law, they *transgressed* the ancient one, handed down from their ancestors

and held sacred by the people, and they did not stop short at bloodshed either, if that bloodshed . . . were of use to their cause. . . . In short, I maintain that the majority, indeed, of these benefactors and leaders of humanity . . . must from their very nature be criminals . . . more or less of course. . . . You see there is nothing new in all that. The same thing has been printed and read a thousand times before. (CP, 254-55)

Early in *Pickpocket*, Michel encounters in a neighbourhood café the police inspector who had confronted him after his arrest at Longchamp. To the inspector's question about his theory of crime, Michel answers, "It's not new! Men of talent and genius are free in certain cases to disobey the law. Society has everything to gain from this arrangement ['Elle n'est pas neuve! Les hommes de talent ou de génie sont libres dans certains cas de désobéir aux lots. Pour la société il y a toutes les bénéfices']." "Who will distinguish them from the others?" asks the inspector. "Themselves," responds Michel. "But they'd never stop," argues the policeman. "You want to turn the world upside down! ['C'est le monde à l'envers!']" "It's already upside down ['Il est déjà à l'envers']," retorts Michel. "It's a question of turning it right-side up ['Il s'agit de le mettre à l'endroit']." Thus, although the economy of the film does not allow for the same degree of development of this dialogue, Bresson repeats the essential terms of Dostoevsky's argument. And in both novel and film this initial conversation will be repeated, though in much abbreviated form, in a later scene: in the novel, in Raskolnikov's interior ramblings, and in the film, when Michel visits the inspector in his office (CP, 269). In both novel and film, criminal and police inspector meet one final time. Dostoevsky's version reads:

No sooner had he opened the door than he stumbled upon Porfiry himself in the passage. . . . How could Porfiry have approached so quietly, like a cat, so that he had heard nothing? Could he have been listening at the door?

"You didn't expect a visitor, Rodion Romanovitch," Porfiry explained. . . . "I was passing by and thought why not go in for five minutes. . . . I came to see you the day before yesterday, in the evening; you didn't know? . . . I came into this very room. . . . Don't you lock your door? . . . You are nervously irritable, Rodion Romanovitch, by temperament; it's out of proportion with other qualities of your heart and character, which I flatter myself I have to some extent divined. . . . No, Rodion Romanovitch, Nikolay doesn't come in! This is a fantastic, gloomy business, a modern case, an incident of today when the heart of a man is troubled. . . . Here we have bookish dreams, a heart unhinged by theories. . . . No that's not the work of a Nikolay, my dear Rodion Romanovitch!"

"Then . . . who then . . . is the murderer?" Raskolnikov asked in a breathless voice. . . .

"Why *you*, Rodion Romanovitch! You are the murderer." . . .

"You are at your old tricks again, Porfiry Petrovitch! Your old method again. . . ."

"What does that matter now? . . . I have not come to chase and capture you like a hare. . . ."

"If so, what did you come for?" Raskolnikov asked irritably. "If you consider me guilty, why don't you take me to prison?" . . .

". . . to arrest you directly is not to my interest. . . . What you need now is fresh air!"

Raskolnikov positively started. "But who are you? what prophet are you? From the height of what majestic calm do you proclaim these words of wisdom?"

"Who am I? I am a man with nothing to hope for. . . . But you are a different matter, there is life waiting for you."

"When do you plan to arrest me?" (CP, 434-46)

Although much more succinct, Bresson's version maintains the essential features of Dostoevsky's:

VOICE-OVER: I hadn't heard him coming.

The Inspector enters Michel's room.

MICHEL: It's you!

INSPECTOR: I already came by three days ago. I waited around for you for a while.

MICHEL: I'd gone out to get some air.

INSPECTOR: It's unhealthy to stay cooped up in this little room ["enfermé dans cette petite chambre"] immersed in your books and notepads.

The Inspector crosses the room to Michel's table and draws his index finger through the dust on a book lying there.

MICHEL: I know you suspect me. If you think you are within your rights to arrest me, go ahead, arrest me! Put hand-cuffs on me! Otherwise don't push me to the limit. I don't want you constantly hanging around ["Autrement ne me poussez pas au bout. Je ne veux pas que vous continuiez à tourner autour de moi"].

INSPECTOR: I left you alone.

Michel throws a book on the floor. That's enough! Enough!

INSPECTOR: Don't shout. Calm down. Control yourself. Don't get crazy ["Ne vous mettez pas la tête à l'envers"]. And sit down. I came because I'm interested in you.

MICHEL: I don't give a damn about your interest.

INSPECTOR: . . . and to let you in on a little fact that I didn't know. . . . A complaint was lodged a little over a month ago . . . (we hadn't met yet) by a girl to the police in the neighbourhood. . . . A small sum of money had disappeared from the home of an old woman living in her apartment building. The next day the complaint was withdrawn. Because often the guilty party turns out to be a relative or old friend who can't be arrested. Anyway, this lady had a son. Well, it's not really stealing to take money from one's mother. . . . Maybe they were living together. . . . And then a month later, the same young man is arrested at Longchamp at the racetrack. The matter is far from clearcut. So I release him. . . .

MICHEL: And who is this young man?

INSPECTOR: It's you!

Michel gets up. You're mistaken!

INSPECTOR: I'm not mistaken.

MICHEL: Curious method!

INSPECTOR: Forget about my method.

MICHEL: You're trying psychology on me, but you're not sure. . . . You kill me! This is really a killer! ["Vous m'assomez! C'est assomant!"] What do you want from me?

INSPECTOR: I wanted to open your eyes! ["Je voulais vous ouvrir les yeux!"]

MICHEL: They're wide open.

INSPECTOR: To yourself. But I was wasting my time. As for the future, for your future. . . .

MICHEL: What's it to you? Are you a prophet? Do you think my future is any of your business? ["Croyez-vous que mon avenir vous regarde?"]

INSPECTOR: Yes, it seems to be my business to an extent. . . . All I have to do is give the order and you will be arrested and sent to prison.

He gets up.

MICHEL: And what are your intentions? I *insist* on knowing them!!!

Although highly condensed, Bresson's version of this scene is surprisingly similar in its development, characterization (both police inspectors are calm, arriving at the accusation through a kind of quiet reason, while the accused becomes highly volatile), and vocabulary (the words "method" and "prophet," among others, are striking repetitions).

Ultimately both Raskolnikov and Michel return to the scene of their crimes, an error that lands them in prison. Finally, each bears his soul to a young woman (Raskolnikov to Sonya, Michel to Jeanne) who seeks him out in prison. There we witness a highly ambiguous final scene that may or may not be interpreted as a "conversion" of the criminal.

There can be no doubt that Bresson intended some reference to Dostoevsky's *Crime and Punishment* in *Pickpocket*. Indeed it can be argued that this novel was also the source of his next film, *Au hasard Balthazar*.[29] And yet, for all its apparent similarities to the Russian model, Bresson's film bears a highly ambiguous relationship to Dostoevsky's masterpiece. Put succinctly, there is just enough resemblance between the two works to cast Bresson's work into a perfectly Dostoevskian ambiguity but not enough to allow an interpretation of the whole of Bresson's film.

Bresson's previous experience in adaptation is well documented. In particular, his *Journal d'un curé de campagne*, adapted from Bernanos's work of the same title, was termed by André Bazin "the kind of fidelity . . . most insidious and the most penetrating kind of creative liberty." Bazin had already termed Bresson's adaptation of Diderot, *Les Dames du Bois de Boulogne*, "a marvellously subtle play of interferences and counterpoint between fidelity and betrayal." As for *Journal d'un curé de campagne*, Bazin argued that Bresson's film "opens a new stage in cinematic adaptation. Until now, film tended to try to replace the novel as if it were an esthetic translation into another language. . . . But *Journal d'un curé de campagne* is something else again. Its dialectic of fidelity and creativity reduces, in the last analysis, to a dialectic between the cinema and literature. It is no longer a question of *translating* . . . but of building *on* the novel *by* the cinema, a work of another order. The film is no longer 'comparable' to the novel or 'worthy' of it, but rather an esthetic being which is like a novel *multiplied* by the cinema." Paradoxically, Bazin argued that the filmmaker's work was more literary and the novelist's more imagistic than its counterpart![30] Thus, even in a work whose title and dialogue were entirely maintained by Bresson, the question of adaptation was at best a highly charged, ambivalent, and even perverse venture.

So perverse, indeed, that although the relationship demands attention, virtually all of the critics who have noted Bresson's allusion to the Russian novel have elected to dismiss the matter. Thus, for example, Roger Tailleur dismisses *Pickpocket* as "Dostoievski written . . . by an abusive disciple."[31] Bresson himself seeks to problematize his relationship to his "model." In an interview with Paul Schrader he stated, "If I make a film from Dostoevsky, I try always to *take out* all the literary parts. . . . I don't want to make a film showing the work of Dostoevsky."[32] What he intended to *save* from the Russian novelist's work may be gleaned from a passage from *Notes sur le cinématographe:* "Proust says that Dostoevsky is original in composition above all. It is an extraordinarily complex and close-meshed ['serré'] whole, purely inward ['interne'], with currents and counter-currents like those of the sea, a thing that is found also in Proust . . . and whose equivalent ['pendant'] would go well with a film" (NC, 63/126-27).

We are truly at sea in this play of Bressonian ambiguities. It is not clear from the context what Bresson may mean by the term "take out"—he could either intend "to remove" or "to include." What is "the work" of Dostoevsky? Is it "un ensemble extraordinairement complexe et serré, purement interne"? Bresson claims numerous times in his *Notes* that his only interest is in the internal drama of his films. On the other hand, what is meant by the "pendant," the equivalent that would "go well" in a film, is also entirely ambiguous. What *is* clear is that the so-called psychological workings of *Crime and Punishment* have been entirely removed from *Pickpocket*. Bresson has effectively replaced Dostoevsky's entire polyphonic and dialogic structure[33] with a cinematographic and purely external display of the work of the pickpocket. One of the effects of this departure is to force our attention back on those aspects of the two works that do coincide. And we are forced, precisely, to consider why Bresson was at such pains to imitate Dostoevsky only in the two overlapping scenes (described above) and in the particular finale, that is, the proposal of a theory justifying the protagonist's criminal activity, the police inspector's cat and mouse game with the suspect, and the so-called conversion to love at the end of both works. What emerges as a *certainty* from the parallelism established by Bresson with the Russian novel is the *ambiguity* of the final scenes of both works.

Dostoevsky's "Epilogue," coming as it does after five hundred sixteen pages of unmitigated psychological turmoil and numerous subplots, involves Raskolnikov in a renewed debate over his "guilt": Raskolnikov "judged himself severely, and his exasperated conscience found no particularly terrible fault in his past, except a simple *blunder* which might happen to any one. He was ashamed just because he had so hopelessly, stupidly come to grief through some decree of blind fate and must humble himself and submit to 'the idiocy' of a sentence. . . . But he did not repent of his crime" (CP, 525). The question of guilt continues throughout the novel to hinge purely on the success of his venture: "Those benefactors of mankind who snatched power for themselves . . . succeeded and so *they were right*, and I didn't, and so I had no right to have taken that step" (CP, 526). In the last two pages of the novel, Raskolnikov is suddenly overcome by love for Sonya. "How it happened he did not know. But all at once something seemed to seize him and fling him at her feet. . . . He knew with what infinite love he would now repay all her sufferings. . . . Everything, even his crime, his sentence and his imprisonment, seemed to him now in the first rush of feeling an external strange fact with which he had no concern. . . . Life had stepped into the place of theory" (CP, 530-31). Taking up a copy of the New Testament that Sonya had given him, Raskolnikov asks himself, "Can her convictions not be mine now? Her feelings, her aspirations at least. . . ." Dostoevsky concludes his novel with the passage that has legitimized an eternal debate on the meaning of his novel:

> He did not know that the new life would not be given him for nothing, that he would have to pay dearly for it, that it would cost him great striving, great suffering.
>
> But that is the beginning of a new story—the story of the gradual renewal of man, the story of his gradual regeneration, of his passing from one world

into another, of his initiation into a new unknown life. That might be the subject of a new story, but our present story is ended. (CP, 532)

The interpretations of this finale leave little doubt as to its ultimate undecidability. Some critics seize on the fact that Raskolnikov grasps the New Testament and wonders whether Sonya's convictions may not now be his. Thus, for example, Maurice Beebe argues that "the revelation that comes to Raskolnikov through love and humility 'in prison, *in freedom*' is inevitable because it is the obverse side, the *pro*, of the will-to-suffering, the *contra*, that has been throughout the entire novel his primary motivation."[34] Edward Wasiolek adds, "If we consider the beginning and end of *Crime and Punishment*, we find that Raskolnikov goes from pride to humility, hate to love, reason to faith, and from separation from his fellow men to communion with them. . . . Raskolnikov is the image of a man pursued by God, condemned by his nature to choose him, yet hating the choice he is forced to make." Yet even Wasiolek concedes that "the epilogue follows logically, but not artistically," from the rest of the novel.[35]

The problem is, of course, that the final two paragraphs do not specifically mention *religious* conversion and are remarkably vague about exactly what "renewal" may mean. Dostoevsky coyly commits the answer to a *never to be realized future*. Thus, even such critics as Konstantin Mochulsky and A. Boyce Gibson, who term Dostoevsky "the great Christian writer," do not see a religious conversion in the final pages of the work. "We know Raskolnikov too well to believe this 'pious lie,'" writes Mochulsky, who nevertheless finds a Christian meaning in the work.[36] Gibson argues that "there is no theology . . . and particularly no theodicy [in this] sidelong approach to a Christian interpretation of man."[37]

Michael Holquist, who makes perhaps the most cogent argument for a religious conversion in *Crime and Punishment*, manages this conclusion only by dividing the work into "two different and opposing types of plot and two different kinds of time, two different ways of understanding, two different modes of interpretation that their traditions presuppose." This dialogic structure permits Holquist the discovery of "a bond between the parts [of the novel] that derives from the direction of time in the two story types that define the novel. . . . The movement of the epilogue is analogous to the wisdom tale in that it points back to the inadequacy of answers that precede its concluding insistence on *another* realm . . . and to the reminder of another and greater mystery."[38] Yet, as convincing as Holquist's dialogic argument may be, it still does not resolve what a majority of critics see as Dostoevsky's decision to unbalance these two forces in such a way that "hope and belief play havoc with the imaginative logic of the work."[39] If there is a truly Christian presentation in Dostoevsky's work, he was not to develop it explicitly for another decade.

We have, in other words, in the model to which Bresson alluded in his film, "the immanence of a revelation which does not occur,"[40] a decidedly problematic (even modernist) analogy. I cannot but conclude that Bresson chose to highlight the ambiguous ending of a novel by a writer that was *not yet* a Christian apologist to convey, through a parallel ambiguity, that his own work was *no longer* comfortable with orthodox Christian solutions. In her study of Bresson and Dostoevsky, Mireille Latil Le Dantec concludes of Bresson's oeuvre as a whole, "A new day can be discerned behind the tragedies of Dostoevsky. But the darkest night invades the final scenes of Bresson and engulfs the steps of an irresponsible criminal steeped in despair. . . . The absurd reigns supreme, and with it a feeling of solitude."[41] Precisely because it does mark such a turning point in Bresson's work, the final scene of *Pickpocket* ends up producing a mirror of the critical controversy surrounding Raskolnikov's sense of renewal.

Indeed, the final scene of *Pickpocket* bears a disquieting likeness to Dostoevsky's ambiguous epilogue. After delighting his viewers with a carnivalesque display of the pickpockets' sleight of hand and digital finesse, Bresson has his protagonist fall too easily into a trap he *knows* has been set for him, with the result that he ends up in prison. Jeanne arrives to visit him in jail, but at her first visit Michel remains cold and aloof. Like his literary predecessor, "he judges himself severely . . . but does not repent of his crime" (CP, 525):

MICHEL: These walls and bars are all the same to me. I don't even notice them. It's the idea.
JEANNE: What idea?
MICHEL: I should have been more careful. I let myself get caught. The idea is unbearable!
JEANNE: You're suffering.
MICHEL: I confessed everything. . . . But I shall deny it all. Why did you come?
JEANNE: You're all I have.
MICHEL: You want me to tell you that I have acted badly and that you win . . . I don't need anyone.
Having returned to his cell, MICHEL: There was something else that I hadn't said. Why live? I had decided nothing as yet.

In his notes for *Crime and Punishment*, Dostoevsky hesitated between two possible endings for his novel, acceptance of suffering and suicide. Ultimately he seems to have kept both, assigning to Svidrigailov, Raskolnikov's double, the option of suicide.[42]

After Michel returns to his cell, Bresson conveys, through a series of dissolves, some passage of time. One of these dissolves produces Michel holding a letter from Jeanne recounting the sickness of her child and concluding, "I will come to see you again." The voice-off narrator recounts, "As I read this letter, my heart beat violently." The guard then leads Michel back to the visiting area. A shot-countershot sequence displays Michel, expressionless, standing behind the bars and Jeanne sitting. She stands. The narrator notes, "A glow illumined her face." They kiss expressionlessly through the bars. The narrative voice-off intones, "O Jeanne, to get to you what a strange path I have had to take ['pour arriver jusqu'à toi, quel drôle de chemin j'ai dû prendre']." A final shot shows Michel and Jeanne standing on either side of the bars, their cheeks pressed together through the bars, their faces expressionless.

If Jeanne is illumined, Michel does not seem to be. His beating heart *may* be a sign of love, but it recalls as much his first essay at pickpocketing, when he notes the beating of his heart, as it implies an emotion that has never seemed more un-likely in a fictional character than in this automat. The ending is remarkably am-biguous, and like that of *Crime and Punishment*, it has engendered a fierce debate.

Those who look for transcendence and religious grace in Michel's evocation of "le drôle de chemin" will find it there as surely as the Christian critics find evi-dence of Raskolnikov's conversion in the epilogue of *Crime and Punishment*. Paul Schrader, for example, argues that "at the close of *Pickpocket* Michel comes to an acceptance of grace in the person of Jeanne. . . . The ending is a 'miraculous event.' . . . This decisive action forces the viewer into the confrontation with the wholly Other he would normally avoid. He is faced with an explicably spiritual act which now requests his participation and approval. . . . It is a miracle which must be accepted or rejected."[43] Daniel Millar agrees that *Pickpocket* is "a spiritual drama," and Richard Roud avers that "what interested Bresson was the road to redemption, not the scenery along that road. . . . *Pickpocket* is an allegory of redemption."[44] Certain French critics are even more categorical: Amédée Ayfre writes, for example, "Grace is there, powerful, even while invisible. In fact there is nothing but grace, its sovereign omnipotence obscures everything else. . . . In the end only God knows."[45] Michel Estève concurs: "Bresson's films illustrate so well what Chantal de Clergerie, Bernanos's heroine, said: 'As for sin, we're all immersed in it, some enjoy it, others suffer from it, but, in the last analysis, we all have to break the same bread at the fountain's edge.' Only Jeanne's true love can deliver Michel and open man's soul to Grace. . . . The beauty of the last scene of *Pickpocket* evokes . . . the defeat of Evil and illumination by redemption."[46] What is regrettable in these several assertions is the rejection of visual evidence ("what interested Bresson was not the scenery along that road," "grace, while invisible . . . obscures everything else") in favour of the invisible and inexplicable.

On the other hand, critics such as Jean Sémolué can point to the fact that like Raskolnikov, Michel has considered and rejected theology: "I believed in God for three minutes," he has told Jeanne earlier in the film. Sémolué argues that "the asceticism evoked here is not necessarily of the Christian variety. . . . We have, rather, an impression of a lapse into ordinariness following on the collapse of Michel's personality. Bresson wanted to paint love as an explosion; one wonders whether we aren't witnessing his defeat, a splintering. . . . The last phrase is spoken in total darkness, the color of salvation in Bresson's ambiguous universe. . . . But I don't feel the plenitude in *Pickpocket's* darkness. Michel's conversion to love seems more a conversion to resignation."[47] Even a critic who situates *Un condamné à mort* firmly within the context of grace notes that Bresson's other works do not incarnate that grace.[48] More bleakly, Louis Seguin writes, "In *Pickpocket* Bresson ends up alone, abandoned to his own resources, i.e., to nothingness," and Roger Tailleur adds, "With Bresson we enter the reign of the hyper-empty."[49] Summing up the undecidability of the ending of *Pickpocket*, Robert Vas notes, "We are further from understanding Michel's pilgrimage and the forces behind it than we have ever been in the case of past Bresson heroes."[50]

If it was Bresson's object to evoke the same ambiguity that reigns at the end of *Crime and Punishment*, he could not have made a better calculation, for the debate that rages about the spirituality of the film is only exacerbated by reference to the enigmatic ending of the Russian model. But the parallels with Dostoevsky's text are not limited to the anecdotal levels of the two works. In fact, despite his aversion to the psychological morass of Raskolnikov's interior debates, Bresson subtly and quietly adopted what Bakhtin has called the dialogic and carnivalistic aspects of Dostoevsky's poetics.[51] Indeed, the reason that the debates continue to rage about the ultimate meaning of the final scenes of both lies precisely in the dialogic structure of the two texts: at least two (and in Dostoevsky's case, many) points of view are presented for consideration. Thus it is no mere coincidence that Bresson included in *Pickpocket* a discussion of morality that throws established rules into doubt. If Michel tells the police inspector that his theory of the superman is "nothing new," he is recognizing that the same tension that existed in Dostoevsky's time between Hegel's *Philosophy of History* and Chernyshevsky's "anthropological principle of history" still resonates today between such thinkers as Nietzsche and Camus, on the one hand, and Marx and Teilhard de Chardin, on the other.[52] When the police inspector objects, "C'est le monde à l'envers," Michel interjects, "Il est déjà à l'envers. Il s'agit de le mettre à l'endroit." This direct allusion to Camus[53] hides another allusion to Dostoevsky: the upside-down, carnivalesque nature of his world.[54]

In assessing Dostoevsky's poetics, Mikhael Bakhtin discovered not only the polyphonic and dialogic structure of his novels but alongside these, "the task . . . of destroying the established forms of the basically monological European novel."[55] Indeed, the most stunning of Bakhtin's discoveries is that these two are aspects of the same urge and intersect in Dostoevsky's "carnival attitude." This latter Bakhtin describes as

deliberate multifariousness and discordance, a mixture of high and low. . . .
The laws, prohibitions and restrictions which determine the system and order
of normal, i.e. non-carnival life are for the period of carnival, suspended,
above all the hierarchical system and all the connected forms of fear, awe,
piety, etiquette etc. are suspended, i.e. everything that is determined by social-
hierarchical inequality among people, or any other form of inequality. . . .
Man's behavior, gesture and word are liberated from the authority of all hierarchical positions (of estate, rank, age, property status) which define them
totally in non-carnivalistic life. . . . Eccentricity is a special category of the carnival attitude which is organically connected with the category of familiar
contact, it permits the latent sides of human nature to be revealed and developed in concretely sensuous form.[56]

Among the Bakhtin discerned in the carnival structure, he lists profanation and the
mock crowning and subsequent discrowning of the king of carnival. He notes,
however, that "carnival is functional not substantive: it absolutizes nothing: it proclaims the jolly relativity of everything." And, continues Bakhtin, because carnival
emphasizes the borderline position between opposites, its spatial metaphors are
thresholds and stairs: thresholds because they are neither in nor out, stairs because
they symbolize the transition upward and downward.

These are precisely the elements shared between Dostoevsky's novel and Bresson's film, and they constitute, beyond the all too evident coincidences of plot, the
deeper structural relationship between the two works. Both Raskolnikov and
Michel are truly *eccentric* characters, most prominently in their disregard for social
and hierarchical relationships, for family, and for social values as expressed through
dress codes, dwelling arrangements, and money. What is more important, they
seek to *profane* not only Christian values (Michel says cynically, "J'ai cru en dieu
pendant trois minutes") but also canonical philosophical texts (Raskolnikov parodies Hegel; Michel Nietzsche, Camus, and . . . Dostoevsky).[57] Both characters see
themselves as latter-day Napoleons, justified in rising above the law because of
their "greatness," but in the context of their acts these fantasies are specifically carnivalesque: the mock crowning and discrowning of the carnival king. Michel parodies this apotheosis early in *Pickpocket* when he proclaims, "Je n'avais plus les
pieds sur terre. . . . Je dominais le monde!" and seconds later he is arrested. And just
as "Raskolnikov lives in essence on the threshold: his narrow room, the 'coffin'
opens directly onto the stairway landing, and he never locks his door," so too does
Michel "live" primarily in transitions between more settled spaces. If "the threshold, the foyer, the corridor, the landing, the stair, its steps, doors which open onto
stairs, garden gates, and aside from this the city: squares, streets, façades, taverns,
dens, bridges, gutters are the space in *Crime and Punishment*,"[58] so Bresson has
trained his camera on stairs and on doorways, merely to try to catch Michel passing

through *his* frame. The characters, the nature of their acts, the structure of their worlds, and the aesthetics of their authors[59] are all characterized by a single word: *prestuplenie* ("transgression," or literally, "overstepping").[60]

It is no accident that virtually all of Michel's transgressions occur at racetracks (a literary and cinematic topos for "le monde à l'envers"), on subway trains, while victims are getting into automobiles or crossing the street. The apogee of all of his activity takes La Gare de Lyon for its stage. Here Michel and his doubles enact the most carnivalesque scene of all: in the great Salle des Pas Perdus and on the train, newspapers are substituted for pocketbooks, hands fly into the most awesome variety of hidden places, and money, watches, wallets, and other valuables are moved so rapidly from hand to hand that the spectator is left dizzy and disoriented. Whereas Bresson's filming with but few exceptions has been remarkably passive until now, the camera leaps into the fray, seeking out the most hidden of gestures, moving rapidly from one subtle gesture to another. The editing likewise takes on a frenetic pace of cutting that itself breaks all the normal rules of film grammar. Everything is turned upside down and inside out. The pace and length of this scene make it abundantly clear that Bresson considers it the "crowning achievement" of his film. Certainly nothing else in the work, and especially not the markedly understated finale, can match it for interest or intensity.

Also, inasmuch as *transgression* is the modus operandi of both character and author in both *Pickpocket* and *Crime and Punishment*, I cannot fail to remark that the very voice-off narrator established to "orient" the viewer's understanding of the film, no less than the *prière d'insérer* inserted at the outset of Bresson's film, is himself part of this carnival. In the hierarchy of narrative authority, one should, traditionally, always be able to count on the narrator. That authority increases as the narrator is distanced from the world of the story: in cinema a voice-off narrator automatically commands our implicit respect, so much more so the image maker. Yet in *Pickpocket* that reliability is called into question repeatedly. We have already appreciated the fact that as image maker, Bresson avowedly destroys the normal cues by which viewers orient themselves in a fiction film and find coherence in its images. Bresson further undermines his authority as image maker in protesting the "weakness" of his character in an adventure "for which he was not made." Our experience of the film hardly corroborates these statements. In introducing a simultaneous voice-off narration and visual journal, Bresson introduces a confusion of point of view that is never resolved. But the most destructive because most obvious breakdown of narrative authority comes through the numerous misstatements pronounced by the voice-off narrator. Since Bresson's voice-over is integrated into the system or the psychology that motivates camera movement in the film by its strict identification with a character whose honesty is immediately in question,[61] the narrative authority is itself carnivalized, rendered topsy-turvy. Indeed Michel frequently omits or misstates information necessary to our understanding of events and in one case blatantly abuses in both voice-over narration and journal the credibility of the viewer.[62] In his last journal entry, Michel writes (and confirms by voice-over narration):

> During the two years I lived in London, I made some handsome strikes, but I lost the greater part of my gains on gambling or wasted it on women. I found myself in Paris again aimless and penniless.

This statement is so wildly out of character for Michel (gambling does not occupy his time in Paris, and his relationships with women are so tortured as to make the statement parodic) that it casts into doubt every other narrative statement he makes. And it is ultimately this degree of doubt that robs of its credibility and power the final voice-over statement of the film: "O Jeanne, pour arriver jusqu'à toi, quel drôle de chemin j'ai dû prendre." Because of this doubt as well, we are forced to turn elsewhere to understand the mystery and enigma of this film.

If the parallel Bresson has established with Dostoevsky succeeds in revealing the carnivalesque nature of *Pickpocket* and ultimately in undermining the believability of Michel's conversion, it nevertheless fails to account for much of the rest of the film. Among the things left unexplained by Dostoevsky's presence in the film is the remarkable shift of registers between Raskolnikov's murder and Michel's pickpocketing. Quite paradoxically and undoubtedly in a way that Bresson could not have foreseen, the allusion to Dostoevsky so foregrounds the presence of an absent text that it appears to screen and virtually render absent a text that is very present in the film. Not a single mention has ever been made in the more than fifty reviews of *Pickpocket* nor in the dozen books that have been devoted to Bresson of the presence of Richard Lambert's *The Prince of Pickpockets* in this film.

While it may perhaps be futile to speculate on the reasons for the suppression of Lambert, that silence is all the more surprising given the insistence with which Bresson has foregrounded this study of George Barrington. The book is presented full-face (title page and frontispiece) to the film viewer when Michel returns to his room after his training at the café with his doubles and finds Jacques sitting on his bed. Jacques holds open to the camera the copy of *Prince of Pickpockets* and says, "Thieves are reprehensible and lazy people." Michel objects, "Barrington wasn't lazy. He spent entire nights reading." "Only to dupe rich people into becoming his friends. He stole from his friends. Do you find that acceptable?" questions Jacques. And he adds, with as much emotion as a Bressonian character can muster, "At least he was courageous. In his day they hung thieves. Now they just go to prison." Michel changes the direction of their debate: "Do you know what prison is?" "I can imagine," answers Jacques. "You can't imagine it at all ['Tu n'imagines rien du tout']."

Not content to leave it there, Bresson reintroduces the book in the second and third encounters between Michel and the police inspector. In their second meeting at the café, the dialogue is as follows:

INSPECTOR: Pickpockets will never improve the condition of humanity.
MICHEL: I never said that. That's absurd.
INSPECTOR: One question: Do you believe there are many of these people among us?
MICHEL: Which people?
INSPECTOR: To whom more is permitted than the others. . . . Maybe you know a person like this?
MICHEL: If I knew such a person, I wouldn't come to tell you about it.
INSPECTOR: Obviously. *Takes* The Prince of Pickpockets *from Jacques.* May I? . . . Barrington, never heard of him. Maybe he's one of these superior men. . . . Come see me and bring this book.

In the scene immediately following, Michel sits outside the inspector's office holding a copy of the book. Upon entering the office he says immediately,

MICHEL: I've brought you the book.
INSPECTOR: What book? Ah yes, Barrington. So this Barrington interests you?
MICHEL: Everything interests me.
INSPECTOR: Of course, a young writer.
MICHEL'S VOICE-OFF: I thought I could discern sarcasm in his expression.
INSPECTOR: He manufactured hooks. *Holding up to the camera an illustration from the book entitled* Barrington Picking the Pocket of J. Brown, esq. This is how he inserted them into people's pockets.
Reaching in desk drawer, the Inspector holds up a crochet identical to that pictured in the book. Look, a worker in Nurenberg made me fifteen of these.
Michel makes a gesture with the hook as if to cut his own pocket. The Inspector closes the book and returns it.
MICHEL: I have to leave. Keep it.
INSPECTOR: Good bye.
MICHEL'S VOICE-OFF: How could I have not realized. It was a trap.

Finally, when the inspector pays an unexpected visit to Michel's room and directly accuses him, it is this same book that Michel throws to the floor "in anger."

"It was a trap," thinks Michel. Indeed, the book can be read as "trap" not just in the sense of diversion of attention but also, by an easy extension of exactly the kind we make in the unconscious, as a metaphoric displacement. We recall that the most egregious of Michel's misstatements or lies is his assertion that he had gone to *England* and has wasted all his money on women and gambling. Now, *The Prince of Pickpockets*, like the title of Bresson's film, is in *English*, a language that would presumably be difficult for Michel, Jacques, and the Inspector. None seems to have difficulty reading it (i.e., translating its meaning into their own idiom).

The presence of *The Prince of Pickpockets* in Bresson's film effectively displaces the register of Raskolnikov's murder down to the apparently trivial activity of the "vol à tire," as Bresson inevitably calls this activity: theft by pulling. Murder, by its violent nature, its utter finality, and the extreme punishment meted out to the criminal, occupies our attention at a level that makes Raskolnikov's original motivation and ambition at least plausible. Picking pockets does not. It is, as Jacques correctly points out, a socially reprehensible and cowardly activity. So why would Bresson have shifted Dostoevsky's ethical register downward in a way that apparently trivializes Michel's status? Barrington himself suggests part of the answer to this question, for as reprehensible as the activity appears, he was a master at transforming it into something it was not! This in two ways. First, like Dostoevsky's Raskolnikov, he argues that by his actions he becomes the equal of the most powerful prince:

> Sovereigns seize on the territories of neighboring princes, whenever they think doing so suits their purposes, without scruple or remorse; people of fashion run in debt and never pay their creditors; bankers and brokers are seldom restrained by conscience in the interest they take, or the charges which they make; merchants, and traders of all kinds are not more scrupulous in the profits which they exact of their unwary customers; and as for lawyers of every denomination, their boundless rapacity is proverbial. The *mode* then of appropriating the property to oneself, and not the *act* of doing so, is the sole difference between the most powerful prince and the most opulent merchant.[63]

In this, Barrington doubles Raskolnikov's argument for the permission to crime. But Barrington's second activity is much more pertinent for its inclusion in Bresson's fictional universe: pickpocketing becomes the pretext for art. Because of the need to pass unnoticed among the finest peers of England, Barrington constantly played at being someone he was not. "Disguise made it difficult to identify him, and everywhere his deportment gave him the *prima facie* advantage of appearing sober and well-bred" (PP, 33). When caught, he repeatedly had recourse to the most extraordinary verbal pyrotechnics in the courtroom and numerous times so articulately and movingly defended his person that the jury was induced to pardon (PP, 110-79 passim). To one jury he exclaimed, "There is no joy but what arises from the practice of virtue and consists in the felicity of a tranquil mind and a benevolent heart" (PP, 183), a monumental hypocrisy, it turns out, since he was back in jail within days for the same illegal activities. What makes Barrington all the more interesting as a model for the character in Bresson's film is that he was a poet and an actor. He is known to have addressed a series of poems to one of the actresses in a theatre troupe he joined to avoid detection. To Barrington are attributed as well the following verses intended to serve as a prologue for a play in New South Wales entirely produced by convicts:

From distant climes, o'er wide-spread seas, we come,
Though not with much éclat or beat of drum:
True patriots all, for, be it understood,
We left our country for our country's good. . . .
But, you inquire, what could our breasts inflame
With this new passion for Theatric fame;
What, in the practice of our former days,
Could shape our talents to exhibit plays? . . .
And sure in Filch, I shall be quite at home.
Unrivall'd there, none will dispute my claim
To high pre-eminence, and exalted fame. . . .
Sometimes, indeed, so various is our art,
An actor may improve and mend his part: . . .
Grant us your favour, put us to the test,
To gain your smiles we'll do our very best;
And, without dread of future turnkey Lockits,
Thus, *in an honest way, still pick your pockets.*
(PP, 245-46)

Barrington's equation of theatrical passion and picking pockets should not go unnoted. I am particularly struck by Philip Rahv's contention that Dostoevsky's novel "depends on the sleight of hand of substituting a meaningless crime for a meaningful one."[64] Bresson's explicit subject, coupled with his insistence on "hiding ideas so that they may be found" (NC, 42/85), suggests how much the Lambert text's invisible visibility may be a metaphor for Bresson's own cinematic activity. In his doubling of Michel's unreliability as narrator, Bresson has already suggested an underlying parallelism between their two arts. But the similarity goes much further.

Bresson once stated that "the subject of *Pickpocket* is in my view a pretext for creating 'cinematic material' ["une matière cinématographique"]."[65] But the pretext has a concretely metonymic relationship with the text. Bresson noted in *Notes sur le cinématographe*, "Your film—let people feel the soul and the heart there, but let it be made like a work of hands ['un travail de mains']" (NC, 12/30). And later he adds, "The things one can express with the hand ['Que de choses on peut exprimer avec la main']. . . . What economy!" (NC, 64/127). Sometimes, to be sure, unconsciously: Bresson (mis)appropriates Montaigne to the effect that "hands are often carried where we direct them not ['La main se porte souvent où nous ne l'envoyons pas']" (NC, 68/133).[66] In any case, his conception of the cinema is "a hand directing everything ['une main qui dirige tout']."[67] In response to a question about the subject of his film, he expounded on "the wonder of pickpocketing. Have you ever felt the disturbance in the air created by the presence of a thief? ['le merveilleux du vol à la tire. Avez-vous déjà ressenti le trouble que met dans l'air la présence d'un voleur?'] It's inexplicable. But the cinema is also the domain of the inexplicable."[68] "Those people," Bresson said of the pickpockets of Paris, "pull off astonishing feats ['des choses merveilleuses!']." And Jean Sémolué adds, linking this evocation of the pickpocket to Bresson's own work, "All that remained was to organize those things into something no less astonishing and marvelous than a well-constructed film, a beautiful object."[69] But somehow, for Bresson, this work of organization had to be carried out on the sly. Indeed, the very way Bresson went about his work on this film suggests this deeper connection to the pickpocket: he has recounted how he began *Pickpocket* filming "in hiding":

> They told me, "Hide, it's easy." I hid. I was soon discovered. We had to employ ruses ["Il fallait user des ruses"]. Shots made from hiding are not very precise. Crowds are chaotic ["un désordre"]. I used this chaos in certain scenes. The sequence in the station was shot entirely in the crowd, during the month of July as the rush was on to leave for vacation. It required an enormously mobile camera and the rapid deployment of our material. In short, I heaped difficulties on myself, not the least of which was working in all that bustle and noise.[70]

We can easily imagine Michel making this same statement when asked to reveal his M.O. Elsewhere, in a moment of cinematic bravado, Bresson writes, "Your camera catches ['attrape'] not only physical movements that are inapprehensible ['inattrapables']" (NC, 53/110). His favourite analogy for the camera is an aggressive one: "For me, the word shot ['prise de vue'] signifies capture. One has to catch ['attraper'] the actor under the play of lights and surprise him ['le surprendre'] and seize from him ['de capter sur lui'] . . . the rarest and most secret things he can produce."[71] Of Claude Laydu, the priest in *Journal* Bresson claimed, "I robbed him of what I needed to make the film."[72] Joël Magny has noted that Bresson imitates his characters not only in this surreptitious activity of the pickpocket but in his very obsessiveness:

> Prey to an idea, a desire, a vocation, the character ends up seeing the world only in terms of the goal to be attained: the only things that matter are obstacles

Pickpocket

or aids to his quest, anything outside his path is a matter of indifference and disappears. This is the state of mind, or better yet the point of view ["optique"], that Bresson wants to create in the spectator.[73]

And in that optic Bresson films. Even to the extent of saying, like Michel, "Laugh at a bad reputation ['Moque-toi d'une mauvaise réputation']" (NC, 62/125). Like Michel, and Raskolnikov before him, Bresson sees himself as a member of a group of solitary visionaries able, nay, destined, to transgress the general rules because of a secret superiority: "The future of cinematography belongs to a new race of young solitaries who will shoot films by putting their last cent into it and not let themselves be taken in by the material routines of the trade" (NC, 62/124-25). As with Michel and Raskolnikov, the real interest is not in material gain but in a goal that always remains aggressively secret and mysterious. "Hide the ideas. . . . The most important will be the most hidden" (NC, 18/42).

And what is this "most important, most hidden idea"? Louis Malle was among the first to suggest the answer to this "enigma." "Pickpocket is also an erotic film, 'le vol à tire' being evidently merely a thinly disguised or transposed symbol of the sin of the flesh. The cold expression and pursed lips of Martin Lassalle and his accomplices evoke Don Juan and le marquis de Sade."[74] Robert Bresson is never so passionate a filmmaker as when he is filming the orgy of pickpocketing in the Gare de Lyon. That orgy is exquisitely prepared by a more private one, when Michel and his doubles are practising their art. Here Bresson lubriciously approaches his camera to a close-up that eliminates faces and leaves only bodies prey to myriad hands that reach inside clothing at both breast and crotch levels, unbutton buttons, pull out secret and preciously guarded objects.[75] Although the scene in the Gare de Lyon is the apex of this frenzy—Jean-Pierre Oudart calls it "a hysterical erotic relationship ['rapport érotique hystérisé']"[76]—the most violently intrusive example occurs just after Michel, waiting in the bank for his next victim, experiences a failure of will. "I was stopped by fear ['J'ai eu peur']," he says as the victim passes through the doors, "he got away ['il m'échappa']." But typically for this narrator, he is wrong. Seconds later we see Michel and his accomplice work the man over with a thoroughness that has all the overtones of rape and is rendered all the more uncomfortable for the viewer by the stop-action editing on certain hand movements that, were they conducted so slowly, would surely have been detected by the victim. The impression given by this "co-operative" camera work and editing is that the image maker enjoys a very Gidean complicity with the thieves in their most intimate activities.[77] Not that there is any *evident* pleasure to be gleaned here.[78] Even the ocular orgasm—Bresson uses the term "ejaculatory force of the eye ['force éjaculatrice de l'oeil']"!! (NC, 6/19)—witnessed at the racetrack in the opening scene is so transient and so ascetic that it seems to signify "erotic" without affording the pleasure normally associated with the erotic.

So much in this film is defence against just such an erotic pleasure that it is small wonder that the explanation of grace seems to have taken hold despite its lack of applicability to the character or to the intertextual supports that lend the film its major resonance. The defence begins, of course, with Bresson's very theory of the cinematograph: if no image has value, and if value is only relative, then we are cast into a world of fragments whose ultimate meaning is always "elsewhere" ("ailleurs"). The defence continues with Bresson's condemnation of psychology: "No psychology!" warns Bresson, in a general approach that sounds more like an illustration of Freud's theory of repression than anything else (NC, 39/83). "Apply myself to insignificant (non-significant) images. . . . Flatten my images (as if ironing them ['comme avec un fer à repasser']), *without attenuating them*" (NC, 6/18). But he seems to understand the visual effects of a repressive camera style: "Production of emotion determined ['obtenue'] by a resistance to emotion" (NC, 65/129). And for a director who will have no truck with psychology, Bresson appears to have an unusual interest in his own unconscious desires: "Your film begins when your secret wishes pass into your models ['Ton film commence quand tes volontés secrètes passent directement à tes modèles']. . . . Impose on it your urges, your orgies ['tes volontés, tes voluptés']" (NC, 43/90, 63/126).[79] In *Pickpocket*, however, the eye may see and the hand may reach, but the ego seems to be able neither to tolerate a direct expression of pleasure in that which is forbidden nor to forgo transgression.[80]

Pleasure in *Pickpocket* is always somewhere else. It must always be located in the fetish as replacement for the desired object. Of course, fetishism is always a kind of theater, as Joyce McDougall reminds us, a drama in which one's "I is a character, an 'actor' in the scene of the world, who, in private, in his internal reality, stages a more intimate theater whose repertory is secret." In all of us, "the I continually settles accounts with the past and so indefatigably reproduces the same dramas. . . . These psychic scenarios are always handicrafts ['artisanales'], sometimes however approaching real works of art." For some, psychoanalysis will be the stage in which these dramas are enacted, employing a cast of characters that the I has dredged spontaneously from the unconscious. For others, this "tireless rehearsal for an anonymous spectator" will be played out in a private drama of fetishism or a public drama of cinema—or both.[81] In this case, the I will often need others for its (private) theatre:

> In the scenarios that derive from (the unconscious), the I attempts to expel and
> thereby externalize its intimate conflicts, but in order to accomplish this, it
> needs the cooperation of the other I's; those others will be called on to play
> the roles of various minor characters, derived from the internal world of the
> subject, having been designed by projection for these identifications of the
> expelled characters, and yet the subject has not the least suspicion that it has

served as *metteur en scène* for these dramas, and the relational tensions that result from them.[82]

Now, to some extent this structure describes all creative artists who draw from their imagination various aspects of their own personalities. But Bresson's application of this tendency is particularly marked. It is by now well known (both from his own writing and from the reports of his "models") that he worked to "wear down the actor, to make him die ['aplanir l'acteur, le faire mourir'],"[83] to reduce his players to virtual automatons. Those who have reported on his techniques, such as M. Monod, refer to the "slightly sadistic advantage gained through discomfiture of others" and to the fact that "Bresson played every part."[84] Bresson himself writes,

> Model. Reduce to the minimum the share of his consciousness ["se conscience"]. . . . You will guide your models according to your rules ["à tes règles"]. . . . It would not be ridiculous to say to your models: "I am inventing you as you are." . . . The cause which makes him say this sentence or that movement is not in him, it is in you. . . . Models: mechanized externally, internally free ["intacts, vierges intérieurement"]. On their faces nothing willful. . . . Your film begins when your secret wishes pass into your models. . . . It is to you, not to the public that they give those things which it, perhaps, would not see. . . . A secret and sacred trust ["Dépot secret et sacré"]. Many people are needed to make a film, but only one who makes, unmakes, remakes his images and sounds, returning at every second to the initial impression or sensation which . . . is incomprehensible to the others. . . . When I listen only to myself, I do wonders ["des merveilles"]. (NC, 8-70/23-136 passim)[85]

Jean-Pierre Oudart goes so far as to assert that "the sadistic relationship between Robert Bresson and his actresses constitutes the repressed of the Bressonian fiction."[86] Beyond his repression of his actors, however, we have become aware of the many other fetishistic aspects in Bresson's work.

Now, fetishism itself, according to McDougall, usually derives from unmanageable fears deriving from the primal-scene experience, which result in what Freud has called *Verleugnung* ("disavowal"). But McDougall argues that this disavowal is compensated by the restructuring of the psyche around fantasies that replace the disavowed parental genitals. The child "takes note and creates in an *autoplastic* way the fantasmatic means for dealing with this unhappy knowledge." This *reworking through fantasy* may include what McDougall calls "denuded representation," which screens not only the "empty sex" of the mother "but also the meaning of that which should have been attached to this discovery."[87] She notes,

In these efforts to know nothing of the truth of sexual relations in order to be able to maintain the fictive introjection of the primal scene, the pervert engages in a no win struggle ["un combat"] with reality. In this light, his erotic behavior is a sort of perpetual and compulsive *acting out*. For the subject has created for himself a mythology whose real meaning remains hidden, a text whose most important passages have been erased ["un texte dont on aurait gommé des passages importants"]. [But] these missing passages are not repressed, for in that case, they would have given rise to neurotic symptoms; they have been abolished, the subject having *destroyed* the meaning.[88]

In essence, McDougall is arguing that fetishism may take the form of a generalized fragmenting of reality into whose ellipses the disavowed meaning has slipped. The result is a recathected *collage*. Masud Khan writes, "One of the results obtained by the collated internal object in the psychic reality of the pervert is that this object gives him the possibility of instituting in his internal reality a paradoxical screen which protects him from the global invasion of his person by the intrusive om-nipresence of the mother in his infantile experience."[89]

"Les idées les cacher, mais de manière qu'on les retrouve. La plus importante sera la plus cachée," writes Bresson. We may begin to perceive, if not exactly *what* is screened off, at least the means by which the "ideas" are hidden. Bresson's cinemato-graph is, as we have had occasion to note, a montage; but in the light of McDougall's analysis of fetishism and perversion, we can see that this montage comes more and more to resemble a perverse collage of individual images each of which has been carefully decathected. "Images chosen in prevision of their *inner* association," writes Bresson, "don't run after poetry. It penetrates unaided through the joins (ellipses) ['Elle pénètre toute seule par les jointures (ellipses)']" (NC, 25/55, 14/35). What is left between these significant ellipses is a system of fragments that, like the fetish, operate primarily by *synecdoche*, what Pierre Jouvet calls "meaningful fractions."[90]

This collage effect, in which each of the images loses its primacy of reference to be subsumed into an overall pattern, results perhaps less in a sense of overall composition than in generalized fragmentation. This again is consistent with the workings of fetishism in general and of the pickpocket, both film and character, in particular. Michel's real crime (like Meursault's in Camus's *L'Étranger*) is against his mother. As the police inspector points out, an identity has been established between the man who stole from his mother and the man who has been picking the pockets of women and then men in the racetracks, subways, streets, and sta-tions of Paris. In both cases a violation that, rather than operating in the repressed realm of sexuality, has taken a "drôle de chemin," a displacement onto fetishized objects, fragments that are slipped deliciously from under the clothes of the other player in this drama into the hands of the fetishizer. The *real* thing has been dis-avowed. The pleasure is always elsewhere: in the hand, in the money, wallets, watches removed from the victims—fragments. Just as in the making of the film the pleasure itself is located in fragmentation, a pleasure of the fetishized eye. "My joy is in *making the film*" exclaimed Bresson to Marjorie Greene.[91] "La force éjaculatrice de l'oeil," he writes (un)cryptically in his *Notes* (NC, 19).

Perhaps this is why the final images of the film focus on Michel carefully separated from Jeanne by iron bars. Perhaps this is why Bresson confesses, "Shooting is going out to meet something. Nothing in the unexpected that is not secretly expected by you ['Rien dans l'inattendu qui ne soit attendu secrètement par toi']" (NC, 52/108). What a strange path, through Dostoevsky and George Barrington Bresson has taken in order (not) to tell us his story.

Notes

1. Jean-Luc Godard and Michel Delahaye, "La Question: entretien avec Robert Bresson," *Cahiers du cinéma* 178 (May 1966): p. 69.

2. Cf. Jan Dawson, "The Invisible Enemy," *Film Comment* 13, no. 5 (September/October 1977): p. 24; and Gilles Gourdon, "Georges Bernanos," *Cinématographe* 41 (November 1978): p. 47. I except Mirella Jona Affron's essay ("Bresson and Pascal: Rhetorical Affinities," *Quarterly Review of Film Studies* 10, no. 2 [Spring 1985]: pp. 118-34) on the parallels between the form and content of Bresson's *Notes sur le cinématographe* and Pascal's *Pensées*.

3. *Notes sur le cinématographe*, pp. 85, 42, in English *Notes on Cinematography*, pp. 40, 18. All further references to this text will be indicated by NC, followed by pagination in the English and the French edition, respectively. It is worth noting that the *Notes* constitutes a connection to Rohmer's work through the mediation of Pascal (see Affron, "Bresson and Pascal," which points up the many connections between Bresson's *Notes* and Pascal's *Pensées*).

4. Quoted in Rui Nogueira, "Burel and Bresson," *Sight and Sound* 46, no. 1 (1976-77): p. 21. Robert Vas confirms this sense of dismay, writing, "With the increasing familiarity of his methods goes a corresponding growing ambiguity of meaning, so that the ending seems as cursory as it is schematically striking. We are further from understanding Michel's pilgrimage and the forces behind it than we have ever been in the case of past Bresson heroes before" ("Pickpocket," *Monthly Film Bulletin* 27, no. 321 [October 1960]: p. 140).

5. E.g., in Jean-Paul Sartre's *La Nausée* (Paris: Gallimard, 1938).

6. The term "distanciation" is of course borrowed from Brecht. For a Brechtian analysis of Bresson see Susan Sontag, "Spiritual Style in the Films of Robert Bresson," in *Against Interpretation* (New York: Farrar, Straus & Giroux, 1961), pp. 177-95.

7. Nick Browne, "Film Form/Voice-Over: Bresson's *Diary of a Country Priest*," *Yale French Studies* 60 (1980): p. 234.

8. Ibid., p. 235.

9. There is, as Browne thus notes (ibid., p. 239), a pairing of "written text"/"performance by voice" that focuses our attention on the battle for supremacy of these two narrative techniques. But what is more important in *Pickpocket*, the narrative voice-off becomes a locus of conflict between what is said (or written) and what the viewer sees. Browne notes of *Diary*, "The relation between voice-over and image in the film is not essentially a difference in tenses, past and present. Within the framework of the film, there is a sense of movement between the pastness of the diary format and the presence of the unrolling image, whether accompanied by voice-over or not. . . . Within the narrative system of character, tense is only an aspect of the general problem of narrative distance. That linkage and control of two points of view is the underlying formal and compositional issue of the film and the basis of its power, becomes clear not so much in sequences accompanied by speech-narration that repeats what the scenes show (transparency) but in the scenes of explicit disjuncture, when the Priest says something to himself that is in conflict with what the image shows (character opaqueness)."

10. I have borrowed Sarah Kozloff's term "image maker" from *Invisible Storytellers*, p. 44. For another "take" on these extra-diegetic elements see David Bordwell, *Narration in the Fiction Film* (Madison: University of Wisconsin Press, 1986), pp. 289-310.

11. The character's facial expressionlessness is matched to the voice-off narrator's cold tone. Bresson argued (NC, 48/101) that "an ice-cold commentary can warm, by contrast, tepid ['tièdes'] dialogues in a film. Phenomenon analogous to that of hot and cold in painting." The term *tiède*, however, suggests that the dialogues themselves will hardly be lively, as indeed is the case in this film.

12. Alan Williams, "The Two Films," in *Max Ophuls and the Cinema of Desire* (New York: Arno, 1980), pp. 17-42.

13. An accusation that might well be levelled at Bresson himself, a hypothesis whose implications I shall explore further on in this essay.

14. And a curious connection with *Les Amants*, where Jeanne and Raoul are pictured in a plane in this same amusement park.

15. Cf. André Targe, "Ici l'espace naît du temps," *Camera/Stylo* 68/69 (February 1989): pp. 88-90, translation mine: "Far from erasing the traces of joins in the service of reinforcing narrative credibility, Bresson emphasizes them in raising the play that they introduce into the fictional continuity. . . . In place of identities or scenic tricks, the eye discerns only *functions*." Targe evokes Eisenstein's famous comparison of montage and orchestral score in writing: "He has invented a new discourse of the image, derealizing its substance in favor of form, playing musically with rhythm and tempo" (p. 98).

16. Ferdinand de Saussure, *Course in General Linguistics*, trans. Wade Baskin (New York: McGraw Hill, 1966), pp. 114-16.

17. Ibid., pp. 119-20.

18. Ibid., p. 116.

19. See André Bazin, "The Evolution of the Language of Cinema," in *Film Theory and Criticism*, ed. Gerald Mast and Marshall Cohen (New York: Oxford University Press, 1979), p. 126.

20. See Susan Sontag, *On Photography* (New York: Dell, 1973), pp. 4-7, pp. 111-22. Sontag's view of photography is closer to Bresson's other project of secrecy. She notes, "All that photography's program of realism actually implies is the belief that reality is hidden. And being hidden, is something to be unveiled . . . a disclosure. . . . Just to show something, anything, in the photographic view is to show that it is hidden" (pp. 120-21). See also Roland Barthes, *Camera Lucida*, trans. Richard Howard (New York: Hill & Wang, 1981).

21. Vincent Pinel notes that "the author's role consists in revealing the deeper personality of his actor. . . . To this end, Bresson uses a mechanical means: repetition. The actor, having reached a certain degree of saturation, forgets that he is 'playing' and becomes himself again. One must 'flatten the actor, make him die ["aplanir l'acteur, le faire mourir"]'" ("Le Paradoxe du non-comédien," *Études ciné-matographiques* 14-15 [1962]: pp. 81-82, translation mine). For further discussions of Bresson's working methods with his "models" see Lars Helmstein, "Le Pont brûlé," *Camera/Stylo* 68/69 (February 1989): pp. 28-46.

22. Marjorie Greene, "Robert Bresson," *Film Quarterly* 13, no. 2 (Winter 1959): p. 7.

23. See Pinel, "Le Paradoxe du non-comédien," pp. 78-83; and Greene, "Robert Bresson," pp. 5-10.

24. Godard, "La Question," pp. 33-34.

25. Georges Sebbag, "Un Simple Crochet," *Camera/Stylo* 68/69 (February 1989): p. 5, translation mine. Sebbag adds, contrasting the usual use of actors with Bresson's, "He is seductive because he overcomes suicide, preserves appearances, and somehow manages to avoid the passage of time. But this long view of his is a disadvantage in the present moment: the current drama is somehow forgotten in the reconstitution of a trajectory that leads the actor outside the film to others he has done or will do. . . . By contrast, in Bresson's film an unknown profile, a strange body, neutralize these other voices that prevent us from authenticating a sequence and prolonging the action" (ibid.).

26. For a discussion of Brando's intertextuality, see my *Bertolucci's Dream Loom*, p. 120.

27. I am not the only viewer to see this allusion. Many of Bresson's critics have noted it in passing, among them René Cortade (*"Pickpocket* ou le roman russe à la glacière," *Arts, Lettres, Spectacles*, 23-29 December 1959, p. 7); Richard Roud ("The Redemption of Despair," *Film Comment* 13, no. 5 [September/October 1977]: pp. 23-24); Lindley Hanlon (*Fragments: Bresson's Film Style* [Rutherford, N.J.: Fairleigh Dickinson University Press, 1986], p. 27ff.); Michel Estève (*Robert Bresson: la passion du cinématographe* [Paris: Albatros, 1983], p. 60ff.); and Mireille Latil Le Dantec

("Bresson, Dostoievski," *Cinématographe* 73 [December 1981]: pp. 11-17).

28. Fyodor Dostoevsky, *Crime and Punishment*, trans. Constance Garnett (New York: Modern Library, n.d.), pp. 328-29. All further references to this novel will be indicated by CP.

29. The scene in *Crime and Punishment* (pp. 56-60) in which Raskolnikov dreams that he witnessed the cruel bludgeoning of a little sorel horse bears striking similarities to the general theme of Bresson's film *Au hasard Balthazar*, about the donkey Balthazar.

30. André Bazin, *"Le Journal d'un curé de campagne* et la stylistique de Robert Bresson," in *Qu'est-ce que le cinéma* (Paris: Cerf, 1985), pp. 114, 119, 126, translation mine.

31. Roger Tailleur, *"Pickpocket*: le pheaurme," *Positif* 33 (April 1960): p. 44. Colin Young argues that Bresson shows "only limited interest in the inspector/suspect relationship—he wishes us to see Michel alone" ("Conventional-Unconventional, "*Film Quarterly* 17, no.1 [Fall 1963]: p. 18). Only Latil Le Dantec's "Bresson, Dostoievski" and Hanlon's *Fragments: Bresson's Film Style* develop the Bresson/Dostoevsky parallel to any great extent. I shall discuss their analyses below.

32. Paul Schrader, "Robert Bresson, Possibly," *Film Comment* 13, no.5 (September/ October 1977): p. 27.

33. Obviously these are Bakhtin's terms as used in *Problems of Dostoevsky's Poetics*, trans. R. W. Rotsel (New York: Ardis, 1973). I shall have occasion to return to them later in this essay.

34. Maurice Beebe, "The Three Motives of Raskolnikov," in *"Crime and Punishment" and the Critics*, ed. Edward Wasiolek (Belmont, Calif.: Wadsworth, 1961), p. 108.

35. Edward Wasiolek, "Structure and Detail," in ibid., p. 115.

36. Konstantin Mochulsky, *Dostoevsky: His Life and Work*, trans. Michael Minihan (Princeton: Princeton University Press, 1967), p. 312.

37. A. Boyce Gibson, *The Religion of Dostoevsky* (Philadelphia: Westminster, 1973), pp. 92, 102.

38. Michael Holquist, *Dostoevsky and the Novel* (Princeton: Princeton University Press, 1977), pp. 75, 100-101.

39. Philip Rahv, "Dostoevsky in *Crime and Punishment*," in Wasiolek, *"Crime and Punishment" and the Critics*, p. 17. See also J. Middleton Murry, "Beyond Morality," in *Fyodor Dostoevsky: A Critical Study* (London: Martin Secker, 1916), reprinted in ibid., pp. 47-53; Ernest J. Simmons, *Dostoevsky: The Making of a Novelist* (London: John Lehmann, 1950), p. 133; and Derek Offord, "The Causes of Crime and the Meaning of Law: *Crime and Punishment* and Contemporary Radical Thought," in *New Essays on Dostoevsky*, ed. Malcolm Jones and Garth Terry (Cambridge: Cambridge University Press, 1983), pp. 41-65.

40. Jorge Luis Borges, "The Wall and the Books," in *Labyrinths* (New York: New Directions, 1962), p. 188.

41. Latil Le Dantec, "Bresson, Dostoievski," p. 17. She is referring to the fact that after *Un condamne à mort s'est échappé*, Bresson's work becomes increasingly bleak and pessimistic. His latest film, *Le Diable probablement*, is a misanthropic tale that ends in the suicide of its protagonist, Michel—the name of the hero of *Pickpocket* and of Gide's *L'Immoraliste*, another novel that resonates dramatically with this film. René Predal adds, "The bleakness of the last films of Bresson is equaled only by that of Godard's works. Enclosed in an armor of iron predestination, his characters find no escape from their despair and die miserable. . . . His heroes are unattached, incapable of forming attachments with others. . . . His condemnation is total, global" ("Bresson et son temps," *Cinéma 83* 294 [June 1983]: p. 10). See also Joël Magny, "L'Expérience intérieure de Robert Bresson," ibid. p. 23ff. Even a Christian writer like Jan Dawson concludes of Bresson, "His vision of Christ is a suicidal one. . . . If he has achieved a state of grace, it is a nihilistic grace" ("The Invisible Enemy," p. 25). Jean Sémolué adds, "To accomplish in front of us the action that will reveal their inner selves, Bresson's solitary characters emerge from the darkness only to disappear into darkness and silence once their action is accomplished" ("Les Personnages de Robert Bresson," *Cahiers du cinéma* 75 [October 1957]: p. 15). Calvin Green likewise concludes, "Bresson's films since *Pickpocket* have all emphasized the same mixed pessimism: grace alienates and mortifies" ("*Ars Theologica:* Man and God at the New York Film Festival," *Cinéaste* 3, no. 2 [Fall 1969]: p. 7). Cf. Estève, *Robert Bresson: la passion du cinématographe*, p. 134.

42. See Wasiolek, "Structure and Detail," p. 115; and Murry, "Beyond Morality," pp. 47-53.

43. Paul Schrader, "Robert Bresson," in *Transcendental Style in Film: Ozu, Bresson, Dreyer* (Berkeley and Los Angeles: University of California Press, 1972), pp. 93, 81.

44. Daniel Millar, "Pickpocket," in *The Films of Robert Bresson*, ed. Ian Cameron (New York: Praeger, 1970), p. 85; Richard Roud, "Novel Novel: Fable Fable?" *Sight and Sound* 31, no. 2 (Spring 1962): p. 86.

45. Amédée Ayfre, "The Universe of Robert Bresson," in Cameron, *The Films of Robert Bresson*, p. 23.

46. Michel Estève, "Permanence de Robert Bresson," *Études cinématographiques* 3-4 (1960): pp. 227-28. Cf. Jean Wagner, "L'Homme derrière l'objet," *Cahiers du cinéma* 104 (February 1960): p. 50: "If there are bars separating the two heroes in the last scene, their souls are united: the wind listeth where it will."

47. Jean Sémolué, "Les Limites de la liberté," *Études cinématographiques* 3-4 (1960): pp. 238-39, translation mine.

48. Allen Thiher writes, "In nearly all his works, be it *Au hasard Balthazar*, *Jeanne d'Arc*, *Pickpocket*, or *Une Femme douce*, Bresson's narrative turns in one way or another on isolation and humiliation, on estrangement and the impossibility of a desired community. Only in *Un condamné à mort* does transcendence seem to be realized in the flesh" ("The Existentialist Moment: Bresson's *Un condamné à mort:*

The Semiotics of Grace," in *The Cinematic Muse: Critical Studies in the History of French Cinema* [Columbia: University of Missouri Press, 1979], p. 136).

49. Seguin, "Pickpocket," *Positif* 33 (April 1960): p. 41; Tailleur, "Pickpocket," p. 44.

50. Vas, "Pickpocket," p. 140. John Russel Taylor concludes, "There is no sense of a process completed, but only of an inexplicable change of character" ("Robert Bresson," in *Cinema Eye, Cinema Ear: Some Key Filmmakers of the Sixties* [New York: Hill & Wang, 1964], p. 135).

51. See above, n. 33.

52. For a discussion of Chernyshevsky's role in Dostoevsky's work see Offord, "The Causes of Crime and the Meaning of Law."

53. The title of Camus's anthology of essays is *L'Envers et l'endroit*.

54. Certainly the theme of carnival goes back a long way. Bakhtin explores it in Rabelais's work, of course (see Mikhael Bakhtin, *Rabelais and His World*, trans. Helene Iswolsky [Cambridge: MIT Press, 1968]), but Curtius notes its presence already in the *Carmina Burana* as well as other works of antiquity (see Ernst Robert Curtius, *European Literature and the Latin Middle Ages* [New York: Harper & Row, 1953], pp. 94-98).

55. Bakhtin, *Problems of Dostoevsky's Poetics*, p. 5.

56. Ibid., pp. 87, 100-101.

57. A comparison of Nietzsche's *Beyond Good and Evil* with Michel's arguments to the police inspector reveals surprising coincidences (see *Beyond Good and Evil*, trans. Walter Kaufmann [New York: Vintage, 1966], pp. 31, 37, 41-42, 44, 55ff.). I shall have more to say about Bresson's relationship to Camus below.

58. Bakhtin, *Problems of Dostoevsky's Poetics*, p. 142.

59. See Mireille Latil Le Dantec, "Le Diable probablement," *Cinématographe* 29 (July-August 1977): p. 32: "The negative gestural asceticism of *Pickpocket* subverts the accepted order of things, which it refuses because, in any case, the world is upside-down ['le monde est a l'envers']." And Jeanne will say to Michel, "You're not of this world ['Vous n'êtes pas dans la vie réelle']." I shall have more to say on this point below.

60. Edward Wasiolek, *Dostoevsky* (Cambridge: MIT Press, 1964), p. 83.

61. See Browne, "Film Form/Voice-Over," p. 236. Browne writes of *Diary of a Country Priest*, "That linkage and control of two points of view is the underlying formal and compositional issue of the film, and the basis of its power, becomes clear not so much in sequences accompanied by speech narration that repeats what the scenes show (transparence), but in the scenes of explicit disjuncture, when the Priest says something to himself that is in conflict with what the image shows (character opaqueness)."

62. This tendency has been noted by Patrick Bensard ("Notes sur *Pickpocket,*" in *Camera/Stylo* 69/69 [February 1989]: p. 113) and by Lindley Hanlon, (*Fragments*, pp. 40, 114).

63. Richard S. Lambert, *The Prince of Pickpockets: A Study of George Barrington Who Left His Country For His Country's Good* (London: Faber & Faber, 1930), p. 34. Further quotations from this text will be indicated by PP.

64. Rahv, "Dostoevsky in *Crime and Punishment*," p. 37. This is a feature, by the way, common to Dostoevsky, Bresson, and Camus, whose presence in this film is also remarkably complex.

65. Jacques Doniol-Valcroze and Jean-Luc Godard, "Entretien avec Robert Bresson," *Cahiers du cinéma* 104 (February 1960): p. 4.

66. The sense of Montaigne's text is, according to Tom Conley (unpublished letter to the author), rather the detached hand, the representation of an absence, following Christian iconography.

67. R. M. Arlaud et al., "Propos de Robert Bresson," *Cahiers du cinéma* 75 (October 1957): p. 7.

68. Arts, 17 June 1959, quoted in Estève, *Robert Bresson: la passion du cinématographe*, p. 63.

69. Sémolué, "Les Limites de la liberté," p. 233. Lars Helmstein, "Le Pont brûlé," p. 36, is also quite explicit about the connection between Bresson's character of the pickpocket and his own approach to the cinema.

70. Doniol-Valcroze and Godard, "Entretien avec Robert Bresson," pp. 6-7.

71. Pinel, "Le Paradoxe du non-comédien," p. 81.

72. Greene, "Robert Bresson," p. 7.

73. Magny, "L'Expérience intérieure," pp. 22, translation mine.

74. Louis Malle, "Avec *Pickpocket* Bresson a trouvé," *Arts, Lettres, Spectacles*, 30 December 1959-5 January 1960, pp. 1, 6. Patrick Bensard develops this angle, if obliquely, in "Notes sur *Pickpocket*," p. 111ff. They are not alone in this observation: Eric Rhode notes that Michel's robberies are for "erotic satisfaction" ("Pickpocket," *Sight and Sound* 29, no. 4 [Fall 1960]: p. 193). Magny comments cryptically, "Sexuality occupies a stronger place in the work of Robert Bresson the more his work becomes pessimistic" ("L'Expérience intérieure," p. 23).

75. Jacques Frenais notes that "*Pickpocket* is constructed like a sexual conquest, like a pick-up ['comme la drague']. In fact, the pickpocket Michel is Don Juan" ("Autour du *Pickpocket* de Robert Bresson," *Cinéma 78* 235 [July 1978]: p. 36).

76. Jean-Pierre Oudart, "Le Hors-champ de l'auteur," *Cahiers du cinéma* pp. 236-37 (March-April 1972): p. 86.

77. Gide's *L'Immoraliste* provides one of the models for this film. Michel, the novel's narrator, watches, like Bresson, with quiet complicity and a secret voyeuristic pleasure, as an Arab youth steals a pair of scissors from him. Patrick Bensard calls *Pickpocket* a "joyless Don-juanism" ("Notes sur *Pickpocket*," p. 113).

79. Not surprisingly, given the fact that he has been in analysis for many years. See Prédal, "Bresson et son temps," p. 10.

80. Jacques Frenais, "Autour du *Pickpocket*," p. 37.

81. Joyce McDougall, *Théâtres du Je* (Paris: Gallimard, 1982), pp. 10, 36, translation mine.

82. Ibid., p. 56.

83. Pinel, "Le Paradoxe du non-comédien," p. 83. For other similar observations on Bresson's treatment of his actors see Jacques Laurans, "Le Choix d'un modèle," *Camera/Stylo* 68/69 (February 1989): pp. 8-10; Helmstein, "Le Pont brûlé," pp. 28-46; and Gourdon, "Georges Bernanos," p. 47.

84. Roland Monod, "Working with Bresson," *Sight and Sound* 27, no.1 (Summer 1957): p. 32.

85. Cf. Joyce McDougall, *Plaidoyer pour une certaine anormalité* (Paris: Gallimard, 1978), 107: "Certain analysands . . . give the impression of repeating indefatigably an old situation in which the former child had to create a vacuum between himself and the Other, denying reality and eliminating unbearable affects"; see also ibid., p. 133ff., translation mine.

86. Oudart, "Le Hors-champ de l'auteur," p. 98, translation mine. See also Oudart's "Un Pouvoir qui ne pense, ne calcule, ni ne juge?" *Cahiers du cinéma* 258-59 (July-August 1975): p. 37. The ultimate repression of the actor, according to Marie-Claire Ropars-Wuilleumier ("Un Mauvais Rêve," in *L'Écran de la mémoire* [Paris: Seuil, 1970], pp. 178-81), occurs in Bresson's *Au hasard Balthazar*.

87. McDougall, *Plaidoyer pour une certaine anormalité*, p. 53. Elsewhere she notes, "It is no longer the disavowal of a *sensory perception* but something infinitely more elaborate and evolved, a disavowal, certainly, but of a different order" (p. 52).

88. Ibid., p. 50. Cf. Bresson's statement: "Cinematography a military art. Prepare a film like a battle" (NC, 9/25). Cf. the following statement by André Targe: "In a universe entirely fragmented, devoid of any touchstone, filmic time breakdown loses the artificial coherence that editing normally gives it" ("Ici l'espace naît du temps," p. 90).

89. Cited in McDougall, *Plaidoyer pour une certaine anormalité*, p. 60.

90. Pierre Jouvet, "D'Homère à Proust: de Griffith à Bresson," *Cinématographe* 32 (November 1977): p. 9.

91. Marjorie Green, "Robert Bresson," p. 7.

Pickpocket

Breaking Silence (Forty Years Later)

Babette Mangolte has made several films over the past three decades, and was director of cinematography on several others (by Chantal Akerman, Yvonne Rainer, and Sally Potter). She currently teaches film at University of California, San Diego. The following is an outline of her current project, a film exploring the profound effect Bresson's *Pickpocket* had on some of the non-professional actors who appeared in it. Less a conventional script "treatment" than a poetic text, Mangolte's synopsis and screenplay reveal the impulse of so many Bresson commentators: to elucidate, as she puts it, "the mystery that surrounds the power of certain works of art that have changed our lives." *Ed.*

Synopsis

A FAMILIAR FACE . . . Where have I seen it before?
I am in the middle of a very Parisian group of people. I feel and come from elsewhere, I know no one here, and in the middle of this crowd, I have the strange feeling that the past is calling me. I have to think back beyond oblivion to something I cannot remember. I ask myself that nagging question: this face, this man, do I know him? from when? from where? From what past, from what life?

I have lived in the United States for twenty-five years. The past, in which I might have met this man, must date back before those twenty-five years, to another life, another me, me as a college student, living in a garret in the Latin Quarter, me as a Cinémathèque mole, a film buff, hanging around in coffee houses, talking all night about American B movies. That life, can I still remember it? Seated across the table at that very Parisian dinner party, I look at this man. His face is as familiar as the face of a close friend I might have lost touch with, forgotten, and was about to rediscover. I decide to come closer.

I discover that it is the face of someone I never knew, or rather that of someone of whom I knew only the film image. That face, that image is of a character in a film, a secondary character. Among all the films I have been moved by, that film, *Pickpocket*, perhaps had the strongest influence on me, not just because it is one of the most beautiful in the history of film, but because I have always felt that it represented my youth as a student who did not study, and that endless waiting peculiar to an age in life which seemed eternal and for which time did not exist. Shot in Paris during the summer of 1959, *Pickpocket* still seems to me to represent the essence of the present, whatever the time (the sixties, the nineties) or the place (Paris, New York) in which I watch it.

Forty years later, I leave New York in search of the Paris of my youth. There I discover the life of a man who, during that summer of 1959, had been hired to play the part of Jacques, the friend of the main protagonist (the traditional role of the confidant), in a film by Robert Bresson. In 1959, that man, Pierre Leymarie, was a medical student who did not intend to be an actor, becoming one only by chance, and only for a few weeks. For him, the shooting of the film had been an interesting though frustrating experience which had since been deliberately forgotten. When the film was released, it was not a popular success, and some reviews had been harsh on its actors. Although one may not be an actor, one will still be treated like one, and bad reviews are taken personally and hurt.

Breaking Silence, a project born out of that chance encounter, is an attempt to recover the forgotten experience of a one-time actor who, one summer, found himself party to a film that is now regarded as a major work, and, by many, as a masterpiece of French cinema, a film as powerful forty years later as it was then, a film that gives an enduring impression of the Paris of its time, and expresses in an uncompromising way the inner experience of an encounter with grace, a subject that today seems impossible to write about.

The question I want to ask is how it is that this film is able to present images as authentic experience, so that, many years later, I can mistake that image of life for life itself. Let's call that question: the enigma *Pickpocket*. Does it have to do with the actor himself, whom Bresson called the "model," with what he is, or seems to be?

I want to investigate the shooting of *Pickpocket*, its participants, the details of their experiences during the summer of 1959, and the consequences in their lives. It is, therefore, a history, but also an examination of a new paradox of the actor.

My purpose is to bring to light, through the remembrances of a past whose influence is still profound today, a way of working that disregarded ordinary standards, a unique method and practice, and to recreate another encounter, the one with an eccentric, demanding, authoritarian and original artist, Robert Bresson.

Pickpocket

Many questions come forth: why did Bresson hire non-professional actors? Is a film actor's interpretation of his part still a relevant concept? Or, instead, should one become the character in order for the spectators to think that what they see involves no interpretation, no control, no thought? Could I ever remember the face of a well-known actor as being that of someone I would have known in real life? Would I have been surprised to discover this man's face I knew only as an image if I had seen it in other movies, or if I had felt he was playing a role, interpreting a part?

But I would also like to find out how a powerful but short-lived experience transformed the life of a student, who acted once, one summer, who later fulfilled his vocation as a doctor, and for whom that summer's adventure was at the time no more than a distraction. How can we define another enigma: what does it mean, to be an actor?

Several themes are intertwined. What is the source of this work that is now recognized as a masterpiece; how did Bresson's aesthetic and system affect not only the film itself, but also the people who took part in its making? An elucidation of the mystery that surrounds the power of certain works of art that have changed our lives.

Is it possible for a movie to change our lives?

Can one summer's experience transform a life forever?

I do not claim to answer these questions, but only to raise them.

Screenplay

A familiar face. . . Where have I seen him? A party in a Paris apartment.

A door, street sounds—although unidentifiable as such, they are an excerpt from the soundtrack of a movie made forty years ago.

The Medical School at Caen. Students are coming and going, empty office.

A Paris street, a bus passing by, view of a carriage entrance left ajar.

Sounds from forty years ago.

A staircase on Place Saint-Michel (this shot is in black-and-white). Sound of footsteps offscreen.

A subway corridor.

The deserted racetrack at Longchamp. Sound gradually fills the screen: excerpt from the soundtrack of the first sequence of *Pickpocket*.

This face, this thoughtful gaze: where have I seen him?

We understand that the face is the one of a dinner guest. The dinner table, people still standing with their glasses, chatting, sounds of a conversation, about ten people (at my friend Michelle L.'s).

This man's face . . .—Have we met before? I ask him. He looks at me and says:—Do you go to the movies?—Yes, sometimes, I answer (with a straight face).—I played in a movie, once, he says.—Really? Which one?, I ask.—A movie by Robert Bresson (a brief pause) *Pickpocket*. I look at him. He looks at me (facing the camera). A silent pause, as if to leave me some time to understand.

The shot from Pickpocket *with Jacques at the door (black-and-white).*

That face in black-and-white is replaced with the same face forty years later (same frame), that of the actor who played "Jacques," Pierre Leymarie. It is the same face.
I think: how strange I could have thought I knew him!
My friend Michelle's voice, saying: Meet Pierre Leymarie. Pierre, this is Babette Mangolte, my friend from New York.—I am very happy to meet you, I tell him. *Pickpocket* is my favourite movie. I would so much like to talk to you.—Let's arrange to meet later, Pierre answers.

Dissolve to next scene.

The gates of the Jardin du Luxembourg, pan and tracking shot around the fountain, Place Edmond Rostand toward the MacDonald's at the corner of Rue Soufflot and Boulevard Saint-Michel.

Dissolve to a black-and-white photograph of the café Mahieu, which stood at that same corner in 1959.

Title: June 1959.

Pierre Leymarie's voice, talking about how he met Bresson at the café Mahieu, where he had come for a casting. I later learned that Bresson always arranged to meet the people he hired as actors in Paris cafés. He also cast *Mouchette* at the café Mahieu and *Au hasard Balthazar* at the café Flore.

Pierre Leymarie is shown in his office at the Caen Medical School, where he is a professor. He explains how he learned about the *Pickpocket* project from a student friend, Philippe Lécolier, who was in charge of the film club at the Cité Universitaire where both of them lived at the time. Lécolier knew Bresson, who had asked him to find people for the movie he was working on in May or June of 1959. Pierre was twenty-four then, and had no intention of becoming an actor. He was a medical student.

In Caen. Pierre Leymarie talks about the casting, and his first impression of the process. There were about ten people at the Mahieu, and each of them was filmed for a few minutes. According to Lécolier, Pierre's screen test was encouraging: "Bresson liked what you did." Pierre was invited to Bresson's house, where the director explained to him his ideas about filmmaking: anything but "canned theatre." "Producers want me to hire stars, but you know, I am the star." Bresson was not very talkative, but he knew exactly what he wanted: "Place your hand here, look over there," or "Let's do it again. A little faster." One could feel he was constructing the movie with the images and sounds he would get from the actors he had chosen through an intuitive process. "We actors never decided anything. We helped the great director to accomplish his work." That is how Pierre remembers it.

We also see Caen and Pierre Leymarie's present life, his relationships with the people with whom he works. We see him from a distance. Contrast between his present position of authority and what he tells about the shooting, when he was not able to decide what to do and when he resented Bresson's control.

In Paris, café Le Cluny (at the corner of Boulevard Saint-Michel and Boulevard Saint-Germain), with Jean Pélégri, who plays the part of the police detective in the movie: Pierre and Jean talk about their memories from the shooting. Kassagi (a professional pickpocket who was hired by Bresson to play himself) teaching them tricks and showing them how to pinch wallets. Jean and Pierre remember the famous scene in which Michel talks about his theory regarding superior men who are allowed more than others. They talk about Bresson's authority, his desire to break the actor's acting through repetition, until acting becomes completely automatic. Doing the same shot forty times over! But camera moves were very complex, I say. Jean tells how Bresson always ended up using the first take. This is not what Bresson said during interviews.

Fade to black.

Excerpt from the movie *Pickpocket* (black-and-white).

Fade to black.

Pierre Leymarie talks about what he understood about Bresson's method as a director of actors. This interview is close up facing the camera with a neutral background (shot indoors in Caen, at Pierre's house). I read him an excerpt from Roland Monod's text on his own work with Bresson, while Monod was shooting *Un condamné à mort s'est échappé*. (That text was published in November of 1956, three years before the shooting of *Pickpocket*.) Had he read the Monod text before meeting Bresson? Pierre says no, but he had seen *Un condamné*, as well as *Journal d'un curé de campagne*. He liked the films. He understood that Bresson was different, was an artist, but he had read nothing about him, and only knew what his friend Philippe Lécolier had told him.

Pierre tells how he had been invited to the first screening of the movie. It had been difficult for him to see himself onscreen, and that experience had not been a pleasant one. He read every review, and now says they were all very bad, except for the one by Louis Malle, published in *Arts et Spectacles*. Actually, most reviews were full of praise, even calling the movie a masterpiece, with the reservation that the story was morally ambiguous. But the movie did not have a large audience. Pierre remembers that a friend of his father told him: "You're not a bad actor, you just don't act!" Bresson would have liked that.

It was not until ten years later, while Pierre, now a doctor, was living in Montréal, that his landlady told him, bowing in front of him: "Ah, sir, I saw you yesterday on television." Gaining your landlady's respect for being on TV! The movie had been shown the day before. He had not known about it, and had not seen it. He saw the film again only recently, because he had been invited to give a talk following a screening of the movie in Caen two or three years ago. Only upon seeing his name on the marquee—"*Pickpocket*, a film by Robert Bresson, introduced by Pierre Leymarie"—did he finally come to terms with that deep and painful experience.

The house where Pierre now lives will be shown at the end, as a conclusion: an ordinary life, though one marked by that moment, during one summer, when an adventure took place, an encounter with a strong and domineering personality, that of Bresson. A movie whose fame has continually grown during the past forty years.

Close-up on hands in black-and-white (the Gare de Lyon sequence).

Here we learn how to see and listen.

The miracle of observation.

Mouchette

"D'où cela vient-il?":
Notes on Three Films
by Robert Bresson

Console-toi, tu ne me chercherais pas, si tu ne m'avais trouvé.
Be consoled: you would not be seeking me, if you had not found me.

— PASCAL, *Pensées*[1]

Pour tout acte, le considérer sous l'aspect non de l'objet,
mais de l'impulsion. Non pas: à quelle fin? Mais: d'où cela vient-il?
Consider any act from the point of view, not of its object but
of its impulsion. Not: to what end? but: where does that come from?

— SIMONE WEIL, *La Pesanteur et la grâce*[2]

ROBERT BRESSON is now the undisputed doyen of French filmmakers, with a career dating back to 1943. His work is among the most readily recognizable in the contemporary cinema—through the stress it places on ellipsis and silence, the tones outwardly bereft of emotion in which the *modèles* (Bresson refuses the term *acteur*) speak, and the unceasing avoidance of any normative "psychological" explanation for the characters' behaviour. Anne-Marie in *Les Anges du péché* courts death from exposure through her nightly praying on the grave of the founder of the religious order that has expelled her; Yvon in *L'Argent*, made forty years later, butchers first a couple, then an entire family, with an axe on his release from an unjustly earned prison sentence . . . Such extremes of behaviour, so hermetically presented, have meant that Bresson's work has aroused extremes of feeling among critics and commentators.[3] But, if there is one point of well-nigh general agreement, it is that Bresson's whole oeuvre is at once riven and structured by paradox.

Paradox, or better paradoxes?—for it is possible to detect and itemize a number of interconnected contradictions in Bresson. He is a Catholic director in whose films the Church figures hardly at all, and then primarily as instrument of oppression or isolation; a Christian artist whose articulation of word and image often works to deny the causal relationship between actions and their consequences, for evil or for good; a believer in a God who is to be looked for between the images rather than found behind them . . . Writers and commentators have approached these contradictions by way of a number of different vocabularies: theological (Louis Malle on *Pickpocket*), mystical (Paul Schrader in *Transcendental Style in Film*), existential-phenomenological (Allen H. Thiher in *The Cinematic Muse*), and psychoanalytic (Jean-Pierre Oudart in *Cinéma et suture*), among others. Sometimes such vocabularies are adopted to clarify or "explain" the films, sometimes on the other hand to emphasize their resistance to any kind of definitive reading. Thus, for Malle, *Pickpocket* is an allegory of the Fall and Redemption of Man, while conversely it is significant that Susan Sontag's essay on Bresson figures in a collection of texts entitled *Against Interpretation*. If these notes incline towards Sontag's approach, this is not to dismiss Malle's as reductive or misleading. His interpretation of *Pickpocket* is among the most important texts on Bresson's work, and suggestions that the film may be understood as a journey away from emotional (especially sexual) confusion, or that Mouchette's suicide by drowning is like a baptism or even a marriage ceremony, have contributed significantly to my thinking about those films. But the richest and most suggestive approach to Bresson seems to me to be concerned with notions of the discontinuous, the unsayable, and the healing of a split too large for a non-contradictory psychological discourse to grasp—notions that are of central importance to (particularly Lacanian and post-Lacanian) psychoanalysis, but also to certain kinds of Christian mysticism.

The importance of the "Christian dimension" may seem unsurprising given that of the three films dealt with here two—*Journal d'un curé de campagne* and *Mouchette*—are based on works of fiction by Georges Bernanos. But it is not as "literary adaptations" that I propose to consider them. Bresson's scrupulous fidelity to the text of *Journal d'un curé de campagne* in particular is of a quite different order from what such a label might imply—a point illuminated by Michel Estève:

> Its surprising success is that it corresponds perfectly to Bernanos's work, not by being servilely literal but by way of a re-creation that rigorously eliminates both the psychological and the social, centering everything on the spiritual drama.[4]

It is this elimination of the "psychological" that constitutes an important link between the world of Bresson's films and that of Lacanian psychoanalysis. Lacan's vigorous onslaughts on the American appropriation of Freud in the interests of harmonious social engineering are well documented; to quote Sherry Turkle,

> Lacan denigrates "humanistic" philosophy and psychology that treat man as an actor who wills his action and instead sees man as a submitting object of processes that transcend him.[5]

Such a statement would (*mutatis mutandis*) be likewise true of Christian theology. The further distinctive contribution of Lacanian psychoanalysis is its stress on the constitutive importance of language, as the fundamental condition of the unconscious and hence of all human psychic activity. In *Fonction et champ de la parole et du langage en psychanalyse*, Lacan refers to the dangerous "temptation of the analyst to abandon the foundation of the word precisely in situations where its use, verging as it is on the ineffable, would require more than ever its examination."[6] Language, for Lacan, not merely touches upon the unsayable, but is coterminous with it, and the "talking cure" of analysis engages with language not as a seamless garment for ideas and meaning, but as a mechanism that produces sense(s) through its errors, hesitations, and silences. The grandiose claims to universality often made (if only, fittingly, by implication) by or on behalf of psychoanalysis, especially since Lacan, cannot obscure its specificity as part of Judaeo-Christian culture. The point has been often enough taken about Freud; but many exegetes or disciples of Lacan have articulated the concepts of psychoanalysis with those of Christianity. Thus, Françoise Dolto, in *L'Évangile au risque de la psychanalyse*, reads the Gospels as psychodramas—in other words, as texts that like any other have their own unconscious. Whether or not it is relevant that Lacan's own brother is a prominent Jesuit theologian, it would appear undeniable that the founding concept of the "Nom-du-Père" in his work is closely connected with the Old Testament conception of the unpronounceable Name of God. Among modern writers in the Judaeo-Christian mystical tradition, Simone Weil places particular stress on the significance of the unsayable, and her observation in *La Pesanteur et la grâce* ("Intelligence can never penetrate a mystery, but it and it alone can assess the suitability of the words to express it.")[7] offers parallels with Lacanian ideas on the relationship between (omnipresent) language and the "real" it seeks to circumscribe but by definition can never express.

In this context, we can see in a new light Bresson's renowned fidelity to the texts on which many of his films are based. "The letter kills, but the spirit gives life"; perhaps it is precisely Bresson's fetishistic literalness that, killing the letter with an excess of devotion, frees the spirit that would otherwise remain imprisoned. André Bazin's essay on *Journal d'un curé de campagne* (hereafter referred to for brevity as *Journal*) draws particular attention to that film's doubling-up of sound and image (or written and spoken text), and describes Bresson's approach as "a

fidelity that sacrifices the letter only with the utmost respect and a thousand preliminary feelings of remorse." The fact that Bresson, to quote Bazin again, "prunes
around the essential,"[8] has a relevance that is metaphysical, even psychoanalytic, as
well as stylistic.

Before starting the analysis of the three films, I shall examine another sense,
more global and more immediately striking, in which Bresson's work is illuminated by the analogies between psychoanalysis and Christian mysticism. The
epigraphs to this article are part of a Christian tradition (dating back at least to Saint
Augustine) where the soul's search for God is at the same time a search (albeit unknowing) for itself, so that the view of salvation as the linear movement of a uni-
tary soul towards a fixed destination or destiny comes to seem inadequate if not
actually misleading. The remark Pascal attributes to his God, like so much else in
the *Pensées*, has habitually been understood in a Jansenist sense; only those chosen
from all eternity will truly seek God, and the search is thus a self-validating proof
of the inevitability of its goal . . . But a more "modern" reading would see the
search as the most important part of the finding rather than as a preliminary to it,
returning us to the notion of salvation or healing as *process*. Christian mystics have
attached the greatest importance to the "silence of God," seen not as a spiritual
void generating despair but as a "speaking silence," attention to which is a vital
part of the redemptive process. The analogy with the "talking cure" mentioned
above should be manifest. The "thinking reed" that is for Pascal[9] man awaiting
and seeking salvation, and the analysand likewise in search of enlightenment
and self-realization, both need to pass through the silence of their God (or God-
surrogate) as part of their journey. The country priest's sense of an abandonment
so total that he cannot even make the gesture of accepting it; Michel the pickpocket's awareness of being caught up in a process he has to accept precisely
because he cannot understand it; the silences that punctuate *Mouchette* and reach
a crescendo, so to speak, just before the girl's suicide—these can all be seen as
instances of the Pascalian paradox.

The epigraph from Simone Weil likewise lends itself to a double interpretation. On one level, it is a hortatory reminder that "God moves in a mysterious
way," and that the faithful should not ask for too much insight into his purposes—
not treat the "Nom-du-Père," that is, as if it were knowable. At the same time, it
calls into question the dissociability of search and goal, of process and *telos*,
through the importance it attaches to the origin—or better the search for the origin—of our drives and actions. The concern of psychoanalysis is not so much to
provide the analysand with explanations of her/his dreams and other behavioural
symptoms as to develop and encourage attention to the deeper, unconscious strata
from which they emanate. "Non pas: à quelle fin? Mais: d'où cela vient-il?" could
serve as counsel for the patient in analysis as much as for the patient believer. Like
the Pascal quotation, too, it is relevant to Bresson's work. Hesitant or sceptical

viewers often wonder what the "point" of the country priest's agony might be, or what "explanation" of Michel's kleptomania or Mouchette's suicide best fits the elliptical, recalcitrant data. Such questions, of course, also present themselves to readers of the Bernanos novels, but less insistently, if only because Bernanos's verbal narration lends itself less readily to ellipsis than the visual and verbal narration of the films. Rather than attempting to answer questions like these, it might be more profitable to ask in return: "Non pas: à quelle fin? Mais: d'où cela vient-il?" To assert that the priest's agony ensures his immediate accession to the Kingdom of Grace (which, theologically, is what is meant by speaking of him as a saint), or that Michel is being borne along by God, with a little intertextual help from *Crime and Punishment*, towards his final rendezvous with Jeanne and grace in the prison, is possible only from a position of transcendental faith that is not available perhaps even to all who would call themselves Christian. Those who cannot occupy that position need to ask themselves a different set of questions, in which the priest's compulsive and infinite sense of spiritual responsibility for those to whom he is "Father," or Michel's self-hatred and tortured relationship with his mother, or Mouchette's consecutive assumption and final rejection of the roles of daughter, mother, and lover, will play important parts. To the dislocation of question and answer *about* the films corresponds (most notably in *Pickpocket*, which is full of questions somebody, generally Michel, declines to answer) a dislocation of question and answer *within* them. Dislocation, indeed—of signifier and signified in Lacan, of seeker and sought in Pascal, of asker and asked-for in Weil—can be described as the central element in the intellectual and spiritual context in which Bresson's work is here situated.

It is thus appropriate that the first aspect of *Journal* to be considered, if only because it has attracted the most critical attention, is the double presentation of the priest's diary, which we see him writing in close-up as his voice reads the text aloud. Bazin says that this

> prolongs the Bressonian dialectic between abstraction and reality thanks to which we finally accede only to the reality of the soul.[10]

The doubling-up, that is to say, paradoxically intensifies our sense of the ineffability of the priest's experience. Similarly, Michel Estève speaks of the film's use of montage as suggesting to us as "the silence of the soul as silence and absence of God."[11] Hostile critics will retort that God's silence is a meaningless concept if one does not believe that He exists, and that the text/image doubling impoverishes the cinematic in favour of the nebulously metaphysical. Yet the perception of language in the journal-writing scenes, like the Lacanian view of language as material, is in one sense at least not metaphysical at all. The priest's simultaneous writing and reading do not give the sense of a key opening (or a window opening on to) the infinity of Truth. Rather, they place before us language in its materiality, with its hesitations and the instruments of its production, so that it is as though the priest were not so much capturing his agony in language as passing through language as an integral part of it. If for "priest" we read "analysand," and think of the expression of symptoms rather than the capturing of agony, the analogy with the psychoanalytic process should become plain. It is interesting too that the long conversation between the priest and the countess—the emotional fulcrum of both novel and film—is marked by pauses, hesitations, and silences that come to dominate the sequence. The countess throws on to the fire a medallion portrait of the young son whose premature death has caused her to turn aside from God and the world in despair. The priest removes it from the burning coals, returns it to her and blesses her, before promising his absolute silence about what has happened. That we are here in the presence of something more than a simple variant of the seal of confession is shown by the fact that Bazin speaks of the silent dialogue of the two souls as "le côté pile de la face de Dieu"[12]—a phrase reminiscent of Gerard Manley Hopkins speaking of the non-believers drowned in "The Wreck of the Deutschland":

Yet did *the dark side of the bay of thy blessing*
Not vault them, the millions of rounds of
thy mercy not reeve even them in?

Bazin and Hopkins are each suggesting that the "face" or merciful presence of God has his silence and absence as its necessary counterpart, much as the presence of syllables, words, and concepts in language depends upon the pauses and silences that punctuate them. The absence is necessary for a presence—linguistic, divine, perhaps both—to be felt. Such a formulation is also helpful in thinking about the end of the film, where the images do not so much "add to" the spoken text as prolong its resonance. The priest's former colleague Dufréty relates his death from cancer of the stomach and dying words, "Tout est grâce," exactly as in the novel, while the image of the Cross fills the screen, where it remains for several moments in silence. Amédée Ayfre observes: "The whole of Bresson's film is in the Cross, which sums it up as well as concluding it"[13]—a judgement made in the context of a study of Bresson's work as "cellulaire," reproducing the whole of itself in the smallest details. This is one of the most important ways in which the Cross functions as a symbol of Christianity, so that there is a sense in which the whole Christian paradox of death, redemption, and transcendence is "in" even the smallest Sign of the Cross or Cross-as-sign. Paul Schrader, following Jean Sémolué, distinguishes three levels of alienation in the film: "(1) sickness—the priest and his body; (2) social solitude—the priest and his parishioners; (3) sacred solitude—the priest and the world of sin."[14] In the light of this too the whole of the film is in the Cross, which marks a final separation from the three levels through an acceptance and transcendence of them. To the image of the Cross (on which Christ's body, while not visible, is none the less suggested by its absence) the priest leaves his body and the world of his parishioners, which he has accepted quite literally to the point of death. It is noteworthy that the scenes Bresson shot but discarded in the editing almost all showed the priest in his relationships with his parishioners (for instance, saying Mass). It is as though the first body to disappear from the film were the institutional Church and the social body of which it forms part. The Cross acts also as a meeting-place of the theological and the psychoanalytic—a statement which may appear sweeping, even inappropriate when we bear in mind how resolutely both Bernanos and Bresson avoid any imputation of a "psyche" to the priest. But Christian psychoanalysts have written about the significance of the Cross as the convergence point of the vocabulary of their faith and that of their clinical practice, and it is in this more global sense that the concept is here used. Françoise Dolto (a former close associate of Lacan's) sees the Passion and Crucifixion as a psychodrama in which the overcoming of an excessive Oedipal dependence (figured by Mary's presence at the foot of the Cross), and the conquest and killing of narcissism, are important elements. Pierre Solignac's work as psychiatric counsellor to priests and those in the religious life led him to write *La Névrose chrétienne*, an indictment of the institutional Church, in which he recounts his analysis of a priest whose passage through acute depression and self-loathing took harrowing psychosomatic forms. The priest's observations to Solignac have echoes of the *Journal*:

> Charity is all too often only a pharisaic caricature of love: "Lord, I give to charity." I can no longer abide that expression: give it to charity. For me it is an insult. The priest's true vocation is to be a man of communication, horizontal but also vertical communication—that, I believe, is one of the symbols of the Cross. His role is certainly not to condemn some in order to reassure others.[15]

If "tout est grâce," and if that is what the final shot of the Cross exemplifies, then the remarks quoted by Solignac appear at once in a theological and in a temporal sense, the latter applicable to the realm of psychoanalysis. The Cross as transcendence of narcissism and emblem of communication with one's own psyche as well as with the world at large is a symbol available outside the world of orthodox Christian belief, and indeed (as the priest's death in the home of an unfrocked former colleague illustrates) often best and most sensitively perceived precisely there. There remains one major stumbling-block in the final sequence, at any rate for non-believers—the concept of "grace," which may seem to reduce ultimately important issues to the level of a raffle for eternity. Pascal's *Pensées* are a key text here, for they transcend the apparent arbitrariness of grace descending incomprehensibly from above by siting its origin equally within the individual who receives it:

> Be consoled: it is not from yourself that you must expect it, but on the contrary in expecting nothing from yourself that you must expect it.[16]
> The figure bears absence and presence, pleasure and displeasure.—The figure has a twofold sense—one clear, one where sense is said to be hidden.[17]

If we understand "grace" as in some sense equivalent to healing (an equation unexceptionable for Christians and helpful for others), the parallel between what Pascal says in the first passage and the operations of psychoanalysis becomes clear. Those who come to analysis frequently do so precisely because they expect nothing of themselves; and it is to the speaking void or hollow within them, as Lacan would say "là où ça parle," that the therapeutic process draws attention. Just as for Pascal grace is like a flow back and forth between two poles—the void of the believer and the plenitude of God as they endlessly interact—so the process of analysis (which can often involve the kind of transcendence of narcissism Françoise Dolto sees figured by the Cross) is situated neither within the analyst nor within the analysand—one answer to the question: "D'où cela vient-il?" In this light, "tout est grâce" appears not as the desperately optimistic last gasp of benevolence, but as a recognition that the Cross as it fills the screen brings with it a perception that transcends the linearity of "common-sense" positivist psychology. The second Pascal quotation is an extraordinary prefiguration of modern linguistic notions about the relationship between signifier and signified, and the centrality of ambiguity and absence to any signifying system (including the cinema). In *Le Titre de la lettre*, Jean-Luc Nancy and Philippe Lacoue-Labarthe tell us that for Lacan the signifier

> is no longer the other face of the sign to the signified, existing only in this association, but that order of spacing in which the law inscribes and marks itself as difference.[18]

This is clearly applicable to the diary-writing scenes in the *Journal*, where the "espacement" between voice and pen acts as the space within which for the priest the "lot" of the divine will inscribes itself. A veritable "game" of presence and absence is at work in the final shot, where to the absence of two bodies—Christ's and the priest's—corresponds the presence of the Cross. The temporal or immanent view of the Cross mentioned by Solignac's priest—as the meeting-point of horizontal and vertical communication—is complemented by the transcendental view of it as mediator between the divine presence on earth and the strivings of the flesh-bound spirit to ascend to Heaven. The triumph of Bresson's ending is to suggest such a host of "absent presences" through the simple presence of the Cross, and such a wealth of voices and languages through the silence around it.

The theological dimension is far less overt in *Pickpocket*, a film that appears to defy its audience to read it, and to solicit a psychological reading which it constantly thwarts. A title tells us: "Ceci n'est pas un roman policier" (which in any event becomes obvious after a few moments), and this taken together with the opening shot of Michel writing in his cell ("D'habitude ceux qui font ces choses ne les écrivent pas, et pourtant je les ai faites") seems to invite us to view the film as a confessional autobiography. Yet such a reading is rendered difficult, if not impossible, by the extraordinary lack of psychological detail of which Jean Collet says:

> Robert Bresson does not want us to know his characters. He does not believe in psychological knowledge, he does not reveal characters, he does not trace a coherent, accessible portrait of the beings who fill the screen. Rather, he asserts that any being is inaccessible, that any character is a mystery, and that one never knows anybody.[19]

This may appear to point to a nihilistic reading of the film, as one variant of the cinema of alienated non-communication (a view reinforced by the fact that we never hear either of Michel's mysterious pickpocketing accomplices utter a word). It may, on the other hand, be seen as a reference to the Christian "mystery of being"—the doctrine of the fundamental unknowableness (other than to God) of each human creature and soul. The second of Collet's sentences is certainly evocative of this, while the first would be equally applicable to the methods of a psychoanalysis which "situates the instance of the ego. . . in the line of fiction, forever irreducible for the individual alone"[20]—which, that is to say, rejects any notion of a pre-existent, non-contradictory individuality or subjectivity and sees the ego as constructed by, rather than determining, the individual's "life-story." Even more than *Journal*, which does not from the outset call its own narrative status into question, *Pickpocket* remorselessly obstructs any linear or transparent view of human motivation. This is not to say that readers of Genet in particular will not be tempted to succumb to the psycho-hermeneutic interpretation well summarized by Daniel Millar:

> Michel's relationship with his mother has been a favourite area for probing, since he refuses to see her until she is seriously ill—in fact, dying—and then expresses affection for her. From here it is a short Freudian step to the Inspector as friendly yet rejected father-figure, and then to the gestures of theft as

surreptitious caresses, so that Michel's final declaration of love for Jeanne becomes his renunciation of his repressed homosexuality.[21]

Certainly the overpowering sense of relief that accompanies Michel's embracing Jeanne through the bars in the final sequence can, as I have earlier indicated, be seen as the culmination of a journey away from emotional and sexual confusion. But it might be prudent to speak of "illumination" rather than "explanation." Bresson's well-documented antipathy to psychology comes through in his comment on his *modèles*—a comment that could well be that of the analyst on his analysands or even of the Creator on his creatures:

> "The thing that matters is not what they show me but what they hide from me and, above all, *what they do not suspect is in them.*"[22]

They do not suspect what is in them; we (on the further side of them from God or the God—surrogates that are the psychoanalyst or the director of a film) do, but what we "understand" is (to go back to Simone Weil) not the end of what is in them, but where this comes from. Thus it is that the movement of the audience in "understanding" *Pickpocket* is likely to be a double one. The more we understand where Michel's actions come from, the less clear it becomes precisely what their end will be. We overcome his blindness to the source of his actions the better to share in his unawareness of where they are taking him, and in his concomitant sense of the inevitability of the voyage. This is in part a simple matter of narration, since a story told in flashback always already comes to us with an air of inevitability. It has partly also to do with the deliberate non-naturalism of certain sequences (most notably Michel's going abroad without a passport and returning after a lengthy absence still wearing the same suit). In a study in which the "speaking silence" occupies so prominent a place, it is important to acknowledge the brilliance of Martin Lassalle's acting, in particular his ability to suggest psychological opacity and spiritual eloquence by facial expression. What all these factors, together with the use of sound (the racecourse and ticket-machines like the mechanism of an inexorable process, the Lully music accompanying Michel's "training" in larceny as if to hint at what that process might be), give us is the sense of a purpose or pattern beyond the reach of immanent rationality. Michel embodies the Lacanian view of "man as a submitting object of processes that transcend him," and this is what underlies Louis Malle's reading of the film as an allegory of the Fall of Man.

For Malle, the thief Michel is as it were "Everyman," the Inspector is God, the ultimately untrustworthy friend Jacques is an inefficient guardian angel, and the divine grace that saves Michel at the end takes on the form of Jeanne. Any hint of facility in this (paraphrased) reading is countered by two important points.

The first is that Malle does not equate the person of Jeanne with divine grace, as he does for instance that of Jacques with the guardian angel. What he says is:

> From one fall to the next, divine grace makes its way within him, taking on the face of a young girl, a little feeble at the beginning but becoming sublime at the end, itself sublime.[23]

Jeanne's *niaiserie* can perhaps be seen as the result of her "expecting nothing from herself," to quote Pascal. Certainly the disconcerting quality of the ending concerns the question of how far Jeanne is the agent of Michel's redemption or healing, and how far she is its instrument. The second interpretation, which Malle clearly endorses, will doubtless be unacceptable to non-believers; yet if we opt for the first it becomes very difficult to take seriously a final shot which verges on a parody of the classic Hollywood "happy ending." We are left oscillating between the two possibilities, as the question: "D'où cela vient-il?" poses itself in its intractable ambiguity. The other major interest of Malle's reading is his equation of Bresson-the-director with God:

> The film gives the image of God's omnipotence not only in its subject-matter, but in its expression. As in the great works of believing artists, form and content are identical, which is to say that the artist for a moment takes the place of God. For the time it takes to show the film, the artist is God.[24]

The director behind the camera, like the analyst behind the couch, can readily be likened to God—superficially absent but everywhere implicit in the world (the film, the discourse) he creates. There is a moment in the film where Michel tells Jeanne that he believed in God once, for three minutes. This is often taken to refer to the scene of his mother's funeral, where a single tear appears on his cheek. Like the final shot, this verges on self-parody if we view it psychologically, as the concentrated essence of filial remorse; but at the same time it is difficult not to grant some place to such an interpretation. If we see the tear as also a recognition that he has perforce transcended the Oedipal anguish of his relationship with the (always-absent/ever-present) mother, and bear in mind Françoise Dolto's view of the Crucifixion as the quintessential Oedipal drama, it is perhaps possible to illuminate the scene by the preoccupations of psychoanalysis and the paradoxical rhetoric of grace without claiming that either perspective "explains" or exhausts it.

There is one other sequence, very near the beginning, to which I believe Michel's reply can be related. This occurs after a racecourse theft; as Michel walks away, we hear him say, in voice-over: "Je n'avais plus les pieds sur terre. Je dominais le monde." A cut to him sitting in a police car between two officers is accompanied by his voice telling us: "Un quart d'heure après, j'étais pris." The text is a distillation of hubris and its inexorable consequences. It is as though, for that brief moment, Michel had the illusion of autonomous subjectivity—believed, in other words, in a God who was himself . . . This goes beyond tragic error to mark the first stage in the inevitable odyssey that neither Michel nor the audience can ever fully comprehend. That incomprehension is the necessary strength of a film that unconsciously invites a transcendental reading while never cutting loose from the contingent world of immanence. The Cross would not have been out of place at the end of *Pickpocket* either, for it is there that the transcendent and the immanent, like the vertical and horizontal axes of communication, meet.

Bresson's second Bernanos adaptation, *Mouchette*, likewise ends on a gesture of withdrawal, at once more theologically dramatic and more clearly determined by external social factors than those which close the other two films. These two distinctions illuminate the parallel between the disappearance of Mouchette's body when she drowns herself and the ending of *Journal*. Schematically, one may say that the priest's body disappears so that his soul may rise upwards towards union with God, while Mouchette's disappears downwards, as if to remind us of the Catholic belief that suicide is the ultimate mortal sin . . . Not for one moment, of course, is it seriously possible to believe that Mouchette has "damned herself." The long-standing tendency of the Catholic novel to reconstruct sinners as saints would of itself be sufficient to see to that, and the use of Monteverdi's *Magnificat* clearly invites us to view Mouchette's death as a form of redemption and rebirth.

This is achieved partly, though not solely, through the overturning of theological orthodoxy in favour of a pathos engendered by the music and the natural harmonies of Mouchette's descent (the branches and bushes in which she becomes caught, the water that reforms over her body as though to absorb her). But the impact of the final shot rests also on a series of "doublings" and eliminations which resume all Mouchette's gestures in the film. Her body vanishes offscreen before it vanishes beneath the water, and it is hardly sufficient to invoke squeamishness on Bresson's part to account for this. To this twofold disappearance corresponds the absence of the voice from the Monteverdi *Magnificat*. The significance of Bresson's choosing an instrumental passage from a primarily vocal work can perhaps be illuminated by the absence of the Body of Christ from the Cross at the end of *Journal*. Both perform a kind of ascesis or *dépouillement* that takes up and amplifies other, similar movements earlier in the film. Thus, just as the structure of *Journal* can be seen as a progressive elimination-through-transcendence of all that is understood, materially but also socially, by the "body," so the double disappearance of Mouchette's body connects with her rejection of the social "body" of the village and of the different roles assigned to her within it. At school, she is a "bad pupil" (when she first does not sing with the others, then sings out of tune), yet alien not only to the "good pupils" at whom she throws mud but also to the other "bad pupils," the boys who expose themselves to her. At home, she is called upon to play mother, not only to her father, her brother, and the baby, but also to her own mother, to whom she brings comfort and a bottle (of gin . . .) in the death scene. In Arsène's shack—a place literally and metaphorically outside the world of the village—the role of sexual partner is thrust upon her, a role that she none the less assumes when telling Mathieu and Madame Mathieu that Arsène is her lover. This is parallelled by her twofold repetition of the word "cyclone" to describe a storm from which she has taken refuge. This demonstrates a curious linguistic stubbornness both childlike and adult. Childlike, because children regard names as necessarily inherent in objects, so that if Arsène calls the storm a "cyclone" then that is what it must be; adult, because the context in which Arsène uses the term ("Il vient. Quand on ne l'entend plus, c'est qu'on est dedans"),[25] makes it equally applicable to his own (emotional/epileptic/alcoholic) turmoil, so that the girl's repetition of it indicates her nascent awareness of the world of psychic disorder. The tissue of contradictions between roles perceived, prescribed, accepted, and rejected has thus by the end of the film become so convoluted that Mouchette's suicide appears as a cutting-free from the complexities of which it is the result. In this context it is not merely rhetorical to describe her suicide as a death to language, or the counterpointing of the gesture of damnation and the attire (white dress and flowers) of salvation as the film's final and most audacious rejection—Bresson's refusal of the orthodox theological labelling of Mouchette as suicide and sinner.

"I identify myself in language, but only by losing myself-as-subject in it."[26] Lacan's formulation would certainly have relevance to Mouchette. The complexity of the relationship it implies between subject, signified, and signifier—the stress on the gaps and absences that at once separate them and hold them together—also resembles that suggested by Pascal, or by Simone Weil in *La Pesanteur et la grâce* for whom a precondition of the ultimate transcendental signifier that is grace is the void necessary to receive it:

Grace fills, but it can enter only where there is a void to receive, and it makes that void itself.[27]

Thus it is that towards the end of the film it is through the cluster of voids and absences already noted that the presence of grace becomes apparent. Mouchette's acceptance-yet-rejection of labels and identities, and the void it engenders, is like a taking upon herself—an empathetic transference—of the evil around her, and the ending perhaps points to a redemption that goes beyond the purely personal.

The Christian world of a Pascal or a Weil is "mystical"—and thus metaphysical; the discourse of psychoanalysis—in particular of its Lacanian avatars—is insistently material. This is a contrast, even a contradiction, but not one which can find no synthesis or resolution. The three Bresson films discussed here are remarkable, not only for their mystical and metaphysical resonances, but for the insistent materiality of their images and soundtracks. The gardeners' raking that accompanies the scene between the priest and the countess in *Journal*, or the scraping of pen across paper in the same film; the noise of machines that accompanies so much of Michel's odyssey in *Pickpocket*; the crackling of the vegetation as Mouchette rolls three times down the river bank, then the sound of her body disappearing into the water—these seem like so many *traits d'union* linking the material and the mystical or metaphysical universes, which can also be seen as converging upon or within the silences and ellipses that punctuate the films.

In the summer of 1982, during the filming of *L'Argent*, I spoke to Bresson, asking him in particular how he understood the concepts of God, grace, and damnation. His reply each time was the same, and each time unsurprising: "je ne peux pas vous le dire." I hope here to have suggested how his films speak the inevitability of such an answer.

Notes

Translations of quoted material are the author's. The citations below refer to the original French texts. *Ed.*

1. Pascal, *Pensées*, Livre de Poche, 1972, p. 246.
2. S. Weil, *La Pesanteur et la grâce*, 10/18, 1948, p. 53.
3. The "Petite Anthologie positiviste de l'anti-bressonisme" in Robert Droguet's Premier Plan volume (now long out of print) distils some of the most venomous negative responses.
4. Quoted in M. Estève, *Robert Bresson*, Albatros, 1983, p. 30.
5. S. Turkle, *Psychoanalytic Politics*, Burnett Books/André Deutsch, 1979, pp. 49-50.
6. J. Lacan, *Écrits*, Seuil, 1966, p. 118.
7. *La Pesanteur et la grâce*, p. 133.
8. A. Bazin, in *Cahiers du cinéma*, no. 3, June 1951, p. 8.
9. Pascal, op. cit., p. 161.
10. Bazin, op. cit., p. 18.
11. M. Estève, *Cinéma et condition humaine*, Albatros, 1978, p. 213.
12. Bazin, op. cit.
13. A. Ayfre, *Conversion aux images*, Éditions du Cerf, 1964, p. 267.
14. P. Schrader, *Transcendental Style in Film*, University of California Press, 1972, p. 72.
15. P. Solignac, *La Névrose chrétienne*, Éditions de Trevise, 1976, p. 26.
16. Pascal, op. cit., p. 232.
17. Pascal, op. cit., p. 213.
18. J.-L. Nancy and P. Lacoue-Labarthe, *Le Titre de la lettre*, Éditions Galilée, 1973, pp. 49-50.

19. J. Collet, *Télédné*, May/June 1960, p. 3.
20. Lacan, op. cit., p. 91.
21. *The Films of Robert Bresson*, edited by R. Durgnat, Studio Vista, 1969, p. 82.
22. R. Bresson, *Notes sur le cinématographe*, Gallimard, 1975, p. 11.
23. L. Malle, *Arts*, no. 755, December 1959.
24. Ibid.
25. R. Bresson, *Mouchette, L'Avant-Scène du Cinéma*, 1968, p. 19.
26. Lacan, op. cit., p. 181.
27. Weil, op. cit., p. 20.

Un condamné à mort s'est échappé

Bresson and Music

I N HIS *Notes on the Cinematographer* Robert Bresson states that there should
be "no music as accompaniment, support or reinforcement. *No music at all.*"
After this italicized emphasis, he adds: "Except, of course, the music played
by visible instruments."[1]

Yet Bresson often uses music in his films and the visible instruments are few,
among them the portable pop in *Au hasard Balthazar*, the café-loudspeakers in
Mouchette, the brasserie jazz in *Le Diable probablement*, the recorded classical music
in *Une femme douce*, the radio guitar in *Quatre nuits d'un rêveur*, the "Benedictus"
and bagpipe in *Lancelot du Lac*, piano-played Bach in *L'Argent*. Most of the other
music in Bresson's films is played by, as it were, invisible instruments: those of
Monteverdi, Bach, Mozart, Purcell, Lully.

Do Bresson's films then contradict his contention that music should not be
used as "accompaniment, support or reinforcement?" Perhaps in writing this
stricture he had in mind the kind of film score he used in his first three feature
films: *Les Anges du péché*, *Les Dames du Bois de Boulogne*, and *Journal d'un curé de
campagne*. All three have conventional scores by an excellent composer, Jean-
Jacques Grünenwald. But such traditional scores were already encountering the
Bresson aesthetic. In *Journal*, the composer's finely thought-out *leitmotiv* system,
with its moving "theme" for the priest, is already confronting difficulties coping
with the director's own score, his meticulously orchestrated "sound effects" (the
squeaky gate, the bicycle noise, the barking dog). Grünenwald's conventional
music collides with the Bresson style because, as the director himself states, there
is "no absolute value in an image. Images and sounds will owe their value and
their power solely to the use to which you destine them."[2]

Bresson therefore subsequently avoided music as "accompaniment, support or
reinforcement," and began to use it more as "information," in the same way as
other sounds were used, so that it was no longer, as he prescribed in his *Notes*, a
"powerful modifier and even destroyer of the real, like alcohol or dope."

Un condamné à mort s'est échappé is not only the first film which Bresson himself wrote (as opposed to adapting the works of others) but is also the first where he was in full control of the music and could use it as he wanted. He employed Mozart, the Kyrie Elieson of the Mass in C Minor, music which had a "colour," he said, matching that of the film. Used sparingly (under the credits, seven times during the film, and at the end) the music, as was the director's intention, underlined elements of the film in a way which an ordinary film score, more or less supportive, could not. Indeed as Jean Sémolué has said, "through the truth of the reality that the whole film shows us, the music establishes the reality of truth."[3]

The Mass indicates a kind of alternative organization, conveying something more basic, more elemental and at the same time otherwise inexpressible. Specifically, this music is used as a means of (and during scenes of) communication. The Kyrie ("Lord, have mercy") announces its theme at the beginning of the film and it does so over a plaque commemorating those who died in the prison in which the film takes place. The music communicates a kind of promise—as does both the title and the co-title (*Le Vent souffle où il veut*) of the film. The Lord will have mercy.

The music is heard in seven sequences, in all of which the prisoners are communicating with the condemned man, times when they are no longer alone. Susan Sontag has observed that "all of Bresson's films have a common theme: the meaning of confinement and liberty."[4] In this film the confinement is solitary.

The Kyrie is heard again during the final moments, telling us that indeed mercy has been had. Of this final music Paul Schrader says: "When Bresson uses music as decisive action, like the use of Mozart's Mass . . . it is not editorializing but like Ozu's coda music is a blast of emotional music within a cold context."[5]

This sequence has been described by Richard Roud: "And when they [the condemned man, Fontaine, and the boy he had to take with him, Jost] finally reach the street, Fontaine's first reaction is to take Jost into his arms; and Jost, in one of the cinema's greatest lines, says, 'If only my mother could see me!'"[6] The adventure is over, the tension is gone, doubt is vanquished, triumph is complete—and the sole spoken sentiment is this painfully inadequate, lovable, profound banality: If only my mother could see me now. Near tears, we are now near laughter, and in this suddenly alienated atmosphere, Mozart's Kyrie emerges on the soundtrack. The two men, free, cross the railway bridge and are wreathed in celestial-seeming steam, great billowings that hide them from us as though in an apotheosis. Yet though the screen darkens, the film is not over. Mozart's music continues alone—for nearly a minute (a very long time in film)—and we attend as the Kyrie comes to its successful but resigned (C minor) conclusion.

There is no triumph. The Mozart sinks in slowly, as the ears finally take over for the eyes, and we understand that this may be a thanksgiving for the escape ("Lord have mercy") but that it retains what Sémolué suggests is its "sorrowful" aspect, one which appeals for those who have not escaped, "beyond the prisoners [remember the plaque?] the entire human race."[7]

Here the director has led us to some place we had not expected to go, but where our arrival seems inevitable. Bresson himself has said that music (and sound in general) can take us into a region no longer merely terrestrial, a place which he says, "I would even call divine."[8]

Bresson's use of Monteverdi in *Mouchette* is similar to his use of Mozart in *Un condamné à mort s'est échappé*. The music's role is sacerdotal; it points to a design beyond that which we are experiencing. It is—as Bresson intends the term—divine. This is indicated in the first minute of the film. Footsteps are heard as Mouchette's mother leaves church—the first of many such sounds, for the track of this film is an extraordinary mosaic of realistic noises—and we hear her relate her worries. In contrast to this expressed anxiety comes the consoling sound of the *Magnificat* from the *Vespro della Beata Vergine*. The score is antiphonal: statement and answer. It answers her questions about Mouchette's fate, and confirms that her fears will be responded to in a merciful way.

The music is not heard again until the end of film (a pattern repeated in most of Bresson's films following *Mouchette*). Here, it accompanies Mouchette's suicide. It may be seen as the answer to the question posed by the girl's mother: "What will become of [her] without me?" The music is like a requiem, the girl is already in her shroud. As Lindley Hanlon has observed: "The death of Mouchette is such a surprise that the music helps us reassess the events of her life . . . and ponder the sum total of their meaning for her."[9] Yes, but is this the mercy that Monteverdi seemed to promise?

The question need not be asked. Both the music and Bresson's style have by this time moved us from the realistic plane of the film into another territory, something beyond realism. The images tell us: lively little girls do not die like this—no struggle, no bubbles, no instant transference to another state. In any event, Mouchette may be a martyr to the way of the world, but the Monteverdi suggests that grace is also there.

The girl has decided that life has no answer for her, yet the *Magnificat* tells us otherwise. God, it says, will exalt and redeem the humble. Solace is, as always in Bresson, extended. "Dying with grace," writes P. Adams Sitney, "is a dominant theme" of Bresson's cinema. Only in six films do the protagonists survive at the end (*Les Dames, Un condamné, Pickpocket, Quatre nuits*—and in *Les Anges* and *L'Argent* they won't survive long, having given themselves up as murderers). Three films also end with suicides (*Mouchette, Une femme douce,* and *Le Diable*). These, adds Sitney, "emphasize the enigma of the human will: they seem insufficiently motivated, but are pure acts of accepting death."[10] Grace is extended to the young suicide Mouchette (a surprising acceptance from a Catholic filmmaker). The mother's fears have been addressed.

Particularly poignant is that Mouchette does not, in a sense, know what she is doing—she is too young to understand. Perhaps it is this which makes Monteverdi's music so apt. Its very simplicity bespeaks innocence.

In *Balthazar* the protagonist is not only young and innocent, but an animal as well, a donkey, alien from the human world he must inhabit. Nor can he speak—except through the music of Franz Schubert. This identification is plainly stated at the beginning of the film when the introduction to the slow movement of the piano sonata (no. 20 D 959) is interrupted by the brayings of Balthazar. The film's opening image is that of the protagonist as a baby, Balthazar being nursed by his mother. The Schubert fades and we hear sheep bells. At the end we will again hear the bells, and as the donkey dies, will realize that the film has encompassed his life.

When Balthazar appears, Schubert appears; this visitation is not invariable but it occurs often enough that we perceive the connection. We can even understand what Schubert is saying. He speaks of a simpler time, of an age gone by, he sings of nostalgia.

Though there are anthropomorphic qualities in the picture, the use of Schubert is not one of them. The music is not speaking to Balthazar, he can't even hear it—it is speaking to us. And when the donkey dies—amid a flock of sheep, black against white—the music stops and only the bells remain, gradually fading. The voice is stilled when what it represented is no more.

Though the music also serves other purposes in *Balthazar*—that wondrously layered experience, that labyrinth of subtle parallels—the identification is important because it points to one of the ways Bresson uses music to create an experience otherwise unobtainable. Nick Browne has rightly indicated the mechanism: "Through an ensemble of means that tie the *story* to the *representation*, the literal level supports and announces a second, figurative, and implied meaning that has transforming significance."[11] This is because, "on the level of the *story*, Balthazar's status as subject or object, the role of circumstance and accident (what the film designates as 'chance') and the meaning of his suffering, are determined psychologically. On the level of the *representation*, Balthazar's meaning is ecstatic, profound, and religious."[12]

Schubert is representative of the otherwise inexpressible. Bresson accomplishes this through his restraint, tact and grace. Charles Barr has written of "the marvelous delicacy with which [Bresson] coordinates images and music, binds together images of sorrow and joy into a serene unity."[13] The director is able to do this precisely because he has separated his means. One of these is music and it does not accompany, support or reinforce. Rather, it is information, sound used as other sounds are used, in order to create a necessary dimension.

As Maureen Turim has observed, however, *Balthazar*'s meanings "are only to be derived from how this expression and structure operate." Balthazar is not

Au hasard Balthazar

Mouchette. Grace is not offered him by Schubert as it is her by Monteverdi. "Many have tried," Turim continues, "to read transcendence or resurrection into Balthazar's death, I think in an attempt to avoid confronting the lack of any comforting closure around any stated positive values."[14] Though the text certainly works to create this desire, the denial of an expected narrative logic, and a lack of any affirmative conclusions, indicate what Bresson is saying, the value he places on what he shows. Schubert surely speaks for the animal but only to remind us. When the animal is dead there is nothing to remind us of. At the end of *Balthazar* I do not cry for the donkey, I cry for myself.

Bresson uses music differently in other films. Both Lully in *Pickpocket* and Bach in *L'Argent* have less commentary. In these films, they are not spokesmen, as Schubert is in *Balthazar*, but are emblematic of intention. They embody probity and rectitude, they are from a world where integrity and justice are presumed to support virtue (ironic counterpoints to the petty thievery in one and the axe murder in the other).

Recall *Un condamné*. Just as the soundtrack of this film (interior sounds: the footsteps, the shouts in German, doors opening and closing; and exterior sounds: the bell of the trolley, the wail of the trains, the sweak of the guard's bicycle) define a space outside the screen which we rarely see, so Mozart indicates a higher plan which we can only glimpse as it unfolds.

One remembers Susan Sontag's comment that "for Bresson film is not a plastic but a narrative experience."[15] For him music is a form of narration.

Notes

1. Robert Bresson, *Notes on the Cinematographer*, London: Quartet Books, 1986, p. 19.
2. Ibid., p. 21.
3. Jean Sémolué, quoted by Leo Murray in Ian Cameron, ed., *The Films of Robert Bresson*, New York: Praeger, 1970, p. 79.
4. Susan Sontag, "Spiritual Style in the Films of Robert Bresson," *Against Interpretation*, New York: Farrar, Straus & Giroux, 1961, p. 186.
5. Paul Schrader, *Transcendental Style in Film: Ozu, Bresson, Dreyer*, Berkeley: University of California Press, 1972, p. 69.
6. Richard Roud, "Robert Bresson," *Cinema: A Critical Dictionary*, ed. Richard Roud, vol. 1, New York: The Viking Press, p. 146.
7. Sémolué, p. 80.
8. Sémolué, p. 81.
9. Lindley Hanlon, *Fragments: Bresson's Film Style*, London: Associated University Presses, p. 149.

10. P. Adams Sitney, "Robert Bresson," *The International Dictionary of Films and Film-makers*, vol. 2, Chicago: St. James Press, p. 65.

11. Nick Browne, "Narrative Point of View: The Rhetoric of *Au Hasard, Balthazar*," *Film Quarterly*, 31, no.1, [Fall 1997] p. 23.

12. Ibid., p. 27.

13. Charles Barr, in Cameron, p. 112.

14. Maureen Turim, "The Textual System of *Au Hasard, Balthazar*," thesis (unpublished), University of Wisconsin, 1975, pp. 162, 165.

15. Sontag, p. 181.

Mouchette

LINDLEY HANLON

Sound as Symbol in *Mouchette*

> The soundtrack invented silence.
>
> — ROBERT BRESSON, *Notes on Cinematography*

B RESSON'S GREATEST ACHIEVEMENT has been the redemption of sound in the cinema from the obscurity of the background and secondary role it has traditionally played. Sound and the absence of sound play a fundamental role in Bresson's films in the structuring and intensification of visual images and as an independent element of composition and signification. Sound is Bresson's most important source of narrative economy, never duplicating an image's message. Sound may even be substituted for that image. The exchange of sound for image relieves Bresson's films of the redundancy of conventional sound realism and frees sound for use as an emblem:

> In addition, I prefer to conjure up the image with the help of a sound, because each time I can replace an image with a sound, I do it. And I am doing it more and more.[1]

Sound functions consistently throughout *Mouchette*, as a basic element in the editing structure and as a major source of emblematic meaning.

Origins

The function of sound in *Mouchette* is very close in certain ways to the function of sound in *Un condamné à mort s'est échappé*. In that film, the hostile presence of the guards is systematically indicated by sounds: the clanking of a key on the iron railing, the opening and closing of Fontaine's door, a whistle, and the rattle of machine-gun fire in the distance. The image of the source of the sound may appear at the beginning of the film, but from then on sound stands alone, without an image, an effect that represents its cause. Leo Murray, in his essay on *Un condamné à mort s'est échappé*, distinguishes several functions of sound in that film:

> The sounds we hear from inside the prison itself assume the quality of signs. These may be signs of menace (the creaking bicycle of the guard who rides around the prison walls at the end of the film), of presence (the rattling of the guard's key on the metal bannister), of communication (the tapping on the walls between prison cells), of death (the machine gun).[2]

Throughout the film, the gauging and interpretation of those sounds and the construction of the escape materials occupy all of Fontaine's attention and efforts. The film is constructed of hundreds of shots of Fontaine as he listens carefully, moving his eyes to judge the direction of the threat. Footsteps tell him when the guards make their rounds to deliver the pitiful soup, a schedule that, once mastered, he can translate into time that can be devoted to his tasks. Fontaine judges the time of day by the sound of the chiming clock and memorizes the schedules of passing trains that will muffle the sounds of their escape, all integral parts of his plan. Fontaine must also judge the noise he makes that could be "read" by the guards as an indicator of the nature of his activities.

Compared with the silence required and the almost absolute silence around him, each sound Fontaine makes shrieks and grates and seems to last an eternity. Bresson achieves this effect by regulating the volume of sound, by juxtaposing sound with absolute silence, and by judiciously extending the time of an activity or motion by breaking it up into a series of shots. It is this ability of sound to signify a threat that Bresson utilizes in *Mouchette* as well.

Entrapment

Mouchette too lives in a threatening, enclosed environment, but her world is a personal, social, and metaphorical "prison," not an actual prison. To convey this metaphorical sense of "prison," Bresson begins the narrative of *Mouchette* with shots and sounds very similar to the analysis of actions I have described in *Un condamné à mort s'est échappé*. Annette Michelson has described the extraordinary intensity of those first moments of the film:

The first twenty minutes of *Mouchette* are composed (it is the only word) in such a manner that seemingly disparate situations, dramatic lines, narrative potentials, separate identities converge upon a central destiny, that of a child. The weight and inexorability with which they do so establish the density and logic of a rural world. The convergence is effected by an editing, a framing, movement, and direction of actors which combine a disjunctive intransigence with an absolute poise.[3]

The estranged outsider, Mouchette will watch and listen to the world around her as Mathieu, the gamekeeper, does in the first shots of the film. Sounds register the threat of that world and her defiance toward it. Sounds register the ritual actions of the life of the community, and music suggests the solace of religious belief and the possibility of another life. There is nothing incidental in Bresson's use of sound. Each sound has a meaning and function in the narrative.

The theme of entrapment is brilliantly evoked on the levels of both sound and image in the first major scene of the film, after the titles. The structural possibilities of sound are introduced in these first shots as well. After one longer shot of Mathieu running through the woods, very close shots of Mathieu, the game warden, next to a tree emphasize the confining aspects of the frame, as he watches Arsène, the poacher, setting his traps. Mathieu's eyes move back and forth furtively like those of a bird, his head still. The rustle of dry leaves and the crunch of footsteps represent what he is watching offscreen. The sound is very distinct and loud as if heard by someone with heightened attention to the sounds as such. These close, flat shots of an as yet unidentified character and intensified sounds are a typically oblique beginning to the film. There is no establishment of a space, time, or narrative connection between this scene and the previous shot of a woman in church. The situation and actions of these people are introduced almost abstractly, abruptly, piece by piece, with no narrative interrelationships and explanations provided. As in *Au hasard Balthazar,* only gradually do we begin to infer the identity of characters from conversations and confrontations between them. The first shot of a man running through the woods simply establishes the rural domain and Mathieu's role as a gamekeeper, a role more familiar to the French. We hear his feet make a crackling sound on the leaves, a sound that will signify by itself, from then on, the presence of someone in the woods. From just the sound of feet on leaves, over a shot of Mathieu watching something offscreen, we can infer what the person is doing offscreen, as does Mathieu himself. Sound will systematically represent action in offscreen space.[4]

Bresson then proceeds to intercut shots of Mathieu spying and Arsène setting traps and making the rustling noise we have heard previously. The sound carries over the cut, bridging the shot change. Dogs bark in the distance, suggesting a world beyond the cramped space to which we have been introduced. A very marked silence ensues as they wait in their separate spaces in separate shots for the game to arrive. Bresson continues cutting back and forth between Mathieu, Arsène, and the partridge. As a partridge is caught in one of the rings of thread Arsène has constructed, loud and long sounds of thrashing in leaves and wings beating break this silence and amplify the horror of the act of capture. The rustling of leaves continues as Mathieu, the gamekeeper, closes in on Arsène, the poacher. Mathieu approaches the bird, which is struggling to free itself from the collar around its neck. As he lets the bird loose, it flies upward and into the distance with a loud flapping of wings.

The sequence introduces a sound trope that recurs throughout the film, along with other strategies, to suggest the similarities between Mouchette and the game stalked.[5] Bresson transforms sound from the realistic effect of an action into a metaphorical device in the narrative structure. Like Fontaine in *Un condamné à mort s'est échappé*, Mathieu assesses the presence of the foe by listening and watching intently. The crackle of leaves and branches signifies the presence of another person or animal as it is trapped. Throughout the film the same crackling is heard as Mouchette hides like an animal in the grass and forest for shelter and listens for threatening sounds around her: the presence of Arsène and Mathieu or anyone else who might discover her whereabouts and enforce their will on her. Once, as Mouchette waits and watches in the forest, a partridge flies up, making the same flapping sound and reminding us of the earlier incident of Arsène trapping partridge, reintroducing the metaphor. The sound of wind and rain close in and assault her as she crouches beside a tree. Later in the film, the crackling of the fire that Arsène builds before the rape scene reminds us of the sound of cracking leaves and adds to our sense of Mouchette as a trapped animal. Arsène pursues her around the room, and she hides under a table on all fours. Although initially an encounter where Mouchette exhibits her warmth and compassion for Arsène, nursing him and singing to him during his epileptic seizure, the communion between them is turned into terror as Arsène forces her back against the fire which, like him, threatens to consume her.

Renard-Georges in his comparison of the film with the Bernanos novel, *Nouvelle histoire de Mouchette*, which Bresson adapted, suggests another source of this heightened use of sound. He points to examples in the text where Bernanos describes Mouchette's animal-like sense of sound, that enables her to hear the threats around her and changes in people's voices that indicate their attitude toward her. Thus Mouchette's sense of hearing, as well as the sounds she makes and hears, develop further the metaphor of the trapped animal:

> *Mouchette*, like the preceding films of Bresson, manifests the sensory sharpness of the filmmaker: sounds, silences, glances, light and shadow comprise the skeleton of the work, but here again correspond to one of the major poetic

features of the novel. Bernanos, under the double influence of his own sensibility and that of his childhood memories of the countryside of Artois, endowed Mouchette with the same faculty of capturing the least sounds and their nuances. Her familiarity with the sounds of nature is made evident in the evening scenes by the precision of Bernanos' vocabulary, which is able to convey all varieties of rain and wind simply by their echo in the landscape: "le crépitement de l'averse (the crackling of a downpour) . . . ; l'immense chuintement du sol saturé, les brefs hoquets de l'ornière (the prodigious hissing of the saturated soil, the brief hiccups of the rut) . . . le bouillonnement de l'eau pressée par la pierre, son sanglot de cristal (the bubbling up of water pressured by the stone, its crystal sobbing)" (1270). But even more incisively Bernanos makes explicit the faculty of wild animals which orients them exclusively around their hearing. In the cabin: "chacun de ses sens parait dormir, sauf celui de l'ouie. Elle n'a pas besoin de prêter l'oreille pour distinguer entre eux les mille bruits du dehors" (1279). ("Each sense seemed asleep, except the sense of hearing. She did not have to listen to be able to distinguish between the sounds of the outdoors.) Similarly Bresson, by rejecting all background music in the body of the film, forcefully puts in relief the sometimes magical, the at other times tragic presence of the sounds of life in the forest and in the house and, by this effect of contrast, the absolute silence of the village on that last morning.[5]

Other metaphorical similarities between Mouchette and animals are suggested in the dialogue of the film. Just before the extended scene of the rabbit hunt that Mouchette watches, Mathieu's wife has compared her with Arsène's game and in doing so suggests the idea to Mouchette:

Moi, ça me brûle le sang de penser qu'une brute à qui tu ne ferais pas grâce d'un lièvre, [countershot of Mouchette], tu ne t'occupes même pas de savoir s'il a saoulé ou non cette petite.[6]

(It burns me up to think that a brute, whom you wouldn't forgive for one hare, [countershot of Mouchette], you don't even care to find out if he has got this girl drunk or not.)

The placement of the word "lièvre" ("hare") just before the cut to Mouchette constructs the simile (Mouchette as game) in the same way relevant dialogue from *Hamlet* appeared over shots of the gentle woman [in *Une femme douce*] and therefore seemed to apply to her. And, like Balthazar, Mouchette is the innocent victim of the adults around her. Visual details continue the analogy: her little pony tails and heavy knit wool stockings make her look a bit like a creature.

Still other sounds convey the sense of her entrapment in spatial terms. Her father returns drunk one evening as she is caring for the baby and her mother. On one side of her, offscreen right, the baby cries loudly. To her offscreen left, her father is stretched out on his mattress imitating the acceleration and shifting of a motor. Sound seems to close in on her from all sides in a situation of hopelessness and entrapment. Similarly, the put-put sound of her father's truck, used to transport contraband liquor, is often heard offscreen to signal his approach and habitual reprimands for using up his liquor to soothe her mother's pain. In response to the sound of the truck and the flash of headlights, she quickly refills the bottle to its previous level with water from the faucet.

Emblematic Sounds

The loudness of these sounds sets off and calls attention to the general silence that pervades the relationships of these people, who seem to have known each other so long that verbal communication is infrequent and concise. Physical sounds become one of the few indicators or transmitters of interpersonal communication. The repeated sound of footsteps as the men enter the bar, the mechanical sound of the habitual placement of glasses on the bar, and the slurping of liquor being poured show, for example, the similar approaches of Arsène and Mathieu to Louisa the barmaid. While unifying the shots, the sounds intensify their competition for her attention. Drinking becomes a continuous ritual in the film, the rhythm of which is recorded in the alternation of the sound of bottles and glasses clanking with the slurp of gin. The clanking of bottles in cases as Mouchette's father fills the truck, stopping as the police notice and then drive on, and Mouchette's camouflaging the gin bottle by refilling it with water reiterate these sounds. For her work in the café Mouchette receives a few coins, which she hands over to her father in exchange for a drink. By emphasizing the ritual of drinking in his use of sound, Bresson implies that this is Mouchette's initiation into a lifetime habit.

Just as the sound of the truck indicates her father's presence, so does the sound of Mouchette's clogs become an emblem for her disposition. The defiant clunk-clunk-clunk of these shoes as she walks across the pavement and hard floors register her rebellious inclinations and heroic defiance. She clunks conspicuously into her classroom where the other girls are much more genteel and obedient. She clunks across the road away from them as they huddle together to gossip, presumably about the boys, who ride away on motorbikes. She turns haughtily away from those same boys, who call her names and mock her with their obscene behaviour, and clatters along down the road. The clogs send mud spattering up around her as she stamps in a puddle in the churchyard in front of her father who shoves her ahead into the church. Finally she has the courage to snap back "Merde!" to her father as she leaves the house. Her shoes make a squirting, gushy sound as she plods through the mud in the woods on her way to Arsène's cabin. When she visits the old lady, who speaks to her of the attractions of death, Mouchette scornfully rubs mud into her carpet with her galoshes. Her clogs seem her one weapon against the hostile world around her.

Mouchette's repeated acts of defiance, to which she seems instinctively drawn, are memorable because of their accentuated sound dimension. In the row of girls singing the song about "hopeful horizons open to those without hope," Mouchette is conspicuously silent. Her silence seems a refusal on her part to sing the words that she, and we, sense in no way describe the dismal life she leads. For her refusal to sing, she is yanked over to the piano where she is forced to sing by the schoolmistress. The wrong note sounds out painfully each time as the schoolmistress sounds out the correct notes on the piano and barks "Chante! Chante! ("Sing! Sing!") at Mouchette. She sings the song correctly only to Arsène, whom she cares for in the cabin, when it expresses her real emotions. When she returns to the line of girls to sing, we hear the wrong note again, and tears moisten Mouchette's cheeks, the sign of her total humiliation.

Action upon action, sound upon sound accumulate as the film progresses and hint at the character of Mouchette. After this ordeal, she leaves the school and crosses the street to crouch down behind the shoulder of the road. She hurls mud balls, which land with a dull thud on the crisp, clean clothing of the girls. At home she efficiently makes coffee in a skilful, carefree way, humming, turning the coffee mill around and around, enjoying the ratchety noise, and clanking the coffee pot and water pot on the stove. She pours the coffee continuously into the four bowls lined up next to each other for that purpose. She repeats the slurping ritual with the warm milk. The actions indicate her amazing spirit amidst such hardship. With greater disdain, she tosses her dish rag into the water as she leaves her job at the café for the day. With the same disdain, she tosses away the croissant that the "charitable" lady has given her following her mother's death, because the woman has called her a slut. These actions and the sounds associated with them define the range of Mouchette's power to influence those around her, a range of actions as limited as Balthazar's, and similarly, violently punished. These sounds ring out as the only traces of her existence registered in the world around her, the continuity and impressions of which are preserved in the film.

Sound, Objects, and Physical Reality

The role of sound, as we have observed, is very closely allied with the role of the objects that produce them in the film. It seems to be an assumption of Bresson that the way we handle objects in our everyday activities indicates the deeper levels of our unconscious more accurately than the words we utter or dramatic actions we engage in. Physical reality, which cinema had supposedly redeemed, has never had a more articulate spokesman than Bresson, through the medium of sound. It is the accentuation of physical sounds that gives the world around the characters in *Mouchette* a hollow, empty, hard, cold feeling, as if these objects and people existed in an empty box filled with sound vibrations and echoes. Bresson's stress on the physicality of these objects and on the materiality of the world, suggests the lack of any spiritual warmth or energy to protect the characters and comfort them in what we might imagine as a sort of existential buffer zone. The harsh, naked quality of the sounds, accentuated by their loudness and by the lack of intermediate, background noise as filler, intensifies the hostility of characters toward each other, as exhibited in their actions. Bresson suggests that neither the natural physical world nor the physical world man has created are benevolent. Mouchette is pelted by rain and wind, which we hear; the moon, in contrast, is silent, dark, and menacing. The crackle of leaves underfoot is as pronounced and unforgiving as the sound of Mouchette's clogs on the paved road or stone floor.

This harsh physical reality that Bresson depicts contrasts with the mixture of realistic detail and supernatural fantasies and memories represented in the Bernanos novel, as P. Renard-Georges has pointed out. Yet I think his conclusions are perhaps overstated with regard to what I consider the profundity and spirituality of Bresson's portrait of Mouchette:

> For Bernanos does depart from the real, yes, but he so undermines its opacity by his mystical and visionary reflection, that he empties it of all objective content, renders it malleable, and what he finally gives us of these beings, of these landscapes, of these events, is what gives the supernatural form. Bresson, *he*, perceives and presents for us to see all the riches of the real, but he does not explore all the profundity, he does not penetrate all the sedimentary layers where, for Bernanos, God waits for Mouchette. His quest for the real does not become a pilgrimage to the real.[7]

I would contend that it is not so much the issue that Bresson does not penetrate those "sedimentary layers" where Bernanos believes God exists, but that Bresson does not believe that the physical world, in this film, *contains* that divinity. Renard-Georges correctly observes at another point that Bresson's characters are "prisoners of reality,"[8] that Bresson does not open up our view of the world to let in an image of the "beyond." It is not that Bresson fails to do so, but that he chooses not to do so. Bresson's images and sounds of the physical world in *Mouchette* suggest that that world is relentlessly cold and profoundly empty. There are special moments when a human being may interact with those physical objects and thereby transform them into signs for an interior state, as when Mouchette expresses a certain lightheartedness as she makes coffee in the morning. Yet ultimately, except in those special moments of grace, and except for innocents like Mouchette, the world and the people who populate it are unenlightened and hostile. As the little girls sing about "hopeful horizons," Bresson shows Mouchette silent to suggest that there are none in sight for her in life.

The world around these characters is as indifferent to them as Bresson describes the camera eye: "l'indifférence scrupuleuse d'une machine" ("a machine's scrupulous indifference").[9] And this is why the rigour of Bresson's narrative structure as a whole and in all its detail is appropriate for the world he depicts. Moment after moment of suffering are set end to end in *Mouchette* like so many empty gin bottles lined up under the bar. Yet that harsh arena through which these characters walk serves all the better to highlight those very rare moments of great warmth and beauty that mark for Bresson the possible spiritual quality of man. As I will describe in more detail, through the sound of the crash of bumper cars, Mouchette's smile radiates for a special moment as her glance meets that of a young man who crashes into her in play. That moment of happiness is brutally ended when her father violently slaps her as she approaches the boy at the next concession. In a similarly paradoxical situation, Mouchette's song seems all the more tender when juxtaposed with the violence of Arsène's fit. These oddly intimate moments of human contact suggest the action of grace that only can fill that void.[10]

The actions of these gentle creatures, which populate all of Bresson's films, seem all the gentler by contrast with the severity of the world around them. Mouchette cares for those around her throughout the film. Their relationship to her, with the exception of the woman, who gives her money for the bumper-car ride, and her mother, consists of the exchange of goods, services, money, and abuse. Mouchette's suicide, like the gentle woman's in *Une femme douce* is clearly an escape from this existence. Mouchette wraps herself in an organdy dress, a buffer against the ground; yet even in this special moment it rips against a branch as she begins her roll to death. The sound of a motor offscreen holds out the one chance Mouchette has of resisting the temptation of death. As she rolls down the hill for the first time, a motor is heard in the distance. She looks up, as the bushes stop her at the water's edge, stands up, and walks up the hill, raising her arm. In a long shot we see a farmer on a tractor driving up the road away from her. She waves and opens her mouth, but the sound of the tractor motor drowns out her voice. In the distance the farmer waves back as if saying hello. The call for help, for rescue is unheard across the space of the field. She rolls down the hill again, and into the water. The water envelops her totally and finally as the screen fades to black. We are left to ponder her motivation, but the chain of harsh sounds add to the chain of other materials from which we can infer connections in the narrative, from which we can infer that death better defines Mouchette's horizon of hope than physical and social reality.

Music

Like the warm, human glances that penetrate the world's void, music in Bresson's films suggests the possible solace of another, future world and "envelops the film in Christianity."[11] The first shot of *Mouchette* shows Mouchette's mother anguished and desolate as she leaves a church. She asks what will happen to her family and says that her chest feels as if there were stone there. Her loud footsteps on the stone floor reiterate that cold, hard reality that pervades the film. Then, in marked contrast, the solemn, rich tones of the Monteverdi *Magnificat* intervene and continue over the titles. The music suggests in its text that her question will be answered mercifully and in its sound that there exists a transcendent beauty to which this image of suffering must be related. The *stile concertante* (concerto style)[12] of the excerpts from the *Magnificat* sets one set of instruments against another as an echo, with an organ continuo. The runs of sixteenth notes played by the strings contrast with the solemn, sustained notes of the voices in a slow, chorale-like setting.[13] This echo effect suggests a certain spatial hollowness and a question-and-answer structure that might represent the humble below (the voices), in this case the woman, beseeching the Lord above (the instruments). The rising lines of sixteenth notes seem to mimic and promise the "exaltation of the humble" stated in the text: "et exaltavit humiles." ("and (He) hath exalted the humble.") For these reasons, the Monteverdi can suggest a final redemption, a horizon of hope for Mouchette and her mother, "the humble," whose sufferings are recorded in the film. The film "exalts the humble."

Occurring at the beginning of the film and after Mouchette's death, the music accompanies much less footage than similar scores in *Un condamné à mort s'est échappé* or *Pickpocket*, where musical phrases would occasionally coincide with special moments in these films as a rich continuo for the image phrases and as a similar evocation of another spiritual world. In a similar fashion, however, in *Un condamné à mort s'est échappé*, the text paralleled the theme of the narrative "Kyrie eleison; Christe eleison." ("Lord have mercy on us; Christ have mercy on us.") The rigour of *Procès de Jeanne d'Arc*, with rolling drums heard at the beginning and end as an austere evocation of execution, is replaced in *Au hasard Balthazar* by frequent lines from a Schubert piano sonata. From *Mouchette* on, Bresson only uses music at the beginning or the end of the film unless the source of the music can emanate from the space and situation of the film narrative. Bresson considers his use of music in the earlier films a mistake, a deviation from his firm economy built on concrete, realistic detail. Yet it seems to me that, whatever the source of the music, whether classical music heard on the record player of the gentle woman, or sensual rock music emanating from Marthe's radio [in *Quatre nuits d'un rêveur*], the music communicates the characters' states of mind and the possibility of metaphysical solace. In the later films, the music is more directly and literally allied with characters and their actions within the fiction of the film. It is a more subtle, less intrusive means on Bresson's part of authorial commentary on the action of the film. Yet, as an indefinite correlative of unspoken thoughts and feelings, and as commentary, its narrative function is the same.

Recurring after Mouchette's death, the Monteverdi seems to function as Bresson's Requiem for the girl who has wrapped herself in shroud-like vestments. The death of Mouchette is such a surprise that the music helps us reassess the events of her life we have seen and ponder the sum total of their meaning for her. Even as she is rolling down the hill we assume she is playing a rather odd game, although she has come from the old woman who has spoken to her of her own affinity with the dead. The music helps us sort out the sudden change in the course of Mouchette's life, the sudden end to which she submits herself. The words of the text of the *Magnificat* here affirm the possibility of another life after death and sanctify the tragedy of Mouchette's decision to escape from the despair of her own life: "deposuit potentes de sede." ("He hath put down the mighty from their seat.") It is as if Mouchette has asked herself the question her mother poses at the beginning of the film: "Sans moi, que deviendront-ils?" ("Without me, what will become of them?") She seems to have decided, from evidence Bresson has set before us as well, that her life holds out no hope of a bearable answer to that question. But, in the words of the *Magnificat*, He hath (and will) exalt and redeem the humble. What touched Bresson about Mouchette's character was just this innocent, unconscious heroism:

Sa résistance à l'atroce, la révélation que cette enfant attend de la mort, mille traits extraordinairement justes.[14]

(Her resistance to atrocity, the revelation that this child expects from death a thousand extraordinarily just rewards.)

The film ends as it had begun in a direct confrontation of the idea and prospect of death. Mouchette joins her mother in death, which has paradoxically robbed the young girl of the one person, her mother, with whom she hoped to be able to speak about her suffering.

Other sounds and snatches of music are as organized and meaningful, although less obvious as commentary, emanating as they do from within the fictional situation. For example, in the bumper-car montage sequence, the carnival music consists of carefully orchestrated phrases, each associated with a particular person and situation, although the music successfully appears to emanate at random from sources on location. At first associated directly with its source, the music functions structurally "offscreen" over several shots, unifying the separate sequences into a coherent whole. The following breakdown of sound and image shows their complex relationship:

Footage	Image	Sound
680	Mouchette washes dishes and leaves to sit with her father outside the café.	OFF Carnival music (a), clank of glasses, voices.
734	MS of Mouchette as she approaches bumper cars; montage of 46 shots in cars; shooting gallery confrontation with her father.	Rock music from bumper-car pavilion (b), cars bumping. Rock (b) + shots from rifles.
855	Mouchette sits down next to her father, tears fall down her cheeks.	(a) + (b) in dissonance.
865	Airplane merry-go-round sequence with Mathieu, Arsène and Louisa.	Merry-go-round concession. music (c).
910	Arsène enters café between father, Mouchette, and Mathieu. Mathieu confronts Louisa.	(a) + (c), a confusing conflict of melodies, (c).

FADE OUT

The music reflects Mouchette's emotional states and underscores conflicts between Louisa, Mathieu, and Arsène, registered in the dissonance of one or more tunes (a, b, and c). Rather lively rock music bridges the forty-six shots of the bumper cars, creating a smooth, continuous flow in space and time, and reflecting Mouchette's amusement. The swiftly changing angles and speeds of the cars are punctuated by the sound of collisions. The scene is a typically perverse and complicated mixture of violence and gentleness on Bresson's part, similar in impact to the shots in *Au hasard Balthazar* of Gérard in his leather jacket singing in the balcony of the church. Mouchette seems to enjoy having another outlet for her energies other than her clogs, and seems to revenge herself playfully on the world around her by crashing into those around her in their cars. On the other hand, the bumper cars also relay back and forth the attraction of Mouchette and the young man to each other. The crashes of the cars take on erotic overtones. When the ride stops, Mouchette leaves the car, and the young man approaches her shyly near the next concession. Her father violently interrupts this momentary communication between them by grabbing her by the shoulders, turning her around, slapping her twice, and shoving her forward. The sound of machine-gun fire coming from an arcade underlines his fiery disposition. Mouchette's reaction to this interruption, as she is forced to sit down next to her father, is shown in her tears and in the dissonance of two musical passages (a and c). This carnival scene and the music associated with it occurs at the exact centre of the film, framed at the beginning and end of the film by highly structured classical music. Between these instances of music, the continuity of highly organized and audible sounds throughout the film works as a rhythmic continuo essential to the structure of the film.

Sound and Structure

While sound in Bresson films is always related to the narrative situation and characters, sound has also provided Bresson with a means of unifying the number of shots that compose a sequence and whose temporal and spatial identity may at first appear unclear. As the aural representation of offscreen space within the context of a shot, sound provides a natural bridge to that shot. A typical aural trope in *Mouchette* consists of a shot that focuses on an empty architectural space, with the sound of footsteps heard offscreen. A person enters the field of the shot, moves through the space of the shot, with the sound of his footsteps continuing over the cut to the next space, perhaps an interior, that the character enters in countershot. There are many examples of the use of sound to unify images structurally: Mouchette's entrance into the classroom and her house, Mathieu's entrance with Arsène's traps, and the continuous sound of her father's truck and traffic outside the house.

In chapter 1 [of *Fragments: Bresson's Film Style*, the book from which this article is excerpted] I speculated on the function of these empty spaces. They tend to make us wonder where the character is, asserting his or her absence, causing us to await his or her presence. Like the hollow sounds that come to symbolize the void in which they are produced, images of empty spaces begin to represent that void as well. The entrance of a character into an empty space underlines the loneliness of the character, her isolation from those around. Further, what lurks beyond the frame is unknown and possibly threatening. Twice Mouchette's father enters the frame and shoves her forward. The schoolmistress moves into the frame and pulls Mouchette over to the piano, holding on to her neck with her fingers, as the collar of Arsène's trap encircles the neck of the bird or rabbit caught in it. As Arsène enters her space to violate her, the shot space represents the character's private zone, where others trespass. In contrast to this aural and spatial void is the bumper-car sequence, which seems the most active and "filled-up" sequence in the film. Music, crashing, smiles, and lots of people surround Mouchette and convey a momentary "fullness" in her life. Her father shoves her out of the one situation in which she was about to make human contact with another, and thereby enforces the isolation and emptiness of her life. In the last shot of the film she has literally dropped out of sight, leaving an empty, uninhabited space that the music enters to fill with a sense of spiritual presence.

Once the identity of the sound and its associated source have been visually established, the sound can then stand alone without recourse to an image of its source. The sound produced by an action offscreen may replace a change of shot to that offscreen space. It is this ability of sound to signify independently that contributes to the density and economy of Bresson's style. Bresson can concentrate the attention of the viewer on an image of Mouchette's face as she fills the gin bottle. The sound of her father's truck, previously established as he loads it with liquor, serves to indicate his approach, possibly in combination with light from the headlights, which flash across the room and Mouchette's face. There is hardly any sound one can think of that does not have a particular and powerful significance in the narrative structure of the film.

Bresson's precise composition of the soundtrack constitutes a type of "*musique concrète*," that Henri Pousseur among others has defined. Pousseur describes the role of everyday noises and sounds in his composition *Votre Faust*, written in collaboration with Michel Butor, in the following way:

We made our first endeavour in this direction with *Votre Faust*, consisting essentially of *a combination of pre-existing elements*: "everyday" realism on the one hand (noises of all kinds, more or less stylized, more or less musicalized, including speech pure and simple and all its applications), "cultural" realism on the other hand, thanks to a vast composition of *quotations*, literary and musical, variable in their dimensions (from simple sound to the complete opera scene) in their degree of distortion or variation, and in the multiple combinations that are realized; at the same time (there are) some musical quotations among them and some quotations with "natural noises," a mobility articulated at different stages permitting the work to become the forum of action for a transsubjective practice in which chance also has its say, its role as proposition and stimulation, surprise and deception to play.[15] (My translation.)

As Noël Burch has pointed out, sound in the cinema seldom achieves this complete independence from the image track.[16] But certainly Bresson's painstaking manipulation of sound, texture, volume, and rhythm in his beloved "*bruiteur*" (sound machine) creates a highly articulated sound composition that interacts with those images. The sounds puncture sequences and dialogue at varying intervals, giving the sequences an aural rhythmic structure about which Bresson has written:

The noises must become music.[17]

Rhythmic value of a noise.
Noise of a door opening and shutting, noise of footsteps, etc., for the sake of rhythm.[18]

The regular sound of footsteps in a series, for example, sets up a pattern, like that of a metronome, into which other sounds intrude to break up that pattern. Those intervening sounds function as accents in the series of footsteps, in much the same way that consonants might break up a chain of vowels in a sentence of poetry. The following chart diagrams that type of regular pattern and its interruptions:

Sound of Footsteps:	1	2	1	2	1	2	1	2	1	2	1	2
Sound of door (D);				D	D					G		G
glass (G):						CUT						

The regular temporal intervals between footsteps are shortened by the intrusion of another sound, occurring as it were on the off-beat. The aural rhythm may in turn continue over the cut as an element of continuity, with the cut functioning as a rhythmic accent. Or the rhythm of sounds and cuts can be aligned, to accentuate the cut, as often happens, we will see, in Bresson's dialogue.

One other sound is very important in Bresson's narrative composition, the sound of the human voice. In *Mouchette* the characters speak to each other infrequently, but when they do speak, the quality and rhythm of their voices add to the aural texture of the film and convey aspects of their character: the short, choppy, hard sentences exchanged between Louisa and Mathieu, punctuated by the clank of glasses on the bar; the snapped command of the schoolmistress: "Chante! Chante!", accompanied by pounding on the piano keys; the low, soft, fading voice of the mother; the sparse phrases of Mouchette and her pretty singing voice; the crude verbosity of Arsène. Traditional dramatic articulation and artifice are absent. It is the human voice that stretches across the emptiness of the world and seeks a response. It is the silence of that voice that indicates the unspeakable humiliation and suffering of the characters. When Mouchette smiles, sings, or swears, her voice conveys the reserve of passion beneath the inscrutable surface of her face. Bresson has commented on the natural alliance of glances and words:

Voice and face.
They have formed together and have grown used to each other.[19]

Like every other sound in the film, the sound of the voice contributes to the rich rhythmic modulations of the soundtrack.

Future Developments

Bresson further exploits and refines the emblematic and structural possibilities of sound in subsequent films. In *Une femme douce*, the husband's footsteps echo over the cuts between past and present and call attention to the death-like silence that pervades their rooms, whether the young woman is dead or alive. The sound of closing doors accents their arrival and departures from one another and his searches for her and for some reason for her death. In *Quatre nuits d'un rêveur*, the tape recorder registers Jacques's fantasy life in a disembodied fashion, a chant that he plays back to himself for consolation and inspiration. In both films, contemporary popular music is sought out as a correlative to the characters' moods, emanating from sources within the film.

In *Lancelot du Lac*, each sound is set off clearly from each other and reappears throughout the film as a haunting reminder of earlier scenes and its symbolic function there. The soundtrack is a set of sound themes and variations: the panting and neighing of horses and the pounding of racing hooves; the clatter and crash of armour; the groans and gagging on blood as a knight is engorged and falls to the ground; the haunting warning of crows and the bird outside Guenièvre's window; the march of drums and flourish of bagpipes heralding the events of the tournament; the horn that signals the time of day; the church bell and singing of a *Benedictus*; and the scrape and echo of footsteps passing through stone corridors. In *Lancelot du Lac*, sound conveys the epic emptiness of an age. The creak and strain of armour remind us, at every moment, of the barriers that men have constructed between them as part of their eternal warfare. The hollow rituals of combat in which they engage are conveyed by the repetition of motions and sounds associated with them: mounting horses, taking the lance, closing the helmet, riding off through the dark woods. The final shot of a pyre of haunted armour suits is Bresson's supreme metaphor for the emptiness of these physical shells of men for whom the spiritual quest is lost. The neighing of horses and gnawing squawk of crows warn these men of the destruction and defeat in store, like messengers from a heavenly realm. The darting eyes of the horses, like Balthazar's, survey and shy away from the repeated follies of man. The juncture of sound and image, meaning and sign, word and phrase in *Lancelot du Lac* is perfect and sums up Bresson's remarkable achievement as a sound composer.

Notes

1. Jean-Luc Godard and Michael Delahaye, "Entretien avec Robert Bresson," *Cahiers du cinéma*, no. 178 (Paris, 1966): p. 39.

2. Leo Murray, *"Un condamné à mort s'est échappé"* in Ian Cameron, ed. *The Films of Robert Bresson* (New York: Praeger, 1970), p. 80.

3. Annette Michelson, "Etc.," *Commonweal*, 29 November 1968, p. 318.

4. Noël Burch, "De l'usage structural de son," *Praxis du cinéma* (Paris: Éditions Gallimard, 1969), pp. 44-55; 133-34.

5. P. Renard-Georges, "Bernanos et Bresson," *Études bernanosiennes 9: Nouvelle historie de Mouchette de Bernanos à Bresson. Le Révue des lettres modernes* (Paris, 1968), pp. 93-94 (my translation).

6. Robert Bresson, *Mouchette (découpage)* in *l'Avant-Scene*, no. 80 (Paris, 1968), p. 30.

7. Renard-Georges, "Bernanos et Bresson," pp. 105-6.

8. Ibid., p. 105.

9. Bresson, *Notes*, p. 14.

10. See Susan Sontag, "Spiritual Style in the Films of Robert Bresson," *Against Interpretation* (New York: Laurel Publishing, 1969), pp. 192-94.

11. Yvonne Baby, "Le Domaine de l'indicible," *Le Monde* 14 March 1967 quoted in "Bernanos et Bresson," p. 104.

12. Leo Schrade, *Monteverdi: Creator of Modern Music* (New York: W. W. Norton, 1950), pp. 254-55.

13. Claudio Monteverdi, *Magnificat* (for seven voices and six instruments) in *Tutte le Opere di Claudio Monteverdi*, vol. 14, *Musica Religiosa 1*, ed. Malipiero, Universal Edition, pp. 285-326.

14. Bresson in "Questionnaire à Robert Bresson," *l'Avant-Scène*, no. 80, p. 6.

15. Henri Pousseur, *Fragments théoriques I sur la musique expérimentale* (Brussels: Éditions de l'Institut de sociologie de l'Université Libre de Bruxelles, 1970), p. 69. See also "Edgar Varèse (1885-1964): The Liberation of Sound" in *Contemporary Composers on Contemporary Music*, ed., E. Schwartz and Barney Childs (New York: Holt, Rinehart & Winston, 1967), pp. 195-208.

16. Noël Burch, *Praxis du cinéma*, pp. 146-47.

17. Bresson, *Notes*, p. 10.

18. Ibid., p. 23.

19. Ibid., p. 33.

Une femme douce

Bresson, Dostoevsky

W HOSE STYLES, at first glance, could appear more disparate than those of Dostoevsky and Bresson? The Russian is the writer of scale, of scope; overflowing dialogue, abundant and confusing intrigues filled with plotting criminals and mystery. The Frenchman is the filmmaker of ellipsis and litotes, of economy of speech, of paring down; disdainful of traditional suspense, he states at the beginning of *Pickpocket*, a film loosely inspired by *Crime and Punishment*, "This is not a detective novel."

"Mystery," for Dostoevsky, is situated elsewhere, on an entirely different level: "I have been called a psychologist. This is incorrect. I am nothing but a realist, in the true sense of the word. That is to say, I paint the human soul in all its depth."

It is no doubt at this level that we must seek, despite appearances, a kinship of inspiration. A kinship based less on the influence of the writer on the filmmaker than on a kind of increasing infiltration as Bresson rids himself of the scoria of literature—Giraudoux, Cocteau—in the dialogue of his early films. Paradoxically, as Bresson comes increasingly into his own, the more he conquers his "writing of images and sounds," ousting theatre from film and banishing acting from the scene, the more he resembles the novelist of passionate dialogues, whose work had so long been considered ready-made for the screen.

Bresson has always claimed to be more sensitive to music and painting—art forms he practised before filmmaking—than to literature. This, however, does not detract from his admiration for Proust, an admiration surpassed only by that for Dostoevsky. Since when has the latter's work been so important for Bresson?

Offences and Scandals

Long before *Pickpocket*, *Une femme douce* or *Quatre nuits d'un rêveur* (drawn from *White Nights*), before *Au hasard Balthazar* and *Le Diable probablement*—films informed by Dostoevskian elements that, as we shall see, give rise to two entirely different, yet deeply personal works—one can discern affinities of inspiration in Bresson's early films. The effort to escape "psychological" codes is already there; subtle, ambiguous relationships between characters are intimated in their stead.

In *Les Anges du péché*, one finds the central theme of *Crime and Punishment*: redemption through love as the criminal gives himself up to the police (the Pickpocket will not imitate Raskolnikov). The film also intertwines a police investigation with the interior adventure of the relationship between two women: one who saves at the cost of her life, and the other who is saved at the cost of imprisonment. The mystical confrontation of these two souls, where one is mercilessly pursued by the devouring zeal of the other before the latter woman's hate is transformed into love and devotion, is not foreign to a Dostoevsky novel.

Equally close is *Les Dames du Bois de Boulogne*, in which an impoverished girl falls prey to a man's lust (derived from *Jacques the Fatalist*). A melodrama so dear to eighteenth-century sensibilities (hence *The Nun*) is dramatized in the Dostoevskian manner of the girl "who had nowhere to go" (like Dounia, Raskolnikov's sister, like la Douce, or Nastasya Filippovna in *The Idiot*). In the character of Maria Casarès, Bresson has made Madame de la Pommeraye far more intelligently perverse. Oddly enough, the "scandal-marriage" (that turns against its instigator), also exists, though consciously and deliberately, in *The Idiot*. The converted liberal (Paul Bernard) ends where Prince Myshkin began: compassionate love has sublimated passionate love and brutal sensuality ("I must own that girl"). Yet critics of the time, even the subtle André Bazin, seem to have missed the impact of Helen's vengeance—seeing only a social question in it (the marriage with a "delicious cabaret singer"). Much more than the arrogance of one's social class, the Ideal has been wounded; that which hides at the heart of sensuality for the angelic and pure girl, "not like the others."[1]

"You have played a trick on me. Well, I have played one on you. A woman with a vengeance, you do not know what this is." Dostoevsky would say: "A man humiliated will seek himself to humiliate."

In this perspective, the author's and filmmaker's characters look like brothers and both fit Gide's description as beings "cut from the same cloth. Pride and humility remain the secret workings of all their acts."

There is positive pride, of course: courage, Mouchette's stoic pride, sitting upright at the coffee table, staring straight ahead to stop the tears. Lieutenant Fontaine (*Un condamné à mort s'est échappé*) who risks execution for a pencil, "all this so as not to give in." The cost of human dignity here touches the very core. The vision of Jeanne d'Arc's chained feet, of a beaten Fontaine with spit on his face, reveal Bresson's ability to use his own—albeit less terrifying—memories of *The House of the Dead*. Dignity, however, for both Bresson and Dostoevsky extends to all living creatures. The deaf sound of thugs kicking Arnold in the stomach (the vagabond in *Au hasard Balthazar*) is no less terrible than the club sounding on the helpless donkey's back. The image of the bridle brutally pulling on the poor animal's mouth evokes Raskolnikov's vision of the moujik torturing the small horse. Animals, are, without a doubt, the absolute degree of innocence. ("He's a saint," says the mother talking of the donkey, something that evokes *The Idiot*; Myshkin's revelation in Switzerland when he hears a donkey braying.)

For both artists, however, the most tragic face of offended innocence is that of the young girl, or of the young girl precociously fallen prey to men: Sonya in *Crime and Punishment*, little Nelly in *The Insulted and the Injured*, Nastasya Filippovna, precociously handed over to her "tutor" Totsky or the "little fiancée" of Svridrigailov. With Bresson, it's Agnès, or Mouchette; or Jeanne d'Arc whose moral resistance is tested ("Thrice an English lord tried to dishonour me") and who must submit to a humiliating "test" of her virginity. It's Marie who does not escape a gang of "black shirts" only to fall into the hands of an old lustful miser (*Au hasard Balthazar*).[2]

The shame felt can be summed up in a single gesture: hands that crawl up Joan's sheets after the dreadful "examination," or Marie's stance, seen from the back, naked, huddled up in a corner of a room where the thugs undressed and beat her. Or of Mouchette, like a frightened wild animal, soaked and hidden in a thicket during a downpour.[3] Because Bresson shares with Dostoevsky the gift of capturing the essence of a single gesture, of a stance.

Humiliation often takes the shape of "a lowered head." Thérèse (Jany Holt), the prisoner in *Les Anges*, is seen head lowered as she is brutally shoved by a guard into the soup wagon. Just as Mouchette, on the stoop of the church, is pushed in the back by her father. And when she plays a false note, the piano teacher shoves her head right down to the keyboard.

Yet the lowered head sometimes serves as a parody of respect: Arnold's apparent deference to the police captain is accompanied by a "die you dirty pig!"

Indeed, the humiliated fight back and defend themselves; delight in masochism rarely appears in Bresson. The slap, so constant in Dostoevsky (Ganya slaps Myshkin, Shatov smacks Stavrogin) is in Bresson, often returned (Marie slaps Gérard, la Douce strikes her husband). In *Les Dames*, a dancing boor blows cigarette smoke in Agnès's face. She, in turn, burns him with her own cigarette. He slaps her in the face. She pushes him violently, knocking over a table and breaking a vase.

From film to film, the scene of the scandal is not only reduced to two or three people, but condensed into gestures and objects. Already in *Les Anges du péché*, in the convent where Anne-Marie rebels, refusing to kiss the feet of her companions, one sees the novice's provocation as she throws the nuns' favourite black cat to the ground. The object thrown to the ground then becomes an increasingly efficient vehicle to convey a scandal endured (humiliation, as the vase broken by Myshkin) or desired (rebellion, as the abandoned Nelly throws the cup to the floor). Humiliation of the broken wine bottle, spread about the floor like an obscene stain in front of the visiting monk (*Journal d'un curé de campagne*). Or Mouchette's bowl of coffee accidentally knocked over in front of the village cronies. Rebellion seen in the glass thrown to the ground by Agnès trapped and tricked during a lunch (*Les Dames*) or in the book tossed onto the floor by the Pickpocket ("Enough!" he orders the police superintendent). Or by the croissant Mouchette tosses—on purpose this time—when confronted with "So, you are breaking my bowl now?" In the flowers suddenly thrown to the ground by la Douce during a stroll with her husband. Or in the siphon Gérard uses to pierce an ice cube in his coffee—only a prelude to the momentous "break"(*Balthazar*). Rebellion in the form of the chequebook thrown to the ground in front of Reich, who had come "to offer protection."[4] Or in the refined insult of the pathetic chinking of the coin, tossed by Charles, in payment onto the desk of the renowned psychoanalyst (*Le Diable probablement*).

Bresson refines various forms of humiliation: the ironic impact of the Sunday schoolgirls' mocking laughter, the perfidious allusions of the "rumours" about the country priest. These "rumours" are reduced to two or three words uttered by the notary who "finishes off" Marie's dying father (in *Balthazar*). Surrounded by jeers, the notary burns him with the brevity of his answers: "A donkey, that's cute," "it's modern." The donkey then crystallizes the obsession with the ridiculous, to which, we already know, only saints are indifferent.

Bressonifying thus the character as the pretext to the initial situation (an innocent man suspected, a girl who has left her parents in *The Insulted and the Injured*), the filmmaker bestows a terrible mutism on the father, more profoundly Dostoevskian. Refusing to "forget the offence" ("He loves his misery more than us," says the daughter to the mother), he dies face toward the wall. When the priest comes, bringing his evangelic consolation, his reply "I suffer perhaps less than you think" has a very "Stavrogian" ring to it.

The humiliated who humiliate in turn, this is also la Douce. She has found the chink in her husband's armour. "But you, you became a financier." More than just a sentence, a simple attitude suffices to provoke the man who was "only seeking to possess her body": naked in the bathtub, a leg casually dangling over the edge, her eyes fixed on him, her hand outstretched toward the soap that has fallen to the ground.[5]

In *Lancelot du Lac*, Mordred's irony provokes a scandal as if the king were somehow surprised by the absence of his best knight.

MORDRED: Love, Sir! Lancelot is in love.
THE KING: Who?
MORDRED: The Queen.
THE KING: He is her knight.

MORDRED: And more.

GAUVAIN: This is the greatest lie ever.

THE KING: You are jealous and you are looking to create a stir.

For the answers to resound as in a Cornelian exchange is not enough. Yet the rapidity of alternating fixed shots of the knights, a visual shock punctuated by another, the sound of lowered visors, prolong and perfect the discoveries of *Procès de Jeanne d'Arc*. There the duel between the judges takes the form of a shot/counter-shot sequence, without ever changing the angle, attacking Jeanne from all sides.

Why evoke *Lancelot*? Because in its stylistic perfection it appears to be the metaphor of the duel, of internal conflict—as dear to Dostoevsky as to Bresson—between love and friendship, violence and gentleness, offence and respect.

Contradictions of the Soul

In Bresson, as in Dostoevsky, we see the same gestures of impulsive, unpredicted tenderness: Jeanne throwing herself into the arms of the thief after he confesses, la Douce coming out of the cinema where she was harassed, seeking shelter in the arms of the husband whom she "wanted to love." The girls as well, throwing themselves around their mothers' necks (Anne-Marie, Agnès, Marthe).

Compassion answers to aggression, respect and humility to offence. Hands care and sympathize: those of the veterinarian on the back of the donkey, those that press the hand of the sick (Jeanne d'Arc, la Douce). Hands that wipe away blood and dirt (*Journal d'un curé de campagne, Une femme douce, Lancelot*), or hands open to others (Séraphita and the priest, the bloodstained hand, offered by the Dreamer to the abandoned girl).

One bows down in front of those who deserve respect, or simply before suffering, as do the starets before Dmitry Karamazov. Crouched on the ground, the novice says her vows; Lancelot kneels in front of the King and kisses the hem of the Queen's dress; a small peasant woman kisses the ground where Lancelot had trodden. Filled with remorse and respect, Thérèse kisses Anne-Marie's feet (like Catherine Ivanovna kisses those of her daughter-in-law Sonya). Mouchette kisses the hand of her sick mother; Marie kisses the hand of her childhood friend Jacques, who had tried to save her. Finally la Douce's husband devotedly kisses the naked feet of his wife . . . But his lips creep up to her knees, and when he utters that terrible phrase, "and I, who thought you were going to leave me," she lets herself fall back into a chair. Idealism and sensuality within the same soul: in *Lancelot,* this is expressed through a contrast between the Queen's lighted window up above and the sighs in the crumpled hay down below.

The internal contradiction at the heart of a human being is manifested just as much on the exterior: one person must make a choice between two others. Natasha must choose between Vanya and Alyosha (*The Insulted and the Injured*); Nastasya between Myshkin and Rogozhin; Stavrogin having to choose between Lisa and Dounia, the latter always ready to play the role of the "nurse," as Lisa nastily describes her.

Jacques in *Balthazar*, Michel in *Le Diable probablement* and, of course, the Dreamer in *Quatre nuits*—but also Gauvain in *Lancelot*—belong to that species of "sacrificing savers," loyal lovers who must destroy their own hearts in order to heal the wounds of love and passion.

Young women who are not lost but who "lose themselves" are aware that they do not love "as one is supposed to love" (Grochenka to Dmitry). "It's you I love, Michel" says Alberte in *Le Diable probablement*; saying this to her devoted friend who implores her not to break her parent's heart (like Natasha and Vanya in *The Insulted and the Injured*). Yet she runs away with Charles, for whom she does not feel "true love." Marthe of *Quatre nuits d'un rêveur* (Nastenka reworked by Bresson) says: "Why can't he be you? Why is he not made like you?"—"He can do what he wants, I don't give a damn"—And "I can only love what I admire and respect." With Bresson, the wounding of the ego, the sensual wound, is far deeper than with Dostoevsky—given a certain liberty of interpretation with respect to the original.

While Bresson's adaptations of Dostoevsky distill the texts to their essence, one must nevertheless ask how the filmmaker translates the intentions of the text. How indeed does Bresson address the painful contradictions that arise from impetuous behaviour—advances and retreats, affirmations and negations—signs of the mystery of a being seeking the Other and the Self. As a filmmaker, Bresson addresses these, not by way of actors, but through the management, if you will, of visual and sound space; a tear running down a cheek, the boy's hand feeling his way up a blouse, a bird's song that breaks the silence. It's the remarkable scene in the 2CV in *Au hasard Balthazar*: Marie "wants to" but "does not want to." Just like in the night scene when, sensing the presence of the young villains, she lets one hand slide along the bench and with the other, clutches her beating heart.[6]

Marie "wants to" and "does not want to" destroy her father's sadness. A father who embraces her like a lover and of whom she says—using a typically Dostoevskian expression—"Papa? He is mad about me."

During the apartment sequence of *Quatre nuits d'un rêveur*, and despite Marthe's tender affection for her mother, one has never seen such power of transgression that is conveyed by a splendid parallel montage: in the locked room the tenant undresses Marthe while the footsteps of the mother resound through the tiny apartment. Onto the naked, standing bodies of the two young people falls a "Marthe, my dear" that echoes the "Marie, Marie" of the poor father looking for his daughter lying in the hay with Gérard (*Balthazar*).

Who does not wish for the death of the father? Blasphemy seems quite a stretch from *Les Anges du péché* (though even there, the nun's difficulty issued from conflicting feelings of filial love and rebellion), to *Lancelot*. However, Lancelot is torn between the King—the greatest of fathers capable of inflicting the most severe punishments—and the Queen (to love the same woman as does one's father, that was Dmitry Karamazov's dilemma and that of the Raw Youth). Incited by Guinevere ("It's almost as though you killed him yesterday"), yet fearing the void of heaven, Lancelot, had he not, before sacrificing himself to loyalty, quashed the secret parricidal desire deep within his heart?

Back and Forth and the Restrictions of Space

The conflict of feelings, the conflict with the father is just as much a conflict in space: to obey or to disobey. To stay or to leave. On the doorstep, Marie hesitates, not knowing which direction to choose. From behind, one foot barely on the ground, she hears her father's voice: "Where are you going?—Nowhere—Then stay."

Beings of desire (physical or mystical, and so often an obscure mélange of the two) are thus found on doorsteps of the paternal home, of the Artus Castle (that "shack" where one risks a suffocating death) or of a condemned prison cell. It's no coincidence that the knocks on the wall, the anguishing creaks pushed to a tense extreme and the "acknowledgement" in the hallway appear in both *Un condamné* and *Quatre nuits d'un rêveur*. It's the science of the beating heart behind closed doors, akin to Dostoevsky.[7] Here we catch a glimpse not only of the attempt to reach the Other (or Others), but of the vertiginous moment of risk-taking (heightened by moral transgression in the second case): to dare or not to dare.

It is very odd to see Bresson's view of space intersect with Dostoevsky's predilection for intermediate spaces, for stairs and doorsteps—so often pointed out by the critics.[8]

The exhausting walks of Dostoevsky's heroes through the city or up and down winding stairwells as they try to solve some mysterious imbroglio are nothing but an detective novel alibi to meet the Other, and a way for the heroes to come to know themselves. Bresson's heroes too, are seeking some chance meeting for love, full of obstacles. Already in his first films—*Les Anges du péché* and *Journal d'un curé de campagne*—a continual transit between two places (the convent and the prison, for example) is employed in order for one to see the unhappy Bressonian character take shape; someone constantly trying to reach "the Other side," always eager to go outside when caught inside, curious to enter when out-of-doors. As well, there is the paradox of closed-off spaces: Hélène's apartment (where the protective friend lives) functions as a trap; Agnès's apartment is an imprisoning space for the young girl as it is a place of desire (and fantasy) for Jean. Long before the adaptations, one could already see the filmmaker, on the deep level of the symbolic unconscious, approaching the writer whose *Journals* are full of such annotations: "Scene in the stairwell"; "Insult"; "Affront in stairwell"; etc.

In the stairwell in *Les Dames*, Jean is rebuffed by Agnès (the scene of the umbrella). Anne-Marie confronts Thérèse on a staircase landing. The country priest is subjected to disapproving glances from above, where height clearly signals power relationships.

Stoops, sills, those places of desire, are just as much places of solitude and anxiety. The Pickpocket refuses to go in to see his sick mother. In contrast, the country priest is pained by closed doors: of the Torcy presbytery, closed in the absence of the vicar; in Lille, the doctor's door that shuts after the fatal diagnosis, only to have a suitcase deposited at its step. And what could be more remarkably Dostoevskian than the scene of the "fraternal correction" in *Les Anges du péché*? Could there be a more painful quest for the Self than that of the young nun? Seeking judgement at the doorstep of each one of her companion's cells, she is answered by door upon door shutting with a different verdict.

But the stoop is also the place of espionage, a place where someone lies in ambush[9]—let us not even address the terribly obvious Judas hole of the prisons. At the carriage entrance in *Les Anges*, the nuns lay in wait for the new recruit, as did Agnès's "admirers" in *Les Dames du Bois du Boulogne*. So did Jean waiting in the rain in the very same film, or the master pickpocket who lay in ambush for his future apprentice. (An equally disquieting situation is found in *Crime and Punishment* and *The Eternal Husband*.) In *Lancelot*, Mordred and his clique spend their time spying on doorsteps.

As with Dostoevsky, only with a visual form, spying for Bresson reveals the need to know, to puncture mystery. But this mystery seeks to go far beyond the simple event, and unlike Dostoevsky, Bresson hates to complicate things—just the opposite: this is not a detective novel.

The key phrases that return in Bresson's dialogues are, to cite but a few: "I had to know" (*Pickpocket*); "I could not but know" (the husband to la Douce); "How can one be sure of anything around here?" (*Un condamné à mort s'est échappé*); "But of whom are you sure?" (says Guinevere to Lancelot).

Questioning

With Bresson, the feeling of enigma is clearly treated differently.

Of Dostoevsky's talkative characters, Henry Bars said: "The more they speak, the more one understands that what is essential cannot be said. As if the premonition of a person's mystery aggravated a kind of need for *effraction** in Dostoevsky and the beings he created." This need for *effraction* was already apparent in the many visual metaphors created by the author of *Un condamné à mort s'est échappé* and *Pickpocket*. Bresson tries to create such a need within the viewer, erasing signs from the "model's" smooth face; taking refuge behind a "mysterious appearance"[10], the model occasionally releases, almost regretfully—and to great effect—an expression. The model's "charm" lies in the fact "that he does not know who he is" and thus his "involuntary expressiveness," the strange music of his "interiorized" voice, oppose the deliberate expressiveness of the professional, he or she who aims to explain.

But the way in which Bresson has the story progress through images also reveals a concern for "protecting complexity" (as Gide once said of Dostoevsky). In the form of a rigorous search for composition, Bresson moves closer and closer to a kind of divested poetic writing, the spirit of which is not unlike what the novelist sought through profusion.

Indeed, in Dostoevsky, Jacques Catteau saw the force, the freedom, and the elucidation of the chronicle at work. In a total refusal of ornamentation, the Russian writer creates a space that is "strictly dependant on the hero's movement and expression." As well, it is both the object of a specific intention just as much as it is the object of a scrutinized vision.[11]

With Bresson, the viewer is frequently bound to a character's steps and actions. Objects, and space, though they keep (and precisely because they *keep*) the weight of reality intact, then become vehicles for a character's "idea" or "dream."

The spoon left on the window sill; the pyjamas sent in a package in *Un condamné à mort*; the slit in the pocket of a vest in *Pickpocket*; or the envelope containing a letter in *Quatre nuits d'un rêveur* have all lost any kind of logical status. They are objects *for* the hero. And, thanks to a precise choice of concrete details, St. Petersburg is at once a city topographically identifiable and at the same time, it is another, different city for Raskolnikov, for the Dreamer, and for the Raw Youth, just as Paris, seen through Bresson's lens, is not the same for Michel the Pickpocket, for the foreign couple la Douce and her husband, for Jacques the Dreamer, or for suicidal Charles. A combination of fossils in a glass cage (the museum scene in *Une femme douce*), dry fish bones displayed in shop windows, and an echo of the couple's alternating footsteps, are ways in which the real becomes the "fantastic."

In *Quatre nuits d'un rêveur*, passers-by, lovers in the square, pigeons, the blaze of the *bateau-mouche*, the close-up of n° 14 on a building, the noise an electric bolt makes, an opening or closing door together form a universe of desires, one of anxiety and happiness combined, in harmony with the state of mind of the narrator in *White Nights*.[12]

---

* A "breaking open." *Ed.*

In *Le Diable probablement*, quays along the Seine, squeaking rubber shoes in a service elevator, a single glass placed on the table of a deserted café, and the night constitute something entirely different: together they form a route leading to death—the anxiety of which is increased tenfold by an interminable sequence in the metro where Charles and the hired assassin wait in silence for the train to arrive at the next station.

But the coincidence of the viewer with a character's interior time (without objective space having to lose any integrity) does not in any way signify that the viewer is swallowed up by that time. A Bresson film, like a Dostoevsky novel, is a questioning of appearances, it is a call to explain what is normally expected of a chronological ordering.

An Effort of Conscience

One cannot help but remark upon Bresson and Dostoevsky's shared predilection for stories "filtered . . . through a narrator."[13] Refusing omniscience, Dostoevsky chooses to filter the novel through letters (*Poor Folk*), through the "recollections" of a dreamer (*White Nights*), through memoirs (*House of the Dead*), or writings (*Notes from Underground, The Dream of a Ridiculous Man*). Bresson goes through a daily journal (*Journal d'un curé de campagne*), a factual account laid out with military sobriety (*Un condamné à mort s'est échappé*), confessions devoid of all commentary (*Pickpocket*, a film that in fact takes up Raskolnikov's primitive diary), or a narrative as a form of self-justification (*Une femme douce*). Dostoevsky's ploy involves questioning the character and her story through her own discourse. In his great novels, a naive narrator with a limited point of view is used so that the need for meaning becomes even greater and more difficult.

In Bresson's films that rely on a voice-over text, the director's intervention into the space around the character never exercises any kind of supremacy. Of course, Bresson often sees more, and better, than his characters. He sees the monk's expression as he stares at the country priest's wine bottle; he sees the police inspector (that fortunate cheating gambler) lurking behind the Pickpocket—momentarily reformed ("the police and I were lost from sight"). In *Une femme douce*, Bresson espies the old maid watching the husband at the very moment in which he interprets his wife's words to his advantage (the form of the husband's story is here a splendid equivalent to the doubt the reader of the Dostoevsky short story feels). In short, this is about questioning the narrator's lucidity without imposing the author's point of view; meanwhile the story, modestly unfolding at the edge of events, only serves to revive the need for meaning. In a narrative, pleonasms and image-text "redundancies" in Bresson[14] share the same function as the myopic narrator in Dostoevsky. They frustrate the viewer and force one to step back in order to understand, and see, what is going on.

The relation of image to spoken text, by uniting the spontaneity of *experiencing* with the privilege of *knowing*, allows Bresson to raise the stakes far above the ordinary rules of "suspense." When the outcome is known, what is questioned, in every shot, is the mystery of freedom.

In *Un condamné à mort s'est échappé,* when Fontaine asks if the sentry boxes are vacant and the text "they were vacant" doubles what is seen on-screen, the viewer is caught within an intense "moment," which presents a new obstacle to overcome, a moment in which chance and freedom are in constant play. The cruelty of *Une femme douce* is derived from a similar principle: images of the past and present are treated "on the same level"—a perfect counterpart to that part of the husband's conscience attempting "to believe in fate."

What happens, conversely, when Bresson adapts *White Nights* in the third person? Dostoevsky's art, conveyed through his naive narrator, of letting a menace hover over the final outcome without revealing it—all the while hinting at the cruel undercurrent of the *roman sentimental*—is transformed by Bresson into his own art. An art that consists of translating an interior rhythm through a "language of things," while at the same time ostensibly *"levelling"* the narrative into four chapters, like a child's picture book. Naiveté is thus introduced into the unanswered question of the final image.

What is remarkable in Bresson's later films is the extent to which the filmmaker's compositional demands not only outstrip traditional concerns of literary adaptation to the screen (with respect to subject, remembrances or the occasional borrowing from the text) but, more importantly, are also in line with the Russian writer's preoccupations.

Such traditional concerns are, however, evident in *Au hasard Balthazar* or *Le Diable probablement,* where one can clearly sense the conscious or unconscious impregnation of *The Idiot* and *The Insulted and the Injured.*[15] One might also suggest that the gang of black shirts recklessly "celebrating" Arnold's inheritance recalls Rogozhin's gang celebrating that of Myshkin. As well, the anarchists who proclaim destruction, read the writings of the revolutionary Bakunin, and who slip obscene photographs into pious books seem to come straight out of *The Devils* (but they are also repetitions of History). Moreover, one can detect a Dostoevskian *air* about the epileptic drunkard Arnold and his "suicide" serving possibly as an alibi to a crime, and about his misfiring revolver, which is similar to Hippolyte's gun. But we are falling prey to the vertigo of interpretation. And even if certain common situations undoubtedly exist (in *Le Diable*, the situation of Charles caught between Edwige and Alberte, the latter consoled by the brave Michel who sits like a loyal dog on the stoop, echoes the relationships of Alyosha, Katya, Natasha and Vanya), it is not at this superficial level that a parallel becomes interesting.

However, as Bresson perfects himself with each new film, one can sense an "aesthetic of chaos" arising from deep within the narrative—akin to the aesthetic that inspired Dostoevsky's great novels.

In *Au hasard Balthazar*, it is the donkey, the naive narrator whose absolute innocence lies outside language. His expression is the interior conscience of the film and the condemnation of the world he inhabits. The only continuous line through human folly is his stoic submission during a tortuous journey up the hillside toward Calvary. This progression toward absurdity and catastrophe, mixing several stories that revolve around the donkey, appears to be the poetic equivalent of the Idiot's universe—one that could only be surpassed by those offered in *The Devils* and *Le Diable probablement*. Here, the world breaks open, into many different "voices" barring all possibility of communication, and even within the sequence (see the religious discussion inside the church), sundry objects (the vacuum cleaner on the red rug, the organ being tuned) do not signify polyphony, but a universal cacophony, total discontinuity. Absurdity rules above all and at its side, solitude.

Charles and Dmitry Karamazov think of the same image as they ponder suicide; they want to see the bullet lodged in their heads. But Dmitry will not kill himself. Having felt guilty not because of the act, but because of the intention, he will, in coming to understand his own liberty, try to "renew himself." There is a dawn somewhere behind Dostoevsky's tragedies. But it's the black night that engulfs the last film of Bresson, swallowing the steps of a desperate irresponsible criminal. That bitter green star, the Absinth star of the Apocalypse foreshadowed by Lebedev in *The Devils*, has it so poisoned the spring of life in Bresson's world that a place for liberty no longer exists?

Translated from the French by Lara Fitzgerald

Notes

1. It is using the idea of the "trampled Ideal" that Dostoevsky (after Coleridge, Gide reminds us) interprets Othello's murdering of Desdemona.
2. The scene has been transcribed in detail in "Bresson et l'argent," *Cinématographe*, no. 27.
3. Marie also arrives during a storm at the miser's home. Thus Bresson increases the feeling of distress and rediscovers an image that haunts Dostoevsky. In *Crime and Punishment* (Svridrigailov), "it's a girl wearing a rain-soaked dress who was crying . . . she had no socks and her shoes with holes were so wet that it seemed as though they had been soaked in a marsh all night." In *The Dream of a Ridiculous Man*, the same thing: ". . . I noticed in particular his torn shoes taking water, I still see them,

they really struck me." As well, when Dounia runs away from Svridrigailov, when Lisa escapes after giving herself up to Stavrogin, they are both drenched by the rain.

4. Just as Volkovsky does to Natasha in *The Insulted and the Injured*.

5. Dostoevsky is just as much an expert when it comes to subtle shows of force: in *The Devils*, the "great writer" Karmazinov drops his wallet to see if the narrator will bend down and pick it up.

6. There is not a single Dostoevsky novel where the heart does not beat violently, or sit in a character's throat. Bresson shows the same intuition: there will be the same gesture with Marthe, hesitating whether to open the door to the tenant. The condemned man felt it before her, and so did the Pickpocket who said: "My heart beat violently."

7. *Crime and Punishment*: Raskolnikov behind the usurer's door.

8. Dominique Arban, *Le Seuil chez Dostoievski, thème, motif et concept*. Cahiers de l'Herne, spécial Dostoevski.

9. Hence the obvious interest of glass doors (*Les Dames du Bois de Boulogne, Une femme douce*) through which people are watched.

10. Robert Bresson, *Notes sur le cinématographe*, éd. Gallimard.

11. Jacques Catteau, *La Création littéraire chez Dostoevski*, Institut d'études slaves 1978, p. 525 "Le héros dans l'espace : visée et vision."

12. In the name of verisimilitude, in his *White Nights*, Visconti eliminated the episode of the letter brought to the unknown "rival" and thus eliminated the character and his story.

13. See Jacques Catteau, op. cit.; "L'élection de la chronique."

14. For example, the famous "I had to lean against the wall" accompanying the gesture, or the Pickpocket's "I went straight to the wicket": an aesthetic of systematic duplication (often triplication when writing in a notebook is involved) where deliberate, methodical naiveté intending to elicit questioning has often been missed by critics!

15. Articles from *Cinématographe*: "Bresson et l'argent" and "*Le Diable probablement*" (nos. 27 and 29).

Lancelot du Lac

KRISTIN THOMPSON

The Sheen of Armour, the Whinnies of Horses: Sparse Parametric Style in *Lancelot du Lac*

The Elliptical Narrative

ROBERT BRESSON'S 1974 FILM *Lancelot du Lac* is at once a very simple and a very complex film. The narrative contains relatively few events; while it depends partially on the fact that virtually any viewer will have at least some knowledge of the Arthurian legends, it also treats some actions so elliptically as to confuse us about certain causal relations. Similarly, the film's style uses techniques sparsely, introducing, and then varying, a number of elements throughout the film. Armour, horse whinnies, birdcalls, the various locales, even the methods of staging and framing shot/reverse-shot segments—all play in rhythmic ways across the film.[1] Although *Lancelot* is a narrative film, not all its stylistic repetitions serve the syuzhet action, or help us to reconstruct a fabula line.* Rather, much of the interest of the film's style remains independent of narrative functions.

---

* One of the most valuable methodological procedures devised by the Russian Formalists for analyzing narratives has been the fabula-syuzhet distinction. Basically, the syuzhet is the structured set of all causal events as we see and hear them presented in the film itself. Typically, some events will be presented directly and others only mentioned; also, events often will be given to us out of chronological order, as when flashbacks occur or when a character tells us of earlier events which we did not witness. Our understanding of these syuzhet events often involves rearranging them mentally into chronological order. Even when the film simply presents events in their 1-2-3 order, we need to grasp their causal connections actively. This mental construction of chronologically, causally linked material is the fabula.

Once we begin to look at *Lancelot's* parametric variations, as well as at how style serves the narrative, the underlying complexity of the film becomes apparent. Limited though the number of elements participating in these patterns may be, Bresson combines and recombines them in ways that are difficult to grasp upon one or two viewings (although they are clearly there and, once noticed, can be seen during a viewing). Hence an apparently simple surface leads us into a convoluted texture.

Stylistically, *Lancelot* is a quintessential Bressonian work. Typically, Bresson is known for the deliberately inexpressive quality of his style: the expressionless performances of his actors, the refusal to establish spaces and to emphasize certain events with long shots, and the like. By doing a period piece, he was able to introduce armour into his panoply of devices for avoiding expressive performances. Not only do his actors deliver lines tonelessly, but often we see their faces or hands or feet sheathed in blank metal. And by equating the horses so completely with his human characters, he can show actions at one further remove by framing only the legs or bodies of the horses. Stylistic techniques similar to ones Bresson had worked with for three decades were used to perfection in this film.

Yet *Lancelot* was, after *Procès de Jeanne d'Arc*, only Bresson's second period piece. His early reputation had been as a great adapter of literature. *Les Dames du Bois de Boulogne* and *Journal d'un curé de compagne* were hailed in France in the early 1950s as perfect cinematic translations of the original texts. As Bresson remarked: "I would like the source of my films to be in me, apart from literature. Even if I make a film from Dostoevsky [i.e., *Une femme douce*], I try always to take out all the literary parts."[2] Bresson seemed to internalize the original, then create the filmic equivalent.

In a sense, *Lancelot*, too, is an adaptation. And if its presentation seems elliptical, we might suspect that Bresson assumed a certain knowledge on our part of the original: the general idea of the Round Table, Lancelot and Guenevere's affair, Mordred's rebellion against Arthur, and so on. The story events themselves are simple; Bresson has eliminated many events included in what I take to be a close source among the Arthurian legends, *La Mort le Roi Artu*, which itself is quite a short book (less than two hundred pages in a recent translation).[3]

The film's action can be segmented as follows:

I. (Shots 1–13). The forest: fights, knights riding (the failure of the Grail quest).
II. (Shot 14). Close-up of the Grail with crawl title explaining the situation; drum and pipe music.
III. (Shots 15–24). The forest: peasants gathering wood encounter Lancelot, lost. The credits.

IV. (Shots 25-40). The castle, night: Lancelot returns, meets Gauvin and others; the wounded arrive; Lancelot and Gauvin's meeting with Artus.

V. (Shots 41-73). The castle, day: Lancelot goes to the forest shed, meets Guenièvre for the first time since his return; he tells her their affair is over.

VI. (Shots 74-76). Castle chapel: Lancelot arrives late for mass, sees Guenièvre with Artus.

VII. (Shots 77-97). The castle: Artus says he will close off the Round Table room; introduction of Mordred.

VIII. (Shots 98-111). The tents: Lancelot and Gauvin discuss Artus's decision; Gauvin says the other men watch Guenièvre's window.

IX. (Shots 112-115). Hallway of the castle: Guenièvre and Gauvin talk; he praises Lancelot as a saint; Gauvin asks Artus for a goal, is told to pray.

X. (Shots 116-147). The forest shed: the second meeting of Lancelot and Guenièvre; she still refuses to release him from his oath to her.

XI. (Shots 148-172). The battlements and tents: Lancelot and others discuss the moon; Lancelot offers friendship to Mordred, who refuses.

XII. Shots 173-182). Lancelot's tent: Gauvin reveals that some of the men are going over to Mordred; Lancelot gives him a jewelled bridle.

XIII. (Shot 183). Castle chapel: Lancelot prays for strength to resist temptation.

XIV. (Shots 184-191). Castle yard: knights arrive from Escalot with a challenge to a tournament; Artus, Gauvin, and Lancelot discuss it.

XV. (Shots 192-208). Castle yard: practice at tilting; training of a horse.

XVI. (Shots 209-240). The forest shed: the third meeting of Lancelot and Guenièvre; Lancelot gives in to Guenièvre; they are spied on by Mordred and others.

XVII. (Shots 241-276). The tents: Mordred and supporters argue with Gauvin and Lionel about Lancelot; Mordred sets up an assassination plot. Lancelot says he is not going to the tournament; others depart.

XVIII. (Shots 277-288). The castle: assassins lurk in the hall as Guenièvre bathes; Lancelot sets out for the tournament alone at night, disguised.

XIX. (Shots 289-304). The forest: while riding to the tournament, Mordred accuses Lancelot to Artus; the others defend him.

XX. (Shots 305-397). The tournament: Lancelot arrives without revealing his identity; he defeats knights from his own side.

XXI. (Shots 398-411). The forest: riding back from the tournament, Gauvin and others chide Mordred for his accusation of Lancelot.

XXII. (Shots 412-433). The castle: the knights arrive home; Gauvin talks with Guenièvre, who thinks Lancelot has gone forever.

XXIII. (Shots 434-444). Castle and tents: two knights set out to look for Lancelot.

XXIV. (Shots 445-452). Castle yard: the two knights return, unsuccessful; a storm begins, which keeps Guenièvre awake.

XXV. (Shots 453-460). The tents: Mordred and others see Lancelot's flag tattered; they assume he is dead.

XXVI. (Shots 461-471). Mordred's tent: Mordred and his supporters play chess at night; Gauvin confronts him.

XXVII. (Shots 472-495). The forest shed: Guenièvre admits to Gauvin that she loves Lancelot; Gauvin prevents Artus from entering, sends out the knights to search again.

XXVIII. (Shots 496-516). The forest: an old peasant woman refuses to answer the knights; she has Lancelot in her cottage; in spite of his wound and her warning, he departs.

XXIX. (Shots 517-523). The castle: Lancelot and his men break in and rescue Guenièvre from a cell.

XXX. (Shots 524-525). Deserted castle: Bors, Lionel, and Lancelot discuss the siege, decide to attack.

XXXI. ((Shots 526-542). A tent at Artus's camp: as Gauvin lies dying, he praises Lancelot.

XXXII. Shots 543-552). Deserted castle: Artus sends a message offering to take Guenièvre back.

XXXIII. (Shots 553-565). Deserted castle: Lancelot and Guenièvre have their final talk; she is resigned to going back, he resists it.

XXXIV. (Shots 566-607). Outside the deserted castle: Lancelot escorts Guenièvre to Artus's camp; he goes back and hears of Mordred's rebellion; Lancelot's men arm and leave.

XXXV. (Shots 608-644). The forest: a riderless horse; knights riding; archers shooting from the trees. Artus is dead; Lancelot, wounded, utters Guenièvre's name and falls, dying.

A detailed comparison of this outline with the events of *La Mort le Roi Artu* would be pointless, since Bresson's version bears so little resemblance to the original. A few examples should suffice to show that little of the film's elliptical narrative can be filled in even by someone completely conversant with the original French prose version; these examples should also demonstrate the direction in which Bresson moved to fashion his narrative structure.

Bresson has simply eliminated most of the original events (e.g., there were three tournaments and an additional battle with the invading Romans), while expanding a few elements greatly. Thus most of the first half of the film comes from one summary sentence in *La Mort:* "Now, though Lancelot had behaved chastely by the counsel of the holy man to whom he had confessed when he was in the quest of the Holy Grail, and though he had apparently renounced Queen

Guenevere, as the tale has related before, as soon as he had come to court, not one month passed before he was smitten and inflamed as much as he had ever been at any time, so that he fell back into sin with the queen just as he had done earlier."[4] This particular passage Bresson elaborates into three separate meetings between Lancelot and Guenièvre (Segments v, x, and xvi) before Lancelot gives in to her and resumes their affair.

The elimination or compression of events in an adaptation is common enough, of course. But Bresson eliminates or compresses some things only partially, leaving bits of puzzling information which seem to hint that we have missed something along the way. In the French prose version, Gawain's brother Agravain is a central figure, the one who first tells Arthur of Lancelot and Guenevere's adultery. Mordred becomes the main villain only late in the narrative, after Agravain's death. Bresson's version combines Agravain and Mordred's functions in Mordred's character alone. Yet Agravain is present, noticeable in one scene only: the argument before the departure for the tournament (Segment xvii). There we can recognize him only because Gauvin addresses him as "brother." At other times he is simply spoken of. Bresson similarly makes fairly important supporting characters of Lionel and Bohort but gives us no clue that they are Lancelot's cousins. As a result, the factions in the infighting among the knights remain confusing. Moreover, Agravain's death at Lancelot's hands during the rescue of Guenièvre of which we learn only when Lionel mentions it after the fact in Segment xxx—performs a major causal function in driving Gauvin to fight Lancelot and receive his fatal wound (Segment xxxi).

Perhaps the most indirectly presented segment of the film, and the one during which the spectator would benefit the most from prior knowledge, is Segment xxix, Lancelot's rescue of Guenièvre. It begins with a shot through a barred window of knights and squires running past; a cut reveals a doorway, with Lancelot entering as Guenièvre's voice calls for help from offscreen. As Lancelot approaches Guenièvre and lifts her, we see that his sword and hands are bloody. Only in the last shot of this seven-shot segment do we see the barred window in the background and realize that the opening shot had been filmed from inside Guenièvre's cell. And finally, as Lionel follows Lancelot out at the end of this shot, we see a tent beyond the doorway and realize further that this scene has occurred within the battlements of Artus's castle; Lancelot has been attacking the castle to rescue Guenièvre. Yet the last time we had seen Guenièvre, she was in the forest shed, with Artus agreeing not to break in upon her. The events of the original version had Guenevere captured and condemned to death by fire; Lancelot and his followers actually rescued her from a pyre in an open space before the castle. (Thus even those familiar with the original will not necessarily be able to follow the action in this scene.) When the rescue occurs in the film, we have no idea that Lancelot needs to rescue Guenièvre, much less that he has attacked and defeated the troops of Artus's castle at this point. Only in the next scene, when Lionel tells Lancelot which knights the latter has killed in the battle, do we grasp what had happened.

Still more elliptically, at the end of Segment xxx Lancelot decides to attack Artus's army, which is besieging Lancelot's castle. (In the original, Lancelot takes Guenevere to his own well-staffed castle, Joyous Guard; in the film, they simply take refuge in a nearby deserted castle.) As he and his men run out to the battle, we hear several seconds of the sound of horses' hooves and armour clanking. This sound stands in for the entire battle; the cut to the next scene depicts its aftermath, with Gauvin dying.

Lancelot contains almost none of the redundancy of the classical Hollywood film. But Bresson's method of avoiding a straightforward presentation of fabula events is not to overload our perception with narrative material, as Godard might. Often he simply does not give us enough cues for us to make the relevant narrative connections. Neither is the difficulty of Bressonian narrative that of obscurity in need of interpretation (à la Bergman or Fellini); this is not a symbolic structure which we can piece together. We simply do not receive enough fabula information to assemble a complete picture.

Difficulties in grasping fabula–syuzhet relations form a pattern across the film. Segment 1's action begins very late in the King Arthur story; in effect, the short scenes with anonymous combatants form a sort of sparse "montage sequence" summarizing the degeneration of the grail quest into brutality. Thereafter we might expect to get references to earlier events scattered through the rest of the film, especially in the early scenes. Instead, the narration introduces a crawl title which summarizes in the most cursory fashion a series of lengthy past actions.

> After a series of adventures which were tinged with the marvelous and of which Lancelot du Lac was the hero, the knights called by King Arthur the "Knights of the Round Table" set out in quest of the Grail. The Grail, a divine relic, the goblet of the Last Supper in which Joseph of Arimathaeas caught the blood of Christ on the cross, would gain them a supernatural power. It was believed to be hidden somewhere in Britain.
>
> The wizard Merlin, before dying, consecrated the knights to this sacred adventure. He interpreted certain signs, which named as leader of the quest, not Lancelot du Lac, the greatest knight in the world, but an extremely young knight, Perceval (Parsifal) the "Very Pure."
>
> Hardly had they left the castle when the knights dispersed. Perceval disappeared. They never saw him again.
>
> Two years have passed. The knights have returned to the castle of King Arthur and Queen Guenevere, having suffered heavy losses and without having found the Grail.

After the end of the crawl title, the major portion of the film—Segments III to XXVIII—involves a much more leisurely presentation of a few events. The intervals between scenes are short, though the durations of those intervals often are not specified. No significant action is left out in this portion, and we see most events directly; the only exceptions are Gauvin's reports to Lancelot involving Mordred's growing influence among the knights and the men's tendency to watch Guenièvre's window. Similarly, few past events are revealed, and most references to the past simply reiterate the failure of the quest and the loss of many knights. Here the exceptions involve Guenièvre and Lancelot, who speak of his past vow to her and of her gift of a ring (Segment V), and Gauvin, who recalls an incident in which Mordred had deliberately splashed Lancelot when crossing a stream (Segment VIII). For the most part, these scenes concentrate on the onscreen debates about Guenièvre and Lancelot's relationship, about the reasons for the failure of the quest, and about the correct future policy for the Round Table.

These scenes are balanced between Lancelot's initial return to Camelot (Segment III shows him lost in the forest on his way there) and his later return (in Segment XXVIII he leaves the peasant hut). Between his departure from the hut and the rescue in Segment XXIX comes the film's first elimination of major causal action through ellipsis—the sentencing of Guenièvre and the subsequent attack by Lancelot's troops. From this point to the end of the film, as we have seen, large ellipses continue: the transition from Segment XXIX to Segment XXX eliminates the rest of the battle and its results; we learn of the death of Agravain in Segment XXX. Another major battle occurs between Segments XXX and XXXI. Both of the next two scenes fill us in with information about it: Lancelot has fatally wounded Gauvin (Segment XXXI) and has deliberately spared Artus's life (Segment XXXII). Finally, the bulk of the final battle is not shown; we see Artus already dead and Lancelot dying. Thus the overall pattern of the film's presentation of fabula information is: severe compression of many events (Segments I-II), leisurely and direct action (Segments III-XXVIII), and highly elliptical and quick action (Segments XXIX-XXXV).

The overall narrative function of this pattern is to concentrate our attention on the characters' doubts and questions, rather than on the excitement and glamour typically associated with battles in classical historical epics. (A similar deglamorization goes on in the elliptical treatment of the tournament scene.) But at the same time, the changing pattern of narrational presentation undermines narrative comprehension in favour of abstract patterning. The film gets us used to one type of fabula-syuzhet relations, then switches tactics near the end, confronting us with events that we suddenly find much more difficult to follow. These two results of the film's overall shape—a narrative function and an anti-narrative function—reflect on a general level the parametric patterning of specific stylistic devices.

Aside from the elliptical plot, another reason for our inability to grasp the narrative completely arises from the opacity of the characterization. We know that Bresson uses non-actors and often withholds from them any knowledge of the entire story. Their expressionless performances have become a recognizable trait of the Bressonian style. Bresson has said that he wanted to eliminate the magical happenings of the original Arthurian legends: "I am going to try to transfer this fairy tale into one realm of feelings, that is to say, show how feelings change even the air that one breathes."[5] And he has also said, "I think the only way to reach the public with historical characters is to show them as if they lived at the present with us."[6] For Bresson, this does not mean that his historical characters behave as real people might in our epoch; rather, his historical characters behave exactly as do his contemporary characters. Jeanne d'Arc behaves similarly to Mouchette, Lancelot similarly to Fontaine. In any cast, Bresson achieves through his nearly expressionless actors a ritualistic sense of acting. A steady rhythm of actions and speech contributes especially to this sense. Bresson seldom reveals psychological motivations through conventional acting; rather, he often concentrates on feet, hands, torsos, and visored faces for the gestures of his action. But he does show us faces as well, and their occasional expressions stand out all the more against the usual neutrality. In fact, Bresson contradicts Schrader when the latter claims that one seldom sees faces in *Lancelot*, that they are covered or kept out of the frame: "When he comes to pray in front of the cross, you see him entirely, you see his face. I don't see what you mean."[7] In this film, the tiniest gestures and glances become expressive. Gauvin's puzzled frown when Guenièvre tells him Lancelot has left them forever becomes a striking moment. The same is true of voice quality, as when Lancelot emphatically tells his men that he will support Artus against the rebellious Mordred. Such moments gain not only in emphasis but in intensity through their comparative rarity. Yet overall there are many moments when we cannot grasp the characters' motivations.

If Bresson has modernized the original legends' narratives by concentrating on characters' feelings, he has also given a very modern ideological bent to his story. *La Mort le Roi Artu* put much stress upon the redemptive power of the characters' penitence. Guenevere became a nun after Arthur's fatal battle with Mordred. Then, upon hearing of her death, Lancelot became a priest and died in bed a few years later. Lancelot's companion, an archbishop, has a vision of Lancelot ascending to heaven and, upon his death, comments, "Now I know well that penitence is of greater value than aught else; I shall never leave off penitence as long as I live."[8] The only hint of any penitence in the characters in the film comes in Segment XXXIII, as Guenièvre insists she must return to Artus, so that she and Lancelot may atone for the bloodshed they have caused. But Lancelot does not agree with her, and we never have any indication that he goes to his death repenting.

The original version of the downfall of the Round Table suggested strongly that Lancelot and Guenevere's adultery was the underlying moral cause, with

Mordred coming in only later in the story to be the immediate cause of the deaths of Arthur and his knights. Bresson shifts the blame to a sort of social corruption creeping into the Round Table and its chivalric values. When Lancelot blames his sin for his inability to find the Grail, Guenièvre responds: "You were all relentless. You killed, plundered, burned. Then you turned on each other, like madmen, without realizing it. And you blame our love for this disaster." Bresson does not emphasize the violence more than does the original, which contains many explicit descriptions of battles and wounds. But *Lancelot* does eliminate much of what had seemed to justify the violence in the original—the chivalric code. Only a few references remain, as when Guenièvre berates Lancelot for sparing Artus's life when he had a chance to kill him. The original tale presents, at great length, a one-on-one duel between Gawain and Lancelot, with Lancelot displaying chivalry by offering to undergo a period of atonement for killing Gawain's brother, in order that he need not fight and kill his friend. In Bresson's film, Lancelot simply kills Gauvin by mistake, offscreen, in the melee of the battle.

In *La Mort*, Arthur's army meets Mordred's on Salisbury Plain (not in a forest), but Lancelot is not present to support Arthur. Mordred's side suffers huge losses but, by dint of vastly superior numbers, finally kills Arthur and the remaining Round Table knights (though Arthur kills Mordred in the process). Bresson attributes Mordred's victory to quite a different cause than does the original—his use of archers hidden in trees, picking off the clumsy knights riding below. Rather than simply going down to defeat, the Round Table becomes the victim of a new age with different technology. Its vanquisher, Mordred, is emphasized, time and again, as being cowardly—the opposite of the chivalric qualities the knights cultivate in themselves. Along with the other magical events of the narrative, Bresson completely eliminates the elements of Arthur's mystical death—the hand in the lake that grasps Excalibur, the boatful of women who transport the dying king to his tomb, and so on. Thus the implications that the values of the Round Table will endure into the future are also eliminated. All this does not imply that Bresson is being realistic or historically accurate (he has said that the setting, costume, and prop designs were deliberately anachronistic). Rather, by taking a mystical set of events and making them seem historically concrete to modern viewers, he has provided a way of enabling us to see their ideological implications without the relatively optimistic emphasis of the original. *Lancelot* adheres to the increasingly bleak outlook of Bresson's later films; rather than finding a religious or moral grace, as in the earlier ones, the characters now lose the grace they have in the face of a corrupt society's pressures.

But Bresson's anachronisms and modern ideology only make the film *seem* historically concrete to us. Other changes wrought by Bresson render the whole thing impossible as well. For one thing, the characters are far too young to have lived through all the triumphs of the Round Table and to be now in a late period of decline. *La Mort* specifies the characters' ages: near the end of the story Arthur is ninety-two, Gawain seventy-six; Lancelot about fifty-five, and Guenevere about fifty. There is no way to insert Bresson's characters into a plausible chronology extending back into the past; by eliminating their earlier lives, Bresson suspends them in a period of decline that holds few hints of the former glories of Camelot. (The effect is once again to emphasize the bleakness of the society and the loss of grace.)

In such circumstances, the love of Lancelot and Guenièvre becomes not a cause of corruption and a reason for chastisement, but the only apparently positive force in the society. From the beginning Bresson emphasizes the impending end of the Round Table: the old peasant woman says all the knights who passed are doomed to death; Lancelot remarks to Guenièvre, "Everything is finished for us here in Britain"; and Artus listlessly refuses to appoint new knights to the Round Table or to undertake any new projects. With the chivalric code already moribund, the lovers seem to have the only vitality in the group.

Given such a situation, the narrative's chief interest comes to lie not primarily in physical action and in quest journeys, but in the characters. This may seem somewhat odd, in view of what I have already said about expressionless performances. But here we come back to Bresson's elliptical narrative. Characters do, in fact, talk a great deal in the film, and they often discuss their feelings and beliefs. Yet there is considerable ambiguity about them as well, especially given the lack of exposition concerning their past actions and motivations. Gauvin is a particularly mysterious character. At first he seems merely a friend of Lancelot's, discontented at the inactivity of the Round Table. But his remarks about the men watching Guenièvre's window, his own glances up at it (three of the four shots of that window are from his point of view), and his increasing role as Guenièvre's defender hint that he is perhaps himself in love with her. This would make him the ideal knight in the traditional terms of chivalry, since he keeps his passion on the platonic level; he also does his duty by battling Lancelot to avenge his brother's death while continuing to admire and defend his opponent. Yet all this remains only a possible set of traits for Gauvin; the narrative withholds so much information that we cannot say anything for sure. The same is true to some degree of Artus, whose reactions to learning of Guenièvre's adultery are not shown. Only Lancelot and Guenièvre's motives are known extensively, and this once again focuses attention on their love as the one positive force amid the social decay in Camelot.

Narrative and Non-Narrative Functions of Style

The indirect presentation of narrative material in *Lancelot du Lac* results in part from its stylistic systems. These sometimes function to serve the narrative; at other

Lancelot du Lac

times the style works by a parametric logic of its own. Bresson introduces a device or pattern, then varies it, often without regard to the causal logic of the scene's action. Trying to interpret such variations symbolically in relation to the syuzhet action usually leads to frustration, or banality.

There are two major systems across the film which Bresson uses to introduce and vary his stylistic devices; I will deal with these and then describe some localized devices. The first overall system is the easier to notice: the limited number of motifs, visual and aural, that recur at intervals. But Bresson also structures whole scenes as variations of each other—to create narrative parallels, or simply to provide abstract variations that are of interest in themselves.

Motifs

Some motifs are so pervasive that they do not require extensive analysis. Armour, for example, appears in every scene of the film and is associated with all the characters except Guenièvre and the peasant and servant classes (though we can assume that the helmeted foot soldiers of the final battle come from these classes). But even within such a ubiquitous device, Bresson works numerous subtle variations. Armour can create narrative connotations; for example, Lancelot wears his armour during his meetings with Guenièvre as long as he resists her, then strips it off as he gives in to her at the third rendezvous. After the first segment, which begins with a beheading, armour carries a suggestion of dismemberment. This motif returns when the peasant child brings Lancelot his leg armour; Bresson frames this low, so that the pieces take on the appearance of legs (Fig. 11.1). And in the final scene, the armour of the dead knights irresistibly suggests a junk heap, a succinct image for the end of the Round Table and the chivalric conceptions behind it.

But the use of armour goes far behind these obvious thematic implications. Much of the film's visual interest lies in reflections, and specifically in the play of light on armour. *Lancelot* is notoriously a dark film, even in 35mm prints. In many shots, the composition consists of patterns of tiny highlights against dark backgrounds. In the bright scenes, the armour changes by reflecting the bright but neutral tans, whites, and greys around it. Bresson has managed to find a costuming substance that makes the figures like chameleons, changing to fit their environment—yet in no case do the suits of armour add strong colour to the scene. Rather, they help produce the muted brown, white, and grey tones that dominate the film, especially in the numerous castle scenes. Against these, the many tiny patches and flashes of bright colour stand out boldly.

The tents serve a similar range of functions. In their simplest form, they are locales for straightforward narrative action. Thematically there is an opposition set up between the knights in their tents and the looming castle walls; the flimsy tents perhaps enhance the pervasive sense of the imminent end of the Round Table. The tents also, however, undergo changes similar to those in the armour. They, too, change colour: white by daylight, glowing orange when lit from behind by a lantern, and utterly black in dark night scenes. This lack of strong colour makes them a perfect blank background against which other elements can be seen. In particular, the various coloured shields and flags over the tents' entrances stand out. For example, as the knights and their squires depart for the tournament at the end of Segment XVII, we see their horses go through the frame and exit; once they are all out we see only two white tents forming an almost solid white field, with a portion of one shield in green, red, white, and black at the upper left, and one with blue and white zigzags at the upper right. For a moment we have a Mondrian-like composition dropped into the middle of a narrative film.

These shields, along with the leggings of the knights, the embroidered reins, and the horses' saddle blankets, provide splashes of colour against the otherwise sombre tones of the film. More than the tents or the armour, these coloured elements become part of an abstract formal pattern largely independent of any narrative function. Each tent has a different shield and flag, yet these are not used as an identification system for the knights. Indeed, we barely learn who most of the knights are—it would be difficult to draw a clear set of connections between them and their shield markings. When Lancelot's flag is shredded by the storm, we need to be told it is his. The green, red, and white shield with black dots is apparently Artus's; we see it near his seat at the tournament and again over his tent as he receives Guenièvre back from Lancelot in Segment XXXIV. Yet one would have to have a good eye for pattern to be able to make the connection on the basis of two scenes—and, at any rate, the association is not confirmed until our last view of Artus alive. Occasionally we do get a colour motif assigned to a specific character. Gauvin's pink leggings identify him for us in those many moments when Bresson frames the characters from the waist down. And Lancelot's orange saddle blanket helps us keep track of him during the fragmented presentation of the tournament scene; but even in this case we must be quick about noticing it, since it appears only in flashes.

Mostly, however, these coloured elements participate in graphic play. The flags at the tournament tell us little; we do not even find out until the next scene that Lancelot has in fact jousted against his own comrades rather than against the Escalot knights. Similarly, the horse blankets are arranged graphically and rhythmically within shots to provide a variety of colours, rather than to let us know who is riding past. In the final shot of Segment XXIX, Lancelot's rescue of Guenièvre from Artus's castle, we see a line of knights ride into the deserted castle which Lancelot will use as his stronghold. The first knight has a bright red saddle, the second a blue, followed by orange and red; Lancelot is next, with Guenièvre behind him in a pink dress under a dark cloak. Finally, four other horses pass with green, blue, orange, and blue blankets, respectively. Again, no knight except Lancelot is identifiable; Bresson, working on abstract colour variations, lines up his colours so that no two horses in a row are the same.

The film's patches of colour tend to be small in the frame because they usually appear in the backgrounds of scenes. (The few exceptions, as when the camera pans or tracks up to a rack of brightly embroidered reins, become virtual explosions of colour.) But the colour so stands out against the prevailing tones that it draws the eye away from the more narratively salient foreground; in general, bright colours always tend to "come forward," even if they are in the background of a shot. Often the colour comes in the form of the shields on the tents, which tend to slide in and out of the frame because there is a good deal of camera movement following the walking knights. But Bresson has a continuing device that also introduces colour; in conversation scenes, people often pass by in the background—squires leading horses in daylight scenes, carrying lanterns in night ones. Their passages seem almost ritualistic, adding a rhythm to the scene rather than simply providing verisimilitude. They would not be particularly noticeable ordinarily, but Bresson often makes them the most colourful element in the shot.

Such movements may serve to punctuate scenes, coming at certain key moments in the action. For example, in Segment XVII, as Lancelot stands in a tent entrance, we see hanging on another tent in the background a black shield with a yellow X on it; just before he announces to the other knights that he will not be going to the tournament with them, a knight passes behind him, leading a horse with a red blanket. (Bresson's use of people passing in backgrounds somewhat resembles a device in Ozu's colour films; there street or alley shots often contain rhythmic movements of people passing back and forth in the depth of the shot—most prominent are women wearing bright red sweaters. Ozu's device usually occurs between scenes, however, and serves to create graphic interest rather than to emphasize moments in the action.) This function of colour as emphasis is, however, somewhat random, since other key moments go unmarked by such motifs, and, given Bresson's pared-down style, there are few gestures or lines of dialogue that are not important. Moreover, at other times, bright colours seem to call attention away from the main action rather than emphasizing it. In one of the film's most extraordinary shots, the establishing view of Artus standing before his tent waiting to receive Guenièvre back, the prevailing colours are the deep green of the forest and the white of the tents; but one horse at the left has a bright red blanket that calls attention off to that side. The horse plays no part in the action, and, indeed, the next cut back to a view of Artus's tent eliminates the horse, and hence the splash of colour, from the frame. (Here Bresson's usage is much closer to that of Ozu.)

I have mentioned that some of the uses of colour punctuate dialogue or action. To some extent, the same is true of the more pervasive sonic motifs. The offscreen whinny of a horse occurs in about half of the segments, as when Gauvin walks across the yard to tell Guenièvre that Lancelot has returned (Segment IV) or when Lancelot looks up at Guenièvre's window and promises he will return from the tournament the next day (Segment XVIII). The sound serves as a mild sort of marker, but, again, it is used arbitrarily; in many equally important passages, there is no such marker. Or in others, the horse whinny may give way to a note on an offscreen horn; this latter sound comes at only five moments: (1) when the other knights welcome Lancelot home, (2) when Lancelot tells Artus he has not found the Grail, (3) over the first shot of the moon, (4) over subsequent shots of men looking up at it, and (5) as the two knights set out to search for Lancelot after the tournament. There seems to be no particular pattern for this usage in terms of creating specific parallels among the types of action thus marked.

Birdcalls form a more specific motif, and there are three different types of calls. The opening scene introduces a cawing sound, as we see crows pecking at two armoured skeletons hanging in the forest. Distant cawing is heard offscreen, primarily during the scenes with the peasants in Escalot, and later as Lancelot lies bleeding after leaving the tournament. This motif culminates in the final scene as we see the crows in the sky, circling above the dying knights. It quickly comes to have a close association with carrion and works in with the many forebodings of the downfall of Artus's knights.

The second type of birdcall comes from the bird perched outside the forest shed where Lancelot and Guenièvre meet. This call is harsher and more prolonged than the cawing. It marks moments in the progress of their affair: as the camera frames Guenièvre's scarf when she leaves it on the bench, and later, when she says she wanted to see Lancelot one more time and raises her eyes to his.

The third type of bird sound comes only once. After we see the knights carrying Guenièvre to Lancelot's stronghold, following the rescue (Segment XXIX), we hear a bird singing. This brief sound provides us with perhaps the only indication of joy resulting from this action; we never witness any rejoicing on the part of Lancelot or Guenièvre. This indirect use of sound to substitute for a scene not shown us would thus be parallel to the sound at the end of Segment XXX that substitutes for the battle. Although all these birdcalls have some apparent narrative function, they often distract us more from the narrative action than their inessential and minimal function would seem to warrant.

Variant Scene Structures

So far we have looked at how Bresson takes visual and aural motifs of a familiar sort and weaves them into parallel narrative and abstract patterns. A similar theme-and-variations method also holds true for the structuring of whole scenes.

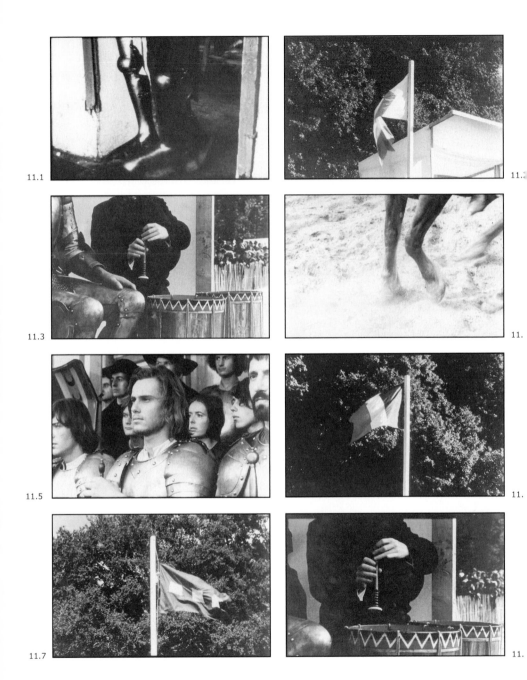

11.1

11.2

11.3

11.4

11.5

11.6

11.7

11.8

11.9

11.10

.11

11.12

13

11.14

15

11.16

11.17

11.1

11.19

11.2

11.21

11.2

11.23

11.

.25

11.26

.27

11.28

29

11.30

.31

11.32

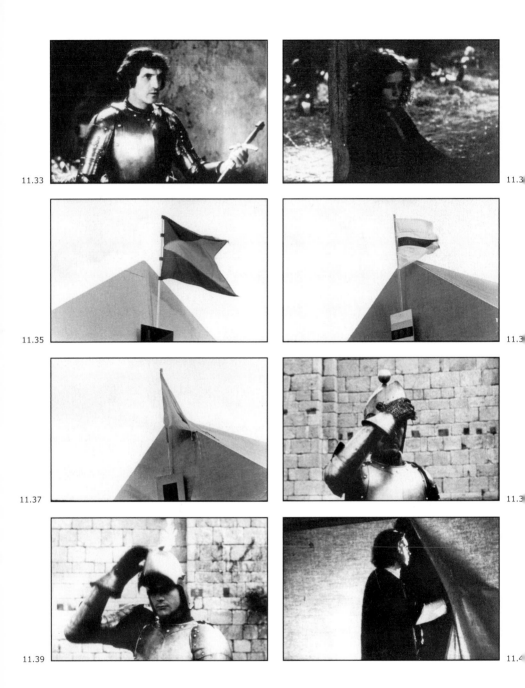

11.33

11.34

11.35

11.36

11.37

11.38

11.39

11.40

Scenes can become variants of each other through the ways that camera movements, framing, and cutting are used, as well as through more straightforward parallels in action. The following layout of the film's segments indicates what I take to be the parallel scenes. (The two main columns follow the film's chronology in a U shape; scenes paralleled out of that chronological order are listed out of line, and scenes that seem to have no parallel with another scene are asterisked.)

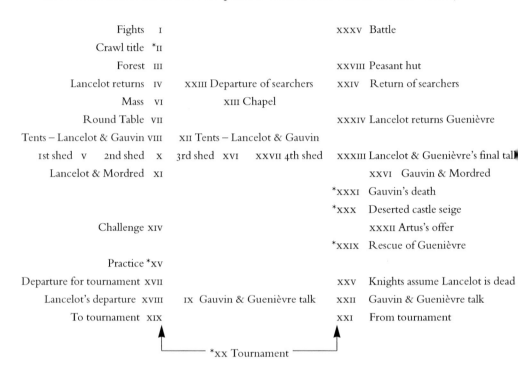

The tournament is the film's structural centre, with the other scenes forming a rough symmetry around it. It is perhaps the most obvious example of a scene that is structured by the introduction and variation of devices. The first four shots of the segment show us the basic elements that will make up the rest of the scene: a flag going up a pole (Fig. 11.2); a bagpiper playing, with a bit of the crowd visible at the rear (Fig. 11.3); a horse's legs against the ground (Fig. 11.4); and Gauvin and Artus among the onlookers (Fig. 11.5). The entire scene contains 93 of the film's 644 shots, and virtually all are variants of these four elements. There are about five framings of the group around Gauvin, all serving the same basic function. The jousts are handled in a limited and repetitive way, with the sound of the bagpipe coming from offscreen, a cut to the piper, and then a shot or two of the joust itself. A few of the bouts contain long shots, but most framings concentrate on the lower quarters of the horses, on lances striking shields, and on the reactions of the onlooking group. Even the flags have a pattern of variation, with the wind apparently reversing directions at intervals (Figs. 11.6 and 11.7). And after giving us six shots at different junctures of the piper with the same framing as in Figure 11.3, there is a cut to a new but similar framing of this action (Fig. 11.8). After this point we do not see the piper or flags again, as Bresson begins a rapid and elliptical montage of Lancelot striking down one knight after another. This kind of abstract patterning becomes more feasible here than in other scenes, since there is no dialogue as such. Only one word is spoken—"Lancelot"—but this is repeated over and over.

The tournament scene forms the film's structural centre for a number of reasons. It comes about halfway through the film and provides an interruption because it is so strikingly different from the scenes around it. David Bordwell argues that in *Pickpocket*, the pickpocket scenes stand out from the rest of the film because of their relative unpredictability; moreover, their difference emphasizes the similarities among the surrounding scenes. The same thing happens in *Lancelot*, with the tournament serving as a sort of pivot to signal the parallels in scenes that precede and follow it. In short, it points up the syuzhet's formal symmetry.

On either side of this highly abstract scene comes a scene that is clearly a variant of the one on the other side: the conversations among the knights as they ride to and from the tournament. The first consists of sixteen similar medium shots, with one knight centred and facing three-quarters front left in each shot (Figs. 11.9 and 11.10). The second contains fourteen shots, beginning and ending this time with an establishing shot (Fig. 11.11) showing the whole line of knights. In between are twelve similar medium shots with the knights now facing three-quarters front right (Fig. 11.12). The actions within the two scenes are also parallel. In the first Mordred accuses Lancelot of adultery with the queen while the others defend Lancelot; in the second they tell Mordred that Lancelot's appearance at the tournament disproves the accusation. Incidentally, one might assume at first glance that Bresson has the knights face left in the first scene, and right in the second, not to achieve formal variation, but simply because they are going toward the tournament initially and away from it later. But Bresson's establishing long shot for the second scene begins with the knights riding in from right to left (i.e., riding in the same direction they had been facing in the earlier scene). Then they come around a bend in the path and ride out foreground right. (Fig. 11.11 shows this later stage of the shot, with knights riding toward the right in the front and toward the left in the rear plane.) The film demonstrates in fact that the direction the knights face in either scene is purely arbitrary in terms of any imaginary geography we may wish to construct for the road between Camelot and Escalot. Graphic considerations remain primary.

The opening and closing scenes of the film also parallel each other, the first being structured around repeated panning shots with three mounted knights, the last around repeated pans with a riderless horse running through a similar forest landscape.

But the most complex parallels and variations among scenes come with the three conversations between Lancelot and Guenièvre in the forest shed (Segments v, x, and xvi), the later scene there between Gauvin and Guenièvre (Segment xxvii), and the argument in Lancelot's castle just before he returns Guenièvre to Artus (Segment xxxiii). The subjects and settings of these scenes are fairly similar (the straw upon which Lancelot's knights sleep in his castle recalling the heaps of straw in the forest shed), but the variations Bresson works upon the stylistic constructions of these scenes has an internal formal logic quite apart from the action.

Segment v begins with a brief conversation between the lovers inside the entrance of the shed; they then go upstairs. Lancelot moves to the space he will typically occupy in these scenes, to the left of the unseen window, the light outlining his face against the dark wall (Fig. 11.13). Guenièvre sits facing him on the bench, the window just off left, with its light picking her out in similar fashion (Fig. 11.14). This shot/reverse-shot pattern continues from shot 55 to 73, the end of the scene; occupying nineteen of these shots is a sustained conversation, during which he tells her of his failure to find the Grail. Early in this conversation, she asks to see his hand. He reaches out of frame right, and on the cut to Guenièvre, his hand extends in at the left. The shot spaces are thus exactly contiguous. Bresson tends to let the pace of the dialogue determine his cutting rhythms; that is, there is relatively little offscreen speech—only two instances in this scene. For the most part, one actor says a line, there follows a cut to the other actor, that actor says a line, and so on. Since Bresson's actors seldom register facial expressions, the concept of the reaction shot becomes less relevant than in a classical film. Conventional cutting usually dictates that a shot/reverse-shot pattern be edited in relation to the ebb and flow of character emotion, with dialogue carrying over cuts as needed. In *Lancelot*, many of the conversations are cut with traditional shot/reverse-shot framings (down to the inclusion of shoulders in the foregrounds of some shots), but the deliberate rhythm of the cuts gives the conversations a ritualistic quality that enhances the relatively flat deliveries of the actors.

Segment x, the second meeting, begins to work more complications into the simple pattern of the earlier scene. Now there is no scene downstairs to establish the situation. Rather, we first see a bird on a branch, viewed through a window, the frame of which is just visible at left and bottom (Fig. 11.15). This framing will be a familiar one later on, but this is the first time it occurs. The shot is from Lancelot's point of view (POV), but we cannot know this yet; all we hear is his voice, offscreen, saying, "Accept." A cut reveals Lancelot, apparently in a doorway, speaking to Guenièvre; we might assume at this point that he is facing her returning his gaze; rather, we move 180 degrees to a shot from behind Lancelot (Fig. 11.17). He turns and begins to pace to the left, with the camera following (Fig. 11.18); he speaks to Guenièvre while looking at the floor. By this time we might suspect that he had not been looking at her in the previous shot, and that the

362

bird shot had been from his POV. As in so many scenes, Bresson avoids using an establishing shot; even the apparently conventional shot/reverse-shots of many of the film's scenes become more problematic when we cannot be sure of the characters' relative positions—as in this case. We hear Guenièvre's offscreen voice, refusing his plea that she release him from his oath to her. But the camera holds on him, panning to the right again as he turns and continues pacing (Fig. 11.19). He crosses the room three times in all before turning and glancing three-quarters front right at her; then he resumes pacing, crossing the room twice more. By this time the space is becoming clearer. This is the same space to the left of the window that he had occupied in the earlier scene; Guenièvre is presumably to the right on her bench again—as we discover to be the case when there is finally a cut to her.

One might assume thus far that Bresson is drawing upon that cliché of naive criticism: when the characters are emotionally separate from each other, they are not shown in the same shot together. It is true to some extent here, perhaps, and certainly in the third shed scene there is a series of two-shots as they finally embrace. But the idea is so simple as to be barely worth pointing out, and besides, it does not always hold here. For after the cut to Guenièvre on her bench, Lancelot sits beside her. A few shots later he resumes his pacing, and again the camera pans with him. Then he sits beside her again in the same twoshot framing. After several more shots, including Lancelot's return to the window and another POV of the bird, the characters move into a new shot/reverse-shot setup, with three-quarters views of each (Figs. 11.20 and 11.21). But almost immediately, within the same first shot of Guenièvre, she turns her face away (Fig. 11.22), so that he and she both face to the right. This situation continues from shot 127 to 142. During all this, Lancelot has been glancing alternatively off at her and at the floor; in shot 142 she looks up briefly at him, re-establishing the double eyeline-match characteristic of shot/reverse-shot, then looks down. This play of glances within shot/reverse-shot situations is characteristic of other conversation scenes in the film as well; it helps offset the expressionless performances of the actors, suggesting ongoing thought processes without specifying what shape these might take. This shot/reverse-shot series continues on to shot 145, then ends as she rises, leaving the scarf on the bench with the camera holding on it after the characters exit.

The parametric structuring of these scenes becomes very apparent by the third of these parallel meetings. After a shot of Lancelot approaching the shed, there is a cut to a *plan américain* of Guenièvre standing to the left of an offscreen window, her head bowed. There then follows a medium shot of Lancelot in the doorway, looking off front right, speaking to Guenièvre. This set-up reverses aspects of the second meeting. Now she is the focus of the opening shot/reverse-shot; her glance is withheld, so that we understand where she is in the framings of him, but we are unsure where he is in the reverse-shots of Guenièvre. Rather than pacing, as he had done, she stands absolutely still. These framings repeat twice each. After the third shot of him (Fig. 11.23), the camera returns to the same framing of her (Fig. 11.24). She says, "I wanted to see you one last time"; after a tiny pause, she raises her eyes and looks directly to the front, with a harsh birdcall from offscreen marking the moment (Fig. 11.25). This shot resolves the question of where Lancelot is; the camera is virtually in his position. As if in response to the birdcall, she looks off right (Fig. 11.26); but in fact she is looking at the stairway, and the camera pans as she moves to it, with Lancelot joining her there. They go upstairs, and a shot/reverse-shot pattern interspersed with eyeline matches follows as she points out to him that the scarf is missing. She then watches as he removes his armour and tosses it on the floor; as in earlier scenes, he occupies the space to the left of the window, she to the right, by the bench.

Their embraces are framed in a way that demonstrates the careful balancing of shots that Bresson employs in these scenes embodying on the local level the principle of balancing scenes across the film. Initially we see her on the left, holding him, as she always does, with her head on his shoulder, her face away from his (Fig. 11.27). Then she pulls away, into an over-the-shoulder shot/reverse-shot situation (Fig. 11.28); a similar shot of him over her shoulder follows, and each is repeated. Then they embrace again, with her head on his other shoulder, at the right (Fig. 11.29). This leads to a series of two-shots, interspersed with a pair of shots out the window, one of Mordred and his followers approaching the shed, one of them leaving; the scene ends with another, similar embrace.

Segment XXVII, Gauvin's visit to Guenièvre in the same shed, is handled more simply. Gauvin enters and joins her upstairs, but he passes along the other side of the trapdoor, thus ending by facing Guenièvre from the side of the room opposite to where Lancelot had characteristically stood (Figs. 11.30 and 11.31).

Finally, in Segment XXXIII, Lancelot and Guenièvre sit on the floor of his stronghold, arguing about whether he should turn her over to Artus. It begins simply enough, with two tracking shots following the feet of a pair of knights, the camera then holding on Lancelot and Guenièvre in medium-long shot (Fig. 11.32). A somewhat conventional shot/reverse-shot pattern then begins, with Lancelot sitting still, looking off at Guenièvre (Fig. 11.33) She sits, opposite him, her face in shadow, looking variously in three directions: off and down, three-quarters front and down (Fig. 11.34), and front at him. These directions alternate from shot 555 to 562. Then, for one of the longest takes in the film, Bresson holds on Guenièvre. This time the cutting does not follow the lines of dialogue. Guenièvre and Lancelot continue to make short statements, but we now hear only his voice offscreen. This reverses the situation of their second meeting, when the camera had held on him, panning as he paced, with her lines coming from offscreen. Now she sits, glancing in different directions. One might posit a narrative function at this point—is her reaction more important than his, so that we would wish to see her face? Yet, aside from the fact that we can barely see her shadowed face which registers no emotion during this shot—Lancelot speaks some significant lines here: "My eyes are made for the impossible"; "How to understand that the woman He made for me was not made for me, and that what is true is false." The choice of framing seems purely arbitrary in terms of what the characters say; we might just as logically hold on Lancelot for a few minutes. The long take seemingly functions primarily to complete a pattern of *découpage* started in the scene of their second meeting, the to-and-fro panning movement with an avoidance of reverse-shots of Guenièvre. The scene ends as Lionel enters and tells them it is time for Guenièvre to go back to Artus.

These formal variations across scenes help create narrative parallels to some extent, but the similarity of the settings, actions, and conversations would be more than enough to do that. More important, these scenes demonstrate that *Lancelot* is organized on every level, from the local to the global, on abstract formal principles that can enhance, coexist with, or even override the narrative logic.

Other Parametric Patterns

There are two other parametric patterns that deserve mention, though they are not as pervasive as the motivic play and the variant spatiotemporal shifts: graphic matching and unclear spatial and temporal relations.

Although it has not been a characteristic of all his films, in *Lancelot* Bresson uses a surprisingly large number of close graphic matches from shot to shot. There are not a great many filmmakers in the narrative cinema who use this device extensively, although it is a staple of abstract films. *Lancelot* shares this trait with the works of Ozu and Kurosawa in particular; specifically, its several series of matches on the movements of knights arming for battle resemble the dynamic graphic matches on moving figures in *The Seven Samurai*.

Segment xix, in which Artus and his knights ride to the tournament, contains no cuts without a graphic match. Every framing presents a centred knight, seen from the waist up and facing three-quarters front left, against a moving background of the dark forest (Figs. 11.9 and 11.10). The parallel scene of the return (Segment xxi) includes a long shot at beginning and end but matches all the other shots in the same way (Fig. 11.12). One might argue that such matching serves a narrative function, but probably the only conceivable interpretation would be that Bresson is trying to suggest that these men are all similar. Yet, in fact, they are opposed to each other, and it would be difficult to demonstrate much similarity between Gauvin and Mordred or Artus. We can only conclude, once again, that these graphic patterns form a purely abstract structure alongside the narrative—a structure with its own partially independent interest.

The same principle holds true for the series of tent shots at the beginning of Segment xxv, the morning after the storm. The first shot frames a tent peak, facing to the left, with a coloured flag flapping above it. Bresson then cuts to a similar shot of another tent, but facing right (Fig. 11.35) and with a differently coloured flag. The next shot again shifts direction and colour, with a third tent facing left (Fig. 11.36). But now the film breaks this pattern of systematic oppositions by cutting to another tent facing left—Lancelot's (Fig. 11.37). The peak and lighting match precisely with the previous tent, but the flag colour is different, and the flag itself is tattered and does not flap in the wind. The cutting does differentiate Lancelot's flag a bit, but since we do not know to whom any of these flags belong until Mordred and his friend speak in the next shot, the point is a small one. On the whole, the systematic nature of the graphic shifts of colour and shape comes forward. The same is true of the various scenes composed of quick shots showing knights leaping onto their horses, squires saddling horses, and knights closing their visors (Figs. 11.38 and 11.39).

The graphic matches depend on our perception of various similarities, but there is another set of devices in *Lancelot* that plays on an uncertainty in our understanding of space and time. At a number of points, Bresson presents a series of cuts or a sound/image juxtaposition that we can perhaps grasp only retrospectively, or that we must understand by inference. The use of sound at the end of Segment xxx to substitute for the battle undermines expectations. Frequently during this film Bresson uses the, by now, common device of bringing up the sound of the upcoming scene several seconds before the end of the current one. Indeed, he bares this device in the film's first dialogue, during the scene among the peasants, when the old woman tells the child that a person is doomed to die if one hears his footsteps (even his horse's) before one sees him (Segment iii). This device of sound off, sound overlaps and sound substituting for events thus becomes one of the many ways of suggesting the fated decline of the Round Table. By the time the battle occurs, late in *Lancelot*, we will be expecting the sounds of armour and hoofbeats to carry us into a battle sequence, since Lancelot is leading his men out to attack. Instead, a straight cut takes us into a scene of the battle's aftermath. Retrospectively, the few seconds of battle sound seem to constitute a tiny separate scene, in a time we never witness, imbedded at the end of the previous scene.

Bresson plays a few spatial tricks on us as well. In Segment viii, Lancelot and Gauvin are seated in a tent, talking; the situation is initially handled in shot/reverse-shot. Then Gauvin stands and moves right to the tent opening, looking through it and to the right (Fig. 11.40); Lancelot is, at that point, offscreen left. Gauvin's POV of Guenièvre's window follows (Fig. 11.41). The scene then returns to the same framing of Lancelot that had been used in the shot/reverse-shot portion of the scene (Fig. 11.42); he continues to look off right. There follows a medium close-up of Gauvin, by the tent flap, now facing left (Fig. 11.43). The logical inference here is that this new framing of Gauvin is from Lancelot's POV; yet suddenly Gauvin looks through the tent flap and Lancelot stands up in the background (Fig. 11.44). We realize that

Gauvin is now standing just outside the tent (having presumably moved there during the preceding shot of Lancelot). Bresson has taken advantage of the neutral backgrounds provided by the tent walls to fool us; it is impossible to tell by his surroundings whether Gauvin is inside or outside the tent, since both positions look about the same. A similar juggling of space occurs in Segment XVII, as the knights argue before departing for the tournament. The scene looks like a conventional over-the-shoulder shot/reverse-shot. But the armoured shoulders and dark hair in the foreground at both sides look much alike, and Bresson makes the space considerably less clear than it might appear. In one shot, he lines Bors, Gauvin, Agravain, and Mordred up in a row (Fig. 11.45). Then he cuts to a reverse angle on Agravain and Mordred, with the same argument continuing; we must infer that the foreground shoulders belong to Gauvin on the left, Bors on the right (Fig. 11.46). Yet when the scene moves next to a new reverse-shot past Agravain's shoulder, we see Lionel and Bors facing him and arguing; there is no indication where Gauvin now stands (Fig. 11.47). We have already seen how the spatial presentation of Lancelot's rescue of Guenièvre impedes our understanding of that whole scene. Such moments demand an active effort to figure out the space, time, and logic of the scene. If we simply wait to have narrative information provided to us in a straightforward way, as in the classical film, we will probably feel a confusion at the moment, then factor out what happened from our construction of a coherent chain of fabula events.[9]

Conclusions

In the mid-1960s, Bresson told interviewers Jean-Luc Godard and Michel Delahaye:

> I attach enormous importance to form. Enormous. And I believe that the form leads to the rhythms. Now the rhythms are all-powerful. That is the first thing. Even when one makes the commentary of a film, this commentary is seen, felt, at first as a rhythm. Then it is a colour (it can be cold or warm); then it has a meaning. But the meaning arrives last.
>
> Now, I believe that access to the audience is before everything else a matter of rhythm. I am persuaded of that.[10]

Whether or not one agrees with Bresson that meaning comes chronologically last among a device's effects on the spectator, the point is that he values form, and especially rhythm. And he considers rhythm, rather than meaning, the key to audience engagement with a film. We would not expect every audience member to respond to Bresson's work as he would wish; he has a reputation as a "difficult" director to all but a small number of film-goers. As is clear from his interviews, he has no wish to win a wide audience if it means having to adopt the prevailing norms of mainstream commercial filmmaking.

Rather, as with other great individualists who create their own alternative stylistic systems, Bresson must force spectators out of their normal viewing habits. His very failure to provide traditionally expressive performances and linear, clear narratives should cue us to look elsewhere for the salient aspects of the film's stylistic interest—the variations, the deliberate, playful difficulties.

But to what end should we shift our viewing habits? What interest might the graphic matches or the limited, repeated motifs hold for a spectator? To some degree, the style does have a general effect on our understanding of the narrative. By forcing an active, deflected concentration on the spectator's part, Bresson creates a sense of intensity that an ordinary film would invest entirely in the actions and expressions of conventional performances. I heard a student remark after seeing the film for the first time that she was surprised how deeply she had come by the end to care about the characters, given that she had been bothered initially by the flat performances. This sense of involvement comes, I suspect, from a complex perceptual engagement with the film as a whole—an involvement we might think of as centring around Lancelot and Guenièvre.

And perhaps our involvement with the film's form does come to some extent through the unique rhythm created by the obsessive theme-and-variations construction. Consider, for example, Penelope Gilliatt's attempt to describe what she calls the "extraordinary" final sequence:

> A dark wood, in the deep watercolors that characterize the film. Two shots of a riderless horse in panic, crashing through the trees. A wounded knight. A riderless horse. A knight, crumpled: wounded, maybe dead. A riderless horse. Lancelot's knights on horseback, riding into an ambush of archers fighting for Mordred. Arrows fired by the archers who are hidden in trees. A riderless horse. King Arthur lying dead, his crown still on his helmet. A great, lone bird, high overhead, coasting in a pale-grey sky. The felled horse and his wounded rider Lancelot, who staggers away to lean against a tree. A riderless horse. Lancelot stumbles away to a pile of dead knights in armor, who have collapsed around King Arthur. "Guinevere," says Lancelot, just before he falls. The bird again. A last movement in the monstrous pile of armor.[11]

This is generally an accurate summary of the scene's shots. But more important, Gilliatt adopts a fragmented, virtually verb-less prose style in order to convey the striking rhythms and repetitions of this sequence; it is difficult to imagine a journalistic reviewer approaching most standard narrative films this way. *Lancelot* draws us into its narrative in part by its insistent repetitions, which do not repeat literally, but vary in subtle, unpredictable ways.

Nevertheless, as we have seen, much of our involvement with the style of the film cannot be reduced to a set of narrative functions. If we assume that interpretation is the primary operation we perform when watching a film, then the permutational structure of *Lancelot* makes no sense. All those variations would have to serve the meaning or fall into a residual category like "excess"; that is, all the *systematic* aspects of style would function to create meaning in relation to the narrative, while the *non*-systematic aspects would simply be those material aspects of the image that escape thorough integration into narrative functioning (texture, colour, grain, etc.). Yet clearly there are systematic stylistic structures here that operate on their own. Unless we want to deal with only parts of films like *Lancelot*, we must make different assumptions and perform other operations than interpretation. Most fundamentally, we should accept the idea that the intensity and complexity of perception itself is also an end in artistic experience—perhaps the *main* end.

This is not to say that independent formal play replaces narrative and meaning. No one would deny that many classical narrative films are deeply engaging without drawing much upon stylistic devices used for their own sakes; similarly, abstract films can provoke complex responses without the use of narratives or specific meanings. Why, then, should we not acknowledge that there exists a set of films which in a sense combine the principles of both? Narrative and abstract patterns for structuring stylistic devices exist side by side in such works. Either may come forward more strongly at any given time. Guenièvre's conversation with Gauvin (Figs. 11.30 and 11.31) would be an instance in which narrative dominates, while the Mondrian-like shot of tents and shields favours the abstract. Other filmmakers who work both inside and outside mainstream commercial filmmaking institutions have blended narrative and abstract structures. While Bresson works in an alternative, less commercially oriented milieu, a filmmaker like Yasujiro Ozu used sparse parametric style while employed in one of the world's most successful commercial film industries, that of Japan.

Such filmmakers' works are valuable, not simply for their originality of style or their interesting subjects, but also because this twofold working upon formal material holds such a potential for great complexity unaccompanied by thematic obfuscations. Whether sparse in style, as are the films of Bresson and Ozu, or perceptually dense, as are the works of Godard and Tati, parametric films exploit a great range of the cinematic medium's possibilities.

Notes

1. In an early review, "Bresson's 'Lancelot du Lac,'" *Sight and Sound* 43, no. 3 (Summer 1974): pp. 129-130, Jonathan Rosenbaum mentioned the basic strategy of these elements; my analysis develops similar points.

2. Paul Schrader, "Robert Bresson, Possibly," *Film Comment* 13, no. 5 (September/October 1977): p. 27.

3. *La Mort le Roi Artu* is the last of the five volumes of the French prose Vulgate Cycle, c. 1230, author unknown. One of the longest extant versions of the Arthurian legends, its other volumes include events connected with Merlin, Lancelot's earlier life, and the quest for the Grail. The translation I have used is J. Neale Carman's *From Camelot to Joyous Guard: The Old French La Mort le Roi Artu* (Lawrence: The University Press of Kansas, 1974).

It has been stated (in Jane Sloan's *Robert Bresson: A Guide to References and Resources* [Boston: G. K. Hall, 1983], p. 88) that Bresson's film is based upon Chrétien de Troyes's "Le Chevalier de la charette" (translated by W. W. Comfort as "Lancelot" in de Troyes, *Arthurian Romances* [New York: Dutton, 1914], pp. 270–359), but I can find no events which the film and this work have in common; de Troyes's account covers an earlier period in the Arthurian legends, long before the Grail quest.

4. Carman, *From Camelot to Joyous Guard*, p. 4.

5. Jean-Luc Godard and Michel Delahaye, "The Question: Interview with Robert Bresson," *Cahiers du cinéma in English* no. 8 (February 1967): p. 27.

6. Ian Cameron, "Appendix—Interview," in *The Films of Robert Bresson*, ed. Amédée Ayfre et al. (New York: Praeger, 1970), p. 134.

7. Schrader, "Robert Bresson, Possibly," p. 30.

8. Carman, *From Camelot to Joyous Guard*, p. 172.

9. Between the initial writing of this essay and its final revision, two analyses have been published which treat aspects of *Lancelot's* parametric form. Lindley Hanlon discusses the dialogue in the film, concentrating on the use of stripped-down, repetitive sentence structures, verbal motifs, and vocal inflections. She essentially analyzes the verbal component of the film as if it were a set of poems (*Fragments: Bresson's Film Style* [Rutherford: Fairleigh Dickinson, 1986], chap. 5, "Chansons et Gestes: Voice and Verse in *Lancelot du Lac*," pp. 157–187).

André Targe takes a different approach, examining the tournament scene's layout of shots, which he says can be studied without reference to the sequence's narrative context or logic (pp. 87, 92). Targe charts the patterns of shots and finds regular alternations and symmetries running through the entire scene. At one point (p. 97) he compares the insistent repetition to Philip Glass's music for the experimental minimalist performance piece *Einstein on the Beach* ("Ici l'éspace nait du temps . . . [Étude détaillée du segment central de 'Lancelot du Lac']," *Camera/Stylo* 5 [January 1985]: pp. 87–99).

These two analyses provide additional evidence that sparse parametric repetitions govern *Lancelot's* dominant. Targe's editing charts in particular show that the symmetries I have found between whole scenes across the film recur in miniature within a single sequence. Also, the fact that three critics independently chose to analyze subtle repetitions and variations in the same film would seem to confirm that a notion of parametric form is relevant to *Lancelot*. In addition, Hanlon and Targe use comparisons to poetry and music in characterizing *Lancelot's* style—precisely the two art forms most heavily dependent on parametric variations.

10. Godard and Delahaye, "The Question," p. 12.
11. Quoted in New Yorker Films' publicity flier for *Lancelot*.

Lancelot du Lac

MICHAEL DEMPSEY

Despair Abounding:
The Recent Films
of Robert Bresson

S PARE, austere, restrained, severe, bleak—words like these typically appear in every description of Robert Bresson's films. Certainly, they all apply. No filmmaker has ever denied us more intransigently so much of what we tend to regard—rightly—as the pleasures of cinema: all those "forbidden" delights of acting, overtly beautiful imagery, styles of editing and camerawork and art direction and scoring and special effects which "vulgarly" manipulate us—all of them bastardized tricks of "filmed theatre," which is what the very term "cinema" means to him. His kind of filmmaking he calls *le cinématographe*;[1] some of its components are monotone line readings, automatic gestures, and untrained "models" instead of actors and their false expressiveness; flat rather than eye-catching imagery; elliptical editing which compresses emotional peaks and often omits even climatic scenes; chaste camerawork which hides faces as often as it reveals them or holds on spaces after characters have vacated them. Whether you call it "spiritual style," like Susan Sontag, "transcendental style," like Paul Schrader, or Bresson's "universe," like Amédée Ayfre, it is a style which portrays life as Calvary, in which mortification is endless and all surfaces, human or material, obdurately resist yielding "insight" or "meaning."

But the hill of Calvary leads finally to eternal ecstasy in the next world for those who are able to climb it. Despite the forbidding chill which any account of Bresson's methods may suggest to people who do not know any of his work, he is actually a fountainhead of faith in the reality of this eternal ecstasy. He marshals his expressive resources toward final shots which seek to draw this same faith from us. The glowing cross and the voice intoning, "All is grace," at the end of *Diary of a Country Priest* testify to Bresson's certainty that the spirit of the impoverished, cancer-ridden young cleric has flown from its prison of flesh and earth to everlasting fulfilment in the bosom of God's love. The last image in *The Trial of Joan of Arc*—the charred stake on which her body has been burnt to ashes—evokes the immortality and the liberation of her soul. In *Les Anges du péché*, Thérèse, murderess hiding in a convent as a postulant, responds to the death of a saintly young nun who tried to help her by reaching out to accept the handcuffs which the police snap onto her wrists. In *Pickpocket*, Michel must be jailed before he can learn what freedom really is. Fontaine's flight from another prison, in *A Man Escaped*, emblemizes the soul's submission to God and his grace, which inspire him to risk his carefully plotted escape by taking a last-minute cellmate, Jost, along with him. Bresson has been the most optimistic of filmmakers; every facet of his fastidiously cultivated technique has striven to show the way to Paradise.

But all this has changed drastically during the past dozen years. During that time, Bresson made his first colour films—*Une femme douce* (1969), *Four Nights of a Dreamer* (1971), *Lancelot of the Lake* (1974), and *The Devil Probably* (1977)—and they all have something else in common: the waning of transcendence and the rise of despair. The importance of this change in tone for a Catholic filmmaker cannot be overstated. In the past, as Marvin Zeman has pointed out,[2] Bresson has often seemed interested in finding exceptions to Catholicism's official condemnation of suicide, which continues to be a major preoccupation in the colour films. But justifying despair is an even more extreme step. To a Catholic, despair is by definition an "unforgivable" sin because it denies that even God has the power to save one's soul—which amounts to a denial of God's very existence, at least as a Catholic defines God. Yet despair suffuses Bresson's recent work, without the compensating imagery of salvation which completes his earlier films.

Instead, the colour films portray the withering away of transcendental hope. One example is especially pointed. In *Une femme douce*, a young wife caught in a destructive marriage kills herself rather than accept her suffering any longer or cling to hope for earthly relief. Yet Bresson offers no sign that, after death, she finds heavenly relief. In the story by Dostoevsky on which he based the film, the tormented woman leaps to her death clutching an icon, which seems to reveal her faith that God will forgive her for the sin of taking her life. This image seems made for Bresson, yet he rejects it; his "gentle creature" has a crucifix, but she leaves it behind. Each of the colour films has an equivalent conclusion; each conveys little or no sense of an afterlife; each implies a God who is either silent, indifferent, or non-existent.

All of this puts a distressing new construction on a major element in Bresson's work: the religious paradox of co-existing predestination and free will. Either a mystery or an absurdity, depending on your beliefs, this conundrum proposes that God, being all-knowing, knows every detail of every human life in advance, in particular whether a given person will be saved or damned; yet, at the same time, human beings have free wills, choose their destinies. To Catholics and some other religionists, what reconciles the halves of this flagrant intellectual contradiction is "grace," that enigmatic soul-illumination through which God indicates his will and inspires—but does not force—us to submit to it. According to theologians, such grace is strictly *unwilled*, *unbidden*, a divine gift; we can do nothing to merit it, though we can refuse it. By accepting it, we accept our predestined fate, God's will for us, yielding superficial liberty to gain profound liberty. Thérèse reaching for the handcuffs; Michel touching Jeanne through the wire mesh of his cell and murmuring, "What a strange road I have taken to reach you"; Fontaine discovering, after he decides not to kill Jost, that he could not have escaped without Jost's help—these are some of Bresson's past embodiments of this reconciliation between predestination and free will. To Bresson, as Zeman puts it, "Life consists of finding out to what we have been predestined"; or, as Paul Schrader states, "The drama is whether or not the character (or the viewer) will accept his predestined fate . . . Man must *choose* that which has been predestined."[3]

Which is fine, if you happened to be predestined to salvation. But this is a theological Gordian knot; for, if we are predestined to a given fate, then we are equally predestined to choose or reject said fate. Not that logic necessarily matters to believers in this creed. When I was a Catholic seminarian, during high school and early college, even the most intelligent priest-instructors avoided or evaded discussing the matter. There is simply no way to deal with it rationally. You either believe that, through grace, Fontaine freely accepts rather than murders Jost, or you believe that this choice is also predestined, hence no real choice at all—which means that you reject the entire paradox and with it Catholicism and perhaps God as well.

While working on *The Devil Probably*, Bresson told Schrader, "I think there is predestination in our lives. Certainly. It can't be otherwise."[4] But without an accompanying sense of transcendence, of "grace abounding," belief in predestination renders life not the hill of Calvary but the mountain of Sisyphus. Both inflict long, intense agony; but the first promises ultimate salvation, while the second offers only ultimate futility. In one respect, Bresson's statement is ambiguous; he does not say *how much* predestination there is in our lives. But whether he believes its role to be partial or total (and how could it be partial?), the change in his manner of dealing with it in his films has been grim. The black-and-white films depict predestination to suffering which culminates in glorious transfiguration. The colour films depict predestination to the same suffering only to have it end in extinction.

Une femme douce—Scenes from a Marriage as Hell

This new predestination without salvation shapes the very structure of *Une femme douce*. Following Dostoevsky, Bresson shows the heroine's suicide at both the beginning and the end of the film, so that there is never any doubt about her fate. In place of Dostoevsky's icon and the film's crucifix, Bresson grants her a secular token of elegy: the white shawl which floats in the air after her body has struck the earth. We wonder if Bresson will show something more the second time we witness the suicide. He does—but it proves to be an image of horror.

Une femme douce is such a baleful film because, in the absence of a transcendental dimension, it must finally make the pain of the heroine and the pawnbroker she marries utterly useless. Between the suicide scenes, Bresson intercuts "present" scenes of the distraught husband pacing around the wife's laid-out corpse and "past" scenes from their relationship. Desperately talking to himself or their maid, he struggles to fathom the tragedy and his own role in it. Not that the answer to the central question—why did she kill herself?—is any mystery. We quickly discover that poverty, not love, drove her into a soul-destroying union with a cold, money-grubbing, stiflingly possessive man who snuffed out all pleasure and hope for her. But if this said everything, *Une femme douce* would be simply a remake of *Gaslight*. Within this level of obviousness is something else that is far from obvious: *what precisely* pushes the wife over the brink? When she kills herself, the marriage seems to be improving. Her husband has blamed himself for all their misery and sworn to make their future bright. This is what haunts him as he paces around her corpse. But her death refuses to yield comforting insight, to him or to us.

This mismatch quickly degenerates into brutal psychological warfare, which takes the form of either caustic words—he attacking her for "overpaying" pawnshop customers, she ordering him to stop dominating her with money—or killing silence. The marriage grows to be so lethal that we look for an excuse to question the film's depiction of it. Unfortunately, Bresson's adaptation has provided one. The notion that the wife (she and the husband are nameless in the film) truly has no other option except pawning herself to this crabbed man is a lot harder to accept in modern Paris than in Dostoevsky's Russia. The mumbo-jumbo surrounding her "sinister" relatives, who never appear but supposedly help force her into the marriage, is just as clumsy. These elements create confusion at the heart of the film. Nearly everything in it pushes us to blame the husband for the whole disaster. Yet the wife's unconvincing motivation suggests, perhaps unintentionally, that the marriage is an act of masochism for her. Yet we cannot tell where this masochism comes from because, as always, Dominique Sanda, who plays the wife, suggests anything but a "gentle creature." Even in this, her first film, she seems much too vibrant and self-reliant to let Guy Frangin's emotionally parched stiffneck shackle her.

Yet this blurriness certainly adds to the atmosphere of opaque incomprehension which seeps through the film like slow poison. Bresson's style undermines even their wedding night, one of their few happy experiences, by pointing up the groom's uneasiness with the bride's mischievous sensuality. Thereafter, sexual passion still flows between them—as Bresson himself has said, the film's colour is keyed to the warm blush of Sanda's skin—but it is rising hatred which fuels the passion, except for some tender moments which she initiates. After one steely encounter, the husband narrates: "That night we made love as usual, but her attitude had changed, and I only wanted to possess her body." Bresson's most grisly touch is running this line over an image of her cadaver as he circles it in anguish. The film builds to one creepily sadistic episode in particular. After an especially sharp quarrel between them, the husband carefully leaves out a pistol before going to bed alone. The next morning, he feigns sleep while, just as he planned, she finds the gun, clicks the hammer, and all but presses the muzzle against his face. This is the closest that Bresson has ever come to conventional suspense; the moment is frightening even though we know that she will not pull the trigger. Afterwards, he is able to play cunningly on both her shame at nearly commiting murder and her uncertainty about whether or not he was really asleep.

This part of the film does suggest *Gaslight*; there is no doubt that, in episodes like this, he is actively working to destroy her psychologically and emotionally. In their new book *Self and Cinema: A Transformalist Perspective*, Beverle Houston and Marsha Kinder declare that everything in the film, including the elements which appear to condemn him (even when he condemns himself, as he often does through his narration), actually reveals him as an endlessly devious sado-masochist totally intent on absolutely nothing besides destroying the wife's sense of her own experience in order to subjugate her ever more profoundly.[5]

This approach to the film yields a lot of fresh insights, but I feel that it also misses the deepest source of its despair. Point of view in *Une femme douce* seems thoroughly confused. Commentators routinely state that the body of the film consists of flashbacks, yet Bresson has stated firmly that "there are no flashbacks in the film."[6] Unless he is simply being perverse, this must mean that, as far as he is concerned, the images of the marriage are *not* being filtered through the husband's subjectivity; instead, they are elliptical but objective pictures of what happened between the couple. Yet the film's structure encourages us to treat them as his distorted, undependable memories, as their *entirely verbal* equivalents certainly are in the Dostoevsky story. Which possibility is true is not just an academic matter. The film's narration unquestionably belongs to the husband, but it is not the entire film the way the narration in the story is the entire story. The imagery of the film is what the story lacks, and that imagery is too distinctively Bressonian to express anyone else's subjectivity, including the husband's. For proof, look at the wife's suicide and her last moments alone in her bedroom; stylistically, they are identical to the rest of the film, even though the husband did not witness them. Why is this important? Because it indicates that, without diminishing the husband's responsibility for the wife's death in the slightest, Bresson is not presenting him as an endlessly devious sado-masochist *only*. If he were, the film would be just a rarefied good girl-bad guy melodrama.

Bresson is after something larger: the fundamental impurity, corruption, and inadequacy of all our motives and acts. A small but key example comes early, when the (future) wife pawns her crucifix. As the pawnbroker weighs it and offers more money than it is worth, he suddenly describes himself with a line from Goethe's *Faust*: "I am part of that force which does evil." Now he may well be, as Houston and Kinder maintain, flaunting his education. But he is also sincerely baring the full acrid depth of his bitter self-loathing, which he longs to escape. When she smiles kindly and adds, "Or good," to the quotation, he feels a sudden freshet of hope for deliverance from his repressed, avaricious nature through union with her (virtually the same deliverance that Jeanne offers Michel in *Pickpocket*). Yet the flaws in his nature are too deep-rooted; he cannot stop viewing her *simultaneously* as an object to be possessed. In *Une femme douce*, such contradictions merge inextricably; he is *both* a cruel manipulator and "a husband pining for love," and she is a willing victim (whether or not Bresson intended this) *as well as* a brutalized innocent.

This byzantine confusion of motives brings about the final tragedy. The husband flings himself at the wife's feet, extravagantly begging for her forgiveness. She reacts with confusion and distrust, just as we do. Is he sincere? Or is this just another power game? When he says, in the present, "What I felt was not pity for her; I was full of enthusiasm; no one can understand my emotion," we see a tear rolling down his cheek, in the past, just before he throws himself at her this way. But can we trust that tear? Why did he feel enthusiastic? Because he had hit upon a clever new way to control her? Or because he truly envisioned future happiness for them both? Why can (note the change of tense) no one—including us, presumably—understand his emotions? Because they are truly ineffable, or because he is rationalizing his perfidy? When she cries, "And I thought you would desert me," is she glad or unhappy? What could break through such an impasse? Only grace, only a leap of faith. Had the old Bresson made this film, grace might have entered precisely at this point—or shortly thereafter, when the husband abruptly embraces the wife "like a madman." Then *Une femme douce* might have been like Roberto Rossellini's *Viaggio in Italia*, in which a similar leap of faith suddenly dissolves the bitter estrangement of another married couple. But, without this possibility, the couple in *Une femme douce* cannot reach one another. Even if his change of heart is totally sincere, it comes too late; she has been too severely damaged for such belated rescue. And during his sudden embrace, to him the act of a tender lover, we see what he cannot see: the distant, responseless pallor of her face as he holds her. Despair and tragedy are inevitable.

The ambiguity surrounding the marriage also envelops her suicide. Seconds before jumping, she smiles at her mirrored image. What does this signify? We can guess, but we will never know. And what are the effects of her death? She escapes unbearable pain, achieves "freedom" and "autonomy" (if such terms have any useful meaning in this context). Yet, as Charles Thomas Samuels told Bresson,

"Her suicide is a hostile act, dooming him to an eternity of grief unmitigated by understanding" (just as killing him would have doomed her). To which Bresson replied, "Of course."[6] He underlines this by having the maid look in uneasily moments before the wife jumps and then observe the death leap too late to prevent it. We may imagine that the maid, whom we have barely noticed throughout the film, will suffer as much as the husband will. The wife obviously never considered this or did not care.

Compare her suicide to the one that climaxes *Mouchette*, which is a spiritual victory, as Bresson treats it. When the mistreated young rural girl splashes off-screen into a pond to drown, he holds his camera on the rings which ripple serenely across the water's surface and adds coolly lovely notes from Monteverdi's *Magnificat* to the soundtrack—signs that God has mercifully embraced her soul. But *Une femme douce* ends with the husband lifting the wife's head as she lies in her coffin, imploring her to open her eyes for just one second, and then—dreadfully— the lid sliding onto the coffin and a hand bolting it down. No comforting music, no icon of redemption, no "freedom" or "autonomy"—just a cadaver locked inside a box to rot. Unlike *Mouchette*, which suggests that its heroine is better off dead, *Une femme douce* suggests that its "gentle creature" would have been better off if she had never been born.

Lancelot of the Lake—The Dark Void

A nightmare of the quick and the dead in a dimming cosmos, *Lancelot of the Lake* immediately violates one of Bresson's primary maxims about filmmaking. Explaining to Samuels why he used the floating shawl in *Une femme douce*, he said, "since I try never to show anything that is impossible, and since, of course, Dominique Sanda does not actually hit the ground. . ." Yet *Lancelot* opens with a gory decapitation in close-up. As the knights continue fighting, their helmets hiding their faces, the neck of the beheaded knight gushes a geyser of blood onto the ground. Later, the tournament at Escalot features crashing combat with heavy lances, and the climax returns to the forest of the opening scene for more slaughter. The sound track reverberates, tersely and harshly, with the clashing of broadswords, the splintering crunch of spears against shields, the penetrating thuds of arrows piercing armour or stabbing horses. In *Lancelot of the Lake*, Bresson's style shows a new crispness, a gnashing, angry snap; even his customary narrative elisions feel unusually draconian. This tougher tone, this willingness to bend old rules, seems to reflect a deepening desperation.

Unlike Bresson's other colour films. *Lancelot* returns to a lost world of courtly ideals and Catholic dominance, only to discover the same malaise there which the colour films isolate in contemporary society. After sketching the tattered end of the disastrous quest for the Holy Grail, the film takes King Arthur and the chastened Knights of the Round Table back to Camelot. During the quest, several knights died; others plundered and pillaged aimlessly—Bresson gives us brief shots of riders wrecking a chapel and a sword sweeping an altar clean. Mournfully surveying the chamber of the Round Table, Arthur resolves to close it permanently, partly out of fear that he and the survivors have outraged God. But, instead of regrouping, the remaining knights form rival factions, one gathering around their greatest hero, Lancelot, who they hope will rally them to renewed glory, the other supporting Mordred, who opposed the quest and now plots against Lancelot.

Grimly, Bresson rips away nearly every vestige of romance, pomp, and magic from the material. As Jonathan Rosenbaum has mentioned, *Lancelot of the Lake* contains no trace of the Lady in the Lake, Merlin's sorcery, or Merlin himself;[7] he might have added, no Excalibur, no "lily maid of Astolat," no "Gaily bedight, a gallant knight, in sunshine and in shadow . . ." We seldom see Bresson's knights out of their armour, which is always creaking and clattering. At first, this touch gets laughs; each time the knights walk or move, they sound like garbage cans banging together. Yet as we grow used to this noise, the armour takes on sinister qualities. Encased inside it, the knights look insectoid, like a strain of humanoid beetles walking the earth following some cataclysm. Helmets mask and unveil already opaque faces according to intricate rhythms; during one argument, knights raise their visors to speak, then lower them after each line. This use of armour underlies the primitivism and the savagery lurking beneath the facade of knighthood—which also emerges from Bresson's references to superstition's infiltration of Catholicism. Spiritually if not historically, *Lancelot of the Lake* parallels *Robin and Marian*; both limn the decay of knightly honour and religious idealism, sending mythic heroes to wintry deaths.

In his colour films, Bresson's religion-rooted style mirrors this sense of lost faith. Like the Catholicism which nurtured it, this style is based upon suppression—of the aforementioned "forbidden" elements of film. But as the power of religious faith has blurred and faded in his work, many of these "forbidden" elements have crept into it: the modern Parisian settings and details of *Une femme douce*, *Four Nights of a Dreamer*, and *The Devil Probably*; the overtly "beautiful" imagery of *Four Nights*; the graphic violence, action, and spectacle in *Lancelot of the Lake*; the uses of nudity and more glamorously attractive "models" (especially women) in all four. In *Lancelot* above all, we feel the conflict between this new interest in the "forbidden," both theological and cinematic, and Bresson's restraining formalism—a conflict which parallels Lancelot's guilt over his attraction to Guinevere. *Lancelot of the Lake* often threatens to burst the steely bonds of Bresson's style and become a Sam Peckinpah film. The resulting tension makes it, purely as a piece of direction, the most exciting of the colour films.

Bresson's handling of the affair between Lancelot and Guinevere reflects this as much as his treatment of the violence does. Unable to regain his bearings after the quest, Lancelot feels torn apart by conflicting loyalties—to God as Lord, to Arthur as Liege, to Guinevere as lover. By renouncing the last, his most secular oath, and reverting to religious asceticism, he blindly hopes to regenerate himself and the Round Table. Bresson uses the stoic, chiselled face of Luc Simon for its craggy aura of angst; his Lancelot cannot hope to make an absolutely correct decision. When he tries, his confusion only grows. After resolving to join Guinevere instead of the tournament at Escalot, he changes his mind and competes anonymously, winning so brilliantly that the onlookers guess his identity and cheer this restoration of his knightly prowess. But the tournament's brutality only deepens his revulsion against the tooth-and-claw viciousness which the knightly code gilds with high-flown talk of honour and God.

The significance of Guinevere (Laura Duke Condominas) is clear the instant we first see her: she is the only character who never wears armour, who is visible from head to foot all the time. So it is she who carries out the film's contrast between the hard imperviousness of armour and the soft vulnerability of skin. But this statement alone is too abstract; her allure is openly sexual. Laura Duke Condominas seems physically slight, in stature a girl-queen, especially when juxtaposed to the armoured knights. But Bresson takes full advantage of her intent gaze and vibrant voice. Whenever she approaches the metal-sheathed Lancelot, he is plainly mesmerized, and so are we; such proximity is tender, comical, and kinky all rolled into one. In another scene, the camera starts on her calves as she stands nude in a wooden tub while attendants bathe her, then rises past her thighs, buttocks, and gleaming back. The lush image contradicts the lives of the knights: bare flesh so enticing that we want to stroke it ourselves, in a world of metal skin; utter defencelessness where dangerous weapons and plots are the norm. Even when the shot ends in close-up on the back of her head as she gazes narcissistically into a small hand mirror, Guinevere looks even more ravishing.

But she is not just a sensual delight; she explicitly challenges Lancelot's knightly code. She condemns his attempt to use the will of God as an excuse to renounce their love. To her, this obsession with serving God ascetically is just masculine vanity, which would possess a divine token like the Grail, or even God himself, like a trophy. Refusing to agree that the disasters which have befallen the knights are God's punishment for their adultery, she intones: "I am the one who was created to help you, the one who will cross this dark void with you," and there is no doubt that she speaks for Bresson. The spare, eloquent image of her lit window against the darkness of the night and the castle establish her as the film's prime beacon of human light: "Our only woman, our sun," the knights call her. Amid God's silence or absence, she assumes the role of grace.

But what she represents cannot save Lancelot or anyone else from chaos. When he rescues her from imprisonment, he only precipitates more carnage, as his forces war against Arthur's loyalists. Bresson elides the main battle, concentrating on its aftermath, particularly the pointless death of Lancelot's staunchest supporter, Gawain, whom Lancelot himself, failing to recognize him in his armour, struck down by mistake. At the height of this new catastrophe, it is Guinevere, not Lancelot, who sacrifices their love by returning to Arthur in order to end the war. As they walk together toward Arthur's camp, the camera catches her bare hand holding his mailed wrist—a melancholy completion of the film's central motif—and then, as they separate for the last time, her palm as it brushes fleetingly over his uncovered hand. After this moment, the final part of *Lancelot* plunges even deeper into despair than *Une femme douce* does. Mordred rebels against Arthur, and Lancelot sets aside his grievances to defend the king. But right away we lose all sense of who is fighting whom; from this point onward, we do not so much as glimpse a human face again. Bresson recapitulates the massacre in the forest from his opening scene, but with a ghastly addition: bowmen raking the knights from the trees, rendering them nakedly vulnerable despite their armour. We sense that one of those pivotal instants in history has dawned, when warfare escalates to previously unimagined levels of destruction—like the advent of new atomic rockets in *The Devil Probably*. At such a moment, values like fealty to lover or sovereign or even divinity seem like tissue paper defences against annihilation.

The old Bresson would still have found a way to pass Lancelot into paradise; now that doorway is sealed. Yielding Guinevere, standing by religion, defending his liege—none of these sacrificial acts assuages his grief or regenerates his sense of divine providence. His is the most chilling death in all of Bresson's films. We see a plainly dying knight, identity hidden by his armour, stumbling to a clearing in the forest, where a pile of other knights, all dead, lies like a scrap heap. From inside his armour, one lofting word finally reveals him: "Guinevere!" He topples onto the fallen knights, the metal wreckage clanking once. Bresson cuts to a silent shot of a gliding bird, then returns to Lancelot as he sags in death, his armour clanking one last time. Perhaps Bresson would maintain that this bird, like the shawl in *Une femme douce*, evokes the presence of God. But what we remember are the piled up knights, their armour now their coffins, and that flat, dull clank. In *Lancelot of the Lake*, it is not grace but death which abounds—death with no life beyond it.

The Devil Probably—Worldwide Suicide

The Devil Probably might have arisen from the concluding clank of *Lancelot of the Lake*. Returning to the modern world, Bresson has made his *Salò*, a shriek of desolation at what he views as humanity's lemming-like rush to extinction. Charles, a young student, drifts toward suicide because he cannot bear the manifold social, political, and ecological horrors of our world. His friends try urgently to dissuade him. Two women, Alberte and Edwige, take turns living with him, offering devotion and love-making. Institutions and activists present more rational-based reasons for staying alive: revolutionaries at a cellar rally; liberal and conservative Catholics debating "Whither the Church?"; a psychoanalyst who minimizes Charles's agony as mere neurosis; another companion, Michel, whose crusading study group monitors ecological rape and promotes science as the key to solving the world's problems. The film, then, covers the pleasures, the dreams, the hopes which keep us believing, against the worst evidence to the contrary, that it is better to go on living than to die. But they are not enough for Charles. "I see too clearly," he tells the shrink. "That is my dilemma." So he hires a junkie, Valentin, to shoot him dead in a cemetery. It is not surprising to learn that *The Devil Probably* was nearly banned in France for "inciting the young to suicide" (and why the young only?); the film is a virtual brief for suicide.

Once again, Bresson has admitted "forbidden" elements into his work, this time direct social comment and footage of ecological disasters, screened by Michel's study group, which appears to have been shot by others. Bresson defines social evil in terms of ecological callousness, represented by these images of fume-spewing factories and jets, poisoned animals and trees, mounds of garbage and trashed car hulks, a grounded tanker polluting the ocean, nuclear explosions, the baby seal hunt in Newfoundland, brain-damaged children of the Minamata mercury pollution. Of the latter, Michel declares, "These pictures can't be shown enough." Bresson heightens the impact of the footage (a first for him, except for short clips from *Benjamin* in *Une femme douce*), putting his own stamp on it, through terse editing and some augmented sound effects, like the smash of the club which slaughters one baby seal. It is startling to find Bresson, so insistent on "abstraction" and "timelessness" in his films, slamming home this topical indictment so bluntly, like a Trappist switching robes with a hanging judge.

Charles and Bresson both despair of any possible cure for this monstrous decadence. The cellar revolutionaries sloganize stupidly for terrorism ("Je proclame la destruction," one shouts repeatedly); the film caricatures and curtly dismisses politics as part of the problem. Religion gets a longer hearing but the same verdict. While the rival Catholics wrangle, in a manner straight from the John XXIII-Second Vatican Council era, Bresson highlights the cavernous emptiness of the gothic cathedral where they meet and the discordant bellows of its pipe organ as a repairman tinkers with it. Later, Charles spends a night there, playing Monteverdi choral music and contemplating the cathedral's grandeur. Earlier, he had quoted Victor Hugo on how God vanishes from a church the instant priests enter it. No priests appear now, but neither does any heavenly illumination, any grace. Psychoanalysis is equally impotent; Charles's shrink offers Freudian clichés and smug preachments about "adjusting" to society. Bresson vents his well-known disdain for "psychology (of the kind which discovers only what it can explain)"[1] on this sub-Mazursky cartoon. But the scene does yield Charles's fiercest outburst, when he opens an ad-laden magazine and cries, "Losing life, I would lose . . ." and then reads off all the consumer goods so rapidly that my pen could not keep up with his passionate torrent. About all Charles has left is some minimal belief in God, who will, he states, not punish him for committing suicide, for not understanding what no one can understand. Yet he has nightmares of being beaten even after death. And again, Bresson renders a suicide worthless in any larger sense. After the opening titles, he cuts to two successive editions of a newspaper, the first claiming that Charles killed himself, the second changing him to a murder victim. The ending explains this discrepancy. After shooting Charles, Valentin places the gun in his hand to make his death look self-inflicted—but forgets to wipe away his own fingerprints. Thus, as far as anyone will ever know (unless his friends say otherwise), this Charles person died not to protest the contamination of the world but because he met a homicidal addict. Even the film's title, which provides a convenient scapegoat, is ironic. The sense of futility is total.

Obviously, all this is intolerable. So we seek to discredit Charles, as we do the portrait of marital hell in *Une femme douce*. We fix on the film's unfair treatment of political action or the "sub-Mazursky" shrink. Or we deny that the film is "really" about all this horror. François Truffaut assures us:

> Ecology, the New Church, drugs, psychoanalysis, suicide? No, these are not the subjects of *The Devil Probably*. Its real subjects are the intelligence, the seriousness, and the beauty of the young people of today, and particularly of these four of whom one could say—quoting Cocteau's remark in *Les Enfants terribles*—"the air they breathe is lighter than air."[8]

Louis Malle (a former assistant to Bresson) tells of sitting next to a note-taking critic during the 1977 New York Film Festival:

> And I imagined that he had a very misconceived idea of what the film was about . . . probably thinking he should talk about ecology, about the old man's vision of the world—everything that has to do with what Bresson worries about a lot, but which for me is very naive, very clichéd. What is fascinating about the film is that it looks like Pascal—it's all about grace, about people with a gift for life, which is something divine . . . it's a completely mystical film. When he deals with the news, it's foolish. And I'm sure Bresson would agree with me. In an interview in a French newspaper, he said: "You know, it's not a statement about the new generation—actually I was projecting some of my own memories about my childhood.[9]

In one respect, these statements are cop-outs; they implicitly dismiss Charles as a misfit, an over-reactor, a whiner, a defeatist. Charles is none of these things, yet the impulse to dismiss his vision *is* justified. What barely makes *The Devil Probably* watchable is Bresson's awareness of this. Just as Luis Buñuel's lack of overt pity for his characters provokes us to pity them (according to André Bazin), so also does the very relentlessness of Bresson's case for suicide goad us to dispute it. And, as Truffaut and Malle discern, despite Charles's airtight logic, he does not have all the arguments on his side.

The young people in the film are indeed fascinatingly beautiful, both physically and spiritually. As Alberte and Edwige, Tina Irissari and Laetitia Carcano suggest light and dark ministering angels, and Henri de Maublanc imparts a handsome gravity to Michel. As for Charles, Antoine Monnier gives him a faintly androgynous allure; he suggests a lark shot out of the sky tracing a lyric curve down to earth. Quoting Leonardo da Vinci, Bresson has urged us to think above all about the surfaces of artworks.[1] In *The Devil Probably* the surfaces are, along with the horrors, these examples of human loveliness, which use physical beauty to highlight spiritual beauty—Charles's probing honesty, the loyalty of his friends to him. At times, the very ineffectiveness of their efforts to "save" him is comically touching, as when Alberte becomes convinced that a shrink is all he needs or when she sobs out her hope that he will regain his zest for living, while he pats her mechanically. After struggling in vain to out-argue Charles, Michel finally snaps in exasperation, "I want to live even if it's illogical." Bresson parallels his steadfastness toward Alberte with hers toward Charles, when she leaves him to live with Charles. Bresson gives special emphasis to their reconciliation: as they walk toward traffic, she suddenly says, "Embrasse-moi," and the camera holds on their embrace for ten seconds or more. It is "illogical" to pose such flimsy intimacy as a counterweight to evil abounding, which is why Bresson does it.

He also repeats his strategy in *Une femme douce* by making the precise catalyst for Charles's suicide uncertain. Why, instead of killing himself directly, does he pay Valentin to do it? This ambiguity is another frail barrier against total nihilism. Early in the film, Alberte and Michel read in Charles's diary: "When will I kill myself, if not now?" But Charles does not kill himself "now." Later, he sits by the Seine at night, examining a bullet before firing it into his brain. But he fires it into the river instead. The idea of paying Valentin to kill him comes, ironically, from the shrink, who tells how ancient Romans contemplating suicide sometimes hired their own executioners. There is something ceremonial about the way that Charles and Valentin walk to the cemetery, as though completing the Stations of the Cross. Does this appeal to Charles? Would dying *alone* be too unbearable? Has he hired Valentin in order to protect the integrity of his logic against last-second, "illogical" fear? We can only wonder. Right up to the final instant, like Rossellini's Socrates, Charles still yearns to speak: "I imagined that my thoughts would be sublime at this moment, but—" The same applies to Bresson; making this expression of his despair, he demonstrates that it is not quite absolute.

The last shot of *The Devil Probably* holds its contradictions—the "logical" case for suicide, the "illogical" impulse to continue living anyway—in precarious balance. After Charles dies, the camera watches Valentin first walk, then jog away into the background, along a path barely visible against the night. Once again, there is no trace of transcendental feeling; the image conjures up Guinevere's "dark void." Yet the shift from Charles to Valentin is revealing. Sick and gaunt, Valentin (Nicholas Deguy) is a negative image of the other characters, a wretched zombie who scorns charity and cares for nothing but his next score of smack. Yet he, too, wants to live, even if it's illogical. Earlier, in the most flamboyant effect of his career, Bresson begins the Monteverdi choral music which Charles plays in the cathedral over a preceding image of a syringe filling with Valentin's blood during a heroin injection. Our minds leap back to this astonishing shot as the camera watches him vanish, then holds on the empty path before fading out silently. Bresson pays tribute, finally, to the tenacity of the life force in a parched, attenuated world, yet how bitter a tribute. And how sad if *The Devil Probably* proves to be his last film.

Four Nights of a Dreamer—The Kingdom by the Seine

Yet his age and the mounting difficulty of funding even the most commercial projects, let alone his kind, make this dire possibility more and more likely. So I wish that somehow chronology could be rearranged to make *Four Nights of a Dreamer* his newest film instead. When it first appeared, Carlos Clarens wrote prophetically: "Because it is noticeably less stark and sombre than any Bresson picture to date, *Four Nights of a Dreamer* is headed for a low place in the director's canon."[10] But, after the renewed desolation of its two successors, it may have more to show us today than was apparent in 1971—a good reason to place it out of sequence here.

None of this makes *Four Nights* exuberant even by Bresson's standards; it, too, dwells on isolation and despair. But, unlike its companion films, it also has not merely moments but long passages of weird, soaring elation. Again, Bresson transposes Dostoevsky to modern Paris (*White Nights*, in this case). Jacques (Guillaume des Forêts), a reclusive young painter, labours in his loft over semi-abstract, cool-hued canvasses and recites into a tape recorder variations on a reverie of "pure and innocent" love in a medieval setting. When he goes outside, he often trails and watches strange women without trying to pick them up. When he finds Marthe (Isabelle Weingarten) poised to jump from the Pont Neuf one night and coaxes

Quatre nuits d'un rêveur

her off the parapet, it is as though his medieval fantasy has unexpectedly come to life. When Marthe tells him that she was contemplating suicide because a lover has failed to return to her, as promised, after completing a term at Yale, Jacques (one might say "chivalrously") tries to sustain her fading hope, while yearning to replace the other man in her heart. However, their four nights of rendezvous by the bridge end when the other man finally does return and Marthe abruptly abandons Jacques. Knowing recent Bresson, we expect him to take her place on the Pont Neuf, even if we also know that *White Nights* ends in a burst of irrational joy. But Bresson follows Dostoevsky; Jacques remains alive—returning to his painting, thanking Marthe into his tape recorder for the love and happiness she brought him, even so briefly, during these "luminous, marvellous nights."

Unlike *Une femme douce* and *The Devil Probably*, *Four Nights of a Dreamer* uses a time-shifting structure *without* predestining its characters by revealing their fates in advance. Bresson has also lightened Dostoevsky's material with odd, frequently awkward comic touches. Jacques is his looniest hero, and our introduction to him is downright wacky. After a pre-titles shot of him hitch-hiking in Paris, we pick him up traipsing through a field, looking resigned to the necessity of communing with nature but plainly having no idea how to do it. So, with stoic determination, he turns two somersaults. It is a "Huh?" moment; we wonder if we are supposed to laugh, until we see some people nearby also going "Huh?" Later, gleeful with hope for a Great Love with Marthe, he tapes cooing pigeons and his own chants of "Marthe," playing the chants everywhere he goes (oblivious to gawkers); then, to his amazement, he starts seeing her name all over the city—in a store window, on a cargo barge. Bresson makes him a giddy Pierrot beneath his dead pan; if it were raining and this were a different movie, he would be singin' in it. Bresson seems to have caught his own whiff of this ether; witness his use of a trip to the movies by Marthe and her mother to stage a nutty *film noir* send-up, complete with gats, George Raft suits, Max Steiner crescendoes, and a perforated gunsel gazing soulfully at a picture of his moll before croaking his last. Of course, this parodies the Grand Passion that Jacques and Marthe seek. But what makes it elusively touching is the very "inappropriateness" of Bresson's style when it confronts the "forbidden" in yet another form—in this case, a spoof which Blake Edwards could have tossed off with ten times his expertise.

But Marthe's story has an eerie erotic expressiveness far surpassing anything else Bresson has done. She becomes fixated on the newest lodger in the apartment which she shares with her mother, yet she fearfully avoids meeting or even seeing him. Then, alone in her bedroom one night listening to music, Marthe becomes so turbulent with freefloating emotional and sexual longing that she suddenly removes her nightgown and begins to preen languidly before a full-length mirror. Bresson films her semi-abstractly, like living sculpture: framing her from the neck down as she slumberously sways and turns, then intercutting her taut, now sensually alive face and loosened, silken hair with her slowly flexing legs, as her absorption in her feelings and her desire-permeated flesh increases. Afterwards, when she has turned the music off, we hear sounds from the lodger's neighbouring room, and Bresson cuts to a shot of his hand rapping on the wall. It is as though their mutual yearning had telepathically mingled through the walls which separate them physically; Marthe feels this so strongly that she covers herself even though she is still alone. The following day, after she goes into the lodger's room, Bresson places them in a standing nude embrace as they hide silently from her mother, who, paranoid about male treachery, prowls and calls for Marthe. Bresson's austerity flowers in a wondrous new way during these frankly sexual scenes. "I believe in the value of concentration in this respect as in any other," he told Clarens,[10] but the enrichment flows both ways. Capturing both the blocked surge of sensual desire and its fragile fulfilment, he makes erotic attraction play virtually the same role here that religious grace plays in earlier films: an *unwilled, unbidden* transfiguration which binds and frees simultaneously. As Jacques proposes telling the lodger in a letter he offers to deliver: "She cannot defend herself against her love for you."

Nor can Jacques defend himself against his own love for Marthe. He tries to live out the fantasy of saving, comforting, and finally winning the adoration of a lovely, mysterious woman. Though fully aware of this perversity, Bresson celebrates the feelings which begin to flow between the two self-absorbed dreamers. Without abandoning his visual precision, he surrenders along with them to the beauty of the Parisian evenings. The iridescence of the life around the bridge recalls the nighttown of *American Graffiti*, and the arrival there of a glowing *bateau mouche* creates as stunning an effect as the landing of the alien spaceship in *Close Encounters of the Third Kind*. Cutting inside the boat to a velvetly seductive Latin band as rainbow colours shimmer, liquid yet ghostly, through the boat's glass canopy and off the river, highlighting the hippie-troubadours who strum along the quads, reflecting the whole enchantment off the faces of Marthe and Jacques, Bresson suggests that the ecstatic tenderness which they want is *not* a mere illusion. No film has ever conjured up a more bewitching vision of rapture.

However, Bresson also points up the cruelty of romantic obsession. As Marthe and Jacques exchange intimate details of their lives, we expect them to drop their misty dreams and fall in love with each other. But Marthe keeps on using the word "love" carelessly, when she means devotion or affection: telling Jacques that she "loves" him because he is not "in love" with her or that he fears the lodger's return lest it reveal this "love" of theirs. She completely misunderstands Jacques's emotions; genuine love for her has overwhelmed him, unwilled, unbidden, just as genuine love for the lodger overwhelmed her in the same way. But, regardless of his wish to do so, Jacques simply cannot arouse in Marthe the same desire that she arouses in him and the lodger arouses in her; such desire, like religious grace, is "the wind (that) blows where it will." Bresson subtly underscores their confusion by sharply separating the parts of his narrative from one another with titles like *Histoire de Marthe*, *Histoire de Jacques*, *Première nuit*—suggesting that, like the stories and the nights, the dreamers will be unable to merge.

Yet they do try, in a way unique to Bresson's films. When, despite her letter, the lodger still fails to appear, Marthe curses him bitterly and hides in the darkness along the river; her romantic dream now looks hollow and ridiculous. Jacques's hesitant approach pushes her into a fury of lamentation which makes him walk away, profoundly depressed. Grasping his true feelings at last, she stops her self-pitying outcries and goes after him. Then comes another of those Bressonian moments which evoke complex emotional interchanges through the simple eloquence of two people touching one another. When Marthe catches up, Jacques calmly opens her cloak, tells her quietly of his love, then embraces and caresses her. After an instant's hesitation, she folds her arm acceptingly around his neck—a muted echo of her nude embrace with the lodger. What makes these gestures, this muted echo, so significant in terms of Bresson's "theology" is that they signal the *refusal* of Marthe and Jacques to submit to "predestined" fates—in this instance, her obsession with the lodger and his inability to evoke the same obsessions with himself from her. Moments later, sitting in a café with Jacques, she sums up this conflict between "unbidden" love and "chosen" love: what she feels for the lodger will fade because she did not choose to feel it, but her new feelings for Jacques will last because she *decided* to feel them. By this point, Bresson's hypnotic depiction of the four nights has induced us to agree; we could happily see the film end now, with each telling the other of the strange roads which have led them to one another.

But this "chosen" love is another fantasy, and Bresson's direction of the next moments destroys it breathtakingly. As Jacques and Marthe leave the café, newly pledged to each other, he renews our pleasure in the nightlife around the Pont Neuf with additional exquisite images: Jacques wrapping a red-and-white gift scarf around Marthe's neck, a candle burning on a street musician's guitar case. Just as we see the candle, Marthe is telling Jacques to come live in the lodger's old room, and he is gazing up at the moon. But she is looking levelly at something else: the lodger approaching through the crowd of night people. He sees her, calls to her. Then, with shocking swiftness: she rushes to him, Jacques looks down to see her reach him, she kisses him, she runs back to kiss Jacques three times, she vanishes with the lodger, Jacques watches. Bresson has never directed a crueler, more piercing moment of disillusionment than this.

Yet he implicitly accepts Dostoevsky's fervent, contradictory concluding lines: "Good Lord, only a *moment* of bliss? Isn't such a moment sufficient for the whole of a man's life?" Instead of quoting these lines, Bresson permits us to notice the reflection of the "luminous, marvellous nights" in the colours of Jacques's paintings. "Call it a happy ending if you wish," Clarens writes.[10] I do, and I will.

But, as we have seen, Bresson moved on to darker endings. *The Devil Probably*, in fact, almost extinguishes several of the most poetic motifs in *Four Nights of a Dreamer*: the *bateau-mouche*, the hippie life along the Seine, the embraces. Will Bresson's art, craft, and reflections, cultivated so mandarinly and so heroically these many years, end here, as Pasolini's did? Had Pasolini not been murdered after completing *Salò*, he might have fallen into creative sterility, unless he could have found a way not to deny but to transcend his despair. So it may be with Bresson. I think of Alfred Hitchcock saying that his love for film was stronger than any morality and hope that Robert Bresson's, even now, remains stronger than any despair.

Notes

Numbering of notes follows the style of the original text. *Ed*.

1. Robert Bresson, *Notes sur le cinématographe*. Gallimard, 1975. (English translation: *Notes on Cinematography*. Tr. by Jonathan Griffin, Urizen Books. 1977)
2. Marvin Zeman, "The Suicide of Robert Bresson," *Cinema* (Beverly Hills), vol. 6, no. 3.
3. Paul Schrader, *Transcendental Style in Film: Ozu, Bresson, Dreyer*. University of California Press, 1972.
4. Paul Schrader, "Robert Bresson, Possibly" (interview), *Film Comment*, September/October, 1977.
5. Beverle Houston and Marsha Kinder, *Self and Cinema: A Transformalist Perspective*, Redgrave Publishing Company, 1980.
6. Charles Thomas Samuels, "Robert Bresson" (interview), in *Encountering Directors*. G.P. Putnam's Sons, 1972.
7. Jonathan Rosenbaum, "Bresson's *Lancelot du Lac*." *Sight & Sound*, Summer 1974.
8. François Truffaut, "Vive Robert Bresson," printed statement distributed during Filmex 1978.
9. Jonathan Cott, "Fires Within: The Chaste Sensuality of Director Louis Malle" (interview), *Rolling Stone*. 6 April, 1978.
10. Carlos Clarens, "Four Nights of a Dreamer," *Sight & Sound*, Winter 1971-72.

Le Diable probablement

KENT JONES

A Stranger's Posture:
Notes on Bresson's
Late Films

"IT IS A CURIOUSLY WIDESPREAD BELIEF that people who say they enjoy [atonal] music must be shamming," writes Charles Rosen in a recent article on the alleged death of classical music. Rosen also notes that in a favourable review of his book on Schoenberg, the reviewer was puzzled over his discussion of the music's emotional content: "He could not believe there was any." This provides a useful analogy with widespread perceptions of Bresson's cinema, which is often thought of in similarly unsympathetic terms. In the music of Schoenberg, Webern or Messiaen (when he is composing atonally), emotion is always present, but it is never manufactured with a potential audience in mind. When we use the word "emotional" to describe an artwork we're usually talking about the feelings brought about by its cultural, sociological and historical reverberations (thus a film like *The Deer Hunter*, a devastating emotional experience but in so many ways a risible and slovenly film). But in the case of a Webern, who never strayed from the strict discipline of the 12-tone row, all of the aesthetic energy goes into rendering the presence, shape and dimension of individual sounds, both individually and in relation to one another, moving randomness and form in thrilling proximity. A single note on the celesta in the *Variations for Orchestra* carries the same density and ontologically thrilling identity as Yvon's red gloves pulling the oil pump out of the pipe in *L'Argent*.

Modernism in film, because of the relative youth of the medium and its never-ending oscillation between art and popular entertainment, between tradition and endless modification by the demands of and shifts within the marketplace, will never be properly understood if film history is seen only on its own terms and never in the context of the other arts, as Orson Welles counselled. Otherwise, Antonioni's fondness for Eliot and Morandi, or Resnais's affinity for the *nouveau roman* are nothing more than isolated cases, matters of personal taste, and Bresson, associate of Cocteau and Klossowski and admirer of Godard, is defined as a Jansenist, an ascetic, an austere transcendentalist, or, worst of all, a Bressonian, rather than one of the greatest of all modernists. Meanwhile, if the severe pronouncements of avant-garde filmmakers like Snow or Frampton are taken at face value, their work forms a counter-tradition that represents the true cinematic modernism, in which narrative can have no part.

I don't want to belabour the comparison with serialism, as though Bresson were interested only in transposing an artistic mutation from one medium to another (which is perhaps truer of Resnais). But I do know that when Bresson says, "I believe that one moves an audience through rhythm, concentration and unity," it could just as easily be Webern speaking. Moreover, acting in the cinema is easily comparable to diatonic scales in music—they are both thought of as intrinsic to their art forms and when they are gone they are severely missed, immediately prompting accusations of cerebral coldness. One must remember that Schoenberg and Webern did not destroy diatonic composition any more than Bresson destroyed acting. Understanding an unprecedented mode of expression as a part of history rather than the end of it is often extraordinarily difficult.

After you've seen a Bresson film, it is still possible to admire the great acting of Robert Donat or Robert Ryan (or the canny use of a limited actor like Gary Cooper to create the effect of great acting). Watching any film is a complex perceptual and evaluative procedure, central to which is the evaluation of how actors mesh with the rest of the film, the way they test themselves against the demands of their roles, the degree to which they balance acting with the appearance of not acting. To lessen the importance of this unconscious procedure in the viewing experience has enormous repercussions: obviously, people are accustomed to the dominant structure, which is why it's not terribly surprising that they will continue to use it as a guide even when they are confronted with a new structure. For example, Charles Thomas Samuels in his book *Encountering Directors*, who harps away at Bresson about acting throughout their interview as though it was the intention of his models to be "flat" and "austere." "But all your models speak in the same Bressonian voice," says Samuels, after which he is duly admonished by Bresson.

There is a striking passage in *Notes on the Cinematographer* in which Bresson comments on a contemporary screen actress whose eyes are supposedly magical but who appears to him to be the incarnation of evil. (I've always been convinced that he was writing about Jeanne Moreau.) Here is the focal point of Bresson's art—the things that we involuntarily reveal about ourselves. He is not alone, but other directors for whom this phenomenon is also important merely exploit it to other ends. Only Bresson makes the ceaseless self-revelation of people both the central event and the lynchpin of his cinema. Manny Farber once identified the private interactions between actor and scene or film as the better part of what we like to call a performance. In any late Tom Cruise performance, for instance, there is an overriding sense of ownership as opposed to participation that is miles from whatever character he happens to be playing, an unpleasant feeling that he is offering himself as a very expensive gift to his paying audience. Cruise almost always kills his good instincts with his politician's vanity. The recognition of this type of vanity and its many gradations is difficult to come by in contemporary film criticism, first of all because the actor and his or her presence is almost always thought to be of secondary importance when discussing a film, ornamental rather than organic (or, at best, merely iconic). But there is also something else that contributes to this lack of acknowledgement of the centrality of acting in cinema (writers James Naremore and Nicole Brenez excepted), something at once more subtle and more troubling. During this supremely litigious moment in history, the very idea of "reading" someone has become a sort of unspoken taboo, done in absolute privacy. It's an obvious remnant of Reagan-era anti-intellectualism—the precise description of facts is often skirted over or bypassed in favour of a pre-established scenario.

Politics and celebrity are loci of close inspection and/or the denial thereof. Any footage of Richard Nixon is inherently dramatic because of his eternal transparency—his profound bodily discomfort, which he is constantly trying to overcome and conceal with a pre-meditated program of smiling, waving, and decisive hand gestures which always appear suddenly, like a weapon being withdrawn from a sheath. And, if there's one film that unwittingly dramatizes the contemporary conflicts between scrutinizing and evading the evidence of human behaviour, it's *Nixon*, which takes one of the most absorbing spectacles of displaced longing in televisual history and spits out a motley collection of footage consisting of frenzied actions and impersonations, with an accompanying set of fashionable and palatable core issues for an agenda. To say that Oliver Stone's cinema is the polar opposite of Bresson's is to state the obvious: there is no rhythm to speak of in Stone's work, the images overpower the soundtrack, and the acting is purely visual and almost entirely grotesque. But the most profound difference of all, which serves to illustrate the alienation many young viewers feel from Bresson's cinema, is in their respective attitudes towards the people who pass before their cameras. Stone applies the various myths, technological marvels and formal change-ups of which he avails himself with abandon over his actors, while Bresson forces the faces and bodies of his models into relief within his shallow spaces, thus exposing their continual, unconscious self-revelations to our probing consciousness. To put it pithily, in the presence of Stone's phantasmagoric murals as well as so much else in modern cinema, the eye and ear have a tendency to become acquisitive, whereas in the presence of Bresson's patiently concentrated cinema they must be inquisitive or nothing.

Bresson's attention to his models seems to me an outgrowth of the attention we reflexively pay to the strangers we see as we walk down the street every day of our lives, people we will never meet but who excite our curiosity. City-dwellers in particular share an instinctive curiosity, a way of staying watchful and yet always removed, a quality that I've always felt in Bresson's work. Most forcefully in the films before *Procès de Jeanne d'Arc*, I have the impression that I'm getting a profound glimpse of a series of strangers who will nonetheless remain strangers. The way that Bresson films the man who walks up and down the prison courtyard in *Un condamné à mort s'est échappé* is so temperamentally and spiritually close to the way that people hold one another's images as they walk through the streets of Manhattan or Paris or Los Angeles—discreetly, secretively, yet fully. In essence Bresson isolates and elevates one of the most constant and beautiful of all human characteristics, curiosity about one's fellow men and women, by practising it with his camera, and reminds us in the process that such curiosity is active rather than passive.

Although I would argue that Bresson is far from a transcendental artist, his carefully measured distance from the action in his films could be likened to "a Godlike remove," resulting in an all but total absence of complicity with his characters. By complicity, I mean a particular kind of interaction between performer, character, director, camera and audience made possible only through acting. Take Jacques Dutronc's performance in Pialat's *Van Gogh*, in which there seems to be a secret pact between the film and the actor, a desire to move according to Van Gogh's slow, langorous rhythms, a shared acceptance of self-destruction as the final outcome of never coming to terms with society and its rules. Such anarchically elongated beauty is unthinkable in Bresson's cinema. Bresson's entire concept of the cinematographer and his models as opposed to the director and his actors is an integral part of his "Christian universe," while other filmmakers whose ideas of life are less certain and more speculative, require the complicity, the attachment, and the self-directed wilfulness of acting.

Within Bresson's "Christian universe," ultimate reality is not imminent but omnipresent, and conventional ideas of moral accountability, the kind that drive Pialat's Van Gogh to anti-social behaviour and finally suicide, make way for what finally amounts to varying degrees of innate moral sense. For Bresson, morality is like a muscle, atrophied by the fruitless workings of the man-made world yet called upon to see past those workings to the acceptance of truth, which manifests itself as a metaphysical solitude. The degree to which the recognition of that solitude is dependent on chance is open to debate. In the early films there is a more pronounced feeling that moral knowledge is within reach and only in need of a crisis before it can press through the barriers of confusion and self-deception; whereas in the later films, the concentration is on the infernal workings of society and the consequent, seemingly endless deferral of the revelation of truth.

To evaluate any Bresson film properly, it is necessary to describe his models carefully, what they give away about themselves, and how it relates to the action. In *Un condamné à mort s'est échappé*, consider the doubt that François Leterrier betrays with his enormous eyes, as he torques his reedy body into a crouch, always appearing to be looking up at the heavens and asking: Will you allow me to meet this challenge? His moral deficiency, a deficiency that most of us share, is this compulsion or instinctive need to pull back and question his fitness for an impossible task, when his soul seems to be resting on his thin shoulder blades as they pull up around his head. The drama of *Un condamné à mort s'est échappé* is not merely one of chance and grace, but of Fontaine's exemplary self-consciousness, the very self-consciousness that has him anticipating every possible misstep throughout his escape. It's fascinating to contrast this crouching hero with the tall and erect-postured Martin Lassalle in *Pickpocket*, a mask of blank confidence designed to breeze past the kind of questions that plague Fontaine, and yet there is the hint of a profound and deeply private nervousness, a striking unsteadiness in his gaze. Which is of course fitting for *Pickpocket*, a film of true moral suspense—how long before the thief recognizes that his identity is a paltry construction? And in *Journal d'un curé de campagne*, the moist-eyed and thin-lipped, secretly disappointed Claude Laydu suggests what James Agee might have become had he gone into the priesthood, always trying to jump to the next spiritual step before it has even appeared, conflicting definitions of piety, pride, spirituality and love swimming through his head (it's much closer to a regular performance than Lassalle's and Leterrier's). While an actor's personal affect is commonly one among several aspects of his or her performance, and while its importance and weight changes according to the different strategies of different films and directors, in Bresson it is singularized, the perpetually stunned response of a non-professional thrown in front of a movie camera. And it is as constant as the sun.

Bresson's rapt gaze at his characters in *Les Anges du péché* and *Les Dames du Bois de Boulogne* is so close to the Borzage of the thirties, particularly *The Shining Hour* and *Mannequin*, or a forties film like *Till We Meet Again*, where the dramatic and visual focus is not as much on bodies as it is on faces, which are studied attentively in anticipation of the climactic moment of emotional/spiritual recognition. In the films that follow, recognition occurs not on a mental but a physical level. Beginning with *Journal d'un curé de campagne*, emotional recognition in Bresson occurs less on a mental than on a physical level. The viewer becomes keenly aware of breath as it contracts and expands the chest, of the beating hearts of the priest, the prisoner and the criminal—one racing from embarrassment, the next from excruciating tension, the third from the sudden intrusion of love into his fortress-like existence. These men discover nothing through merely looking at the world, as in Hitchcock—they mentally apprehend what their senses have already shown them only when the evidence becomes physically overwhelming. The brain is at work but counts for nothing since the heart is the true and final receptor of spiritual evidence. How many times in each of these films, all narrated in the first person, does the hero describe his precise physical sensation during a moment of crisis?

As Bresson begins to depict contemporary reality, the hope of spiritual recognition for his heroes dims and his camera's relationship to the human body becomes increasingly allegorical. Beginning with *Procès de Jeanne d'Arc*, in which he consciously chose a young woman who represented the youth of 1962, moral suspense and the possibility of enlightenment withdraw into darkness as resignation, narcissism and suicide are illuminated. (There is not much moral suspense for Joan of Arc, whose spiritual knowledge is, after all, a given). The whole body is registered more fully, but with a singularity bordering on caricature—the litheness of Dominique Sanda in *Une femme douce*; François Lafarge's taut, shifty moves in *Au hasard Balthazar*; and Anne Wiazemsky's impossibly painful delicacy, like a flower in a tornado, in the same film; Nadine Nortier's stunted, combative, arrhythmic comportment in *Mouchette*. (Think of the terrible contrast between her clunky legs wrapped in wool and Sanda's doe-like prancing from bath to bed.)

It was during this period that Bresson eased up on his practice of finding moral resemblances between his models and his characters. "In the past this method consumed a good deal of my time," he told Carlos Clarens in a 1971 *Sight and Sound* interview. "Today I go much faster. I rather trust my instinct and believe in luck and random chance," a remark that is revealing given his increasing emphasis on the representation of youth. *Quatre nuits d'un rêveur* represents the real beginning of this last, most despairing phase of Bresson's career. His previous depictions of contemporary culture had been off-handed and somewhat beside the point; it's only in retrospect that one realizes that Martin Lassalle in *Pickpocket* would have fit rather snugly into the universe of Chabrol's *Les Cousins* or Rohmer's *Le Signe du lion*, or in the paranoid free-for-all of Rivette's *Paris nous appartient*. As the axis of Bresson's cinema shifts from an ahistorical enlightenment to direct impressions of young people in the contemporary world, the possibilities for individual change and self-revelation become less certain, and the question of exact moral resemblance becomes less and less germane. It's impossible to determine what was the cause and what was the effect of this shift, but I suppose that it was Bresson's exhaustion with the exacting process of choosing his models that opened up his vision to the world around him and deepened his resignation over its apparent rootlessness. It's the strangest sensation to observe the growth of this process, from a few snatches of rock music on a transistor radio meant to signify Gérard's careless sense of destruction in *Balthazar* to the full-blown, horrified vision of *L'Argent*.

When I was a teenager, during the seventies, my father used to criticize me for my stooped posture. I know I was not alone; "Stand up straight!" was a parental litany in those days. Just before I left for college, when my mother prompted him to give me some piece of far-reaching advice, he said, "Stand tall and always show your full posture." As I look back on it now, what seems most interesting is not his viewpoint but my response—a silent, passive-aggressive, mumbled "Okay," as though any suggestion that there was something in the world worth standing up straight for was patently absurd and that there was no way he could possibly know that since he was fixated on questions of physical posture. Our bodies meant nothing to us at that moment, and I am still astonished whenever I see an adolescent boy talking about going to the gym, or worried about his appearance in any context other than following contemporary standards of cool. Our weapon was a "knowledge" that the world was, if not awful, then terminally ridiculous. Our parents, our teachers (except the "cool" ones), politicians and TV stars (this was before youth culture took over the airwaves and the movies) were all unwitting pieces in the mosaic of absurdity. As I look back on it now, it's no mistake that many of us who held on to this sense of resignation went into the arts, so profound was our sense that real political change had ceased to be possible: change had to be total or it was meaningless. It is often said that our despair resulted from "the failure of the sixties," but I tend to think that it was something more mysterious, of which that over-hyped idea was only one part. Change was occurring everywhere as we were growing up, but we shared a sense of isolation that seems to me to have been the result of being alone in our rooms with our music—the drugs and drinking, the manifestos of anarchism, strike me now as mere accompaniments to our profound solitude. Our perception of the sixties was not so much one of failure as much as a never-ending project we had internalized and kept alive not by action but by inaction, by dreaming. The collective sunken posture of our generation as we drifted through the world was a kind of insurance against anything affecting us that we did not want to enter our psyches, and a precursor of the contemporary pull towards the organization of life around various information technologies—fax machines, cell phones, PCs and DVD players—whose relationship to their owners Bresson would have filmed so well.

It's strange to look back at *Quatre nuits d'un rêveur*, one of the least appreciated of Bresson's films, and recognize the external features of that moment in history captured with such astonishing accuracy, coupled with such quiet derision. From the moment that Guillaume des Forêts walks down the street and into the country and performs his lackadaisical somersault, I feel like I'm watching myself and my friends so many years ago, captured under several thick layers of glass and preserved for eternity. It's fascinating that the one filmmaker who captured the physical stance of that generation was the one who cast the coldest eye on them. Des Forêts and Isabelle Weingarten are prototypes for the young people in *Lancelot du Lac* (in which an old cherished project takes on echoes of May '68 through the casting of people who look like they have just come from the barricades: when

Lancelot tells Guinevere, "I want the impossible!" the spirit of '68 is unmistakable) and for the even more confused and despairing crew in *Le Diable probablement*: stoop-shouldered young men shuffling along in what seems like an endless straight line and aquiline young women possessed of a delicately compulsive narcissism. The extraordinary sequence in *Quatre nuits* where Weingarten examines her naked body in the bathroom mirror as music plays on the radio, unlike anything else in Bresson's cinema or modern cinema in general, gains its power not from lyricism but from an endless, crystalline quality: the many, many layers of self-consciousness (you have the sense that Weingarten is examining herself as she examines herself examining herself) are remarkable, and there's a subtle chill to the ritualized quality of the action. To say that Bresson's vision of youth in the early seventies is conservative is no doubt just, but the clarity of the vision betrays, if not a sense of connection, then a sort of paternal empathy engendered by the spectacle of such rootlessness. I think it is clear that Bresson is no reactionary, that by his reckoning it's the forces at work in the world that leave young people with no sense of hope, as opposed to any inherent laziness.

Bresson made this implicit position explicit in *Le Diable probablement*, a fascinatingly awkward, thematically burdened film that tests the idea of whether young people can withstand the monstrous man-made death drive of capitalism when they have been denied a belief system. By the time Bresson made *L'Argent* six years later, the posture (in both the literal and figurative senses of the word) of the bright middle-class youths played by des Fôrets in *Quatre nuits* and Antoine Monnier in *Diable* gives way, for the first time in his work since *Au hasard Balthazar*, to the presentation of an Everyman. Physical comportment is no longer a locus of moral fitness, and there is nothing left but the hard fact of being. Christian Patey's Yvon in *L'Argent* is not a brilliant disaffected youth like Monnier's Charles or a self-consciously carefree one like des Fôrets's Jacques, but a guy who must work for a living and put food on the table (interesting that Yvon represents the first time Bresson has filmed an urban manual labourer). And physically, Patey is a singularity in Bresson's career, whose gallery of male models (no pun intended) is otherwise entirely made up of lithe, delicate men whose faces and bodies are strongly suggestive of Modigliani. Patey is not exactly a hulking monster, but he is physically in another universe from Monnier-Lafarge-Leterrier: bigger-boned, more noticeably muscular, his affect suggesting entrenched, depressed sluggishness rather than darting attentiveness or soulful compassion.

In *L'Argent*, the man-made world is a ruthlessly efficient machine fueled by money in which everyone is potentially disposable. The viewer is drawn to little traces of activity and sensual detail that the characters don't even notice—Yvon's gloved hands as he pumps oil (a devastating cut: it is our introduction to him, and we've just left the owners of the photography shop discussing how they can palm off their counterfeit bill), the heavy-footed walk of the old woman as Yvon follows her from town to her house in the country, the dog frantically running through the house as the final murders are committed. Bresson makes his camera as implacable as the position of modern society itself, and with the most extraordinary calm and dispassion makes a film about the genesis and final realization of a tragedy, over which neither he nor anyone else has any control. *L'Argent* is just as frightening a film as Pasolini's *Salò*, except that it is less toxic, informed by a terrible resignation rather than a profound anger. Yvon's solidity (there is the saddest hint of a bygone innocent youth in his face and his movement) is no match for the society that is systematically destroying him. In an interview with Michel Ciment, Bresson said that Yvon's redemption was not really felt at the end of the film because it would have disrupted the rhythm. But when he speaks of rhythm in this particular case, one wonders if he's thinking of the film's rhythm or the rhythm of inhuman obliteration that the film is treating, and whether or not they are the same.

What led to Bresson's increasing need to focus on desperation and hopelessness in the years between *Un condamné à mort s'est échappé* and *L'Argent*? But then, can it really be said that *L'Argent* or *Le Diable probablement* are pessimistic films? That different outcomes seem almost impossible for either Charles or Yvon is less important than the fact that, beyond the despair felt by each character, the world continues: the events of both films, awful as they are, occur in the same Christian universe where the flowing of water through a stream and the hanging of clothes on a line (the clicking of those clothes-pins!) imprint themselves on the eye and ear, acquiring a pure, heightened beauty that approaches the ecstatic. Just as Pasolini left his vanity behind when he made *Salò* to focus his audience's attention on the cruelties of the world in the most direct way he knew, Bresson ended one of the most adventurous and heroic careers in the cinema by filming a real-life horror story. But whereas Pasolini withdrew any possibility of redemption from his film and left all responsibility to his audience, Bresson kept his faith in an ultimate reality behind the veil of modern callousness by trusting his own senses to perceive its beauty, and in the sensitivity of his camera and his Nagra to record it. "I love life," Bresson said in a 1986 conversation with Brian Baxter, and that love is evident in every frame of *L'Argent*, perhaps the only film ever made that allows the horrors of mankind and the beauty of the world that contains it to coexist without irony or bitterness. As Yvon sits in the café having his last drink as a free man, his head slightly cocked, his brow furrowed, his body almost inert, the acts he has perpetrated are inseparable from the extreme beauty of his being.

Le Diable probablement

The Devil Probably:
The Redemption of Despair

FRANÇOIS TRUFFAUT has described *The Devil Probably* as "voluptuous." Voluptuousness is not a quality generally associated with the films of Robert Bresson, although one can find it in *Les Dames du Bois de Boulogne* and, to a lesser degree, in *Balthazar*. But Truffaut is not being provocative, nor is he simply trying to "sell" the film. "Two beautiful girls," he writes, "and two handsome boys animate the film . . . and I am insisting on their beauty because it is in part the subject of the film: wasted beauty, wasted youth. Bresson plays with these four beautiful faces, deals them out like face cards in a card game."

This doesn't mean we're deprived of our usual Bressonian ration of doorknobs and doorjambs, low-rise waist or belt shots, but this paraphernalia of daily life only serves to set off the beauty of the faces. And Truffaut, perhaps characteristically, prefers to see the doomed beauty of adolescence as the subject of the film.

But the film can be seen in many other ways—and that is why I found it his best film since *Pickpocket*. Actually it is a kind of reverse *Pickpocket*, for our hero Charles is *not* saved by love, does not find grace. (Oddly enough, the non-actor who plays Charles—and who is Henri Matisse's great-grandson—looks a little like Marika Green, the girl in *Pickpocket*.) Bresson seems to feel that, given the state of the world today, private solutions are no longer possible. Love is no more the solution to the destruction of the earth and its resources than the remedies that society proposes: the revolution, the church (whether traditional or "progressive"), psychoanalysis. And so, although Charles doesn't want to die, his hatred of life as he sees it around him is so great that he hires a junkie friend to shoot him.

In some rather cruel scenes Bresson disposes neatly of an omniscient psychoanalyst who tried to explain to Charles that his disgust with society is rooted in the occasional spankings his father used to give him. The "new" Church and left-wing politics are treated no more gently: progressive Catholicism is dismissed with Montesquieu's remark that the Catholics would conquer Protestantism and then become Protestants themselves. As for the revolution, Charles declares bluntly that "There won't be any revolution"—meaning that there will be none worthy of the name.

To find a solution to a problem, one must first discover who is to blame. And in the bus scene (the most extraordinary single sequence of the film), we hear snatches of conversations from the various passengers. One says "Don't blame the government, we are governed by the masses—in other words by ourselves." Another asks, "Who is really in charge?" "Obscure forces," murmurs someone; another adds "The Devil, probably." Suddenly, the bus slams on its brakes and everyone is thrown backward; there is a shot of the driver's hand on the door-opening button, and we see him getting out of the bus.

What has happened? We never find out, nor is it important to know. But somehow it's appropriate: this ending to a sequence which began calmly but spookily with repeated brief shots of passengers' fingers on the stop-button, and shots of the sign which has lit up in response saying "Stop requested." On the one hand, such a sequence is "pure cinema," on the other it is a paradigm of the film itself. The mechanical gestures, with their mechanical responses, correspond to the mechanistic view of life which Bresson believes prevails today. And the conversations, which aren't really conversations but alternating monologues, are emblematic of the life of his characters who never seem to be talking to each other but rather *at* or *away from* each other—as is the contrast between the almost desultory rhythm of these various remarks and the dynamic workings of the bus and its gadgets. The remark, "The Devil, probably," just before the bus jams on its brakes, can be taken either literally (religiously) or as an exasperated sense that the only answer has to be an unrealistic one. Since we have no idea of who or what is responsible, why don't we just blame it on the devil, and then forget about the whole thing?

Bresson, though, doesn't let us forget anything: he has included supposed (and some real) stock shots in the film of all the ecological horrors: thermonuclear missiles, DDT-destroyed trees, oil slicks, the killing of baby seals, automobile graveyards—pollution in every form. But pollution implies that there was something pure in the first place to be polluted, and this is one of the reasons why the film, which sounds as if it ought to be depressing, is not.

It is not the only reason, however. Bresson has achieved such a degree of emotional involvement with his characters, and his artistic control has created such a perfectly realized film, that one comes away from the film feeling uplifted. It may be the portrait of the end of a civilization, and I am sure Bresson wants it to be that; but when a civilization can produce a work as exalting as this one, then it is hard to believe that there is no hope. *The Devil Probably* is no more a downer than *King Lear* or *Oedipus*, no matter how bleak and hopeless their pictures of life. And isn't that what great art is all about?

But how does Bresson achieve this effect? Not through presenting us with lovable characters. Many will find Charles insufferable. And Alberte, the girl friend who is convinced that Charles can be saved if only she can get him to a psychoanalyst, is rather stupid. But though they may be silly, they are silly like the rest of us. Alberte's faith in psychoanalysis appears more touching than dumb; Charles may be "spoiled," but, as Truffaut remarked, he is beautiful.

And this beauty is more than skin-deep. One of the most affecting moments in the film comes toward the end when Charles, on the way to Père-Lachaise cemetery to be murdered, pauses in front of an open ground-floor window. A few snatches of Mozart can be heard coming from a radio inside: he hesitates a few seconds before continuing, but those few seconds are heart-stopping because they express his and our sense of everything he is about to give up. He has already told us in the psychoanalyst's office that he can't stand the idea of not seeing or hearing any more; but suddenly, now, we *feel* what he means. And when he gets to the cemetery, there is one of those inexplicably moving moments when he says to his hired assassin, "You know, I was sure I'd have some sublime thought at a moment like this, but what I'm actually thinking about is. . . ." And then the gun goes off, and we are left to ponder what he might have been thinking of. The scene has that same ring of elegiac truth as the one in *Citizen Kane* when Mr. Bernstein (Everett Sloane), in reply to someone who suggests that Rosebud couldn't just be some girl Kane once knew casually tells us about getting off the ferry from New Jersey to Manhattan one morning and seeing a girl walking toward him getting on the boat to go the other way. That was thirty years ago, he says, but there's hardly a day I don't think of that girl and remember her.

The ratio of emotion to abstraction in most of Bresson's films since *Pickpocket* has been somewhat over-balanced in the direction of abstraction. *The Devil Probably* readjusts the balance. I should also add, for whatever it's worth, that this is Bresson's most original script. Not an adaptation of Dostoevsky, Bernanos, or Diderot; not based on historical material like *Joan of Arc*, *Lancelot*, and *A Man Escaped*; not using dialogue by Giraudoux or Cocteau; not even suggested by elements from another work (the echoes of *Crime and Punishment* in *Pickpocket* or of *The Idiot* in *Balthazar*). As far as I can tell the script is totally his. But perhaps there are always "echoes" in a Bresson film. When I asked him why he chose the rather uncommon name of Alberte for the leading girl, he replied that he wanted a girl's name that was derived from a masculine name—and then added that of course he also had Proust's Albertine in mind.

I am not sure that the originality of the script is that significant. But it is the single most important material difference between this film and the others. Bresson, at seventy, is now so fully in command of his medium that he no longer needs any kind of crutch. And, having thrown his crutches away, he not only can walk: he can soar higher than ever before—and take us with him.

L'Argent

L'Argent

T OLSTOY'S SHORT STORY, "The Counterfeit Note," dates from the beginning of the century. This is when Tolstoy becomes truly Tolstoyan, in other words, when he draws a religious idea from his work—an idea that for the most part had always been there—and devotes all his art to the service of this idea. In "The Counterfeit Note," a short story cluttered with characters and events, Tolstoy follows the subterranean and picaresque trail of a counterfeit bill. Irresponsibly put into circulation by two rascals from good families who need money, the counterfeit note sets off a series of crimes, from pickpocketing to plundering, right up to gratuitous murder—conceived, apparently, as an end in itself. But does the note directly instigate the crimes or is it simply a pretext? Tolstoy responds to this question in a typical Tolstoyan manner: had the two boys believed in the forces of "good," nothing would have occurred. But why had they not believed? Here, Tolstoy provides a clear answer: he attributes "evil" to what lies at the core of bourgeois society: atheism and materialism. Yet at the same time, Tolstoy seems to hold a strange conviction that every society creates evil according to some kind of natural secretion, as certain molluscs produce pearls. The bourgeoisie would then be nothing other than a large mass of innumerably wicked molluscs. The humble and the simple then, society made of those without culture, in other words, "non-society," escape "evil" and are even "good."

Robert Bresson has based his latest film on this Tolstoy short story and given it a title redolent of Zola: *L'Argent*. It's not the first time that Bresson has taken to such grafting: in *Pickpocket*, there was already the echo of *Crime and Punishment*. In *L'Argent*, Bresson has left "good," that is Tolstoy's view of "good," in the shadows, in order to concentrate on "evil" and to undertake a precise and impersonal study of the way in which this inevitable social secretion is formed. The golden thread that guides us through the diabolical labyrinth is, of course, the counterfeit note. Here lies an odd contradiction however, because for Bresson, the note is counterfeit from the very beginning; even if it were real, its watermark remains the horned and sardonic effigy of the devil. "Evil" then, let us not forget, is embedded within the very existence of money, regardless of its being counterfeit or real.

Bresson, of course, has his own idea of "good" and it comes across clearly in the film. Curiously enough, both Tolstoy and Bresson see "evil" as something that exists outside of national borders, yet both define "good" in a "national" framework. For Tolstoy then, good is essentially Gerasim, the typical Russian peasant who comforts the dying "bourgeois" Ivan Illyich; it is the Sarmathian serfs, bound to the soil, including even the terrible habitual murderer Stepan. They are "good" because they are Russian to the core of their beings, and can be nothing else but Russian. As for Bresson, he finds "good" in the ancient virtues of French civilization, that traditional mix of rigour, close analysis, and rational-ism—the distinctive mark of national genius. In other words, "good" becomes "style." From this we arrive at the curious conclusion that evil is found in life, and good in the way in which life is represented. The blood-stained axe the murderer uses to kill his victims is an evil object, but the image of the axe is beneficent. In short, style exorcizes evil.

It seems superfluous to emphasize the "puritan" beauty of certain shots, of certain details. The actors play their roles with a hallucinatory sobriety, in a strange atmosphere halfway between the era of banknotes and the era of credit cards.

Translated from the French by Lara Fitzgerald

L'Argent

Mouchette

RAYMOND DURGNAT

The Negative Vision
of Robert Bresson

ROUND THE TIME OF *Lancelot du Lac* (1974), Bresson was said to have declared himself "a Christian atheist." This ambiguous phrase covers a multitude of positions, some fairly common among religiously minded people. Many agnostics firmly believe that no God exists, yet steadfastly maintain some key Christian ideas. And "modernist" Christians believe in a God, or some indefinable Equivalent, whom it's nonetheless impossible to really *know* (a view converging with Zen Buddhism, an often atheistic religion).

Not only "Christian atheist," but many other religious labels, accommodate enough ambiguity to bedevil (that's the word!) debate. And to confound my long-cherished yearning, to tease out from Bresson's films some clearer idea, if not of his beliefs exactly (for art more often explores experiences than beliefs), then some doctrinal *tendencies*, or issues that preoccupied (or tempted?) him. His tight, controlling style suggested his ideas might be more narrow, precise, sombre, and strange than usual in Christian movies, which so often settle for "Love," or "the Power of Good," or "Miracles" of some safely obvious kind.

Actually, every doctrinal hint I thought I found seemed, in the end, to lead *away* from intellectual exactness—while remaining firmly within a *sacred* sphere (not a merely "psychological" one). Bresson, like Dreyer and Tarkovsky, generates a sense of "the profane *as* sacred"—whether in itself (as part of God's Creation), or because flesh and spirit are so interwoven, so symbiotic, that neither is "complete" without the other. Earthly life needs some spiritual values to complete itself; and yet, the spiritual *needs* life on earth, in the flesh. Thus Matter is an *aspect* of Spirit, even when it also *hides* it; "faith versus the flesh" is not a binary opposition (like either/or, good/evil, etc.), but a dialectical one (a new, "higher" synthesis).

This "trinity" of Christian directors takes a rather sombre view of "the material world" (which would include much that is social and psychological). Dreyer and Tarkovsky present matter, society, and psychology in a dense, solid, way; Bresson's style is more ethereal, elusive. His sense of "life on earth" as *both* "a veil" *and* "a glass darkly" is my subject here.

1. Bresson and the Hidden God

Bresson's style being tight-lipped and severe, and its sense of God's grace, though intense, obscure, Bresson is not infrequently called "Jansenist." The Roman Catholic Church having declared Jansenism a heresy, might Bresson be a candidate for excommunication?

An interesting question, in these days of political correctness.

Bishop Jansen, and his, mostly French, followers, *circa* 1640, had affinities with Calvinism (hard-core Puritanism), of which Jansenism is sometimes described as a Catholic adaptation.[1] English Protestantism being the religion I know best, I sometimes find myself wondering about Bresson's affinities with its most sombre form, Calvinism.

Jansenism and Calvinism both stressed, among other things: (a) the total depravity of fallen man, and (b) double predestination (God created us knowing we would choose sin and be damned. His justice is incomprehensible). Man cannot *deserve* God's grace, and the slightest sin is a mortal one: "A man can drown in two inches of water." "If a man is damned, his virtues serve only to make him damn himself more thoroughly." Salvation requires a very special grace, which, being divine, is irresistible: so, the saved deserve no credit for that either. Both doctrines shared a bleak view of man, and the hopelessness of his situation— as befitted their own origins, in a long era of wars, civil wars, occupations, and resistances.

Within Roman Catholicism, the Jansenists' great antagonists were the Jesuits. In Buñuel's *The Milky Way* the two aristocrats, duelling with sword and dagger, swapping theological propositions as they thrust and parry, emblemize the power-struggle between their lay supporters.

Jesuit doctrines were relatively easygoing. God left fallen man with sufficient grace, and freedom of will, to respond to grace, which God distributed rather freely. For noble pagans, like Plato, who, living before Christ, hadn't really had a fair chance of salvation, God might well make special arrangements. Indeed, Jesuit optimism about pagans being not all bad encouraged missionary activity. Hence, in Joffé's *The Mission*, a Jesuit anticipates modern Third Worldism and liberation theology.

Nowadays, of course, some Christianities are unrestrainedly optimistic: God doesn't ask much; He's grateful to be allowed to help us feel good about ourselves.

However, serious Christian thinking broadly agrees that the "dialectic" of God's severity and God's love is difficult, uncertain, and logically "absurd." Secular morality shares related problems: for example, "Double Predestination versus Free Will" reappears in humanism as "Determinism versus Freedom." The arguments of Pascal, a leading Jansenist, about freedom, history, logic, pleasure, and purity, still loom large in French culture: the central "Act" of Rohmer's *Ma nuit chez Maud* is a polite, but serious, discussion, of his (Jansenist) ideas, between an earnest (but sinful) Catholic, a Marxist, and an agnostic lady doctor.

Bresson's *Les Dames du Bois de Boulogne* (1945) features a Square Port-Royal. As Port-Royal was long the centre of Jansenist influence, this might indicate a certain, if not position, then special interest. Similarly the subtitle of his *Un condamné à mort s'est échappé, Le Vent souffle où il veut* ("The wind bloweth where it listeth"), *might* hint at Jansenist leanings, for it *might* imply that God decides, in an entirely arbitrary way, whether to send His grace our way. (The less severe line would be that though man has no claim on grace, the faithful, even if sinful, can confidently hope for it, as a gift. The sacraments, the Church itself, "institutionalize" that confidence.)²

Jansenism, with its pessimism about man, its uncertainty about "the hidden God," was already a kind of negative theology. Which would help account for the revival of interest in it—even among film critics. It wasn't completely heretical. Whatever its errors, it contained much truth about one kind of Christian experience. Its heresy lay, less in the experience itself, than in a doctrinal one-sidedness: its denial of the other, "laxer," truths which maintained the "orthodox" balance.

I suspect that Bresson gets called "Jansenist" only by a very vague association. His view of man seems, and may well be, sombre, austere, stand-offish: too fastidious to be gregarious, maybe even reclusive. Especially compared to, say, Father Bing Crosby and Sister Ingrid Bergman in *The Bells of St. Mary's*.

However, it's not heretical to say, like Saint John of the Cross, "The soul cannot be possessed of the divine union, until it has divested itself of the love of created beings." For the devotional and the doctrinal may differ extensively (like experience and ideology).

Film culture too often treats movies as doctrinal, as "ideology," as general statements, even when they concern a very specific, individual, case. Generalizations may seem more important, more profound, than individual stories. But truth in films is often intimate, very modest. It may be "Two or three things I know about my kinds of Christian experience." It's not instruction in what to think, it's witness to how an artist thought. In understanding that art is often a particular experience, and not "a philosophy in case-history," Catholicism, even at its most dogmatic, is more liberal than much political correctness.

It's possible too that Bresson's films have doctrinal deviations. Many churchgoers, these days, hold quite odd opinions, without alarming their co-religionaries.

Nonetheless, some popular sloganizing—about democracy, "togetherness," sexuality—can make a certain Bressonian aloofness between people seem cold, unkind, or even wicked. And for Marxism, so influential in film culture, whatever isn't social is a form of alienation.

At any rate, it's worth brooding over something not unlike (though maybe different from) a "Jansenist" misanthropy in Bresson's films.

Christian Misanthropy

Protestant theologian Reinhold Niebuhr distinguished two kinds of Christian: "the children of light" and "the children of darkness." The first are affirmative about man; the second inclined to despair (nausea?). When Buñuel deals with religion, it's the "children of darkness," the abused or tormented ones, on whom he focuses (cf. *El, St. Simon of the Desert, Viridiana, Tristana*). Might Bresson take the same events, with many of the same dark experiences, yet put a different "inner drama" within them?

The nuns of *Les Anges du péché* (1943) have withdrawn from the world. But it's to achieve a closer community with one another. They sally forth to involve themselves with prostitutes, more aggressively and optimistically than respectable —and even worldly, cynical—people do. In a sense they're "private eyes," going down mean streets. They're detectives of, not crimes, but of innocence.

The very title, "Angels of Sin," has a hint of paradox. It intimates an indulgent picture of sinners as rather kindly really—good-hearted prostitutes, perhaps? But Bresson's strict pure nuns only venture amongst streetwalkers.[3] A Freudian interpretation might take the ambiguity as symptomatic: "Why would nuns seek out prostitutes? Surely to vicariously gratify their own unconscious, which they redeem by lovingly reforming one sinner after another . . ."

Or maybe their vocation is unconsciously lesbian—they're a "closed order" of women, saving other women from being sexual objects for men. Is *Les Anges* a Christian-Lesbian film?

Some Catholic psychoanalysts might allow such sexual possibilities, but only in specific cases, not as an automatic supposition. Whereas much film-culture Freud is amateur psychoanalysis, and addicted to film-cultural generalizations. "The religious choice of celibacy is usually (or always!) motivated by sexual repression."[4] But the same logic would propose: "Social workers are usually (or always!) motivated by sexual repression." And even "Freudian theorists are usually (or always!) motivated by sexual repression." Freudian theory, dogmatically applied, is more Jansenist than Jansen . . . (Is this another reason for Jansenism being so fashionable a reference?)

Amazing Grace, How Sweet It Sounds

Jansenism, in its milder, non-heretical forms, was less obsessed with weighing particular sins than one might expect. Indeed, "committing a sin" risked implying that apart from one's sin, one was innocent. Moreover, when God intervened, He tended to do so irresistibly. Hence, though one little sin was a sure sign of being damned "all through," sinfulness was less to do with a specific act which one committed than with a general state which one's whole soul was in. The difference between being one of the Damned or one of the Elect was a global, impalpable thing.

Catholic institutions—confession, the Sacraments, religious communities—made forgiveness of sins, therefore salvation, relatively available, obvious, physical. Puritans, lacking such institutions, found forgiveness harder to be sure of, and were more prone to feel crushed by their sins, like Christian in *The Pilgrim's Progress.* One might say that Calvinism was less severe, but more anxious; Jansenism was less anxious, but more severe.

Another difference: most Calvinists felt obliged to be "a monk in the world"; Jansenism was more easily contemplative, withdrawn, aloof from social engagement.

On all these counts, Bresson seems more Catholic than Calvinist. Though sins, and states of sins, are sensitively noted, his films are not obsessed with sins, particular or accumulating, as Calvinism so often was. The lyricism suggests guilt or grace imbuing the world, or welling up within from the soul, like "awareness dawning." There isn't the Calvinist emphasis on The Will. The moral tenor, though sombre, is calm, refined, patient. There's more confidence in some ultimate outcome.

Fatalism

Keith Reader compares the hero of *Un condamné* to "a broken spoon in the hands of God." Apt phrase. Fontaine is resigned to God, but not to man. In Fontaine's hands, the broken spoon works like a chisel, and a lever. His watching and waiting is active, not passive. He takes his chance from God, like a relay runner takes the baton, and runs with it. Active, passive—same difference. He doesn't wait for society to rescue him. (In 1943 society itself was a broken spoon—even more obviously than usual.) What he really trusts is, "Do the right thing," instinctively, without agonizing—a rare privilege.

Predestination

Determinisms, Jansenist or materialist, share a common problem. Since everything's predested, why try? Why not relax and enjoy moral rape by destiny?

Logical empiricism has one answer. However predetermined the future may be, nobody knows what the determination will turn out to have been. So we're condemned to think, feel and behave exactly as we would, were everything still to be decided. Christianity puts this in terms of Duty. As children used to sing, "He has no hands but our hands. . . ."

This applies within our own minds too. As practically every psychologist for two hundred years has insisted, we only know one-tenth of what goes on in them. So we don't always know what we're going to do, until we've done it. Moreover, we're still changing. That's what the present is: absence of closure. We're not our past, we're what we're becoming. Simply to discover what binds us is to become something else (as psychoanalysis promises). We remake ourselves as we go along, as a jazz player improvises on a theme. From the basic song, a stream of surprises.

That's nothing to get triumphalist about. Our "freedom" is very limited. Though it's not "illusory," in the usual sense, it does depend on the fact that nobody knows much: which should keep us humble. Often, our demand for "freedom," is really a demand for omnipotence. But maybe fate and freedom are, not the same thing exactly, but a package deal. As Sophocles' Oedipus says: "Our freedom lies in accepting our fate—in understanding it." Or, as Christianity says, more boringly, "Thy will be done."

Bresson catches a kind of indeterminacy between fatalism and freedom, active and passive. A kind of "letting go."

Body and Soul

Protestantism, being somewhat individualistic, emphasizes a person's will. Since true religion is somewhere in the mind, there's no point in mortifying the flesh. The body does what ideas tell it to. Protestantism is often austere, but it's rarely ascetic. Jansenism was more ascetic, and sometimes sought to mortify the flesh. In this respect, Bresson may be closer to a Protestant turn of mind. A touch Huguenot?

For Protestants, Communion bread and wine are only symbols of Jesus' body and blood. But for Catholics, they really, materially (though not sensorially) become Jesus' flesh and blood. Protestants watching Bresson's *Journal d'un curé de campagne* (1951) may overlook a paradox (clearer in the novel). The young priest's galloping stomach cancer means he can hardly eat, so, without realizing it, he's living on the sacramental bread and wine. But because he's on the wine, he's becoming an alcoholic.

That's real materialism.

A similar paradox inspires a much grosser Catholic film, *Le Défroque* (Leo Joannon, 1954). An ex-priest (Pierre Fresnay), now an aggressive atheist, is a real thorn in the side of Mother Church. Making fun of the faith, he consecrates a quantity of wine in a restaurant. But suddenly, he can't bear to see Christ's blood thrown away, so, he drinks it all himself. He feels drunk and ill. But, his faith is respect for material reality when that's imbued by *love*.

Matters Arising

Most religious films, for example Attenborough's *Shadowlands*, focus on a clearly definable issue, doctrinal or practical, such as The Problem of Evil, or grief as a reason to doubt God's existence. Bresson's films seem less concerned to argue a specific issue; they're not "religious problem" films, like "social problem" films. Though they involve many fascinating sins, and obstinate problems, their deeper thrust is a more global relationship, between "the material veil," and being imbued by Grace. Which man can't compel, or will, or possess, or demand. It's not property, nor is it a human right. Rather, "The quality of Mercy is not strained; it falleth like the gentle dew from Heaven." You're "surprised by joy." Infiltrated by calm.

Bresson's films are rarely stories about temptation or struggles with doubt or for "reasons to believe." They're more about subliminal resistance to, or discovery of, grace. The grossest sins aren't usually the deadliest. In *Les Anges*, for example, prostitution is a sin all right, but the deadliest danger is spiritual pride, such as the rebel nun may suffer from. In *Pickpocket*, Jeanne, through Michel's eyes (and ours) is a quietly, effortlessly erotic, not object, but presence. That's not his sin (nor is it ours, since Bresson is showing her in Michel's context). Sometimes eroticism = sexual love purified by soul, by unconditional responsibility (which is self-giving).

In Catholicism, the sexual act itself is not a sin, but sexual pleasure is. This puts sexual—erotic—thoughts in a rather peculiar position, somewhere in between. Often, sexual pleasure is treated as not a sin in itself, but as a sort of animal innocence, something to thank God for, like, say, winning the lottery, even though greed is a sin.

In Protestantism, sexual pleasure, in marriage, is not a sin: if it's not actually a grace from God, it was nonetheless instituted by God as a "consolation." Which makes eroticism, if it's responsible, "a gift from God." Is Bresson being a touch Protestant here?

Perhaps. Or just—a modern Catholic?

"O Jeanne," says the reformed pickpocket, "what strange paths I had to follow, to reach you." The form of words echoes a form of words about God (it's sexual idolatry). Through responsibility, Michel reaches Jeanne and God together.

When Godard uses Anne Wiazemsky in *La Chinoise*, it's to make Maoism look smart, sensitive, rich and sexy, that is classy, bourgeois.[5] When Bresson uses her (in *Au hasard Balthazar*), she's a sad and serious young woman concerned about a mere, funky animal.

Spiritual pride is especially dangerous, being disguised as, and often behaving like, real goodness. It may camouflage itself as shame ("How shameful to be no better than other people! To not have fulfilled one's enormous potential!"). Michel's often blank, furtive, lowered eyes look to me like pride masquerading as shame—the arrogance underlying moral masochism, a Freudian might say.

The problem is that morality does require self-respect, of which spiritual pride is perhaps a kind. Similarly, the same guilt may be healthy or morbid, depending on what other attitudes it is associated with.

Mouchette looks rather Jansenist, less in its gloomy view of French life (which is orthodox pessimism) than in its young heroine's fate. Obstinately rejecting one unworthy human relationship after another, her very purity drives her to something like suicide. Three times, she lets herself roll down a steep bank, towards deep water.

Suicide, proverbially, was the one unforgivable sin (despair in life was despair of God). Actual Christian judgements were more flexible, but nonetheless, suicides were, in principle, refused churchyard burial (hence the coroner's rider on suicide verdicts, "while the balance of mind was disturbed").

Yet the deliberateness of Mouchette's suicide is uncertain. Is she merely tempting fate? or tempting God? or giving the Devil a chance (never a good idea in Christianity)? Is it a sort of Russian roulette, less suicide exactly, than running the risk of it? They're all sins, no doubt, but maybe not mortal, if you reflect that "Between the stirrup and the ground,/ He mercy sought, and mercy found."

Moreover, topography in Bernanos can be intensely "spiritual." In *Sous le soleil de Satan*, another young innocent (Gérard Depardieu in Pialat's film) strays from his usual path at night and feels physically and mentally "lost" in a confusing "wave of earth," which gives him physical and spiritual vertigo.

Is Mouchette's "semi-suicide" the negative version of that? She abandons herself to topography—to vertigo, to fate? She hasn't found what she hardly knows she wants, and she fears she never will, but, she still won't settle for not having it. She rejects a soul-destroying future. In a sense that's despair, so she's damned; but in another sense, she's saving her "divine discontent." So perhaps her rejection of a "soul-destroying" future is the intention of saving her soul as best she knows? And maybe that intention is enough to save her—like "mercy sought"?

Is her seeming despair really a "Negative Theology"?

Why didn't God intervene, to save her from herself? I recall a photograph, widely sold as a picture postcard between the wars, and much studied by religious people. Called *L'Inconnue de la Seine*, it showed the profile of an unknown young woman, found drowned in Paris, and thought to be a suicide. Her face is as peaceful as an angel.

Maybe I'm too soft on suicide, as modern secular thought tends to be. But to me, Mouchette's end suggests a renunciation not of life, but of a wilfulness— of her own negativity. It's her "negation of the negation" (to borrow a phrase beloved of Hegelians and existentialists alike). She'd be a sort of Christian atheist, like, in a different way, Godard's Virgin in *Hail Mary*.

Bresson's films don't "tell us exactly what happened." They respect the mystery. He doesn't want authorial omniscience about his characters. Indeed, claiming to share God's omniscience, God's total and spiritual judgement, even about fictional characters, might seem presumptuous. (That was Sartre's complaint about Mauriac.)

This ambiguity may seem modernist, but never knowing who's damned or not is the traditional Christian position. Not only may virtuous pagans, like Plato, be saved, but so may honest atheists who actually heard The Word, and *still* rejected it. For they understood The Word semiotically, but, for whatever reason, they couldn't understand its full reference. They were victims of "invincible ignorance." In the same indulgent spirit, some Jesuits argue that, though Hell undoubtedly exists, maybe there's nobody in it.

Bresson offers us severity, fastidiousness, aloofness, yes, but also "Invincible Uncertainty." Not by dodging issues, but by not loading them one way or the other.

2. Bresson and Bazin:
Two Strains of Christian Realism?

———

Whenever I think of Bresson, I think of André Bazin, and vice versa. They're both French Catholics, of similar generations—born 1907 and 1918, respectively. (Bazin died forty years ago—poignantly, for he's the younger of the two, by eleven years). They're also both extremely visual, that is, sensitive to the material, physical world.

In a rare attempt to link film theory and religious theory, Bazin starts with the Holy Shroud of Turin.[6] His arguments might usefully be not repeated, but redeveloped, here, with Bresson's aesthetic in mind.

For Bazin, photography, when it's an art, is no mere "mechanical reproduction of the physical world." It's an interaction between three points in space: the photographer's mind, the scene before his camera, and the photographic negative inside the camera. In this "triangulation," both the photographer's mind and the physical scene before him, are links with God. For God created the photographer's soul, and God sustains the physical scene before him. Through photography, the divine in Man communes with the divine in Matter. The photographer, if he's an artist, and a seeker after Truth, contemplates God's being-in-the-material-world.

In this "Fallen" world, Man and Creation are *separated* from God. Photography, as contemplation, and potentially, religious art, depicts Creation as it is—fallen, damaged. Though sustained by God's presence, it shows also the ravages of God's "Absences." To which the neo-realist films Bazin loved are poignant testimony.

In this view, the essence of photography is *not* some coldly objective camera-eye scrutinizing its subject from a distance, in a mechanistic or voyeuristic way. But neither is the artist's subjectivity projected onto the outer world, in an anthropomorphic, fantasizing way. The photographer's vision serves to perceive real aspects of the external scene before him. This "communication" between reality and vision is the essence of "realism," whatever the medium. Photography—or, more exactly, the "photorealism" that concerned Bazin—is a loving interaction, an amorous anxiety, about Creation.

Forget Vertov's "kino-eye" and its pseudo-objectivism; the Shroud of Turin is the better paradigm. Supposed to have enwrapped Christ's body after the crucifixion, it preserved His image, thanks to some miraculous process, some unknown chemistry with the body it cherished.

The process resembled photography, in being a chemical process. Admittedly, photographs work with light, whereas the "shroudograph" process involves something else, some bodily exudation. The Shroud is, so to speak, a "sweato-graph." But both processes are "chemographic."

The Shroud might be called "sweat photography," much as we speak of heat-photography (even though heat is not light), and X-ray photography (even though X-rays aren't light either). Similarly, radar, and radio-telescopes, respond to material emanations/transmissions, which encounter a responsive medium. None of these processes is "passive"; they're re-active. Like the human senses: sight, heat-sensitivity, hearing, etc.

Another difference: the photographic camera is conspicuously distant from the scene, whereas the Shroud was wrapped around it. But if the image on the photographic negative arose from "action at a distance," it would be magic. What actually happens, is that the scene and the negative have touched—through the lens. Light rays that were in the scene have moved into the camera. A part of the scene has directly touched the negative. To be sure, this light was only part of the scene; and what usually interests us is not this light itself, but the surfaces that reflected, or emitted, it, and that, remaining in the scene, send only indirect traces to the negative.[7] Nonetheless, the action of light rays that were in the scene but move onto the photographic negative is—very literally—"photo-synthesis." And if plants do it, it's natural, *not* mechanical! Photography may be a "mechanical" process, but like all mechanical processes, it's a specialized application of a natural process. As usual, human artifice simply borrows from Creation.

The Shroud of Turin is actually a sort of "contact print," like a Man Ray "rayograph."[8]

Human seeing likewise depends on touching. Light, having bounced off a visible surface, touches the eye, and what's more, enters it. Then, by a further relay of other perceptual processes, some still mysterious, but all partly chemical, it "enlightens" the brain-mind. To see is to be touched—indeed, entered!—by light. As language attests: to "see" an idea is to "grasp" it; "to see" is to "understand" (which means in one sense: stand right beside). Seeing is nothing to do with voyeurism; it's feeling, exploring, finding out.

Nonetheless, realism is not reality (any more than a picture is what it's a picture of). And photorealism is limited to the visible surfaces of reality. (And less than that: for the camera sees only one particular angle, at one particular moment; that is to say, it sees from only one of 360x360x360 degrees spatially [without counting internal views of the subject], for only 1-n^{th} of a second, and it severs the scene from almost all its material (including causal) connections. Moreover, the whole visible world is only tiny fragments of material reality, nine-tenths of which is invisible (heat, energy, electromagnetism, etc.). Narrative itself is ninety-five percent invisible, since all we see are phenomena (events, actions, facial expressions, etc.) from which we deduce the connections which the very concept of "story" requires. It's because most of secular reality, including emotions, values, and the purposes people have in mind, are invisible most of the time, that the "invisibles" of religion give photorealism no special difficulty.

Visible reality, *tel quel*, makes not much sense by itself. Neither does photography, which needs a cameraman's mind to apply its knowledge of the world, to the world, at the same time as discovering new things about it. One might almost say: realism = discovery (a usual connotation of the term in art history).

Bazin's photorealism is *in-sight*ful. It doesn't just show already known truths about the world, at work *in* the world; it explores the world, enters it, embraces it, seeks to *enwrap* it, to see it "in the round," as The Shroud enwrapped Christ's bodily material. It enwraps so as to *show*. Despite its name, it doesn't shroud the truth; it shows a structure, "hidden within" the material. (Bazin, who though Christian wasn't puritanical, discusses at length another interesting case of enshroudment as display, of the invisible becoming unignorable. It's Jane Russell's bosom in *The Outlaw*.)

If photorealism can't exactly see reality's hidden, invisible aspects, its more abstract forces and relations, it can nonetheless trace them through patterns, illustrate them, as, for example, a pattern of iron filings makes visible the electromagnetic forces that arrange it.

Bazin's photorealism is thus a kind of "Christian realism" (odd term—like "Christian atheism"). It's a kind of transcendentalism. Not an "inspirationally optimistic" kind, such as looms large in popular worship ("All Things Bright and Beautiful," Pangloss, Emerson, etc.). Bazin's transcendentalism is affirmative, but not optimistic. He acknowledges the tragic (as neo-realism did). To that extent, Christian realism stayed closer to social realism than to metaphysical speculation. For Bazin, the material world is by and large a production by God; his Christian Socialism, like critical realism, notes failures of compassionate fraternity.

Thus Bazinian photorealism is Franciscan in spirit. "The world, the flesh, and the devil" don't have man helplessly in their grip. It leaves man a rather large margin of liberty. It's a congenial, fairly orthodox theology, in which God gave man liberty by a partial, local, withdrawal of Himself from the world; and then, when man chose Evil, and Creation "fell," a second withdrawal took place; nonetheless, enough of God remained everywhere, at least to keep a little divine spark alive in man, until Christ's sacrifice clinched it.

Crucial for Bazin is the compatibility of (a) realism and liberty (as distinct from, say, Zola's "social realism" which emphasized determinism), and (b) hope (therefore progress, reformism, etc.) and compassion (which acknowledges the normalcy of suffering).

The combination of realism and liberty helps explain the importance for Bazin of Wyler's deep-focus. He thought it left spectators freer than tight cutting, to choose for themselves what they wanted to look at. Thus American deep-focus was more democratic than montage, the Soviet, Leninist aesthetic, which minimizes the spectator's choices, in dictatorial fashion. Bazin's preference has a political dimension.[9]

Freedom apart, deep-focus respected certain continuities of reality: not just time-space, but the social co-presence of people; whereas montage was a chronic "fragmentation" of every relation. Deep-focus was one way of respecting continuities; neo-realists tended the same way, for De Sica and Rossellini made much use of steadily panning long-shots, through which the world is "continuously unrolled," and with much "free space"—clouds, street-perspectives, passers-by, of "other people."

"Shroudography" apart, Bazin's photorealist theory appeals to a phenomenological tradition, whereby reality is so extensively perceptible, that something rather noumenal can be, if not explored, then at least sensed, like Bergson's sense of a life-force . . . or Wordsworth's, of "something more deeply interfused" (or, as Bazin argued, Jane Russell's bosom in *The Outlaw*). Bazin's photorealism is another such "spiritual realism," so tender that it's practically Franciscan.

As is the neo-realism of De Sica and Rossellini (who devoted a film to Saint Francis and his "little flowers"). Saint Francis loved animals, and Bazin, it seems, loved strange pets, like snakes. I wouldn't be surprised if he *relished* the strange forms which the life-force, an aspect of God, comes up with, much as Blake loved the tiger, tiger, burning bright, Wordsworth loved daffodils dancing in the breeze, and Christopher Smart loved his cat, whose self-grooming he likened to an order of worship.[10] None of these things *prove* God; all of them help you imagine what he might be, through whichever aspect of reality catches your own imagination.

Bazinian photorealism adumbrates subsequent doctrines of *cinéma vérité*. But some differences are crucial. *Cinéma vérité* is a valuable addition to our repertoire. But *cinéma vérité* theories are *non-* or *anti*-Bazinian when they contrast *vérité* and artifice, truth and interference, and indulge obsessional doubt about selectivity, sometimes implying that truth requires a hands-off, know-nothing procedure.

Bazin never objected to artifice *as such*, and he championed Olivier's *Henry V*, whose medieval perspectives exploit, and exalt, painterly unrealism. (Bazin argued ingeniously that such unrealism is actually fidelity to the realities of another medium.) While admiring Wyler's deep-focus for not cutting, he makes no objection to all the times when Wyler does cut. He has little to say against the eye- and mind-jolting montage in *Citizen Kane*. He never forbids montage generally; he only wants to justify not cutting, as a positive choice, in certain circumstances, and to show that montage, far from bring the acme of film art, was often a bad habit.

He never criticizes the conspicuously "tight" set-ups and close-ups that make Bresson's *Journal d'un curé de campagne* visually dynamic, and give so many of its shots the look of a montage film. He much admired its extremely "artificial," and long-held shot of a conspicuously "abstract," and virtually non-diegetic, cross. Its "abstraction" is all the more striking, since the setting gave Bresson every opportunity for naturally realistic crosses, crucifixes, etc.

It's about this cross that Bazin wrote his much ridiculed sentence, "There is nothing more that the image has to communicate except by disappearing." This is indeed a negation of photorealism, and neo-realism alike. But, Bazin never said photo-realism was the only way to understand the world. He wanted its aesthetic qualities, its creative strategies, to be appreciated. Its relative "transparency" was not "failure to edit," not "naive realism," but an exploration, a showing-forth. It refrains, not from "artifice" generally, but from certain habits of artifice. Neo-realism and deep-focus were pragmatics, which generated a special syntheses of "photorealism" and "art(ifice)." The long-held cross in *Journal* is a "solo spot" for an instrument of artifice. It owes much of its power to its contrast with the different richness in the preceding shots. Its "un-photo-realism" draws on the rich photorealism preceding.

Every film director, if he's an auteur, establishes his own angle on reality. But his angle on it may also be an aspect of it. The "slice of life" he sees may be "subjective," in the sense that it's *now* in his mind. But it's not merely subjective, if it's also in the scene itself, objectively. Subjective and objective, auteurism and realism, aren't mutually exclusive.

Photorealism, like art generally, deploys two complementary processes. It puts the important things in and it keeps irrelevancies out. It's both "additive" and "subtractive." Often, "less is more"; but "less" must leave *enough*—just as the meaning of silence in music depends on the quality of the music. If the music is poor, the silence is empty. Moreover, minimalism and maximalism may co-operate. Neo-realism was maximalist in some respects (e.g. real locations, and their wealth of evidence, of meaning), and minimalist in others (dialogue, "eloquent" acting, etc.). Similarly, Bresson's aesthetic is terse (minimalist), but intense (maximalist).

Bresson's style has many neo-realist aspects, notably his remarkable sensitivity to locations, of which more anon. Neo-realist, too, is his treatment of his actors as "models," chosen for some "reality" which their appearance seems to *exude*—like "sweatography." Something "on the surface" also runs deep—like, say, a lifetime of habits, which have shaped body and soul alike. It's not necessarily the "reality" of the model himself, for it also involves what film forms do to his appearance, and how the film diegesis recontextualizes it. Often, though, I suspect, it's a part of the model's reality—an element, whose functioning in his real life depended on its combination with other traits, which Bresson's rigorously "subtractive" aesthetic keeps out. The model's appearance in the film isn't a description of him as a whole person; but, he has given the film something of himself, though "he didn't know he had it in him." The man who played the curé of Torcy in *Journal* was Bresson's psychoanalyst.[11] The "Englishman" in *Procès de Jeanne d'Arc* (1962) was a kindly and perceptive lecturer at the St Martin's School of Art, with whom I had the pleasure of sharing an office for some years. What Bresson saw in him, and brought out, so as to misuse, was a streak of hurt indignation, sensitively contained, yet volatile. In preventing his "models" from acting, and in not using the same model twice, Bresson is the strictest of the neo-realists (Rossellini used stars galore).

In 1951, when Bresson shot *Journal*, minimalism was avant-garde, not yet the routine it has since become. Most religious filmmakers, even that other purist, Dreyer, deployed heavy visual artillery to get their effects; Bresson sought to hear *only* "the still small voice." He found Dreyer's grand histrionics all too obvious. Though, come to think of it, Dreyer often chose his actors for some "character-atmospheric"; which no-one else could "see." (The casting of *Vampyr* is thoroughly "Bressonian," a major strength of a film which is more neo-realist than its fantastic elements may suggest.)[12] And wasn't Dreyer's severity towards Falconetti—keeping her kneeling for hours, talking her into a "state"—a psychosomatic, an "involuntary," level of feeling, of being—a different means to a Bressonian end—and, quite literally, "sweatography"?

Bresson is neo-realist also in his use of locations. In some ways, though, he's a neo-realist painter, rather than a photographer. Is this a radical difference, or one of method?

Photographers take pictures; painters make pictures. Bresson seems to use a half-and-half method. Like a painter, he seems to assemble "little scenes," from fragments. He constructs little conjunctions of reality, often very small (close-ups of hands turning keys in locks . . .). They can suggest "the hand of God"—something more local, more special, than Bazin's sense of "God as the ground of the canvas." For Bresson, God is less "widely" given; the world is more often an obstruction, a thick veil, and weighs upon us, like a lead-grey sky. Many materialistic details seem both ominous and stonily devoid of "meaning," spiritual or otherwise. Often, oppressiveness and emptiness coincide. Or a deadpan expression coincides with a *temps-mort*.[13] As a jazzman said of the "notes left out" by pianist Thelonious Monk: "It's like falling down an elevator shaft." Where Bazin inclined to "open-plan," Bresson tends to compositional "enclosure," further sectionalized by editing, and sometimes reminiscent of "grid-structures" in certain modern paintings. Bazin rarely treats images as abstractions. Bresson advises: "See your film as a combination of lines and of volumes in movement, apart from what it represents and signifies."[14]

As striking—and in a sense radical—as these differences are, the affinities are equally important. As different as photographic taking and painterly making may be, they can overlap. After all, movie sets are both constructed and photographed. If movie people usually talk about making pictures (not taking them), it's because the preparation and construction of scenes, and even the duration of the shot itself, are so often so gradual, so elaborate, so slow, as to be more like painterly "making-and-remaking" than "spot-and-snapshot" thinking. So finally, perhaps, painting versus photography is a matter of process, not spirit.

Bresson and Dreyer both favour hard, angular compositions. In Bresson they're veiled by grey-on-grey tonalities; Dreyer's figures are more volumetric, more sculptural. Dreyer carves out spaces; Bresson's spaces, though gaping when you look at them, are softened by grey-on-grey. Bresson likes "miniaturist" details, Dreyer is more partial to larger canvases. Both men are so painterly, that almost any frame-still looks powerful on the page. On the screen, Dreyer is the master of camera-movements, whereas Bresson's editing accumulates more quietly, steadily, intensely.

Stefan Sharff opened my eyes to the virtuosity of *Une femme douce* (1969) by applying what he called "the door test." (Doorways are spatially paradoxical: they join yet divide spaces, while making an action-space of their own). How a director manages doors, and moves his actors through them, is an excellent test of skill. *Une femme douce* is almost a "nest of doors," negotiated with virtuoso variety, which remains "subliminal" (*ars celare artem* . . .), while avoiding minimalism's main risks, weakness and monotony. (When Michel Ciment asked Bresson about the doors in *L'Argent*, he replied: "If I choose why can I not have ten times more doors in my films? Doors opening and closing are magnificent, the way they point to unsolved mysteries. What's wrong with doors? They have a music to them, a rhythm.")

Bresson's style is intensely formal, aesthetic, with its monotonal shades (grey-on-grey), its hard, locked compositions, its small, firm, arcs of movement. Eyes are lowered like quietly stubborn refusals (because we'd like to know the thoughts). A man's shoulders, head, direction of look, and the frame-edges, make a quietly tense set of angles. Shots are "diagonalized," not monotonously, with rigid ninety-degree zig-zags tilted all over the place, but diversely, more like Degas. During a street conversation, cars stream by in the depth of the shot like a barrier of blind cages. Many a shot is a "knot" of thrusts, angles, vectors.

Editing extends such effects throughout the films, and successive shots "snap" against each other, their strong compositions and minimal movements making "hard" cuts, even as softly contrasted grey tones soften them slightly. Whence a curious effect, as of "an iron hand within a velvet glove."[15]

If movement is film's "third dimension," editing (the succession of shots) is a fourth. A Bresson film as a whole is a sort of "serial painting," working on juxtaposition of images. But with a difference. Serial paintings are juxtaposition in space, with the images placed side by side. Film editing is juxtaposition in time, as a succession of shots replace one another in the same space. The succession is very different: more kinetic and more evanescent (for though the images are "juxtaposed," you don't see two at once). Sometimes Bresson's conjunctions suggest a kind of spiritual constructivism: conjunctions of details make—linkages . . . ? like Fate? Providence?

As with constructivism, however, form is relatively free of symbolism, even, perhaps, uncongenial to it. Symbolism involves a correspondence between a particular detail, and some other, usually deeper meaning. The one-for-one correspondence between the object (as signifier) and the concept (as signified) risks localizing the latter, restricting it to the qualities of the former—and abstracting it from the world as interactivity. Bresson keeps the symbol and the concept relatively close, even tautological: a key is liberty, a cell is imprisonment, etc. The concept is so close to the object that it collides with its obstinate materiality. This little steel shape in the palm of one's hand is "a lifetime of liberty." Object and concept repel each other, even as they're kept together. The spiritual can't pull away from the drama, nor even from the interaction of material details, which becomes a sub-drama, of a *chosiste* kind. The spiritual level ("higher" or "deeper," depending on which paradigm you fancy) is reached, not through inert, defined objects, but through interactions on material planes. Though the material leads to the spiritual, it can't be kicked away, like a ladder you've climbed up; the film is about sensing the higher meaning in relation to the whole of the lower action. Not as "part of it": there *is* a certain separation, a difference of levels. But there's a humility before the material—even if it's sometimes ambivalent.

Our vision shouldn't stop at the lower action; and there is a certain asceticism in Bresson, who is not, perhaps, Franciscan like Bazin. His materiality, his worldliness, have a severer, bleaker, more desolate feel. The material world is not unlike purgatory, perhaps: we go through it because we must. But we *must*.

Journal d'un curé de campagne has all the issues needed to make a solid, social realist drama, as was probably intended in an earlier adaptation of the Bernanos novel, by Bost and Aurenche. Bresson, without excluding, without simplifying, without de-realism-izing, that social drama, soft-pedals it, minimalizes it, leaving room for an emptiness, a sense of God withdrawn. God isn't symbolized: indeed, to symbolize Him would make him all too obviously "present." Instead, the drama as a whole, remains material (with elements like the curé's imploring eyes . . .). They express a complexity about God which no single symbol for Him could. A concept defined is a concept *idea*-lized; but a concept in the context of dramatic action is a concept *real*-ized. The word "God" is hopelessly general, ambiguous; but to find Him by embracing duty, cancer, and helping a handful of lost souls, makes Him less indefinite.

Several neo-realists—Rossellini, Fellini, De Sica—had Christian "tendencies," or at least interests. Are they also "Christian atheists"? Or "Christian nostalgics"? Are neo-realism and Christian realism two movements, which sometimes overlap, sometimes keep their distance? Is Christian realism too sectarian a term, for what might be called spiritual realism? What affinities might exist with poetic realism? Alongside such similarities, the distinguishing characteristic of spiritual realism might be the quasi-religious, faith, or hope, that the mind is not only the creator of certain values, which it then projects out there, but also the detector of something out there that gives our lives valid meanings, other than the self-centredness which various forms of materialism so easily encourage. Spirituality is not just fantasy: it's a linkage, of internal and external worlds.

Bresson's films might leave non-Christians cold, were it not for their evident stylishness, their unsentimentality, and, perhaps, for something else. Every mind (especially the atheistically inclined, like this writer's) feels, at some level or another, a host of mental pressures, too obscure and unfocused to qualify as thoughts, with names like "nagging anxiety," "restlessness," "unfocused anxiety," "terrible emptiness," "nameless dread." They're elusive yet brutal, like ghosts. Bresson's films resensitize us to such phenomena. Their dearth of the usual, secular labels and references, creates a "zone of alienation," in which, to our surprise, *even* God is *thinkable*. . . . From an agnostic's angle, they're studies in "alienation," like Antonioni's *L'Avventura*, and Resnais's *Last Year at Marienbad*.

They're surprisingly congenial to our ultra-sceptical era, in which even Marxism, once brashly materialistic, now genuflects to structuralist and post-structuralist theories whereby reality, internal and external, if it exists, is unknowable by us, since linguistic labelling makes us up. In such a void, *anything* can be asserted, even the hypothesis of God. Bresson's minimalism chimes in with that (post-modernist?) ambiguity, where belief in *nothing* allows belief in *anything*.[16] And Christian atheism makes God thinkable!

Bresson's style—both "realistic" and "artificial"—has its "poetic," its mental atmosphere. It's a "cloud of connotations," not unlike a belief-system (with all its sensed incoherences). It's apprehended, not just emotively (lyricism), nor as a "purely subjective entity" (like, say, God = Superego), nor as a series of propositions (philosophy), but as "a corner of nature [or, more exactly, *external* reality] seen through a temperament." In other words, "the workings of the world, as grasped through a frame of mind."

3. Bresson and the Times of His Time

Bresson's films mix traditional Christian attitudes with contemporary experiences, traditional ideas with new.

Realisms: Zola, Courbet, Bresson

As our comments on Bazin suggest, realism generally seeks a certain objectivity, but doesn't seek to abolish subjectivity. It's not purist; it's impurist.

That formidable realist, Zola, discussing another realist, Courbet, defined a work of art as "a corner of nature seen through a temperament." Zola was a Socialist and scientific realist, Courbet was an Impressionist one, or at least labelled as such.[17] Both were intensely moralistic, pessimistic, and rather *noir*, and both were emphatic realists, yet also visionaries: their emphasis on material detail gives material a force, a tendency, a spirituality (usually dark, oppressive). Bazin's theory of photography is likewise "material," and realistic, and though the force, the tendency, is more affirmative, here too "the real is spiritual." The same is true as Bresson, insofar as his use of photography is painterly (and gloomily lyrical).

Though Christian art and expressionism are both concerned with soul-states, Christian art tends rather to realism: since the world is created by God, it's imbued with His spirit, not distorted by it. The world belongs, not to one's own feelings, but to God, and therefore to all men, to one's neighbours, and, in art, to "the people in the picture."

Compared to expressionism, most realisms, Christian or humanist, seek a calmer balance of observation and empathy. Van Gogh is one of the exceptions, but has his calmer moments, as John Berger emphasized. A Bressonian mood, of enigmatic anguish, is, perhaps, as near to expressionism as a realism can get. But Bresson's affinities with Bazin put him, I think, on the realist side of the fence.

Between expressionism and realism, Impressionism occupies a special niche. It's clearly "a corner of nature seen through a temperament." But where expressionism upfronts empathy, Impressionism upfronts perception, and its sensorily more delicate operations. Expressionism suits a certain German temperament (soulful, philosophical, aggressive, generalizing, impatient with particularities). Impressionism is more congenial to a French delicacy of perception: as in Impressionist (and Cubist) painting, in "stream of consciousness" in literature, in analytical phenomonology (Bergson, Merleau-Ponty), and in many 1920s' avant-garde movies. Their scenarios, or optical effects depict, not so much "deep soul-and-world states," like Caligarism, as the finer, more fleeting, mercurial details of perception, or memory, or consciousness, of the mind within re-presenting the world around.[18]

In these Impressionist styles, the flaws in the glass distort the scene, and yet we know enough about scenes to see the distortion—and to deduce the presence of a glass. This interest in the external, material world as interpreted by an internal, mental one, implies a sort of "contested primacy." Which Bresson often achieves, as his dark lyricism fights it out with a kind of *chosisme*—"the object *tel quel.*" Is Bresson a kind of post-Impressionist using photography, not just for convenience, but because it's congenial to his vision; its grey tones, its sharp angles, its successive angles in time evoke cubism, but focused not on a single object but on the shot as a fragment of a jigsaw puzzle. Only God sees the big picture.

For some purposes, humans must sharply distinguish internal subjectivity from external objectivity. For other purposes, we need to remind ourselves that they usually work together. Subjectivity *proposes*, objectivity *disposes*. But subjectivity does much of the reconnaissance.

As Sartre observed, thought is always thought about *something*—"pure thought" is unthinkable. After all, thought itself crosses that great divide, between mind and matter. The brain is internal matter, the physical sensations in the nerves are already thoughts, that is, mind.

The 1930s: Bresson and René Clair

Bresson's first film, *Les Affaires publiques* (1934), is often likened to Clair's satires, notably *Le Dernier milliardaire* (1934), and Bresson worked on Clair's never filmed 1939 project *L'Air pur.* Clair fused an avant-gardist delicacy of perception, a tender-hearted poetic realism and a satirical pessimism. His visual style emphasizes "the spaces between people": little figures in long shot, panes of glass silencing them, plot mistimings (a wryly comic dada-cubism). It's easy to believe the report that Clair's depressive tendencies required a long retreat in a Benedictine monastery. As guest, not monk, I hasten to add, but still, nearer Bresson territory than categories like "comic" and "religious" might suggest.

The 1940s: Bresson and the Vichy Régime

An exodus of established directors followed the fall of France in 1940, opening the studios to a "New Wave" of directors. Many, notably Cocteau, Clément, Clouzot, and Bresson inclined to sombre, claustrophobic withdrawals from a bleak world.

Bresson's first two features, *Les Anges du péché* (1943) and *Les Dames du Bois de Boulogne* (1945), are classic examples of this mood. So cold, austere, *withdrawn* did they seem, that when export markets reopened, and even Clouzot's scandalously *noir Le Corbeau* (1943) found foreign distribution, Bresson's films did not. MGM bought *Les Anges*, but not to show it, only to remake it—just imagine, say, Ingrid Bergman and Lana Turner in the leads . . .

Though *Les Anges* is not *specifically* Pétainist, Pétainism would strongly approve of its "corps of nuns," a tight, socio-moral order, almost a militia, dedicated to rescuing "fallen women," fitting symbols for a fallen France, doomed by its immoralities. The heroine's disobedience of her religious superiors is not subversive, since she's faithful to their common ethos, which has made her what she is. Saints as rebels as renewers are well understood in Christian tradition; and we can all understand rebel/authority adversariality as simultaneously co-operative—especially when God oversees the Grand Design. Catholicism, unlike Leninism, allows a plurality of party lines. *Les Dames*, though shot during the Liberation, may have been an earlier project. That its "fallen woman" finds redemption in a decent marriage would not offend French Catholic attitudes towards sexuality, but simultaneously challenge and deepen them.

These affinities with Vichy moralism, though worth noting, aren't the whole story, and don't "deconstruct" Bresson's films, whose moral appeal is much wider. The scenarist of *Les Anges* was playwright Jean Giraudoux, now best known for *The Madwoman of Chaillot*. Neither fascist nor weakling, he was Propaganda Minister when France declared war, and approved the slogan, "We will win, because we are the strongest." As propaganda goes, it was a good try. It was (a) true (as far as equipment and resources went), (b) aggressively unsentimental, and (c) avoided French disunity. Properly virile stuff.

Les Dames was written by Jean Cocteau. In the guise of a society drama and a "woman's film," it focuses on several of his obsessions. Maria Casarès is a dominant female, possessive/destructive, a Mother/Death figure, as recurrent in Cocteau (not Bresson).

Both films are "soul-fights," primarily between women, which should interest feminists, especially those who suspect that feminine authority and power function much like masculine authority and power. For Christians like Bresson, are sex and gender spiritual categories, or only secular ones? Is the soul itself sexed or gendered—or only the body? Christianity wavers between both tendencies.

Meanwhile, in this world which we think we know, Bresson's women are as forceful as his men.

In *Les Anges* a cat and a caretaker are agents of chaos, or malice, even, perhaps, of the devil. The association, I think, is poetical, not typical. It's not that Bresson associates cats, or males, or working-class males, with wickedness. Rather, cats have a purely poetical association with loners, with selfish malice. (And with witches: so is this cat the "Original Sin" which the nuns have almost, but not quite, eliminated from themselves?) As for the caretaker, his was a famously grouchy, misanthropic profession in every country.

Bresson and Neo-Realism (cont.)

The style of *Les Anges* and *Les Dames* is relentlessly precise, and as studio-bound as Carné's poetic realism, with its exquisite haze of lights. Bresson's third feature, *Journal d'un curé de campagne*, moves into neo-realism, with barer lighting, and a surprising sensitivity to locations. No doubt technical progress has been a factor here.

Bresson once said that every shot should correspond to something seen in his mind's eye. This might seem to require the total control of studio conditions. According to reports, however, Bresson could improvise very quickly. Perhaps his eye could soon find, wherever it looked, some Bressonian detail—rather as cubists can see *everything* as cubes.

Improvisation would have been facilitated by his eye for a few small inert objects or details, or relatively small areas, or of simple configurations, like a grey face against grey sky, or, easier still, grey wall. These "little" scenes could be swiftly set up, leaving space, time and budget enough to satisfy his multiple-take perfectionism. *Une femme douce* was reputedly shot in interiors which, though re-dressed, were not even re-lit; yet it's as immaculately Bressonian as *Un condamné à mort s'est échappé* (1956) where studio artifice was used. Using "models," not professional actors (let alone stars), might cut a budget by two-thirds.

It's sometimes assumed that, since religion is an illusion, neo-realism, and other social realisms, can't take religious experience seriously. Nonetheless, religious experience is a psychosocial reality, and neo-realism was rather sympathetic to it. Rossellini explored it—sceptically in *The Miracle*, lyrically in *The Little Flowers of St. Francis*, anti-moralistically in *The Machine That Killed Evildoers*, and dramatically in *Stromboli*, which, as a "conversion experience," is a "Bressonian" subject, interpreted very differently. De Sica's *Miracle in Milan* mixes neo-realism and fantasy in a style whose reminiscences of René Clair might throw some light on the problems of *Les Affaires publiques*. Whether Rossellini's *Miracle* is Christian or anti-Christian is a moot point, but either way French Catholic critics welcomed its essentially Franciscan sensibility. Christian nostalgias are evident in Fellini too, from *La Strada* to *La Dolce Vita*, while the *Fellini-Satyricon* depicts a search for spiritual purity through a social sprawl not unlike some neo-realist narratives. As for Pasolini's *The Gospel According to St. Matthew*. . . .

If neo-realism implies a sense of social networks, *Journal* is ambiguously neo-realist and pointedly aloof from it. On one hand, the village is a community of sorts; its village priest is a social functionary; his parishioners, harsh, secretive loners, personify a much criticized aspect of "la France profonde." On the other hand, each soul makes its own decision, rather than some "communal experience" uniting them, for good or ill. They are and they aren't a society.

Here again, Bresson's ambiguity reflects Christian orthodoxy, as it tries to keep a balance between opposite tendencies, both of which are necessary. One "opposition" is Christian fraternity versus selfish aloofness. The other is worldly sociability versus Christian interiority. But often in Bresson, isolation from God and isolation from others go together. Such is the intensity of solitude, that fraternity seems more discovered, or earned, or achieved, than "natural." And yet, a Christian pessimism about other people remains. Salvation may sometimes require some "act of solidarity" with one's neighbour—but won't come through it, or him, if he's as wicked as oneself, which he very likely is.

This view is more severe, more puritanical, than a "dominant" modern view, which equates religion with "love of others," with a general idea that togetherness is next to Godliness, and with its political corollary, the Social Gospel. Doesn't Christianity entail a sombre, maybe despairing, view of, not just "bourgeois society," but of all possible human societies?

Bresson and Post-War Uncertainties

One might expect Bresson and his contemporaries, as a wartime "New Wave," to share a generational style. Yet Bresson seems closer to three directors who start a few years later, and remain, like him, slightly apart from mainstream cinema.

Bresson, Tati, Melville, and Franju are four poets of solitude.

To bracket Bresson's *Journal* with Tati's *Jour de Fête* is a bit eccentric, no doubt. Yet, both mix neo-realism with high-intensity auteurial style; curé and postman are "inspired loners," in rural "everyday life," which is seen as stagnant. In *Journal*, "la France profonde" is a spiritual mire. Tati adores its spiritual contentment. (His comic style, too, brings us back to René Clair.) Tati and Bresson's musical use of sound and silence, and their critiques of modernity, different in tone but similarly embodied in their visual treatment of machinery and mechanisms, also suggest an affinity.

In Bresson's *Journal*, Nicole Ladmiral, as the deeply troubled girl, links us with Franju's documentary, *Le Sang des bêtes* (1949). She speaks the film's voice-over, and her calmly desolate voice is an "exudation" of her spirit, for, soon after *Journal*, she committed suicide. Though Franju was a hard-line atheist, his version of *Thérèse Desqueyroux*, after Mauriac's religious novel, fits the curé's "world-mood." (How alike, too, are the barrenly beautiful landscapes of *Journal* and *Thérèse Desqueyroux*, the latter shot on Mauriac's estate.) And Franju's *Judex* is a childlike dream, with angels . . .

Melville is another "cat who walks by himself"—in a world of outsiders. His protagonists are more criminal than religious, but the two men can swap subjects. It's Melville who makes *Léon Morin, prêtre*, and Bresson *Pickpocket*. Many critics have called Melville's style, particularly in such films as *Le Samourai*, Bressonian in its austerity, ritualized gesture, visual formalism, its abstract use of sound and silence, and its non-expressive acting. Melville, bridling at the suggestion that his style was influenced by Bresson, claimed it was the other way around: "Look at *Journal d'un curé de campagne*," he said, "and you will see that it's Melville. . . . [It's] *Le Silence de la mer!*"

Though Bresson's *Journal* is often praised for fidelity to the novel by Georges Bernanos, it strikes me as, not a close translation, but an "opposite equivalent"— reaching the same destination by an entirely different route. The "home key" of Bresson's style is cool, quiet, often "immobilist"; Bernanos's prose describes turbulent energies, verging, at times, on a tormented transcendentalism. Pialat approximates it more closely in his adaptation of another Bernanos novel, *Sous le soleil de Satan*, where vast, lowering landscapes, like latent tidal waves, frame the Devil's attack on a man's soul, which includes confusing his sense of simple, physical space. Bernanos's descriptions, which are even more expressive than his narrative, carry an (expressionist?) metaphysic. Mind and Matter are two states of the same energy, restless, turbulent. The Devil looms large, but in unexpected forms: he's never the snake over your shoulder, whispering "Enjoy . . . ," but rather an energy of negation, like an avalanche, tearing aside Creation (which is constructive Order—a higher state of Energy). An agnostic might say that Bernanos describes the experience of libido—the energy of hatred—pure, motiveless, oceanic—better than any Freudian literature (which is too rational to "let itself go").

In *Journal*, it's true, Bernanos's style is dryer, more curt, than usual, as if taking its cue from the curé's simplicity. But still, Bernanos is all about irresistible forces; Bresson, about immoveable objects. Bernanos feels in terms of country muscularity, energetic as a ploughman's; Bresson's thought is urbane, like fine calligraphy. His quick suave mind quickly finds final positions, of whose sophistication only his quiet finesse reminds us. But it's not soft: its quiet aloofness is also a dreadful obstinacy. When his characters are tempted to damn themselves, it's less through worldly selfishness, or some obvious "deadly sin" (lust, covetousness, etc.), than for some spiritual sin, sometimes deceptively close to saintliness, like some quiet core of resistance to everything except itself. Evil, in Bresson, is a force of inertia, dark, icy, static.

The curé experiences a rare moment of worldly exhilaration, while riding pillion with a soldier of the Foreign Legion, who has perceived the curé's strength of soul. This would certainly have appealed to Vichy, which sought consolation for defeat in its empire overseas. But here, too, "deconstruction" must tread warily. Colonialism was still the norm throughout the non-Communist left. (Not all Communists, and very few Socialists, were anti-colonialists.) The right was just as diverse. Bernanos, though Catholic and a royalist, was militantly anti-Franco, and a Foreign Legion general. As for Christianity itself being dominated by "ideology," a currently popular dogma in film culture, Christian Socialists would have something to say about that.

The Foreign Legion detail was not ideologically or economically determined, nor *Beau Geste*-type pulp, but Christian respect for the "hard" virtues, as well as the "soft" ones preferred by Christian sentimentality. The "hard" virtues—courage, initiative, determination, stoicism, self-discipline—are a perennial problem in Christian ethics, for they look more like "power," and very wicked people may possess them. Much Christian preaching discusses the "soft" virtues exclusively, thus reinforcing Christianity's reputation as a "femininizing" and "bourgeois" religion. But some Christian theories attribute even "amoral virtues" to God, like, for example, William Blake's "Tyger! Tyger! burning bright," whose "fearful symmetry" is energy and a dangerous order.

The "Foreign Legion" virtues impose in Bresson's next film, *Un condamné à mort s'est échappé* (1956). Here they serve a cause universally approved, the French Resistance. The film's consensual aspects, and obvious suspense, put Bresson back on the map commercially. It evokes Becker's *Le Trou* (1960), whose escapees are all criminals, and improvise a kind of "anarcho-solidarity" with some strict moral aspects.

Bresson's subtitle, *Le Vent souffle où il veut* ("The wind bloweth where it listeth") establishes the religious theme, and avoids any "equalization" of the moral and amoral virtues.

Nonetheless, its protagonist, Fontaine is another criminal, or, at least, "outlaw." This was significant since the Vichy government, which bowed to the Germans, was impeccably legal and constitutional, and, given the complicated circumstances, might have had a democratic majority, even as late as the film's action (1943). Strictly speaking the Resistance were "terrorists." However, Fontaine is more a prisoner of the Gestapo than of the French authorities—which may well be a crucial difference.

Christianity, even when law-abiding, is in a sense an "outlaw" code, for its inner, other-worldly, purposes are beyond the ken of "the law," or "Caesar," or "the body politic," or even "social justice." *Un condamné* contemplates the surprisingly difficult problem of fraternity, a fine-sounding, but actually quite elusive attitude. It's as highly ambiguous as "brotherly love," "loving one's neighbour," "social responsibility," "solidarity"—and "limited co-operation," for "enlightened self-interest." It's often very intense, while it lasts, and yet contingent on some common purpose, like being in the same boat or the same prison. With Bresson, perhaps, its principal motive is more some inner moral drive, than affection for the others. It is, or becomes, more than "Survival": Fontaine seems driven less by fear than by duty.

The film emphasizes "fraternity at a distance," "fraternity through stone walls." Fontaine responds to a knocking sound through a cell wall—a human presence verging on abstraction. He exchanges moral support with a Protestant pastor (a gracious touch in 1956, when official Roman Catholicism was still hard-line about heresy). He helps a depressed, inarticulate, old peasant. He trusts a young fascist militia-man. Thus he "transgresses" cultural "walls."

And yet, it seems to me, the contacts are more like commitments than personal encounters. Moral support comes from human spirituality, rather than human personality.

One might of course argue that the impersonality, of *Un condamné* comes not from Bresson, but from the story, which was based on André Devigny's autobiography, and which allows only "minimalist" relations. In asserting, even here, a force that is like fraternity, even if it isn't that exactly, is Bresson asserting a kind of "Resistance humanism"?

But from another angle, did Bresson choose the situation, as a metaphor for the human predicament more generally? Is that prison this world, and confinement in a cell like being in the body? Is *Un condamné*, with its ambiguities of aloofness and dependence, of contingent fraternity and "inner duty," all we should hope for?

Bresson and *Cahiers du cinéma*

Bresson's Christianity was highly congenial to *Cahiers*—to Bazin, obviously, but also to Bazin's "children," who became the French New Wave. *Cahiers* in the 1950s had strong religious tendencies. Chabrol and Rohmer discerned in Hitchcock a strictly Christian moral metaphysic (and *The Wrong Man* does have some near-Bressonian aspects—for example, "Christian realism," questions of passivity versus providence). Jean Douchet read Hitchcock differently, but also in a deeply spiritual (gnostic?) sense. Truffaut's attack on *le cinéma de papa* zeroes in on Aurenche and Bost, condemning especially their moral disrespectfulness. Chabrol's attack on "big, important subjects," as inferior to "little, personal" ones, effectively downgraded the "social consciousness" demanded by liberals and socialists alike. Chabrol's *Le Beau serge*, breakthrough film of the *Cahiers* set, is overtly

Catholic, à la Mauriac. Rohmer's *Ma nuit chez Maud* revolves around Pascal's Jansenism, and his *Perceval le Gallois* has affinities, as well as differences, with *Lancelot du Lac*.

Moreover, Bresson's films are auteurial in every way. Their fusion of auteurial style with neo-realism exactly anticipates Truffaut's analysis of the New Wave as Lumière (realism) + Delluc (formalism as subjective vision). *Hiroshima mon amour* (Resnais, Duras) is Bressonian in its purity, its solitude, its craving for suffering as rebirth, the suavity of its style. Several films by Louis Malle—*Lacombe, Lucien*, *Le Feu follet*—share with *Mouchette* a quiet despair about the impossible confusions between integrity and hopeless obstinacy. Not that Malle's is a "religious" spirit, but, on the worldly level, he and Bresson share a certain pessimism, about worldliness and its spiritual emptiness. Bresson's *Les Dames* describes mondanity very exactly.

Bresson and the Advanced Mainstream

Un condamné looms large in Gilles Jacob's *Le Cinéma moderne* (1964), for its *secular* interest. Its solitary protagonists, trapped in a spiritually empty world, prefigure the "cinema of alienation"—*L'Avventura, Last Year at Marienbad*; Fellini and Bergman re-introduce God in "negative" form in *La Dolce Vita* and *The Silence*. You don't have to be Christian for Bresson to hit a nerve; you only have to understand *Waiting for God(ot)* . . .

Formally too, as Jacob points out, Bresson was first to *melt* narrative into a succession of moments, to fragment a storyline into short swift chunks, like a narrative jigsaw, to dissolve cause and effect into enigmatic pressures. Another instance of "reactionary," not progressive, ideas driving modernism (e.g. Marinetti, Joyce, Pound, Eliot).

Bresson and The New Hollywood

Paul Schrader, whose book *Transcendental Style in Film* shows a deep understanding of Bresson, borrowed aspects of his style, but imbued them with a whiff of sulphur.

Schrader and Scorsese's Taxi Driver is a Bressonian hero—of a "diabolical" kind. His spiritual mission is warped and twisted, his cage-like taxi-cab and mean room are Bressonian "cells," his "training diet" (actually junk food) a loony asceticism, his vigilante crusade a sort of one-man Foreign Legionism. All the same, doesn't his despair strike a chord in our spirit? Hasn't his bungled suicide a touch of soldierly selflessness? When, "all passion spent," he reverts to normal—or nearly—

he's sane enough to be a touch uneasy about being thought a hero. Which makes him, in a way, more lucid, more *realistic*, than society.

We may even wonder if his hatred of vice is a kind of negative virtue. To be sure, it's vicious, demented, and "diabolized" by his own frustrations, but then, "Nobody's perfect," as Joe E. Lewis once memorably pointed out. Is his behaviour more O.T.T. than the Wrath of God in some Old Testament passages? But then again—is hatred, even of vice, the Devil's form of virtue?

Taxi Driver combines (a) virtues meriting damnation, and (b) a "righteous cynicism" about this world, where all activity is more or less corrupt (pleasure, politics, direct action). These attitudes, unusual in religious films, are heavily emphasized in strict Calvinism (Schrader's religious background) and in Jansenism (of which Bresson is often accused).

Schrader's "Hollywood" aspects can distract attention from his protagonists' inwardness. The parade of glossy shirts in Schrader's *American Gigolo* (1980) infuriated me, but there's a (modest) precedent in *Pickpocket*. The drug dealer of his *Light Sleeper* (1991) diligently keeps a journal, like the country priest. It's part of his spiritual effort, ordering his thoughts, a modern, cooler version of a "soul-fight,"as Puritans might have called it.

Some recent films have asserted "the new pessimism" more prettily. The elegantly spiteful socio-sexual intrigue of *Dangerous Liaisons* (Frears 1989) and *Valmont* (Forman 1992) evokes Bresson's *Les Dames*. Indeed, the original stories are culturally related. The Bresson occurs in Diderot's *Jacques le fataliste* (*circa* 1784); the others are based on Laclos's *Les Liaisons dangereuses* (1782). All express the dark underside of The Age of Reason (like the Marquis de Sade).

Bresson and Recent Avant-Gardes

Godard's *Hail Mary* (1985) could be his version of a Bresson heroine. She's half-Joan of Arc, half-Mouchette—and a projection of Godard himself, of course. He had fetishized on Old Father Marx; she fetishizes on Jesus her Son. Godard admires, mocks, envies, her subjective belief in a virgin birth—an old Christian miracle—and her fierce indifference to Scientific Truth. Thus naive Christianity chimes in with post-modernist relativism. She insists on faith *in her own flesh*; she doesn't generalize. Bresson rarely generalizes, and when he does it's to assert Christianity's Uncertainty Principle: "The wind bloweth where it listeth." He's more severe, and purer, than Godard in what he rejects, and mellower in affirming less.

Is "Christian atheism" a post-modernist religion?

4. From the Death of God to the Death of Man

Bresson's style, minimalist yet intense, reflects his sense of God.

Christian doctrine forever hesitates between two tendencies. One is to describe God and everything about Him as fully and definitely as possible. The other fully accepts the unknowability of His nature, and His *modus operandi* ("The wind bloweth where it listeth"). The first tendency might be called "positive" (or "maximalist," since it's maximally discursive). The second is "negative" (or "minimalist," since it seeks to assert only *just enough* for intense communion).

"Official" Christianities tend to "accentuate the positive," sometimes becoming logico-legalistic. Usually however, they defer, if only in the end, to God's mysteriousness. "Negative" theologies, though equally traditional, tend to be less assertive, conceptually at least. Protestantism, and *a fortiori* Puritanism, were "minimalist" in their rejection of elaborate ceremonies and baroque metaphysics. Pietism and Quakerism sought to hear the "inner voice" *alone.*

I thought of naming this section "Bresson and the Cloud of Unknowing," after the fourteenth-century devotional text, whose "agnostic" title summarizes its love of "conceptless communion" with God. But its "God-shaped cloud" is joyful, mystical, very unlike Bresson's, drier, more guarded, more material, mysticism.

Modern materialism has encouraged Christian minimalism. The less Christianity asserts about the fine detail of God's operations, the less vulnerable it is to logical empiricism, cultural relativism, and other "modern" (eighteenth-century) ideas. Some modernist theologians long ago took scepticism on board, and sought to de-mythologize, de-historicize, de-tribalize God. Rather as lizards sacrifice their tails to save their vital organs.

Often enough, "negative theology" dispenses with God as a reality, except as an idea, a yearning, "a God-shaped hole" in our mind. *Honest to God* (1963) by Anglican Bishop John Robinson expounds "South Bank Christianity"—not the first, but the most accessible, version of "radical minimalism." Here, the very *yearning* for God is a sort of *functional equivalent* of Him. It's stripped of His material powers, of miracles, etc., yet *sufficient* at least for enlightened souls. We're not so much *obeying* a God Who Is, as *giving Him our being.* Another kind of self-sacrifice.

In Jungian terms, the idea of God belongs with "Oceanic Experiences" in which all mental boundaries dissolve, in an exquisite sense of unity. In Lacanian terms, God belongs with The Other—a mental structure that irrationally but powerfully unites The Imaginary and The Symbolic, the Self, other people, and the external world.

For Christians, the self and the outside world are mystically "equalized." God loves us, but not more than He loves everybody else, even our enemies. To really love God (as distinct from asking him to do us special favours) is to renounce any priority in His eyes, to see ourselves as He does, understandingly but ruthlessly, impartially, objectively.

"Negative" theology may evoke Zen Buddhism, often described as an atheistic religion. But Christianity is essentially vitalist, whereas Zen seeks liberation, not only from consciousness, but from life itself.

Is *Au hasard Balthazar* (1966) a meditation on "Christian vitalism" versus "Buddhist-like" nihilism? It contemplates, without clearly answering, a perennial Christian problem: animal versus spiritual. Do animals have souls? Or are they only objects for our use, like plants and stones? Is Balthazar the animal in us? Or is he rather like us—mind with purpose but no meaning? Are donkeys to us as we are to the angels? "I always hoped there'd be dogs," says David Niven in *A Matter of Life and Death*, seeing a black dog in Heaven. Will Balthazar's young mistress meet him in Heaven? Is Bresson's film his dourer, darker version of Franciscanism? Of Rossellini's Saint Francis film?

Maximalism often makes Evil a furiously energetic force, all sex, horns, and libido, like Mr. Hyde. Minimalism inclines to a quieter, more intellectual tradition in which Evil is the *absence* of God. God is the Creation and Preservation of Structures; Evil is their degradation. Evil is Entropy, God is Information. In Bernanos, Satan is Entropy plus Hate.

When God destroys things, or lets them be destroyed—the curé by cancer, Saint Joan by fire—it's so they can serve some higher purpose (or "reintegrate their highest self into a higher structure"). It's because God is this terrifying, though creative, tension, that it's so difficult to *assert* anything about him. Often, the only attitude is acceptance—resignation—"Mother Mary says to me: Let it be." Whether or not the curé's cancer is in itself evil, destructive, entropic, it's "Nearer My God to Thee."

Since less assertion means less dissension, minimalisms rather favour ecumenical tendencies. Bresson's work is "ecumenical," not by being blandly non-committal, but in the sense of depending on few, if any, ideas to which Protestant viewers would strongly object. They might well disagree with his Catholic specificities, like the curé's belief in transubstantiation, but they wouldn't want to take issue with them. They're well used by now to "making allowances" for doctrinal differences, and treating other beliefs as other roads to Heaven.

It's hard to say when Bresson *respects* a belief, and when he *holds* it. He deeply respects very simple, very conventional, fundamentalist, maybe very "narrow" faiths, like the country curé's, or Joan of Arc's. Her trial, in his film, is a sort of "Pilgrim's Progress," starting with a "naive" faith, a mixture of crusading assertion (maximalist?) and doctrinal innocence (minimalism?), and finding a more interior, shattered, yet noble, one (an ultimate minimalism?). Which parallels the "inner drama" of the Crucifixion: God abandons His Son.

Artists in the maximalist tradition often favour conversion stories: the lost sheep finds God, specifically, in a face-to-face kind of way, or helped by obvious miracles. Minimalisms often incline to redemption stories, whose protagonists "find God" under some human alias, or in a moral rebirth, which might seem, to them, only secular. Michel the Pickpocket finds Responsibility, Fontaine finds Freedom. Are Responsibility and Freedom mutually exclusive? Well, God is opposite things to opposite souls.

Maximalist artists often favour Big Strong Events, with obvious "oppositions." When Bresson's stories involve such things, as religion often must, he treats them in minimalizing fashion, as if to equalize, or prioritize subtler, more interior issues. The freedom into which Fontaine escapes is almost as dark as the prison itself; it's Fog, Night, and The City (a dangerous, maybe wicked, place); and, to continue in the Resistance is to live in fear still. Bresson's version of *St. Joan* forgoes Dreyer's sense of her animal fear of burning. His characters seem not so much to save or damn themselves, as to find, or fumble, their chance of Grace. Does Bresson believe in an afterlife? Probably, but his films are more about minimalist knowing down here, than earning points for up there. Does he believe in Hell? With flames, or just remorse? His films don't say for sure.

Minimalism about such things may or may not be sceptical. Many quite simple, straightforward Christians take their articles of faith as metaphors, for they-don't-know-what. "Something like that sort of thing, in a way, if you know what I mean." That's not just inarticulacy; often it's authentic vagueness, a profound minimalism.

Bresson's films concern not "reasons to believe," but rather "the experience of belief." And not "*all* experiences of belief," just the two or three kinds that he happens to know about. After all, we don't expect love stories to prove the existence of love, or generalize about all loves. They simply increase our overall understanding of Love, by modestly describing some, possibly unusual, or narrow, kind of it.

Richard Attenborough's *Shadowlands* is a love, and a religious, story, of the maximalist kind. It concentrates on Big Problems, in strong, four-square, terms (senseless physical pain, faith-destroying grief). Bresson is more oblique; often, it seems, his characters don't know what's troubling them; their real problem is not some "issue," but obliqueness to God.

5. From the Death of Man to the Death of Reality

Before Bernanos's novel came Bresson's way, a screen adaptation of *Journal* had been prepared by Jean Aurenche and Pierre Bost, the writing team denounced in Truffaut's swingeing attack on much French cinema. A & B had a steady, if somewhat hostile, interest in religion (A had belonged to André Breton's Surrealist group, B was of Protestant stock).[19] Truffaut loathed both their disrespect for his kind of morality and their adaptational method, which, if sometimes too methodical, was nonetheless intelligent. Mainstream movies being a primarily dramatic form, as novels are not, A & B would invent new dramatic scenes, partly to paraphrase points implied by the novel in non-narrative ways (descriptive asides, prose style, etc.), partly in a spirit of loving infidelity (after having respected the novel's main substance, they would "link" it to their bitter-sweet vision of the world).

They were dramatic maximalists. To describe a character's Christianity, they'd go into detail about his whole secular world—his social background, its moral codes, his personal psychology, his personal moral code, etc. It's a pre-modernist, realist procedure (but still mainstream, still effective. Long after the New Wave was spent, Bertrand Tavernier commissioned scripts from Aurenche-Bost).

Bresson adopted the opposite strategy, an anti-dramatic minimalism. He gives just enough secular circumstance to "ground" a religious experience—seen as inexplicable. The *super*-natural seems everywhere and nowhere, intense, but elusive.

Surprisingly perhaps, this brings Bresson close, in certain ways, to existentialism. Its anti-humanist, atheistic, and Communist strains have attracted much attention, but its development owed much to Christian thinkers—Dostoevsky (twice filmed by Bresson), Kierkegaard, Gabriel Marcel (Bresson's co-religionary and older contemporary [1889-1973]).

Existentialisms contrasted with essentialisms, in which man is dominated by some particular, built-in "essence," whether a soul (as in Christianity) or "human nature" (as in humanism), or a set of instinct and drives (Freud). In existentialism, man is shaped or profoundly reshaped, by his experience in the world, with all its accidents, which make him, and life, meaningless. Man must make his own morality, in the teeth of the Absurd.

Existentialism is so diverse, it's probably better to speak of existentialisms, in the plural. But they all, atheist, or Christian, or a little of each (like "Christian atheist"?), share the long spiritual crisis which followed "the death of God," (the nineteenth-century loss of faith), and led straight into "the death of Man" (a sceptical relativism, depriving him of soul, essence, of intrinsic meaning). It was sharpened, for French thinkers, by all the moral and spiritual problems of defeat in 1940 and four years of Resistance. *Un condamné*—a Resistance subject, ambiguously Christian and secular—has an existentialist feel, as does *Procès de Jeanne d'Arc* (1962), another Occupation/Resistance story.

Existentialism didn't actually *inspire* the spirit of the French Resistance (which developed from thoroughly traditional motives). But their historical association was reinforced by a certain congeniality. The Resistance had to improvise, discover, construct itself as it went along—in the teeth of some potent moral principles ("human life is sacred," "no one should take the law into his own hands," etc.).[20]

Un condamné has the Resistance feel. It's not "pure" existentialism, but the affinities provoke reflection, along with the differences.

Existentialist. Fontaine is faced with "choices" which no rationality can resolve. He's locked into extreme humility, in a brutally material world (concrete, sounds, a broken spoon). He's caught between intense solitude and a dangerous solidarity (for treachery is always possible). The solidarity between people isn't "love," Freudian, Christian, or sentimental.[21] It's respect, born from a succession of swift reciprocal judgements, as to moral character. There's no dependence on a "special" person, only solidarity, not traded, but freely exchanged, for a "common meaning." The freedom Fontaine attains has an existentialist *angst*: fog, night, duty . . .

Essentialist. Fontaine brings his own specific "authenticity" into the prison with him. His survival instinct is very alert, very sensitive, very intelligent (about simple things). It's almost like "low selfishness," yet it's also a compulsion, a sacred duty, unthinking obedience to a "categorical imperative." It's not so much conscience as a duty that comes naturally. He doesn't seem driven by fear of pain or death, and he's quite ready to kill a weary German sentry whose squeaky bike has a kind of pathos (à la Tati?).

Does Fontaine's escape mark him as a special person, a moral hero? Does he in some way deserve, or at least elicit, God's grace? Then why should Fontaine's cellmate, a fascist militiaman, also qualify for escape? God moves in mysterious, apparently unjust ways.

Thus, the existentialist response to the Absurd; "negative" theology and absurdism have an affinity: a kind of moral stoicism.

Oddly enough, it's Sartre the atheist who explores the afterlife, as if searching for "rewards" and results. In *Les Jeux sont faits* (directed by A & B's collaborator, Jean Delannoy, 1948), life after death offers two lovers a second chance, which they flunk (because foreknowledge isn't freedom, though they do a little good before dying again). *Huis clos* (Jacqueline Audry, 1954), with four ill-suited people locked together for eternity, is Sartre's classic statement that "Hell Is Other People."

Cocteau's *Orphée* (1950) is another "afterlife" fantasy, by an agnostic, with much play on Resistance imagery (underground tribunals, etc.) and, a final touch of existentialist *nausée*. An angel, contemplating the reunited lovers, remarks, "They had to be put back in their mud."

Meanwhile, Bresson's Christian films remain realistic, materialistic, earthbound![22]

From an essentialist angle, Bresson's films are about the near-impossibility of distinguishing soul from psychology, and happenstance from Providence. From an existentialist angle, they're about finding freedom within contingency, and meaning despite the Absurdity of everything, even moral feeling.

Gabriel Marcel often concentrates on "I-Thou" dialogue. In Bresson, such exchanges, though not insincere, are "minimalist." Michel the Pickpocket accepts "other people" (one or two) and "God" (it seems) together. Mouchette rejects everybody and "God" (perhaps) together . Little or no explanation of feelings goes on. It's radically unlike American "togetherness."

In *Pickpocket*, Michel's hand slides into pockets, almost mechanically, his eyes blank. Cunningly veiled intention? Inauthenticity? Conditioning by habit? Might pickpocketing symbolize an all-round kind of bad faith: are we all pickpockets, sidling around one another, slyly stealing one another's ideas? After all, if "Property is theft" then so is theft.

Some critics suspect a bisexual subtext. The thief's hands, slyly gliding into purses and pockets, would be sexual gropings. His victims are not "authority figures" exactly, but people "authorized," by having money, to have socio-sexual "standing." Michel feels deprived (castrated), so he's castrating his victims in turn.

It's always possible (most Freudian speculations are),[23] but so is something else. Consider a comic parallel: Harpo Marx sneakily hikes his thigh over other people's hands, usually in the vicinity of their thighs and belly. It's a sort of reverse-pickpocketing; he gives them something more intimate than they know what to do with. If, as Freudians like to do, we assume a precise sexual analogy; then he's sneaking his cock up on them.

Is that what we "unconsciously" read? Or do we, rather, read an infantile solicitation of physical contact which, being as yet undifferentiated sexually, isn't "bi" or even sexual? Is thieving really about relating to "other people" generally—in a spirit more "global," i.e. more existential? From this angle, Harpo is propositioning people, not with his leg as a phallic symbol, but as an infantile demand for indulgent attention. Like a hug. When is a hug unconsciously sexual—and when is it a sensory metaphor for something existential?

Michel's kleptomania is socio-moral. It's about feeling socially excluded, but actually being socially *self*-excluded. Pickpocketing is a palliative, which exacerbates his disease, estranging him ever further from reciprocity with "the others." Imprisonment seems to help him, as if relieving his debt to society (or other people). Similarly, psychoanalysts consider payment for treatment, however nominal, a constituent of their patient's personal dignity. To sexual attraction Michel responds *responsibly*. *Pickpocket* involves sexuality, but it's about reciprocity, on which an existentialist analysis, unlike a Freudian analysis, would focus. It would also concentrate on the morality of the ongoing behaviour as the key to self-analysis. If sexual overtones are there, which is possible, the moral components of the sexual might matter more than the sexual components of the moral. As Sartre implies in *Saint Genet* (1954), analyzing a criminal's moral, sexual, and socially masochistic deviations in terms of "bad faith." Sartre (half-ironically) calls Genet a saint, for his ruthless rejection of "bourgeois" hypocrisy, which Sartre thinks was the real, though hidden, executioner.

Pickpocket might almost be Bresson's Christian retort to all that. When Michel goes straight, he starts to fly right. Not because "conventional values are best after all." Nor because "in bourgeois society, bourgeois-type honesty pays off." Nor even because "Thou shalt not steal." But rather because not stealing is accepting responsibility, accepting reciprocity, enlarging oneself by accepting the subjectivity of other people. Other people are no longer "Hell." They're subjectivities like one's own—but different. [24]

Earlier, Michel rattled off a Dostoevskian psychological analysis of himself. Many critics take it literally, but maybe it's "bad faith." He has read the books, knows what's plausible, what induces sympathy, what's perversely grand.

Mostly, though, his introspection is not like that. He doesn't look within himself for something corresponding to some accepted explanation or judgement. Rather, he seems to listen to himself, almost like listening out for some quiet prompt.

From time to time, we hear a brief, spare, burst of music, as if to celebrate an achievement, an indefinable realization. Is it Bresson's non-diegetic comment, or does it also express a psychic tremor in Michel's mind, nameless, convincing?

We often find our thoughts surprisingly elusive. We often surmise our motives, from the books we've read, or from other knowledge about ourselves. Or our motives and associations may be clumped together, indistinguishably. Thoughts often strike us, like a physical jolt, but we're not so sure what the specific message is. Or we feel a broad splash of emotion, plus a mish-mash of half-ideas, as a whole network of associations fires off. Or a mood poleaxes us, for no reason we're aware of. Massive affect, no "thought."

This applies even to the so-called conscious mind. Its "stream of consciousness" is typically chaotic, irrational, even absurd. So much so that ninety-five percent of the time we ignore it for a much narrower kind of "conscious" thought— the "systematic" thinking that follows the decision, or attempt, to think about something. Such thinking is usually rational, in a very loose sense, but it's rarely tightly logical. It's a fairly directed use of some of our consciousness. Insofar as it's learned, it's artificial, but it's not unnatural.

It's as if not much conscious thinking needs to reach consciousness. Not because it's Unconscious in the Freudian sense. It's not repressed, or uninhibited, or not about reality. It can work quite rationally and efficiently, and often, trying to become conscious of its operations, messes it up completely.

Even our Freudian Unconscious itself hoves into consciousness, routinely, rationally, and usefully. Quite apart from Freudian slips, many conscious wishes, many "good vibrations," are the Unconscious speaking. It never speaks, but it purrs. Or it thunders. Just like all those "non-repressed" feelings we sense, but can't speak.

If Freud shifted attention to the Unconscious, Sartre shifted it back to the conscious.

Isn't our sense of self more "seismographic" than education teaches us? Do we present to ourselves more as mood and style than as statement? Is music more like how the mind works, than are words?

Here, as often, existentialism and phenomenology go together—with Merleau-Ponty as a sort of "middle term" between Sartre and Bazin.

Phenomenology of the Spirit

Phenomenology fits a long French tradition of rational introspection. It runs from Descartes's "I think therefore I am" to the Symbolist movement in poetry, which loved to juggle with the subtlest traces of thoughts. It surfaces in the French flair for Impressionism, which, as "a corner of nature seen through a temperament," is also "subtle realities of perception, projeted upon a corner of nature." When you look at a Cézanne, you *see* perception working. Impressionism's literary counterpart is stream of consciousness. They both extend realism from the external, material world to the internal, mental world.

Proust is perhaps the great symbolist realist. His photographic memory "enwraps" an entire social stratum, an entire life-history. *À la recherche du temps perdu* is his "Shroud of Turin"!

For other Symbolists—Mallarmé, Huysmans—poetic and religious contemplation had much in common. Bresson's concern, that his photopaintings be true to the visions in his mind, might be an application of Symbolist fastidiousness.

Symbolist introversion infuriated Bernanos, who thought such absorption in one's own thoughts, such self-indulgent self-reflexivity, verged on self-worship, that is, Satanic Pride. Sartre's dictum, that "thought is always about *something else*," and his insistence that imagination is always poorer than reality, likewise deplore Symbolist retreats to private mental realms and ivory towers. But then again are such analyses of "bad faith," though put to socially moralizing use, somewhat Symbolist in their very finesse? And, fascinating as that finesse is, is it always convincing? Are his condemnations of rebellious minds—Baudelaire, Flaubert, Genet—another way of "playing God"?

His studies of these great loners are intricately analytical, as Bresson's visual explorations of secret, aloof minds cannot be. Bresson's thought, like his medium, film, is a hybrid—part painterly, part-performance, part-literary. It's more a synthesizing than an analyzing form, more presentational than explanatory. Yet, his formalist photorealism asserts a spiritual plane, a kind of Suprematism.

He intimates his meaning much as painters, photographers, or musicians do: in forms, patterns, traces, ways of seeing, here mixed with the richnesses of film—acting, story, a few words . . . The world of Sartre is thoroughly minced by language; Bresson's worlds are ruled by silence, by brief bursts of music, most enigmatic (and moving) of the arts.

After Existentialism

Existentialism was a heroic, but a very vulnerable, "realism." Its two-decade hegemony over Paris fashions was ended by linguistic-based structuralisms. They assumed that linguistic forms structured everything—mental, moral, sexual, interpersonal, social, and material. After "the death of God," and "the death of Man," came "the death of reality." Language is all.

In a rich essay on Bresson, Keith Reader links a key scene in *Journal* with Jacques Lacan's insistence on verbal language. The dying priest's diary fills the screen, while his voice overlaid repeats the words left by the nib: a "linguistic" world has supplanted the visual-physical world.

Yet much of the physical world remains. For this voice, its textures and intonations, are very expressively physical (though *non*-linguistic). Voice is not language: it's a vibration of the body (just as the expression of the face is a *non*-linguistic physicality). It's "vocography," like "sweatography." It's "audiorealism" like "photorealism." It's Bazinian cinema.

The curé's handwriting, with its childlike diligence, and even the page itself, a simple schoolbook, have a minimalist force. Handwriting, too, is graphic, not verbal. For unlike words, which are arbitrary signs, calligraphy is indexical of, and analogical with, the physical movements which the hand performed. It's a muscular kinetic. It's expressive like dance. Insofar as it's expressive of the mind behind the hand—it's abstract expressionist.

Calli*graphy* is a *graphic* art—like *graphic* design, like pho*tography*. It has nothing in common with verbal language, except meaning.

The "little details" of voice and writing are by no means marginal to the words which the curé writes. The words are correct, bland, inexpressive. It's the "little details" that make them eloquent—by reference, context, expressive form.

The words don't explain the film; the film explains the words.

Lacan's enthronement of the word entails a blank denial of the pictorial and the graphic:

Unless we are to deny the very essence of psychoanalysis, we must make use of language as our guide through the study of the so-called pre-verbal structures. Freud has shown us and taught that symptoms speak in words, that, like dreams, they are constructed in phrases and sentences . . . in an article of 1927, Freud introduced us to the study of the fetish by indicating that it has to be deciphered . . . like a symptom or a message. He tells us even in what language it has to be deciphered. This way of presenting the problem is not without significance. From the beginning, such an approach places the problem explicitly in the realm of the search for meaning in language rather than in that of vague analogies in the visual field. (Such as, for example, hollow forms recalling the vagina, furs the pubic hairs, etc.) . . . The problem is not one of repressed affects; the affect in itself tells us nothing. The problem concerns the denegation of an idea. With this denegation, we find ourselves in the realm of significance, the only area where the key word "displacement" has significance. A fundamental province of human reality, the realm of the imaginary . . . Language is thus the symbolic activity par excellence: all theories of language based on a confusion between the word and its referent overlook this essential dimension. Does not Humpty Dumpty remind Alice that he is master of the word, if not of its referent?[25]

To Lacan's Humpty Dumpty logic, what might Bresson reply?

Perhaps: "Ten properties of a subject, according to Leonardo: light and dark, colour and substance, form and position, distance and nearness, movement and stillness."

And: "Your film must resemble what you see on shutting your eyes."

Whatever Lacan seems to think, the psychoanalysis of visual structures is solidly established in mainstream psychoanalysis: Freud on Leonardo, Adrian Stokes, Anton Ehrenzweig, for example. (Intriguingly, Lacan's denegation of the visual would abolish not only vaginal symbolism, but phallic symbols also!)

Throughout his work, Lacan effectively substitutes for "other people" The Other, a socio-linguistic conglomerate within oneself. Just as those structuralisms that "abolish the subject" also abolish "other people," as subjects existing for themselves.

Nonetheless, Reader's *rapprochement* of Bresson and Lacan is wonderfully perceptive. If only in one respect, Bresson and Lacan, like Rosie O'Grady and the Colonel's Lady, are "sisters under the skin." The skin of Bresson is painterly, that of Lacan, verbocratic. Both establish a distance, an aloofness, from "the others." Slightly like scrutinizing them through a third party (God, The Other). Or through a camera obscura. Rather as the brain surgeon-cum-psychologist surveys the villagers in *A Matter of Life and Death* (another film about loneliness and Heaven). There's not much touching in Bresson—not many hugs. . . .

The distance from "other people" of Bresson's protagonists, and perhaps of Bresson himself, is not arrogant, not judgemental. It's delicate, fastidious. It's akin to existentialist *noir*. Friendship certainly exists, but it's highly selective. Some might think such selectivity elitist, or alienated. Or is it simply sensitive?

Alienation from other people—in Antonioni, as in Marx—is usually involuntary; like neurosis, it's an illness. In Bresson it's deliberate and selective. It's a protection from errors. Like negative theology, negative psychology. Purity, by itself, seems and perhaps is somewhat "negative."[26] It's reluctant to say too much, as Bresson thought Dreyer's actors said too much (and as A & B's religious adaptations certainly did).

Another, "lower" kind of negativity, is culturally conspicuous today. It's an unselective, destructive, rejection of any adult reality. Both kinds, inextricably entangled, inspire a range of artistic phenomena: minimalism, the new novel (a.k.a. the anti-novel), Negative Dialectics, Writing Degree Zero. And, of course, films of absence (Bergman's *The Silence*, Antonioni's *L'Eclisse*) and of inauthenticity (Tarkovsky's *Solaris*). Robbe-Grillet describes the world as "traces" with no, or only derisory, meaning—like a negation of Bazinian "Truth." The very title of Samuel Beckett's *Waiting for Godot* implies a "negative theology." As does Bresson's title, *Le Diable probablement*. Don't those words evoke those moods in which one thinks: "Does God rule the word?—"No, the devil, more probably . . ."

Bresson's modernist affinities risk making him seem less "Christian" than he is, or was. Often, minimalism = purity + intensity. *Journal* ends on a note of "Tout est grâce . . ." ("All is Grace—Even the cancer which is killing me"). It implies: "I've given up trying to *define* Grace, as this but not that . . ."

6. Christendom's Last Stand

One might divide Bresson's spiritual journey into three phases:

1. Up to and including *Pickpocket*, the drama is substantially interpersonal.
2. Thereafter, it seems to become more intrapersonal, more "agnostic." *Au hasard Balthazar* is an audacious conception (a meditation on "the animal Creation"—including Man as dumb animal, as beast of burden), though it seems to split awkwardly between Balthazar's story and the human story.
3. *Lancelot du Lac* (1974) is eerily materialistic. After a battle, suits of armour lie about, evoking the smashed bodies inside them, but they're only smashed metal. Scrap metal. Junk heaps. No ghosts in these machines.

The knights get ambushed in deep forest, by men like jungle guerillas. I thought of Viet Cong tactics, defeating first the French Foreign Legion, then "the West." Will this be The Decline of the West? the Fall of Christendom? Which, although unworthy, had at least a vision of Christ?[27]

Notes

1. Most such movements have many forms, degrees, and syntheses with other movements; a certain schematization is unavoidable, and fair enough.
2. For more detail on such knotty questions, from an atheist point of view, cf. *Thou Art Peter: A History of Roman Catholic Doctrine and Practice*, Watts & Co., London, 1950.

3. Wim Wenders' *Wings of Desire* is another "angel" film whose equivocal title suggests sexual ecstasy; but it's actually about purity. Bresson is less of a loner than one might think. Some Christian films, like *Journal* (Bresson), *Ordet* (Dreyer), *The Gospel According to St. Matthew* (Pasolini), *The Last Temptation of Christ* (Scorsese), *Shadowlands* (R. Attenborough), *The Apostle* (Duvall) stay close to traditional concepts of the Christian God. Others, like Bresson's *Balthazar* (if I've understood it aright), *Teorema* (Pasolini), and *Wings of Desire* (Wenders) sustain a kind of "post-Christian" nostalgia, for—a God shaped McGuffin, as Hitchcock might say.

4. Similar assumptions would yield, for instance, "Child-care workers are usually unconscious paedophiles." But all such generalizations are too sweeping. A feminist-existentialist might retort that "generalizing about the unconscious desires of nuns makes them objects of sexual reductionism."

5. Oddly enough, Wiazemsky is the granddaughter of François Mauriac, the dour Catholic novelist, who came off worst in a famous controversy with Sartre. A Mauriac novel stated that its protagonist, after dying, went to Hell. "Authorial omniscience" pushed as far as this infuriated Sartre: "God is not a novelist, and neither is Monsieur Mauriac."

6. André Bazin, "Ontologie de l'Image Photographique" (1945), in *Qu'est-ce que le cinéma? I; Ontologie et Langage,* Éditions du Cerf, Paris, 1958.

7. I wouldn't accept that "indexicality" is a major factor in "illusionism." "Indexicality" is a process of production; "illusionism" centres on the perception of the forms themselves.

8. In semiotic jargon, it's *both* an indexical sign (a trace) *and* an analogic one (a picture). Moreover, it's a direct trace (unlike *indirect* traces, like, say, cigarette-ash). And it's richly descriptive (unlike, say, a footprint, which is a *direct trace* but a picture so limited to the foot, that we couldn't call it a picture of a man).

9. Bazin's "anti-Leninism" was not, as some Leninist critics have assumed, "reactionary." His Catholicism was solidly left-wing, as Chris Marker, his co-editor on *L'Esprit*, later turned Marxist, attests.

10. Wordsworth is usually classified as a "romantic," but, as the preface to the *Lyrical Ballads* declares, Coleridge wrote the "fantastical" poems, and Wordsworth the "realistic" ones, which depicted poor simple souls in their social and physical *materiality,* in verse whose simplicity sought a kind of "transparency." This realism being heavily social, and programmatic in intent, Wordsworth qualifies as a "proto neo-realist," a "proto-Zavattini" (less effective, alas, than in other fields). Here, for a while at least, realism and romanticism developed together; it's late Victorian realism which decided to *contrast* them.

11. I'd be most interested to learn what analytical school he adhered to; was it, perhaps, the Jungian-cum-Christian school of the journal *Psyché,* influential in Catholic circles around this time?

12. Bazin, in praising realism, never denounced artifice. Nor did neo-realism. Neo-realist fantasies include Rossellini's *The Machine Which Killed Evildoers* (1948). De Sica and Zavattini made *Miracle in Milan* (1951) to demonstrate that neo-realism and fantasy were compatible. Pasolini synthesized neo-realism and "spirituality" (doubtless more pagan than Christian).

13. A *temps-mort* ("dead moment") is a moment of trivial or no dramatic significance; often, the characters' minds are a "blank."

14. Bresson's distinction between "representation" and "significance" implies a rather careful theory.

15. Stefan Sharff's *The Elements of Cinema: Toward a Theory of Cinesthetic Impact* (Columbia University Press, 1982) has some brief but brilliant comments on the synergy of Bresson's editing.

16. Cf. Paul Feyerabend, *Against Method: Outline of an Anarchistic Theory of Knowledge*, NLB, London, 1975.

17. They're actually Socialist Realists, a term pre-empted, alas, by Stalinist idealism.

18. The affinities of basic film forms and cubism are well explored in Wylie Sypher's magisterial *Rococo to Cubism in Art and Literature: Transformations in Style, in Art and Literature from the 18th to the 20th Century*, Vintage Books, New York, 1960.

19. A & B's "religious" adaptations were *La Symphonie pastorale* (1946) and *Dieu a besoin des hommes* (1950) (both directed by Jean Delannoy, reportedly another Protestant whose chilly style sometimes reminds me of David Lean's), and *L'Auberge rouge* (1951), directed by the scandalously anti-clerical Claude Autant-Lara, a particular target of *Cahiers du cinéma*.

20. Fascist existentialism is an intellectual possibility. Nietzsche, Heidegger, Ernst Junger, and some justifications of terrorism, might exemplify it, and Sartre's defences of Stalinism and Maoism arguably involved a fascism of means (if not ends).

21. Cf. "Existentialism," in Charles Rycroft, *A Critical Dictionary of Psychoanalysis*, Nelson, London, 1968.

22. One Sartre-based film is very earthbound, however. It's *Les Orgueilleux* (1956), co-written by Aurenche and Communist pessimist Yves Allégret.

23. Freudians often forget that possibility isn't probability, let alone uncertainty. "If I've worked out how it *might* be true, I've demonstrated that it *is* true," a logical fallacy very popular among "theorists."

24. The Ten Commandments are *not* about loving one's neighbour. They're about *respecting* him. As regards loving man, they're a "negative theology."

25. Jacques Lacan and Vladimir Granoff: *Fetishism: The Symbolic, The Imaginary and the Real,* in Sandor Lorand & Michael Balint, *Perversions: Psychodynamics and Therapy*, Gramercy-Random House, London, 1966, pp. 266-9.

26. André Green, *Le Travail du négatif*, Les Editions du Minuit, Paris, 1993, especially Chapter 1, "Pour introduire le négatif en psychoanalyse."

27. The King Arthur theme often implies the Fall of a Christian order. Hence six thoughtful films with Holy Grail imagery: *Lancelot du Lac* [1974], *Monty Python and the Holy Grail* [Gilliam and Jones 1975], *Perceval le Gallois* [Rohmer 1978], *Apocalypse Now* [Coppola, 1979], *Excalibur* [Boorman, 1981], *The Fisher King* [Gilliam, 1991].

Au hasard Balthazar

The Question

Interview by Jean-Luc Godard
and Michel Delahaye

F OR THOSE OF US who had the privilege of seeing *Au hasard Balthazar* some
weeks ago, there is no doubt that we witnessed one of the most significant
events of the cinema, astoundingly meaningful both in its own right and as
a fusion of themes from previous Bresson films. Therefore we asked Jean-Luc
Godard and Michel Delahaye to meet Robert Bresson. The following interview
is one of the longest we have ever published, and the most significant statement
by Bresson himself up to now. In future issues, we will continue our criticism of
Au hasard Balthazar, an extraordinary film, with other instruments of investigation, among them, a round-table discussion. *Eds. Cahiers du cinéma*

JEAN-LUC GODARD: I have the impression that this film, *Balthazar,* reflects something that goes back a long time, something you had been thinking about for
fifteen years, perhaps, and to which all the films that you made then were
tending. That is why one has the impression of finding again in *Balthazar* all
your other films. In fact: it was your other films that prefigured this, as if they
were fragments of it.

ROBERT BRESSON: I had been thinking about it for a long time, but without
working on it. That is to say that I worked on it by fits, and it was very hard. I
wearied myself at it rather quickly. It was hard, too, from the point of view of
composition. For I did not want to make a film of sketches, but I wanted, too,
for the donkey to pass through a certain number of human groups—which
represent the vices of humanity. So it was necessary that these human groups
overlap one another.

It was necessary, too—given that the life of a donkey is a very even life, very serene—to find a movement, a dramatic rise. So it was necessary to find a character who would be parallel to the donkey, and who would have that movement; who would give the film that dramatic rise that was necessary for it. It was just then that I thought of a girl. Of the lost girl. Or rather—of the girl who loses herself.

GODARD: In choosing that character, were you thinking of characters from your other films? Because, seeing Balthazar today, one has the impression that that character has lived in your films, that it has passed through them all. I mean that, with it, one meets, too, the pickpocket, and Chantal . . . Consequently your film seems the most complete of all. It is the total film. In itself, and in relation to you. Have you that feeling?

BRESSON: I did not have that feeling in making the film, but I believe that I have been thinking about it for ten or twelve years. Not in a continuous way. There were periods of calm, of complete non-thought, that might last two or three years. I took it up, that film, dropped it, took it up again. . . . At times, I found it too difficult, and I thought that I would never do it. So you are right to think that I had been reflecting on it for a long time. And it may be that one finds again in it what was, or what was to be, in other films. It seems to me that it is also the freest film that I have made, the one into which I have put the most of myself.

You know—it is so difficult, ordinarily, to put something of oneself into a film that must be accepted by a producer. But I believe that it is good, that it is even indispensable, that the films we make partake of our experience. I mean, that they not be works of *mise en scène*.

At least what people call *mise en scène*, and which is the execution of a *plan* (and I mean *plan* in both its senses, a shot and a project). So a film must not be the mere execution of a *plan*, even of a *plan* that is your own, and still less that of a *plan* that would be another person's.

GODARD: Would you have the impression that your other films were more films of *mise en scène*? As for me, I do not have that impression.

BRESSON: That is not what I meant. But, for example, when I took as ground of departure the *Journal d'un curé de campagne*, which is a book by Bernanos, or that narrative of Commandant Devigny that is the basis of *Un condamné à mort s'est échappé*, I took a story that was not by me, that was accepted by a producer, and into which I tried my best to put myself.

Note well that I do not think it a very serious matter to start from an idea that is not by you, but, in the case of *Balthazar*, it is possible that the fact of starting from a personal idea, on which I had already worked a great deal in thought, even before the work that I had to do on paper, it is possible that that fact is responsible for the impression that you had—and which pleases me very much—to know that I have truly put myself into this film, still more than in my other films.

GODARD: I met you once during the shooting, and you said to me, "It is very difficult; I am more or less in the process of improvising." What did you mean by that?

BRESSON: For me, improvisation is at the base of creation in cinema. But it is true
also that, for a work so complicated, it is necessary to have a base, a solid base.
For one to be able to modify a thing, it is necessary that, at the start, that thing
be very clear and very strong.

Because if there has not been, not only a very clear vision of things, but
also a writing on paper, one risks getting lost in it. One risks getting lost in that
labyrinth of extremely complex *données*. On the contrary, one feels all the
more freedom toward the very foundation of the film because one has compelled oneself to encircle that foundation and to build it firmly.

GODARD: To take an example: I have the impression that the scene of the sheep
who are dying, at the end, was one of the things that was more improvised than
the others. Perhaps at the start you had thought of only three or four sheep?

BRESSON: That is true as to the improvisation, but not as to the number. For
there, in fact, I had thought of three or four thousand sheep. Only, I did not
have them. It is here that the improvisation came in. It was necessary, for
example, to confine them between fences so that the flock would not appear
too meagre (a little the problem of the forest of which one can give the illusion with three or four trees . . .), but, in all cases, it seems to me that what
comes abruptly, without reflection, is the best of what one does, as it seems to
me that I have done the best of what I have done when I found myself resolving with the camera difficulties that I had not been able to overcome on paper,
and that I had left blank.

And when that happens often—now I have grown accustomed to it—one
understands that the sight of things abruptly found again behind the camera,
when you have not been able to arrive at them by words and ideas set on
paper, makes you discover or rediscover them in the most cinematographic
way there is, that is to say in the strongest and the most creative.

MICHEL DELAHAYE: You seemed to say a little while ago that there was something
more in your last film. I believe that a director always sees or puts something
more in the latest film that he has made, but it seems that you were thinking of
some specific circumstances that made it possible for you to put into *Balthazar*
things that you had not put into your other films.

GODARD: And then, I believe that one can say that, for the first time, you tell or
describe several things at once (without my putting into that the slightest pejorative meaning), when, until now (and in *Pickpocket*, for example), everything
happened as if you were seeking or following one thread, as if you were exploring a single vein. Here there are several veins at once.

BRESSON: I believe that, in fact, the lines of my other films were rather simple,
rather apparent, while that of *Balthazar* is made of many lines that intersect

one another. And it was the contacts among them, even chance, that provoked creation, at the same time that it provoked me, perhaps unconsciously, to put more of myself into this film. Now, I believe very much in intuitive work. But in that which has been preceded by a long reflexion. And notably by a reflection on composition. For it seems to me that the composition is a very important thing, and perhaps even that the film is born first from its composition. That said, it can be managed that this composition be spontaneous, that it be born from improvisation. But in any case, it is the composition that makes the film. In fact, we take elements that already exist; so what counts is the relations among things, and thereby, finally, the composition.

Now, it is at times in these relations—sometimes intuitive—that one establishes among things, that one best orients oneself. And I am thinking of another fact: it is also by intuition that one discovers a person. In any case, more by intuition than by reflection. In *Balthazar*, the abundance of things, and the difficulties that, for that reason, the film represented, perhaps made me try my best; first, at the time of the writing on paper, then, at the time of the shooting, for everything was extremely difficult. Thus, I had not realized that three-quarters of the shots of my film were exteriors, situated in open air. Now, if you think of the downpour of last summer, you see what that could represent as additional difficulties. The more because I was trying to take all my shots in sunlight—and actually, I shot them in sunlight.

GODARD: Why did you insist so on sunlight?

BRESSON: It is very simple: because I have seen too many films in which it was grey or dark outside which, moreover, could give rise to beautiful effects—and in which suddenly one entered sunlit rooms. Now, I have always found that unendurable. But that often happens when one passes from interiors to exteriors, for in the interior there is always added light, artificial, and when one passes to the exterior it is no longer there. Whence an absolutely false shift. Now, you know—and you surely feel as I do on this point—that I am a maniac for truth. And in the slightest of things. Now, a false lighting is as dangerous as a false word or a false gesture. Whence my care to balance lights in such a way that, when one enters a house, there is always all the same less sunlight than outside. Is that clear?

GODARD: Yes, yes. That is clear.

BRESSON: There is also another reason, which is perhaps more precise, deeper. You know that I go, I think moreover without seeking it, toward explicit at once: I believe that simplification is a thing that one must never seek; when one has worked enough, simplification should come of itself. What is very bad, is to seek simplification, or simplicity, too soon; which leads to bad painting, bad literature, bad poetry . . . So I go toward simplification—and I scarcely realize it—but this simplification requires, from the standpoint of taking photographs, a certain strength, a certain vigour. Now, if I simplify my action, and at the same time the image fails (because the contours are not sufficiently encircled, or the relief is not sufficiently marked), I risk a total failure of the sequence.

I am going to give you an example, chosen in my last film, *Balthazar*. If, in the love scene in the 2 CV—actually, of the beginning of love in the 2 CV—the photography had failed, had become grey, the action, which is extremely simple, which results from elements, hangs on very subtle threads, would have failed completely; there would no longer have been a love scene. But I believe, as you do, that photography—or cinematography—is a pernicious thing for us, that is to say too easy a thing, too convenient, for which one must almost have oneself pardoned, but which one must know how to use.

GODARD: Yes, it is necessary, if one can say so, to violate photography, to push it in its . . . But as for me, I go about it differently, for I am—let us say more impulsive. In any case, one must not take it for what it is. I mean, for example, that because you wanted sunlight so that the photography would not fail, by that you were, in a sense, forcing it to keep dignity, rigour . . . Which three-quarters of the others do not do.

BRESSON: That is to say that you must know exactly what you want to have plastically—and do what is necessary to have it. The image that you have in mind, you must foresee, that is to say, see it in advance, literally see it on the screen (while taking into account the fact that there risks being a disparity, and even an entire difference, between what you see and what you will have), and you must make that image exactly as you want to see it, as you see it, as you create it . . .

GODARD: Generally they say of you that you are the cineaste of the ellipsis. On that, when one thinks of people who see your films according to that idea, it is certain that with *Balthazar* you break all records. But I take an example: in the scene of the two automobile accidents—if one can say that—since one sees only one—had you the feeling of making an ellipsis in showing, precisely, only the first? As for me, I think that you had the feeling not of having eliminated a shot, but of having put one shot after another shot. Is that true?

BRESSON: Concerning the two automobile skids, I think that, since one has already seen the first, it is useless to see the second too. I prefer to have it imagined. If I had had it imagined the first time, at that point, there would have been something missing. And then, as for me, I rather like to see it; I think that it is pretty, an automobile that turns round on the road. But after that, I prefer to have it imagined with the help of a sound, for every time that I can replace an image by a sound I do so. And I do so more and more.

GODARD: And if you could replace all the images by sounds? I mean . . . I am thinking of a kind of inversion of the functions of the image and of the sound. One could have the images, of course, but it would be the sound that would be the significant element.

BRESSON: As to that, it is true that the ear is much more creative than the eye. The eye is lazy; the ear, on the contrary, invents. In any case, it is much more attentive, while the eye is content to receive—except in the rare cases when it invents, but then in fantasy. The ear is a much deeper sense, and very evocative. The whistle of a locomotive, for example, can evoke, imprint in you the vision of an entire railroad station, sometimes of a specific station that you know, sometimes of the atmosphere of a station, or of a railroad track, with a train stopped . . . The possible evocations are innumerable. What is good, too, with sound is that it leaves the spectator free. And it is towards that that we should tend—to leave the spectator as free as possible.

GODARD: And that is what many people say—Resnais, for example . . .

BRESSON: You must leave the spectator free. And at the same time you must make yourself loved by him. You must make him love the way in which you render things. That is to say: show him things in the order and in the way that you love to see them and to feel them; make him feel them, in presenting them to him, as you see them and feel them yourself, and this, while leaving him a great freedom, while making him free. Now, this freedom, precisely, is greater with sound than with the image.

DELAHAYE: In your films, especially in *Balthazar*, this amount of freedom that one has toward sounds and images, is in fact engaged in the deep sense of your vision, goes in a well determined direction that is your own. You said a little while ago, for example, that you wanted to paint the vices of humanity. So you impart in the spectator a certain vision of humanity and its vices.

BRESSON: Yes, of course. And I come back to what I said a second ago: the principal thing . . . In the end it is not a matter of working for an audience. There is nothing more stupid, more vulgar, than working for an audience. Well. That said, it is necessary to do what it is necessary to do. And, with respect to that— *le public, c'est moi.* I mean that if I try to represent to myself what the audience will feel, I cannot help but say to myself: The audience, it is I. So, one does not work for an audience. But what one tries to do should be able all the same . . . For we find, ultimately, the same chances of acceptance by the audience as a painter, for example, but after some time. Thus the other day someone asked me the question, "Do you believe that a single film of yours could affect people?" It can, perhaps, affect some people, but I do not believe that a single painting by Cézanne has made people understand or love Cézanne, has made them feel as Cézanne did. It takes a great many paintings! Imagine a painter painting a Cézanne under Louis XIV. Absolutely no one . . . In short: they would have put the painting in the attic!

So it takes us several films. And, as we go on making films, it is good, and it is agreeable, to feel that the audience, suddenly, is trying to put itself in our place and to love what we love. To sum up, it is a matter of making ourselves loved.

Loved, in what we love, and in the way in which we love things and people.
. . . But from what point had we set out?

DELAHAYE: From the vision that you had of things, from the direction that you imprinted on your vision.

BRESSON: Good. But then, there, we enter . . .

GODARD: In humanity, why precisely the vices? Besides, as for me, I did not see only the vices.

DELAHAYE: I took up again that expression that you had at the beginning, describing *Balthazar*, and that struck me.

BRESSON: The film started from two ideas, from two *schemata*, if you will. First schema: the donkey has in his life the same stages as does a man, that is to say, childhood, caresses; maturity, work; talent, genius in the middle of life; and the analytical period that precedes death. Well. Second schema, which crosses the first or which starts from it: the passage of this donkey, who passes through different human groups representing the vices of humanity, from which he suffers, and from which he dies.

There are the two schemata, and that is why I spoke of the vices of humanity. For the donkey cannot suffer from goodness, or from charity, or from intelligence . . . He must suffer from what makes us, ourselves, suffer.

GODARD: And Marie, in that, is, I dare say, another donkey.

BRESSON: Yes, precisely: she is the character parallel to the donkey, and who ends by suffering like him. Example: in the miser's house. One refuses food to her (she is even forced to steal a pot of jam) in the same way that one refuses oats to the donkey. She undergoes the same jolts as he. She undergoes lust, too. She undergoes, not rape, perhaps, not exactly, but something that is almost a rape.

In the end, you see what I sought to do, and it was very difficult, for it was necessary that the two schemata about which I have just spoken to you not give the effect of a system, it was necessary that they not be systematic. It was necessary too that the donkey not return like a theme with his judge's eye, and look upon what humanity does.

That was the danger. It was necessary to obtain a thing rather structured, but which would not appear so; just as the vices must not appear to be there in order to be vices and to harass the donkey.

If I said vices, that is because at the start it was indeed vices, and from which the donkey must suffer, but I attenuated this systematic aspect that the construction, the composition could immediately take.

GODARD: And the character of Arnold? If it were necessary to define him . . . It is not that I would want to define him at all costs, but, in the end, if one had to do so, if one absolutely had to give him some keys, or to have him represent some things rather than some others, what could one say of him?

BRESSON: He represents drunkenness a little, that is to say, gluttony, so he represents that particularly, but at the same time for me he represents nobility, that is to say, that freedom toward men.

GODARD: Yes. For, when one sees him, one is compelled to think of certain things . . . Thus, he has a little of the look of Christ.

BRESSON: Yes, but I did not seek that. Not at all. He represents first of all drunkenness, since when he is not drunk he is gentle, and when he is drunk he beats the donkey, that is to say, reveals thereby one of the things that must be the most incomprehensible for an animal, to know that the same person can be changed by swallowing a bottle of liquid. And that is a thing that must astound animals, the thing from which they must suffer the most.

At the same time, in this character, I felt nobility immediately. And perhaps too a parallelism with the donkey: they have in common a certain sensitivity to things. And that, one can perhaps find with certain animals, very sensitive to objects—for you know that an animal can flinch, can shy at the sight of an object. Then that is because objects count very much for animals, all the same, more sometimes, than for us, who are accustomed to them, and who, unhappily, do not always pay attention to them.

Then, there as well, parallelism. I felt it, but I did not seek it out. All that came spontaneously. I did not want to be too systematic. But as soon as there was nobility, of course I felt it. I did not press it, but I let it act.

It is very interesting to start from a rather strict schema, and then to discover how one handles it, how one ends in something much more subtle, and even, at a certain moment, intuitive.

GODARD: I think, all of a sudden, that you are someone who loves painting very much.

BRESSON: I am a painter. And perhaps it is there, precisely, that you find your idea. For I am scarcely a writer. I write, yes, but I force myself to write, and I write—I realize—a little as I paint (or rather, as I painted, for I no longer paint, but I will paint again): that is to say that I am unable to write a continuous strip. I am able to write from left to right, and thus to align some words, but I cannot do it for a long time, or in continuity.

GODARD: To make cinema, precisely, one has no need of that. It is the cinema in itself that constitutes the strip. One has it from the start; one absolutely no longer needs to concern oneself with it.

BRESSON: Yes, but then you are speaking of the general composition of the film. As for me, when I write, I write as I put colour: I put a little on the left, a little on the right, a little in the middle, I stop, I start again . . . and it is only when there begin to be some things written, that I am no longer annihilated by the blank page, and that I begin to fill the holes. You see: it is not at all a strip that I write. So, the film is made somewhat in this way. That is to say that I set some things at the start, some others at the finish, others still in the middle; I took notes when I thought about it—every year, or every two years—and it is the assemblage of all that that ended by making the film, as colours on a canvas end in assembling to give the relations of things with one another.

But the great risk of the film was its lacking unity. Fortunately, I knew the dangers of dispersion that lie in wait for a film (and that is the greatest danger that it can run, the trap into which it almost always falls); I was very much afraid that mine would not find unity; I knew that this unity would be very difficult to find.

Perhaps it has less than the others, but perhaps that is, as you were saying a little while ago, an advantage.

GODARD: As for me, I only wanted to say that your other films were straight lines, and that this one is made rather of concentric circles—if it is necessary to give an image to compare them—and of sets of concentric circles that cut across one another.

DELAHAYE: Everything happens as if there were several films in one, several subjects of films brought to their unity.

BRESSON: That is a little what I feared—and if you feel that, it does not much please me, for—that was really the great difficulty, with the danger that it involved a loss of attention on the part of the spectator. In fact it is very difficult to catch the attention of the spectator when one takes a character, drops him, takes another, returns to the first—for the attention dies. I know that this film has less unity than the others, but I tried my utmost to let it have one all the same, thinking that, thanks to the donkey, in spite of everything, in the end the unity would find itself again. I could not do otherwise than as I did.

The film has perhaps also a unity of vision, a unity of angle, a unity in the way in which I cut up the sequences into shots . . . For all that can give unity. Including the way of speaking.

That is, moreover, what I always seek: that the people almost all speak in the same way.

To sum up: it is through form that one finds unity again.

DELAHAYE: As for me, I wanted, a little while ago, to stress, not the plurality, but the unity. And I wanted to say precisely that, beyond the diversity of the elements—and it is fabulous—all the same one finds unity again.

BRESSON: Then, in that sense, that pleases me.

GODARD: And how do you see questions of form—if one can say that? I know indeed that one does not think about that so much, in any case at the time, but one thinks about it before, and one thinks about it afterwards. For example, when one makes a *découpage*, one does not think about it. At the same time, I always ask myself, afterwards: why did I cut there rather than there instead? And with others as well, that is the one thing that I do not succeed in understanding: why cut or not cut?

BRESSON: I believe, as you do, that that is a thing that must become purely intuitive. If it is not intuitive, it is bad. In any case, for me it is the most important thing.

GODARD: It must, all the same, be capable of analysis . . .

BRESSON: As for me, I see my film only by the form. It is curious: when I see it again, I no longer see anything but the shots. I do not know at all if the film is moving or not.

GODARD: I believe that it requires a very long time to reach the point of seeing one of one's own films. One day you are in a little village, in Japan or somewhere else, and then you see your film again. At that moment, you can receive your film as an unknown object, in the same situation as an ordinary spectator. But I believe that that requires really a very long time. It requires, too, not being prepared to receive the film.

BRESSON: As for me, and I come back to it, I attach enormous importance to form. Enormous. And I believe that the form leads to the rhythms. Now the rhythms are all-powerful. That is the first thing. Even when one makes the commentary of a film, this commentary is seen, felt, at first as a rhythm. Then it is a colour (it can be cold or warm); then it has a meaning. But the meaning arrives last.

Now, I believe that access to the audience is before everything else a matter of rhythm. I am persuaded of that.

So in the composition of a shot, of a sequence, at first there is the rhythm. But the composition ought not be premeditated, it ought to be purely intuitive. For example, it arises especially when we shoot out of doors, and when we approach a setting absolutely unknown the day before. In the face of novelty, we must improvise. That is what is very good: the necessity to find, and quickly, a new equilibrium for the shot that we are making.

To sum up: I do not believe in too long reflection there either. Reflection reduces things to being no longer anything but the execution of a shot. Things must happen impulsively.

GODARD: Your ideas on cinema—if you have any—have they evolved, and how? How do you film today, in relation to yesterday or to the day before? And how do you conceive of cinema after your last film? As for me, I realize today that in the past, three or four years ago, I had ideas on cinema. Now I no longer have. And to have any, I am forced to continue to make cinema, until I give myself new ones. Let us say then: how do you feel yourself in relation to cinema? I do not say in relation to the cinema that is made, but in relation to the art of cinema?

BRESSON: Yes, however, actually I must tell you how I feel myself in relation to that which is made. Only yesterday, someone said to me (it is a reproach that people make to me sometimes, without intending it, but it is one): "Why do you never go to see films?" For that is absolutely true: I do not go to see them.[1] And because they frighten me. Precisely, and quite simply for that reason. Because I feel that I separate myself from them, that I separate myself from present-day films, from day to day and more and more. And that frightens me extremely, for I see all those films accepted by the audience, and, beforehand, I do not at all see my films accepted by the audience. And I am afraid. Afraid to offer a thing to an audience that is sensitized to another thing and that would be desensitized to what I do. But there is this in it too—that going to see a film from time to time interests me. In order to see what disparity there is. Then I realize that, without intending it, I move farther and farther away from a cinema that, in my opinion, has set off on the wrong foot, that is to say, is sinking into the music hall, into photographed theatre, and that is losing completely its strength and its interest (and not only its interest, but its power), and that is going toward catastrophe.

Not that films cost too much, or that television is a rival, no, but simply because this cinema is not an art, although it pretends to be one; it is only a false art, that tries to express itself under the form of another art. Now, there is nothing worse and more ineffective than that kind of art.

As to what I myself try to make, with images and with sounds, of course I have the impression that it is I who am not mistaken, and that it is the others who are mistaken. But I have, too, the impression, at first that I am in the presence of too numerous means (which I try to reduce, for what kills cinema equally is profusion of means, luxury—and luxury has never contributed anything in the arts), and then, that I am in possession of extraordinary means.

That leads me to say something else to you: it seems to me that the arts—the fine arts, if you will—are on their decline, and even approaching their end. They are in the process of dying.

GODARD: I think so too, yes.

BRESSON: Already there scarcely remains anything of them any longer. Soon, they will no longer exist. But, curiously, if they are killed by cinema, radio, television, it is precisely this cinema, this radio, this television that kill them that in the end will remake an art, will remake the arts—but in a completely different way, of course, and perhaps even the word "art" will no longer be used. In any case, it will not be the same thing.

It is by cinema—and I will say, by cinematography, because I like to make the distinction, as Cocteau made it, between cinema, that is to say current films, and what is all the same the cinematographic art—so it is by cinematography that the art that cinema is in the process of killing will come to life again. The culprit, the culprits in this death of the arts, are the present day mechanical means of diffusion. About that, the other day Ionesco said something rather lovely, in any case very exact: we are faced with miracles. Cinema, radio, television, are miracles; it is films, television transmissions, radio reportages that are not miraculous. So, art is behind.

Perhaps it is not very exact to say that art is behind miracles. It would be necessary to say more exactly that art is killed by miracles, but that it should come to life again thanks to those miracles.

GODARD: I would not have expressed it that way, but I too think that it is the end. Only, I absolutely do not know . . .

BRESSON: How it is going to start again?

GODARD: Yes, how it is going to start again?

BRESSON: As for me, I feel, not in cinema, but in cinematography, an extraordinary art, marvellous, but which is absolutely not taken in hand. Which, I try to take in hand. It is not I who am marvellous, it is the means that are at my disposal. I try to profit by these means, and while shutting the door—double-locking it—to theatre, which is the deadly enemy of cinematography.

And I can say that to you, who make use of actors, and who know how to make use of them . . .

GODARD: You mean: theatre is the enemy of cinematography, but not on the stage . . .

BRESSON: Obviously. Theatre is theatre. Indeed it is because of that that theatre people who want to change the theatre never will change it. It exists, you cannot change it, or then it would be something else than theatre. For in wanting to change the theatre, in wanting to marry it to the cinema, one kills both, cinema and theatre. There is absolutely no possibility of mixture.

Each time that the theatre sticks its nose into the cinema, it is catastrophe, and reciprocally, each time that the cinema sticks its nose on to the stage. See the result, when people want to have those extraordinary noises, those projections, those plays of images . . . What is that? Not theatre!

GODARD: A little while ago you were talking about actors . . .

BRESSON: Actors? Well . . .

GODARD: I do not see the difference between an actor and a non-actor, since in any case he is someone who exists in life.

BRESSON: But there, to my mind, there is the point, it is about that that everything turns . . .

GODARD: If one has a theatre actor, then one must take him . . . good Lord, as what he is: an actor, and one can always succeed . . .

BRESSON: Nothing can be done about it . . .

GODARD: A moment comes, yes, when nothing can be done about it, but there is a moment, too, when one can do something.

BRESSON: I have tried, in the past. And I almost succeeded in doing something. But I realized that a gulf was being hollowed . . .

GODARD: But it is all the same a man, or a woman, that one has there, before one.

BRESSON: No.

GODARD: No?

BRESSON: Because he has acquired habits.

But I think that we are sinking into far too many subtleties, abstractions. It would be necessary . . . In short: I am going to finish those notes, that book, that I am in the midst of writing, and in which I will explain all that. And I will need many pages to explain what happens, to explain the difference that there is between a professional actor who tries to put himself, tries to forget himself, tries to . . . and who arrives at nothing.

GODARD: But can one not simply consider an actor a little as . . . let us say: an athlete, or a runner, that is to say a man who has a certain training to do something; and can one not make use of that training to obtain something, even if one does not wish that . . .

BRESSON: But believe that if I could obtain what I want with an actor, I would not give myself all this trouble! For all that I do gives me enormous trouble. And if I had been willing to accept actors, stars, I would be rich. Well, I am not rich. I am poor.

That is because there is there, at the start, something that has stopped me and that has made me reflect. Not during the work, but after.

GODARD: It is true: a moment comes when actors are rotten, but, finally, when you take a non-professional, from the fact that you take him to have him do certain things in a film, he is acting. In one way or another, you are having him act.

BRESSON: No. Not at all. And there indeed is the point.

GODARD: Finally . . . let us understand each other about words: you are having him live.

BRESSON: No. And then there, we arrive at an explanation . . . which I would prefer to leave for another time. I have said to you that I was writing about that. Then I would prefer, if you will, to give you, when my book is published, the notes that I reproduce, and that will show this—that there is an absolutely uncrossable gulf between an actor, even trying to forget himself, trying not to control himself, and a person, virgin of cinema, virgin of theatre, considered as crude matter that does not even know what it is and that surrenders to you what it did not intend to surrender to anyone.

You see by that that here there is something very important, not only with respect to cinematography, but even with respect to psychology. With respect to a creation that then becomes . . . that is a creation, with its body, with its muscles, with its blood, with its spirit, that rejoins your creation. For you find yourself mixed into this virgin person. That is to say you arrive at putting yourself inside, and in a way . . . that I do not want to explain now because that would take us too far away, simply: you arrive at being present in your film, and not only because you have imagined it, because you have put into it words that you had written, but because you are in it.

You cannot be inside an actor. It is he who creates. It is not you.

GODARD: When you say "virgin of all experience" I understand very well, but as soon as he has done something, as soon as he has filmed one twenty-fourth of a second, he is less virgin by that one twenty-fourth. To make a comparison: he is a little like a non-Christian who, once plunged into the water, will be baptized, and theoretically Christian. The same way, a non-actor: there is something that he does not have, but he is going to acquire it, as soon as he is plunged into cinema. That said, fundamentally he is still a man like others.

BRESSON: No, not at all. I am going to tell you . . .

GODARD: Then I do not understand you . . .

BRESSON: No, you do not understand . . . One must understand what an actor is, what his profession is, his playing. First, the actor never stops playing. Playing is a projection.

GODARD: One can break that, destroy it, prevent the actor from . . .

BRESSON: No, you cannot prevent him. Oh, but I have tried! . . . You cannot prevent him from playing. Absolutely nothing can prevent him from playing.

GODARD: Then, one can destroy him.

BRESSON: No, you cannot.

GODARD: Yes. In the final analysis one can destroy him, the same way that the Germans destroyed the Jews in the concentration camps.

BRESSON: You cannot, you cannot. . . . Habit is too strong. The actor is an actor. You have before you an actor. Who effects a projection. That is his movement: he projects himself outside. While your non-actor character must be absolutely closed, like a container with a lid. Closed. And that, the actor cannot do, or, if he does it, at that moment he is no longer anything.

For there are actors who try, yes. But when the actor simplifies himself, he is even more false than when he is the actor, when he plays. For we are not simple. We are extremely complex. And it is this complexity that you find with the non-actor.

We are complex. And what the actor projects is not complex.

GODARD: But why do you deny the actor . . . Finally it is all the same a human being who is the actor, however bad he may be, and this human being is necessarily complex. Why do you deny to the actor his aspect of human being?

BRESSON: That is because he has acquired the habit of being an actor to such a degree that, even in life, he is an actor. He cannot be otherwise. Live otherwise. He cannot exist otherwise, than exteriorizing himself.

GODARD: But, after all, to be an actor is no worse than to be a blacksmith or . . .

BRESSON: Why do you use the word "worse"? I do not at all hold it against him for what he is.

GODARD: No, but I meant: just as you take a blacksmith for what he can do, and not for playing a notary or a policeman, so you can take an actor, if the worst comes to the worst, at least for playing an actor.

BRESSON: But not at all. There you have all the same someone from whom you want to extract a certain thing. Imagine, for example, that you wanted to do an operation. You calm the patient so that he will not contract, so that he will not make movements that would prevent you from taking hold of the tendon or the nerve that you are to attend to. It is exactly the same thing with the actor: his actor's personality prevents you from reaching what you wanted to attain. Moreover, he projects himself . . . In the end it is very simple—if we could go to see some films together, I would show you: there are actors who are marvellous on the stage, who pass for very good film actors, and who are empty! . . . For they are empty. And you realize that when you put the actor under a magnifying glass. Of course in the theatre you do not see him under a magnifying glass, and, moreover, the actor knows what he is doing, and the theatre is an illusion . . .

GODARD: But that moment when he is empty, when he becomes a human cell again can that not be interesting? The actor, as human cell . . .

BRESSON: Not at all. There is no longer anything inside. He is uninhabited. He is a marionette who makes gestures. And that goes so far that, for me, now (and it is also because of that that I so dislike going to the cinema), most films appear to me as competitions in grimaces. Really. I am not exaggerating a thing. I see grimaces. I see strictly nothing else than the spirit that has caused these grimaces to be made, but I do not see the deep thing that has nothing to do with grimaces. I do not see it.

So, this kind of perpetual mimicry (and I am not speaking of gestures of the hands, which are intolerable, or of movements of the eyes, of looks), all that which makes the whole of theatre, appears to me, seen in close-up, impossible!

Then, why want to mix these two things? Why want to use beings that are formed for the theatre, whom people have formed like that, for the other? One must know what dramatic schools are!

GODARD: Yes. That is frightful!

BRESSON: And the voice, moreover! That tone that gives an absolutely false voice! But on what is their voice based? And what makes them pretend that they speak rightly? In the name of what do they think they can affirm it? When I think that sometimes someone says to me that in my films people speak falsely! Me, I would have people speak falsely! But what makes that person believe that he himself speaks rightly?

For there you have a voice that must agree with feelings which are not your feelings. Are you going to pretend then that your voice is going to be fixed exactly on that and that it is not going to waver? But your speech wavers all the time! There is not a single intonation that is precise!

I say, on the contrary, that mechanics is the only thing, as with the piano. It is by doing scales, and it is by playing in the most regular and the most mechanical way, that one captures emotion. It is not by trying to plate on an emotion, as virtuosi do. There it is: actors are virtuosi. Who, instead of giving you the exact thing for you to feel, plate on their emotion for you, to say to you: that is how you must feel the thing!

GODARD: Yes. It is enough to understand each other about words. I mean: actors are perhaps, in fact, virtuosi, but for me they represent, let us say, a certain kind of poetry, once one takes them as they are, as virtuosi. Antonin Artaud, for example, who is the limiting case, was a poet and an actor.

BRESSON: He was an actor, and as for his voice, he did not know how to make use of it.

GODARD: What interests me, in the fact that he was an actor, is that he was a poet.

BRESSON: What is good, in any case, is that you see the problem. You have reflected on the case of the actor. You know what he is. He is your raw material. Good. And you take actors as actors. That is probably a means that serves you, but as for me, I can no longer make use of it.

GODARD: I mean that ultimately, when I take actors, it is a question of ethics. And it is perhaps, too, a little out of cowardice, because I find that cinema corrupts people, those who are not prepared. Thus, all the people whom I have known, whom I loved in actual life, and who have made cinema without being actors and I think too of Nicole Ladmiral—are people who ended badly. Either the girls became whores, or the boys killed themselves . . . In any case, the least thing that happened to them, was to become less good than they were before. And even sometimes when I had actors play . . . A boy like Jean-Pierre Léaud, for example, in my last film, I was saddened at having him play, because I felt . . . that he was living too much, and that it was something important for him, and I was a little ashamed toward him . . . Then, is it not a question of ethics?

BRESSON: As for me, I am not in that situation, for I do not have them play. That is all the difference.

GODARD: Yes, in a sense, that is true.

BRESSON: Then for me the question does not pose itself. On the contrary. The people that I take in my films are delighted at having taken part in them and say that they have never been so happy as in doing it—someone said that to me again yesterday—and, afterwards, they are delighted to go back to their profession. But they have not played for a second. For nothing in the world would they be actors, for the good reason that they have never been actors.

I do not ask them to experience such-and-such a feeling that they do not have. I simply explain the mechanics to them. And I enjoy explaining it to them. So I say to them, for example, why I make one shot close rather than another, and how. But as for having them play, I do not ask that of them for a second. You see the difference. The two realms remain absolutely separate.

GODARD: One could say that to be an actor is to be romantic, and not to be an actor, classical.

BRESSON: That is possible. But see all that there is behind that. I have said nothing and done nothing lightly. I have been led to reflect on all that because I began by trying several solutions. It happened, at the time when I was beginning to take non-professionals, it happened that suddenly I said to myself: All right! That scene I can have played by an actor, a good actor. I am going to try. Well. I try. I botch it. I say to myself then: it is my fault. And then . . . Well, the scene, I botched it three times in succession . . . And it was only afterwards that I said to myself: but what happened?

And now, when I think about a film, and I write on paper, and people say to me: you should take an actor . . . But it is obvious to me that what I am in the process of writing will fail completely, if I take an actor. The result will no longer have anything to do with what ought to be. And if I took him, then I would have to rewrite everything, to transform everything, for what an actor is going to do already implies, even at this stage, a completely different writing.

Finally, when I arrive at a simplification such that it is a matter of finding a flash on a face, and it is necessary to find that flash, well, that flash, an actor will not give it to me.

GODARD: There I think that it is as if a painter, instead of a model, took an actor. As if he said to himself: instead of taking that laundress, let us take a great actress who will pose much better than that woman. In that sense, of course, I understand.

BRESSON: And note well that that is not all to diminish the work of the actor. On the contrary, I have an enormous admiration for the great actors. I think that the theatre is marvellous. And I think that it is extraordinary to manage to create with one's body. But let there be no mixing!

GODARD: Would it interest you, for example, to make a film about an actor? And if you had it to make, how would you make it? I mean a film on the act of playing. For, definitively, it is the act of playing that does not interest you, if this playing is to serve as base for creation, the act of being oneself and of not being oneself, but, in the case of a film made about the act of playing? . . . Because there is already a little of that in *Balthazar*. I am thinking of Arnold. He is a little a character of an actor.

BRESSON: You mean that he represents an actor?

GODARD: He could represent the theatre and nobility.

BRESSON: There, no, I do not follow you. He did not know. He did not know a thing. When he was to say a sentence, it was absolutely mechanical. To say the sentence in the most mechanical way possible, that is all that I asked of him.

GODARD: I am not speaking of the person who plays, but of the character as one sees him in the film.

BRESSON: The character? Yes, maybe, because he is picturesque. Then, maybe, that way, yes. Because he has more relief than the others.

GODARD: Perhaps that is one of the vices about which you did not think . . .

BRESSON: He has a more conspicuous relief.

GODARD: In relation to the others, he is something that they are not. And he, more than they, could represent the theatre.

BRESSON: That is to say that he is a much more mysterious character; then he is at the same time more definite, almost tangible. Thereby he is a character of fiction.

GODARD: What I call playing, is not being an actor or not, it is doing what Arnold does in your film, for example: saying goodbye to the kilometre marker and to the telegraph pole. That is sublime, but it is something else, it is . . . Ultimately that is what I call playing, or being romantic. Now, none of the other characters, exactly, would do that. They are in different worlds.

BRESSON: Perhaps that is it: we enter a different world, which is the world of poetry—too much perhaps. Nevertheless, as for me, I have seen boozers, drunken fellows, speak to road signs and to trees . . .

GODARD: Oh, yes, but they are poets.

BRESSON: Yes, of course, but I mean that there I did not try to enter a poetic, theatrical, or romantic domain. You know: everything in this film—with some arrangement—comes ultimately from reminiscences and personal experiences. Thus, when I have him speak to the marker, it is really that I have seen analogous things. I remember, in the past, during my childhood: at the time, there were a great many fellows like that, who passed on the roads, in the country, and to whom one gave shelter, whom one put up for the night . . .

DELAHAYE: Vagabonds . . .

BRESSON: Yes, vagabonds. Well, I have seen some of them speak to objects, to plants . . . Yesterday, I saw a fellow on the Avenue de Wagram speak to a *pissoir*. I did not understand what he was saying very well, but it must have been curious . . .

DELAHAYE: You said at the very first, and you have just said it again, that you put yourself into your films. Well, you said too that you put yourself into them thanks to the actor—rather, to the non-actor. Then, these characters, whom you take because they are not actors, do you not take them all the same for the characters, exactly, that they are already in life, with what they may have for you of the near, of the familiar?

I take Pierre Klossowski, for example. Even before your film, he was a character. When you had him enter the film, did you not take him in virtue of what he had written?[2]

BRESSON: Of course, that is one factor, but the particular factor . . . For one can very well have led an entire life and . . . Ultimately you know how different—

and I am not the first to speak of it—the life of a writer can be from what he writes, and how mistaken one can be about him. It is all the story of the criticism of Proust. Must one look at the life of someone to judge his work? This is his work. And that is his life.

I mean by that that one must pay attention. What is important is to see him, to feel him manoeuvring, to arrive at a moral resemblance. That is all. But the moral resemblance may very well have nothing to do with the profession, with the work of the person in question.

DELAHAYE: But if Klossowski had not written books, if he had not made himself known as he is, you would perhaps not have known him, so not have taken him.

BRESSON: I would not have known him because people would not have made me think of him, would not have brought him to my house. You see what I mean? The same way Anne Wiazemsky, the Marie of the film, was brought to me by Florence Delay. You see how an earlier work leads to another. And Florence Delay had been brought to me by a friend, with whom I had made some tests, who had spoken to me of her, had told me what she was like, what she was. In that, there is a great deal of intuition, but there is also a kind of search, deep, interior, and not at all exterior.

There we enter the realm of sound. I say that the voice is not only what people say—noises. The voice is the most revealing thing that exists. All the people that I take, I would prefer to have known at first over the telephone, rather than see them enter my house without having heard them. On that I have had extraordinary experiences. I have seen, once, someone whom I liked very much; have even seen several people at different intervals whom I believed that I knew. And then, one day, I heard them over the telephone. Then, there, my opinion was completely changed. And that, too, is why we must always take into consideration what is the sound and what is the image.

Yes: a voice over the telephone is already something extraordinary. Then I listen a great deal to people talking. It is the voice that informs me most about people. Moreover, when I choose characters, I see the friends who brought them to me, I speak of them, I see if they correspond, and in fact, sometimes I have some luck. Until now, I have rarely been mistaken. Now, this person about whom you are finally certain, about whose personality, whose character, whose interior life, you are certain that you are not mistaken, if, at the moment when you put him into your sequence . . . All right. So you put him into it. And this happens: something goes wrong. Then there, if something goes wrong, there is something wonderful happening: as it is you who are mistaken, the result is that you correct yourself in relation to the person, instead of its being he who corrects himself in relation to you. It is there, in that way, that one: enters cinematographic creation, a way that can lead very far.

That is to say that the character does not change only in relation to me. If you will: I am enlightened with his light and he is enlightened with mine. It is a mixture, a kind of fusion. It is a wax . . . It is two waxes that melt into one another, and at a point . . .

But it was little by little that I realized that, and it is only now that I see it well, that I see there an extraordinary mine, but all that is possible only with non-actors.

DELAHAYE: But cannot a non-actor also reveal in a film something of himself that he does not reveal in actuality, a thing that he himself, perhaps, does not suspect is in him? For example, a man, spineless in life, may be, in a film, without his having sought it, hard or courageous.

BRESSON: That is possible, yes. It shows then a hardness that he has never let be seen. And it is that that is wonderful. For we are complex. That is why, when you want to show a spineless man in cinema it is a mistake to make him spineless. For he has the opposite in him as well.

But the audience is in love with the false. Why? Because the habit of theatre is a habit whose loss will require a very long time to bring about, and that the act of going to the theatre . . . I mean that there would be no theatre if there were not a fixed choice of the false on the part of the creator. For there is no theatre without falseness. And even the falseness of the actor is indispensable. All right. But then, let us not put this false actor in front of a camera that is a miracle, and that catches things that neither your eye nor your ear could catch. Why give it the falsified? Give it the true! It is of no interest to say to a gentleman: I am taking a documentary on you, that I am going to put in the archives, and people will say later: that is how they acted plays in 1966.

But that is not at all to go against what you do and against what you feel, you, Jean-Luc Godard. It is only that you questioned me . . . You know that I like very much what you do, and that it refreshes me a great deal to go to see your films.

But there, you too are in a domain that is not the ordinary domain of cinema. That is still something else. No doubt you make use of cinema a little to do what you do, but what you do is really your own. And nothing of what I have said was said to advance what I think or to . . .

GODARD: Oh, but I believe, I have the impression, compared with you, of not making cinema. I do not mean at all that I have the feeling of making things that are not interesting, but, compared with you, I have the feeling of not making cinema. Although that is not the word that fits. Let us say cinematography.

BRESSON: There is another reproach too that people have made me. People have said to me: it is from pride that you do not take actors. But what does that mean? I reply: Do you believe that it amuses me not to take actors? For not only does it not amuse me, but it represents a terrible amount of work. And then I have only ever made six or seven films . . . Do you believe that it amuses me to remain thus at a standstill? To be unemployed! Me, I do not find that funny at all! I want to work; I would prefer to work all the time. And why have I not managed to film more? Because I was not taking actors! Because thus I was ignoring a commercial aspect of the cinema, based on stars. Then, to say things like that, is absurd!

And I think, moreover, that criticism, bad criticism, which ultimately represents the majority, not only turns the audience away from a better course, but makes bad directors of those who could be less so. There is at the start the optics of the theatre, that people accept too much, and, too, this policy, very bad, of constant praise . . .

GODARD: One must say that the theatre is older. It has existed for so long a time that one has difficulty in not referring to it.

BRESSON: Yes. And when one thinks that there still exist people who think, and sometimes write—I read it again recently—that a silent film is pure cinema! To think that we are in that state!

GODARD: They say that, yes, but that does not prevent that, when they see a silent film, they can no longer endure it!

BRESSON: And what I was saying goes even farther: there was no silent cinema! It never existed! For in fact they had the people talk, but they talked in the void, one did not hear what they said. Then, let one not say that they had found a silent type. No. It is absurd! There are people like Chaplin and Keaton who found, for themselves, a style moreover, wonderful—of pantomime, but the style that they gave to their films was not a "silent style." On that, too, I will say some things in my book. For I think that that is really the moment for saying them. Only to do things in addition, besides, I need time. And each time that I set to work at it . . . I do not succeed. That is because a film, for me, is not only to work on the film, but to be in the film. I think about it all the time. And all that I live, that I see, situates itself in relation to the film, passes through the film. To go off to the side is like changing country.

So, this book does not go forward. However, I must do it. And I am very impatient to do it. I believe that this is the moment. For cinema is falling. And it is such a fall!

Yesterday, I went into the Cinerama. For you know that one has access to it from the Studiorama.[3] And often I go to sit in the balcony, where there is no one, and when one sees that immense screen, that covers everything, that makes an effect! . . . And the trains . . . that start from one end and come back on you! It is magnificent, that invention! People start from your right pocket and return to your left pocket. Then, when it is a train that returns to you! . . . That is marvellous! Yesterday, then, in the balcony (and there were a pair of lovers who moreover were absolutely not looking at the film)[4], yesterday I saw that cinema and it stupefied me.

GODARD: The same thing happened to me, four days ago, at the Studiorama. I went to the washroom, which is at the level of the balcony of the Cinerama, and I sat down in the balcony. And it is true: one enters a theatre . . . I saw some images from the film: crazy characters who were jumping around. It is there that one sees that cinema is not the same thing as cinematography.

BRESSON: Absolutely! Well, that is the cinema, now.

DELAHAYE: Can you say, exactly, what impression you had at that moment?

BRESSON: A horrible impression! The impression of the absolute of the false, the false being seized by a miraculous apparatus, and again reinforced. For there one has a deliberate reinforcement of the false to make it enter well into the head of the spectator. And when they have that in their heads, I guarantee to you that it is difficult to get it out of them!

DELAHAYE: What you have just said reminds me of the point from which we set out half an hour ago, of knowing the disparity that there is between what you make and the cinema. Now, that makes me think of another disparity: the one that there is between the things that you show and the real elements of which you were speaking. I take as an example an element of *Balthazar* (borrowed from a contemporary reality a little like "The Wind blows where it lists," which started from specific facts): the episode of the young hoodlums, the *blousons noirs*, black jackets. In both cases you seem to want purposely to disengage, from specific facts or elements of the present, a general significance that goes beyond them. With you these realities are purified of all the elements to which people attach themselves this very day, and to which another director would attach himself. And what one sees in your film is a reality that is indeed ours (for the disparity is in a sense a false disparity and you return to the reality), but which has become the support . . . in a way of a timeless fable.

BRESSON: I think that the disparity is situated here especially: cinema copies life, or photographs it, while as for me, I recreate life starting from elements in as natural, as crude a state as possible.

GODARD: One could make what was said a little while ago more specific by saying that cinematography, contrary to cinema, is moralistic.

BRESSON: Or, if you will: it is the system of poetry. To take elements as disparate as possible in the world and to bring them together in a certain order that is not the usual order but your own order. But these elements must be crude.

Cinema, on the contrary, recopies life with actors, and photographs this copy of life. So we are absolutely not on the same ground. When you speak of the present, let us say of contemporaneity, as for me I do not think about it at all. And if the reference to the period asserted itself, then perhaps I would think about it, in the sense that I would say to myself that, as a matter of fact, I prefer to be outside the period. Starting from the moment when I try to go rather deeply within people, that is one of the dangers that I must avoid.

Here I add another thing that I have not yet said and that is important: the great difficulty in what I try to do, in what is, to sum up, a penetration into the unknown of ourselves, the great difficulty is that my means are exterior means, and that therefore they are in relation to appearances, all appearances, the appearance of the person himself as well as the appearance of what surrounds him. So the great difficulty is to remain in the interior, always, without passing to the exterior; it is to avoid the sudden occurrence of a terrible disconnection. And that is what happens to me sometimes, in which case I try to repair the fault.

I take an example in my film: that of the young hoodlums. When they pour oil on the road and the cars skid, there I am completely on the outside. And that is a great danger. Then I recover myself as best I can to catch people again in what they have of an inside.

DELAHAYE: Here I make what I wanted to say more specific: at present, when the cinema shows, for example, *blousons noirs*, we see that too as a sociological documentary, which implies that these boys are conditioned by certain things, and, rightly or wrongly, one takes that into account, which brings about that in the limit everything can be explained and one can no longer judge.

While with you, it seems that these boys are one of the possible incarnations of Evil.

BRESSON: I did that saying to myself that it was dangerous, without damaging too much, without too much dispersion. For that is dispersion: passing from one point of view to another, that is to say, as I was saying a little while ago, from an interior to an exterior point of view.

And it is because of that that I believe, that I am persuaded, that, in cinema, one can no doubt make a group work with scenarist, dialogist, adapter, decorator, and so on, but that this work leads necessarily to divergence. Each goes in his own direction and the thing to which that must lead is, in advance, totally dispersed, moreover, reduced. That is to say that, starting from a Victor Hugo idea, one arrives at a Hemingway novel, and it is equally because of that that at the end of the operation one can as well say that Hemingway resembles Victor Hugo.

In any case, one obtains a cinema-novel that no longer has anything to do with anything. It is that, this absolutely regular cinema, that, in short, bores everyone because it is always alike.

But in the end, I believe that I repeat myself and that I harp on the same things . . .

GODARD: That is inevitable, but it is the tone of the conversation, and that is why at last I believe that it is necessary to keep this tone.

DELAHAYE: You were saying a little while ago that sometimes you remained on the exterior (in the case of the young hoodlums, for example). Then, can one not say that, from the point where you are, you render a moralist's judgment to take up again the term used a little while ago by Jean-Luc Godard? For it is somewhat to that that I was referring a little while ago.

BRESSON: I say that then, it is because of that that I give some people the impression of attaching myself to all that to which others would not attach themselves, that is to say, of choosing, among ten things to do, exactly those that the others would not take. Why? Because the others are exterior, because they photograph something, and, as for me, I know that the other things would disperse me, and the one that I do is the only one that could be appropriate for me.

People have been able to say, for example (I do not know if they were right), that what I made were experiments, attempts (but that experiment that I made, from Bernanos, was truly an attempt). Well, people said to me then: that is odd, you have taken of this novel everything that appeared not to be cinematographic, and you have left all the rest. I said: Of course! since I was seeking something else completely! So, it is normal that the others take what they want to take, when they make their customary films, and that I take, without otherwise intending it, what can serve me to make my own film.

It is not to speak of originality in relation to me, I would rather speak in relation to anyone else at all rather than me. But there is, in this connection, a definition of originality which is magnificent and which could perhaps serve us—but perhaps by transforming it, by rewriting the thing—it is: "Originality is wanting to do as others do, but without ever succeeding." That is a marvellous saying and extraordinarily true.

Now, there is a little of that with me. I am awkward. I tried perhaps at the start to do as others do. In fact: I took actors, I made, or tried to make, films as others did, but I did not succeed. Or rather: I realized that if I did as the others, I would not be able to say what I have to say, because I did not succeed in making use of those means.

GODARD: There are two tendencies in you (and I do not know which seems to you to correspond to you the better): you are, on the one hand, a humanist, on the other hand, an inquisitor. Is that reconcilable, or . . . ?

BRESSON: Inquisitor? In what sense? Not in the sense . . .

GODARD: Oh, not in the sense of the Gestapo, of course. But in a sense, let us say . . .

BRESSON: Not in the sense of the Inquisition? Saint Dominic? . . .

GODARD: Oh, yes, all the same . . .

BRESSON: Oh! . . . No. No . . .

GODARD: Or then, let us say particularly: Jansenist.

BRESSON: Jansenist, then, in the sense of austerity . . .

GODARD: Yes, but all the same, there is something else, and the word inquisitor . . .

BRESSON: Really, Inquisitor! You do not mean that I assert my way of seeing things. For yes, I assert—I cannot do otherwise—my way of seeing, of thinking, my personal view, but as everyone who writes does . . . In the end, if Inquisitor there is, I would say then that I go seeking in people what I find that is most subtle and most personal.

GODARD: Yes, but there is at the same time a frightening aspect . . .

BRESSON: The Question, then?

GODARD: Yes, The Question.

BRESSON: As you say: of course, I put the Question.

GODARD: There!

BRESSON: The Question that will bring out the response. But we live, we put questions, and, perhaps, we ourselves give responses, or we await responses. But it is certain that this manner of work is a questionnaire. Only it is a questionnaire in the unknown that is to say: give me something that will surprise me. That is the stratagem. And if you have actors, you will not succeed at it. There are too many things that interpose themselves. There are screens.

DELAHAYE: I come back to Jansenism. Do you not believe that beyond the question of austerity, there is a deep agreement between your vision and the Jansenist vision of the world, for example, and precisely, on Evil? With you, the world seems condemned . . .

GODARD: And, exactly, Pascal is an Inquisitor, and, to me, if there is a film that is Pascalian it is indeed *Balthazar*.

BRESSON: You know, to my mind Pascal is so great, but he is great to everyone's . . . But, in Jansenism, there is perhaps this, which is an impression that I have as well: it is that our lives are made at once of predestination—Jansenism then—and of *hasard* chance. So, *hasard* (we find again the *hasard-Balthazar*), perhaps it is indeed that (and, there now, I realize it) that was the point of departure of the film. Very strictly, the point of departure was a lightning stroke vision of a film whose central character would be a donkey.

GODARD: Like Dostoevsky—whom you cite in the film—who all at once saw a donkey and had the revelation of something. And that little passage, in two words, says so much . . .

BRESSON: Yes. It is marvellous. You think that I should have set it as exergue?

GODARD: No . . . No. But it is well to have put it in . . .

BRESSON: Yes. I marvelled when I read that. But I read it after having thought of the donkey, you see. In short: that is to say that I had read *The Idiot*, but that I had not paid attention. And then, two or three years ago, reading *The Idiot*, I said to myself: But what a passage! See the admirable idea!

GODARD: That is it: you thought about it, like Myshkin . . .

BRESSON: Absolutely admirable, to have an idiot informed by an animal, to have him see life through an animal, who passes for an idiot but is of an intelligence

. . . And to compare this idiot (but you have it in your mind: you know that in fact he is the subtlest and the most intelligent of all) to compare him to an animal that passes for an idiot, and that is the subtlest and the most intelligent of all. That is magnificent.

Magnificent that idea of having the idiot say, when he sees the donkey and hears him bray: There! I understood! . . . that is extraordinary; that is genius.

But it is not the idea of the film. The idea came, perhaps, visually. For I am a painter. The head of a donkey seems to me something admirable. Visual art, no doubt. Then, all at once, I believed I saw the film. Then I lost it, and the next day, when I wanted to set myself at it again . . . Later I found it again.

GODARD: But when you were little you did not see . . .

BRESSON: Yes! I saw a great many donkeys.

GODARD: Yes, and then, in Protestant settings, there are always many donkeys.

BRESSON: Yes, of course I saw some . . . And childhood too plays all the same a very important part.

GODARD: Leenhardt too saw many donkeys in his youth . . .

BRESSON: But you know that a donkey is a marvellous animal. And then, there is another thing that I can tell you, it is that I was very much afraid, not only while writing on paper, but while shooting the film, that that donkey would not be a character like the others, that is to say would appear a trained donkey, a performing donkey. So I took a donkey that knew how to do absolutely nothing. Not even how to pull a cart. I even had a great deal of difficulty getting him to pull the cart in the film. In fact everything that I believed that he would give me, he refused me, and everything that I believed that he would refuse me . . . he gave me. Pull a cart, for example, one says to oneself: a donkey will do that. Well, not at all! . . . And I said to myself: when it will be necessary to train him for the circus . . . And what happened, is that I stopped the film, with the donkey untrained, and that I sent him to the trainer so that he would be able to make the circus sequences. I had to wait two months before shooting them.

GODARD: Yes: in the circus scene, it was very necessary that he know how to stamp his hoofs.

BRESSON: So, I waited two months for him to be prepared. Moreover that is why the film is a little late. But at the start I was very worried. And what I have said to you somewhat rejoins if you will, what I was saying to you about actors a little while ago. I wanted that animal to be, even as an animal, crude matter.

And perhaps the looks that the donkey gave at certain moments, at the animals, for example and also at the characters, perhaps they would not have been the same if it had been a trained tame donkey. But I discovered—or rather verified—something that contradicts everything that people think about the donkey (and, although it did not surprise me, all the same it astonished me): to know that the donkey is not at all a stubborn animal, or, if he is, that he is much more intelligent and sensitive than the others; when someone makes a brute of him, he stops as a brute and no longer does anything. Now the trainer (who is an intelligent man and an excellent trainer) told me immediately, as I asked him if the donkey is not more difficult to train than the horse: it is exactly the contrary. The horse, which is stupid, is rather difficult to train, but the donkey, provided that you do not make the gesture that you must not make, understands immediately what he has to do.

GODARD: All at once I think of another point of view, the formal one. It is the angle or the distance from which it was necessary to film the looks in order to render them well.

BRESSON: Of course.

GODARD: The donkey looks sideways, while we have our eyes in front.

BRESSON: Yes, of course.

GODARD: And one had to be certain . . . In short, one had to be not a millimetre too much to the left or to the right . . .

BRESSON: There is yet something else: I did not have at all the obstacles that I expected with that animal, but others, of another order. For example, when I shot outdoors, in the mountains, or near Paris, I worked with a small camera, and it made noise. Well, as soon as this camera was too near the donkey, it kept him from doing whatever it might be. You see the difficulties in which I could be! So it was necessary to distract him by something else, to try to catch his look. But it happened too that I made use of exactly that attention to the noise to catch some looks.

In any case, difficulties of that sort, moreover the rain, all that made the film very difficult, and I had to improvise all the time. All the time I kept finding myself having to upset everything. I could not do this thing this way or at this place, I had to do it that other way, and at that other place.

During the last scene, that of the death of the donkey, I had a terrible anxiety, for I feared never being able to reach what I wanted. I had enormous difficulty to get the donkey to do what he was to do, what I wanted him to do. And he did it only once, but in the end, he did it. Only, I had to provoke him to do it, in another way than the one that I had thought about. In the film that is situated at the moment when the donkey hears the bells and pricks up his ears. It was by catching something at the last moment that things worked: he had the reaction that was necessary. He did it only once, but it was marvellous. That is the kind of joy that filming sometimes gives you! One is in terrible difficulties and, all at once, the miracle occurs.

DELAHAYE: And *hasard* . . .

BRESSON: Yes, and chance . . . And I love the title. Someone said to me: I do not like that repetition! I replied, But that is marvellous, a rhymed title.

GODARD: Yes it is marvellous, a title like that.

BRESSON: And, moreover, how exact, in relation to the film, this *Hasard-Balthazar*...
And we come back to Jansenism, for I really believe that our lives are made of
predestination and of chances... When one studies the lives of people, of great
men for example, that is a thing that one sees very well. I think of the life of
Saint Ignatius, for example, of which at one time I thought I could make a
film—which I did not make. Well, studying the strange life of this man who
founded the greatest religious order (the most numerous, in any case, and one
that has spread throughout the entire world), studying his life, one feels that he
was made for that, but everything, in his course toward the foundation of that
order, was made of chances, of encounters, through which one feels him little
by little coming to what he was to do.

That is, too, a little the case of the escaped man, in *Un condamné à mort s'est
échappé*: he goes towards a certain point. He absolutely does not know what
will happen there. He arrives at it. And there, he has to choose. He chooses.
And he arrives at another point. And there, again, chance makes him choose
another thing.

For Saint Ignatius, it went exactly the same way. Everything that he did,
he did not do himself. He did it thanks to his encounters.

DELAHAYE: In the *Condamné*, the journey of the hero makes one think of the
spiritual journey of Saint John of the Cross.

BRESSON: Yes, yes. Because, at the very bottom, if we are willing to turn our
attention to it; everything in life has a resemblance. Even the simplest, flattest
lives resemble another life, of another man. But with different chance events,
different chances... In the lives of great men, that is apparent, because one
speaks of them, because one knows the details, but I am persuaded that the
lives of all of us are made in exactly the same way, that is to say made up of
predestination and of chances. It is well known that we are made at five or six
years. At that age, it is finished. At twelve or thirteen years, that is apparent.
And afterwards, we continue to be what we have been, making use of the different chances. We use them to cultivate what was already in us, and perhaps if
that had not been cultivated, nobody would ever have seen what there was.

DELAHAYE: That is all the problem of vocation. Then vocation would be made of
all that we are let us say, at eleven years old, a kind of unchangeable depth that
makes use, more or less well, of that sum of chances about which you were
speaking.

BRESSON: Yes. That is to say that you arrive at a crossroads where you find chance.
But you do not even have to choose. A chance makes you choose to turn to
the right rather than to the left. Then, you arrive at another crossroads, which
is your destination, and another chance works, you go in another direction,
and so on. As for me, I am certain that we are surrounded with people of talent

and of genius, I am certain of it, but the chance of life . . . It requires so many coincidences for a man to succeed in drawing something from his genius.

I have the impression that people are much more intelligent, much more gifted, but that life flattens them. Look at the children, in the middle class . . . I take the middle class because that is exactly where they flatten them. Immediately, people flatten them because there is nothing more frightening than talent or genius. People are terribly scared of it. The parents are scared of it. Then, they flatten them.

And among animals, there must be some very intelligent ones that people flatten by training, by blows . . .

GODARD: In your projects, do you still think of *Lancelot*?

BRESSON: Yes. I hope to make the film. But in two languages. In French, of course, and in English. It is the very type of the film that one must make in two languages (and, ordinarily, I should make it in German, too), because the same legend is part of our mythology and of that of the Anglo-Saxons. Moreover, at their origin those stories were written in the two languages. We have the transcription of the *Chevalier à la charrette, The Knight of the Cart.*[5]

Then, there was Perceval le Gallois, and Tristan, too . . . In short: it is from those first poems, sung and recited, that the legend of the Grail came, rewritten then by the scribes and by the monks who added the religious elements.

DELAHAYE: Yes, but a very ancient common Celtic fund pre-existed all that, that is what bought about that, at the time of formation of French and of English, the two languages adapted what constituted their common possession. For Tristan, for example, it seems indeed that the first known trace of the theme is to be found in the Cornwall tradition—whose language has disappeared today.

BRESSON: That is what interests me: to take up again an old legend known in all Europe. And if I can make the film in English, I will have a little more money at the start, which is important, since I cannot make the film with France solely . . . Unless I take stars. And French stars. Well, I will not. But indeed I hope to make it in both languages.

Nevertheless, I will not take up again the purely fairy-tale element of the legend; I mean the fairies, Merlin, and so on. I am going to try to transfer this fairy-tale into the realm of feelings, that is to say to show how feelings change even the air that one breathes.

In any case, I think that today people would not believe in that fairy-tale. Now, in a film, it is necessary to believe. Moreover that is one of the reasons why one must not do theatre; in: theatre, one does not believe. So I will try to make the fairy-tale aspect pass into the feelings, and to bring about that these feelings have an action even in the episodes of the plot of the film. So now, if people have confidence in me a little, I am going to be able to work.

And I would like, too, as an experiment, an exercise, to make *La Nouvelle histoire de Mouchette*. It is a very harsh story, of course.

GODARD: The character of Marie, in *Balthazar*, much resembles Chantal of another Bernanos novel: *La Joie*—which, moreover, in the past I wanted to make.

BRESSON: Yes, perhaps. I must, in fact, have read *La Joie*, but, you know, I read few novels . . . However, I must have read at least some passages. The end, perhaps . . . And the novel ends, if I remember well, on the death of a priest.

GODARD: Yes, that is it.

BRESSON: But the character of the *Nouvelle Mouchette* is something marvellous in this sense that it is still childhood—a period between childhood and adolescence—caught in the harshness. Not caught in the silliness, but really in catastrophe. That is admirable, and that is what I am going to try to render. And there, on the contrary, instead of dispersing myself (if I can say that, for I try always not to disperse myself) in a swarm of different lives and beings, I am going to try to be constantly, absolutely on one face: the face of that little girl, to observe her reactions. Then I will take her, yes, the most awkward little girl, the least an actress, the least a player of roles (now children, little girls especially, are often that terribly much). In short: I will take the most awkward girl that exists, and I will try to draw from her all that she does not suspect that I am drawing from her. It is on that account that that interests me, and, obviously, the camera will not leave her.

GODARD: Will it interest you to give her an accent? For Bernanos spoke with his frightful Picard accent.

BRESSON: No. Certainly not. I do not like accents . . . Bernanos has marvellous flashes. He wrote in a slightly heavy way, but there are two or three things that he found, that he says, about the little girl, that are extraordinary. And it is not psychology . . .

GODARD: Yes, I remember. Thus, he said, that at the moment when one spoke to Mouchette of death, it was as if one had said to her that she could have been a great lady under Louis XIV . . . In short there was a kind of fabulous rapprochement. And exactly, that was not psychology. Although at the same time it rejoins psychology, but it is something so profound . . .

BRESSON: It is not psychology, but as a matter of fact I think, in that connection (and there we come back to what can be so interesting for us), that psychology is now a well known thing for us, admitted, familiar, but that there is perhaps an entire psychology to draw from a cinematograph that is the one of which I think, and in which the unknown happens to us, all the time, in which this unknown is recorded, and that, because a mechanics has made it arise, and not because one intended to find this unknown, which cannot be found, because the unknown is discovered and not found.

Here, we come back to that saying of Picasso, who said that one finds at first, and then one seeks. This is it: one must find . . . One must at first find the thing, and, afterwards, one seeks it. That is to say: one must at first find it, since one wanted to find it, but it is by seeking that one then discovers it.

So, I believe that one must not make a psychological analysis—and psychology is too a priori, a thing—one must paint, and it is in painting that everything will rise.

GODARD: There is an expression, that people no longer use, but it was said in the past; it is: the painting of feelings. That is what you are doing.

BRESSON: Painting—or writing, in this case, it is the same thing—in any case, more than a psychology, it is, I believe, a painting. (Conversation tape recorded)

Translated from the French by Jane Pease

Notes

1. Bresson goes to see all the films (French *Cahiers* editors' note).
2. Pierre Klossowski is a novelist: *Roberte ce soir, La Révocation de L'Édit de Hantes.* (JP)
3. The Studiorama projection room communicates with the Empire Cinerama Theatre. (French *Cahiers*)
4. Blake Edwards's *The Great Race* (French *Cahiers*)
5. *Lancelot* of Chretien de Troyes. (JP)

Pickpocket

Robert Bresson, Possibly

I N 1972 ROBERT BRESSON, in response to my recently published book, *Transcendental Style in Film*, wrote me, "I have always been very surprised not to recognize myself in the image formed by those who are really interested in me." It's equally a shock for a critic to meet a director whom he has respected from a distance and whose films he has studied and interpreted. The critic-interviewer is often quite surprised to discover that "his subject" has a rather different interpretation of his films, their value and meaning. The director will explain patiently and emphatically, for example, that he used a particular tracking shot for an entirely different reason from the one the critic has proposed in two articles and a monograph-in-progress. The critic finds himself with the uncomfortable choice of becoming an obliging Boswell or trying to converse across a widening chasm.

It was with these trepidations that I interviewed Bresson last year—trepidations, the following interview demonstrates, which were fully justified. For I not only respect Bresson, but consider him the most important spiritual artist living (now that Rothko is dead)—a spiritual artist who has forged a style so singular it resists imitation. I had corresponded with Bresson several times from 1969 to 1972 and had fantasized that, upon meeting, we would burst like old friends into eager debate.

The interview indicates something quite different. Bresson was earnest, sincere, hospitable; he continually struggled to make his thoughts clear. Yet there was never the rapport I had hoped for. His answers were not in tune with my questions, or my questions with his answers. It felt as if each idea was fighting to assert itself through a fog of misunderstanding. Perhaps this distance was due to the peculiar nature of a first meeting, or perhaps it was a by-product of the barriers of age, culture, and language. But more likely it was because Bresson cannot (or will not) understand why I respect him, and I cannot (or will not) accept his interpretation of his films.

We talked for four or five hours and although we were rarely on the same wavelength, the discussion often became animated and passionate. I left with my respect for Bresson intact, eager to read the transcribed interview.

Several months later, I sent Bresson an edited copy. He wrote back saying he preferred not to have the interview published. *The Devil Probably* had been shut down for lack of funds, and he was despondent that "it is not possible to make a film in France without a major star or to make a film which is something more than an actor's performance." "Despite the fact that your questions were extremely pertinent," he wrote, "I find the interview flat and uninteresting. Without any doubt I was that day in crisis against everything regarding my profession and fighting against my disgust toward it."

A year later, after the release of *The Devil Probably*, and at the urging of Stéphane Tchalgadjieff, his producer, Bresson relented and agreed to let *Film Comment* publish the interview.

The interview was conducted on May 17, 1976 at Bresson's austere apartment on Quai de Bourbon, Île St. Louis, Paris, overlooking the Seine and in the shadow of Notre Dame. Bresson was preparing to direct *The Devil Probably*. I was in Paris for one day (my first), enroute to Cannes where *Taxi Driver* was to be shown. The interview was arranged by Richard Roud (for *Film Comment*) and Stéphane Tchalgadjieff. Roberta Nevers assisted as interpreter, although once Bresson began speaking in English he needed little assistance. After the interview I prepared to take a photo of Bresson, whereupon he picked up a tan upholstered Louis Quinze chair and pretended to hide behind it.

Saints without Theology

PAUL SCHRADER: I would like to ask you some personal questions, rather than professional ones. Questions I am trying to answer for myself. When I first saw your films, I felt I understood them immediately. No one needed to explain them to me. When Jost comes in to the cell in *A Man Escaped* and Fontaine decides not to kill him, I immediately knew that the film was about grace and redemption. That was the way I was educated. I saw it as a phenomenology of grace, that is: we must choose grace as it appears to us, and, therefore, we will escape, even though we are predestined to escape. (Predestined, because it says in the title he will escape.) We can't escape unless we choose the grace which is offered to us, in this case, the young boy. This seemed natural and logical to me. But in your last three films, the colour films, *Une femme douce*, *Four Nights of a Dreamer*, and *Lancelot*, I feel a new direction in your films which I don't fully understand and . . .

ROBERT BRESSON: Because they are in colour?

SCHRADER: No. My supposition is that in the earlier films there was an effort to create, if not saints, the possibility of saintliness in a world without God, to use Camus's phrase, and I sense that in the most recent films that you are trying to create a kind of saintliness in a world without theology.

BRESSON: You can't say that about *Lancelot*.

SCHRADER: I feel that from *Country Priest* to *Balthazar*, you were working off a given theology, and now you are foraging new terrain. I can understand creating a saint without God, but I can't understand creating a saint without theology. Does this make any sense to you?

BRESSON: No, no, because the more life is what it is—ordinary, simple—without pronouncing the word "God," the more I see the presence of God in that. I don't know how to quite explain that. I don't want to shoot something in which God would be too transparent. So you see, my first films are a bit naive, too simple. It is very hard to make a film, so I did it with great simplicity. The further I go on in work, the more I see difficulty in my work, the more careful I am to do something without too much ideology. Because if it is at the beginning, it wouldn't be at the end. I want to make people who see the film feel the presence of God in ordinary life, like *Une femme douce* in front of death. I think back to the five minutes before she is going to kill herself. There is something there ideological. That death is there and mystery is there, as in *Mouchette*, the way she kills herself, you can feel there is something, which, of course, I don't want to show or talk about. But there is a presence of something which I call God, but I don't want to show it too much. I prefer to make people feel it.

SCHRADER: Do you sense this change?

BRESSON: The change in my work? Of course. I said that in the first film it was too obvious. I don't want it to be.

SCHRADER: Maybe that's what I mean when I say that in your later films, I don't feel a sense of theology.

BRESSON: Not in *Lancelot*?

SCHRADER: You seem to be creating your own theology rather than work off a previous theology.

BRESSON: I see another way to answer your question. Ideology is the moral. I don't want to be ideological. I want to be true, I want to have a certain way of being on top of life, and I don't want to show you anything especially. I want to make people feel life as I do: that life is life, and in everything, the most ordinary, the most material, I see ideology.

SCHRADER: In your book, *Notes on Cinematography*, you write that ideas derived from reading will always be book ideas. In the Godard *Cahiers* interview years ago, you spoke of Jansenism, and in an interview three years ago in *Transatlantic*

Review you also spoke of Jansenism. Do you feel at this point that Jansenism is "book ideas"?

BRESSON: There are two translations of "Jansenism": Jansenism itself, the religious doctrine; or the style which is too cold and too strict. That's what they mean by Jansenism when they call me Jansenist. I don't agree with this at all.

SCHRADER: When you spoke of Jansenism in the interviews?

BRESSON: I did? I don't remember.

SCHRADER: Yes. You spoke of it in distinctly religious terms. You were talking about the concept of chance in *Balthazar*. You said in Jansenism there is a concept of grace by chance.

BRESSON: Yes, I said I would rather be a Jansenist than Jesuit. I don't want to go too deep in abstract conversation. But I think there is predestination in our lives. Certainly. It can't be otherwise.

SCHRADER: I believe that also. Is Jansenism among those "ideas derived from reading which will always be book ideas"?

BRESSON: I want to be as far from literature as possible, as far from every existing art. That's why I say books because I did take my ideas from books, Dostoevsky and others, but I am a bit shy. I don't like to say it so much. It is not because of laziness, but because I wanted to work. It takes me two or three years of thinking to write a film. It takes too long. If I want to work quickly, I have to ask if the producer will take this idea. Until now, I have found only two writers with whom I could agree: Georges Bernanos, a little, not too much, and, of course, Dostoevsky. I would like the source of my films to be in me, apart from literature. Even if I make a film from Dostoevsky, I try always to take out all the literary parts. I try to go directly to the sentiments of the author and only what can pass through me. I don't want to make a film showing the work of Dostoevsky. When I find a book I like, such as *Country Priest*, I take away what I can feel myself. What remained was what I could have written myself.

Suicide

———

SCHRADER: I want to ask you about *The Devil Probably* because it's again about suicide.

BRESSON: How do you know?

SCHRADER: Stéphane told me. Do you pass judgment on the suicide of others?

BRESSON: First of all, there are thirty different suicides for different reasons, and you could as well ask me if I could kill myself. If I agree with suicide, that's what you are saying.

SCHRADER: Yes.

BRESSON: I don't know if I agree, but you know that for Catholics suicide was absolutely forbidden thirty or forty years ago. Priests would refuse to have sacraments if the person committed suicide. But now it has changed. I don't know if it comes from Rome, I am not sure, but I know they are much easier with it now. I try to understand people's sentiments aside from religion. For myself, there is something which makes suicide possible—not even possible but absolutely necessary: it is the vision of void, the feeling of void which is impossible to bear. You want anything to stop your life. I don't know so much about it, but I think two-thirds of the suicides come from this impossible way of living. For that I would be very understanding. There are still many other reasons. Because you are ill without any hope. I think these are very frequent. Somebody who can't bear the idea of dying at a certain date. Like Montelant, who was going blind, who was alone, he couldn't bear it; he lived a very lonely life. I don't know if I was going blind if I wouldn't commit suicide, but I think that the determination to kill yourself comes when it is impossible to do otherwise. I never thought about suicide so deeply, but now I could tell you that there is not one kind of suicide that I could not agree with. Like the young boy of about twenty or twenty-two who killed days ago in the street. But he killed himself after that.

SCHRADER: Stéphane told me that your new film was going to be about a young man that kills himself—no, that arranges for his own death by protest. And I replied, I find it very hard to believe that any character in a film by Bresson would kill himself for anything other than internal reasons.

BRESSON: You know, there are young people who kill themselves for this same reason that he does in my film. I think in the whole world things are going very badly. People are becoming more and more materialistic and cruel, but cruel in another way than in the Middle Ages. Cruel by laziness, by indifference, egotism, because they think only about themselves and not at all about what is happening around them, so that they let everything grow ugly, stupid. They are all interested in money only. Money is becoming their God. God doesn't exist anymore for many. Money is becoming something you must live for. You know, even your astronauts, the first one who put his foot on the moon, said that when he first saw our earth, he said it is something so miraculous, so marvellous, don't spoil it, don't touch it. More deeply I feel the rotten way they are spoiling the earth. All the countries. Silence doesn't exist anymore; you can't find it. That, for me, would make it impossible to live. The way this young person wants to die—he doesn't kill himself, himself—he makes himself be killed. The old Robin Hood people used to commit suicide with the help of friends. He kills himself for a big purpose.

SCHRADER: Does he kill himself for personal reasons or to make the world better?

BRESSON: Yes, there is both in his reasons. Yes, to be an example. Yes, to be martyred.

SCHRADER: I hope you will be able to see *Taxi Driver* because it is also about a man who realizes the void in his own life, and knows that life has no meaning, but he doesn't understand that he can kill himself, so he tries to kill the president, thinking that he will be killed in return. He fails, but the feeling is the same.

BRESSON: When we talked about void, I didn't mean when somebody thinks his life is nothing. The void is a total absence of something. You are talking about a feeling which I could very well imagine, if he thinks his life is nothing, that he asks for nothing, that what he does is absolutely uninteresting—there is a void in that. But the void I was talking about with people who commit suicide is something terrible.

SCHRADER: A spiritual void?

BRESSON: Yes. But, of course when I do write something—I am not a writer, my friend, at all—but I make a great effort to write because making a film is not interesting if you don't write it yourself. Perhaps I would make a mistake if I were a novelist. But this way of wanting to die is many things: it is a disgust with life, with people around you, with living only for money. To see everything which is good to live for disappear, when you see that you cannot fall in love with people, not only with a woman, but all the people around you, you find yourself alone with people. I can imagine living in disgust with so many things which are against you around you, and then you feel like suicide.

SCHRADER: Does the void come from within or does the void come from without?

BRESSON: Both. The void around you makes the void within you.

SCHRADER: In *Notes*, you quote da Vinci as saying in an artistic context that all that matters is the end. The ends of your films are very spare—*A Country Priest, Balthazar, Lancelot*—very simple, and, although Leonardo writes in an artistic context, it's also true in a religious context. In religion we are taught the only thing that matters is the end: how you die, like the thief on the cross. Which brings us back to the question of suicide. You are a man who seeks to completely control his artistic world, yet the most crucial decision, which is the end of life, cannot be controlled because it is, most often, whim or accident. One never dies in the way one hopes for oneself, and if the end is the most important, then suicide is an artistic decision as well as a religious one.

BRESSON: Perhaps, perhaps not. Because quite often what is important in the life of a man who creates, an artist, would not be the end of his life, but the middle, so the way he dies does not count so much. Let's take somebody I knew a little bit, Montelant. He thought that life was finished for him so he made it a little shorter himself. I mean, his life was not in his death. His life was living. When he decided to die, he said, my life is finished.

SCHRADER: One can control his life, yet the ultimate decision is never his own.

BRESSON: No, but if I would one day feel that all that is interesting in life is finished and I can't work any more, I'm not sure what I would do. But it has nothing to do with my new film. I am not twenty-two years old. You know there are more suicides among young people; they said this in the paper the other day. In France—I don't know why—when they are young, about twenty or twenty-two, they are much more fragile, sensitive. They have nothing to live on, especially religion. The collapse of the Catholic religion, this reason and others, can work very strongly on the mind of a young person.

The young man in my film is looking for something on top of life, but he doesn't find it. He goes to church to seek it, and he doesn't find it. At night he goes to Notre Dame, to find God, alone. He says lines like this, "When you come in a church, or in a cathedral, God is there"—it is the line of his death—"but if a priest happens to come, God is not there anymore." This is why, although I am very religious—was very religious, more or less—I can't go to church in the last four or five years when these people are making their new mass. It is not possible. I go inside the cathedral and sit down. There I feel God, the presence of something divine which doesn't exist anymore in the mass. The young man cannot feel God's presence in the daytime with people moving about and the priests there. He goes to find something which he could rely on, but something happens. The police come. I am sure there are young people who commit suicide because they can't find this anymore.

SCHRADER: What will happen to you when you die?

BRESSON: (Laughter.) You know, I can't take my mind off the fact that I believe you still feel things. You feel the loneliness, you feel the darkness of your coffin, you feel the cold. Resurrection is a most difficult thing to believe. The resurrection of the body: what is it? I don't know. But you know, I feel that I feel it. I have this certitude that there is something different than earth where we live which you can't imagine, but you can imagine that you could imagine. Sometimes I have had in my life, not now, something like a presence. Of what, I don't know, but I have felt it. It was very short, but I was very much impressed by it. It is something that I cannot explain. I go very often to the country on weekends when I feel the trees, the plants. I can't understand people who say there is no God. What does it mean? That everything is natural for them?

SCHRADER: If you feel even for one moment that there is a presence of something else, then it is hard to believe that when you die, you will be completely lost.

BRESSON: Yes, except that one day you believe in the middle of the day and at night, you don't. You know what I mean, one day you believe and one day you don't. Faith is a shock. It is something you get; you don't know how. But belief is something else. Your intelligence tells you to do something. I think I

Lancelot du Lac

am in the middle, between faith and believing. In my film, when the woman is going to die, I want it to appear there is something else after death. That's why when people become so materialistic, religion is not possible, because every religion is poverty and poverty is the way of having contact with mystery and with God. When Catholicism wants to be materialistic, God is not there.

SCHRADER: A good minister will say the same thing you say in *Notes*, which is: I am only a way to the mystery. Therefore, my personality and the personality of the actors are not important; it is only important that I enable you to see what there is. But then, most ministers are like actors. They are very bad and they are interested only in themselves.

BRESSON: I don't know what they are trying to do now, the Protestants. They are trying to explain what is not explainable. That is why many young people try to find something idealistic in Tao—because they need something to live.

Camera Style

SCHRADER: Have you seen any of Ozu's films?

BRESSON: No, I don't go anymore to see movies. I may have seen one a long time ago.

SCHRADER: Ozu's career is very much like yours. He was known as a comedy director, but as he grew older, he stopped moving the camera and he started closing in on the drama. Finally he made films in which the camera doesn't move, very similar to your films. He concentrates on the face, on the composition, on the flatness of life, and lets the intercutting of the events be the story. It is interesting that both he and you began in light comedy.

BRESSON: It was completely bad, what I did in comedy.

SCHRADER: When Antonioni saw his first Ozu film, he walked out and said, "What is there for me to do?" So, perhaps it is better that you have not seen his films.

BRESSON: All the time, the camera moves, but very discreetly. I can't bear it in a film when you see it used as a broom. There are two things that are bad: when the camera moves—like this [making sweeping gesture]—or when you shoot something that is impossible for the human eye to see. What they all do very often.

SCHRADER: You say in your book: make rules, but don't be afraid to break them.

BRESSON: Yes, yes. I don't think much of technique, or making technique a part of things. If you find a new way to catch life, nature, this could change details, but not the whole. I don't think so much of what I do when I work, but I try to feel something, to see without explaining, to catch it as near as I can—that's all. And that's why I don't move so much. It's like approaching a wild animal. If you are too brusque about it, it will run away. I think you must think a lot in the intervals of working and writing, but when you work, you mustn't think anymore. Thinking is a terrible enemy. You should try to work not with your intelligence, but with your senses and your heart. With your intuition.

SCHRADER: I absolutely agree. Symptoms are universal, causes are particular. Symptoms are more interesting because we all have the symptoms, but we have different causes. Movies should be about symptoms rather than about causes.

BRESSON: It is very difficult to see things. So many times you go walking in the street, you look at things, but you don't see them. If you see the look in a man's eyes and at the same time see the reason why he is looking as he is, you are not touched.

SCHRADER: If movies provide the symptoms truly, the viewer will supply the causes.

BRESSON: I want people to guess, to think. But it must be very clean and sharp, not fuzzy and confusing. Today movies make people want to know everything in advance, to be shown everything in a way I don't understand.

SCHRADER: What I love about movies is that if you and I are here talking and if you re-cut so that we are now talking in New York, the audience will assume that somehow we got from Paris to New York. You can do the very same thing in spiritual ways. If you show a situation and if you cut to another place, the audience will make the leap with you. The audience will jump across the ocean with you.

Pornography

BRESSON: Yes, but if you don't show a succession of things exactly as they are in life, people stop understanding. Pornography has brought that to the cinema, that you must see everything. So the public is now conditioned to films where you show everything. It is terrible, I can't work anymore. If I can't make people guess, if I am obliged to show everything, it doesn't interest me to work.

SCHRADER: I think that movies and pornography are different. I, personally, am not threatened by explicit movies. In *Notes* you say "the nude, if it is not beautiful, is obscene." Do you feel that the explicit is by its very nature wrong?

BRESSON: When it is explicit, it is not sexual. The same as mystery. If you don't make people guess, there is nothing there.

SCHRADER: I believe that sex is mysterious whether you see it or not.

BRESSON: Yes, but when you see too much, it is not mysterious anymore.

SCHRADER: Even if you see it all, it is still mysterious.

BRESSON: Only what is lovely—sexual life is beautiful—but how they do it in pornographic films is ugly and dirty.

SCHRADER: But could you not show pornography—show people fucking—and also be mysterious? It is no less mysterious than watching me drink from the glass.

BRESSON: Not by showing things, but by my sensation of things. Making people feel how I feel. The most important and the most real is my way of feeling— to make people have the same sensation that I have in front of things.

SCHRADER: Would you not agree that you learn no more about sexual feeling from seeing pornography than you learn about what cognac tastes like by watching me drink this?

BRESSON: You are quite right. There is no art in only showing things as they are, in a filmed succession of things. An idiot could see what is in front of his eyes and that's all. If you try to make people feel and think instead of hearing and seeing, then it is artistic.

SCHRADER: Do you oppose pornography on moral grounds or on artistic grounds?

BRESSON: Not on moral grounds.

SCHRADER: Artistic grounds?

BRESSON: Yes.

SCHRADER: If you could use the new eroticism, would you?

BRESSON: No. Pornography is false sexual life.

SCHRADER: But all films are false.

BRESSON: Not to love. Not with a work of art. I tried to see a few pornographic films, but I left because they turned sexual life into something horrible which doesn't exist. Perhaps for some people, but not for me.

Violence

SCHRADER: It's like violence; it has to be used in a certain way. There is a parody of violence in *Four Nights of a Dreamer*. The suicides are always non-violent; why?

BRESSON: Because I do not like violence. When you see violence in a movie, you know that it is false. It doesn't touch me at all.

SCHRADER: Suicide is a very violent act.

BRESSON: It's very violent inside you, but it's not very violent to watch.

SCHRADER: For me, the notion of suicide is one of violence. It's the idea of blasting things out of your head which are destroying you; you don't really want to die, you want to destroy the way you are thinking. Suicide involves a lot of violence, a lot of blood, it's an explosion inside your head. I see suicide much more violently than you do. I'm moved when Mouchette rolls, when Femme Douce leaps, when Balthazar falls. I'm moved when the cross comes up in *Country Priest*, but to me, giving oneself to death is a very violent act, and I would never kill myself in a non-violent way.

BRESSON: I couldn't show violence, the blood, and those terrible things, because it would have been faked for the movie. People would say, "How did they do that?"

SCHRADER: I understand your objection.

BRESSON: Sometimes you see things well done of this sort, but it is not moving—because you know it is false, because it is forced. But what you can do is have the sensation of death. You can be moved by death if you don't show it, if you suggest it. But if you show it, it's finished. The same thing about love. You don't feel love if you see two people making love.

Iconography

SCHRADER: I sense a progression in your films: from the exterior to the interior life, from Anne-Marie to Thérèse in *Les Anges du péché*, from the countess to the priest in *Country Priest*, finally to the object itself in *Balthazar*, to purely the external like a graphic object. Ozu did the same thing: he turned to a vase. So many movies are based upon the two-dimensional image of the face—the icon of the face. One thing that bothered me about *Lancelot* is that you don't see the faces.

BRESSON: I don't know what you mean.

SCHRADER: This has to be a conscious decision, because many times in *Lancelot* the frame line is just below the face. Then when you see the face, it is often covered by a helmet.

BRESSON: When he comes to pray in front of the cross, you see him entirely, you see his face. I don't see what you mean.

SCHRADER: In your other films, one always remembers the faces, but in *Lancelot*, one doesn't.

BRESSON: Because the face is not special. It doesn't work. His face was a very difficult face to take.

SCHRADER: Are you saying that the reason the camera doesn't focus on Lancelot's face is because you weren't happy with the actor.

BRESSON: No, I didn't say that. I say that there are faces which are different from others.

SCHRADER: I think it's very clear that you are not as interested in Lancelot's face as you were in Michel's, or Fontaine's, or even Joan of Arc's.

BRESSON: I understand what you mean, but it is not proof for me. I don't see how you can say that.

SCHRADER: Are you less interested in faces?

BRESSON: On the contrary. I am more and more interested in faces. You say in *Lancelot* you don't see his face?

SCHRADER: So often the mask is over it.

BRESSON: The way it was photographed, perhaps. Maybe the difference between black-and-white and colour.

SCHRADER: I also have a sense that in past films you did actions in three's. In *Lancelot*, everything was done in five's.

BRESSON: I don't understand what you mean.

SCHRADER: You usually did things five times. If it was the jousting combat, you would see the lance five times. Or the horses' feet: in past films you would see a shot of the feet three times, in *Lancelot*, five times.

BRESSON: It was unconscious. I needed it five times. I don't know why. Perhaps it was a hidden reason. I did not show it five times instead of three on purpose.

SCHRADER: Do you love iconography?

BRESSON: I like to start with a flat expression, as flat as possible, so that the expression comes when all the shots are put together. The more flat it is when I am shooting, the more expressive it is edited.

Conclusion

BRESSON: When you come back from Cannes, are you going to pass by Paris?

SCHRADER: No, unfortunately I have to get back. This is a strange trip for me because I was too busy, actually, to make it.

BRESSON: But you are pleased with your film, *Taxi Driver*?

SCHRADER: Extremely.

BRESSON: Are you going to have the big prize at Cannes?

SCHRADER: I think so.

BRESSON: You are pleased with it?

SCHRADER: Yes. Although it is not directed the way I would direct it. I wrote an austere film and it was directed in an expressionistic way. I think that the two qualities work together. There is a tension in the film that is very interesting.

BRESSON: Why didn't you shoot it yourself?

SCHRADER: I hope to direct shortly. I am still very young and it takes a while. In *Taxi Driver*, I had great faith in the director and the actor, who are friends. I believed in what they would do.

BRESSON: So I will see it and write to you.

L'Argent

I Seek Not Description But Vision: Robert Bresson on *L'Argent*

MICHEL CIMENT: People always refer to asceticism in connection with your film-making. It's become a kind of cliché. But what strikes me is the vigour.

ROBERT BRESSON: Vigour comes from precision. Precision is vigorous. When I am working poorly, I am imprecise. Precision is another form of poetry.

CIMENT: Vigour and speed. Your screenplay, directed by someone else, would have made a 13 minute film, not an 85 minute film.

BRESSON: That is a question of composition. I use the word "composition" as opposed to the word "construction." I listen to my films as I make them, the way a pianist listens to the sonata he is performing, and I make the picture conform to sound rather than the other way round. Transitions from one picture to another, from one scene to the next are like shifts in a musical scale. Our eyesight occupies a large proportion of our brain, perhaps as much as two-thirds. Yet our eyes are not so powerful a means of imagination, not so varied and profound as our ears. And so, as imagination is a critical element in any creative process, how could one not privilege the sound aspect? It used to be that in between films I stopped thinking. Then I started taking notes—I even published them. I was interested in what made me work the way I do. The answer is that it is entirely a question of instinct. It is not a matter of choice. I made my first film, *Les Affaires publiques*, in the 1930s. You could call it a burlesque, although the description is not really accurate. "Burlesque" is a term that was applied to certain American films at the time. Painters, me included, would rush to the movies precisely because they moved, the leaves moved. The last scene of *Les Affaires publiques* depicted a ship being launched. I'd obtained footage of the launch of the *Normandie* from the Cie Transatlantique. The boat slipped into the water, sank down and the bottle wouldn't break. Just a matter of chance. I trust in chance. There was a clown in this film called Béby who was unbelievable.

He didn't act. I let him do as he pleased. Which is how I realized that a film is not a matter of acting, but of successive inventions.

When I came to make my first full-length feature, *Les Anges du péché* right at the start of shooting, I was appalled. I had only female actresses, playing nuns. I said, *if that's the way it is, I'm quitting, the movie is over.* Their delivery and gestures were all wrong. Every night, the producer sent me a telegram asking me to ensure they acted. Every night, there were tears and lamentation. They were delightful ladies and they did their best to comply with what I wanted. And even then, it was my ear, rather than my eye, which hated what they were doing. The intonation, the modulations were harder to alter than their way of moving.

Equally, I was very slow to notice that mysteriously invisible orchestral scores were contrary to the essence of film. I was slow to realize that sound defines space on film. A voice treated like a sound effect seems to give the screen an extra dimension. People who experimented with 3D cinema were barking up the wrong tree. The third dimension is sound. It gives the screen depth, it makes characters seem tangible. It makes it appear that one might walk amongst them.

CIMENT: Is your interest in sound the reason why there is so little depth of field in your films?

BRESSON: Maybe. But also because I use only one lens. I like to stand the camera at the same distance as the eye in real life. Which is why, in my films, the background is sometimes out of focus. Which is unimportant because once again it is the sound which gives a sense of distance and perspective.

CIMENT: To go back to my initial question, *L'Argent* is unfashionably short. Why are today's films so long?

BRESSON: Because filmmaking has grown slovenly. Soon films will be three hours long because they don't know, they've stopped looking. It is a form of rest, a holiday for directors who are really theatre directors. I don't understand why it is that those who can write—and many of them can—don't write their own screenplays. I have a hunch the reason they use screenwriters is that, if film-making is an art, if the filmmaker is responsible for everything he does, then constantly he undermines himself, it is a desperate business, whereas having a mate write the screenplay removes every last scrap of uncertainty, leaving you free to work more lazily.

I'd like to have a studio full of young filmmakers with something to say. You know what Degas said, "When you know nothing, life is easy." In other words, the sooner one knows, the better. But when you start shooting, it is important to forget everything you know, make yourself empty and naked before your will. Cézanne used to say, "I paint, I work. I am free of thought." Cinema has got some way to go. Let it! Maybe it will turn out to find what it needs among actors. I doubt it, though. The strength of an art is in its purity. I have noticed that some directors choose non-professional actors and then get them to act. But you saw that in *L'Argent*, no one acts. That's why it seems so fast. What they say is not what matters. Sometimes, I have found it hard to get non-professional actors to speak in a way that the audience's ear might find satisfactory. This time, I think that the dialogue is spoken "right," but with infinitesimal modulations. All the different elements of a film must have something in common if they are to match at each transition. That is true of pictures as well as of sound. Non-professional actors must speak in a way that is entirely their own but which at the same time must not differ significantly from the way in which the others speak. If you charted the way actors speak on a graph, there would be enormous variations in the intensity of their speech, whereas in my films, speech-patterns are more even. So that it all fits together properly. The same is true of the picture. I once said, I flatten the image as though I was ironing it. I do not deprive pictures of meaning, but I minimize it so that each picture loses its independence. The same is true of actors who, in most films, spend their time trying to emphasize their difference, proclaiming their personas, even though that persona does not really exist, is pure invention, an artificial self, not a real one.

CIMENT: You also say that powerful pictures and a powerful soundtrack must not go hand-in-hand.

BRESSON: True, when sound and picture support each other, the sum is bland and weak. But things are not quite that simple. What enters our eyes during a film-shoot emerges from two supposedly perfect copying-machines, which are in fact nowhere near perfect. One of them, the camera, gives us a misleading notion of the appearance of people and things. The other, the sound-recorder, gives us an exact transcription of sound. If a film was to be entirely coherent, the camera would have to steal a bit of reality off the sound-recorder, which is too realistic. The audience would then get so much more out of film. Instead of which, audiences are only interested in how good the actor is and in the modulations of the actor's voice. At the end of *L'Argent*, I tried to capture the force in the air just before a storm. It is not something you can describe in words. I get it by not thinking about anything. There may be some kind of calculation going on, but if so it is not conscious. You have to go with your sensibility. There is nothing else. I've been called an intellectual, but of course I'm not. Writing is unbelievably difficult but I have to do it, because everything must originate with me. I've been called a Jansenist[1] which is madness. I'm the opposite. I am interested in impressions. I'll give you an example, taken from *L'Argent*. When I'm on the Grands Boulevards,[2] the first thing I think is *How do they impress me?* And the answer is that they impress me as a mass of legs and a sound of feet on the pavements. I tried to communicate this impression by picture and by sound. Then people complain about my focusing on the bottom half of people's trousers. Brilliant! They made the same complaint about horses' legs in *Lancelot du Lac*. I showed the horses' legs without showing the riders, in order to draw the audience's attention to their muscular power when they back up at the start of a tournament. There's no point in showing the rider then. It would confuse everything. It would bring something else into play. People would look at the rider and think, "I wonder what he's going to do next?" In everyday life, we often look down at the ground as we walk, or perhaps a bit higher, but we don't necessarily look everyone full in the face, unless they're a pretty woman and we want to see what she looks like. I know why people expect films to show everyone full in the face. It's part of a theatrical tradition because in theatre you can see everything.

CIMENT: You no longer choose your "models" for their moral resemblance to your characters.

BRESSON: So long as there is nothing in their physical appearance, in their voice or their way of expressing themselves, the decision is quickly taken. People are so full of contradictions, of oddities, the kind Dostoevsky almost turned into a system. I enjoy working with strangers, they surprise me. I am never disappointed by my models. They always give me something new, that I would not have been able to think up and which suits my purpose. In any case, I believe in accidents, happy accidents. Lucien, the photographer's employee, like Yvon, the protagonist, is a combination of happy accidents and intuition. My intuition.

CIMENT: You've never used a writer, except for your first two films which were written by Giraudoux and Cocteau, no less!

BRESSON: I owe them a great deal. Afterwards, I was in a position to be sole craftsman, from writing to screening. But at first, I had to find help. Giraudoux worked with me and I was overawed, like a schoolboy. I'd say, "It ought to be something like this," short, or long, and so on, and he would obey, he worked terribly fast. I'd laboriously written three-quarters of the dialogue for *Les Dames du Bois de Boulogne* when I asked Cocteau for help. I'd tried in vain to work with Paul Morand, Nimier, Supervielle . . . it never came to anything. In the meantime, I wrote the dialogue myself, because I knew that in the end one has to do everything oneself. Then Cocteau solved all my problems in an hour-and-a-half, scribbling on the corner of a tablecloth in his apartment.

CIMENT: What is the difference between your adaptations—even if the adaptation is very loose—from Bernanos, Dostoevsky, Tolstoy and your original writing like *Au hasard Balthazar* or *Le Diable probablement*?

BRESSON: There is very little difference, I think. For *L'Argent*, I started with a short story of Tolstoy's called "False Coupon," and the idea it is based on, which is an account of how evil spreads. Then I let myself get carried away by my own daydreams until the end, where I slip in the notion that the protagonist is redeemed, that he can save himself, which does not come at the same point in the short story. There comes a point when I let everything go, like a horse with its reins loose, and I let my imagination lead wherever it wants. Tolstoy's story is quite different. "False Coupon" is a magnificent short story, but right at the start Tolstoy refers to God, to the Gospels. I couldn't go down that route because my film is about today's unconscious indifference when people only think about themselves and their families. I made *Le Diable probablement* against the same indifference, except that in that case I was concerned with the world at large. Perhaps you recall that at that time quite a few young people were burning themselves alive. Not any more. The present generation is not remotely interested in that. Very odd. To them it's all normal. They belong to an era in which the fact that we are ruining this earth of ours is not shocking. At the time of *Le Diable probablement*, someone told me about a boy who had burnt himself alive in his school playground, somewhere in the North of France. I wrote to his parents asking them to let me see his diary. I didn't use it. I wanted to find out what had gone inside the head of this chap who didn't express his thoughts very clearly, but who had got into a panic about what we were doing to the world.

CIMENT: How is it that you decide that a story you are reading is worth making into a film?

BRESSON: Regarding "False Coupon." *I* knew right away. I saw the film immediately because it related to my wanting to make a film about a chain reaction leading to a major disaster. A banknote that ends up murdering loads of people. Why did Julien Sorel kill Madame de Rénal? Did he know five minutes before doing the deed that he was going to do it? Of course not. What happens at that precise juncture? The forces of rebellion are suddenly unleashed within one, all the hidden hatred that builds up inside. I was more interested in Tolstoy's account of all that, than in his religious ideas, fascinating though these are, because one cannot discuss religion in the same way today.

CIMENT: Tolstoy's story has a complex structure, you combined several characters into the one.

BRESSON: I simplified everything, first by elimination on paper and then, much more so, during shooting, so as not to overburden the pictures, so as not to render them opaque, which perhaps lends the film its consistency—in the sense Edgar Allen Poe uses the word in *Eureka*. The poetry, if there is any, comes from the tautness. It is not a "poetic" poetry, but cinematographic poetry. It arises out of my simplification, which is only a more direct way of seeing people and things.

CIMENT: In your *Notes sur le cinématographe*, you write in big letters ORDER AND DISORDER AT A RESPECTFUL DISTANCE, which relates to your method in that you prepare everything very meticulously, and then leave room for accident.

BRESSON: Shake the tree, as Charlie Chaplin used to say. Not too much, in my opinion. You need a bit of disorder, because it is real. Oddly enough, some of my films look very meticulously preproduced but weren't at all in fact. Like *Pickpocket*, written in three months and shot in big crowds, in a very short time. I also shot *Procès de Jeanne d'Arc* very rapidly, though that was easier in that there was a unity of place and characters. Regarding *L'Argent*, I was wary of the large number of locations, the crowds, and I was worried I might lose my thread. But I managed to move from one scene to the next using sound connections—perhaps I should say musical connections. In the old days, I used to fade through from one scene to the next, but an aural transition is so much better. No one does it. People say I drag out the end of each scene because nowadays as soon as the speaking is over, either they bring the music in or another scene's dialogue begins. Otherwise, they say there is a gap!

CIMENT: It is hard to imagine, knowing your films, how much in them is improvised.

BRESSON: In my previous films, as in *L'Argent*, I never tried to settle in advance what I would do nor how I would achieve it. There has to be a shock at the moment of doing, there has to be a feeling that the humans and things to be filmed are new, you have to throw surprises on film. That's what happened in the scene on the Grands Boulevards which I mentioned earlier, I could feel the steps, I focused on the protagonist's legs, and that way I could propel him through the crowd to where he needed to be. That's the Grands Boulevards, as far as I am concerned, all the motion. Otherwise, I might as well have used a picture postcard. The thing that struck me when I used to go to the cinema was that everything had been *wanted* in advance, down to the last detail. The actors prepared their performances, etc. Painters do not know in advance how their picture is going to turn out, a sculptor cannot tell what his sculpture will be, a poet does not plan a poem in advance . . .

CIMENT: How do you find your titles? *L'Argent*, for instance.

BRESSON: It seems obvious. Right away: *L'Argent*. I don't even think about it. If someone had said, you can't use that, it's taken, I should have replied that I didn't care . . . All anyone cares about is money, whether private individuals or governments. The only thing that people consider about a fellow human-being is, is he wealthy? is he worth a great deal? I was astonished to see a poster in the Metro which said *France's best-selling electric cooker*. Best-seller . . . The film that grosses the most is the best. Do you see? Money is what counts. With *Au hasard Balthazar* I was looking for a Biblical title. Balthazar is one of the Three Wise Men. I liked the rhyme of *hasard* and Balthazar. *Le Diable probablement* came to me, early on, as I was writing.

CIMENT: In *Le Diable probablement* there is a similar relationship between pre-determination and free-will.

BRESSON: I am more and more convinced, I have a feeling that, increasingly, what people expect of film stars is that they should explain the psychologically inexplicable. Non-professional actors must not explain anything because they don't know themselves. If they did, they'd be geniuses and they'd serve another purpose. Non-professional actors are a complete mystery, like everyone I meet. Wanting to get to know someone is of interest. What is contained behind that forehead, those cheeks, those eyes? The most fascinating thing in life is curiosity. I want people to want to know, I want them to want to explore the mystery that is life, a mystery not to be imitated, only imagined.

CIMENT: Your films respect fragments of reality, but those fragments are assembled in a certain order.

BRESSON: Fragments of the real. The expression is in the relationship between them, in how they are put together not in mimicry, in the intonations of actors as in the theatre. In a film, sound and picture progress jointly, overtake each other, slip back, come together again, move forwards jointly again. What interests me, on a screen, is counterpoint.

CIMENT: You emphasize what differentiates your filmmaking and theatre. But you, who are a painter and who was born to paint, do not believe that there is any kind of competition between cinema and fine art.

BRESSON: I love theatre. But I do not believe that cinema ought to be photographing theatre, nor is it a synthesis of all the other arts. I like to quote Stendhal, who said *The other arts taught me the art of writing*. That's what I tell young people. One must acquire an eye and an ear.

CIMENT: Your pictures have a strong plastic quality but they never put one in mind of painting. Are you not concerned that cinema might be contaminated by painting?

BRESSON: No. If I ever think of painting, it is as a means of escape. I mean escaping picture postcards. That is not the reason I forego my painterly eye when composing pictures for films. You will have noticed that in *L'Argent* there are a series of close-ups whose only function is to add sensation. When the father, a piano-player, drops a glass, his daughter is in the kitchen. Her dustpan and sponge are ready. I do not then enter the room, but cut immediately to a close shot which I like very much, the wet floor with the sound of the sponge. That is music, rhythm, sensation. I am going to show a man entering a room, like in the theatre, or in most films. Only a door handle turning. You will have noticed, too, that the protagonist is not immediately described. First his legs are seen, then his back, then a three-quarter profile, then suddenly, walking alone, he reveals himself.

CIMENT: Contrary to general opinion, your camera moves a great deal, but always in an almost imperceptible way. There are no ostentatious tracking shots or pans.

BRESSON: Because they seem totally false. When do we see lamps and tables move? That's the effect sudden camera motion has. I seek not description but vision. A sense of motion comes from building a series of visions and fitting them together. It is not really sayable in words. Increasingly, what I am after—and with *L'Argent* it became almost a working method—is to communicate the impressions I feel. It is the impression of a thing and not the thing itself that matters. The real is something we make for ourselves. Everyone has their own. There is the real and there is our version of it. When I started out, with *Les Dames du Bois de Boulogne*, I was after something different, a kind of coherence, that's all. Nowadays, I show a basketful of potatoes as an old lady picks them, not her face. There's no need, because immediately after, we see her doing something much more significant, when she comes up and is going to leave. This is also the only time she receives the young man's assistance.

CIMENT: You have worked with five different directors of photography: Agostini, Burel, Lhomme, Cloquet and De Santis. Was it a break every time?

BRESSON: Not really. We always got on well. I've never been influenced by their methods. They always agreed to everything I asked, knowing what they were capable of. I like De Santis because we see human beings and objects the same way. If I ever make *Genesis*, which I hope to do, I will no doubt work with him. He achieves what I like, which is to show people in the round, in their convexness.

CIMENT: Do you talk to him before a shoot?

BRESSON: I tell him roughly what I want, the overall impression of the film. Details come as a surprise, but they do not affect our initial agreement. Light is often defined on the spur of the moment. For instance, when Lucien stands at the cash machine, the script said he saw by the light of a streetlamp but when we shot it, I realized that the bright colours of a luminous sign would be much better.

CIMENT: In *L'Argent* you give a harsh description of the bourgeoisie, with the people who sell frames, the schoolboy Norbert's parents . . . The positive characters are Yvon, who delivers fuel oil and the old lady who is taken advantage of.

BRESSON: Naturally. That's how I see it. But it is not an anti-bourgeois film. It is not about the bourgeoisie, but about specific people. I am a bourgeois myself. I simply happened to have observed people like that. That's what I liked about the Tolstoy story. People from other classes can behave in the same way, for the love of their children. They are not intrinsically evil, but their behaviour has evil consequences.

CIMENT: The neat thing is how Tolstoy's story is made contemporary, with schoolchildren, photography frames and so on.

BRESSON: I wanted to preserve the initial point of view, because it is accurate. I simply transposed it to France and to our own times. I kept the photographer so that we could have a dark room for him to hide in.

CIMENT: Do you collect a large number of sounds prior to the dub?

BRESSON: I do as many live takes as I can. If I hear something I like, I get it recorded—some water, a bird's wing flapping. The trouble with shooting out of doors is that there is so much noise. When I am not too tired I shoot in the evenings, or at night. That's how we got the water sounds in *L'Argent*.

CIMENT: The beauty of the murder scene in *L'Argent* is in the emotion of the dog's lament.

BRESSON: Many animals are exquisitely sensitive and we show very little interest in this. I wish I had used this more often. It is like another facet of our own sensitivity, an extension of our own joys and sorrows.

CIMENT: Of all the many doors in *L'Argent,* the last, through which the prisoner passes, remains open.

BRESSON: If I choose why can I not have ten times more doors in my films? Doors opening and closing are magnificent, the way they point to unsolved mysteries. What's wrong with doors? They have a music to them, a rhythm. But habit is lethal! Perhaps it is too symbolic, but I love passers-by who stare into nothingness. Once upon a time, we had everything. Now we have nothing.

CIMENT: You say you are a jolly pessimist, but your recent films are more sombre than *Pickpocket* or *Un condamné . . .* which culminated in a kind of jubilation.

BRESSON: I am sorry that in *L'Argent* I was unable to linger on Yvon's redemption, on the idea of redemption, but the rhythm of the film, at that stage, would not stand for it. Perhaps I do see the world more sombrely than I used to, unintentionally. There is something to that.

CIMENT: You rarely commission film composers, preferring classical musicians like Mozart, Lully, Monteverdi, Schubert or Bach.

BRESSON: That is of no importance now that I have completely done away with atmospheric music in my films. It took me a long time to see how nefarious it was, particularly if it is glorious music. Immediately, it makes the pictures seem flat, whereas a sound effect will give them depth.

CIMENT: Why did you choose, in *L'Argent*, Bach's "Chromatic Fantasia"?

BRESSON: Because I wasn't going to have my pianist play anything sentimental. Not just before a storm. As it is, it is too sentimental, though Bach is not. I made a slight mistake . . .

CIMENT: But Schubert's Sonata no. 20, which you use in *Au hasard Balthazar* is definitely sentimental.

BRESSON: Unfortunately! Apart from braying and the sound of hooves. I did not know how to fill the silences. I used this piece as a kind of language for the donkey's soul, a *leitmotiv*. But I am not proud of doing so and it is the last time I ever used music from an unexplained source.

CIMENT: Which of your films are you most satisfied with?

BRESSON: I don't know. I never see them again, or almost never. I got joy from all of them, while they were being made. Some, like *Pickpocket*, were made fast and easily. I like the way it moves and the way one scene moves into the next. *Au hasard Balthazar* has got some inspired moments in it, as well as imperfection. It takes a series of unthinkable, mad coincidences to make the impossible come right. In *Quatre nuits d'un rêveur*, I like the theme: "Love is illusion, so let's get on with it!" That's hardly pessimistic. But no film is perfect.

CIMENT: The sudden transition to the countryside is magnificent in *L'Argent*.

BRESSON: I was very worried about the change in location. I was worried it would disjoint the film and that I should lose my thread. There is a reason for it, though. Prisons tend to be on the outskirts of towns, near the countryside. Yvon goes for a walk there and, not knowing what to do with himself, enters the first hotel he sees. Which is how it all begins. The house or murder and the washing-place were locations I knew, near my house at Epernon.

CIMENT: Yvon is a kind of exterminating angel.

BRESSON: He is forsaken by society. The carnage is an expression of his despair. What was interesting about his meeting the little lady was that it was a meeting between acceptance and revolt. What would come of it? What I want is to get at the moral core, not just tell a tale.

CIMENT: But all your films are about a collision between predestination and free-will, between chance and necessity.

BRESSON: Which is how we are. Three times out of four, chance governs us. And our will is absorbed by predestination. In *La Vie de Saint Ignace*, which I came close to filming a long time ago, there is an idea of predestination. Ignatius Loyola turns up by accident, does not achieve much himself, but finds the right people to surround himself with and founds the Jesuit order.

CIMENT: Your profession confronts your predetermined intention and the chance occurences of a film-shoot.

BRESSON: There have been times when my willpower failed me, which was bad, but now it's soaring. I feel that I have so much to do that I shan't be able to do it all. I am in a rush to get down to work. I'd like to write another book too.

CIMENT: One of the characters says, "Money, a visible God." A false idol then, since what matters to you is the invisible.

BRESSON: Money is an abominable idol. It is everywhere. The only things that matter are invisible. Why are we here? What are life and death? Where are we going? Who is responsible for the miracle of animal and vegetable life? The two are considered very similar nowadays. I should like to include that in *Genesis*.

CIMENT: Can you picture your film before you make it?

BRESSON: Yes, and I carry on picturing it and hearing it all the time I am shooting it, as it comes to life. I do not aim for purity, nor to reproduce the ascetic quality of the screenplay. That is not the point. The trouble is that one cannot conceive of things in disorder. One cannot see a single leaf on a tree. In order to gain an impression of something, one must let one's spirit strip away all that prevents one from grasping it. If an image is over-burdened, it will not follow on smoothly from the previous image. There must be a notion of simplicity. But you know, I've said it before: photography is a lie. Light someone two different ways and you see two different people. In *L'Argent*, my protagonist has three different faces. Sometimes he is very handsome, sometimes he looks like he is eighteen years old. I found Christian Patey by chance. My wife knew him from where she used to live. He was a neighbour of hers. He came by to ask a favour. She thought he would be right for the part. He is unique. He must be strong, violent, but not look it. He cannot be a Parisian.

CIMENT: You came to colour very late.

BRESSON: It was too expensive. As soon as I could afford to, I was delighted to use it. Colour is light, it is in itself light. All day long, my eyes paint, I watch shapes and form and colour. The switch to colour was easy, it made no difference to the way I composed or the way I looked at people. Whatever people say, a painter has a ready-made drawing, at least the principal lines, in black-and-white. Sometimes I need a bright colour to set off duller shades.

CIMENT: Do you still paint?

BRESSON: No. I haven't painted for a very long time. I believe that painting is over. There is nowhere to go. I don't mean after Picasso, but after Cézanne. He went to the brink of the what could not be done. Others may paint because they are of a different generation, but I felt very early on that I must not continue. When I stopped, it was horrible. At first, cinema was only a stop-gap, to occupy my mind. It was the right choice, I think, because cinema can go beyond painting. Unfortunately, though, cinema implies waiting for finance. And I don't like the fact that it is not manual. But for those who have something to say, cinema, or rather the Cinematograph, is tomorrow's writing or painting, with two kinds of ink, one for the eye, one for the ear.

CIMENT: Do you like poets like Francis Ponge? Your films remind one of him, and his *Parti pris des choses*.

BRESSON: Yes. I no longer see Ponge, unfortunately, as he has moved to the South. He wrote me some remarkable letters about my films and about cinema. I like his fondness for objects, for inanimate things. In one of his plays, Cocteau has one of his characters say "objects follow us around like cats." My films remind one of Le Clézio too perhaps. He wrote me a superb letter about *L'Argent*. And painters and musicians wrote to me as well. They see what I see.

CIMENT: Which stage do you like best? Writing? Shooting? Or cutting?

BRESSON: The hardest is writing on paper. You sit there between four walls filled with doubt—as I was saying earlier—and I find writing very hard. Now, I've changed my method. I write as I walk down the street, or swimming in the sea. Then I take notes. During a shoot, the trouble is that you have to move fast. The crew is astonished that sometimes I may have to stop for ten or fifteen minutes to have a think. Years ago, in Italy, where oddly I never managed to make a film, there were some directors, I remember, who would say—and no one thought this was odd—"I am not inspired today, I'm off." Wonderful. But if I pace up and down, if I change angles, everyone seems surprised. All because cinema lives off pre-production. Everything is settled in advance. Everyone knows what angle has got to be shot, in what corner of the studio, because it usually is in a studio. And the result is a mish-mash of realism and a lack of it.

The magic is in the cutting-room, when suddenly images and sounds align. Life comes to life. From start to finish, films are a series of births and resurrections. What lies dead on paper is reborn during the shoot, and dead images are reborn in the cutting room. That is our reward.

CIMENT: In your book, you describe the eye as capable of ejaculation.

BRESSON: It can create. Eyes demolish what they see and reassemble it according to a preconceived idea—a painter's eye according to his taste or his ideal.

CIMENT: Are not your characters motivated by desire?

BRESSON: A desire to live. And a will too. A desire to have what one loves pass before one's eyes. My characters are taken to the brink of themselves. I cannot do otherwise, or they would seem dead. If I were to paint a flower, I should not paint a bud, but a mature bloom, at its most mysterious.

CIMENT: *Un condamné à mort s'est échappé*, with its stubborn protagonist, is like a new *Robinson Crusoe*. In his cell, he tackles a series of technical problems, like how to saw through the bars on his window. He does not indulge in metaphysical despair. He seeks the will to live within himself.

BRESSON: You'll find much of the same in *Genesis*, pre-production for which will begin in a few months' time. Adam is like a shipwrecked sailor setting off to discover an unknown island. The beauty of Genesis is God asking Adam to name things and animals. I find that magnificent. And when he reaches this unknown island, everything is ready and waiting. I am reconsidering this project, which I gave up fifteen years ago. It will take at least one year to prepare. There is the question of getting birds, insects, big animals, a tree. There is the question when to set it. It is unending. The screenplay is progressing well, but it is still incomplete. It is a gigantic task. I am like someone from Marseilles: tired out before I begin.

CIMENT: Where does *Genesis* end?

BRESSON: Either at the Flood or with the Tower of Babel and the invention of language. It will be a long film, for television and spoken in Ancient Hebrew, which is a beautiful language, with bits of Aramaic. Adam cannot speak in French or English, he must speak in a language almost no one can understand.

CIMENT: Will it be even more musical than your other films?

BRESSON: Absolutely. Imagine all the animal sounds, not just at the Creation, but in the ark, during the Flood. A concert performance! The emotion. Silence too, sometimes. I want to do it so badly. I'll rush at it the way one rushes into the ocean. We'll see what happens.

CIMENT: Where will you shoot it?

BRESSON: I don't know yet. Neither in Palestine nor in any other Middle Eastern country. I do not want stylized landscapes and anyway they've never mattered to me much. I'd rather see a camel on top of the Puy-de-Dome[3] than on a sand dune. I'd like to shoot in the Auvergne, which is where I was born, because the landscape is so varied.

Translated from the French by Pierre Hodgson

Notes

1. Jansenist. In common parlance, a Puritan. In the seventeenth century, Jansenists, such as Pascal and Racine, were eventually condemned as heretics. They practised an austere form of Catholicism, and were the Jesuits' principle enemies.
2. For over a hundred years, a part of Paris where working-class people go for a night on the town.
3. Extinct volcano in a somewhat wet part of central France.

Procès de Jeanne d'Arc

Burel & Bresson

Interview by Rui Nogueira

S TARTING OUT as an apprentice photographer after studying at the École des Beaux Arts, Léonce-Henry Burel, the Cameraman with the White Gloves—a trademark initially adopted as a protection against a slight haemophilic condition—entered the cinema in 1912. Rapidly graduating out of the darkroom, he made (as director/cameraman) a number of pseudo-scientific documentaries distributed under the auspices of the celebrated Dr. Comandon, simultaneously learning how to direct actors on a series of comedies featuring a character called Zizi.

In 1915 Burel was invited to join the prestigious Film d'Art company as a cameraman, and the first director he was assigned to was Abel Gance. Although Burel no longer remembers the title of the film (and denies having worked on *La Folie du Docteur Tube*, usually cited as the beginning), their association was long and fruitful, continuing through Gance's most creative period (*Les Gaz mortels*, *La Zone de la mort*, *Mater Dolorosa*, *La Dixième symphonie*, *J'Accuse*, *La Roue*, *Napoléon*) and ending with the final flourish of *La Vénus aveugle* in 1941.

In between times Burel spent four years with Jacques Feyder (*Crainquebille*, *Visages d'enfants*, *L'Image*, etc.). And by the end of the silent era the list of directors with whom he had been associated begins to sound like a roll call of the most interesting talents working in France: Maurice Tourneur, Léonce Perret, L'Herbier, Tourjansky, Volkoff, Rex Ingram. The sound period, however, tells a rather different story. Scrabbling hopefully through a long catalogue of forgotten men and hack directors, the best one can up with for twenty years is Duvivier, Delannoy, Decoin, Gréville.

Burel, born in 1892 ("Hélas!"), and by conviction an old-school anarchist (cf. his opinion of *Pickpocket*), would probably go along with this division of his career into two uneven parts: "Time was when the cameraman really was the director's alter

ego. They were inseparable, dependent on each other, trusting each other completely. Crews were small, and although the director was the boss you made the film
together, really just the two of you, discussing everything, seeing what you could
and what you couldn't do. And the cameraman was in total charge of his camera."

"Things began to change even before sound came in. I remember asking
Gance for an assistant, on *La Zone de la mort* I think, because the equipment was
too heavy for me to carry; and this assistant took over some of my other duties as
well, loading, doing stills, and so on. But it was with sound and then colour that
the changes really came. Crews grew ever larger, with all sorts of electricians and
technicians and assistants to assistants. The cameraman became . . . not exactly
secondary, but merely one element among many; and the operator was now
closer to the director than he was."

"I really loved my profession because you had everything to do, everything to
discover. Nowadays everything has to be safe. They don't take risks any more.
They never fail. But a great cameraman, to my mind, has the right to be wrong.
And a great director is one who lets you try for things. Feyder was like that; for
me he was the greatest. Gance was like that as well (although he had a little too
much violin and double-bass in his range of effects for my taste). And Bresson . . .
he was the last of the species."

For in 1950, in fact, aged fifty-eight, Burel again took up the voyage of discovery interrupted twenty years previously, and pursued it through four consecutive Bresson films. After his disappointment with *Procès de Jeanne d'Arc* ("I would
have liked to finish on a note of beauty"), Burel did in fact go back to filming:
Chair de poule (Duvivier, 1963), *Un drôle de paroissien* (Mocky, 1963), *Le Dernier
tiercé* (Pottier, 1964), *Les Compagnons de la Marguerite* (Mocky, 1966).

Tom Milne

L.H. BUREL: One day while I was at my villa in Cap Ferrat, I received a telephone
call from a producer at U.G.C., a very nice man with whom I'd worked several times, asking if I'd come to Paris to test for a film. "Test?" I said, "An old
dog like me with a hundred films behind him? You can't be serious." But he
explained what a predicament he was in, with a director who was going to
make an extraordinary film and who wanted something extraordinary but
couldn't explain exactly what. "I've suggested all your most distinguished colleagues, and none of them is what he wants. So please come, as a personal
favour to me. I'll pay your expenses, and if nothing comes of it I'll pay you
anything you like. Just come, so that I can say I've done my best."

In the circumstances I said yes and caught the first train to Paris. The director was Robert Bresson, who was preparing *Journal d'un curé de campagne* for

U.G.C. and had apparently been making tests with everybody: Matras, Lefèvre, Thirard. Not the usual tests of a hundred feet or so, but real Bresson tests, a thousand feet long. And each time he said, "No, no, that's not how I see it." So it really was as a last resource that the producer had telephoned me. I met Bresson the night I arrived in Paris, and he said, "I'm going to show you something, my dear Burel. It isn't what I want, but it is something like it. Or at least, it may give you some idea . . ." and so on and so forth. Then he took me to see Carol Reed's *The Third Man*. I thought it was awful—I don't like that kind of photography—and I said to Bresson, "Listen, if that's the kind of photography you want, then I'm not the man to give it to you. I don't like that high contrast style, with no half-tones and no detail. Perhaps I could do it for you, but it would give me no pleasure and I wouldn't do it well."

I rather regretted turning it down, because I had just decided to reduce my activities to one film a year, preferably an interesting one, and this was interesting from every point of view. Even at that time working with Bresson was quite something, U.G.C. was a good company to work for, and since I was arriving on the scene as a saviour, I could dictate conditions. The film also had a generous budget and a lengthy schedule (as a matter of fact it turned out to be the only Bresson film that *did* have a long schedule). Nevertheless I did turn it down. Bresson, however, said that since I was there we might as well do some tests.

I read the script that night. The next day, when Bresson asked me what kind of lens I was going to use, I said I was thinking of 50mm. It doesn't give you much depth, which he evidently didn't want anyway, and it concentrates the action. I also told him I would use relatively powerful diffusers in order to get the extreme contrasts he liked. Now, I had brought along my own diffusers which were made specially for me and which were in effect cylindrical additional lenses. We shot various tests using 50 and 75mm lenses. But the man who was acting as my assistant wasn't used to these diffusers and he must have changed them while changing lenses, getting them on back to front. When I saw the rushes I was appalled; it wasn't diffused, it was out of focus. At which point Bresson came rushing up excitedly, saying, "That's it! You've got it, my dear Burel. That's exactly what I want for my film." So much for *The Third Man* and the high contrast stuff!

He immediately wanted to have me signed up, but I wasn't having any. I like diffused effects and I don't like high definition, but I wasn't going to make a film that was to be entirely out of focus. However, we lunched, we talked, we looked at those rushes over and over again. Finally he said that perhaps we could compromise, meet each other halfway over what he wanted and what I refused to do. I agreed, provided I was given the freedom to do what I liked. I always have done what I liked, even when I hadn't a penny, and now that I didn't *have* to earn my living I didn't see why I should do something I would hate. "I'll let you do what you like and I won't say a word," he said, "only do give me something like those rushes . . ."

So I shot the whole film with a 50mm lens, and in addition to the diffuser, used a very light gauze. But since Bresson was making demands on me, I also made demands on him. I told him I saw the film entirely without luminous contrasts, as something rather insubstantial or immaterial which I wanted to handle without any suggestion of shadows. All right, he said, but how? Since he had the budget to do it, and since there usually isn't much sun in the north anyway (the film was shot on location in the Pas-de-Calais), I suggested that we should shoot without the sun, doing the exact opposite of what everybody usually does and shooting indoors whenever the sun did come out. That way I thought we could give the film a texture, a style, an entirely new feel.

So off we went and spent nearly two months getting up before dawn—agony for me as I have always been a night person—to do up to thirty retakes of the priest setting off to join his flock and so forth. All the scenes inside the church were done in the local church at Hesdin. It was still consecrated, with Mass being said there every Sunday, and every time the crew passed in front of the altar while setting up a scene they would bare their heads. Some of them even genuflected, and the work just wasn't getting done quickly enough until I spoke to the abbé who had been assigned as adviser to ensure that Bresson didn't commit any blunders or heresies. He saw my point that it had to be either a church or a studio, and promptly settled the matter by removing the Holy Sacrament from the altar. After that the crew came, went and swore as usual.

I must say that Bresson was marvellous about my idea of shooting without sun. Despite all the money that had been spent on tests—you can imagine the costs in raw stock and laboratory charges when tests are counted not in feet but in miles, when every take that might be possible must be printed up, and when he is so demanding about finding exactly what he wants—we simply set off and shot for a week without seeing any rushes whatsoever (chiefly because the local cinema had no facilities for double-headed projection, and Bresson wanted to hear the soundtrack as well as see the images). It didn't bother me, because after doing those tests I knew exactly how much diffusion I needed. But when we finally did see the first week's rushes—not much definition, but it was bearable—there was Bresson on one side of me saying, "Yes, my dear Burel, but it isn't . . . you know . . . it's very fine and I'm very pleased, but . . . it isn't at all what we agreed on." And on the other there was the production company saying, "But my dear Burel, what on earth are we going to do with that? We couldn't possibly show that in a cinema."

U.G.C. were so worried that they sent down a technical adviser—a cameraman who had made something of a name with UFA but hadn't been in work much recently . . . need I say more?—who echoed the predictions of catastrophe and ruin. Finally I said that I was going to do the film the way I wanted or I wasn't going to do it at all. And since I hadn't signed a contract—I've never signed a contract in my life—and U.G.C. were tearing their hair with visions of starting again from scratch, they gave in. So the film was completed in those conditions, with nobody agreeing about anything and even the laboratory people getting into the act and trying to correct the contrast in developing. It was awful. The result? The film was awarded the Grand Prix for photography at the Venice Festival. After that I was a god for U.G.C. Only Bresson still had reservations. A few. But he was very proud because he got a Grand Prix as well.

If you watch the film carefully, by the way, you will notice three or four occasions where the camera is outside, moving in to a closed window which opens. It looks simple enough to do but it isn't, because the camera and crew (not to mention any light you have to use) get reflected in the glass. I fiddled and experimented endlessly to get the effect. I had to, because that was what Bresson wanted. Every time he asked me to do something difficult he would simply say sweetly, "But my dear Burel, if you can't do it then I can't make the film." How I sweated!

For me, *Un condamné à mort s'est échappé* (1956) is by far the best thing Bresson has done. It's a masterpiece and it proved that he was one of the really great French directors, on a par—although all three are very different—with Feyder and Gance. And coming from me that's no small praise, believe me. Furthermore the film is a challenge, it throws down the gauntlet. To start by saying this man had escaped and I am going to tell you how, and then to do so entirely without artifice or dramatic effects, in absolute simplicity . . . well, that is mastery.

The filming caused me a lot of headaches for a very simple reason. Which was that many scenes had to be shot in studio sets, and these same scenes would begin or end in the real setting of the prison at Lyon. My problem was to ensure that the spectator could never say this bit was shot in a studio set, and that bit in the Montluc prison. But that's my job, and I did it by studying the lighting in the cells at Montluc, then repeating the light exactly in the studio. The scenes done at Montluc were the ones in which the prisoner came out of his cell into the gallery; there had to be a correlation between the cell and the much more brightly illuminated corridor, and the cell itself had to be lit to match exactly the one I had lit in the studio.

I had to be extremely careful, too, because photographically speaking, I was living dangerously by filming almost without light. When you are working within a comfortable range, a little more or a little less doesn't really matter; but when you're stuck at one end of the scale, then the slightest error can mean catastrophe. For the scenes with Fontaine and Jost in their cell, which is illuminated only by a fanlight, it would have been ridiculous to show them with shadows, especially as the fanlight is right above them. As you don't actually see it until later, I wanted to suggest that the whole cell was illuminated by this fanlight you hadn't seen but which you would know was there. So I think I was one of the first cameramen to use reflected instead of direct light. I threw the light on to a sort of large white shield, so that instead of falling directly on the actors it was reflected on to them. It became an ambiance, an atmosphere, and though directed, came not from a particular point but from an extensive surface. It was easy enough really because Bresson works so much in close-up and because there were never more than three actors in shot. With a big set or a wider field, I could never have done it.

When Fontaine comes out into the corridor, on the other hand, I used directional light to suggest illumination from much larger windows. Nothing was left to chance. The escape scenes were shot at Montluc at the dead of night and I used an absolute minimum of light. Sometimes there's a bit of light and you can just barely see the two of them; but since there was almost nothing else on the screen, you knew they were there.

With *Pickpocket* (1959) the problem was different. Bresson wanted to film in the streets, as far as possible without anybody noticing. Whole sequences of the film, not just a few scenes. It would be easier now, but I had an idea I'm quite proud of. The first high-power lamps, which could be overrun to 2,800-3,000 watts, had just become available in France. In order to be able to use them, I hid car batteries to make up the 110 volts on a little camouflaged cart. After Bresson had rehearsed ten, fifteen, twenty times, my operator came along during the final rehearsal with his camera—we were using a hand camera, an Arriflex—to check his focus and get a good look at the location and action. Then, as the take started, I switched on the lights I had previously hidden in trees or places like that where people wouldn't notice them. So, using the fastest available Gevaert stock, we were able to film almost candid camera style, because people didn't have time to realize what was going on. That way we got scenes around the Madeleine and the Opéra, the café in the Place Pigalle (part interior and part exterior, which was a problem), and the one at the corner of the Boulevard Saint Michel.

For the Gare de Lyon sequence, which was rather more complex, I was able to light practically a whole street by running off the circuits in the local bars and cafés; I would signal with a torch and the lights would all be switched on at once. This was the sequence that was a sort of documentary of ways of picking pockets, and the "technical adviser" had been a professional pickpocket, fantastically clever with his hands. As the filming was rather more complicated than usual, we had been given four or five gendarmes to help. At the technical adviser's invitation, these cops went to a bar to have a drink with him after we had finished—and there he gave them back the keys, wallets and watches he had lifted from them while they were going about their business during filming! Afterwards, being too well known to resume his profession, he went on the halls with a marvellous act.

Including rehearsals which went on for hours and hours, *Pickpocket* was shot in barely seven weeks. I wasn't at all in agreement with Bresson about the film because I didn't care for the way he turned his hero into a lousy little swine (even if he did love his mother). The character is basically a rebel, after all, something of an anarchist, and yet Bresson has him steal only from ordinary people, with never a hint of elegance or altruism to offset the ugliness. I didn't understand what he was trying to say. As a matter of fact, I don't think anybody ever has understood, really. Who is this "pickpocket," why does he steal, and so on? What Bresson did was his business and I didn't interfere, but we used to have long discussions about the film before starting and I made this point over and over again. But unlike Feyder when we had a disagreement about ideas or camera angles (sometimes he would give way and sometimes I would), Bresson wouldn't listen and it never made any difference. He just goes ahead with what he has in mind.

I don't really want to talk about *Procès de Jeanne d'Arc* (1961) because I think it's an entirely botched film. I'd rather forget it. And I think Bresson might prefer to forget it too . . .

My wife, who died a few years later, was already gravely ill and I had really decided not to make any more films. But Bresson wrote to me, very flattering letters, and in the end I agreed. My reasoning was as follows: Bresson, after all, is a very religious man, a sincere believer; he doesn't say so in so many words, but I know he is because we have discussed these things. I'm not a believer myself but I respect sincere beliefs; and as he really wants to make this film, it is going to be marvellous. Joan of Arc as seen by a very talented, very intelligent man who sincerely believes: we can make a great film together, *Un condamné à mort* all over again but seen from a different angle.

Bresson's art director, Charbonnier, had found a wonderful natural setting for the film under the observatory at Meudon. Charbonnier, incidentally, is a very nice man and a very talented painter even though I don't understand his talent. We get on well, but we don't talk the same language. It's like Picasso: I just don't understand, and it's neither his fault nor mine. Anyway, these vaults he had found, huge and full of nooks and angles, were absolutely perfect as a medieval decor. I rubbed my hands, thinking what a joy it was going to be. We tested about a dozen girls, all of them very pretty, and Bresson chose one with great possibilities. Charming, absolutely right for the Maid, and with eyes that were extraordinarily intelligent, limpid, and pure.

Then we started. And he didn't use the setting at all. He stuck me in front of a wall covered with cloth hangings to represent the tribunal where most of the action takes place. And bang up against the hangings—and on a little dais to boot—were the judges. You'd have thought it was a church pageant or something. I said to him, "Robert, why haven't you left me anything behind so I can convey the feeling that we're in an enormous room? What do you expect me to do with this?" "Ah," he said, "But you see I want it to be simple and spare. I don't want anything to distract the eye." That was our first disagreement.

Next we simply turned everything round, still with that wretched dais, and shot the girl. You never saw Joan and her judges together, not once. No interrelation. For me this is Bresson's kippered herring; you get a nice clean set of bones but nothing to eat around them. I saw it very differently, and quite honestly I think I could have done something with it. Second disagreement.

Our third disagreement had me curled up into a ball and showing my prickles, because it concerned me professionally. Here we had this sweet, simple, charming girl with the most marvellous, beautiful eyes, and Bresson would never let her look up at the camera. Never. She always had to look down, even when she was answering her judges. I told Bresson that if I believed in God, which I don't, I would look up when I thought of Him. If I believed, He wouldn't be beneath me but above me. Yet here Bresson was making Joan behave like a shifty hypocrite. And it wasn't even a sign of humility in her, because Joan was not humble or humbled. She was a mystic, a visionary . . . you have to be to lead soldiers into battle without even knowing how to use a sword. I was so furious I really let myself go, and Bresson didn't like it. He didn't want to have Joan look up because Dreyer had done that.

Anyway, that was our great quarrel, and since Bresson will never admit his mistakes—as he is perfectly entitled not to—he held it against me. I had humiliated him, so he wanted to humiliate me. That, however, isn't easy to do. In fact it is probably impossible. I'm an arrogant man; not vain but arrogant, terribly arrogant. That's the way I was born, that's the way I'll probably die, and there's nothing to be done about it. On two or three occasions he found fault with the way I was lighting things. The first time I thought, well, maybe he's right; it was an arguable point. The second time I said, "But it won't match with what we've already done." And the third time I told him he had a week to find a replacement for me. "But why, my dear Burel?"

"Because you're making a mess of your film. Because I expected so much more of you. Because working on it no longer gives me any pleasure. It's the last film I'll ever work on, and I would have liked to finish on a note of beauty.

I'll never forgive you for not letting me have that girl's eyes. I could have given you a face of ecstasy, a face that audiences would treasure in their memories."

Men with writs coming to the set, endless special delivery letters from Bresson and from the producer Agnès Delahaie, pointing out that although as usual I had not signed a contract, I had made a verbal agreement. So I stayed and finished the film after writing a letter to "Dear M. Bresson" (no more Robert) explaining that I didn't want to run the film or the company into any more trouble, and that I would complete it on two conditions. One, that no scene was to be shot until his formal approval had been recorded on the clapperboard. Two, that I would attend screenings of rushes only in working hours. And that was how we finished the film. I left him alone and he left me alone.

Translated from the French by Tom Milne

Pickpocket

Filmmakers on Bresson

F RANÇOIS TRUFFAUT quickly had to disavow his assertions that "to think that Bresson will be an influence on French and foreign contemporary filmmakers seems highly unlikely," and that "the future existence of a 'Bresson school' would shake even the most optimistic observers. A conception of cinema that is so theoretical, mathematical, musical and above all ascetic could not give rise to a general insight." In fact, aside from Godard, one cannot think of another post-war French director who has been as influential (unless it is Renoir, whose influence is pervasive but so transparent as to seem invisible). Bresson's style (and, less so, his vision) have been absorbed and transformed by the directors who worked as his assistants (Miller, Malle). One need not know, for instance, that Louis Malle intended his debut, *Elevator to the Gallows*, as an hommage to Bresson to be able to discern the influence of Malle's mentor: its hero hanging from an elevator cable readily recalls Fontaine's escape in *Un condamné à mort s'est échappé*, made the year before with Malle as one of four assistants to Bresson. Malle's *Le Feu follet*—despite the Satie on the soundtrack, which breaches Bresson's tenets about the use of music in film—is even more Bressonian in its clenched fatalism. (And, as T. Jefferson Kline notes in his essay on *Pickpocket*, there is "a curious connection" between the scene in which Jacques and Jeanne "take a plane ride" with a scene in Malle's *Les Amants*, "where Jeanne and Raoul are pictured in a plane in this same amusement park.") The French New Wave and its heirs have all demonstrated their debt to Bresson in their films. (Oddly enough, Marguerite Duras is the only one of the Left Bank Group, the New Wave's counterpart [Marker, Resnais, et al.], to be markedly influenced by Bresson, though one can detect Bressonian elements in Agnès Varda's *Vagabond*.) The tableaux structure of Godard's *Vivre sa vie* owes as much to *Pickpocket* as it does to Brecht, for example, and Rivette's abstinent *Jeanne la Pucelle*, with its diminutive Jeanne d'Arc, absurdly spare battle scenes, exaggerated natural sound, and disorienting narrative ellipses, follows the path established by Bresson's own life of Joan.

Outside of France, Bresson has influenced experimental filmmakers (Elder, Snow, Markopoulos, Sonbert) and new narrativists (Akerman, Mangolte); political filmmakers from Germany (Reitz, Farocki, Fassbinder) and British independents (Douglas, Forsyth, Davies); cinematic poets from Canada to Kazakhstan (Egoyan, Sokurov, Tarkovsky, Bartas, Saless, Angelopoulos, Tsai, Costa, Tran Anh Hung, Tarr, Lefebvre, Shinozaki, Yanagimachi, Omirbaev); and American directors belonging to or associated with what was once called "the cinema of loneliness" (Schrader, Mann, Scorsese, Siegel, Hellman). Cursory though it is, this catalogue illustrates that Bresson's influence has extended across several generations, numerous countries and disparate cultures, and several incompatible aesthetics. Just how extensive his effect has been is evident in the divergent styles of the directors who have acknowledged his influence: from the quiet, contained artistry of Victor Erice and early João Botelho to the operatic aesthetics of Werner Schroeter and Bernardo Bertolucci, the stringent humanism of Gianni Amelio to the stylistic exhibitionism of Leos Carax and Arnaud Desplechin.

Inferring influence is a treacherous practice, and one has to wonder, for instance, how much of the glum, deadpan quality of recent American independent cinema is third generation Bresson (the suppression of emotion, actors as blank models) or mere post-modernist posturing, impassivity being the most appropriate demeanour for a generation numbed by incessant irony. However, it cannot be denied that Bresson's influence is both conspicuous and ubiquitous in contemporary cinema: in the dire vision, studied compositions and elliptical editing of Pedro Costa's *Ossos*; in the "flattened" images of Alexander Sokurov's recent films; in the automatism of actors in Atom Egoyan's early work, and the gallery of doleful "models" in Olivier Assayas's cinema. Bruno Dumont's *La Vie de Jésus* is unthinkable without Bresson. (Dumont wrote the master a beautiful letter, which ends with the phrase: "*Un homme clair. Je vous aime beaucoup.*") The pachinko parlour sequences in Yanagimachi's *About Love, Tokyo* and the gambling montage in Scorsese's *Casino* show a debt to *Pickpocket*, while Darezhan Omirbaev's *Killer* seems an extended hommage to *L'Argent*. (Omirbaev, however, denies a conscious inspiration; when asked about Bresson's influence on his work, he replied: "I don't know. Perhaps others can see? The person who is inside the building cannot see its outside, roof, etc.") The now legendary cat-killing sequence in Béla Tarr's *Sátántangó* invokes the suicide of Mouchette, and Tarr's doomy minimalism can generally be traced back to Bresson. Aki Kaurismäki, one of Bresson's greatest admirers, initially imitated the master's terse style, deriving his first feature, *Crime and Punishment*, from the same source as *Pickpocket*. He then slowly managed to absorb the influence, so by the time he reached *The Match Factory Girl*, in which, he said, he attempted "to make Robert Bresson seem like a director of epic action pictures," and which he later called "90% Bresson, 10% me," Kaurismäki had transformed the Bressonian style into his own kind of plangent comedy. This inventory of influence could extend to dozens of other examples.

The following texts—from a single line to interview excerpts and, in a few cases, full-scale essays—illustrate the profound influence Bresson has exerted on successive generations of filmmakers. Surprisingly, there is little of the daunted reverence one might expect from these directors. Indeed, certain entries surprise by their irreverence: Kaurismäki's wry comparison of Bresson to Sirk, John Waters admiring the austerity of *Lancelot du Lac* for perverse reasons and Chris Marker's characteristically mischievous observation about the same film, and Straub's refutation of Bresson's late films (though Straub continues to refer to Bresson as "mon vieux maître"). Some approaches are philosophical or theological (Elder, Malle), while others are purely formal (Farocki). Some are reminiscences, Bertolucci's amusing, moving memories of Bresson at a dinner party in Rome, for instance, or Mani Kaul's account of his visit to the set of *Le Diable probablement*, which extends into a lovely rumination on the perils of imitating Bresson and the necessity of measuring the distance between his style and one's own (a sentiment echoed in the text of Marco Bellocchio).

Themes and motifs recur: the force of revelation that Bresson's work had on directors (cf. Assayas, Erice, Schrader, Tarkovsky) and their subsequent fealty to his work; the role of Bresson as "a supreme teacher" as Egoyan calls him, of his cinema as "an exemplary text" from which to learn (one thinks of both Patti Smith's punk poem that ends, "who was your teacher? robert bresson" and of Rohmer's elegant caveat: "Bresson n'est pas un maître, il est un exemple"); and the irreproachable independence, the utter isolation—or, to use Cocteau's phrase, the apartness—of Bresson. The excerpt from an interview with Tarkovsky emphasizes that autonomy (spiritual, philosophical, formal, even economic) as a kind of ideal, and reminds one of Tarkovsky's *cri de coeur* in his diary: "Where have all the great ones gone? Where are Rossellini, Cocteau, Renoir, Vigo? The great—who are poor in spirit? Where has poetry gone? Money, money, money and fear . . . Fellini is afraid, Antonioni is afraid . . . The only one who is afraid of nothing is Bresson."

— James Quandt

Chantal Akerman

In a recent self-portrait, Chantal Akerman chose *Pickpocket* as "the film of her life." *Ed*.

Visually, ethically and aesthetically, it is extraordinary. Recall the ending: "Oh, Jeanne, what a strange way I have taken to reach you at last." That's all. No need to add anything.

Michelangelo Antonioni

[When I was starting out as a director] I really liked Bresson's *Les Dames du Bois de Boulogne*. I liked his way of "dodging" the main scenes; he let you see only the consequences of the main scenes. What also seemed extraordinary was his way of enhancing the characters against the environment. Certain full shots of Maria Casarès remain unforgettable. Maybe this was also because Casarès was an actress who was gifted with a unique presence.

Olivier Assayas

1.

The truth of my feelings about the cinema of Robert Bresson is very simple. When walking out of a screening of *Pickpocket* as a young man, with close friends who hadn't understood a thing about the film, who had missed what seemed so incredibly obvious to me, I felt, deeply, that it had let me see into the inner beauty of cinema in a way that would someday allow me to make films myself.

There are a lot of filmmakers I admire: Bergman, Fassbinder, Cassavetes, Visconti, Mizoguchi, Rohmer, Scorsese, Dreyer, Rossellini, Pasolini, Renoir, Tarkovsky, just to mention the few that most naturally come to mind.

But Bresson is, for me, in a category of his own. He is what keeps me faithful to what cinema can achieve. In moments of discouragement, he reminds me how great films can be . . .

And I don't think I would be making films if not for him, or certainly not the same films.

2. *L'Argent*

When it came out in 1984, *L'Argent* had a profound impact on me as few films had ever done, probably because it brought together all of what I expected from modern cinema, or a cinema to come. . . .

The work of Bresson in particular . . . ever since I discovered it on television as a teenager, has given me the conviction that filmmaking as an art form *is worth it*. Because he had been able to reach such a summit, to express what is essential in the world with such force, this art form *had to be* the modern art form par excellence, the art form one could devote one's life to: if there was only one little chance to reach the height which Bresson attained with such supreme authority.

L'Argent is a masterpiece of formal audacity, of pure beauty dedicated to showing raw truth, a harrowing and almost unearthly light that pierces the world with its lucidity. Faith is no longer there, idealism seems meaningless, nothing transcends the actions of humanity. All that is left is a cold material world, a desolate land where humanity wanders in bondage to diabolical evil.

L'Argent is the testament of a director in his eighties. It is also the film of a radical young man, which dares everything, without compromising with the taste of the time, its eyes wide open to reality. Look at the picture it leaves us: the world that is ours.

Iradj Azimi

Night in Robert Bresson's Work

I have often wondered from where comes the music flowing through each film of Robert Bresson, a music which has never left me.

To try to define it is impossible, for it seems to emanate from an invisible source, yet is intensely present throughout his films.

The characters carry with themselves their mystery, a sort of interior darkness, a sort of chaos. Bresson gives us some inkling of these interior nights. The inklings which are rare and striking, like lightning.

Here is precisely Bresson's art: he renders visible and evident the night within his characters, in broad daylight.

Of course it is possible to evoke here what one calls a style. But Bresson has never aimed for a style, and still less his own style. He has never been haunted by inventing one either. After all, did Dostoevsky have a style when he was rendering Raskolnikov bending over the bridge, gazing down at his murderous thoughts?

Bresson is the watchman of interior chaos. The watchman of darkness. Beyond any epoch or territory: the closest character to Lancelot is Michel, the pickpocket. They carry with themselves the same darkness, the same music.

Besides their shadows and beauty, the films of Robert Bresson have a documentary aspect: a documentary on the beyond, on interior darkness. A documentary on the invisible.

For this reason, Bresson's music, although haunting, will remain forever indescribable. And this is undoubtedly how it should be.

Marco Bellocchio

Notwithstanding my immense admiration and profound emotion for some of Robert Bresson's masterpieces—I remember always having advocated his stylistic genius in debates in which I confronted Bresson and Antonioni about their various methods of working with actors: different, yet in both there is an aloofness, seemingly cold, monotonal, a refusal to enter into a passionate realism or what could be called "true caricature," close to Diderot or Stanislavsky—in practice, I have not imitated nor have I adopted the manner of Bresson so that I could progressively detach myself from his style. This is rather strange because traditionally, at the initial stage of one's art, a great master can easily influence the imagination of those who admire him, and invest in them an artistic identification, a recognizable imitation.

An explanation could be Bresson's religious rigour, but fiercely anti-Catholic in the sense of his intolerance to Catholic hypocrisy. His Jansenist attitude frustrated me in my early years. This could have been because of my inclination toward a sardonic manner, characteristic in Italian cinema, which associates all humanity with a kind of infamy or collective corruption, with many sentimental distractions that are totally unimportant. This frustration made me deviate from the conventional path of universal ridicule (it is reassuring that the foundation of *La commedia all'italiana* is for every Italian director "the house of the father"), and pushed me instead to accord foremost importance to style, and to moral rigour, without converting me to the faith that was behind it; moreover, without sharing the pessimism about humanity, or the idea of inextricable sickness which is characteristic of a Christian ideology.

Two films by Bresson particularly moved me: *Pickpocket* and *Un condamné à mort s'est échappé*, which I have seen and reviewed many times. Maybe because these more than the others leave the atheist the freedom to be moved without believing in God, as though the presence of God in these two films wasn't something dictatorial. In fact they talk about the cure for an obsession, one about the madness of a single man, the other about the heroic resistance to, the radical refusal of, mass insanity (Nazism). In both films, life triumphs over death without God's intervention. The madness of a man, or many men, is defeated by other men (and a beautiful woman), who are not mad.

Translated from the Italian by Ramiro Puerta and Dorina Furgiuele

Bernardo Bertolucci

In the last ten years the name Bresson has become a pure word, an entity, a kind of film *manifesto* for poetic rigour. Bressonian meant for me and my friends the ultimate, moral, unreachable, sublime, punishing cinematic tension. Punishing because his movies are strong sensual experiences with no relief (apart from the aesthetic relief, itself a devastating pleasure).

One day I heard that Bresson was in Rome giving a talk at the Centro Sperimentale di Cinematografia. I rushed over arriving in the middle of the lecture. Standing behind a wall of students, I could just see the immaculate crown of Bresson's head moving slowly. He never used the word *"cinéma,"* but *"le cinématographe."* Everything else was *"théâtre filmé."* When I caught sight of his face, for perhaps only three seconds, it reminded me of a hypnotic rabbit. My legs were shaking with admiration. Was it 1964 or 1965?

That evening, Mauro Bolognini invited me to a dinner in honour of Robert Bresson who had been in Rome for the last few weeks preparing an episode of *The Bible*, a movie produced by Dino de Laurentiis with various directors. Bresson had chosen Noah's Ark. Before I was introduced, Bolognini told me that Bresson was in a rather bad mood and briefly explained why.

That morning, while Bresson was lecturing, Dino de Laurentiis had gone to the studio and witnessed huge cages containing wild animals arriving in pairs: two lions, male and female, two giraffes, male and female, two hippos, male and female, etc. A few hours later, Dino told Bresson that he was excited to be the only producer on earth able to bring the elevated Maestro down to earth, to produce a film with real production values . . .

"On ne verra que leur traces sur le sable (One will see only their footprints in the sand)," Bresson whispered to Dino. An hour later he was fired.

Here I am, in front of Robert Bresson. It is early summer and we are standing on a terrace in Via San Teodoro. Behind him the back of Palatino hill, spots of white ruins in the dark. I must have mumbled something like, "Before I put a bomb in De Laurentiis's studio . . . can I ask you if . . . maybe there is somebody . . . in the history of . . . the *'cinématographe'* . . . you like more . . . do you have a favourite film . . . or many . . . ?"

He looked away. *"Non."*

Then with a tremendous sense of accuracy he corrected himself: " . . . Maybe some shots of Chaplin. But when Chaplin doesn't act." I told him I adored *Les Dames du Bois de Boulogne*. He hadn't yet made *Au hasard Balthazar, Mouchette, Lancelot du Lac, Une femme douce, Le Diable probablement, Quatre nuits d'un rêveur, L'Argent*.

Writing this today, Bresson is suddenly the name of a person again. French. Or Taoist?

Jean Cocteau

In filming his *Pickpocket*, Robert Bresson was seized by one of those inspirations that could have been a simple *tour de force*, had Mozart and Lully not given us the example of how apparent lightness can be an apt expression of a soul that is both simple and profound. It presents the opportunity for misunderstanding, for the kind of confusion that led to *Don Giovanni* being taken as a work to be listened to with half your attention, and Lully as a "petit maître" at the behest of the prince.

Robert Bresson was right to choose Lully to accompany the ballet of thievery and the terrible anxiety an amateur pickpocket experiences. He has elicited acting nothing short of a miracle from a novice, who not only pilfers wallets with long fingers that might belong to a pianist, but he has also endowed his hero with the sort of appalling existence of an animal who stalks his prey all the while afraid that he is also being stalked. A police trap saves the novice pickpocket and recalls the poignant tale of the murderer who returns every night to the place of the crime, waiting to be arrested, and faints with joy when he is finally handcuffed. Bresson shows us without any narrative artifice the compulsion that drives the thief into the lion's maw, and the power of love that frees him, despite the bars of his cell.

I suppose that admirers of *Dairy of a Country Priest*, of *A Man Escaped*, of *Les Dames du Bois de Boulogne*, will rush to applaud a ballet and a drama that seems to have had Oliver Twist as its godfather and Moll Flanders as its godmother.

Bresson is isolated in his terrible profession. As a poet does with his pen, he expresses himself cinematographically. Deep is the abyss between his nobility, silence, gravity, dreams, and the rest of the world, where they are taken to be uncertainty and obsession.

Translated from the French by James Quandt

Marguerite Duras

COMBAT: Do you think *Au hasard Balthazar* an intellectual film?

MARGUERITE DURAS: It is not intellectual, it is total; it is also much more sensual than people think. If you will, what has been accomplished in poetry, in literature, Bresson has done with the cinema. One might say that, until Bresson, cinema was parasitic, derived from other arts. With him came a pure cinema . . .

It is perhaps the only film I've seen that best represents a solitary, therefore exact, kind of creation.

COMBAT: But Bresson's universe is not a simple one, one must enter into it, cleave to it, open oneself to it, believe in it.

DURAS: Belief is totally alien to me and yet . . . There was for me a spectacle . . . absolute, that is the precise word. . . . as if there were such a thing as the Middle Ages, if you will . . . modern and archaic. . . . All current cinema—even good cinema—compared to this seems conventional, thin. . . .

COMBAT: Bresson has a very particular way of approaching language, speech, actors' diction; have you been shocked by these elements [of his style]?

DURAS: No, I always marvel at this in Bresson; I think he has attempted to break the mould of language, well, let's say to . . . depunctuate language . . . For example, I have heard in Bresson an irreproachable language which is French . . . One no longer hears French because it is so thoroughly cast in a mould.

Interview excerpt translated from the French by James Quandt and Lara Fitzgerald

Atom Egoyan

Notes on *L'Argent*

No one responds the way we expect them to. Bresson is entirely comfortable in showing the banal indifference which characterizes most of our actions.

Nothing is as thrilling as we want it to be. A bank robbery is almost cruel in its apparent sense of visual deprivation.

If education is formulated on making us understand the relationship of action to consequence, Bresson is a supreme teacher.

He is intolerant of the casual viewer.

Our sense of morality is aroused by having so little with which to immediately identify.

We enter because of an apparent void, only to find that decisions have been made without our consent.

This is alarming yet completely transcendent.

R. Bruce Elder

What I Admire in Robert Bresson's Films is His Method

Erat nubes tenebrosa et illuminans noctem.

Even before Robert Bresson made, in his middle age, the works that brought him a modicum of recognition, Susan Sontag recognized, with characteristic perspicacity, that the central concern of his oeuvre is "the meaning of confinement and liberty"; she also proposed that this is the core meaning of Bresson's films, and that "imagery of the religious vocation and of crime are used jointly" to suggest what constrains the self. Her claims strike me as, perhaps, only half right. For confinement and liberty, I suggest, are analogues of the spiritual conditions of opacity and transparency—of the states that make individuals impenetrable to the love and light that might redeem them or that, conversely, allow them to be penetrated by love and light.

The ideas of opacity and transparency are central notions around which Bresson's thinking coils. Bresson's emphasis on these concepts makes his imagery neither of religious vocation nor of crime simply metaphors of his concerns; rather they are the very substance of his thought—its warp and woof. Bresson counsels himself to "Hide the ideas, but so that people find them. The most important will be the most hidden."* Bresson intends this comment to allude to the interpretative endeavours he hopes to elicit, but the hermeneutical stance he strives to engender simply recreates, in order to reveal, our natural relationship with reality and with other people; for in life, too, what is darkest and most mysterious also provides the greatest illumination. Saint John of the Cross knew well the paradox and its centrality in the life of the spirit, for at the beginning of his *Spiritual Canticle*, he wrote: "He that has to find some hidden thing must enter very secretly into that same hidden place where it is, and when he finds it, he too is hidden like that which he has found."

Possibly the most renowned feature of Bresson's style is that the narrative's point of view on the protagonist fluctuates, so that the protagonist is now presented directly, in first person, and now is presented as an objective narrative agent—as a token that circulates through the narrative economy (the title of Bresson's *L'Argent* actually evokes the metaphor of silver, though of course the film, which is based on a short story of Tolstoy, "The Counterfeit Note," concerns the circulation of other types of money too), without having much insight into either

---

* Robert Bresson, *Notes on Cinematography*, trans. Jonathan Griffin (New York: Urizen Books, 1975), p. 18. All further references to this book are indicated by NC.

his/her own motivations or the realities of the larger forces that determine the system of exchange in which he or she participates. Bresson writes, "Models [the correlative in the good object that Bresson calls "cinematography" of actors in that institution which Bresson thinks of cinematography's negative, *viz.*, the "Cinema"] mechanized externally, internally free. On their faces nothing wilful. *The constant, the eternal beneath the accidental*" (NC, 25).

This alternation is so familiar a feature of Bresson's films that it is sometimes hard to remember that Bresson only systemized its use in *Au hasard Balthazar* (though, of course, individual scenes in every one of his earlier films foreshadowed the development in some way). The first-person viewpoint, as Bresson uses it, suggests self-knowledge, that is to say, the self's transparency to self-inquiry, and so, by implication, both the liberty that follows from self-knowledge and the freedom that is self-identity, as one's active self comes into coincidence with one's true being; while the objective viewpoint, as Bresson uses it, suggests the self performing in a system beyond the protagonist's ken, and, ultimately, the self as impenetrable by self-scrutiny.

Though a dialectic of this sort between self-identity and alienation is clearly suggested in Bresson's films, they finally do not propose that redemption can be achieved by overcoming *mauvais foi*—Bresson never conceives redemption in such simple terms. Bresson understands that self is never given to itself through introspection. Accordingly, even his protagonists' efforts at self-scrutiny invariably involve a measure of self-deception and self-alienation—not even the country priest's journal, his exercise in self-reflection, is a logbook of self-understanding. The greater the involvement in self-analysis, the greater the deception.

Conversely, it is on rare occasions, when the strictures on the self are most severe and the self is least able to realize itself, that insight sometimes occurs; thus at the end of the *Pickpocket*, when Michel, through the bars of the cage that confine him, looks at Jeanne and reaches out to barely touch her hand (touching it really, for the first time, we think) says, "what a strange way I have taken, Jeanne, to come at last to you." "Faith is dark night to the soul," Saint John of the Cross writes in *The Ascent of Mount Carmel*, "and it is this way that it gives light; and the more [the soul] is darkened, the greater light comes to it."

The question whether the self is revealed in the light of a self-scrutiny that allows its true nature to emerge, or whether it reveals itself through an automatism that serves to protect the self's essential inscrutability recurs throughout Bresson's oeuvre. Thus, although Bresson pithily characterizes his "models" as "mechanized externally, internally free," about this mechanization he also quotes Montaigne's remark, "*Tout mouvement nous descouvre*"; and, further, to this he appends, "But it only reveals us if it is automatic (not commanded, not willed)," (NC, 67); it should be pointed out that *Notes on Cinematography* is a similarly fragmentary work that presents a series of luminous observations whose relationships to one another remain rather obscure. He even offers the yet more radical assertion, "The words [your models] have learned with their lips will find, without their minds' taking part in this, the inflictions and the lilt proper to their own natures. A way of recovering the automatism of real life" (NC, 32). No methodological assumptions could drive a wedge more deeply than this does between ideas of self-reflection and the true individuality that is freedom.

Yet despite what seems, at times, the self's essential inscrutability, despite its (sometimes) reluctance to engage in acts that disclose itself, nonetheless occasions inexplicably erupt when humans become transparent one to another (though, to be sure, in Bresson's films, as in life, these moments are few and fleeting). And these occurrences truly are inexplicable, for, as we realize when Fontaine puts his arm around Jost at the end of *Un condamné à mort s'est échappé*, times when individuals become transparent to one another arise not only when people acknowledge their status as captives, but also when they assume their freedom. Such moments are infrequent, to be sure, and for the most part the meaning of people's actions remain as alien and opaque to those who perform them as they do to other's ratiocination—indeed, to reason itself, whether psychological or theological; the deadpan manner in which Bresson's characters ordinarily perform highlights the essential poverty of people's self-understanding, for it makes his characters' actions seem as though they were the product of drive that belongs to some Other, that has almost nothing to do with themselves. Hence Bresson's refusal to explain his characters' behaviour through psychology, a feature of Bresson's narrative construction that renders his characters' actions all the more inscrutable (and hence, too, Bresson's Jansenism, for the theology is no higher psychology in this regard—on this matter one recalls the famous remark of Jansenism's spiritual founder: *"le coeur a ses raisons que la raison ne connaît point"*).

At times, self-examination conceals the self even as it shines a light upon it. About such occasions (and they abound in Bresson's films), one might be tempted to say that the self prefers to dwell in the realm of obscurity, and conclude that the automatism Bresson's characters frequently exhibit is to reveal their deeper natures precisely by protecting the self's need to hide itself. We remember, for the physically exuberant sequence of thieving in the Gare de Lyon in *Pickpocket* impresses the fact indelibly on our consciousness, that in Bresson's films self-awareness can be a burden, while unselfconscious participation (which participation in fact involves only the slightest measure of any sort of awareness) can be a form of exhilaration, akin, almost, to *participation mystique*; Bresson makes the same point, and just as forcefully, in the mute and totally unselfconscious commitment to his project that Fontaine displays. We might be tempted to conjecture that Bresson has faith in the automatism's powers of self-disclosure, were it not for our understanding how compromised such revelations really are. For the self in Bresson's work exhibits a type of structure that I have come to term "apophantic," that is one in which every revelation is partial, for it belongs to the soul's essential nature that any feature that is revealed, and exactly by showing itself, conceals another feature; as one feature becomes evident, another is eclipsed by that revelation. But this is the way it is with faith, too, which is always both certain and obscure, for it reveals God by hiding Him and by hiding reveals Him. By faith we know what is beyond understanding.

The alternation between the inwardness of the first-person point of view and the utter unselfconsciousness of the third-person point of view is matched by another duality; but this duality, unlike the alternation of the narrative's perspective on its protagonist, was present in Bresson's work from the beginning—or least, from 1943 onward, after *Les Anges du péché* (which anyway is more typical of the world of French filmmaking of its time than of Bresson's subsequent work). The duality I refer to is that between past and present, between memory and actuality. Bresson's films typically present their events as recollections. Yet the images of the events virtually compel us to take them as present. Bresson is explicit about the way the retrospection becomes immediate in his works: "Return the past to the present," he proposes. "Magic of the present" (NC, 26).

One reason we are moved to accept what we see as belonging to the present is that Bresson's work impresses us with the sense that shots are formed of blocks of time that resist carving, and this gives them a quality of reality. The sense of the image's immediacy is reinforced by the realistic, that is to say, quasi-documentary quality of Bresson's shooting and by his frequent use of non-actors—generally, by the evidence that, as precise as his system of his finished films is, the elements that the system incorporates nonetheless involve chance as a factor: "To shoot ex tempore, with unknown models, in unforeseen places of the right kind for keeping me in a tense state of alert" is one of his methods, Bresson tells us (NC, 12). And he avows as a purpose, "Catch instants. Spontaneity, freshness" (NC, 13). Or again, in praise of cinematography, "CINEMA draws on a common fund. The cinematographer is making a voyage of discovery on an unknown planet" (NC, 12). And, in the same vein, "Sudden rise of my film when I improvise, fall when I execute [on the basis of preconception]" (NC, 19).

The formal rigour of Bresson's films makes evident that Bresson does not conceive of improvisation as a loose process; indeed formal rigour and improvisation are associated in thinking in as complex a relation as that between discipline and freedom in the realms of art and of the life of the spirit—for only in the realms of art and of the life of the spirit is the saying that discipline is essential to freedom anything more than a platitude. By "improvisation," Bresson probably means setting aside the schemes that the mind constructs; and only in artistic and spiritual endeavours is it necessary to empty ourselves of what we know so that mystery might emerge; only in artistic and spiritual endeavours do we willingly turn away from light and set out on a dark way.

What importance does Bresson's method accord improvisation? Saint John of the Cross acknowledges that our intelligence arrives at truth through the senses, our natural knowledge derives from concepts abstracted from the images of things; so even the revelation of the beauty of things can serve a higher end. Saint John of the Cross writes:

> When as soon as the will finds pleasure in that which it hears, sees and does, it soars upward to rejoice in God—to which end its pleasure furnishes a motive and provides strength—this is very good. In such a case not only need the said motions [of pleasure] not be shunned when they cause devotion and prayer, but the soul may profit by them and indeed should so profit. . . For there are souls who are greatly moved by objects of sense to seek God (Saint John of the Cross, *The Ascent of Mount Carmel*, bk. III, c. 34).

Sensory experience can light the path towards knowledge of higher matter. Knowledge offered by the senses is not the highest form of cognition; and indeed, luminous sensory experience may occlude the soul's deeper knowledge. As Saint John of the Cross went on to say, human intelligence also "has a faculty for the supernatural, when Our Lord may be pleased to bring it to supernatural action." That is to say, the intelligence can know supernaturally supernatural truths, truths that lie outside of the realm the senses can comprehend; still, the knowledge the senses provides prepare the soul for supernatural revelation. So it is with Bresson's careful, quasi-documentary purpose for, in a similar vein as Saint John of the Cross was thinking, for Bresson the purpose of improvisation is not, as might be expected, the revelation of truth; rather, it is the revelation of mystery, "[w]here not everything is present, but each word, each look, each movement has things underlying" (NC, 12). The senses reveal what the mind, unillumined from above, cannot know; so the filmmaker turns his attention to the precise look of things. He does so not in order to apprehend them in themselves; instead he strives (as the extraordinary formal rigour of Bresson suggests) to grasp relations between things—in a word, their conaturality.

But the peculiar dialectic between past and present in Bresson's films also has a basis in the peculiar ontology of representation. A representational image comes into evidence as the double of the object just as the object withdraws—this is the very meaning of representation. An image is the appearance that an object leaves behind as it departs. Every representation, as Bresson suggests, "returns the past to the present." The tendency to think of words and images as essentially alike since both belong to the genus of representations has pernicious effects. An image differs from a word (at least most words) insofar as it refers through resemblance, and resemblance confers on the referring object a density of its own. The unique phenomenology of resemblance is evidence in those occasional moments when a word's reference is achieved though its likeness to the what it represents, in "ono-matopoeia." When instances of onomatopoeia occur, language thickens with the presence of the (absent) other it represents—we say "the murmuring brook" and the word "murmuring" takes on a gravity (to use Simone Weil's Augustinian term), a weightiness, a substantiality profoundly different from that of the article or the noun it qualifies. This substantiality arrests the mind, makes it take the referring item as an object in and for itself. It is both a representing token and actual object—it belongs simultaneously to the past and to the present.

The duality between past and present, between memory and actuality charac-teristic of Bresson's films, the tension between the events which are presented as though they were recollected and events which are presented as though they are being lived through parallels, and is often embodied in, the alternation between the scenes of protagonists reflecting on their lives and those of them living through its events in all their immediacy. And the latter dialectic, as we already noted, parallels the fluctuation in viewpoint between first and third persons. There is, then, in Bresson's work an intricate homology of structures and this homology serves to ensure that the attributes of Bresson's temporal constructions support and enrich, and at the same time convolute, the tension between narra-tive viewpoints, which, in their turn, support and enrich, but are also enormously complicated by the polarity between the deeper spiritual conditions of opacity and transparency that is fundamental to Bresson's work.

P. Adams Sitney, taking a philological approach to Bresson's work, has shown us, with the lucid precision of a fine classics scholar, that Bresson's style is really a compound—one is tempted to write, "the mathematical sum"—of the rhe-torical figures he deploys; and anyone who watches even a few minutes of a Bresson film bearing the principles of his commentary in mind can readily enumerate the tropes the filmmaker favours: ellipses (who cannot notice, even after cursory attention to five minutes of any Bresson film the extraordinary disintrication of events: Jeanne d'Arc is interrogated in the courtroom, and after a longer or shorter time passes, the scene fades out; Jeanne is alone, the scene fades out); synecdoche (Bresson's framing so as to show only the essential gesture, and not the environment in which it is performed is legendary); elision (one event is abutted with a similar gesture); and reversal, when the first significance of an event turns into its opposite (as when Gérard and Marie in *Au hasard Balt-hazar* exchange slaps, then, inexplicably, go off listening to pop music on the radio) which makes us acutely aware we have no access to the character's interior lives.

Bresson's rhetorical figures have the function of adding density—"gravity" to use Simone Weil's very apposite term—to the events his images depict and, in-deed, to the images themselves. Sontag was correct again to assert that "in reflec-tive art, the *form* of the work is present in an emphatic way" and that "in the film, the master of the reflective mode is Robert Bresson." In considering the reflective quality of Bresson's work, one thinks of the fact that the narrative mode of most of his films is that of recollection. But there is much more to think about in this regard, for to assert that "the form of the film is present in an emphatic way" is to say that the form is especially palpable, that it impresses itself particularly strongly on the viewers'/listeners' consciousness. Bresson's use of rhetorical figures achieves precisely this. The narrative mechanism of the conventional cinema is designed to carry us along, believing that we are observing a process unfold. Nothing must disrupt that sense, lest the film's construction obtrude upon our consciousness. Like his refusal to elicit suspense, Bresson's manner of employing ellipsis, synecdoche (the spatial equivalent of what ellipsis is temporally) arrests forward movement, ejects the spectators from their scoptic identification with the represented diegetical content, and makes them aware of the image as a weighty, palpable entity set over against them, an entity that in some measure remains alien, its meaning illegible, since its being preserves pockets that are not illuminated by meaning. Like Bresson's emphasis on the autonomy of each individual—on each shot as an independent atom in the film's overall chemical structure—these ellipses elicit a sense of mystery. Consequently, in Bresson's films, as in the films of Marguerite Duras, form becomes graver and more substantial as its content becomes slighter.

Bresson's actors have a deadpan manner; they speak their lines, but never in a manner that makes the language seem like emotions made tangible: "To your models: 'Don't think what you're saying, don't think what your doing.'" (Could there be surer confirmation of the importance of the idea of unself-consciousness in Bresson's filmmaking than this?) And also: "Don't think *about* what you say, don't think *about* what you do" (NC, 8). This performance style ensures that we are not carried along a vector of emotion, from scene to scene. The singular lack of emotional momentum that characterizes Bresson's works strengthens the narrative disjuncture, so that the relationship between successive shots remains mysterious, opaque. The performance style Bresson favours contributes further to this. A remark Bresson offers in *Notes on Cinematography* indicates the effect (even though he probably intended something different by it): regarding his use of what he calls "human models" he remarks, "The thing that matters is not what they show me but what they hide from me and, above all, *what they do not suspect is in them*" (NC, 2). Yet, no sooner does he assert this than he turns around and proposes that what for the most part is obscure is occasionally illuminated by an extraordinary form of cognition that breaks the self out of its self-enclosure, to escape (if only for the briefest moment) that state in which, to use Saint Augustine's memorable phrase, "every heart is closed to every heart." "Between them and me: telepathic exchanges, divination." Or, again: "Shooting. Put oneself into a state of intense ignorance and curiosity; and yet see things *in advance*" (NC, 8).

Similarly, "Draw from your models the proof that they exist with their oddities and their enigmas" (NC, 11).

As important a place as ellipsis has in Bresson's methodological repertoire, we must not overemphasize its importance, for a form of prolongation has an equally important role, and just as impressive an effect. I refer to Bresson's manner of focusing on a space before, and of remaining focused on that space after, the narrative action has taken place (the occurrence of which it would be the purpose of a shot in a conventional film to convey). Indeed we can consider Bresson's focusing on the life of the donkey in *Au hasard Balthazar* as he is passed from owner to owner, as a means to convey the real subject of the film (that is the life of the characters in the world surrounding the donkey), to be a formidable narrative extension of this spatial principle.

In Bresson's films prolongation, paradoxically, has the same effect as ellipsis, for it breaks apart that fusion of movements that endows conventional film constructions with seamlessness, accords the represented content greater impact, but at the cost of the palpability of the representing form; through creating a disruption, this device brings the film material into evidence. It interpolates a hiatus between two points of narrative significance and cleaves them apart. Furthermore, this device, by attenuating drama and by indicating that objects possess a theophantic dimension that surpasses that character's psychology (that, indeed, lies beyond the realm he or she understands), at once renders the narrative construction more palpable and the object's significance more mysterious since it is not comprehended by the narrative machinery. "*Equality of all things*," Bresson emphasizes. "Cézanne painting with the same eye and the same soul a fruit dish, his son, the Montagne Sainte-Victoire" (NC, 70). One could point as well to Bresson's manner of ensuring an equality of fullness and emptiness, i.e., of an equality between the action that fills a space and the space itself.

The doubling that is such a hallmark of Bresson's style (and as Susan Sontag also pointed out) relates to the opacity or transparency of the soul that is his central theme. In *Pickpocket*, we see the protagonist writing, and we hear his voice reading, his memoirs. Then we see what Michel just described. Of course, such doubling has different effects in different scenes; but a common effect of the trope is nearly double-sided almost to the point of paradox. On the one hand, hearing a description of the event prior to the event makes the event seem all the more lucid—and we relate this effulgence of lucidity to the protagonist's self-awareness; yet on the other hand, the slight discrepancy in quality between the description and the lived experience makes us aware of how all experience is misrecognition and self-deception, and so renders both the lived experience and its description darker and more obscure.

Sometimes the visual precedes the commentary upon it. A remarkable instance of this occurs in *Journal d'un curé de campagne*. The young priest wheels his bicycle up to the vicar's door, the housekeeper answers the door (we cannot hear their exchange), then the would-be visitor turns his back to the door and leans on it. Then—only then—we hear him say, "I was so disappointed, I had to lean against the door." The exchange between the priest and the housekeeper is opaque (mysterious), as is his action after she leaves. When the explanation is presented ("I was so disappointed . . .") the enigma of what we have just seen is momentarily clarified—but it seems transparent (explicable) only retrospectively and only briefly. For a moment, the light of meaning flickers over the action, but only for a moment, for no sooner do we feel ourselves in possession of the meaning of the action than we recognize that we must not overestimate this transparency; for what *exactly* the curé feels, and what *exactly* his motivations for seeking out the vicar of Torcy are remain in some measure inscrutable, despite the gloss attached to them.

This doubling of text (usually presented orally) and image, whether or not of the sort that are instances of hysteron proteron, arrests whatever forward momentum the narrative possesses (in Bresson's oeuvre it typically possesses rather little) and so they contribute to the form's episodic character; the interruptions (disruptions) make the form so much weightier and more palpable. Such doublings introduce spacings between points which advance the narrative; thus they have a similar effect to his use of elision. Bresson uses repetition to a similar end. The time of repetition is not the time of narrative (as Gertrude Stein's writing makes abundantly clear). As does his way of employing doubling and prolongation, Bresson's use of repetition introduces spacings between narrative advances (that accounts for what many feel to be a lento pacing); and the effect of this spacing is to concentrate our attention on what we actually perceive, in the moment of presence, and to lessen the roles that retention and protention play.

But Bresson uses repetition to another end: think of the repetition—indeed ritualization—of the scenes of prisoners' morning ablutions in *Un condamné à mort s'est échappé*, commencing with their descending the staircases to empty their slop buckets, or the round of Michel's life in *Pickpocket*, from room to street to café to room. The same actions are played out, over again, in the same spaces; spaces themselves appear and reappear, and so seem to take on significance and to become suffused with meaning, though what this significance actually is we cannot say. Here repetition serves to invest actions with a wholly new and wholly other significance that is divulged only to close attention (and even when it so discloses itself remains in some measure obscure). Such repetitions reveal the theophantic dimension of objects and actions—but Bresson also refuses to interpret that dimension through the means of narrative development.

Bresson employs his rhetorical method with such severity and insistence that his narrative sometimes moves towards the pole of abstraction. The *energeia* that carries Bresson's work toward abstraction arises out of Bresson's conviction that the effect of an art must be achieved by its form, not by its content: "Do not try, and do not wish, to draw tears from the public with the tears of your models, but with this image rather than that one, this sound rather than that one, exactly in their place" (NC, 71). (This conviction is what imparts such musicality to Bresson's films.) The space of each image, the colour of each image, the sound accompanying (or omitted from its natural position as its accompaniment) each image has its meaning only through its relation to other images, whether adjacent to it or remote from it. (It is the remoteness of some of these connections, along with the precision of Bresson's forms that hold each element in its exact place, that conditions the synoptic temporality of Bresson's films.) To do this, Bresson understood that the intrinsic significance of the image or sound must be reduced: "If an image, looked at by itself, expresses something sharply, if it involves an interpretation, it will not be transformed on contact with other images. The other images will have no power over it, and it will have no power over the other images. Neither action, nor reaction. It is definitive and unusable in the cinematographer's system. (A system does not regulate everything. It is a bait for something)"(NC, 5). Or again, "No absolute value in an image. Images and sounds will owe their value and their power solely to the use to which you destine them" (NC, 11). And, further, "The power your flattened images have of being other than they are. The same image brought in by ten different routes will be different ten times" (NC, 17).

Bresson's thoroughly kenotic conception of image is much in keeping with the principal tenets of modernism, to be sure. At the same time, the reduction of the intrinsic meaning of the image often converts what would otherwise be a transparent representation into a somewhat mysterious, somewhat opaque element, while the relation between the images, when apprehended, reverberates to luminosity, but one whose effulgent significance cannot be converted into objective precision. Indeed, the fluctuating relation between realism and abstraction also reflects this relation between self-consciousness and its lack, which in turn reflects the relation between the first- and the third-person points of view, which in turn reflects the very convoluted relation between the spiritual conditions of transparency and opacity. For as Bresson's narratives approach the condition of abstraction, they seem ever more like a system of intricate parts whose significance eludes us (as the significance of the narrative systems within which they operate eludes the characters of Bresson's films).

P. Adams Sitney quotes Robert Bresson from a long interview Jean-Luc Godard and Michel Delahaye (*Cahiers du cinéma*, no. 178) conducted with the artist; "Well, in Jansenism there is perhaps this, which is an impression that I have as well: it is that our lives are made at once of predestination—Jansenism, then, and of chance (*hasard*)." The relation between predestination and chance is homologous with that between the conditions of being transparent to consciousness and of being opaque to cognitive or hermeneutical enterprise—or, to put it differently, between intuitive understanding and mystery. Both relations seem to be relations between polar opposites, yet in both relations the two terms partake of one another's natures. For whether it operates through an election whose workings are tantamount to determinism or through a method as arbitrary as grace, the Divine Will remains inscrutable, yet only knowledge of Divine Will, and especially its essential goodness, can illuminate the world in which we live. The phenomenology of religious experience is an odd one, for it is one where darkness illuminates and light obscures; the Pseudo-Aereopagite wrote in *The Mystical Theology* of the darkness that is the vault of the

> immutable mysteries of theology [that] are veiled in the dazzling obscurity of the secret Silence, outshining all brilliance with the intensity of their Darkness, and surcharging our blinded intellects with the utterly impalpable and invisible fairness of glories surpassing all beauty.

The paradox of a darkness born of light and that of a darkness that lights the way are implied in Bresson's method of converting the everyday into the mysterious and of bringing the mysterious to bear on the everyday.

Two conundrums lie at the heart of the religious sensibility: the first is that whatever moves (and this includes time) has its meaning, indeed its being, in what does not move; and the second is that we are most free when we are bound by subservience to an Other. Both irresistibly obtrude on consciousness and, willy-nilly, become the backdrop against which the rest of our thought moves; and in so imposing themselves upon us, they render the significance of our being undecipherable. Both are evoked by special tropes in the repertoire of Bresson's rhetorical forms (or by what commentators insist on continuing to call Bresson's spiritual style), the first by the precision of the form itself and by its enhanced palpability, and the second by the oscillation between the two points of view through which the narrative presents the protagonist (from a first-person perspective and from a third-person perspective, as an objective agent in narrative economy). What is more, they are evoked as well as by the thematics of some of Bresson's films. For example, Fontaine is liberated through being bound by and to his project (and, as we him watch go off who knows where, we sense that he may never be more free than when he was driven by the task that, perhaps, he elected for himself or, perhaps, circumstances imposed upon him).

Such conundrums contribute to making the meaning of a life—any life—inscrutable as it is. ("Respect man's nature without wishing it to be more palpable than it is," Bresson writes.) But these conundrums—these dark, mysterious pockets in Bresson's oeuvre—make for its splendid luminosity, as wondrous as the lucid harmonies of forms that Bresson crafts.

Hence it follows that for the soul this excessive light of faith which is given to it is thick darkness, for it overwhelms that which is great and does away with that which is little, even as the light of the sun overwhelms all other lights whatsoever, so that when it shines and disables our powers of vision, they appear not to be lights at all (Saint John of the Cross, *The Ascent of Mount Carmel*, bk. II, c. 3).

Victor Erice

A Testimony from a Spanish Bressonian

I'm not entirely sure of the date and the place, but I believe the first time I saw a film by Robert Bresson, *circa* 1958, I was surrounded by my oldest friends at a public screening, perhaps in Madrid, or under the banner of an international film festival, probably in Valladolid. What I do remember was the unforgettable title: *Un condamné à mort s'est échappé*. Unforgettable because the image it conjured constituted for me a kind of revelation, that is to say, a type of mental experience that changes one's perception of cinema.

In the latter part of the fifties, not one film of Robert Bresson's had ever been shown in Spain, which was not out of the ordinary, considering the cultural atmosphere in the country, characterized by alienation and lack of freedom. Despite this, we were exposed to Bresson's films by a Jesuit cinephile, Felix Landaburu, at the ciné-club we used to frequent. Besides being one of Bresson's greatest fans, Landaburu was involved in trying to help him on a project about Saint Ignatius of Loyola, which never came to fruition.

The philosophy behind *Un condamné à mort s'est échappé* reinforced an old desire of ours, and at the same time repudiated many of the mostly conventional ideas we had about the film's maker. The film created a fissure in the system of classical representation, emphasizing its limits, and at the same time making it very clear that this was a film that was unlike any other we had seen on screen. From its images and sounds came a concept that called into question the status of the cinematic image, which we thought until then to be valid; it robbed us of decrepit concepts that had been formulated out of inertia or laziness. The most important aspect, however, was that it created a new faith. From then on, going to a Bresson film was a special occasion, a ritual, a rite.

Soon we knew that Bresson was for us a name that was inextricable with film history. His most essential and differentiating quality was that he was a "Cinematographer," or, as he said, he "wrote with moving images and sound." That for us was the ultimate word for him, an emblem of a new faith, against all the odds of disenchanted youth. After that, and spontaneously, my friends and I formed a new secret society, without rules or statutes, full of the fervour of youth and sacredly devoted to the author of *Un condamné à mort s'est échappé*. All of us were confessed Bressonians, just as there were confessed Kafkains, as if this would suffice to define our place in the world. We were only seventeen, eighteen years old . . .

The Secret Bressonian Society grew in the sixties and seventies, diversifying as it multiplied, disclosing itself to the public, as the Master's works were shown in many places, having secured more stable commercial distribution. The passage of time only confirmed what we knew to be true all along; the decisive influence that his ideas had on the birth of what was to be called Modern Cinema.

During this time, a few young Spanish Bressonians transformed themselves into filmmakers. For that, they inevitably had to choose their own path, and in the majority of cases this path lead them to a common ground where "le cinéma" (and its present disfiguration: the audiovisual) reigns absolute. A tale as old as time, where the incurable solitude of the Master projects, like an echo on those who were once his disciples, to keep reminding them of an unforgettable dream: "I dreamt of my film becoming, under watchful eyes, like a painter's canvas which is eternally fresh."

No one was able to speak to young filmmakers of yesterday like Bresson, and in the same way, no one like him can speak to young filmmakers of today. His naked words, essential, will always be like the images and sounds that gave form to his work: a poem that traces in the air the dream of a dawn that has no end.

Translated from the Spanish by Nuria Bronfman

Harun Farocki

Bresson, a Stylist

One can count the elements which form the basis for Bresson's cinematic style.

No Long Shots

Bresson almost never uses long shots *and* never in order to give an overview of something before the details have been examined. In *Au hasard Balthazar*, there is only one scene in which the entire village landscape where the action takes place can be seen, and in this instance only because the camera looks toward the sky where a storm is brewing. The camera looks to the sky only because the stingy farmer had just said that he would keep his donkey just until the rain came. In *Le Diable probablement*, the highway is visible only once and is filmed so that one can see neither the horizon nor the sky. There is nothing of the freedom and open space to which a highway normally leads in a film. There is, however, a long shot at the end of *Lancelot du Lac*. The camera makes a broad jump, far back from the action and one sees the kind of pitiful little forest in which the knights slaughter each other. The slaughter loses its existence and its importance as it acquires an edge and does not fill the space of the image. *Lancelot* is a historical film, a costume film, and Bresson shows through this long shot the limited range which history has in the film. This use of long shots opposes its usual use—usually a long shot is used in a costume film to show how large the costumed and staged world is and that this world has no limits and also that the landscape is sought out and photographed in a way so that it is suited as a setting. This manner was often used in filming the mountains and deserts of the United States.

When Wim Wenders outlined a film in *Filmkritik*, which was to be made up entirely of long shots, he was concerned with the monstrosity of the long shot. With a long shot, one can hardly show more than the fact that a carriage moves— how it moves, with whom and where and what it is all supposed to mean—for that one needs closer shots. Godard often uses long shots to go against his own narrative and representational intentions. He creates something and then moves it into the distance of a long shot so that the how and where and what all that is supposed to mean is diminished.

Bresson Uses Close-ups

In *Le Diable*, when Charles looks up to a window behind which his girlfriend is with a man, only a few metres of the hotel facade can be seen and not the entire airport terminal building. From this small segment, I (as a film tourist) was able to recognize the hotel in Paris. Charles doesn't care about how the cities are starting to look today, he sees only the window behind which his girlfriend is with another man.

Bresson concentrates on his subjects and their work, or that which occupies them. One can't always say that city dwellers work, but they are occupied; their actions can be empty ones, but they are carried out with an even larger sense of naturalness. When a man loves a woman in Bresson's films, he simply pursues her as if performing a task, something often misunderstood as coldness. But whoever works (or does some kind of work) doesn't necessarily stop to look around while doing it. For that you need a nervousness and futility which doesn't exist here. When I saw Kurosawa's *Dersu Uzala*, I noticed that this film about someone living in the nature of Siberia had shots of landscape which were narrow. Since then, the panoramas showing the land of the American farmers and cowboys of the West have seemed touristy to me.

Bresson's actors can't even really look around when they are standing there. If they aren't looking at a particular point, then their heads are slightly bowed (a zero position, they don't let their gaze wander). When their hands aren't doing something, they are simply hanging at their sides (a zero position, they don't grasp absently for things around them). The hands aren't completely open, the arms aren't completely extended: that would be something for soldiers.

A script by Bresson is full of notes like P.M. (*plan moyen*, medium shot) and G.P. (*gros plan*, close-up). P.M. stands for shots which show a person from head to waist and for shots which show a group of people from head to toe with space around them. *Le Diable*, shot 64: *Panoramique* (pan, Bresson doesn't say anything about shot size here). Alberte climbs in triumph to Charles and Edwige and leaves. You could say this picture is a long shot, but one in which the total picture can be seen and only the total picture. Bresson frames his characters narrowly, he doesn't allow the camera autonomy. It is as though one were writing literature in statements. This is an art: Bresson demands that every value appear as a statement. Through this grammatical metaphor, every scene, every object becomes a derivation. Paris becomes "Paris," or as in a mathematical interpretation, a cup becomes "a cup." And because his skill couldn't be used to its best advantage in *Lancelot*, where the scene of costumes, props and constructions appeared as if it might look too prepared, he used the contrast of the long shot of the forest.

How the Persons / Characters Face One Another and How the Camera Records It

Bresson's camera places itself between the characters; it almost stands on the axis of the action. The axis of the action is the name for the conceived line which runs between two characters who relate to each other. It refers to the procession or course of glances, words, gestures. This line is like a river in geography (and like a river in military strategy), an orientation and a frontier (here a "natural" one, even if the river is a rivulet). It is important on which side one has his point of view and one must change the term with the changing of sides. Because Bresson's camera stands nearly on this axis, the characters look a little bit past the camera. This little bit irritates: the camera shoots the character frontally—the character does not return the glance, but dodges the attack. The presence of the camera is clearly apparent and the glance of the character denies it. Now the countershot comes, the image of the character standing opposite. The camera changes its point of view almost 180 degrees and again a character appears whose gaze evades the eye of the camera. This dodging conflicts with the composed firmness of Bresson's actors.

In short sequences, when the setting appears only once, the orientation is made more difficult, as in the beginning of *L'Argent* as Norbert asks his father for money. Here, both of them not only look past the camera, but also past one another. As far as I know, only Ozu has shot opposites in a similar manner, at least since the advent of sound.

What we can do with shot/countershot has been most completely explored in the classic American talkie (*circa* 1930-60). In this system, a rule is enforced that a shot is all the more subjective when it comes from the line of vision of the opposite character. The close-up, from which the star should be recognized, is usually an *en face* shot. The important actor steps into this ramp, only his eyes do not look into the camera, and affirms the continued context. Bresson adopted some of this concept.

Bresson did not adopt the contrasting of "subjective" and "objective." But Bresson does not withdraw from a character, only later to bring the character closer in an erratic way. He denies himself the whole rhetorical repertoire of variation. Usually the shot sizes change—perhaps not from shot to countershot, but during the course of a sequence. For this reason one stages the movements of the characters in dialogue—someone goes farther away and a medium shot is created—someone comes closer and a medium close-up is created. Bresson does the opposite: when the characters move he tries to keep the shot size constant through a pan or an accompanying camera. Once again, the camera is not given any autonomy. At the same time, the takes are missing a reason from the work of the articulation: from which angle and at which cut, that is a tenet for Bresson.

If Bresson cuts from one person to another, then the cut is like the support point on a scale. The operation of weighing makes the opposites equal, things which are fundamentally different become equivalents. Bresson often did this to the point of creating mirror images. In *Balthazar*, Gérard and Marie run around the donkey—Gérard, the pursuer, Marie, the quarry. The film dismantles this pattern and shows one person at a time behind the donkey, the opposite appraised and then in movement, so often that one does not know where the action began. (Before Marie gives up the protection of the donkey and falls into the grass, the image of Marie running around the donkey is assembled twice; the image of Gérard is missing, but the viewer is already too dizzy to perceive this effect.) In *Une femme douce*, a man and a woman sit silently across from each other eating a meal. They are eating soup. Bresson cuts from the descending soup spoon of the one person to the rising soup spoon of the other. The movements of the spoons connect the man and the woman like the spokes of the wheels of a locomotive.

Shot/countershot, an element in film language which is often criticized—Bresson criticizes it by using it even more intensely.

Bresson always liked cutting together surprising things, deriving movements from similarities and contexts. In *Lancelot*, he cuts the folding down of visors one after another in ever-shorter intervals. (In other films, it would be something vulgar.) In *Balthazar*, when he cuts from the door which Marie closes to the window which she opens, it is fantastic. One can go through the door, one can see through the window. Marie looks only at Gérard who lures her—the film montage shows how the one relates to the other, or that the houses have eyes and feet. To show is not the correct word; Bresson includes the spoken word, without pausing or wandering.

In *Le Diable*, Michel and Alberte meet again and again in the small apartment where Alberte has moved to be with Charles. Alberte sits down and Michel stands up, these two movements appear to be related, as if they were mechanical—scale, seesaw, machinery—connected to one another. Often the image of Michel is like a rhyme of the image of Alberte. Through these meetings or contrasts, Bresson works out a harmony or unison between the two. Later they embrace in a narrow shot, they stand next to a tree, behind them the wheels of the Paris street traffic, they have the large space for themselves.

The Shots of Objects and the Shots of Actions

Continuously looking at the importance of speaking people (with words and with facial gestures) is unbearable, even if the camera is placed before the most elaborate thing. Before Bresson shows a close-up of a face, he shows the close-up of a hand. With passion, he cuts off the head and with that the face, and concentrates on the actions of the head (or the foot).

In *Un condamné à mort s'est échappé*, there is a prisoner who makes materials for escape out of things in his cell. He sharpens a spoon handle into a tool, he breaks up the wire netting of his bed frame and wraps the netting with shirts and rags to make a cable. Such a film about work and what work means has hardly ever been made before.

> Tools and machines are not only signs of imagination and creative capabilities of human beings, they are certainly not only important as instruments for transforming and bending the earth to man's will: they are inherently symbolic. They symbolize the activities they make possible, which means their own use. An oar is a tool for rowing and it represents the capability of the rower in all its complexity. Someone who has never rowed before cannot see an oar for what it really is. The way in which someone who has never seen a violin views that instrument is different from the perception of a violinist. A tool is always a model for its own reproduction and an instruction for the renewed application of the capabilities which it symbolizes. In this context, it is an educational instrument, a medium, for teaching people in other countries, who live at another level of development, the culturally acquired methods of thinking and acting. The tool as a symbol in every way transcends its role as a practical means for a definitive end: it is constructive for the symbolic remaking of the world through human beings (Weizenbaum).

Bresson made two black-and-white films in the countryside. *Mouchette* and *Balthazar*—here this symbolic power is evident. A moped is as incredible as a donkey. Bresson shoots objects and actions with a slight top plan view from the place which corresponds to the object and the action. There is no derivation in the sense that the camera comes out of the eye level of the standing viewer/participant and, as with the low positioned camera of Ozu, apparently from the seated Japanese.

It says something about Bresson's courage that he went into the city and shot in colour. Colour is less a tone of humility than is black-and-white. In his images, Bresson attempts a clarity without reaching for the manifest remedies, contrast and space. (He often chooses one colour and a 50mm lens.)

Bresson's city dwellers, often idlers, bohemians, cannot dive into the stream of the history of human work. They try by their actions: stealing something, giving something, taking themselves by the hand, making dinner, making tea, touching a revolver, killing someone with a hatchet—nevertheless, a "symbolic remaking of the world through human beings." They become the acolytes of their own lives.

In *L'Argent*, Yvon is accused by a waiter of circulating counterfeit money. He doesn't want to let the waiter confiscate the money, so he grabs the waiter and pushes him away. We see his hand grabbing the waiter and pushing him away. While the sound of the waiter falling against a table is heard, Yvon's hand pauses. It shakes from the strain. A hand, as if it had just thrown a pair of dice. Dice are an image of fate as well as of killing time.

Rainer Werner Fassbinder

1.

At the age of twenty-three, Rainer Werner Fassbinder wrote the entrance exam for the recently opened Deutsche Film-und Fernsehakademie Berlin, which he failed. Applicants were asked to analyze the opening sequence of Bresson's *Un condamné à mort s'est échappé*; the film and director were not identified. The following is Fassbinder's analysis. *Ed.*

The filmed sequence shows a prisoner's unsuccessful escape from a prison van, from the first attempt to the last consequence. The sequence consists of about forty set-ups, each one clear and simple, with no regard for superficial beauty.

Each set-up makes sense only in connection with the preceding one and the one that succeeds it.

The necessary prerogatives for the escape—the fugitive, his hand, the door handle inside the car, a vehicle and a streetcar which force, or almost force, the prison van to stop—are clearly shown in their interrelationships. In relatively quick succession, we see first the fugitive, who stares ahead; then the road, where in a moment a vehicle may force the prison van to stop; then the fugitive's hand, reaching for the door handle.

Up to the moment of the escape, the set-ups change fairly rapidly; later they markedly slow down, as the main character is forced from activity into passivity. He has had little time for his flight, the police have ample time for his punishment.

The immense power of the police and the actual importance of the escape is less evident in the last set-ups with the battered fugitive than during the flight, where the other two prisoners don't even turn their heads when the shots ring out behind them.

With great sensitivity, the director refrains from showing the brutality visited on the escapee, who is carried, covered up on a stretcher. It is left to the viewer to use his imagination to picture the beaten-up man, so that later, when he sees the distorted, bloody face, he is not totally overcome by horror but is able to reflect on his attitude to such treatment.

The sequence has been thought through down to the smallest detail. It has been stripped of everything superfluous. The director sticks to the essentials.

2.

In 1977, Fassbinder was a member of the jury at the Berlin Film Festival, and threatened to walk out with British critic Derek Malcolm unless their support for Bresson's *Le Diable probablement* for the top prize was made public. *Le Diable* ended up sharing the second prize, the Silver Bear, with two minor films. The following is from an interview conducted at the time. *Ed.*

RAINER WERNER FASSBINDER: Robert Bresson's *Le Diable probablement* . . . is the most shattering film I've seen in this Berlin Festival. I think it's a major film; but then people say—but what if you show a film like this to the man in the street and he doesn't understand it? First of all, I think that's wrong. But even if it's true, doesn't it mean that in the future—and this world will probably last for another few thousand years—this film will be more important than all the rubbish which is now considered important but which never really goes deep enough? The questions Bresson asks will never be unimportant.

CHRISTIAN BRAAD THOMSEN: What about the problems raised in Bresson's film— are they rejecting all existing political forms?

FASSBINDER: Yes, rejecting every commitment. Because commitment for the film's young characters—whom he seems to understand so well—is mainly an escape into an "occupation" which keeps that commitment alive. An escape from the awareness that everything goes on regardless of you and your commitment.

Michael Haneke

Terror and Utopia of Form
Addicted to Truth
A Film Story about Robert Bresson's *Au hasard Balthazar*

> Must we, therefore, eat from the tree of knowledge once more,
> to fall back into the state of innocence?
> Most certainly, that is the last chapter of the history of the world.
>
> – Heinrich von Kleist, *On the Puppet Theatre*

The first film I can—dimly—remember going to see was Laurence Olivier's *Hamlet*. Since the film was shot in 1948, I must have been at least six years old. Of course I saw it again several times, so I cannot exactly separate what I experienced that first time, and what I remember from later viewings. But I remember precisely the theatre, already gloomy with its dark panelling, growing darker as the screening began, the majestic lifting of the curtain, and the gloomy images of the castle of Elsinore surrounded by surging waves, accompanied by a similarly gloomy music.

I also remember that my grandmother, who was with me in the theatre that day, told me years later that she was forced to leave with me after less than five minutes, because I was screaming in fright at those lugubrious images and sounds.

Soon after—it must have been the same year, as I had not yet started school—I spent three months in Denmark as part of an aide programme for children from countries that had lost the war. It was the first time I was away from home for an extended period, and I was miserable. In an effort to distract me, my Danish foster parents took me to the movies. It was a grey, rainy, late fall day, cold and cheerless, and the film, the title and plot of which I've forgotten, took place in the jungle and savannah of Africa. Again, I can remember exactly the narrow, gloomy theatre with doors along the side that opened directly on to the street. The film comprised a number of travelling shots, obviously filmed from inside a jeep, before which fled herds of antelope, rhinoceroses, and other creatures I'd never seen before. I was seated in that car, captivated with astonishment and joy.

Finally the film came to an end and the lights went on, the doors were opened on to the twilit streets; the noise of traffic filled the theatre, outside rain was pouring down, and the movie-goers opened their umbrellas and walked into the evening air. But I was still in a state of shock: I could not understand how I, who scant seconds before had been in Africa in the sun amidst the animals, had been transported back there so quickly. How could the theatre, which for me was like a car I was travelling in, have driven back—and especially so quickly—to northern, cold Copenhagen?

Coming of Age and Enchantment

When I think about the directness and intensity of these first two movie memories, I am always reminded of those remote tribes to whom, shortly after being "discovered"—that is, shortly after their initial confrontation with so-called civilization—films were shown with a screen and projector set up in the middle of the jungle. According to the westerners' accounts, the "savages" fled in panic, and could barely be calmed down. When they asked the reason for this reaction, the natives told them after a long, terrified silence, that for them, the framing of the images appeared as a real mutilation of the people shown in the film, who they perceived as actually being there. For them, the close-up of a head was really the talking, moving, amputated head of a person who was physically present, and who, given such dismembering should have been long dead!

The knowledge of those magical living images, with their power to evoke horror and delight equally, has, in a world that accustoms even infants to the constant presence of virtual reality in their living-room television set, largely fallen into oblivion.

Years later, in my last year at the *Gymnasium* I saw Tony Richardson's screen adaptation of Fielding's *Tom Jones*. The film relates the eventful story of an orphan boy growing to maturity in eighteenth-century England; it was directed with wit and a sure sense of pace, and succeeded in its efforts to make the viewer into an accomplice of its fun-loving hero. Suddenly, perhaps a third of the way into the film, in the middle of a hair-raising chase sequence, the protagonist stopped in his tracks, looked into the camera (that is, at ME!), and, before resuming his flight from his pursuers, commented on the difficulty of his predicament, thereby making me aware of mine.

The shock of recognition of this moment was in every way equal to the terror of my childhood movie experience. Naturally I had long since grasped that the movies were not real, naturally I had long since distanced myself physically and probably mentally by ironic observations from the unnerving immediacy of a thriller, but never before this shocking discovery of my constant complicity with film protagonists had I experienced the dizzying immediacy that separates fiction and reality; never before had I physically experienced to what extent I and my fellow humans—that is, the audience—were largely victims and not partners of those whom we paid to "entertain" us.

Nonetheless, my hunger for stories was not sated—I wasn't sure what I was looking for in the movies. It was no doubt a form of film art that still offered the experience of being directly touched, the wonderful enchantment of the films of my childhood, but which did not thereby turn me into the helpless victim of the story being told and its teller.

I was able to see Bresson's film while still a student, thanks to a film course at our university that gave students the opportunity to become familiar with some of the films that, as uncommercial "art works," were very unlikely to reach our theatres. The film crashed into our seminar like a UFO fallen from a distant planet, and divided us into fanatic supporters and fierce opponents. Provocative, foreign, and surprising, it broke with all the golden rules of mainstream cinema on both sides of the wide ocean, as well as those of so-called European "art film," and was at the same time in an absolutely frightening way perfect in its absolute unity of content and form. I grasped only later that this perfection had its own story of maturation behind it, when I had the opportunity to see Bresson's previous films. Nonetheless, and despite the masterpieces that came after it, *Au hasard Balthazar* remains for me the most precious of all cinematic jewels. No other film has ever made my heart and my head spin like this one. What was, what is so special about it?

Balthazar is a donkey. The film tells the story of his life, his suffering and his death. And it tells—in fragments—the story of those whose path Balthazar crosses.

The beginning: the screen still dark, before the fade-in of the first picture, the tinkling of the bells of a herd of sheep. Then the first shot: close-up, the baby donkey drinks from between its mothers legs; in the background we sense the herd of sheep more than we see it; only their bells are heard ringing softly and serenely. Then a child's skinny arm wraps itself around the animal's neck, tugs it away from its mother, the camera pans along and we see the little girl tenderly hugging the donkey, a boy about the same age also bending over and patting it, and between them, in the background, a man. They are all dressed lightly, it is summer. "Can we have him? Please, Daddy!" "What do you want it for?"

Long shot: the children are running beside their father, who is pulling the little donkey down into the valley from the mountain pasture. The sheep's bells have fallen silent.

Close-up: with a small pitcher one of the children pours water over the donkey's head and says, "Balthazar. I baptize you in the name of the Father and the Son and the Holy Ghost. Amen."

The ending: Balthazar is burdened with the loot of a pair of smugglers—they are going over the border in the mountains. It's night. Suddenly the "Don't move!" of a border guard. The smugglers run back the way they came. As we hear shots, the camera lingers on Balthazar's face, then he, too, takes off, downhill, in the direction where his masters, who tormented him constantly, have just fled.

Daylight. Balthazar is standing quietly between the pine trees on the mountain. Close-up: his shoulder—blood is seeping from a bullet wound. He begins to move, wanders out from under the sheltering trees, into the pristine alpine pastures, still burdened with the smugglers' loot on his shoulders. The sound of a herd. We see the sheep approaching, black sheepdogs jump around them, barking, the bells ringing. A shepherd. Shots of individual dogs. Then the herd stands around Balthazar, we can barely make him out through all the sheep surrounding him, we hear the bells from up close. The black dogs. The sheep begin to move off, slowly revealing the donkey, who is now sitting on the ground. Again the dogs. Then the sheep have retreated into the background—Balthazar in the foreground. The music comes in—the deathly sad andantino from Schubert's Sonata in A Major, which has accompanied Balthazar's life story throughout the film, offering pity and at the same time consolation. Slowly, very slowly, Balthazar's head sinks. Then, completely filling the frame, only the herd—it's in motion, leads us back to Balthazar, who is lying there, stretched out on the grassy pasture, not moving anymore. The music stops. Only the sound of bells. The sheep wander off into the background, disappearing into the mountain landscape. In the foreground: Balthazar is dead. The bells become softer. The end.

In between lies a life that, in its sad simplicity, stands for those of millions, a life of small pleasures and great efforts, banal, unsensational, and because of its depressing ordinariness, apparently unsuitable for exploitation on the silver screen. In fact, the film is not about anyone, and thus about everyone—a Donkey has no psychology, only a destiny.

The title is the precise reflection of the film's intention: "By chance, for instance, Balthazar." It could be anyone else, you or I. Bresson chose the name, he says, for its alliteration. That sounds arbitrary and a platitude, but is actually just the opposite.

Bresson's "model" theory, his systematic rejection of professional actors in favour of aptly chosen amateurs has often been discussed and still more often criticized—this is also the reason behind his films' lack of financial success. Here, in *Balthazar*, the motive for this theory is most easily seen and finds its clearest and most coherent expression: the screen "hero" is not a character who invites us to identify with him, who experiences emotions for us that we are allowed to feel vicariously. Instead, he is a projection screen, a blank sheet of paper, whose sole task is to be filled with the viewers' thoughts and feelings. The donkey does not pretend to be sad or to suffer when life is hard on him—he does not cry, we cry for an icon of imposed forbearance, precisely because he is not like an actor peddling his ability to exteriorize emotion. The animal Balthazar, along with the knights in the director's later *Lancelot du Lac*, locked up in their clattering suits of armour to the point of being unrecognizable, are Bresson's most convincing "models" simply because they are unable to pretend.

Not that Bresson's "model" concept has always worked well. Amateurs can be cast just as inappropriately as actors. That notwithstanding, the "non-acting" of his always painstakingly, even lovingly chosen amateurs, the monotony of their manner of talking and moving, their presence—reduced to mere existence—was and is a liberating experience (far more than the casual "naturalness" of the young actors in the cerebral fireworks and more intellectual jokes of his younger colleague Godard). It gave back to the people in front of the camera their dignity: no one had to pretend anymore to make visible emotions that, because acted—could only be a lie anyway. It had always struck me as obscene to watch an actor portray, with dramatic fury, someone suffering or dying—it robbed those who were truly suffering and dying of their last possession: the truth. And it robbed the viewers of this professional reproduction of their most precious possession as viewer: their imagination. They were forced into the humiliating perspective of a voyeur at the keyhole who has no choice but to feel what is being felt before him and think what is being thought. Cinema has missed out on the opportunity it has, new in comparison with literature, to represent reality as a total sensory impression, to develop forms that maintain and even for the first time enable the necessary dialogue between a work of art and its recipient. The lie that pretence is reality has become the trademark of cinema—one of the most profitable in the annals of business.

One senses in *Balthazar*, as in all Bresson's films, its author's almost physical aversion to any type of lie, especially to any form of aesthetic pretence. This passionate aversion appears to be the driving force behind his entire oeuvre. It leads to a purity of narrative means unique in the history of cinema.

While reading the description of the beginning and end of the film, for a reader unfamiliar with Bresson's films, the impression may creep in of "poetry," affected beauty, pretentious stylization. There is none of that in the film: documentary simplicity in framing, an almost manic rejection of the "beautiful," that is, pleasing images (as were occasionally to be found in his earliest films, and as are mastered by today's art cinema—as well as American big budget films and TV advertising)—indeed one could venture to say that Bresson invented the "dirty" image in the field of art cinema. Alongside the ever perceptible desire to show things as clearly and simply as possible, an infallible instinct saves him from the danger of sterile stylization; for all the precision of their framing, his pictures always give the impression of being frayed, ready for when reality breaks the rules. Herein lies the source, I think, of his well-known conflicts with his cameramen, such as De Santis, all famous for the beauty of their images.

Precision rather than beauty—each shot shows only the absolute essential, each sequence is compressed to its most intense form; even so the length of the shots and cuts are, even for the period when the film was made (1965), unusually calm. Pauses never create room for sentimentality; in its simplicity everything gives the impression of having developed naturally and is never, although in the service of a rigorous aesthetic concept, the victim of the latter. All actions and events retain the richness of real life—the author never takes sides, the spectator is always called on to use his own personal judgement, free to choose, to find his own truth and interpretation. Bresson intended to personify the seven deadly sins in his characters—but against a declaration such as this can be placed a sentence from his *Notes sur le cinématographe*: "Hide the ideas, but in such a way that they can be found. The most important will be the best hidden." Elsewhere he writes, "Production of emotion obtained by resistance to emotion." In support, he cites the pianism of Lipatti: "A great pianist, not a virtuoso, one like Lipatti, relentlessly hits the notes the same way: half-notes, the same duration, the same intensity; fourth-notes, eighth-notes, sixteenth-notes, etc., *idem*. He doesn't pound the emotion into the keys. He waits for it. It comes and takes over his fingers, the piano, him, the concert hall."

I have a video tape of the awards ceremony from the 1983 Cannes Film Festival, where a Special Jury Prize was jointly awarded to the then seventy-six-year-old Bresson for his last film, *L'Argent*, and to Andrei Tarkovsky, for *Nostalghia*. As Bresson, called up by Orson Welles, stepped on to the stage, a tumult broke out, a furious acoustic battle between those booing and those acclaiming him; the audience was asked for calm a number of times—only as Tarkovsky was invited on stage did the storm of protest abate.

What in Bresson's films caused this behaviour in the Cannes auditorium—which represented, or claimed to, the behaviour of audiences around the world? It could not have been the content. Films that tell of the lamentable state of the world are in abundance at every festival; the more cosily and stylishly they settle themselves in our anguish, the greater their chance the jurors and journalists will thank them for it.

The Pain is Exorcized

What is so different about his way of using image and sound that Bresson found it necessary to resurrect for himself a term that had fallen into disuse, "cinematograph," because he no longer found a common language and a common meaning with that which called and calls itself cinema?

A decade before *Au hasard Balthazar* was made, Adorno wrote, in his essay "The Position of the Narrator in the Contemporary Novel," on the subject of Kafka: "His novels, if indeed they even fall under the category, are an anticipatory response to a state of the world in which the contemplative attitude has become a mockery because the permanent threat of catastrophe no longer permits any human being to be an uninvolved spectator; nor does it permit the aesthetic imitation of that stance." And elsewhere, referring to Dostoevsky: "There is no modern work of art worth anything that does not delight in dissonance and release. But by uncompromisingly embodying the horror and putting all the pleasure of contemplation into the purity of this expression, such works of art serve freedom—something the average production betrays, simply because it does not bear witness to what has befallen the individual in the age of liberalism."

The illusion that reality can be depicted in an artifact, and is not always only an agreement between the artist and his recipient, had become—since being called into question by Nietzsche—at the very latest since the incommensurable horrors of the Nazi reign, the Holocaust and the World War, obsolete for everyone who sought to participate even somewhat consciously in this field of activity. The verdict, that no more poems could be written after Auschwitz, demarcated the horizon of consciousness of the survivors and future generations as much as did the retraction of the Ninth Symphony together with all of western culture in Thomas Mann's *Doktor Faustus*.

Only the cinema, the most expensive form of artificial communication and the one most dependant on money, firmly withstood every reflective renewal. The newer subjects, positions, or putative findings were presented in the old, long disavowed forms. And the supposed distinction between the most overtly self-assured anaesthetizing schmaltz of right- or left-wing provenance and the so-called "progressive art film" remained but a self-justifying farce of the artists and actors who live off the film industry.

For the contents and crises of meaning of a shattered world, new forms had to be found, on behalf of the financiers, that betrayed these contents by making them fit for consumption—otherwise the films would not be made. Naturally such forms were found. They were refined and compiled, and in the course of this process the majority of those involved forgot why they had been undertaken in the first place.

A polemic oversimplification? I think this is required in order to express why Bresson, this scandal-monger, was and is such a provocation in the world of moving pictures.

In order to be and to remain active in the feature film world (to avoid the term "film business"), even those who saw through and despised the rules of the game described above found themselves forced to subscribe to them, even to place themselves in their service. To what extent they did so while consciously distancing themselves from them, or were influenced unconsciously by them—is visible in their attempts to playfully circumvent these rules of the game. If individual works overlooked this unspoken agreement—restored thanks to economic necessity—as to the necessity of artistic inconsistency, they were overlooked—shortened, re-edited, castrated as the one-time, and therefore just barely forgivable, *faux pas* of their makers—relegated to the realm of the experimental film (and thus no threat to the market), or at best halfheartedly tolerated by certain critics as exceptions that prove the rule. The most exciting and most truthful of what the cinema has to offer can be found in this category of exceptions: Pasolini's *Salò*, Tarkovsky's *The Mirror*, a few films by Ozu, Rossellini, Antonioni, Buñuel and Resnais, Kluge and Straub, and a handful of others.

What happens in them? The films are as different as their authors and the cultural circles from which they originated. What they have in common, and what differentiates them from the great mass of film production, and even from other films by the same author, is their successful unity of content and form. They shatter the dubious consent between those depicted, the mediators, and recipients, and, like the optical torture chair in Kubrick's *A Clockwork Orange*, prevent us from closing our eyes, and force us to gaze in the mirror. What a sight! The horror! Spectators accustomed to and luxuriously installed in the lies, leave the theatre aghast. Starved for a language capable of capturing the traces of life, and with hearts and minds suddenly opened, the remaining spectators wait for renewed developments of the stroke of luck that has unexpectedly taken place.

Few of the above-mentioned authors achieved more than once this unity of what is depicted and how it is depicted. They found their way back to more easily trodden paths—the storm warnings of failure must be heeded, the fidelity of one's fans rewarded. And the bigger the following, the wider and more well-worn the path. But it's the builders of freeways who earn the most.

In such a context, Bresson's continuity seems almost miraculous. After his two-and-a-half tentative first steps, which contain the thematic catalogue of his later works (a short, *Les Affaires publiques*, and his two first features, *Les Anges du péché* and *Les Dames du Bois de Boulogne*), his formal vocabulary is fully developed with *Journal d'un curé de campagne* in 1950, and he remains unwaveringly committed to it for the duration of his output (another ten films in thirty-two years).

Of almost all the great directors it is said that they have always made the same film over and over. Of none is this so accurate as of Bresson. To be addicted to truth—one has no choice. "Do not think of your film beyond the means that you have chosen for yourself," he writes in his *Notes*. And indeed, it is impossible to tell, while watching his films, if the means have determined the content, or the other way around, they are so very much one and the same. Their unity leaves no room for ideology or an interpretation of the world, commentary or consolation. Everything dissolves into pure relationship, and it is up to the viewer to draw conclusions from the sum of the arrangement.

Reduction and omission become the magic keys to activating the viewer. In this respect, it is precisely the hermetic aspects of Bresson's works that seek to make the spectator's role easier: it takes him seriously.

Left out is the gesture of persuasion of models with whom we can identify emotionally.

Left out is the (all too) condensed meaning of the connections of sociological and psychological explanations—as in our daily experience, chance and contradiction of fragmentary splinters of action demand their rights and our attention.

Left out is the pretence of any kind of wholeness, even in the depiction of people. Torso and limbs come together for only scant moments, are separated, are treated like and at the mercy of objects, the face is one part among many, an immobile, expressionless icon of melancholy at the loss of identity.

Left out is the unusual, because it would defraud the misery of everyday existence of its dignity.

Left out, finally, is happiness, because its depiction would desecrate suffering and pain.

And it is precisely this universal retraction (not so unlike that of Mann's Faust), this tender respect for people's capacity for perception and personal responsibility, that conceal in their gesture of refusal more utopia than all the bastions of repression and cheap consolation.

The unity of content and form redeems a premonition of the interrelation of the senses that has been lost to the described world. By leaving out the portrayal of happiness, wishing grows wings, and for the happy moments of viewing, pain, through its depiction, is made bearable.

Translated from the German by Robert Gray, Kinograph

Hal Hartley

GRAHAM FULLER: The elliptical treatment of the human body occurs in Robert Bresson's films. There's a compositional austerity in your work that also reminds me of Bresson.

HAL HARTLEY: I am very affected by Bresson and, more and more, I am consciously using that knowledge—whatever that means. Sometimes it's just an emotional clarity that I sense in his films, that I try to bring to mine when I'm writing. When I'm shooting too. Bresson cuts right past everything that's superfluous and isolates an image that says exactly what it's meant to say.

In *Surviving Desire*, I show Jude's hand reaching across a table to almost touch Sofie's hand. My treatment of that action struck me as Bressonian. Recognizing that the gesture itself was expressive. Nothing else was needed. It's about getting rid of the superfluous and the presumptuous—that's what keeps coming up in my notebooks. A lot of my experience over the past four or five years as a filmmaker has been in finding out what I need and what I'm going to look at in order to tell a story. And this approach of getting rid of what's unnecessary requires being totally alive at the moment of photography. I always thought that this particular shot in *Surviving Desire* would be done in

close-up or two matching singles. I thought it was their faces that were important at that moment. But it wasn't. It was their hands and nothing else. . . .

FULLER: You've been compared to Harold Pinter and David Mamet, because
there's a similar stylized accent on the words in your films.

HARTLEY: I'm flattered by the comparison, though I don't really know a whole lot
about either of them. Their work is primarily in theatre. Specificity is something I like about Mamet's movie *House of Games*. It's also why I like Bresson.
He doesn't waste time on things that don't convey meaning. Every single
frame of his films conveys meaning, even if it's an image of someone sitting
with nothing to say. Everything Bresson shows you says something. I figure
that's what films does best—convey those moments of meaning in action.

Agnieszka Holland

I saw *A Man Escaped* for the first time in a ciné-club in Warsaw in the sixties. I was
about fifteen years old, and I *felt* this film like no previous film. It is difficult to
express, but the experience was a kind of awakening for me—the film expressed
such essential truths. After that, the next Bresson film, *Pickpocket*; then *Balthazar*,
Mouchette, and later *L'Argent*. Following each screening there was that feeling of
great clarity, mixed with—now that I was making my own films—a little jealousy. That someone can achieve such perfection in a film! For me, Bresson is one
of the giants of the last fifty years of cinema. Maybe *the* giant.

Mani Kaul

An effortless encounter brought me face to face with him. I had imagined meeting him. I thought he was a phone call away. He was. I carried a phone number
for Bresson. With the help of Henri Micciollo, I phoned him. He set a time. He
was casting *Le Diable probablement*.

On the Champs Elysées, on the third or fourth level of a building, the space
was divided by glass walls. Young men and women stood in a line that inched
towards a figure that could be seen behind seven transparent layers. An alchemist
of medieval aspect. Almost. He stood up each time the "model" approached.

A production hand wondered what we (Henri Micciollo, Lalitha Krishna and I)
were there for. Before long Bresson noticed us.

"Gesture comes before meaning," Bresson said in English in answer to a question about his repetition of takes. The mechanism was a trap, which at the end must disappear. These words never left me afterwards.

You find followers of his films, at least one in every country you chance upon. Yet you come across not one who has entirely renounced the "actor," or acting for that matter.

Semblance to Bresson turns into appearance and not into nature; the posture is made meaningful before it attains meaning. The more intellectual the film, the more caricatured. How on earth can the profound find a "posture?"

If one were to attempt to follow or imitate any master, it would be impossible to do so entirely; therefore there is no danger in it, at least in the initial or formative years of one's work. The difference between the master and your imitation of him, the subtle difference, the exact distance/angle of the disparity, will lead you to understand things about yourself. The natural incapacity to imitate someone else perfectly leads to a realization of your own inner and original strivings. All the so-called "mistakes" in following/imitating the master are the first crevices that will open into a chasm of difference between his work and your own. Your imagination then becomes your own. Like the master, but different in that it makes possible your unique expression of emotion as documentary.

Aki Kaurismäki

Robert Bresson—A Wolf

As lonely as Mr. Bresson is in his damned profession, he still isn't totally isolated. He had a brother called Douglas Sirk (or Detlef Sierck) who continually challenged Bresson in the field of melodrama. However deep Bresson wants to hide behind the Catholic term of mercy, he still can't deny that he is a melodrama filmmaker. With his companions—above-mentioned Sirk—and Yasujiro Ozu (who in surface seems to be nearer to Bresson, but let us not be fooled by the surface) he has, in his calm way, continued the tradition of Lubitsch.

Only Mr. Bresson has taken his style so far that there aren't any elements (traditionally and visually) which would connect him to this style of cinema. In fact there might not be any style in any art he would like to be connected with. Here we go back to the beginning; Bresson is a lonely wolf.

Without mercy he denies everything, including life, and I couldn't agree more. Maybe James Agee would have something to say about this but he can't, not in this world. He is already and safely outside of suffering and under mercy.

What I am really trying to say is that Bresson is not only a melodrama director, but also a comedy filmmaker, who could—if needed—easily challenge any Lenny Bruce on the stage. But the man is hiding.

The very same man who wrote that music is not needed in cinema and the next day used one instrumental guitar piece in *Mouchette*. Altogether, I would never have survived in this God-forgotten world without the realistic lies of Mr. Bresson, for which I will always be thankful until I die and thereafter.

Jean-Pierre Lefebvre

Like a falling snow, Bresson blurs defined shapes and gives them a sensual metaphysical geometry. For just as snow buries a landscape, Bresson leaves the richness of the seasons to the viewer's imagination as a subject for thought and meditation. A cinema of pure signification where once the door to appearances is opened, the key to representation is thrown to the wind. A cinema without cameras. A cinema of meaning.

In Paris in 1962, I had the rare privilege of attending the *avant-première* of *Procès de Jeanne d'Arc*. It was pouring rain. Dissatisfied with the projection, Bresson made us wait outside for more than two hours. His films require the same patience, the same asceticism. They force spectators to re-examine their own ethics, and elicit an acute questioning of the images they are absorbing. This is why Bresson, more than anyone else, has influenced so many directors of so many different cultures. He is the unwritten page, the blank screen, the island closest to the midnight sun, and certainly the polar opposite of the all too frequent shots of actors—a description Bresson himself has applied to cinema in general.

When I despair that film has become the opium of the people, when I despair at seeing the seventh art throwing millions at some self-conscious disspelling of illusions, I make a point of seeing once again *Un condamné à mort s'est échappé* or *L'Argent*. It is then that I rediscover the deep and fundamental meaning of my craft as a filmmaker, just as much as I rediscover the craft of being human—for filmmaking is, above all, a most humanistic craft.

Translated from the French by Lara Fitzgerald

Marcel L'Herbier

The February Revolution

Since February 7 [1951], a film has taken its place in our theatres. And it will never lose its place in our memories.

Is this to say that it has from the outset imposed itself on cinematographic history as a triumph of art, or a best-seller, a *film maudit*, an avant-garde, experimental film, or as one of those radiant *classics* whose means and ends are united in a Gordian knot of perfection?

No. It turns its back on all such glory. It enters the special history of the talking film only to project, on the history of "all" film, an originality so revolutionary that it is without precedent—I weigh my words—in any work for the screen of any country in the world.

Which is why this extraordinary film cannot be said to represent, on the road of the "cinematograph," merely a fortunate turning point or even a summit. Because it is the first to discover the mysterious juncture of thirty years of silent films and twenty years of talking films, it takes its place as victor of an unexplored territory. From there, stupefying our predictions, crushing our disbelief, it offers us the fascinating revelation of a film that, following upon those that were silent and those that rattled on—in being ITSELF—is neither the one nor the other.

It will be clear which film I'm talking about. Indeed, *Journal d'un curé de campagne*, which Robert Bresson claims merely to have *adapted* from the masterpiece by Bernanos, does not present itself as an extension of the prestigious race of seminal films that, from *Potemkin* to *The Bicycle Thief*, from *Thérèse Raquin* to *Le Diable au corps*, from *The Passion of Joan of Arc* to *Peter Ibbetson*, have opened the visual art to the premonition of an absolute.

It places itself in an entirely different sphere. Sheltered from their heritage. Worlds apart from their hegemony. And by a miracle that could soon recreate filmic creation, it lays itself open to being their opposite, the better to remain their equal.

It is this unique marvel that urgently demands we shed light on it, for a better understanding of history and, more modestly, to guide unaware spectators, whose indulgence may be sorely tried in the labyrinth of its originality.

God judges the righteous. This supreme belief of the priest of Torcy echoes from Bernanos's soul to Bresson's. May we not believe, with the same faith, that a film that is so "right" can be judged only on its own terms? And by the justice of a future judgement. In this sense, a work whose infinite rightness is worthy only of a final judgement should be spared the pros and cons of an immediate assessment.

Yet should the media nonetheless demand a premature review of a film, of which time alone *will refine the gold*, let us recall that this review appeared in these very pages [the French magazine *Combat*]. And that it expressed itself—by power of attorney from the future—in excellent terms.

But after it, after Julien Green, François Mauriac, Albert Béguin, after all those who so expertly keep score in the combat of films with their initial audience, after the oracles of the Prix Louis Delluc and the diviners of festivals, it would be purely gratuitous to heap praise on theirs.

Yet other considerations appeal for our intervention. To speak openly: this overwhelming film has placed filmmakers on a state of alert. They realize that, through it, an awesome process of cinematographic salvation is underway. Some already see it as compromised. Others console themselves that it will fail. Many fly to the passive defence of the routines that it overturns. All are fearful of its consequence.

For those of us who hope for its success, it is essential that we face up to it. To bring this work nearer to its destiny, to uncover paths to its mystery, and to extend the effects of its revolution to everything it is capable of fertilizing in a cinematographic world that is foundering.

But in what way does the humble priest of Ambricourt, with his silences and his agony, thus deserve to be mobilized in a profane battle: a "bataille d'Hernani" or a palace revolution?

We shall attempt an answer.

There are three degrees of rarity, three singular virtues, there are three victories in *Journal d'un curé de campagne*, the work by Robert Bresson.

In order of importance, they are:

For the first time, thanks to this film, the cinematograph and literature find themselves on an equal footing—in both spirit and form—in the game of art. This equal value, this aesthetic balancing out, have always been, in themselves, and for all time—a law without exception.

Music is the equal of poetry. As is painting, music or architecture. No one art has an advantage over another. No coefficient of favour for any masterpiece. Beethoven equals Michelangelo, and Shakespeare, Goya. The currencies of the absolute are exchanged at par.

The cinematograph, a latecomer, and sometimes seen as an upstart, sometimes as an (intellectually) poor cousin, in the financial fraternity of artistic creation, has constantly been refused the privilege of equality. From their native Parnassus, the major arts look down on it. And let us admit this has been just.

In fact, one might have believed that Albert Thibaudet had made incontrovertible, once and for all, the famous phrase: *The cinematograph is (in the sense that one speaks of the degradation of energy), the degradation of literature.* Let us admit that, for fifty years, filmmakers for their part have done their utmost so that the recurring depredations of the monuments of theatre and literature justify this excommunication.

Madame Bovary, The Charterhouse of Parma, The Red and the Black, just like *Anna Karenina, The Divine Comedy*, and *Great Expectations*, seem to have been adapted for the screen by impenitent directors only to bear out Thibaudet's judgement, and to dig each time a little deeper the trench along the original demarcation line between cinematograph and literature.

Finally Robert Bresson comes along . . . And Albert Béguin can proclaim this truth: "An unprecedented fact until now, a masterpiece of literature has given birth to an adaptation that, because it is entirely free, is a masterpiece of cinema."

No doubt this praise is partially developed on a fragile argument. It is not because it is "entirely free" that the transposition of the *Journal d'un curé de campagne*, taken from a masterpiece, has led to a masterpiece. It is because it is entirely successful. The screen versions of Flaubert's *Salammbô* and Faulkner's *Sanctuary* used far more "entire" freedom in their day. However, we know what the result was, or rather, the end of the line, the landing point, which made all the more glaring the "degradation" of these novels.

But Albert Béguin's assessment remains key. He is expressing a truth. *Journal d'un curé de campagne* is the first film in the world to translate word for image, speech for silence, eloquence for evocation, a work that is less novelistic than philosophic, a work of such lofty inspiration and literary quality that their very emergence seems to inviolably defend it against a perfect transposition from its original art to a till-then minor art.

And herein lies Bresson's first victory. The exception that his film constitutes will soon confirm a rule that will give rise to other miracles. Starting today, the cinematograph receives its letters of nobility. It enters into a state of grace. Its youth no longer exposes it to the hurtful discredit of the immemorial arts. One film sufficed. It proves with a stroke of light that which, for fifty years, remained to be proved: that a work of pure literature can, without suffering a vile betrayal, pass unscathed from its world of verbal beauty to the rough, concrete representation of the skies, roads, horizons of the earth and the faces of men. This is more than one of those masterful strokes of which autonomous films, born alone of the cinematograph, had already given us the example: *Potemkin* or *The Bicycle Thief*. This is the miracle of a revolution.

Bresson's second victory is his making, for the first time, a film that is entirely a talking and just as entirely a silent film.

François Mauriac was not wrong when he recognized in the face of Claude Laydu, "a minor priest in agony with his God," this expression of the soul, this epiphany of inner life whereby the cinematograph, a silent art, triumphed over theatrical rhetoric. Whereby it also continues to show, in our modern world, "devourer of man," the essence of its specific mission: to stop man from fleeing before the human face, that faithful mirror of unspeakable dramas, which is perhaps but the "replica of an eternal and divine model."

But the systematic, intensive, and cruel use of the haunting face of this crucified child—from which "the soul is overflowing from everywhere" so much that you "would think you could touch it"—is not the only thing that links Bresson's aesthetic to the most efficient eloquence of the silent film. The entire film uses, so to speak, a language that comes from so far that it is but an ancient absence of speech. It is fundamentally, from the first shot to the last, fashioned and developed on silence.

In this, Bresson, no less than Bernanos, follows Saroyan's mysterious advice: he does not relate the story with words. He relates without words. He films with silence.

Admittedly silence is still part of human language. But whoever refuses to speak, thus challenging language, appears more silent than silence. And the priest of Ambricourt allows himself to make this challenge. He knows how to express that about which he keeps silent. And, in keeping silent, he still speaks—either with the silence of the dramatic world that determines him, or with the isolated words that have the infinitude of an absence. He also speaks from the depths of his conscience, and his voice thus no longer adopts the living inflections of language. It rises up from the silence of eternity.

Thus, by the exhaustive union of that which speaks and that which doesn't speak, Bresson's second victory is stunning; and it is enriched with innumerable cinematographic consequences that we will have to define one day. In any case, it clearly proves that the silent film's rich heritage can no longer be rejected out of hand, and that, at the same time, the use of human language can lead to a cinematography that is neither silent nor spoken, but goes beyond the surface, to be raised to the same level of the arts, to what Brice Parain calls: the expression of a "superior silence."

Finally, let us say a few words about Bresson's third victory. That his work is, as one great critic affirms, "the first film of inner life," will not be questioned by an objective spectator, or even a fan of Bernanos. But is that saying enough? *Brief Encounter* comes close to expressing, and rather subtly, a sort of elementary inner life. Other films have also tried to do so. Nonetheless, *Journal d'un curé de campagne* remains the only film, and the first one, to express in often admirable figurative equivalencies the near-inexpressible drama of a "higher" inner life.

This is what Julien Green notes: "It required courage to give us a film of such intransigent purity." And the novelist who gave us *Adrienne Mesurat*—she, too, so intransigent—which, in 1949, almost became a film constructed with exactly the same faithfulness as Bresson's—quite naturally comments on the qualities shown by the one "based" on Bernanos, noting "that a work composed exclusively of inner life can be transposed to the screen without the slightest concession." An exceptional equilibrium that ensures that a film's faithfulness does not become a betrayal of literature.

These three victories of Bresson confer on his achievement its revolutionary character. Thanks to them, his film appears to present traditional films a challenge, a temptation, a threat, and an example. A palace revolution? Perhaps, thanks to which the values that were yesterday ensconced on the throne risk being tomorrow cast to the old moons of Méliès or of art film. "A bataille d'Hernani?" No doubt. The battle waged against the dust of traditions by the new romanticism of life that is alive, defined, captured, printed boldly on film stock that is more sensitive than ever.

To this great, profound rekindling of the profound forces of production, Bresson adds his subsidiary successes, which, though of a more narrowly technical nature, are no less substantial, and whose lessons will never cease to be commented on.

It's first of all his success against the defigurations of characters, thanks to his elimination of stars; then his success against the contamination of artifice, thanks to his radical elimination of the studio.

About these two advantages of singular importance, one would have to speak at great length to begin to say enough.

One need only imagine, to assess their significance, what *Journal d'un curé de campagne* would have been if histrionic convention had been substituted for the purities of the novices' faces—and if the roads of Ambricourt had been "faithfully" depicted in the sham of sets and models!

What can be said in conclusion except that, in every way and for all its contributions, Robert Bresson's film represents that which should accurately be called an avant-garde film.

And if we are then surprised that these discreet images bear no resemblance to the acrobatics formerly praised in this category (from *L'Étoile de mer* to *Ballet mécanique* or *L'Âge d'or*), we must assure ourselves that such typical films were in no way avant-garde for the simple reason that they were never truly cinematographic. Despite this erroneous categorization, they were but the mask of a literary avant-garde, behind which surrealism, simultaneism, and other intellectual games for a time amused themselves in expressing themselves using the occasional means of cinema. This is why *Le sang d'un poète* did not open a road. It closed behind itself the golden doors of a quintessence; it even closed them so well that *Orphée* found before itself not an open road, but a dead end.

And it is to Robert Bresson's purely revolutionary film that today reverts the supreme privilege of opening up, at the avant-garde of cinematography, a new infinity.

Translated from the French by Robert Gray, Kinograph

Louis Malle

1.

ANDREW HORTON: You have worked with Robert Bresson as assistant director on *Un condamné à mort s'est échappé*. Is he an influence on your work? I am thinking particularly of *Mouchette*.

LOUIS MALLE: It's interesting that you mention *Mouchette*. I'm still an enormous admirer of Bresson, and I think I'm the only filmmaker that he cares to see, and we've kept up a very good relationship. Bresson is supposed to be a very austere filmmaker, but I feel *Mouchette* is a very *sensual* film. The end of the film where she is rolling down the hill to her death made me cry. I literally cried and I very rarely cry when filmmakers want me to cry. And *Balthazar* was also very much about an experience of the senses. That's what I admire about Bresson: that he has managed to create these sensual moments. When I worked with him on *Un condamné à mort s'est échappé*, Bresson was interested in me because I came from documentaries. He asked me to take care of all of the details such as the spoon with which the prisoner was digging—all of these details which had to do with the escape. I was very impressed with all of his close-ups of such details and with his concern to show a sense of touch.

The soundtrack for the film was also remarkable. I saw it again recently and it is extraordinary. He manages to create a world of sensation that he conveys. In that sense I feel very close to him.

2.

PHILIP FRENCH: I'd like to backtrack to Robert Bresson. What was it you wanted— you felt that you had served half an apprenticeship making documentaries, and you wanted to work with a feature-film director?

MALLE: I never really wanted to be an assistant director. With Cousteau I'd started as a technician, a cameraman, an editor, a sound man. I was not really tempted to come back to Paris and pursue a career as an assistant director. The only reason I worked with Bresson was because I admired him. I put him on a pedestal, much higher than any other French director. I had great admiration for Renoir, but Renoir was not working in France at that time. I was lucky enough to meet Bresson through a friend. He liked *Le Monde du silence* very much and was intrigued by this very young man, so he said, "Why don't you come and work with me?" which was great. I don't think I would have worked with René Clément—I'm not passing judgement, it's just that I admired Bresson and was convinced that Bresson's was the only way of making films. I've changed my mind about that, but in those years I was pretty rigid about it.

FRENCH: What was your role in *Un condamné à mort*?

MALLE: I suppose Bresson found me interesting because I came from a completely different background, a background in documentaries. When I started working with him he was finishing the revisions of the screenplay and he was seeing people for the cast, so I worked with him on that. Early on he put me in touch with the man on whose wartime experiences the film was based. His name was Devigny. He was a Resistance hero, an officer. Bresson said, "You're going to work with Devigny, and you're going to prepare all the props and all the details. I want everything to be absolutely authentic; it's going to help me tremendously." It was shot in the studio, *Condamné*, except for a couple of weeks on location in Lyon for the outside of the prison. But everything else— the cell, the corridors—was a set. I was in charge of the authenticity of the physical appearance of the shooting. I worked on that in pre-production and the first few weeks of shooting, which took place in the cell.

Then Cousteau asked me to go to America for a film about the *Andrea Doria*, so I told Bresson, "I think I'm going to go because Cousteau needs me and also, frankly, because it's exciting." It seemed to me that before the shooting started I was useful to Bresson, and his methods of preparation and casting were fascinating and taught me a lot. When he was shooting, I noticed—that's why I never wanted to be an assistant director—that you don't really learn much from a director. The process of making a film, especially for somebody like Bresson, is so mysterious. He was so secretive about his approach. We would do twenty-five takes, and at some point I could see that he was satisfied, but it was hard for me to understand *why* he was satisfied. And so I told him I was going to leave, and he said, "Well, I'm not going to keep you, I think you're right. I never was an assistant director, I don't think you can learn anything from being assistant director, so you must go your own way." But I kept on good terms with him.

Un condamné à mort was the beginning of his greatest period. He then did *Pickpocket*, *Balthazar*, *Mouchette*, and all those great films over the next decade. When I met him he had done only—well, they were great films—*Les Anges du péché, Journal d'un curé de campagne*, and *Les Dames du Bois de Boulogne*. For me he was the ultimate.

3. With *Pickpocket* Bresson Has Found

Pickpocket is Robert Bresson's first film. The ones he made before were only sketches. Which is as much as saying, if one is familiar with the director's worth, that the release of *Pickpocket* is one of the four or five great dates in the history of cinema.

It is remarkable that, in contrast to Bresson's preceding films, this new one was conceived, written, shot, edited, and *released* all within ten months, as if the period of trial and error were past. *Pickpocket* is a profoundly inspired film, a free film, instinctive, burning, imperfect, and overwhelming. It resolves every misunderstanding; if you deny this film, it is cinema itself as an autonomous art that you call into question.

In *Pickpocket*, there is no more *anecdote*, that is, pretext foreign to the real subject of the film that, more often than not, hides it, what producers call "a good subject," "a good story," with psychology thrown in, dramatic progression, etc. There are only symbols, of a luminous simplicity, that make up an allegory, or, more precisely, what is called in the gospels a *parable*. Turning his back definitively on dramatic construction, Bresson has made a contemplative film, a film of moral reflection, which is to traditional cinema what Pascal is to Balzac.

What does Bresson seek to tell us? Don't hope to find the answer in the thick press kit to his film. "Eyes have they, but they see not. They have ears, but they hear not."[1] *Not one critic* has said (or wanted to say) what a child of twelve with even a slight knowledge of the catechism would grasp immediately: the thief is *Man*, he is you, he is me; he is in the hands of God—this policeman with an indulgent or terrible look—but he revolts, pride, the supreme sin (the parable is Pascalian). He is ill protected by his guardian angel, the simplistic friend, and, from downfall to downfall, divine Grace makes its way in him, taking the face of a young girl, somewhat artless at first, but who becomes sublime in the dénouement, itself sublime.[2]

If you possess these simple keys, Bresson's film opens up before your eyes like a painting by Giotto or a cantata by Bach. Bresson's art has the naive strength, the sly candour, the worried and worrisome certitude characteristic of the great artists in the Christian tradition. To quote him: "I follow a road. I do not seek, I find. It is when I find that I am happy."

How does he proceed? He starts by strangling realism by the throat, that touchstone of cinema which, quite often, is still only an instrument of reproduction. Bresson is held to be revolutionary because he works with *everything*, image, sets, faces, gestures, voices, the generally accepted way of reproducing a sound environment. Allow me to explain: if you set up a microphone in the street, you will not capture the sounds of the street, but an auditory chaos, formless and inexpressive. That's how it is. And that's acknowledged.

So men of art proceed by analysis, selecting real sounds that they record separately and then match in proportion, which are "mixed." Everyone does that, with better or worse results, and Bresson does it better than anyone. But what is acknowledged for sound, an abstract concept without much in the way of realistic references, shocks and surprises when Bresson *alone* applies the same principle to *all* reality. "I take reality, pieces of reality, which I then place together in a certain order." That which he omits or rejects is, obviously, the picturesque, the gratuitous detail, even, and especially, if it "looks real." Just as a soundscape is reduced to its essential components, so will a voice, a gesture, be stripped away of all flourishes, all suspicious embellishments.[3]

What he shows us, finally, is not a false universe, but a corrected, rectified universe, an original universe from which is missing convention, the convention of the "right" gesture, of the "right" voice, theatrical convention. All this is obvious, and we are aghast that this freedom to interpret reality, which we grant so readily to a painter, is still denied to a filmmaker. When we go to a museum today, it is not to see apples; yet Bresson is criticized because his hero doesn't change his shirt.

"His actors play badly." The term "play," by its very ambiguity, is significant. The point is, his actors do not play.[4] Bresson plays with them.

What is indeed admirable in this film, and unique, is that its author, seeking to describe the conflict of a soul struggling with divine grace, has substituted himself for the latter. The film expresses the image of God's omnipotence, not only in its content, but also in its expression. As in the greatest works of the religious artists, form is identified with content, in other words, for an instant the artist takes the place of God. For the duration of the projection, Bresson is God.

The construction of *Pickpocket*? Reread Pascal. "What a chimera then is man! If he praises himself, I humiliate him; if he humiliates himself, I praise him; and contradict him always, until he understands." The film begins with a dazzling experience of Evil ("My heart was beating so hard I thought it would break") to end on a dazzling experience of Good ("My heart beat violently"). Between these two carefully identified extremes, the hero does battle with Pascal's twin perils: despair and pride.[5] His greatness is obvious: he is, in the Christian tradition, the very image of man, a bit of God, a "dispossessed king," at the same time both protagonist and victim of the great mystery of Grace. Hence the film's surprising rhythm, these brusque accelerations, repetitions, contradictions, pauses, sudden surprises, an entire "sense of rhythm," intuitive and learned, which evoke the irregular beat of a heart. "The ways of the Lord are unfathomable."

Bresson goes further still. Finding a masterful solution to what till then seemed to him an insoluble contradiction of cinema, the irritating, favoured, overly clever presence of the camera in the action, *he assigns it the role of the Eye of the*

Creator. The film is seen by Him in all his Omnipotence and Omnipresence. That it is always at the right spot, and demonstrates an improbable virtuosity, that it foresees and determines what takes place no longer shocks us, but rather illustrates Bresson's message. Watch the film carefully: you will see that the characters are *compelled* by the camera, pulled, pushed, held back by it. Look at those admirable backward tracking shots that suck along the characters, lead them.[6]

Everything is beautiful in this film, because everything is necessary. The sequence in the Lyon train station is not a bravura piece: ballet, orgy, revelry, it illustrates perfectly "this sort of sad frenzy that sin procures."[7] The cold gaze, the pursed lips of Martin Lassalle and his accomplices evoke Don Juan and the Marquis de Sade. The camera, more present here than anywhere else in the film, precedes and leads the gestures and looks. The Hand of God, here, is like a vice.

There is the ending, so misunderstood, where, suddenly, all the values are inversed: the prudish young woman is an unmarried mother, the guardian angel a seducer, the thief an honest man; the police, now Jehovah-God of vengeance, *provoke* the lapse and arrest of the hero. Then comes imprisonment, a sequence in the form of purgatory, with its waiting, its false exits, the doors that are closed, the halls that are crossed, all this mystery, this apparent disorder, this suspense of the soul, to finally open onto the Revelation, sudden and unexpected, like it should be. Thus the parable is accomplished: "The wind bloweth where it listeth . . . , [but thou] canst not tell whence it cometh, and whither it goeth."

By the simple and definitive relationships it establishes between content and expression, *Pickpocket* is a film of dazzling originality. On its first viewing, it risks burning your eyes. So, do like me: go back to see it again every day.

Translated from the French by Robert Gray, Kinograph

1. A review in *Radio-Cinéma* is titled: "Is There a Way Out of Bresson's Prison?" Surprising to read in a crypto-Christian weekly!

2. That this is the very subject of *Crime and Punishment* (and many other works) is obvious. Accusing Bresson of plagiarism is absurd; one might as well accuse Mozart, after listening to *Don Giovanni*, of plagiarizing Molière.

3. How much talent must one not have, let it be said in passing, to "reorganize" reality to such a degree in a film, two-thirds of which takes place outside the studio, in the streets, cafés, subway—those places where filmmakers are usually condemned to documentarism.

4. Let me note in passing that any student at IDHEC [the French film school], any editor at the *Cahiers du cinéma*, can get an actress to "play." You just have to stay out of her way, she'll do her little act, and have a great deal of respect for her director.

5. The whole film is thus constructed. Look at the beginning: he commits his first robbery, he exults, "his feet are no longer on earth." Three seconds later, he is arrested.

He is immediately released, gets back the money he's stolen, triumphs again. The next sequence: he goes to see his mother, does not dare enter: once more, shame, despair. Then comes the Lafcadio-like challenge, perfectly naive, and so on . . .

6. One could oppose this typically Bressonian kind of tracking shot with Resnais's "imaginary" forward tracking shots, which are man's lucid gaze on the universe.

7. Not so paradoxically, *Pickpocket* is "also" an erotic film, pickpocketing obviously being but the barely veiled symbol of the sins of the flesh (example: the spasm the first robbery provokes in the hero).

Babette Mangolte

Looking at Bresson's films, several years or even decades after they were made, I see works which are as current as if made yesterday. They have a directness which transcends fashion, and they have a great efficacy of means. The emotion is contained, insidious, digging inside you, and like a cancer, it grows. It takes you a while to realize that Bresson made you think, by weaving for your eyes and ears a fabric of effects. But our thinking is done after viewing the film. Bresson shows you the immanence of fleeting fragments.[1] He takes the distinction and separation of image and sound out of film. He literally merges the two. We hear what we see and we see what we hear. He doesn't illustrate but manufactures a machine for your use. He makes you think that you can use it for yourself.

When I see his films, I feel empowered with feeling. It is as if what I have seen is now part of my own past life, has been integrated into my own experience. It stops being a movie. I despair with Mouchette. I am living the country priest's last agony and ecstasy, the completeness of Balthazar's death high in the mountains with the sound of the bells, the tension produced by an unfamiliar sound on the body of a man preparing his escape, the orgasmic fascination of the pickpocket and the pleasure of skilled work and fun in a successful partnership in petty crime.

At the "heart of the heart" of his films, there is an enigma which the film does not resolve.[2] The film proposes a mystery. We do what we want with it. No film of Bresson is simply about one thing in spite of its clarity. With his directness comes a sense of the complexity of life and of its moral ambiguity.

A Bresson film is a mosaic where every piece (shot) is small with indefinite shade, but when you look back at the finished whole (film), the colours are vibrant, the project clear, the emotion unmistakably there.[3]

Who is he? A moralist, yes, like the people he reads: Montaigne, Montesquieu, Pascal. Born with the century, he values his instincts more than his thoughts. Of his times, he understands the value of his own observations. Good material to work with, he would say. He started as a painter and still thinks like one. He became a filmmaker. He is a filmmaker's filmmaker.

His reflections on his practice exposed in *Notes on the Cinematographer* are curt, elliptical, provocative, polemical, authoritarian and prescriptive. They are the ones of an embattled man who fights for recognition. His films are the opposite. They imply. They avoid drama. They are lyrical, painfully true, open to multiple interpretations. The films are complex. Robert Bresson, the filmmaker, remains a mystery.

1. From Bresson's book *Notes on the Cinematographer*, "that's and that's not it, at the first glance. Reasoning comes afterwards" p.124. "Let the cause follow the effect, not accompany it or precede it" p. 92.
2. Ibid., p. 37.
3. Ibid., "Your creation or invention confines itself to the ties you knot between the various bits of reality caught. There is also the choice of the bits. Your flair decides" p. 64. "Films where expression is obtained by relations of images and of sounds, and not a mimicry done with gestures and intonations of voice (whether actors' or non-actors'). One that does not analyze or explain. That re-composes" p. 9.

Chris Marker

Watch carefully *Lancelot* and Roger Corman's *The Red Baron*. They tell the same story.

Gregory Markopoulos

Robert Bresson: A Brief Survey

Bresson's first film was an experimental film made ten years ago. The concluding scene in this experimental film showed the christening of a ship; but instead of the champagne bottle being broken against the ship, the ship itself was broken.

Les Anges du péché

The film has that rare inspiration which we seldom find in works of our age. Its miraculous unity of style is in accord with both the cadence of the images and the dialogue. Each sequence is complete in itself. From the opening scene of the convent's garden, the bell ringing; the next scene of Sylvie as La Prieure, hurrying to a prison to be present at the release of one of the inmates; the hurried scene through the night (all filmed on location) and the two men following La Prieure and the released woman; the lamps along the street, the taxi hurrying away; the scene of Anne-Marie putting away her worldly belongings; the stunning blacks and shimmering whites of Agostini; and when finally the police are introduced, as a matter of course, to solve a murder which has been committed, their scenes are short (for they are of the outside world). Then, again, Thérèse as portrayed by Jany Holt, while in prison, sending a food-truck filled with soup down the steps of the prison when she becomes irritated with her superior, and the ensuing shots as she attempts to escape from prison: the automatic doors closing, the alarm; to Thérèse killing her lover: she purchases a gun she sees in a window, the sound of automobiles is heard, but never the cars themselves seen; never the proprietor of the store; further, Thérèse arriving at a door, knocking, stepping back, the door opening, the shadow of a man thrust against the wall; the shot. Now, the nuns sewing, eating, working, or walking in a garden with all its exquisite lighting is reminiscent of the garden in von Sternberg's *The Scarlet Empress*. Toward the end of *Les Anges du péché*, we enter into the world outside of the convent in the scene of Anne-Marie chasing Thérèse in the cemetery. The final dazzling brilliance in this work by Bresson culminates in the scene of the death of the character Anne-Marie as portrayed by Renée Faure . . . the police are just entering the convent, but the camera follows a group of sisters as they mount some stairs; the hallway is filled with kneeling nuns, and they begin to chant: Anne-Marie lying upon a bed of boards. Thérèse kisses the tiny feet of Anne-Marie, and the camera trucks away to the chanting of the nuns; down the hallway, the police handcuff her: the exaggerated sound of the handcuffs fades out, and the music of Grünenwald continuing even through the darkness of the screen.

Les Dames du Bois de Boulogne

Bresson borrowed the idea from Diderot's *Jacques le fataliste et son maître*. The idea was transported to the twentieth century and with the aid of Cocteau the dialogue was resurrected. The Garden of the King in the Diderot was changed to the Bois de Boulogne and the former tale of Madame de la Pommeraye and the Marquis des Arcis, was converted to a far crueller history than the original of Diderot.

Bresson has never been pleased with his second film. Alain Cuny was unobtainable at the time, and Bresson had to substitute Paul Bernard. It is a horrible jar to the psyche of a film creator when an essential soul in his film work is unobtainable. With *Les Dames du Bois de Boulogne*, Robert Bresson utilized his exaggerated sense of sound. For example, when Paul Bernard is waiting during a downpour for the young danseuse (he doesn't know what her profession is), we hear the constant tooting of automobile horns, the voices of pedestrians, but see neither automobile or pedestrian; only, the danseuse crossing the street, her footsteps and the rain. Another example is the scene of the danseuse in the cabaret which is completely concerned with the sound of her tap-dancing, the accompaniment and then fade out. This scene is followed by another in which Maria Casarès follows the danseuse to the latter's apartment: the extraordinary close-ups of Maria Casarès against the panes of a glass door, the danseuse dancing, suddenly becoming angry with her partner, slapping his face, the ensuing clatter, broken champagne bottles and ice on the floor; the scene of the danseuse and Paul Bernard meeting in the Bois de Boulogne in the rain: the sound of the rain, the footsteps, and the final echoing of voices as the two disappear into the depths of a kind of cavern. In the final footage, the bridegroom returning to his bride who has suffered a stroke (the bride being the danseuse), and again the heavy footsteps as he enters the house; walks through the empty hallway—which that afternoon had been filled with wedding guests.

Les Dames du Bois de Boulogne seems to surpass Bresson's earlier film, *Les Anges du péché*, as far as film construction is concerned. The minor themes are knit closer. The action is more precise, yet not deliberately studied. The dialogue reaches a brilliant high pitch; from the elevator sequence in which Hélène stops the elevator by opening a part of the door on her level, her lover trapped midway; then the descending and ascending contrasts of elevator and Hélène; of Hélène's dialogue with her lover, with Hélène running down the flight of stairs as the elevator descends. This contrasted with the figure of Hélène dressed in black sitting on a love seat awaiting Paul Bernard; waiting to continue the spinning of his inevitable fate; extending her human revenge by marrying Paul Bernard to the young danseuse who is ill. After the ceremony, at the reception, Hélène tells her lover that he has married a danseuse.

Basically there is little difference between the final scene of *Les Anges du péché* (in which Anne-Marie, the saint, dies and Thérèse, the revoltee, returns to the outer world) and the final scene of *Les Dames du Bois de Boulogne*: the death of the young danseuse, Agnès, on the day of her marriage. The bridegroom returns to her chamber where she is lying, her gown spread around her:

"Are you there . . . perhaps this time you will pardon me. . . . ," speaks the bridegroom.

"In rest," replies the danseuse, his wife.

The camera with the effect of a *dies irae* rises from Agnès's bedside; perhaps one can even hear director of the cinema Robert Bresson saying to his actress: "*Chaud*, Élina, *chaud!*"

Jonas Mekas

On Bresson and *Une femme douce*

Here is what I thought, walking home from *Une femme douce*. *Une femme douce* is a film about diagonals. Diagonal angles, diagonal glances. About eyes that never really meet. A film without a single frontal shot. A film about three-quarter spaces. About the sound of closing doors. About the sound of footsteps. About the sound of things. About the sound of water. About shy glances. About unfinished glances. About the sound of glass. About death in our midst. About light falling on faces. About lights in the dark, falling on faces. About blood on forehead. About unfinished playing records. About a white crêpe blouse. About blue. About flowers picked and never taken home. About the roaring of cars. About the roaring of animals. About the roaring of motorcycles. About green. About how life and death intercut with each other. About hands giving and taking. About hands. About bourgeois pride. About pride. About lights on the door. About lights behind the door. About doors opening and closing. About bourgeois jealousy. About jealousy. About lamps turned out. About brown and yellow. About yellow. About indirect glances. About glances. About one peaceful glance (in the gallery, Schaeffer?). About unfinished records. About doors opening and closing. About doors opening very gently. About a half-opened door. About people standing behind glass doors and looking in. About fool's hopes. About hopes. About a window which doesn't lead into life. About a red car seat. About a red shop window. About standing behind the door, looking in. About a green bed and green curtains. About one happy smile in the mirror, at oneself. About eyes which do not look even when asked. About the sound of metal. About sleep. About two diagonal lives.

Jacques Rivette

The beauty of Robert Bresson's two most recent films [*Pickpocket* and *Procès de Jeanne d'Arc*] is one of pure information: the minimum of relays remain, and the greatest possible reduction in entropy is sought. It seems that no other filmmaker has ever pursued—so ardently—such direct communication with the viewer (that is, a relation of equality, not one of submission as with Hitchcock). Next to Bresson, in this aspect, even Buñuel and Rossellini seem rhetorical.

Here then are the most "public" films, the most commercial films that could possibly exist: it is clear what we are dealing with. And everything continues on as though the public were not actually interested in the truth, but in its rhetorical alibis, not in the message, but in that part of entropy that muddles it. Take for example a film like *Le Doulos* which is nothing but pure entropy and, through an accumulation of relays and fossilized signifiers, it pleases amateurs such that they exclaim: Now, that's cinema! This of course is due to the fact that they are accustomed to this type of film, having developed a conditioned aesthetic reflex; Pavlovian cinema for cinephiles.

That being said, is pure communication the aim of art? The real world is expansive, it is a *mélange* of scattered, partial and sometimes contradictory information of ceaseless overlap and transfers secreting a cancerous, constantly renewing entropy; a confusing mix where the only exceptions are a few brief moments of illumination (the revelation of love, a masterpiece, or certain landscapes). Is art made to mirror the world or to try and put a little order into it, to improve it in its own way? Another question that cannot really be addressed here, but I simply wanted to point out the meaning behind such a search that has no equivalent other than what a Braque, a Fautrier or especially a Webern seeks (like many paintings, *Procès de Jeanne d'Arc* can be said to be as beautiful as a wall—albeit a wall of signs). And if Bresson reaches out toward the white screen (or rather to the modulated grey screen into which he never slips), it is not because he has nothing more to say, but rather everything to say. Or, at least to say one thing absolutely: one word perhaps, yet spoken so completely that it becomes the sign and the meaning of all.

Translated from the French by Lara Fitzgerald

Paul Schrader

I can pin-point the moment my film sensibility was galvanized: April 1969, when I, as a film critic, saw Robert Bresson's *Pickpocket* (it had just been released in Los Angeles). I wrote about it for two consecutive issues, then went on to write a book about Bresson.

I had been drawn to films as a college student (film-going at the time was forbidden by my church). One never forgets one's first love, and my first love in the movies was the intellectual European cinema: Bergman, Resnais, Godard, Antonioni, Buñuel.

I "studied" these films. They touched my mind more than my heart.

Pickpocket moved through my mind into my heart. It was as if my soul was deflowered. Strange to say, Bresson "loosened me up." A weight of High Art fell from my young shoulders. Films could be spiritual *and* profane. I was free to enjoy both.

Martin Scorsese

It's a strange experience to watch a Bresson film at this particular moment in history, because a great deal of today's popular cinema is so big, loud, kinetic and, in many cases, grotesque. In other words, the antithesis of Bresson's cinema. I saw *A Man Escaped* again recently, and it's such a completely pure experience, with absolutely nothing extraneous—it functions like a delicate and perfectly calibrated hand-made machine. I have to wonder whether or not young people who have grown up on digitally engineered effects and DTS soundtracks can actually find the patience required to watch a film by a Bresson or, for that matter, an Ozu or an Antonioni. In a way, it seems impossible: it's as though they're from different worlds. To be honest, I also find Bresson's films difficult at times. But once I settle into his particular orbit, the experience is always rewarding, because he focuses on things that are beyond the reach of most movies. You can call it transcendental but perhaps it's simpler to say that Bresson focuses on the moments that happen between the ones that appear in most other movies. But he is also an incredibly dynamic filmmaker, and I learn a lot each time I watch one of his pictures. There's a cheap dynamism that's easily attainable through the many recent technological advances in movies, but in Bresson you get a true dynamism generated by the most elemental relationships between image and sound. He's created some of the most breathtaking set-pieces in cinema—the pickpockets at the racetrack in *Pickpocket*; Joan's burning at the stake in *The Trial of Joan of Arc*; the final massacre in *L'Argent*. Once Elvis Costello said that whenever he's writing a song he asks himself: is it as tough as Hank Williams? Meaning: is it ruthlessly pared down, as direct, as unflinching in its gaze at aspects of life I might feel more comfortable ignoring? Young filmmakers might ask themselves: is it as tough as Bresson?

Makoto Shinozaki

Bresson's Universe

The austerity and freedom that come with simplicity. The graceful movement of hands and fingertips. A gust of wind to bend trees and to rustle a donkey's mane or a young girl's hair. The creak of a closing door. Footsteps that fade into the distance. Suddenly a short, piercing melody, and silence. A strength hidden deep within his characters' eyes, neither resigned nor despairing. The score that these sounds and images have composed creates emotions strong enough to make the body tremble.

In Bresson's hands, the screen is transformed into a universe. And much like the riddle of the universe, Bresson's films, refusing analysis and interpretation, simply are. Whether we find them beautiful or cruel, these convictions are nothing more than arbitrary human impositions. Like when we look up to the flickering stars of the night sky, there is nothing for us to do but stare breathless at their brilliance.

Jean-Marie Straub

JOEL ROGERS: You would count Bresson as a great influence on your work, wouldn't you?

JEAN-MARIE STRAUB: I have great admiration for *Les Dames du Bois de Boulogne* and *Diary of a Country Priest*, and he has certainly influenced our work. But his later movies I don't like at all. *Lancelot du Lac*, for example, holds no interest for me at all. It's difficult to talk about my influences. Richard Roud always says that my culture is German culture, which is not true. I have the cultural training of a French university student, and no specific or deep training in German literary culture. I learned my German in first grade, during the war, did my extensive studies in French literature, amd was in Germany really for the first time in 1956. And then on the contrary he says I have a French cinematographic culture, citing Bresson and Grémillon as influences. Grémillon interests me very much, as a true communist filmmaker. But I haven't had a chance to look at his films carefully at all. And with Bresson I saw those two early films, and I'm sure they influenced me greatly, but I'm not able to say just how. So I will leave such comparisons to people who know all of both our work.

Andrei Tarkovsky

JURRIËN ROOD: How did you come to know Bresson's work?

ANDREI TARKOVSKY: In 1957 and after my film studies, I spent a lot of time in the Moscow cinematheque called "Bielye Stolby," the White Columns. There I studied the work of Mizoguchi, Bergman and Bresson; it was there in fact that I came to know him. We studied western films at the Institute, but the films that interested me were other films I found myself in the archives.

   The Trial of Joan of Arc was the first Bresson film I saw. I found the film extremely touching and I understood that Bresson was the only director who knew how to captivate and surprise me. I was particularly touched by the absolute independence of the spectator in regard to this film. A total independence in the sense that the film never appears to be a spectacle, but rather nature, life itself. If one wants to watch, one watches, if one doesn't, one doesn't. If one wants to see it as art one may, otherwise not. Such a strong independence from public and critical opinion remains for me the exemplary attitude of a director towards his audience.

ROOD: What do you consider the importance of Bresson?

TARKOVSKY: There are many reasons I consider Bresson a unique phenomenon in the world of film. Indeed, Bresson is one of the artists who has shown that cinema is an artistic discipline on the same level as the classic artistic disciplines such as poetry, literature, painting and music.

The second reason I admire Bresson is personal. It is the significance of his work for me—the vision of the world that it expresses. This vision of the world is expressed in an ascetic way, almost laconic, lapidary I would say. Very few artists succeed in this. Every serious artist strives for simplicity, but only a few manage to achieve it. Bresson is one of the few who has succeeded.

The third reason is the inexhaustibility of Bresson's artistic form. That is, one is compelled to consider his artistic form as life, nature itself. In that sense, I find him very close to the oriental artistic concept of Zen: depth within narrowly defined limits. Working with these forms, Bresson attempts in his films not to be symbolic; he tries to create a form as inexhaustible as nature, life itself. Of course this doesn't always work. In fact, there are episodes in his films that are extremely symbolic and, therefore, limited—symbolic and not poetic. An obvious but banal example of this is the rabbit hunt in *Mouchette*.

The original way that Mouchette chooses to die in the film—the repeated suicide attempt that does not work until the third try—that is for me perfect, very original, because of its profundity, the impossibility of interpretation and its singularity. That which is shown in the film cannot be recounted.

The first episode for me is an example of parts of his films that are symbolic and thus not very meaningful; the second is an example of those parts that are non-symbolic, political and profound.

ROOD: Was your own filmmaking influenced by Bresson?

TARKOVSKY: Without a doubt. But there are artists whose influence you couldn't possibly define. For me Bresson stands as an ideal of simplicity. And from that point of view, I, just like everybody else who strives for simplicity and depth, can't help but identify with what he has achieved in this field. But on the other hand, even if Bresson would never have existed, we would have eventually come across this notion of a lapidary style, simplicity and depth. And when people tell me during the shooting of my film that a certain scene is in some way reminiscent of Bresson—and this has happened—I will immediately change the approach to avoid any resemblance. If there's such an influence, it doesn't show on the surface of my work. This is an influence of a deeper nature. It's a moral influence between artists, without which art cannot exist.

ROOD: At the 1983 Cannes Film Festival you were in direct competition with Bresson. How did that feel?

TARKOVSKY: It didn't feel uncomfortable, because any director can come to Cannes and compete. But I disliked the festival from the start. It was nothing like an art festival; it turned out to be thoroughly commercial.

I was surprised that Bresson came to present his film. I had not expected that. I received an invitation for a screening and I went. Sadly, the only films I saw during the festival were Bresson's *L'Argent* and my own film. After the screening we met. They've told me that I am the only director Bresson wanted to speak to. I've known him for a long time. We met in Paris long ago, and since then I've always held a great respect for this master.

So I liked to be, so to speak, on equal footing with him. [Bresson and Tarkovsky received a joint Special Jury Prize—J.R.] But I do not know if he felt the same way.

Translated by James Quandt and Jurriën Rood.
Jurriën Rood is a Dutch filmmaker among whose films is
The Way to Bresson *made with Leo de Boer.*

François Truffaut

———

Les Dames du Bois de Boulogne

Not quite ten years ago, on an afternoon when I was dying to be at the movies rather than in school, our literature professor came into the classroom and said, "Last night I saw the stupidest film in the world, *Les Dames du Bois de Boulogne*. There's a character in it who resolves his romantic problems by driving eighty miles an hour. I can't think of anything more grotesque." The critics were not any kinder. The public didn't come, or if they did, it was only to smirk at every one of Cocteau's lines. The producer, Raoul Ploquin, was ruined, and it took him seven years to recover.

The Cinéma d'Essai has just put Bresson's film on the program as part of a retrospective, and I hear that the attendance is greater than for any other film, that the audiences are quiet, and sometimes even applaud. To quote Cocteau, the movie "has won its case in the appeals court." After its spectacular commercial failure, *Les Dames du Bois de Boulogne* was shown in film clubs and almost all the critics made their amends. Today, now that *Journal d'un curé de campagne* has won over the last holdouts, Bresson is considered one of the three or four greatest French filmmakers.

His first film, *Les Anges du péché,* from a screenplay by Father Raymond Bruckberger, with dialogue by Jean Giraudoux, won universal approval when it appeared in 1943. In *Les Dames,* Bresson started from an episode in Diderot's *Jacques le fataliste*—the adventure of Madame de la Pommeraye and the Marquis des Arcis. The adaptation is faithful and very restrained. It is faithful to the degree that entire sentences of Diderot remain unchanged. It is common to underestimate the importance of the role of Cocteau, who was on this occasion a rewriter of genius. One example: Diderot: "The history of your heart is word by word the history of mine." Cocteau: "The history of your heart is word for word the sad story of mine." If we read the two sentences aloud, it has to be admitted that Cocteau improved on Diderot; he added the music.

In Diderot's story, all the characters are base. Madame de la Pommeraye is vengeance itself, a pure Racine character (pure in the sense that Phèdre is pure), and Madame Duquenoi and her daughter, the pious ladies, push duplicity to the point of going to confession assuming that the Marquis will corrupt their confessor and find out everything. When Diderot's hostess finishes her tale, Jacques's teacher says, "My dear hostess, you tell the story very well, but you still have a long way to go in dramatic art. If you want your young girl to be interesting, you must teach her simplicity, and show her to us as the innocent victim, against her will, of her mother and of Madame de la Pommeraye, and show us that the cruelest things are done to her. . . . When you introduce a character into a scene, his role must be singular. You have sinned against the rules of Aristides, Horace, Vida and Le Bossu." What is most astonishing about Cocteau's and Bresson's adaptation, why it is at the same time faithful and unfaithful, is that they took the observations of Jacques's teacher into account: in the film, Agnès is unequivocal, she is the innocent victim of Hélène. The lion's share of responsibility goes to Cocteau; from the very first exchange, his mark is everywhere: "Have I not succeeded in distracting you? Are you suffering?" And later: "There is no such thing as love, only its proofs." And further: "I love gold, it is like you: hot, cold, clear, sombre, incorruptible." But if one doesn't know Diderot's text, this could easily be missed. Just as Giraudoux gave *Les Anges du péché* its dynamism, Cocteau endows *Les Dames* with life. We cannot fail to be struck by the similarities between the films that Cocteau has himself made since 1945 and this one. The relationship between Paul Bernard and Élina Labourdette in *Les Dames* is exactly the same as between Josette Day and Jean Marais in *La Belle et la bête.* There is between them a love that leads to total submission and devotion. Maria Casarès reminds us inevitably of Nicole Stéphane in *Les Enfants terribles* as she pronounces those sentences that are Cocteau's trademark: "And above all, don't thank me" or "Don't pull down my supports."

To get away from the monotony of the usual labels that are applied to Cocteau, we should think hard about his realism. It starts with the "spoken" side of his dialogues, which sometimes make us smile: "I can't receive you, come in." The sharp sense of realism, when it's pushed to its limits, introduces the eccentric. Twenty years after *Les Enfants terribles,* Cocteau can film it without changing a word of the dialogue and the actors can deliver it with extraordinary truth. An excellent example, which borders on the baroque but without being ridiculous, is a scene where Maria Casarès walks down a staircase talking to Paul Bernard, who is escaping by the elevator: "Why are you leaving? I don't like the piano. . . ."

Bresson's part is not negligible, however. Though it was begun before the Liberation, the film was abandoned, then taken up again and completed to all intents and purposes, then really started again, several months later. The direction remains, despite the intervening years, very abstract. Cocteau himself remarked: "This isn't a film; it's the skeleton of a film." We are seduced by Bresson's intentions rather than by his execution. *Les Dames* is an exercise in style, like the book *Madame de. . . .* But if, with Louise de Vilmorin, our admiration is easily and facilely elicited, it is the opposite with Bresson, whose stubbornness and laborious work of refining finally commands our respect.

I think *Journal d'un curé de campagne,* in which every shot is as true as a handful of earth—the earth of Georges Bernanos, its author—is Bresson's best film. We shall have to wait for *La Princesse de Clèves,** which he's going to make next year, to know Robert Bresson's own real personality at last and assess his talent, on his own this time, without Giraudoux, Cocteau, and Bernanos.

Un condamné à mort s'est échappé

1.

The importance of this film will make it worth returning to more than once in the coming weeks. I do not expect to do justice to this major work with these notes written hastily after a first viewing. In my opinion, *Un condamné à mort s'est échappé* is not only Robert Bresson's most beautiful film but also the most important French film of the past ten years. (Before I wrote that sentence, I listed on a piece of paper all the films that have been made by Renoir, Ophuls, Cocteau, Tati, Gance, Astruc, Becker, Clouzot, Clément, and Clair since 1946.)

---

* Bresson never made *La Princesse de Clèves;* it was directed in 1961 by Jean Delannoy, adapted and with dialogue by Cocteau.

Now I regret that I wrote a few months ago, "Bresson's theories are always fascinating but they are so personal that they fit only him. The future existence of a 'Bresson school' would shake even his most optimistic observers. A conception of cinema that is so theoretical, mathematical, musical, and above all ascetic could not give rise to a general insight." Today I must disavow those sentences. *Un condamné à mort* seems to me to reduce to nothing a certain number of accepted ideas that governed filmmaking, all the way from script writing to direction.

In many films nowadays we find what is commonly called "a touch of bravura." What that means is that the filmmaker was thought to be courageous, that he tried to surpass himself in one or two scenes. By this token, *Un condamné*, which is a stubborn film about stubbornness, made by a stubborn native of the Auvergne, is the first movie of utter bravura. Let us try to see how it differs from all the others we've seen over the years.

Bresson's remark, "Cinema is interior movement," is frequently quoted. Did he make the statement, rather too hastily interpreted as his profession of faith, for the pleasure of leading the theoreticians down the garden path? The commentators have decided that it is his characters' interior lives, their very souls, that preoccupy Bresson, while in fact it may be something more subtle: the movement of the *film,* its rhythm. Jean Renoir often says that cinema is an art more secret than painting, and that a film is made for three people. I haven't the slightest doubt that there are not three people in the world who don't find Bresson's work mysterious. It took a complete lack of awareness on the part of the daily reviewers to talk about the weaknesses of the actors in *Journal d'un curé de campagne*. However, the actors' work in a Bresson film is beyond notions of "correct" or "wrong." Their work essentially suggests a timelessness, a certain posture, a "difficulty with the fact of existing," a quality of suffering. Probably Bresson is an alchemist in reverse: he starts from movement in order to reach immobility, he screens out the gold to gather the sand.

For Bresson, films both past and present are only a skewed image of theatre, and acting is exhibitionism. He thinks that in twenty years people will go to see movies to see how "the actors played in those days." We know that Bresson directs his actors by holding them back from acting "dramatically," from adding emphasis, forcing them to abstract from their "art." He achieves this by killing their will, exhausting them with an endless number of repetitions and takes, by almost hypnotizing them.

With his third film, *Journal d'un curé de campagne*, Bresson realized that he'd prefer to do without professional actors, even beginners, in favour of amateurs chosen for their appearance—and also their "spirit"—new creatures who don't bring any habits with them, or false spontaneity, bringing, in fact, no "art" at all. If all Bresson did was kill the life and the actor that's inside every person in order to bring before his camera individuals who recite deliberately neutral words, his work would be an interesting experiment. But he goes further. With amateur interpreters who know nothing about theatre, he creates the ultimately real character, whose every gesture, look, attitude, reaction and word—not one of which is louder than the other—is essential. The whole takes on a form that *makes* the film.

Psychology and poetry have no part in his work. It's all about obtaining a certain harmony out of the various elements which act on each other, providing an infinity of relations: the acting and the sound, looks and noises, settings and lighting, commentary and music. It adds up to a Bresson film, a kind of miraculous success that defies analysis and, when it works perfectly, arouses a new and pure emotion.

It is clear that Bresson's films, because he takes a direction that is radically different from that of his colleagues, have a harder time making contact with the public than those films that arouse emotion by less noble and more facile, more theatrical means. For Bresson, as well as Renoir, Rossellini, Hitchcock, Orson Welles, cinema is spectacle, certainly, but the author of *Journal* wants his spectacle to be very particular, to have its own laws, not follow borrowed rules.

Un condamné à mort is a minute-by-minute account of a condemned man's getaway. Indeed, it is a fanatical reconstruction of an actual event, and Commander Devigny, the man who lived the adventure thirteen years ago, never left the set, since Bresson kept asking him to show the anonymous actor who portrayed him how you hold a spoon in a cell, how you write on the walls, how you fall asleep.

But it isn't actually a story, or even an account or a drama. It is simply the minute description by scrupulous reconstruction of what went into the escape. The entire film consists of close-ups of objects and close-ups of the face of the man who moves the objects.

Bresson wanted to call it *Le Vent souffle où il veut* (The wind blows where it will), and it was a perilous experiment; but it became a successful and moving film, thanks to Bresson's stubborn genius. He figured out how to buck all existing forms of filmmaking and reach for a new truth with a new realism.

The suspense—there is a certain suspense in the film—is created naturally, not by stretching out the passage of time, but by letting it evaporate. Because the shots are brief and the scenes rapid, we never have the feeling that we have been offered ninety privileged moments of Fontaine's sentence. We live with him in his prison cell, not for ninety minutes but for two months, and it is a fascinating experience.

The laconic dialogue alternates with the hero's interior monologue; the passages from one scene to another are carried out with Mozart's assistance. The sounds have a hallucinatory quality: railroads, the bolting of doors, footsteps, etc.

In addition, *Un condamné* is Bresson's first perfectly homogeneous film. There is not a single spoiled shot; it conforms to the author's intentions from beginning to end. The "Bresson acting style," a false truthfulness that becomes truer than true, is practised here even by the most minor characters. With this film, Bresson is acclaimed today by those who hissed *Les Dames du Bois de Boulogne* eleven years ago.

2.*

To the degree that *Un condamné à mort s'est échappé* is radically opposed to all conventional directorial styles, it will, I believe, be better appreciated by audiences who go to the movies only occasionally, say once a month, than by the non-movie-loving but more assiduous public whose sensibilities are often confused by the rhythm of American films.

What is striking when one sees the film for the first time is the constant contrast between what the work is and what it would be, or would have been, if it had been made by another filmmaker. At first all one sees are its deficiencies, and for a while one is tempted to redo the cutting and indicate additional shots so that the film would resemble "what a film is supposed to be."

Indeed, everybody pointed out the lack of any establishing shots—one would never know what Fontaine saw through his tiny window or from the roof of the prison. Thus, at the end of a first viewing, surprise might win out over admiration. And André Bazin felt moved to explain that it was easier to describe what the film was *not* than what it was.

It really must be seen again to appreciate its beauty perfectly. On second viewing, nothing any longer gets in the way of our keeping up, second by second, with the film's movement—it's incredibly swift—and walking in Leterrier's or Bresson's still-fresh footprints, whichever of them left them.

Bresson's film is pure music; its essential richness is in its rhythm. A film starts at one point and arrives ultimately at another. Some films make detours, others linger calmly for the satisfaction of drawing out a pleasant scene, some have noticeable gaps, but this particular film, once set on its perfectly straight path, rushes into the night with the same rhythm as a windshield wiper; its dissolves regularly wipe the rain of images at the end of each scene off the screen. It's one of those films which can be said not to contain a single useless shot or a scene that could be cut or shortened. It's the very opposite of those films that seem like a "montage," a collection of images.

Un condamné à mort s'est échappé is as free-style and non-systematic as it is rigorous. Bresson has imposed only unities of place and action; it's not only that he has not tried to make his public identify with Leterrier, he has made such identification impossible. We are *with* Leterrier, we are at his side; we do not see everything he sees (only what relates to his escape), but never do we see anything more than he does.

---

* This second article was written three weeks after the preceding one.

What this amounts to is that Bresson has pulverized classic cutting—where a shot of someone looking at something is valid only in relation to the next shot showing what he is looking at—a form of cutting that made cinema a dramatic art, a kind of photographed theatre. Bresson explodes all that and, if in *Un condamné* the close-ups of hands and objects nonetheless lead to close-ups of the face, the succession is no longer ordered in terms of stage dramaturgy. It is in the service of a pre-established harmony of subtle relations among visual and aural elements. Each shot of hands or of a look is autonomous.

Between traditional directing and Bresson's there lies the same space as between dialogue and interior monologue.

Our admiration for Robert Bresson's film is not limited to his wager—to rest the entire enterprise on a single character in a cell for ninety minutes. The *tour de force* is not all. Many filmmakers—Clouzot, Dassin, Becker, and others—might have made a film that was ten times more thrilling and "human" than Bresson's. What is important is that the emotion, even if it is to be felt by only one viewer out of twenty, is rarer and purer and, as a result, far from altering the work's nobility, it confers a grandeur on it that was not hinted at at the outset.

The high points of the film rival Mozart for a few seconds. Here, the first chords of the Mass in C Minor, far from symbolizing liberty, as has often been written, give a liturgical aspect to the daily flushing of the toilet buckets.

I don't imagine that Fontaine is a very likable personality in Bresson's mind. It isn't courage that incites him to escape but simply boredom and idleness. A prison is made to escape from, besides which, our hero owes his success to luck. We are shown Lieutenant Fontaine, about whom we shall know nothing more, in a period of his life when he is particularly interesting and lucky. He talks about his act with a certain reserve, a bit like a lecturer telling us about his expedition as he comments on the silent movies he has brought back: "On the fourth, in the evening, we left the camp. . . ."

Bresson's great contribution clearly is the work of the actors. Certainly James Dean's acting, which moves us so much today, or Anna Magnani's, may risk our laughter in a few years, as Pierre-Richard Wilm's does today, while the acting of Laydu in *Journal d'un curé de campagne* and of Leterrier in *Un condamné* will grow more forceful with time. Time always works for Bresson.

In *Un condamné* the Bresson style of directing achieves its finest results. We are no longer offered the quiet voice of the little parish priest of Ambricourt, or the gentle look of the "prisoner of the holy Agony," but the clear, dry diction of Lieutenant Fontaine. With his gaze as direct as that of a bird of prey, he hurls himself on the sacrificial sentinel like a vulture. Leterrier's acting owes nothing to Laydu's. "Speak as if you were talking to yourself," Bresson commanded him. He exerts all his effort to filming the face, or, more accurately, the seriousness of the human countenance.

"The artist owes a great debt to the countenance of man; if he cannot manage to evoke its natural dignity, he should at least attempt to conceal its superficiality and foolishness. Perhaps there's not a single foolish or superficial person on this earth, but simply some who give that impression because they are ill at ease, who have not found a corner of the universe in which they feel well." This marvellous reflection of Joseph von Sternberg's is, to my mind, the most apt comment on *Un condamné*.

To think that Bresson will be an influence on French and foreign contemporary filmmakers seems highly unlikely. Nonetheless, we clearly see the limitations of the *other* cinema to the advantage of this film. The risk is that it may make us too demanding of the cruelty of Clouzot, the wit of René Clair, the carefulness of René Clément. Much remains to be discovered about film art, and some of it can be found in *Un condamné*.

Translated from the French by Leonard Mayhew

John Waters

Lancelot du Lac

Another maddening art film that really impressed me. Bresson meets the Knights of the Round Table, sort of, since this film is told almost entirely in close-ups or medium shots of armour, helmets, boots, horses' hooves, and very, very few human faces. In fact, although it seems like a cast of thousands, it is actually only a handful playing many different roles. Since you are introduced to a character from a rear view or by their footwear, Bresson could really save money by having one actor play twenty different parts. If ever there was an anti-star movie, this is it. Students of film budgets ought to watch this great screen economy at work and marvel at what the Screen Actors Guild might think.

Wim Wenders

Around seventy years ago, someone built for the first time a film camera. He made images move in succession, such that later on, he recognized on a screen something he had already seen through the lens: a head turning, clouds moving across the sky, blades of grass trembling, a face expressing pain or joy.

He would have understood Bresson's film *Mouchette*.

He would have rejoiced in the fact that he had invented something that was used in such an incredibly beautiful way.

Translated from the French by Lara Fitzgerald

Mitsuo Yanagimachi

I remember. Scenes from one of Bresson's most unique and beautiful films, *Pickpocket*. Scene one: a woman who is standing in line to purchase a ticket at a train station counter, when her handbag is cleverly stolen by a switch of a magazine for the handbag. The bag is then passed hand to hand amongst the pickpockets and the money is quickly taken. Scene two: in a train, a wallet is picked from a passenger's suit pocket, the money is taken and the empty wallet is returned to the pocket. Both scenes are filmed in close-up, following only the movement of the objects— the shots flow in a single stream of wallet, money and fingers—excluding story, drama, and the emotion of the actors. This breathtaking method expresses both an unbelievable reality and an extremely minimalist simplicity in a single moment. Creating this movement and filming the scenes are an extraordinary, perhaps one could say divine, accomplishment. The scenes leave one with an overwhelming impression of perfection and supreme beauty.

It has been pointed out that the main feature of Bresson's films is simplicity of expression. Although this is a common feature of many great film creators, Bresson is conspicuous as one who pursued simplicity as a means of expressing truth; implemented it, and pushed it to the extreme. Bresson's films have no embellishments or exaggerations; his sole intent is to depict objects as they exist in real life. As a natural consequence, his films are indifferent to comedy, sorrow, violence, fantasy, or eroticism. Once again, Bresson's sublime sensibility allows the viewer to respond to the basic substance of things.

Bresson once said, "I exclude the method of drama which requires expression by action, gesture or speech. There is no need for stories or the guise of human nature in films." Bresson has always made his actors' facial expressions deadpan, even during extreme moments of emotional turmoil, as when an actor kills or is killed. I am reminded of Japanese Noh and Noh masks when watching Bresson's films of formal, expressionless actors. In Noh plays, actors minimize their actions and gestures. However unchanging, Noh masks can clearly express changes in the outward appearance of joy and anger to more complicated inward expressions of a character's depth of consciousness. A stylized, simplified and changeless mask can make evident the profoundness of a human's soul. The same method is employed in Bresson's films.

As I keep company with the outwardly expressionless people in Bresson's films, I can tell that they have tumultuous passions inside, and it is not so difficult to read the profoundness within their souls. Their very lack of expression creates an intensely, deeply and keenly felt sense of complexity, profundity and loneliness.

Noh is one of the prototypes of every Japanese performing art in existence today. Simplicity is the key rule, and style is attained under this rule. It can also be said that Bresson's films are the prototype of all films, for he has proven that by pushing the rules of simplicity to the extreme, he has in turn created the limits of the rules. Films can easily become slaves to convention, compromised and negatively altered by the changing of the times. However, whether world cinema is thrown into chaos or not, Bresson's films will forever remain one of the ideal models for film.

Translated from the Japanese by Koto Sato and Noriko Saito

Filmography

Affaires publiques (1934)

Production Company: Arc-Film
Screenplay: Robert Bresson
Cinematography (black-and-white): Nicolas Toporkoff
Editor: Robert Bresson
Art Director: Pierre Charbonnier
Music: Jean Wiener, Roger Désormière
Running Time: 25 minutes (fragment; the three songs in the film have not been found)
Cast: Béby (the chancellor); Andrée Servilanges (the princess of Miremie); Marcel Dalio (the speaker, the sculptor, the fire captain, the admiral); Gilles Margaritis (the chauffeur); Simone Cressier (Christiane); Franck Maurice (a sailor)

Les Anges du péché (1943)
English Titles: **Angels of Sin**;
Angels of the Streets

Production Company: Synops-Roland Tual
Screenplay: Robert Bresson, R. L. Bruckberger (based on an idea of R. L. Bruckberger)
Dialogue: Jean Giraudoux
Cinematography (black-and-white): Philippe Agostini
Editor: Yvonne Martin
Art Director: René Renoux
Music: Jean-Jacques Grünenwald
Running Time: 80 minutes
Cast: Renée Faure (Anne-Marie); Jany Holt (Thérèse); Sylvie (the prioress); Mila Parély
  (Madeleine); Marie Hélène Dasté (Mother Saint-Jean); Yolande Laffon (Anne-Marie's
  mother); Paula Dehelly (Mother Dominique); Silvia Monfort (Agnès); Gilberte Terbois
  (Sister Marie-Joseph)

Les Dames du Bois de Boulogne
(1945)
English Title: **The Ladies of the Bois
  de Boulogne**

Production Company: Les Films Raoul Ploquin
Screenplay: Robert Bresson (based on *Jacques le fataliste et son maître* by Denis Diderot)
Dialogue: Jean Cocteau
Cinematography (black-and-white): Philippe Agostini
Editor: Jean Feyte
Art Director: Max Douy
Music: Jean-Jacques Grünenwald
Running Time: 90 minutes
Cast: Maria Casarès (Hélène); Élina Labourdette (Agnès); Paul Bernard (Jean); Lucienne
  Bogaert (Agnès's mother); Jean Marchat (Jacques)

Journal d'un curé de campagne
(1951)
English Title: **Diary of a Country Priest**

Production Company: Union Générale Cinématographique
Screenplay: Robert Bresson (based on the novel by Georges Bernanos)
Cinematography (black-and-white): Léonce-Henry Burel
Editor: Paulette Robert
Art Director: Pierre Charbonnier
Music: Jean-Jacques Grünenwald
Running Time: 110 minutes
Cast: Claude Laydu (the curé of Ambricourt); Jean Riveyre (the count); Armand Guibert
(the curé of Torcy); Nicole Ladmiral (Chantal); Martine Lemaire (Séraphita); Nicole
Maurey (Mlle Louise); Marie-Monique Arkell (the countess); Antoine Balpêtré
(Dr. Delbende); Léon Arvel (Fabregard)

Un condamné à mort s'est échappé ou le vent souffle où il veut (1956)
English Title: **A Man Escaped**

Production Companies: Gaumont; Nouvelles Éditions de Films
Screenplay: Robert Bresson (based on the account by André Devigny)
Cinematography (black-and-white): Léonce-Henry Burel
Editor: Raymond Lamy
Art Director: Pierre Charbonnier
Music: Wolfgang Amadeus Mozart
Running Time: 98 minutes
Cast: François Leterrier (Fontaine); Charles Le Clainche (Jost); Maurice Beerblock
(Blanchet); Roland Monod (Rev. de Leiris); Jacques Ertaud (Orsini); Jean-Paul
Delhumeau (Hébrard); Roger Tréherne (Terry); Jacques Oerlemans (chief warden);
Klaus Detlef Grevenhorst (German intelligence officer)

Pickpocket (1959)

Production Company: Agnès Delahaie
Screenplay: Robert Bresson
Cinematography (black-and-white): Léonce-Henry Burel
Editor: Raymond Lamy
Art Director: Pierre Charbonnier
Music: Jean–Baptiste Lully
Running Time: 75 minutes
Cast: Martin Lassalle (Michel); Pierre Leymarie (Jacques); Jean Pélégri (the police inspector); Marika Green (Jeanne); Kassagi (the first accomplice); Pierre Étaix (the second accomplice); Dolly Scal (Michel's mother)

Procès de Jeanne d'Arc (1962)
English Title: **The Trial of Joan of Arc**

Production Company: Agnès Delahaie
Screenplay: Robert Bresson
Cinematography (black-and-white): Léonce-Henry Burel
Editor: Germaine Artus
Art Director: Pierre Charbonnier
Music: Francis Seyrig
Running Time: 65 minutes
Cast: Florence Carrez/Florence Delay (Joan of Arc); Jean-Claude Fourneau (Cauchon); Marc Jacquier (Jean Lemaître); Roger Honorat (Jean Beaupère); Jean Gillibert (Jean de Chatillon); André Regnier (d'Estivet); Michel Herubel (Frère Isambart de la Pierre); Philippe Dreux (Frère Martin Ladvenu); Richard Pratt (Warwick); Harry Sommers (Bishop of Winchester); Gérard Zingg (Jean Lohier)

Au hasard Balthazar (1966)

Production Companies: Argos Films; Parc Film; Athos Films; Swedish Film Institute; Svensk Filmindustri
Screenplay: Robert Bresson
Cinematography (black-and-white): Ghislain Cloquet
Editor: Raymond Lamy
Art Director: Pierre Charbonnier
Music: Franz Schubert; Jean Wiener
Running Time: 95 minutes
Cast: Anne Wiazemsky (Marie); Walter Green (Jacques); François Lafarge (Gérard); Philippe Asselin (Marie's father); Nathalie Joyaut (Marie's mother); Jean-Claude Guilbert (Arnold); Pierre Klossowski (the grain merchant)

Mouchette (1967)

Production Companies: Argos Films; Parc Film
Screenplay: Robert Bresson (based on *Nouvelle histoire de Mouchette* by Georges Bernanos)
Cinematography (black-and-white): Ghislain Cloquet
Editor: Raymond Lamy
Art Director: Pierre Guffroy
Music: Claudio Monteverdi; Jean Wiener
Running Time: 82 minutes
Cast: Nadine Nortier (Mouchette); Marie Cardinal (the mother); Paul Hébert (the father); Jean-Claude Guilbert (Arsène); Jean Vimenet (Mathieu); Marie Susini (Mathieu's wife); Liliane Princet (the teacher); Raymonde Chabrun (the grocer)

Une femme douce (1969)
English Title: **A Gentle Creature**

Production Companies: Parc Film; Marianne Production
Screenplay: Robert Bresson (based on a story by Fyodor Dostoevsky)
Cinematography (colour): Ghislain Cloquet
Editor: Raymond Lamy
Art Director: Pierre Charbonnier
Music: Henry Purcell; Jean Wiener
Running Time: 88 minutes
Cast: Dominique Sanda (She); Guy Frangin (He); Jane Lobre (the maid); Claude Ollier
(the doctor)

Quatre nuits d'un rêveur (1972)
English Title: **Four Nights of
a Dreamer**

Production Companies: Albina Productions; Victoria Film; Film dell'Orso; Gian Vittorio
Baldi; ORTF
Screenplay: Robert Bresson (based on a story by Fyodor Dostoevsky)
Cinematography (colour): Pierre Lhomme (Ghislain Cloquet for the gangster film
sequence)
Editor: Raymond Lamy
Art Director: Pierre Charbonnier
Music: Michel Magne; Groupe Batuki; Christopher Hayward; Louis Guitar; F. R. David
Running Time: 83 minutes
Cast: Isabelle Weingarten (Marthe); Guillaume des Fôrets (Jacques); Jean-Maurice Mon-
noyer (the lodger); Jérôme Massart (the visitor); Patrick Jouanné (the gangster); Lidia
Biondi (Marthe's mother); Groupe Batuki (musicians on *bateau-mouche*)

Lancelot du Lac (1974)
English Title: **Lancelot of the Lake**

Production Companies: Mara Film; Laser Productions; ORTF; Gerico Sound
Screenplay: Robert Bresson
Cinematography (colour): Pasqualino De Santis
Editor: Germaine Lamy
Art Director: Pierre Charbonnier
Music: Philippe Sarde
Running Time: 85 minutes
Cast: Luc Simon (Lancelot du Lac); Laura Duke Condominas (Guenièvre/Guinevere);
Humbert Balsan (Gauvain/Gawain); Vladimir Antolek (Artus/Arthur); Patrick Bernard
(Mordred); Arthur de Montalembert (Lionel)

Le Diable probablement (1977)
English Title: **The Devil Probably**

Production Companies: Sunchild GMF/Michel Chanderli
Screenplay: Robert Bresson
Cinematography (colour): Pasqualino De Santis
Editor: Germaine Lamy
Art Director: Eric Simon
Music: Claudio Monterverdi; Wolfgang Amadeus Mozart
Running Time: 97 minutes
Cast: Antoine Monnier (Charles); Tina Irrisari (Alberte); Henri de Maublanc (Michel);
Laetitia Carcano (Edwige); Régis Hanrion (the psychoanalyst); Nicolas Deguy
(Valentin); Geoffroy Gaussen (the bookseller); Roger Honorat (the police officer)

L'Argent (1983)
English Title: **Money**

Production Companies: Marion's Films; Eos Films; FR3
Screenplay: Robert Bresson (based on a story by Leo Tolstoy)
Cinematography (colour): Pasqualino De Santis; Emmanuel Machuel
Editor: Jean-François Naudon
Art Director: Pierre Guffroy
Music: Johann Sebastian Bach
Running Time: 85 minutes
Cast: Christian Patey (Yvon); Caroline Lang (Élise); Sylvie van den Elsen (the older
  woman); Michel Briguet (the woman's father); Vincent Risterucci (Lucien);
  Béatrice Tabourin (the woman in the photography shop); Didier Baussy (the man in the
  photography shop); Marc-Ernest Fourneau (Norbert)

Selected Bibliography

Works in French and English
Compiled by Robin MacDonald

Works by Bresson

Bresson, Robert. *Notes on cinematography.* Translated by Jonathan Griffin. New York: Urizen Books, 1977. Originally published as *Notes sur le cinématographe* (Paris: Éditions Gallimard, 1975).

———. "Notes on Sound." Translated by Jonathan Griffin. In *Film Sound: Theory and Practice,* edited by Elisabeth Weis and John Belton, 149. New York: Columbia University Press, 1985.

———. "Qui? Pourquoi? Comment?" *Cahiers du cinéma,* nos. 161–162 (January 1965): 14, 23.

———. "Réponse de Robert Bresson à François Leterrier." *Cahiers du cinéma,* no. 67 (January 1957): 1.

Special Issues and Catalogues

"Mouchette." *Avant-Scène Cinéma,* no. 80 (April 1968).

Robert Bresson. Ramsay-Poche cinéma, nos. 68–69. N.p.: Camera/Stylo, 1989. Originally published as "Robert Bresson," *Camera/Stylo,* no. 5 (January 1985).

Robert Bresson: Éloge. Milan: Edizioni Gabriele Mazzotta; Paris: Cinémathèque française, 1997.

Prédal, René. "Robert Bresson, l'aventure intérieure." *Avant-Scène Cinéma,* nos. 408–409 (January/February 1992).

Works about Bresson

Adair, Gilbert. "Lost and found: Beby re-inaugurates." *Sight and Sound* 56, no. 3 (Summer 1987): 157-158.

Agel, Henri. "L'Ascèse liturgique." In *Le Cinéma et le sacré*. Paris: Éditions du Cerf, 1954.

Amengual, Barthélémy. "*Les affaires publiques*." *Cinéma 72-92*, no. 294 (June 1983): 18.

———. "Les pouvoirs de l'abstraction: Sur *Journal d'un curé de campagne* et *Procès de Jeanne d'Arc*." *Positif*, no. 430 (December 1996): 79-84.

Amiel, Vincent. "«Des jambes de fourmis à l'infini». Fragmentation et représentation chez Bresson." *Positif*, no. 430 (December 1996): 85-87.

Andrew, Dudley. "Desperation and Meditation: Bresson's *Diary of a Country Priest* (1951), from the novel by George Bernanos." In *European Filmmakers and the Art of Adaptation,* edited by Andrew Horton and Joan Magretta, 20-50. New York: Frederick Ungar, 1981.

———. "Private Scribblings: The Crux in the Margins around *Diary of a Country Priest*." In *Film in the Aura of Art*. Princeton, N.J.: Princeton University Press, 1984. Originally published in a slightly different form in *European Filmmakers and the Art of Adaptation* (New York: Frederick Ungar, 1981).

Arlaud, R. M. et al. "Propos de Robert Bresson," *Cahiers du cinéma*, no. 75 (October 1957): 3-9.

Armes, Roy. "Innovators and Independents: Robert Bresson." In *French Cinema since 1946*. Vol. 1. Cranbury, N.J.: A.S. Barnes, 1966. Republished in a slightly different format in *Great Film Directors: A Critical Anthology*, edited by Leo Braudy and Morris Dickstein, 91-96 (New York: Oxford University Press, 1978).

———. "Robert Bresson: An Anachronistic Universe." In *The Ambiguous Image: Narrative Style in Modern European Cinema*. London: Secker and Warburg, 1976.

Arnaud, Philippe. *Robert Bresson*. Cahiers du cinéma. Collection "Auteurs." Paris: Cahiers du Cinéma, 1986.

Assayas, Olivier, Jean-Claude Brisseau, Benoît Jacquot, André Téchiné, Thierry Jousse, and Serge Toubiana. "Autour de *Pickpocket*." *Cahiers du cinéma*, no. 416 (February 1989): 26-32.

Baud, René-Claude. "Panorama critique: Robert Bresson." In *Le Cinéma et sa vérité*, compiled by Amédée Ayfre, 208-213. Paris: Éditions du Cerf, 1969.

Baxter, Brian. "*L'Argent*." *Films and Filming*, no. 347 (August 1983): 27-28.

———. "Robert Bresson." *Films and Filming*, no. 396 (September 1987): 13-15.

Bazin, André. "Marcel Carné's *Les Visiteurs du Soir* and Robert Bresson's *Les Anges du Péché*." In *French Cinema of the Occupation and Resistance: The Birth of a Critical Esthetic*, translated by Stanley Hochman, 43-51. New York: Frederick Ungar, 1981. Originally published as *Le Cinéma de l'occupation et de la résistance* (N.p.: Union générale d'édition, 1975).

Becker, Jacques. "Hommage à Robert Bresson." *Positif*, no. 430 (December 1996): 102. Originally published in *L'Écran français*, no. 16, 7 October 1945: 3, 14.

Ben-Gad, Shmuel. "Robert Bresson: A Bibliography of Works by and about Him, 1981-1983." *Bulletin of Bibliography* 51, no. 3 (1994): 295-301.

Bergala, Alain et al. "*L'Argent* de Robert Bresson." *Cahiers du cinéma*, nos. 348-349 (June/July 1983): 6-15.

Bordwell, David, and Kristin Thompson. "Sound in the Cinema. Functions of Film Sound: *A Man Escaped*." In *Film Art: An Introduction*. Reading, Mass.: Addison-Wesley, 1979.

Brenez, Nicole. "«Approche inhabituelle des corps»: Bresson avec Jean Eustache, Philippe Garrel et Monte Hellman." *Positif*, no. 430 (December 1996): 88-92.

Briot, René. *Robert Bresson*. Paris: Éditions du Cerf, 1957.

Browne, Nick. "Narrative Point of View: The Rhetoric of *Au hasard, Balthazar*." *Film Quarterly* 31, no. 1 (Fall 1977): 23-31.

Cameron, Ian. "Interview with Robert Bresson." *Movie*, no. 7 (February/March 1963): 28-29.

————, ed. *The Films of Robert Bresson*. New York: Praeger, 1970.

Cardinal, Serge. "Le Lieu du son, l'espace de la source. Autour d'*Une Femme douce*. (France, Robert Bresson, 1969)." *Canadian Journal of Film Studies* 4, no. 2 (Fall 1995): 3-15.

Cardullo, Bert. "Bresson's *Une femme douce*: A New Reading." In *Indelible Images: New Perspectives on Classic Films*. Lanham, Md.: University Press of America, 1987. Originally published in the *New Orleans Review* 9, no. 3 (Winter 1982): 5-12.

Christensen, Jerome C. "Versions of Adolescence: Robert Bresson's *Four Nights of a Dreamer* and Dostoyevsky's 'White Nights'." *Literature/Film Quarterly* 4, no. 3 (Summer 1976): 222-229.

Clarens, Carlos. "*Four Nights of a Dreamer*." *Sight and Sound* 41, no. 1 (Winter 1971-72): 2-4.

Cocteau, Jean. "*Les Dames du Bois du Boulogne* (dialogue)." *Cahiers du cinéma*, no. 75 (October 1957): 16-23.

Comolli, Jean-Louis, Michel Delahaye, André S. Labarthe, Jean Narboni and François Weyergans. "Balthazar au hasard: table ronde." *Cahiers du cinéma*, no. 180 (July 1966): 32-35, 76-79.

Corliss, Richard. "Stations of the Cross." *Time*, 15 February 1999, 72-74, International edition.

Crowther, Bosley. "On Editing Imports: French Film Man Vexed At a Usual Practice." *The New York Times*, 2 May, 1954. Republished in *The New York Times Encyclopedia of Film 1896-1979*. Vol. 5, edited by Gene Brown (New York: Times Books, 1984).

Daney, Serge. "*Le diable probablement* de Robert Bresson: L'orgue et l'aspirateur (La voix off et quelques autres)." *Cahiers du cinéma*, nos. 279-280 (August/September 1977): 19-27.

————. "Rencontre avec Robert Bresson." *Cahiers du cinéma*, no. 333 (March 1982): vii, between 34 and 35.

Daney, Serge, and Serge Toubiana. "Entretien avec Robert Bresson." *Cahiers du cinéma*, nos. 348-349 (June/July 1983): 12-15.

Darke, Chris. "*Lancelot du Lac*." *Sight and Sound* 4, no. 11 (November 1994): 56.

Dawson, Jan. "*The Devil Probably*: II. The Invisible Enemy." *Film Comment* 13, no. 5 (September/October 1977): 25.

Delmas, Jean. "*Lancelot du Lac*: Robert Bresson et ses armures." *Jeune Cinéma*, no. 82 (November 1974):19-24.

Doniol-Valcroze, Jacques, and Jean-Luc Godard. "Entretien avec Robert Bresson." *Cahiers du cinéma*, no. 104 (February 1960): 3-9.

Douchet, Jean. "Bresson on Location." *Sequence*, no. 13 (1951): 6-8.

Droguet, Robert. *Robert Bresson*. Premier plan, no. 42. Lyon: Société d'Études, Recherches et Documentation Cinématographique, 1966.

Durand, Philippe. "Le drôle de Chemin de Robert Bresson." *Image et Son*, no. 156 (November 1962): 3-13.

Durgnat, Raymond. "*Diary of a Country Priest*." *Films and Filming* 13, no. 3 (December 1966): 28-32.

———. "*Pickpocket*." *Films and Filming* 7, no. 1 (October 1960): 25-26.

Ehrenstein, David. "Bresson et Cukor: Histoire d'une correspondence." Translated by Michelle Herpe-Voslinsky. *Positif*, no. 430 (December 1996): 103.

Estève, Michel. "Bresson et Bernanos." *Cinéma 72-92*, no. 294 (June 1983): 12-17.

———. *Nouvelle Histoire de Mouchette de Bernanos à Bresson*. La Revue de Lettres Modernes, nos. 175-179. Paris: Lettres Modernes, 1968.

———. *Robert Bresson*. Cinéma d'aujourd'hui, no. 8. Paris: Éditions Seghers, 1962.

———. *Robert Bresson: la Passion du Cinématographe*. Paris: Albatros, 1983.

———. "Trois cinéastes spiritualistes." *CinémAction*, no. 49 (October 1988): 137-143.

Fawell, J. "Sound and Silence, Image and Invisibility in Jacques Tati's *Mon Oncle*." *Literature/Film Quarterly* 18, no. 4 (October 1990): 221-229.

Fraser, Peter. "*American Gigolo* & Transcendental Style." *Literature/Film Quarterly* 16, no. 2 (April 1988): 91-100.

Gabaston, Pierre. *Pickpocket de Robert Bresson*. Crisnée, Belgium: Yellow Now, 1990.

Green, Marjorie. "Robert Bresson." *Film Quarterly* 13, no. 3 (Spring 1960): 4-10.

Guérin, Édith. "Le coeur a ses raisons dans le cinématographe de Bresson." *Revue de la Cinémathèque*, no. 14 (December/January 1991-92): 6-9.

Guth, Paul. 1989. Reprint. *Autour des "Dames de Bois de Boulogne": journal d'un film*. Ramsay-Poche cinéma, no. 67. Paris: Ramsay. Original edition, Paris: Juillard, 1945.

Hanlon, Lindley. *Fragments: Bresson's Film Style*. Rutherford, N.J.: Fairleigh Dickinson University Press, 1986.

———. *Narrative Structure in the Later Films of Robert Bresson*. Ann Arbor, Mich.: University Microfilms, 1977.

Herpe, Noël. "Bresson dans le temps." *Positif*, no. 430 (December 1996): 76-78.

Hoberman, J. "The Cure." *Village Voice*, 8 November 1994, 59.

Hodara, Philippe. "Entretien avec Robert Bresson." *Lumière du cinéma,* no. 6 (July/August 1977): 15-17, 80.

Hourigan, Jonathan. "On Two Deaths and Three Births. The Cinematography of Robert Bresson." *Stills* 1, no. 3 (Autumn 1981): 27-38.

Houston, Beverle, and Marsha Kinder. "Experience and Behavior in *Red Desert* (1964) and *Une Femme Douce* (1969): A View from Inside Out." In *Self and Cinema: A Transformalist Perspective.* Pleasantville, N.Y.: Redgrave, 1980.

Jacob, Gilles. "*Au Hasard, Balthazar.*" *Sight and Sound* 36, no. 1 (Winter 1966-67): 7-9.

Johnson, William. "*L'Argent.*" *Film Quarterly* 37, no. 4 (Summer 1984): 18-21.

Jones, Kent. *L'Argent.* London: BFI Publishing, 1999.

Jones, Kent et al. "Robert Bresson." Parts 1 and 2. *Film Comment* 35, no. 3 (May/June 1999): 36-62; no. 4 (July/August 1999): 36-54.

Kelman, Ken. "The Structure of Fate (Bresson's *Pickpocket*)." In *The Essential Cinema: Essays on Films in The Collection of Anthology Film Archives.* Vol. 1, edited by P. Adams Sitney, 209-215. New York: Anthology Film Archives; New York University Press, 1975.

Kovacs, Yves. "Entretien avec Robert Bresson." *Cahiers du cinéma,* no. 140 (February 1963): 4-10.

Lambert, Gavin. "*Un Condamné à Mort s'est Échappé.*" *Sight and Sound* 27, no. 1 (Summer 1957): 32-33, 53.

———. "Notes on Robert Bresson." *Sight and Sound* 23, no. 1 (July/September 1953): 35-39.

Lane, Anthony. "A Man Entranced." *New Yorker,* 25 January 1999, 82-85.

Latil Le Dantec, Mireille. "Bresson et l'argent." *Cinématographe,* no. 27 (May 1977): 15-19.

———. "*Le Diable probablement.*" *Cinématographe,* no. 29 (July/August 1977): 31-35.

———. "Du faux coupon au faux coupable." *Cinématographe,* no. 90 (June 1983): 7-12.

———. "Robert Bresson: Du cinéma au «cinématographe»." *Études: Revue mensuelle d'opinion et de référence* 387, no. 6 (December 1997): 667-676.

Le Fanu, Mark. "Bresson, Tarkovsky and Contemporary Pessimism." *Cambridge Quarterly* 14, no. 1 (1985): 51-59.

Leterrier, François. "Robert Bresson l'insaisissable." *Cahiers du cinéma,* no. 66 (Noël 1956): 34-36.

Linklater, Richard. "*L'Argent.*" In *Projections 4½: In association with Positif. Film-makers on Film-making,* edited by John Boorman and Walter Donohue, 243-245. London: Faber and Faber, 1995.

Loiselle, Marie-Claude. "Poétique du montage." *24 Images,* no. 77 (Summer 1995): 12-15.

Lopate, Phillip. "Films as Spiritual Life." *Film Comment* 27, no. 6 (November/December 1991): 26-30.

Lyons, Donald. "Priests." *Film Comment* 31, no. 3 (May/June 1995): 80-83, 85.

Magny, Joël. "L'expérience intérieure de Robert Bresson." *Cinéma 72-92,* no. 294 (June 1983):19-26.

———. "L'image de l'argent." *Cinéma 72-92*, nos. 295-296 (July/August 1983): 42-45.

McNeece, Lucy Stone. "Bresson's 'Miracle' of the Flesh: *Mouchette*." *The French Review* 65, no. 2 (1991): 267-279.

Merleau-Ponty, Maurice, and Jean-Luc Godard. "Le testament de Balthazar." *Cahiers du cinéma*, no. 177 (April 1966): 58-59.

Mettey, Marcel. "*Au hasard Balthazar*." *Image et Son*, no. 269 (1973):15-29.

Milne, Tom. "Angels and Ministers." *Sight and Sound* 56, no. 4 (Autumn 1987): 285-287.

Monod, Roland. "Working with Robert Bresson." *Sight and Sound* 27, no. 1 (Summer 1957): 30-32. Originally published as "En travaillant avec Robert Bresson," *Cahiers du cinéma*, no. 64 (November 1956): 16-20.

Oms, Marcel. "Quatre Bernanos au cinéma: La grâce sous la braise." *CinémAction*, no. 49 (October 1988): 89-93.

Oudart, Jean-Pierre. "Bresson et la vérité." *Cahiers du cinéma*, no. 216 (October 1969): 53-56.

———. "Cinema and Suture." Translated by Kari Hanet. *Screen* 18, no. 4 (Winter 1977-78): 35-47. Originally published as "La suture," *Cahiers du cinéma*, no. 211 (April 1969): 36-39; no. 212 (May 1969): 50-55.

———. "L'idéologie moderniste dans quelques films récents (3): Le hors-champ de l'Auteur. (*Quatre nuits d'un rêveur*)." *Cahiers du cinéma*, nos. 236-237 (March/April 1972): 86-89.

———. "A Lacking Discourse." Translated by Joseph Karmel. In *Cahiers du Cinéma 1969-1972: The Politics of Representation*, edited by Nick Browne, 276-86. Cambridge, Mass.: Harvard University Press, 1990. Originally published as "Un discours en défaut," *Cahiers du cinéma*, no. 232 (October 1971): 4-12.

———. "Modernité de Robert Bresson." *Cahiers du cinéma*, nos. 279-280 (August/September 1977): 27-30.

Pipolo, Tony. *The Films of Robert Bresson*. Forthcoming.

Polhemus, Helen M. "Matter and Spirit in the films of Robert Bresson." *Film Heritage* 9, no. 3 (Spring 1974): 12-16.

Prédal, René. "Bresson et son temps." *Cinéma 72-92*, no. 294 (June 1983): 4-11.

———. "La dimension plastique de l'œuvre de Bresson." *Jeune Cinéma*, no. 201 (May/June 1990): 4-11.

———. "Entretiens. Léonce H. Burel." *Cinéma 72-92*, no. 189 (July/August 1974): 104-108.

Prokosch, Mike. "Bresson's Stylistics Revisited." *Film Quarterly* 25, no. 2 (Winter 1971-72): 30-32.

Puaux, Françoise. "1975: Robert Bresson et la théorie du «cinématographe»." *CinémAction*, no. 60 (July 1991): 202-205.

———. "La figure de l'âne chez Robert Bresson." *CinémAction*, no. 80 (3d quarter 1996): 122-126.

Pym, John. "Madame Tolstoy and the Axeman." *Sight and Sound* 52, no. 4 (Autumn 1983): 273-275.

Reader, Keith. *Robert Bresson*. Manchester: Manchester University Press, 2000.

Reif, Tony. "Robert Bresson and the Drama of Interiority." In *Innovators of the French Cinema*. Ottawa: Canadian Film Institute, 1965.

Rhode, Eric. "Dostoevsky and Bresson." *Sight and Sound* 39, no. 2 (Spring 1970): 82-83.

———. "Robert Bresson." In *Tower of Babel: Speculations on the Cinema*. London: Weidenfeld and Nicolson, 1966.

Rohmer, Eric. "Le miracle des objets." *Cahiers du cinéma*, no. 65 (December 1956): 42-45.

Rosenbaum, Jonathan. "Bresson's *Lancelot du Lac*." *Sight and Sound* 43, no. 3 (Summer 1974): 128-130.

———. "Working with Bresson: Two Nights of an Extra." *Village Voice*, 29 April 1971, 76, 86.

Roud, Richard. "The Early Work of Robert Bresson." *Film Culture*, no. 20 (1959): 44-52.

———. "Novel novel; Fable fable?" *Sight and Sound* 31, no. 2 (Spring 1962): 84-88.

———. "Robert Bresson." In *Cinema: A Critical Dictionary. The Major Film-makers*, Vol. 1, edited by Richard Roud, 141-153. New York: Viking Press, 1980.

Samuels, Charles Thomas. "Robert Bresson." In *Encountering Directors*. New York: Capricorn Books, 1972.

Sarris, Andrew. "The Devil Certainly." *Village Voice*, 4 October 1983, 61.

———. "Thoughts on Bresson and Hitchcock." *Village Voice*, 10 April 1984, 41.

Schofer, Peter. "Dissolution into Darkness: Bresson's *Un Condamné à mort s'est échappé*." *Sub-Stance*, no. 9 (1974): 59-66.

Schrader, Paul. *Transcendental Style in Film: Ozu, Bresson, Dreyer*. Berkeley and Los Angeles: University of California Press, 1972.

Sémolué, Jean. "*L'argent*: note pour une approche." *Cinéma 72-92*, no. 294 (June 1983): 27-30.

———. *Bresson*. Paris: Éditions Universitaires, 1959.

———. *Bresson, ou, L'Acte pur des Métamorphoses*. Paris: Flammarion, 1993.

———. "Le Film bressonian, bel objet; *Les Dames du Bois du Boulogne*: éléments d'un dossier critique." *Avant-Scène Cinéma*, no. 196 (November 1977): 5, 75-78.

———. "Les personnages de Robert Bresson." *Cahiers du cinéma*, no. 75 (October 1957): 10-15.

———. "Robert Bresson: du mouvement et des sons." *CinémAction*, no. 72 (3d quarter 1994): 60- 66.

Skoller, Donald S. "*Praxis* as a Cinematic Principle In Films by Robert Bresson." *Cinema Journal* 9, no. 1 (Fall 1969):13-22.

Sloan, Jane. *Robert Bresson: a guide to references and resources*. Boston, Mass.: G.K. Hall, 1983.

Taylor, John Russell. "Robert Bresson." In *Cinema Eye, Cinema Ear: Some Key Film-Makers of the Sixties*. London: Methuen, 1964.

Tomlinson, Doug. "Performance in the Films of Robert Bresson: The Aesthetics of Denial." In *Making Visible the Invisible: an anthology of original essays on film acting*, edited by Carole Zucker, 365-390. Metuchen, N.J.: Scarecrow, 1990.

Vecchiali, Paul. "*Procès de Jeanne d'Arc*: Les fausses apparences." *Cahiers du cinéma*, no. 143 (May 1963): 35-39.

Virmaux, Alain, and Odette Virmaux. "Revisitation des *Anges du péché:* (à propos d'un livre de Jean Sémolué sur Bresson)." *Jeune Cinéma*, no. 225 (January 1994): 47-49.

Vitoux, Frédéric, and Michel Sineux. "L'armure sied à Bresson (*Lancelot du Lac*)." *Positif,* no. 163 (November 1974): 72-74.

Walter, Anne. "L'angoisse de la certitude." *Cahiers du cinéma*, no. 104 (February 1960): 47-48.

Westerbeck, Colin L., Jr. "The Dark Night of the Soul of Robert Bresson." In *The Emergence of Film Art*, 2d ed., edited by Lewis Jacobs, 480-493. New York: W.W. Norton, 1979. Originally published as "Robert Bresson's Austere Vision," *Artforum* 15, no. 3 (November 1976): 52-57.

Winston, Douglas Garrett. "*Diary of a Country Priest*: Robert Bresson and the Literary Adaptation." In *The Screenplay as Literature*. Cranbury, N.J.: Associated University Presses, 1973.

Young, Colin. "Conventional-Unconventional." *Film Quarterly* 17, no. 1 (Fall 1963): 14-30.

Zeman, Marvin. "The Suicide of Robert Bresson." *Cinema* 6, no. 3 (Spring 1971): 37-42.

Sources

Affron, Mirella Jona. "Bresson and Pascal: Rhetorical Affinities," *Quarterly Review of Film and Video* 10, no. 2, copyright © 1985 Gordon and Breach Publishers. Reprinted by permission of Gordon and Breach Publishers.

Ayfre, Amédée. "The Universe of Robert Bresson," from *The Films of Robert Bresson*, edited by Ian Cameron, copyright © 1970 Praeger Publishers, New York. Reprinted by permission of Greenwood Publishing Group.

Barthes, Roland. "On Robert Bresson's Film *Les Anges du péché*," translated by Richard Howard, copyright © 1998 by Farrar, Straus & Giroux, Inc. Reprinted by permission of Farrar, Straus & Giroux, Inc., New York. To appear in a selection from *Oeuvres Complètes*, by Roland Barthes, to be published by Hill and Wang, a division of Farrar, Straus & Giroux, Inc., in 1998. All rights reserved.

Bazin, André. "*Le Journal d'un curé de campagne* and the Stylistics of Robert Bresson," from *What is Cinema? 2 Volumes*, University of California Press, edited and translated by Hugh Gray, copyright © 1967 The Regents of the University of California. Reprinted by permission of The Regents of the University of California.

Browne, Nick. "Film Form/Voice-Over: Bresson's *The Diary of a Country Priest*," *Yale French Studies* 60, copyright © 1980 Yale University. Reprinted by permission of *Yale French Studies*.

Ciment, Michel. "I Seek Not Description But Vision: Robert Bresson on *L'Argent*," from *Projections 9*, edited by Walter Donohoe and John Boorman, translation Pierre Hodgson, copyright © 1998 by Faber and Faber Limited. Reprinted by permission of Michel Ciment and Faber and Faber Limited, London.

Dempsey, Michael. "Despair Abounding: The Recent Films of Robert Bresson," *Film Quarterly* 34, no.1, pp. 2-14, copyright © 1980 by the Regents of the University of California. Reprinted by permission of the Regents of the University of California.

Durgnat, Raymond. "The Negative Vision of Robert Bresson," copyright © 1998 Raymond Durgnat. Printed by permission of the author.

Godard, Jean-Luc and Michel Delahaye. "The Question," *Cahiers du cinéma in English*, no. 8, copyright © 1967 British Film Institute. Reprinted by permission of British Film Institute Publishing, London.

Hanlon, Lindley. "Sound as Symbol in *Mouchette*," from *Fragments: Bresson's Film Style,* copyright © 1986 Associated University Presses. Reprinted by permission of Associated University Presses.

Johnson, William. "*Affaires Publiques*," *Film Quarterly* 50, no. 4, pp. 35-6, copyright © 1997 by The Regents of the University of California. Reprinted by permission of The Regents of the University of California.

Jones, Kent. "A Stranger's Posture: Notes on Bresson's Late Films," copyright © 1998 Kent Jones. Printed by permission of the author.

Kline, T. Jefferson. "Picking Dostoevsky's Pocket: Bresson's Sl(e)ight of Screen," from *Screening the Text: Intertextuality in New Wave French Cinema,* copyright © 1992 The John Hopkins University Press. Reprinted by permission of The John Hopkins University Press.

Latil Le Dantec, Mireille. "Bresson, Dostoevsky," *Cinématographe,* no. 73, copyright © 1981 Mireille Latil Le Dantec.. Translation copyright © 1998 Lara Fitzgerald. Printed by permission of the author.

Mangolte, Babette. "*Breaking Silence (Forty Years Later),*" copyright © 1998 Babette Mangolte. Printed by permission of the author.

Moravia, Alberto. "*L'Argent,*" copyright © 1983 Flammarion. Translation copyright © 1998 Lara Fitzgerald. Printed by permission of Flammarion.

Nogueira, Rui. "Burel & Bresson," *Sight and Sound* 46, no. 1, copyright © 1977 *Sight and Sound*. Translation and introduction © 1977 Tom Milne. Reprinted by permission of *Sight and Sound* (British Film Institute).

Pipolo, Tony. "Rules of the Game: On Bresson's *Les Anges du péché*," copyright © 1998 Tony Pipolo. Printed by permission of the author.

Prédal, René. "Robert Bresson: L'Aventure intérieure,"*L'Avant-Scène*, nos. 408/409, January/February 1992; copyright © 1992 René Prédal; translation copyright © 1998 Robert Gray. Printed by permission of *L'Avant-Scène.*

Reader, Keith. "D'où cela vient-il?: Notes on Three Films by Robert Bresson," *French Studies* 40, no. 4, copyright © 1986 Keith Reader. Reprinted by permission of the author.

Richie, Donald. "Bresson and Music" copyright © 1998 Donald Richie. Printed by permission of the author.

Rosenbaum, Jonathan. "The Last Filmmaker: A Local, Interim Report," *Chicago Reader* (26 January 1996), revised 1998, copyright © 1998 Jonathan Rosenbaum. Reprinted by permission of the author.

Roud, Richard. "The Devil Probably: The Redemption of Despair," *Film Comment* Vol. 13, no. 5, copyright © 1977 *Film Comment*. Reprinted by permission of Richard T. Jameson, *Film Comment.*

Schrader, Paul. "Robert Bresson, Possibly," *Film Comment* 13, no. 5, copyright © 1977 *Film Comment*. Reprinted by permission of Richard T. Jameson, *Film Comment.*

Sitney, P. Adams. "Cinematography vs. the Cinema: Bresson's Figures," from *Modernist Montage* by P. Adams Sitney, copyright © 1989 Columbia University Press. Reprinted by permission of the publisher.

Sitney, P. Adams. "The Rhetoric of Robert Bresson," from *The Essential Cinema*, edited by P. Adams Sitney, copyright © 1975 P. Adams Sitney. Reprinted by permission of Georges Borchardt, Inc. for the author.

Sontag, Susan. "Spiritual Style in the Films of Robert Bresson," from *Against Interpretation* by Susan Sontag, copyright © 1964, 1966 and copyright renewed © 1994 by Susan Sontag. Reprinted by permission of Farrar, Straus & Giroux, Inc.

Thiher, Allen. "Bresson's *Un condamné à mort*: The Semiotics of Grace," from *The Cinematic Muse: Critical Studies in the History of French Cinema* by Allen Thiher, copyright © 1979 by the Curators of the University of Missouri. Reprinted by permission of the University of Missouri Press.

Thompson, Kristin. "The Sheen of Armour, the Whinnies of Horses: Sparse Parametric Style in *Lancelot du Lac*," from *Breaking the Glass Armor: Neoformalist Film Analysis,* copyright © 1988 Princeton University Press. Reprinted by permission of Princeton University Press.

Filmmakers on Bresson

Akerman, copyright © 1998 Chantal Akerman; Antonioni, copyright © 1998 Michelangelo Antonioni, reprinted by permission of Michelangelo and Enrica Antonioni; Assayas (1), copyright © 1998 Olivier Assayas, translation copyright © 1997 James Quandt; Assayas (2), copyright 1998 Olivier Assayas; Azimi, copyright © 1998 Iradj Azimi; Bellocchio, copyright © 1998 Marco Bellocchio, translation copyright © 1998 Ramiro Puerta and Dorina Furgiuele; Bertolucci, copyright © 1998 Bernardo Bertolucci; Cocteau, copyright © 1979 the estate of Jean Cocteau, translation copyright © 1998 James Quandt; Duras, copyright © 1966 *Combat*; translation copyright © 1998 James Quandt and Lara Fitzgerald; Egoyan, copyright © 1998 Atom Egoyan; Elder, copyright © 1998 R. Bruce Elder; Erice, copyright © 1998 Victor Erice, translation copyright © 1998 Nuria Bronfman; Farocki, copyright © 1984 Harun Farocki, reprinted by permission of Farocki and Goethe-Institut; Fassbinder (1), copyright © 1997 The Film & Video Department of the Museum of Modern Art, New York and The Rainer Werner Fassbinder Foundation, Berlin, reprinted with their permission; Fassbinder (2), copyright © 1976 British Film Institute Publishing, reprinted with their permission; Haneke, copyright © 1998 Michael Haneke, translation copyright © 1998 Robert Gray, Kinograph; Hartley, copyright © 1992 Graham Fuller, reprinted by permission of Hal Hartley and Graham Fuller; Holland, copyright © 1995 Agnieszka Holland and the Toronto International Film Festival; Kaul, copyright © 1998 Mani Kaul; Kaurismäki, copyright © 1998 Aki Kaurismäki; Lefebvre, copyright © 1998 Jean-Pierre Lefebvre; L'Herbier, copyright © 1951 the estate of Marcel L'Herbier, reprinted by permission of Marie-Ange L'Herbier, translation copyright © 1998 Robert Gray, Kinograph; Malle (1), copyright © 1979 Andrew Horton, reprinted with his permission; Malle (2), copyright © 1993 Louis Malle, reprinted by permission of Philip French; Malle (3), copyright © 1959 *Arts*, translation copyright © 1998 Robert Gray, Kinograph; Mangolte, copyright © 1998 Babette Mangolte; Marker, copyright © 1998 Chris Marker; Markopoulos, copyright © 1962 the estate of Gregory J. Markopoulos, reprinted by permission of Robert Beavers; Mekas, copyright © 1969 Jonas Mekas; Rivette, copyright © 1963 *Cahiers du cinéma*; Scorsese, copyright © 1998 Martin Scorsese; Schrader, copyright ©

Photo Credits